A Companion to
the British and Irish Short Story

Blackwell Companions to Literature and Culture

This series offers comprehensive, newly written surveys of key periods and movements and certain major authors, in English literary culture and history. Extensive volumes provide new perspectives and positions on contexts and on canonical and post-canonical texts, orientating the beginning student in new fields of study and providing the experienced undergraduate and new graduate with current and new directions, as pioneered and developed by leading scholars in the field.

Published recently:

37. *A Companion to Mark Twain*   Edited by Peter Messent and Louis J. Budd
38. *A Companion to European Romanticism*   Edited by Michael K. Ferber
39. *A Companion to Modernist Literature and Culture*   Edited by David Bradshaw and Kevin J. H. Dettmar
40. *A Companion to Walt Whitman*   Edited by Donald D. Kummings
41. *A Companion to Herman Melville*   Edited by Wyn Kelley
42. *A Companion to Medieval English Literature and Culture c.1350–c.1500*   Edited by Peter Brown
43. *A Companion to Modern British and Irish Drama: 1880–2005*   Edited by Mary Luckhurst
44. *A Companion to Eighteenth-Century Poetry*   Edited by Christine Gerrard
45. *A Companion to Shakespeare's Sonnets*   Edited by Michael Schoenfeldt
46. *A Companion to Satire*   Edited by Ruben Quintero
47. *A Companion to William Faulkner*   Edited by Richard C. Moreland
48. *A Companion to the History of the Book*   Edited by Simon Eliot and Jonathan Rose
49. *A Companion to Emily Dickinson*   Edited by Martha Nell Smith and Mary Loeffelholz
50. *A Companion to Digital Literary Studies*   Edited by Ray Siemens and Susan Schreibman
51. *A Companion to Charles Dickens*   Edited by David Paroissien
52. *A Companion to James Joyce*   Edited by Richard Brown
53. *A Companion to Latin American Literature and Culture*   Edited by Sara Castro-Klaren
54. *A Companion to the History of the English Language*   Edited by Haruko Momma and Michael Matto
55. *A Companion to Henry James*   Edited by Greg Zacharias
56. *A Companion to the British and Irish Short Story*   Edited by Cheryl Alexander Malcolm and
                                                                                            David Malcolm

For a full list of titles available in the *Blackwell Companions to Literature and Culture* series, please visit www.blackwellpublishing.com/literature

A COMPANION TO

THE
BRITISH AND IRISH
SHORT STORY

EDITED BY
CHERYL ALEXANDER MALCOLM
AND DAVID MALCOLM

WILEY-BLACKWELL
A John Wiley & Sons, Ltd., Publication

This edition first published 2008
© 2008 Blackwell Publishing Ltd

Blackwell Publishing was acquired by John Wiley & Sons in February 2007. Blackwell's publishing program has been merged with Wiley's global Scientific, Technical, and Medical business to form Wiley-Blackwell.

Registered Office
John Wiley & Sons Ltd, The Atrium, Southern Gate, Chichester, West Sussex, PO19 8SQ, United Kingdom

Editorial Offices
350 Main Street, Malden, MA 02148-5020, USA
9600 Garsington Road, Oxford, OX4 2DQ, UK
The Atrium, Southern Gate, Chichester, West Sussex, PO19 8SQ, UK

For details of our global editorial offices, for customer services, and for information about how to apply for permission to reuse the copyright material in this book please see our website at www.wiley.com/wiley-blackwell.

The right of Cheryl Alexander Malcolm and David Malcolm to be identified as the authors of the editorial material in this work has been asserted in accordance with the Copyright, Designs and Patents Act 1988.

Library of Congress Cataloging-in-Publication Data

A companion to the British and Irish short story / edited by Cheryl Alexander Malcolm and David Malcolm.
    p. cm.—(Blackwell companions to literature and culture)
  Includes bibliographical references and index.
  ISBN 978-1-4051-4537-4 (hardcover : alk. paper) 1. Short stories, English—History and criticism. 2. English fiction—Irish authors—History and criticism. 3. Short stories, English—Themes, motives. I. Malcolm, Cheryl Alexander. II. Malcolm, David, 1952–

  PR829.C64 2008
  823'.0109—dc22

                                         2008008104

A catalogue record for this book is available from the British Library.

Set in 11/13 pt Garamond 3 by SNP Best-set Typesetter Ltd., Hong Kong
Printed and bound in Singapore by Utopia Press Pte Ltd

1 2008

Contents

Notes on Contributors   ix

Preface   xv

Part I: 1880–1945   1

Introduction   3

1   The British and Irish Short Story to 1945   5
     Cheryl Alexander Malcolm and David Malcolm

Topics and Genres   17

2   The Story of Colonial Adventure   19
     Mariadele Boccardi

3   Responses to War: 1914–1918 and 1939–1945   35
     Richard Greaves

4   Irish Short Fiction: 1880–1945   51
     Patrick Lonergan

5   The Detective and Crime Story: 1880–1945   65
     Jopi Nyman

6   The British and Irish Ghost Story and Tale of the
     Supernatural: 1880–1945   81
     Becky DiBiasio

7   Finding a Voice: Women Writing the Short Story (to 1945)   96
    Sabine Coelsch-Foisner

8   Rudyard Kipling's Art of the Short Story   114
    David Malcolm

Reading Individual Authors and Texts   129

9   Robert Louis Stevenson: "The Bottle Imp," "The Beach of
    Falesá," and "Markheim"   131
    Michael Meyer

10 Thomas Hardy: *Wessex Tales*   140
    David Grylls

11 Joseph Conrad: "The Secret Sharer" and "An Outpost of Progress"   149
    Christopher Thomas Cairney

12 The Short Stories of Hector Hugh Munro ("Saki")   157
    Sandie Byrne

13 Paralysis Re-considered: James Joyce's *Dubliners*   165
    Richard Greaves

14 H.G. Wells's Short Stories: "The Country of the Blind" and
    "The Door in the Wall"   174
    Sabine Coelsch-Foisner

15 D.H. Lawrence's Short Stories: "The Horse Dealer's Daughter" and
    "The Rocking Horse Winner"   183
    Kathryn Miles

16 Virginia Woolf: "Kew Gardens" and "The Legacy"   193
    Stef Craps

17 Katherine Mansfield: "The Garden Party" and
    "Marriage à la Mode"   202
    Jennifer E. Dunn

18 Frank O'Connor: "Guests of the Nation" and "My Oedipus Complex"   211
    Greg Winston

19 The Short Stories of Liam O'Flaherty   221
    Shawn O'Hare

20 W. Somerset Maugham's Ashenden Stories   227
    David Malcolm

21 Elizabeth Bowen: "The Demon Lover" and "Mysterious Kôr"   236
    Sarah Dillon

Part II: 1945–the Present 245

Introduction 247

22 The British and Irish Short Story: 1945–Present 249
Cheryl Alexander Malcolm and David Malcolm

Topics and Genres 261

23 New Identities: The Irish Short Story since 1945 263
Greg Winston

24 Redefining Englishness: British Short Fiction from 1945
to the Present 279
James M. Lang

25 Scottish Short Stories (post 1945) 294
Gavin Miller

26 Hybrid Voices and Visions: The Short Stories of E.A. Markham,
Ben Okri, Salman Rushdie, Hanif Kureishi, Patricia Duncker,
and Jackie Kay 308
Michael Parker

27 The Anglo-Jewish Short Story since the Holocaust 330
Cheryl Alexander Malcolm

28 Feminist Voices: Women's Short Fiction after 1945 342
Michael Meyer

29 British Gay and Lesbian Short Stories 356
Brett Josef Grubisic

30 Science Fiction and Fantasy after 1945: Beyond Pulp Fiction 372
Mitchell R. Lewis

31 Experimental Short Fiction in Britain since 1945 384
Günther Jarfe

Reading Individual Authors and Texts 399

32 The Short Stories of Julian Maclaren-Ross 401
David Malcolm

33 Alan Sillitoe: "The Loneliness of the Long Distance Runner" 409
Michael Parker

34 The Short Stories of Elizabeth Taylor 416
Robert Ellis Hosmer, Jr

35   The Short Fiction of V.S. Pritchett   423
     Andrzej Gąsiorek

36   Edna O'Brien: "A Rose in the Heart of New York"   431
     Sinéad Mooney

37   Doris Lessing: *African Stories*   440
     Don Adams

38   The Desire for Clarity: Seán O'Faoláin's "Lovers of the Lake"   448
     Paul Delaney

39   The Short Stories of Muriel Spark   456
     Robert Ellis Hosmer, Jr

40   Jean Rhys: "Let Them Call It Jazz"   464
     Cheryl Alexander Malcolm

41   George Mackay Brown: "Witch," "Master Halcrow, Priest,"
     "A Time to Keep," and "The Tarn and the Rosary"   472
     Gavin Miller

42   William Trevor: Uncertain Grounds for Assured Art   480
     John Kenny

43   John McGahern: *Nightlines*   488
     Stanley van der Ziel

44   The Clinking of an Identity Disk: Bernard MacLaverty's
     "Walking the Dog"   498
     Jerzy Jarniewicz

45   Angela Carter's *The Bloody Chamber*: A World Transformed
     by Imagination and Desire – Adventures in Anarcho-Surrealism   507
     Madelena Gonzalez

46   J.G. Ballard: Psychopathology, Apocalypse, and the Media Landscape   516
     Mitchell R. Lewis

47   The Short Stories of Benjamin Okri   524
     Wolfgang Görtschacher

48   James Kelman: *Greyhound for Breakfast*   532
     Peter Clandfield

49   Hanif Kureishi: *Love in a Blue Time*   541
     Patrick Lonergan

Index   550

Notes on Contributors

Don Adams is an Associate Professor of English at Florida Atlantic University. He has published critical work on a variety of modern authors, including James Merrill, Ronald Firbank, and James Purdy.

Mariadele Boccardi is Senior Lecturer in English at the University of the West of England in Bristol. Her research is in the area of contemporary British historical fiction, with particular focus on questions of nationhood, empire, and representation. Her monograph on the subject will be published by Palgrave in 2009.

Sandie Byrne is formerly Fellow and Tutor in English at Balliol College, Oxford. She is the author of a number of books and articles on nineteenth- and twentieth-century literature. Her most recent publication is *The Unbearable Saki: The Work of H.H. Munro* (Oxford University Press, 2007).

Christopher Thomas Cairney has taught at the Catholic University of Ecuador, National University in Korea, the University of Balamand in Lebanon, and Doğuş University in Istanbul. He is currently teaching at De Anza College (California). A dedicated Conradian, he is also interested in Celtic Studies. His most recent article is "Gaelic Borderlines and Borderlands in the New Cultural Geography of Scotland," in *Re-Visioning Scotland: New Readings from the Cultural Canon* (Frankfurt am Main: Peter Lang, 2008).

Peter Clandfield teaches in the Department of English Studies at Nipissing University in North Bay, Ontario. Among his main interests are contemporary Scottish literature and culture, urban development and redevelopment as represented in fiction and film, theoretical and practical questions concerning censorship, and issues of racial and cultural hybridization and mixing.

Sabine Coelsch-Foisner is Professor of English Literature and Cultural Theory at the University of Salzburg and Head of the Interdisciplinary Research Centre on

Metamorphic Changes in the Arts. She is the author of award-winning *Revolution in Poetic Consciousness* (2002) and has published widely on Romantic, Victorian, and twentieth-century literature, with a special focus on the relations between literature and the arts. Books (co-)edited by her include *Elizabethan Literature and Transformation* (1999), *Private and Public Voices in Victorian Poetry* (2000), *Theatre Practice and Drama Translation* (2004), *Metamorphosen* (2005), *Fiction and Autobiography* (2006), and *Fantastic Body Transformations* (2006). She is currently working on the literary fantastic.

Stef Craps is a postdoctoral Fellow of the Flemish Research Council affiliated with the English Department at Ghent University. He is the author of *Trauma and Ethics in the Novels of Graham Swift: No Short-Cuts to Salvation* (Sussex Academic Press, 2005) and of various articles on modern English literature in both journals and books. His current research focuses on the ways in which postcolonial literature bears witness to the suffering engendered by colonial oppression.

Paul Delaney is a Lecturer in the School of English, Trinity College, Dublin. He is the author of a number of articles and reviews on different aspects of Irish culture, and is the editor of Daniel Corkery's short fiction (2003). He is also the editor of a forthcoming collection of essays on Colm Tóibín, to be published by Liffey Press (2008).

Becky DiBiasio is Associate Professor of English at Assumption College in Worcester, Massachusetts. She teaches courses in Gothic and Medieval Literature, and Mass Communications. She has written articles on the teaching of Victorian Fantasy Literature and is currently compiling an anthology of ghost and horror stories by Edith Nesbit, Charlotte Riddell, Vernon Lee, and Mary Elizabeth Braddon.

Dr Sarah Dillon is Lecturer in Contemporary Fiction at the University of St Andrews. She is the author of *The Palimpsest: Literature, Criticism, Theory* (2007) and has also published on Jacques Derrida, H.D., and Maggie Gee. She is currently working on *Future-Fiction: Studies in Contemporary Narrative*, an analysis of the use of science fiction by contemporary mainstream British writers, including Maggie Gee, Michel Faber, and David Mitchell.

Dr Jennifer E. Dunn teaches English Literature at the University of Oxford. Her research interests include women's writing, intertextuality, and postmodernism. She has published articles on twentieth-century fiction, contemporary authors, and the gothic. Her current research projects include a monograph on the British author Emma Tennant, and a co-edited essay collection on rewritings of Henry James.

Andrzej Gąsiorek is a Reader in Twentieth-Century Literature at the University of Birmingham. He is the author of *Postwar British Fiction* (1995), *Wyndham Lewis and Modernism, J.G. Ballard* (2005), and, with Edward Comentale, co-author of the edited volume *T.E. Hulme and the Question of Modernism* (2006).

Madelena Gonzalez is Professor of English Literature at Avignon University. Her latest publications are *Fiction after the Fatwa: Salman Rushdie and the Charm of Catastrophe* (2005) and *Translating Identity and the Identity of Translation* (2006). Her research interests include contemporary culture, theater, and the novel, and she is currently editing a volume of articles on minority theater.

Wolfgang Görtschacher is Assistant Professor at the University of Salzburg. He is the author of *Little Magazine Profiles: The Little Magazines in Great Britain 1939–1993* (1993) and *Contemporary Views on the Little Magazine Scene* (2000). Recently he co-edited *Fiction and Literary Prizes in Great Britain* (2006), *The Author as Reader*, and *The Romantic Imagination: A William Oxley Casebook* (both 2005). He is the owner-director of the press Poetry Salzburg and edits the literary magazine *Poetry Salzburg Review*.

Richard Greaves is the author of *Transition, Reception and Modernism in W.B.Yeats* (Palgrave, 2002). He has taught English at Liverpool Hope University College, Royal Holloway, St Mary's College, Strawberry Hill, and Loughborough Grammar School. He is currently an Associate Lecturer with the Open University.

Brett Josef Grubisic lives in Vancouver, Canada, and lectures at the University of British Columbia. He specializes in popular culture and contemporary Canadian and UK fiction. The author of a novel, *The Age of Cities*, he also edited *Contra/diction: New Queer Male Fiction* and co-edited (with Carellin Brooks) *Carnal Nation*, an anthology of Canadian fiction. Forthcoming volumes include *Understanding Beryl Bainbridge* and *National Plots: Interrogation, Revision, and Re-Inscription in Canadian Historical Fiction, 1832–2005* (co-edited with Andrea Cabajsky).

David Grylls is Director of the Literature programme at Oxford University's Department for Continuing Education and a Fellow of Kellogg College, Oxford. He has written books on Gissing, Dickens, and Victorian parent–child relations, and edited Gissing's *Born in Exile*. He reviews regularly for *The Sunday Times* and has lectured widely in America, as well as in France, Sweden, Italy, and Greece. He is currently writing a book on the representation of sex in Victorian fiction.

Robert Ellis Hosmer, Jr is Senior Lecturer in English Language and Literature at Smith College. He published the Guide to the seventh edition of *The Norton Reader* (1988), and edited *Contemporary British Women Writers: Narrative Strategies* (Macmillan, 1993). His scholarly interests center on the work of Virginia Woolf, Anita Brookner, Penelope Fitzgerald, Edna O'Brien, and Muriel Spark. He has contributed numerous essays, articles and reviews to the *Dictionary of Literary Biography*, *Paris Review*, *New York Times*, and *Chicago Tribune*, among others. *Shall We Say I Had Fun with My Imagination: Essays in Honor of Muriel Spark* is forthcoming.

Günther Jarfe is Professor of Literary Pedagogy and the Methodology of Teaching English at Passau University where he has taught since 1985. He studied English and German in Freiburg im Breisgau and Hamburg. He obtained his PhD from Freiburg

University and his *Habilitation* from Hamburg University. His main research areas are Victorian literature and culture, Modernism, and the British short story. Among his publications are books on D.G. Rossetti's *The House of Life*, *Young Auden*, and *Understanding the Modern Short Story*.

Jerzy Jarniewicz is a Polish poet, translator, and literary critic, who lectures in English at the universities of Łódź and Warsaw. He has published nine volumes of poetry, six critical books on contemporary British, Irish and American literature (most recently studies of Seamus Heaney and Philip Larkin), and has written extensively for various journals, including *Poetry Review*, *Irish Review*, and *Cambridge Review*.

John Kenny lectures in the English Department, National University of Ireland, Galway. He specializes in contemporary fiction and the theory and practice of literary journalism. He is a principal reviewer of Irish fiction for *The Irish Times*. His books, *John Banville* and *The John Banville Sourcebook*, will be published by Irish Academic Press in 2008–9, and he is currently writing a book on Patrick McCabe. He is Academic Director of the John McGahern International Seminar and Summer School.

James M. Lang is an Associate Professor of English at Assumption College in Worcester Massachusetts, where he teaches courses in creative writing and twentieth-century British literature. He is the author of *On Course: A Week-by-Week Guide to Your First Semester of College Teaching* (Harvard University Press, 2008), *Life on the Tenure Track: Lessons from the First Year* (Johns Hopkins University Press, 2005), as well as numerous articles about twentieth-century British fiction.

Mitchell R. Lewis received his PhD in English from the University of Oklahoma and currently teaches British literature at Elmira College in upstate New York. His research interests include modernism, twentieth-century British fiction, science fiction, gothic fiction, and literary and cultural theory. He has published essays on Michael Moorcock, Patrick McGrath, György Lukács, and cultural studies. His current project is a study of gender, sexuality, and authorship in the work of D.H. Lawrence.

Patrick Lonergan is a Lecturer in English at National University of Ireland, Galway. He is a theater critic for publications including *The Irish Times*, and has published widely on Irish literature and drama. He is the Director of the Synge Summer School, and serves on the Executive of The International Association for the Study of Irish Literatures (IASIL). His book *Theatre and Globalization – Transformations in Irish Drama* will be published by Palgrave Macmillan in 2009.

Cheryl Alexander Malcolm is Associate Professor of English Literature in the Department of American Studies at the University of Gdańsk in Poland. Her books include *Jean Rhys: A Study of the Short Fiction* (Twayne, 1996), with David Malcolm; *Understanding Anita Brookner* (University of South Carolina Press, 2002); *Eros. Usa: Essays on the Culture and Literature of Desire* (University of Gdańsk Press, 2005), co-edited with Jopi Nyman; *British and Irish Short Fiction Writers, 1945–2000*, volume 319 of the *Dictionary of Literary Biography* (Gale, 2006), co-edited with David Malcolm. Her latest book is *Unshtetling Narratives: Depictions of Jewish Identities in British and American Literature and Film* (Salzburg Anglophone Critical Studies, 2006). Her essays have appeared in numerous journals in the USA and Europe, including *Studies in American Jewish Literature*, *MELUS*, and *English Studies*.

David Malcolm is Professor of English Literature in the English Institute at the University of Gdańsk. His publications include studies of the fiction of Jean Rhys (with Cheryl Alexander Malcolm), Ian McEwan, Graham Swift, and John McGahern. He co-edited (with Cheryl Alexander Malcolm) a volume of the *Dictionary of Literary Biography* on *British and Irish Short Story Writers, 1945–2000*. He has also co-edited volumes of essays on Ronald Firbank, Sylvia Townsend Warner, and Rebecca West.

Michael Meyer teaches Anglophone Literatures at the University of Koblenz-Landau (Germany). He is the author of monographs on Charles Tomlinson's poetry, on Gibbon's, Mill's, and Ruskin's autobiographies, and on studying English and American Literatures. He edited a book on the teaching of literature, Salman Rushdie's short stories (*East, West*), and co-edited an interdisciplinary volume on trust and credibility. His research focuses on poetry, colonial and postcolonial novels, short fiction, gothic fiction, and visual representation.

Kathryn Miles is Associate Professor and Director of Writing at Unity College, Maine. She has written extensively on Virginia Woolf's writing and on ecology-related topics.

Gavin Miller is Research Fellow in the English Research Institute, Manchester Metropolitan University. He is the author of *R.D. Laing* (EUP, 2004) and *Alasdair Gray: The Fiction of Communion* (Rodopi, 2005). He has published also in journals such as *New Literary History*, *Journal of Narrative Theory*, *Journal of the History of the Behavorial Sciences*, and *Scottish Studies Review*. His research interests include contemporary Scottish Literature, the history of psychoanalysis, and science fiction.

Sinéad Mooney is the author of *Samuel Beckett* (Northcote House, 2006) and the editor of *Edna O'Brien: New Critical Perspectives* (Carysfort, 2006), as well as a number of essays on Beckett and twentieth-century Irish women's writing. She is currently working on a study of Beckett and self-translation. She is a lecturer in the Department of English of the National University of Ireland, Galway, teaching primarily in the fields of modernism and women's writing.

Jopi Nyman is Chair and Professor of English at the University of Joensuu in Finland. His most recent books include the collection *Reconstructing Hybridity: Post-Colonial Studies in Transition*, co-edited with Joel Kuortti (Amsterdam: Rodopi, 2007). He is currently completing a monograph on home and identity in contemporary diasporic fiction to be published by Rodopi (2008).

Shawn O'Hare is an Associate Professor of English at Carson-Newman College in Jefferson City, Tennessee. He is the founding editor of the scholarly journal *Nua: Studies in Contemporary Irish Writing* and has published essays about the works of Samuel Beckett, Roddy Doyle, Jennifer Johnston, Deirdre Madden, Frank O'Connor, Joseph O'Connor, and James Plunkett, among others.

Michael Parker is Professor of English at the University of Central Lancashire. His publications include *Seamus Heaney: The Making of the Poet* (Macmillan, 1993), *The Hurt World: Short Stories of the Troubles* (Blackstaff, 1995), *Contemporary Irish Fiction: Themes, Tropes, Theories*, co-edited with Liam Harte (Macmillan, 2000), and *Northern Irish Literature: The Imprint of History 1956–2006* (Palgrave, 2007). His next project will be another interdisciplinary study, *Literature and Politics in Britain Since 1979*.

Greg Winston is Associate Professor of English at Husson College. His research focuses on modern Irish and British literatures, especially their intersections with postcolonial history and geography. His publications have appeared in *Colby Quarterly*, *Études Irlandaises*, and *James Joyce Quarterly*, among others. He is currently writing a book about James Joyce and militarism.

Stanley van der Ziel is currently completing a PhD dissertation on the works of John McGahern at University College Dublin, where he also teaches. He has published several articles on different aspects of McGahern's work.

Preface

This volume is aimed at a wide readership – students, teachers and scholars, and whoever is interested in the serious discussion of the British and Irish short story. The volume is divided into two parts. Part I covers the period 1880 to 1945, Part II that of 1945 to the present. The decision to start the coverage of the development of the short story in Britain and Ireland after 1880 is based on the scholarly consensus that, while early nineteenth-century and high-Victorian authors wrote short fiction, they neither took it very seriously nor thought about it in any focused manner. There seems to have been little consciousness in mid-Victorian Britain or Ireland (as opposed to the situation in the USA) of the short story as a discrete kind of text with substantial artistic potential. The fluid social and cultural climate of the late nineteenth century, however, provided fertile ground for an explosion in short-story production and thinking about the short story in Britain and Ireland. The starting point of 1945 for Part II also immediately suggested itself. World War II is a major watershed in British history; at its end Elizabeth Bowen (wrongly, as it turned out) foresaw a glowing new future for short fiction in the post-war world; political, economic, and cultural developments beginning in the late 1940s have created a context for British and Irish writers in the early twenty-first century that is radically different from that of the first half of the twentieth century. However, the division between pre- and post-1945 is sometimes misleading. Elizabeth Bowen, Jean Rhys, and Julian Maclaren Ross, for example, could figure in either section.

Each part of this volume is organized in a similar fashion. Both aim to move from a general to a more particular focus. Each starts with an introduction, which attempts to chart the evolution of short fiction in the period, and to give a sense of the social and literary context relevant to the short story. Then follow essays on specific topics and genres, such as the development of the short story in Ireland from 1880 to 1945, women's writing in both periods, the detective story to 1945, or the science fiction and fantasy short story in Britain after World War II. The third section of each part is made up of discussions of the work of particular short-story writers, or even in some cases of particular short stories, for example of Hardy's *Wessex Tales* or O'Brien's "A Rose in the Heart of New York."

Authors have been encouraged to select the texts they thought most relevant to the overall scheme of the book. They have also been allowed to follow their own approaches to the topic, genre, author, or text under discussion. Thus, some essays are contextual, placing short fiction within its political and social circumstances; others are more biographical in their focus; others still concentrate on technical aspects such as narration or setting. This seems to us desirable. Within limits, the humanities are a matter of dialog. Neither formalist nor historicist has the answer to all questions. It is to be hoped that these essays and the collection as a whole have a dynamism precisely because there is not a uniformity in vision or voice. Further, it should be noted that many essays refer to the subjects of other essays. Several discuss the same authors or texts, although differently. Others imply cross references to essays that precede or follow them. This is surely desirable, and is part of the internal dialog that we wished this book to have. All essays are, however, distinguished by the fact that they are interested in the specifics of specific concrete texts.

Limits of space (even in a volume of a quarter of a million words) have entailed cruel choices. No separate essays on Walter de la Mare, Sylvia Townsend Warner, Mary Lavin, or Graham Swift. No A.E. Coppard, no H.E. Bates, no Naomi Mitchison, no Kate Roberts, no Graham Greene. And so on. Further, there proved to be no space for discussion of the Welsh-language, the Scottish Gaelic, and the Irish-language traditions in short fiction. But a volume like this cannot be comprehensive, and perhaps no volume should be. There are omissions of individual authors that are unfortunate, but in compensation there are general essays on women's short fiction, for example, or gay and lesbian short fiction, or post-war fantasy short stories that open up new perspectives on the short story in Britain and Ireland.

Although the short story is not quite the despised stepchild of scholarship that some commentators suggest it is, short fiction in Britain has never enjoyed the sustained scholarly attention that the novel has. In addition, in Britain, although not in Ireland (and one of the aims of this volume is to emphasize the difference of the development of the short story on the two sides of the Irish Sea), the recurrent disdain of publishers for short fiction is a commonplace, but nonetheless true. The few times in which this has been different – the *fin de siècle*, the period of early twentieth-century modernist experimentation, the paper-strapped early 1940s – do not make up for decades of discouragement and neglect. We hope that this collection of essays may do something to right the balance. The history of the short story in Britain and Ireland is a rich and complex one. There are very many canonical and non-canonical writers of short fiction whose work needs to be looked at carefully. The short story itself, by canonical and non-canonical hands alike, is a form of great achievement and possibilities. This collection of essays aims to point out those things, and to encourage further work on British and Irish short fiction, both in its moments of glory, and in its more neglected times.

Cheryl Alexander Malcolm
David Malcolm

Part I

1880–1945

Introduction

1

The British and Irish Short Story to 1945

Cheryl Alexander Malcolm and David Malcolm

1

It is a commonplace of literary studies that the British short story (although not the Irish variety) has been largely neglected by scholarship. "[E]ven now it seldom receives serious critical attention commensurate with [its] importance," Ivan Reid wrote in 1977 (Reid 1977: 1). "For a complex of reasons the short story has been largely excluded from the arena of contemporary critical debate," Clare Hanson suggested in 1989 (Hanson 1989: 1). In the same year Mary Eagleton stressed the short story's non-canonical status (qtd in Hanson 1989: 62). In 1993, Birgit Moosmüller described the British short story as "auch heute noch ein Stiefkind der Forschung" (even today a step-child of scholarship) (Moosmüller 1993: 11). Thomas H. Gullason entitled his influential essay from 1964 "The Short Story: An Underrated Art" (Gullason 1964: 13), and in an interview in 1976 V.S. Pritchett declared that "The short story is a subject that has been entirely neglected" (Pritchett 1976: 425).

However, although there has been scholarly neglect of the British short story (and it must be stressed again that this is less true of Irish short fiction), this neglect has been relative rather than absolute, and, indeed, in the last decade there has emerged a substantial body of commentary on British short fiction. The scholars quoted above, Reid, Hanson, Moosmüller and Gullason, have themselves done much to efface the neglect of which they write. In addition, T.O. Beachcroft (1968), Walter Allen (1981), Joseph M. Flora (1985), Dennis Vannatta (1985), Valerie Shaw (1983), and Dominic Head (1992) have edited or written important and widely read books about British short fiction. Several volumes of the *Dictionary of Literary Biography* have been devoted to British and Irish short-story writers (the most recent was published in 2006). Barbara Korte's excellent *The Short Story in Britain* was published in 2003, Arno Löffler's and Eberhard Späth's thorough collection of essays, *Geschichte der englischen Kurzgeschichte* appeared in 2005, and Andrew Maunder's comprehensive *The Facts on File Companion to the British Short Story* came out in 2007. Further, the pages of *Studies in Short Fiction* and the *Journal of the Short Story in English* contain many essays on British short fiction. The history of British and Irish short fiction has been closely examined by Korte (2003) and by Harold Orel (1986), while Alastair Fowler dedicates considerable parts of his 1987 *A History of English Literature* to the late nineteenth- and twentieth-century short story and its Romantic and Victorian predecessors (Fowler 1987: 302–10; 335–42). Theoretical aspects of short fiction (its distinctive features, its relation to time, to human psychology, and to the social world) have also been dealt with, for example, by Reid (1977) and, notably, by Charles E. May (1976, 1984, 1994, 1995). But even if there have been elements of neglect in scholars' approach to British short fiction, this is not the case with regard to its Irish equivalent. In twentieth-century anglophone literary studies, the Irish short story has long enjoyed canonical status, and general studies such as those of Patrick Rafroidi and Terence Brown (1979) and James F. Kilroy (1984) are supplemented by an extensive scholarly literature on, for example, the work of James Joyce, Seán O'Faoláin, Mary Beckett, Edna O'Brien, John McGahern, William Trevor, Bernard MacLaverty, and Eilis Ní Duibhne. The short story in Britain, and certainly in Ireland, is not quite the stepchild of scholarship that Moosmüller writes of, and, as Maunder observes, "The acknowledgement of the short story's place in Britain's literary history is one of the most striking developments of recent years" (Maunder 2007: v).

However, there are surprising complexities within studies in short fiction, many to do with the defining features of the short story and its status as a genre. Reid entitles the first chapter of his monograph on the short story "Problems of Definition" (1977: 1), and Valerie Shaw judges that "It seems reasonable to say that a firm definition of the short story is impossible. No single theory can encompass the multifarious nature of a genre in which the only constant feature seems to be the achievement of a narrative purpose in a comparatively short space" (Shaw 1983: 21). A sense that the short story is difficult to define is widespread among its critics, who worry about how long or short a short story can be, whether the story materials of short stories are distinctive in any way, or whether short stories tend to focus on particular kinds of characters and experiences. There is, however, a considerable amount of helpful theoretical discussion of the short story (the work of Charles E. May is a notable example). Most short stories, one can conclude, are clearly considerably shorter than most novels (although there are cases open to doubt, for example, Joseph Conrad's "Heart of Darkness" or Ian McEwan's *The Cement Garden*). Anthony Burgess's suggestion that prose fictional texts can be best understood as existing on a cline from the simplest and briefest anecdote to the longest *roman fleuve* is useful (qtd in Monod 1984: 31). The short story's shortness influences the story material it can contain and the depth in which it can explore its characters. As we argue elsewhere: "Story material must be less complex and extensive than that of the novel; characters can not be developed as they can in novels" (Malcolm and Malcolm 2006: xv). Various commentators (from Poe onwards) have also pointed to the way in which the short story often patterns events to build a highly integrated whole, reminiscent of the lyric poem. They have also argued that the brevity of the short story does not prevent it functioning as a type of synecdoche or metaphor, suggesting that it is part of or illustrates a character's life, a community, or a society. Indeed, many commentators point out that an elliptical suggestiveness is characteristic of most short stories. In addition, a number of theorists of the short story have argued (taking their cue from Frank O'Connor) that the fragmentariness of the short story means that it is particularly good at embodying the voices and the fragmentary experiences of those who are outside the mainstream, the authoritative and comprehensive discourses, the dominant power structures, of their worlds – the poor, the humble, the alienated, the provincial, the colonized, the psychologically disturbed, children, adolescents, or women. Once again, this last (the bodying forth of the marginal voice, the fragment of experience) suggests a connection between the short story and the lyric poem (a connection indicated by writers as diverse as Elizabeth Bowen, Muriel Spark, and John Wain) (Bowen 1937: 7; Spark 1989: 12; Monod 1984: 51).

Many of the problems of definition with respect to the short story apply equally to the novel. However, they do seem to frustrate commentators on the short story more than those who theorize about the novel. Indeed, also like the novel, the short story can only with difficulty be classed as a genre, although the usage is widespread in English-language scholarship. The short story is too capacious a kind of text for that, including as it does texts of widely differing length, subject matter, and conventions. If the sonnet and science fiction are genres, the short story cannot be, but must be denominated differently. It is surely no more, and no less, than an amorphous category or kind of prose fictional text, marked by relative brevity, that embodies concise examples of the well-established genres of literary history and the literary present – *inter alia*, science fiction, the detective story, social-psychological fiction, the beast fable, the supernatural (or horror) story, historical fiction, gothic fiction, the parable, or the legend. Arthur Conan Doyle's "The Adventure of Silver Blaze," Rudyard Kipling's "They," V.S. Pritchett's "When My Girl Comes Home," J.G. Ballard's "Thirteen to Centaurus," Michael Moorcock's "Sojan the Swordsman," Maeve Binchy's "The Ten Snaps of Christmas," and Angela Carter's "The Courtship of Mr Lyon" are all short stories, but they belong to different genres and operate with quite different literary conventions.

The history of the short story in English (in Britain and Ireland) is now quite well understood. Short fictional prose narratives are a very old type of text, and pieces of short fiction have existed in Europe since classical times. (In the medieval period, many short narratives were written in verse, but they are still seen by scholars as part of the history of the short story.) R.C. Feddersen notes that:

> After the fall of Rome in the fifth century A.D., many classical tales (including those of Ovid's *Metamorphoses*) were submerged or Christianized, but short didactic tales thrived in medieval times (often transmitted orally) and encouraged religious devotion. The *contes dévots*, believed to have originated with the early Christians, were pious tales in French verse meant to succor the lagging spirit. Later, *exempla* (short narratives used to illustrate sermons) became latter-day parables for the clergy. In the thirteenth and

fourteenth centuries, *exempla* were compiled into volumes and indexed. (Feddersen 2001: xvi)

Korte provides a discussion of some of the main landmarks in the early development of short fiction in the British Isles: the *Hundred Merry Tales* (1526), cony-catching pamphlets (Elizabethan crime fiction), stories set within the proto-bourgeoisie of the late sixteenth century, short narratives from the Restoration, essays with narrative elements, and character sketches (Korte 2003: 35–47). Korte also writes in detail of the development of short narratives in the eighteenth and early nineteenth centuries. She points out the importance of periodicals of varying kinds in providing an outlet for short fiction. Daniel Defoe, Samuel Johnson, Joseph Addison, Oliver Goldsmith, Leigh Hunt, the Lambs, Mary Wollstonecraft, and a host of lesser-known writers produced short prose narratives in this period, and various kinds of clearly defined short narrative emerged: the character sketch, the short didactic anecdote, socially critical stories, stories of sentiment and education, the gothic tale, and tales of provincial life (Korte 2003: 47–72). This picture is confirmed by John R. Greenfield (Greenfield 1996: xii).

The fullest discussion of the development of "abbreviated fiction" (Orel 1986: 1) in the nineteenth century is given by Harold Orel in his authoritative *The Victorian Short Story: Development and Triumph of a Genre*. He insists that "short stories matured as a genre during the Victorian period" (1), and in separate chapters deals with the work of William Carleton, Joseph Sheridan Le Fanu, Charles Dickens, Anthony Trollope, Thomas Hardy, Robert Louis Stevenson, Rudyard Kipling, Joseph Conrad, and H.G. Wells. Orel's discussion of the presence of short fiction in early and mid-nineteenth-century periodicals is of great interest (8–11). Orel's work and that of Greenfield and Korte make it clear how widespread the writing of short fiction was among mid-nineteenth-century authors. Major writers wrote short narratives, although they did not make substantial sums of money by doing so (Baldwin 1993: 29–31). Early and high Victorian short fiction, like the novel, takes the form of social-psychological texts, gothic and sensational fiction, crime stories, and stories of colonial adventure. Many of its practitioners were women (Korte 2003: 72–89; Greenfield 1996: xiii–xv). The short story was a prominent and important kind of text for the first eighty years of the nineteenth century. Indeed, Orel makes a strong case for the quality of these pieces of short fiction (1986: 4).

But, as critics point out, in Britain for much of the nineteenth century short fiction was undervalued and scarcely reflected on by its practitioners and readers. Reid is wrong when he says of major Victorian writers that "their output of short fiction during the nineteenth century was virtually negligible" (1977: 28–9), but for the Victorian writer and publisher (even of a periodical), the novel or the serial novel was the preferred type of fictional text (Korte 2003: 74). Before 1880, one can observe, above all, a lack of interest in short fiction among authors, even when they write it. Of short-fiction writers between 1800 and 1880, Greenfield declares that they "made unique contributions to the short-fiction form, even though none of them probably would have identified himself or herself as primarily a writer of short fiction" (1996: xiii). Of Dickens's relation to short fiction, Orel notes that he "worked without a clear definition of the genre" (1986: 64), and "His short stories . . . were evidently by-products and on occasion only filler materials" (1986: 64). "Trollope," Orel observes, "like Dickens earned his bread and butter from his novels, and thought his short stories commercially viable, but on the whole marginal material for the making of a reputation" (1986: 79). Writers in Britain appear not to have reflected on the nature of the short story at all, and had little sense of it as a discrete kind of fiction. In an influential essay, entitled "The Tardy Evolution of the British Short Story," Dean Baldwin argues that "One of the more curious anomalies of literary history is why the short story was so late to blossom in Britain" (1993: 23). He contrasts the interest from the mid-nineteenth century in short fiction in the USA and in continental Europe with the disregard or relative ignoring of it in Britain. In the 1840s Edgar Allan Poe was already reflecting on the nature and aims of short fiction (although he used the terms "tale" and "sketch" to discuss it (Reid 1977: 25)), and, even in the 1880s, the American Brander Matthews developed Poe's ideas in influential articles (Baldwin 1993: 31). Commentators relate the importance of short fiction within the US literary world to the domination of British novels within the fiction market; the relative neglect of short fiction in Britain has a similar cause – the prestige of the long novel, and the economics of the publishing world which made such novels profitable. Most scholars agree that, in the 1880s, technological change, changes in periodical publishing, the development of a much larger reading public as a result of education reform, and the exhaustion and automatization of the traditional three-volume novel, produced circumstances in which the short story could become widely written, published and (at least more than earlier) discussed. Even Orel, who thinks highly of pre-1880 Victorian short fiction, and who sees the roots of much of the late nineteenth- and early twentieth-century short story in that short fiction, endorses the scholarly consensus as "substantially correct" (1986: 11). After 1880 (approximately) it makes sense to talk about the short story in Britain as a discrete type of text which is taken seriously and, to a degree, thought about by writers and critics (Hanson 1985: 8).

The last two decades of the nineteenth century and the early years of the twentieth were certainly a time of considerable political, social, intellectual, and artistic ferment, conducive to a revision of literary hierarchies. "Disaffection is indeed a key term in reviewing the climate of the closing years of the century in which the short story flourished," notes Clare Hanson (1985: 12). The reconsideration in the 1880s and 1890s of Victorian values in art and social conduct, and the contemporary challenges to the status quo from organized labor, women, and nationalism among colonized peoples have been thoroughly documented by literary historians. Bernard Bergonzi has written particularly clearly on the complex tensions of *fin-de-siècle* and pre-1914 Britain and Ireland (1965: 30–1). This is a period which sees an explosion of production of and interest in short fiction, and a clear idea of the short story as a discrete kind of fictional text. The term itself began to be widely used in the early twentieth century (Korte 2003: 115–18; Reid 1977: 1).

As the essays in the first part of this volume demonstrate, the short story in the late nineteenth and early twentieth centuries took several forms. Very rapidly it continued developments in the high Victorian period and diversified over a wide genre spectrum – psychological studies, social criticism and commentary, detective fiction, supernatural tales, proto science fiction, and stories of imperial adventure. In addition, the modernist writers Joseph Conrad and Virginia Woolf offered radical experiments in narration, narrative, and language use in their short fiction (Head 1992: 36, 205; Hanson 1985: 55–81). The role of women writers in this period was particularly marked. The Irish short story followed its own line of development, although this interwove with that of mainland Britain (Rafroidi 1979: 27–38; Norris 1979: 39–62).

The period after the Great War of 1914–18 remained one of some vitality in the short story. The disruptions of Irish history and the developments of Irish society during the war against the British, the Civil War, and the period of national reflection that followed proved particularly stimulating for the short story. In Britain, Korte notes substantive commentary on the short story in the *Times Literary Supplement* in 1925 and 1936, and also comments on the space given over to short fiction in avant-garde publications in the 1920s and 1930s. Further, anthologies of short stories were common in this period and the short story found a welcome in a wide range of journals (Korte 2003: 115–18). H. Gustav Klaus discusses the presence of working-class short fiction in the 1920s (1986: 29–42), and the role of fiction magazines in the 1930s in promoting short fiction is documented by Peter Martin (1979: 233–40). Elizabeth Bowen's influential collection of short stories, *The Faber Book of Modern Stories*, was published in 1937. In her introduction, Bowen sees the short story as a modern form, a fiction of and for the fragmented, disturbed and disturbing twentieth century. She concludes by insisting that "The present state of the short story is, on the whole, healthy: its prospects are good" (Bowen 1937: 18).

This prediction was almost immediately borne out. World War II was good for the short story in Britain. Bergonzi presents the situation thus:

> During the war the preferred form for new fiction writers was the short story, or the prose sketch that draws directly on experience but may lightly fictionalize it. If they were lucky they might get published in *Penguin New Writing* or even in *Horizon*, which published fewer stories and was more choosy but also came out more often, monthly rather than three or four times a year. But for those who could not make it in these prestigious publications there were many other outlets in magazines that survived from before the war, or in the irregularly appearing literary miscellanies that were launched subsequently. It is a sobering thought that in the midst of war despite the effects of bombing and an acute shortage of paper as well as other commodities, there were far more publications where a new writer could hope to place serious short stories than is the case fifty years later. (Bergonzi 1993: 40)

Bergonzi notes the main varieties of short fiction during World War II: accounts of army life, texts dealing with the violence of the bombing of British cities, and stories by women about their experiences during the war (1993: 40–5). In 1945 Bowen herself saw wartime London as an especially fruitful site and source for short stories (qtd in Beachcroft 1968: 212). H.E. Bates had gone even further in 1941 when he predicted that the short story would be "the essential medium" for writing about the post-war world (qtd in Beachcroft 1968: 212). How right or wrong he was will be seen in the second half of this volume.

The period 1880–1945 is particularly rich in short stories. Major writers gave their attention to short fiction; some made their reputation through it. The essays that follow aim to indicate this richness and discuss some of the central short stories of the period. However, it is particularly striking how many largely non-canonical writers also produced short fiction of considerable merit in these years. In the remainder of this essay we will analyze work by two partially forgotten, certainly underrated and underdiscussed, short-story writers – Hubert Crackanthorpe and Alun Lewis – each from a different end of the period under discussion. The commentary that follows on their texts should suggest the riches of the non-canonical short story between 1880 and 1945, and provide stimulus for further research.

2

"Of the lesser-known fiction writers of the nineties . . . the most talented, the most important and the most undervalued is Hubert Crackanthorpe," declares William Peden (Peden 1977: vii). In his short life (1870–96), Crackanthorpe published three volumes of short stories, *Wreckage: Seven Studies* (1893), *Sentimental Studies and a Set of Village Tales* (1895), and *Vignettes* (1896). One volume, *Last Studies*, was published posthumously (with a laudatory preface by Henry James). He was also closely involved with avant-garde literary periodicals of the 1890s, *The Yellow Book* and *Albemarle*. The reception of his work was and has been mixed, but he is certainly seen as a significant short-story writer of the 1890s, and his work has been compared to that of Maupassant, James, and Lawrence (Fisher 1994: 61; Peden 1977: ix–x). His work in the short story is very much part of the 1890s, a decade in which, as Crackanthorpe himself wrote, "Books are published, stories are printed . . . which would never have been tolerated a few years ago" (qtd in Frierson 1942: 43).

Crackanthorpe's short fiction is marked by complexity and innovation, both in terms of narrational and narrative technique and of subject matter. A representative and substantial story is "Profiles" from Crackanthorpe's first collection *Wreckage*. "Profiles" starts a sequence of stories in *Wreckage* that deal in powerful tensions between male and female characters. Several involve the destruction of one or more of the central figures. "A Conflict of Egoisms" ends in despair and suicide. "The Struggle for Life" involves violence and forced prostitution, "Dissolving View" extra-marital pregnancy and death, and "A Dead Woman" adultery and jealousy. In "When

Greek Meets Greek" two of the protagonists overcome the tensions between them, although a third is disgraced and ruined; and in "Embers," despite its depiction of the cynical exploitation, almost to the point of ruination, of one character by another, the end is not entirely negative. Over half the stories are set in low and sordid milieus.

"Profiles" is, similarly, a story of passion, violence, and betrayal, in which the innocent Lilly, after beating her abusive aunt senseless, runs off to London, where she abandons her betrothed, Maurice, for the saturnine charms of another lover. Cast off by the latter, she rejects Maurice and, despairing, descends into casual prostitution in London. This lurid subject matter is presented with a great deal of technical skill and complexity. The material for a Victorian three-decker is condensed into fifty-three pages.

The narrator's language is appropriate to the story's brevity: paragraphs are frequently short, sentence fragments abound, and sentences are often simple or compound. There are very few examples of a high style (the inverted "Quite pale was her skin . . ." is unusual (Crackanthorpe 1969: 2)). Lexis is relatively informal or neutral, especially in the extensive passages of dialog. Narrative strategy is also consistent with abbreviation: the story is full of ellipses, in which action is omitted (this frequently occurs between the numbered sections of the story). The narrator runs a gamut of observation, analysis, and summary, but never directly comments on the characters' actions. There is no condemnation of Maurice, Lilly, or Safford for their behavior. Frierson sees this narrational neutrality as part of Crackanthorpe's inheritance from French naturalism (1925: 269). In keeping with the narrator's non-intervention in the text, the story includes long passages of almost narrator-free dialog, and substantial sections in which the narrator adopts the principal characters' points of view, and even at times moves into free indirect speech. The narrator does, however, often describe settings in brief but striking detail, and, at times, the text seems the verbal representation of a painting. See, for example, the story's opening scene (1–2), or the description of Safford's and Lilly's rooms (30, 47).

The story's subtle and innovative narration is matched by a frank and complex treatment of character. This is particularly true in the case of Lilly. The protagonists are driven by passion. Lilly loathes her aunt and does violence to her in anger (6, 11). Maurice reflects that she has become a "slave" to her "passions" (19). In her last conversation with Maurice, she speaks "bitterly" and "almost fiercely," and her voice is "hard and reckless" with "a savageness" (51). Further, the story makes no attempt to disguise the sexual nature of the characters' relations. Maurice and Lilly kiss passionately (8) and have sex in London (17–18). Lily, indeed, develops "a desperate sensuality" that frightens Maurice, and she is drawn to Safford's bull-like charms (24). But characters are not simple; they are marked rather by a dynamic instability. Maurice feels "an annoyance, vague but real" on learning of Lilly's beating of her aunt (18), and the woman's "sensuality" disturbs him (19). Lilly is both irritated by Maurice and inclined to laugh at him when he reveals his emotions to her before returning to Guildford (25). Lilly's mental state is, at times, confused and complex (26), and her feelings about Maurice, once she has told him about her relationship with Safford, are a mixture of dislike, contempt and some affection (40–2). Maurice's own attitude to the fallen Lilly similarly has conflicting elements (45, 47).

"Profiles," in its brevity, its narrational sophistication, and its open and complex treatment of sexual relations, represents Crackanthorpe's short fiction at its best. His is a body of work that embodies the strengths of British short fiction in its first period of flowering, and it deserves to be much better known.

3

"The most talented of the writers whose stories arose directly out of military life was, I believe, Alun Lewis. He is better remembered as a poet, but in my view his major gift was for fiction," declares Bergonzi (1993: 41). Lewis (1915–44) published two volumes of poetry during his life, and one posthumously. His volume of short stories, *The Last Inspection*, appeared in 1942. The types of stories in this collection are varied. It is divided into three sections. Part One is made up of stories of army life, but these are different in purpose and in subject matter. (In their presentation of the shabby and unheroic side of army life, they recall Julian Maclaren-Ross's tales of military inertia and incompetence.) "The Last Inspection" and "Private Jones" are critical of the officer class and its attitude to the war and the working-class ordinary soldiers. "It's a Long Way to Go" is a detailed account of a soldier's return home on leave. "Lance-Jack" consists of musings about army life and the psychology of soldiers waiting to go abroad. Part Two comprises stories of civilian life, often involving child characters. In Part Three the stories are all about military life and involve complex and usually unhappy relations between men and women. In "Acting Captain," for example, the eponymous Captain Cochrane treats a young woman very badly; the private Curly treats her much better, but to no avail; Private Thomas returns to Swansea to see his mortally ill wife, who then dies in an air raid. In "Ballerina" a working-class Welsh private meets an upper-class English girl; he sings for her; she dances for him; and they part.

"They Came" (which Bergonzi describes as "one of the strongest" of the texts in *The Last Inspection* (1993: 41)) tells the story of an unnamed Welsh soldier's return to his unit after some days of leave. About a third of the way through the text, the reader learns that his wife has been killed in an air raid during his leave. The story details the milieu of the army billet and some of the other soldiers. Towards the end, the protagonist gives an account of his wife's death to his friend Nobby. The story is an extremely moving one, in which terrible events and a distraught psychological state are recounted without sentimentality. "They Came" is also a rich combination of social observation, psychological detail, eyewitness testimony, and lyric prose.

The story covers a few hours of the protagonist's life, although he recalls the events of a few nights previously when his wife died. Its focus on the mundane actions of the soldier's return make the enormity of his grief even more apparent. The characters are a range of working-class soldiers, most of whom are unsavoury and unglamorous, pettily nasty non-commissioned officers, and older soldiers, one of whom is clearly deranged. The only positive characters are the young Welsh soldier and his working-class London friend, Nobby, to whom he tells the story of his wife's death, and who has the words of comfort that allow him to go on. Narrational technique, which has the text focus on the young soldier's experiences, through point of view and direct speech, underlines the separation of the protagonist from most of what surrounds him. Settings are similarly opposed. Much of the text is set in the army billet, and this is drab and sordid. However, large sections of the story are set in a much more attractive nature: on the lane down which the soldier walks, and on the "flat upland ridge" with its "dead-white grass" (Lewis 1942: 236, 241) where he talks to Nobby and where he has some kind of epiphany.

The story is rich in psychological detail, especially in its presentation of the grief-stricken protagonist, but also in the incidental portraits of the other soldiers, especially that of the insane Fred. In addition, the text functions as a piece of social observation – of social discrimination against private soldiers, of the vulgar décor of a wartime hotel, and of the sycophantic behavior of a socially-mobile sergeant. Further, the protagonist's account of his wife's death is absorbing, disturbing and moving, and surely captures some of the horror of the home front in World War II. The text's richness is completed by passages, at the beginning and end of the story, in which the prose takes on aspects of poetry and the mode is lyric, rather than narrative. Lexical and syntactic parallelisms, orchestration of sound, and a density of metaphor make these powerful passages, suggesting the possibility of beauty, recovery and transcendence in a drab and horror-filled world. The stories of *The Last Inspection*, like those of Crackanthorpe's volumes, show the deep strength of the British short story in the years between 1880 and 1945, and suggest that there is much scope for further scholarship in this area.

REFERENCES AND FURTHER READING

Allen, W. (1981). *The Short Story in English.* Oxford: Clarendon Press.

Baldwin, D. (1993). "The Tardy Evolution of the British Short Story," *Studies in Short Fiction* 30/1 (winter): 23–33.

Beachcroft, T.O. (1968). *The Modest Art: A Survey of the Short Story in English.* London, New York and Toronto: Oxford University Press.

Bergonzi, B. (1965). *Heroes' Twilight: A Study of the Literature of the Great War.* London: Constable.

Bergonzi, B. (1993). *Wartime and Aftermath: English Literature and Its Background, 1939–60.* Oxford and New York: Oxford University Press.

Bowen, E. (ed.) (1937). *The Faber Book of Modern Stories.* London: Faber.

Crackanthorpe, H. (1969). *Collected Stories (1893–1897),* ed. W. Peden. Gainesville, Florida: Scholars' Facsimiles and Reprints.

Feddersen, R.C. (2001). "Introduction: A Glance at the History of the Short Story in English," in E. Fallon, R.C. Feddersen, J. Kurzleben, M.A. Lee, and S. Rochette-Crawley (eds), *A Reader's Companion to the Short Story in English,* pp. xv–xxxiv. Westport, Conn., and London: Greenwood Press.

Fisher, B.F. (1994). "Hubert Crackanthorpe," in W.B. Thesing (ed.), *British Short-Fiction Writers, 1880–1914: The Realist Tradition. Dictionary of*

Literary Biography, vol. 135. Detroit, Washington, DC, and London: Bruccoli Clark Layman/Gale Research.

Flora, J.M. (ed.) (1985). *The English Short Story, 1880–1945: A Critical History*. Boston: Twayne.

Fowler, A. (1987). *A History of English Literature: Forms and Kinds from the Middle Ages to the Present*. Oxford: Blackwell.

Frierson, W.C. (1925). *L'influence du naturalisme français sur les romanciers anglais de 1885 à 1900*. Paris: Marcel Girard.

Frierson, W.C. (1942). *The English Novel in Transition, 1885–1940*. Norman: University of Oklahoma Press.

Greenfield, J.R. (ed.) (1996). *British Short-Fiction Writers, 1800–1880*. Dictionary of Literary Biography, vol. 159. Detroit, Washington DC, London: Bruccoli Clark Layman/Gale Research.

Gullason, T. (1964). "The Short Story: An Underrated Art," *Studies in Short Fiction* 2/1 (fall): 13–31.

Hanson, C. (1985). *Short Stories and Short Fictions, 1880–1980*. London and Basingstoke: Macmillan.

Hanson, C. (ed.) (1989). *Rereading the Short Story*. Basingstoke and London: Macmillan.

Head, D. (1992). *The Modernist Short Story: A Study in Theory and Practice*. Cambridge: Cambridge University Press.

Kilroy, J.F. (ed.) (1984). *The Irish Short Story: A Critical History*. Boston: Twayne.

Klaus, H.G. (1986). "The Other Short Story: Working-class Tales of the 1920s," *Journal of the Short Story in English* 7 (autumn): 29–42.

Korte, B. (2003). *The Short Story in Britain*. Tübingen and Basel: A. Franke Verlag.

Lewis. A. (1942). *The Last Inspection*. London: George Allen and Unwin.

Löffler, A. and Späth, E. (eds) (2005). *Geschichte der englischen Kurzgeschichte*. Tübingen and Basel: A. Franke Verlag.

Malcolm, C.A. and Malcolm, D. (eds) (2006). *British and Irish Short-Fiction Writers, 1945–2000*. Dictionary of Literary Biography, vol. 319. Detroit, New York, San Francisco, San Diego, New Haven, Waterville, London and Munich: Thomson/Gale.

Martin, P.A. (1979). "The Short Story in England: 1930s Fiction Magazines," *Studies in Short Fiction* 16/1 (winter): 233–40.

Maunder, A. (ed.) (2007). *The Facts on File Companion to the British Short Story*. New York: Facts on File.

May, C.E. (1976). "The Unique Effect of the Short Story: A Reconsideration and an Example," *Studies in Short Fiction* 13: 289–97.

May, C.E. (1984). "The Nature of Knowledge in Short Fiction," *Studies in Short Fiction* 21/4 (fall): 327–38.

May, C.E. (ed.) (1994). *The New Short Story Theories*. Athens: Ohio University Press.

May, C.E. (1995). *The Short Story: The Reality of Artifice*. New York: Twayne.

Monod, S. (1984). "Quatre auteurs en quête d'un genre," *Journal of the Short Story in English* 2 (January): 11–76.

Moosmüller, Birgit (1993). *Die experimentelle englische Kurzgeschichte der Gegenwart*. Munich: Wilhelm Fink Verlag.

Norris, D. (1979). "Imaginative Response versus Authority Structures: A Theme of the Anglo-Irish Short Story," in P. Rafroidi and T. Brown (eds) (1979), *The Irish Short Story*, pp. 39–62. Gerrards Cross, Bucks: Colin Smythe; Atlantic Highlands, NJ: Humanities Press.

Orel, H. (1986). *The Victorian Short Story: Development and Triumph of a Literary Genre*. Cambridge: Cambridge University Press.

Peden, W. (1977). "Foreword," in D. Crackanthorpe, *Hubert Crackanthorpe and English Realism in the 1890s*. Columbia and London: University of Missouri Press.

Pritchett, V.S. (1976). "An Interview," *Studies in Short Fiction* 13: 423–7.

Rafroidi, P. (1979). "The Irish Short Story in English: The Birth of a New Tradition," in P. Rafroidi and T. Brown (eds) (1979), *The Irish Short Story*, pp. 27–38. Gerrards Cross, Bucks: Colin Smythe; Atlantic Highlands, NJ: Humanities Press.

Rafroidi, P. and Brown, T. (eds) (1979). *The Irish Short Story*. Gerrards Cross, Bucks: Colin Smythe; Atlantic Highlands, NJ: Humanities Press.

Reid, I. (1977). *The Short Story*. London: Methuen; New York: Barnes and Noble.

Shaw, V. (1983). *The Short Story: A Critical Introduction*. London and New York: Longman.

Spark, M. (1989). "An Interview," *Journal of the Short Story in English* 13 (autumn): 11–22.

Vannatta, D. (ed.) (1985). *The English Short Story, 1945–1980: A Critical History*. Boston: Twayne.

Topics and Genres

2

The Story of Colonial Adventure

Mariadele Boccardi

There is an interesting coincidence of dates between the period generally identified as the age of empire and the emergence, flourishing and establishment of the short story as a codified and recognizable form. The former broadly extends from 1876 (the year Queen Victoria received the title of Empress of India) to 1914, when the outbreak of World War I diverted both political attention and the public imagination away from the farthest territories under British rule and back to the heart of Europe. The stages in the development of the short story can be traced firstly to 1882, to Brander Matthews's theoretical engagement with the form and the coining of the term "short story"; then to the mid-1890s, when the appearance on the publishing scene of magazines such as *The Yellow Book* and *The Strand* offered an outlet to short-story writers; and finally to the last years of the nineteenth century and the first decade of the twentieth, when the authoritative and long-established *Edinburgh Blackwood's Magazine* gave simultaneous space to tales set in the empire and to political and philosophical essays on the nature, scope, and direction of the British colonial enterprise. The short story of colonial adventure is thus a particular instance of a broader re-thinking of narrative genres at the turn of the century, which led to the programmatic and self-conscious adoption of short narrative forms. The form of the short story gave literary form to specific assumptions with regard to the nature of perception, the limitations and artificiality inherent in shaping a story according to a beginning-middle-end structure, and more generally the perspective from which the subject of representation is approached (see Shaw 1983). At the same time, as Martin Green makes clear in his seminal study of the adventure genre, the literature of adventure had had a hold over the national imagination ever since *Robinson Crusoe* and had performed an ideological function as "the energizing myth of English imperialism" (1980: 3). Without distinguishing systematically between full-length novel and shorter tale, Green suggests that the inherited "great tradition" of Austen, Eliot, James, and Lawrence (in other words, the feminine domestic novel) is in fact misleading as an index of popularity and influence on the reading public. Rather, an alternative tradition (with masculine adventure as its subject matter), encompassing Defoe, Scott, Stevenson, and Kipling, held sway in the public imagination.

Two aspects emerging from the intersection of the respective implications of the form (the short story) and the subject matter (the colonial adventure) help to define this essay's engagement with a third literary genealogy, that of the colonial adventure short story, which goes from Kipling and Stevenson to Conrad, Buchan, and Somerset Maugham. The first aspect refers to the relationship between ideology and popular culture; the second to the predominantly textual experience of empire on the part of the British public. Following Green, Richard Phillips has confirmed that "[a]dventure was perhaps the most popular literature . . . of the modern period" (1997: 10). This popularity necessarily entails a complex relationship with the forming and directing of the opinions of a large part of the British public, whose first-hand experience of adventure was minimal, but who were nevertheless granted the sense of being part of a common enterprise – the conquering of far-away territories and the bringing of those territories under the "civilized" umbrella of the British Empire. Thus, "during the growth of popular imperialism in the mid-to-late nineteenth century" colonial adventure stories "became myths of nationhood itself, providing a cultural focus around which the national community could cohere" (Dawson 1994: 1). The adventure genre's role in simultaneously projecting and imposing a hegemonic attitude towards the imperial enterprise is outlined by Jeffrey Richards: "Popular fiction is one of the ways by which society instructs its members in its prevailing ideas and mores, its dominant role models and legitimate aspirations. It both reflects popular attitudes, ideas and preconceptions and it generates support for selected views and opinions. So it can act – sometimes simultaneously – as a form of social control . . . and as a mirror of widely-held popular views" (Richards 1989: 1). This ideological function of literature, which manifests itself as the propagation of "[e]nergizing ideas and propaganda," was as important to the shaping and preserving of the empire as "railways, canals, and the Maxim guns" (Boehmer 1995: 31–2).

Colonial adventure fiction thus provided an overarching framework for individual and state-sponsored acts of exploration, expansion, and the claiming of new territories; the framework offered a morally defensible motive for the imperial enterprise and allowed readers to enjoy the "series of events that outrage civilised or domestic morality" (Green 1993: 4) without feeling guilty. Indeed, the imperial theme generated a plethora of non-fiction writings that contributed to the scaffolding of the framework. Conrad's tale "An Outpost of Progress" articulates the ways in which agents of a colonial company whose motives and goals were wholly economic and exploitative find a *raison d'être* for their existence in an isolated African station in an article on "Our Colonial Expansion," which "spoke much of the rights and duties of civilization, of the sacredness of the civilizing work, and extolled the merits of those who went about bringing light, and faith and commerce to the dark places of the earth" (1992b: 44). The attitude towards the colonial enterprise the article expresses is symptomatic of an ideological sleight of hand, whereby trade and morality are conflated, with the help of a careful rhetorical arrangement that places "rights" before "duties", "light and faith" before "commerce," and borrows equally from the discourses of humanitarianism and evangelicalism. The effect of the reading is remarkable, as the two agents, otherwise hapless in all practical matters and wholly inadequate as colonists, see themselves as the founders of "civilization . . . and virtue" (44) in that remote corner of the world. Even more interestingly, they imagine themselves as the subject of writing for future colonists, who "will read that two good fellows, Kayerts and Carlier, were the first civilised men to live in this very spot" (44). Where Kayerts and Carlier take the "high-flown language" (44) of the article at face value, and themselves seriously, Conrad's tale is charged with irony arising from the discrepancy between the colonists' view of themselves and what the narrator shows them doing. In the process, the story points to a tension between words and deeds that serves to probe the role of ideology as self-delusion in the men's failure. By the end of the tale, when they are both dead, these would-be harbingers of civilization have suffered the loss of their enslaved workforce in exchange for ivory, have experienced near-starvation, and have finally gone mad. Both literally and metaphorically, they have been first degraded and then killed by the very commerce that they accepted was synonymous with their civilizing mission: not only is the need for ivory in order to maintain their post with the company the cause of their starvation, since they are unable to do anything without the workers they have sold in exchange for it; the Director of the Company's cynicism in sending them to a remote outpost, while aware of their inadequacy, is also at the origin of events and is compounded by his slowness in visiting the station.

If textual production informed the colonial enterprise for those that were involved with it, it did so even more pervasively for the great majority of the public, who were not direct participants in territorial expansion, control, and administration and had never set foot outside Britain, but nevertheless were "eager to participate even if vicariously in the excitements of British power abroad" and satisfied this desire by "a voracious appetite for missionary and explorer travelogues and adventure romances" (Boehmer 1995: 31). The reverse also applied, as colonists stranded in far-flung places in an age where travel was expensive and time-consuming gained their sense of still being part of the society they left behind in the imperial metropolis by the exchange of public news. The event that the arrival of six-week-old newspapers from Britain constitutes in the lives of civil servants and planters is a recurrent theme in Somerset Maugham's Malayan stories. It is an interesting paradox, however, that while the expectation is for news from "home," it is in fact the colonial territory that provides the material and condition for storytelling, as exemplified by the very stories in which the longing for a textual contact with Britain is portrayed. As Kipling illustrates early in the colonial short-story tradition with his long tale "The Man Who Would Be King" just when the narrator (a journalist in a colonial paper) is waiting for an item of news to arrive from home so that he can shut down the presses for the day, a *story* walks into the office from the colonial territory itself; the British news is forgotten and the narrator takes up this new colonial tale to be offered to his readers both in India and in Britain (1987e: 250–1). Life in a colonial outpost, where people find themselves isolated with only sporadic contacts with other colonists, but at the same time experience the stifling incestuousness of a narrow social circle which feeds on gossip, results in "an atmosphere that is abuzz with narrative" (Boehmer 1995: 48). A characteristic of Kipling's and Buchan's tales (as well as Maugham's) is thus their open reference to the oral nature of the stories and the importance of the act of narration itself. Interestingly, Maugham reflects on his own (and the genre's) tendency to reproduce an actual narrative exchange between men by relating it to an elemental adventurous situation – primitive hunting: "It is natural for men to tell tales, and I suppose the short story was created in the night of time when the hunter, to beguile the leisure of his fellows when they had eaten and drunk their fill, narrated by the cavern fire some fantastic incident he had heard of" (qtd in Shaw 1983: 83). The word "beguile" points to the underlying romantic traits of primitive adventure, which, however, the stories show to be as irretrievable as the original "situation of communal storytelling" among a "homogenous group" (84). The narrative situation provides a frame for the story and a strategy of containment for the "shadowy nature" of the story's subject (Hanson 1989: 87). It frequently has an interpretive function, as the narrative becomes an effort to make sense of circumstances beyond the narrator and listener's control; in turn, this operation is symbolic of the colonial experience, whose framework of meaning is granted by its re-elaboration in textual form, as "An Outpost of Progress" illustrates, even if this framework does not match the experience.

The irony that pervades Conrad's tale is only an extreme and explicit instance of a widespread approach to their subject in the authors under consideration. Arguably, the most compelling common feature in their stories is the depiction of the progressive shrinking of the landscape and condition for adventure and the latter's debasement and corruption, either as trade or as bureaucratic administration. Adventure in Kipling is open almost exclusively to "loafers" like Dravot and Carnehan in *The Man Who Would Be King*, while the responsibilities of administering the empire according to established rules are inimical to the trespassing of boundaries that adventure demands. Dravot and Carnehan's own adventure ends in disaster at the very moment when they embrace the responsibilities of their roles as kings. The contours of this paradox inherent in imperial adventure are given more definite lines in John Buchan's "Fountainblue." Its protagonist, Maitland, is an adventurer explicitly engaged in expanding the frontiers of the Empire and therefore broadening the reach of British civilization; yet he cannot himself fit within the confines of Britain, as is made clear when he attempts to woo an upper-class young woman. The story suggests that his discomfort in society is the result of having crossed the line that separates civilization and savagery and being aware of how flimsy the distinction between the two is. His ultimately self-defeating aim is "to destroy the conditions for heroism which made [his] life tolerable" (Kruse 1989: 30).

The short story, born in competition with the realism of the mid-nineteenth-century novel, thus finds itself having to negotiate the relationship between a form that emphasizes elusiveness, a generic tradition belonging to romance, and a subject matter that traces the impossibility of escaping the reality of the conditions for empire. Conrad's long tale "Youth" is the most self-conscious in exploring the gap between romantic expectations of adventure and mundane day-to-day life in a money-making enterprise. Nostalgia for adventure is embedded in the initial narrative situation as Marlow, with the customary mediation of a nameless narrator, tells the events of his first voyage in "the Eastern seas" (1992c: 151): an older, more experienced, but also disillusioned man thus attempts to recapture in the telling the beguiling experience of an innocence which consists of ignorance of the economic motives for colonial travel. The ironic tension between the narrative frame and the story is compounded by the fact that his audience is made up of "a director of companies, an accountant, a lawyer" (151), all representatives of the practical commercial organization of empire. The young Marlow's understanding of the voyage to the East is colored by the romantic echoes evoked in him by the destination of the ship, Bangkok, a "[m]agic name, blessed name" (160). Even as he dreams of the East, "the owner, the underwriters, and the charterers squabbled amongst themselves in London" (160), a juxtaposition that encapsulates the contrast between romance and commerce that pervades the story. The voyage *is* adventurous, as the crew have to deal in succession with a leaking hull, a fire on board, and an explosion on deck, but each occurrence is largely the result of a need to complete the voyage and keep the cargo safe so that investors will not suffer excessive losses. The contact with an exotic land *is* romantic: the East presents itself to Marlow's expectant eyes as "a high outline of mountains, blue and afar in the morning; like faint mist at noon; a jugged wall of purple at sunset. [. . .] And I see a bay, a wide bay, smooth as glass and polished like ice, shimmering in the dark". (176) However, this beguiling vision is soon shattered by the prosaic sound of shouting and cursing from a nearby ship, and, tellingly, "the East spoke . . . , but it was in a Western voice" (178), confirmation that the land of adventure and romance has already been contaminated by material interests. Ultimately, what is left of the experience is the very self-awareness that engenders and permeates the tale, whose subject and concluding words is "the romance of illusions" (180). In other words, and paradoxically, the story of adventure is the result of the demise of adventurous action.

A landscape of romance welcomes Wiltshire on his arrival to Falesá in Stevenson's "The Beach of Falesá": "I saw the island first when it was neither night nor morning. The moon was to the west, setting, but still broad and bright. To the east, and right amidships of the dawn, which was all pink, the daystar sparkled like a diamond" (1999a: 3). Wiltshire, however, is on the island as the agent for a large okra trading company, so that from the start his romantic approach to his surroundings clashes with the economic motives and aims that are at the basis of his being there. Under the spell of the South Seas scenery, he is prepared to accept advice on the island's customs from Case, an established trader but also an unscrupulous competitor, and it is this relationship that provides Wiltshire with the elements of an adventure. On his first night on the island, Case persuades Wiltshire to marry a native girl in a mock ceremony, without telling him that she is "taboo" and association with her will mean the inhabitants of the island will refuse to trade with him. The adventure of which Wiltshire becomes the hero unfolds from this point over two fronts: on the one hand, he shows the moral integrity in the face of obstacles of the British hero (albeit a commercial one) by officially marrying the girl at the first opportunity; on the other hand, he engages in the destruction of Case by showing up for simple tricks the apparent portents with which the trader kept the islanders under his influence. This aspect is a counterpart of the imperial ideological pitting of reason against superstition and the colonial enterprise's aim of the one triumphing against the other. In spite of these staple features of imperial adventure, however, Wiltshire (and the story) ultimately confirm the economic basis for colonial adventure, and have to bow to the real consequences of mixed marriages: while on the island, Wiltshire sticks to his pledge to "deal fairly with the natives" (70), in other words not to cheat them out of their okra, but as a result his accounts (the reason for his being on the island) are not satisfactory. He is therefore "glad when the firm moved [him] on to another station, where [he] was under no kind of a pledge"; commercial principles ultimately prevail. As to his romance with Uma, it lasts into middle age, but means that Wiltshire cannot, in the established adventure tradition, return Home in glory, as his children are "only half-castes" (71) and he freely admits that "they are better here than what they would be in a white man's country" (71). If the setting of "The Beach of Falesá" (a trading post) favors the commercial overtones of the plot, Stevenson's interest in the pairing of exotic location and economics is confirmed in "The Bottle Imp," whose fantastic subject (the proverbial genie in a bottle) is treated with a wink to market forces, as the condition for the transferring of the bottle before its evil effects become manifest is to sell it at a price lower than that at which it was bought.

Both Conrad and Buchan propose a variation on Stevenson's exploration of the potential conflict between adventure and romance. Conrad's "The Lagoon" shows a young native warrior having to choose between love and heroism, and tells of his regret at abiding by the former and letting his brother die as a result. The story presents two interesting features. Firstly, the narrator–listener exchange is between a white man and a Malay, whose equality is the result of having shared a military adventure in the past; the story thus points to adventure as a factor that can affect the racial and social boundaries around which empire is constructed. Secondly, the narrative situation sees the two men standing outside the hut where the woman at the root of the conflict outlined in the story lies dead. At the death of romance the Malay vows to engage again in adventure and avenge his brother, but, in a characteristic move for Conrad that echoes the stance in "Youth," the story sees this wish, just as much as the earlier dream of love, as unachievable, part of "a world of illusions" (1992a: 37). Buchan, on the other hand, proposes romance as a form of adventure, if other avenues are closed. The protagonist of "Basilissa" has been convinced from a young age, following a prophetic dream, that his destiny was to prove himself in an adventure. The opportunity arises during a voyage along the Greek coast, when he rescues a girl from superstitious villagers and a predatory warrior, in a situation that brings out the characteristics of the adventure hero (reason and honor). The location and the story's references, however, point to ancient history and myth, as man and woman call each other Perseus and Andromeda: the successful completion of adventure is the result of the protagonist's textually influenced understanding of adventure. The historical and social reality of empire as the ground of adventure is here abandoned in favor of the consummation of a timeless and universal desire for it, expressed in the dream that opens the story and in the words that conclude it, "I . . . have been waiting on you from the beginning of the world" (Buchan 1997c: 33).

The colonial adventure short story engaged with existing fiction that had accompanied Britain's progressive acquisition of new territories, and which is broadly encompassed within Green's parameters of adventure literature. By the 1880s, the novel set in colonial outposts and detailing the adventurous deeds of a model Englishman (frequently a boy imbued with the ethos of the public school he has just left behind) had already given rise to its own tradition, particularly in the domain of juvenile literature. Authors such as R.M. Ballantyne, G.E. Henty, and Captain Marryat had established a successful and ideologically unambiguous formula whereby a young representative of the public school-educated middle classes chose, or was forced, to make his way in a colonial outpost. The young man's ultimate triumph over anything the unfamiliar territory may throw his way is never in doubt: his race, resourcefulness, and Christian manliness, attributes he possesses from the start as a combination of genetic make-up and the nurture of the school sports grounds, ensure his success. Conversely, his success validates the social ideology of which he is both home product and representative abroad, and which he shares with his readers (White 1993: 82). The prize of the adventure is a return home (importantly, the colonial territory is a testing ground for character and the means of winning wealth and status to be brought back to England, and rarely a long-term living option), a space which is always implicitly present, if only by contrast, in the adventure narrative, "as the motive and reward of the Empire-builder [. . .,] the inspiration and justification of empire" (Bratton 1996: 78 and 87).

The juvenile adventure tradition was perpetuated in what is arguably the most successful juvenile publication of the turn of the nineteenth century, the *Boys' Own Paper,* whose first issue dates to 1879 and which, at its height at the turn of the century, boasted an estimated circulation of 665,000 copies a week (Dunae 1989: 23). The magazine specialized in serialized school stories and tales of exciting deeds; it therefore pursued the twin elements that characterized the novels of Marryat, Henty, and Ballantyne, namely, the public-school ethos and the pluck inherent in being British. James Joyce's *Dubliners* tale "An Encounter" offers intriguing and timely (the volume was published in 1914) evidence of the persistent hold over the juvenile imagination of adventure fiction in serialized form. "An

Encounter" testifies to the popularity of boys' magazines modeled on the *Boys' Own Paper*: It tells the fascination that the world evoked by papers exercises on two boys, who attempt to replicate the daring deeds they read: the story mentions "*The Union Jack, Pluck* and *The Halfpenny Marvel*" (2001: 12), whose "chronicles of disorder" fulfilled a "hunger . . . for wild sensations" and "opened doors of escape" (13). Apparent in this description are the seeds of a contradiction common to the adventure genre generally and to turn-of-the-century colonial short stories particularly: their attraction rests on their breaking of the ordered social life of the mother country, whose stifling of heroism is implicitly acknowledged even as the ostensible purpose of the adventurous action is precisely to extend the boundaries of that social order, and the reward of successful adventure is a return to the mother country. The boys' plans for action inspired by their reading peter out before they can be put into practice. While this failure to act is typical of *Dubliners* and makes this story representative of the collection's exploration of the paralysis of Irish life, it also goes to confirm the impossibility of adventure within the confines of the imperial city – even of a city as ambiguously placed with respect to the empire as Dublin.

There is a potential for subversion in the adventure situation which juvenile literature polices by marking strict boundaries within which adventure is allowed. As I pointed out earlier, the formula for boys' adventure stories sets a return to Britain and the taking up (or alternatively the regaining) of the young man's allocated place in society as the satisfactory goal of the protagonist; the adventurous deeds take place in an alien territory which is left behind both spatially and temporally. In the late-Victorian short stories of Arthur Conan Doyle, however, the policing necessary to preserve the colonial metropolis's social order becomes the focus of the action, a strategy that, while superficially reassuring, in fact reveals the precariousness of that order and the morally and socially brittle nature of the interaction between the center of the empire and its vast territorial extent. Although they are not strictly speaking colonial tales, a significant number of the Sherlock Holmes stories are concerned with the repercussions and reverberations of imperial adventure on British society. "The Boscombe Valley Mystery" is, in this sense, a good example. In it, Holmes is summoned to clear a young man of the murder of his father, a former settler in Australia. From the available clues Holmes retraces what amounts to a colonial adventure story: the victim's neighbor, also returned from Australia, had made his money as part of a gang of highwaymen and had killed to prevent his criminal (colonial) past from resurfacing in his established (metropolitan) present. This newly acquired wealth, whose colonial provenance made it unsuspicious, allowed him to "settle down to a quiet and respectable life" (2001: 91) and establish himself as a country squire, until the victim recognized him for a robber and began blackmailing him. The story thus raises a number of relevant questions about colonial adventure. Firstly, in his colonial exploits the future murderer "had a wild, free time of it" (90), enjoying the looseness of boundaries between legality and illegality offered by the colonial environment; it is this permeability of boundaries that allows for the trespassing that constitutes adventure, so the story places a spotlight on the commonality of colonial adventurous deeds, on the one hand, and the threat to the metropolitan social order posed by crime, on the other. Secondly, the fact that Turner can remain part of Boscombe society undetected is an indication that there is no intrinsic quality in the social order, whose foundation is purely wealth masquerading as moral integrity. Finally, the story's ending reveals that the internal weakness of society must remain undisclosed, as Holmes grants the murderer freedom until his imminent death from illness. This convenient way out avoids the exposure of Turner's deeds and, with it, the potential disruption of the social order; its neatness, however, is a little too pat to dispel the sense that the imperial foundations of British life are in danger of being shown up as shallow.

It is no coincidence that Robert Baden-Powell, close friend of Kipling, founder of the Scouts movement and himself involved in person in imperial adventure in the Boer War, should have recommended that would-be scouts read Conan Doyle. Holmes provided a model for the all-seeing power that "carefully notes every tell-tale detail, and then, if something is amiss . . . is equipped to report it to the authorities" (Bristow 1991: 189). Baden-Powell saw scouting as the culmination of the spirit of colonial adventure placed at the service of the state and therefore normalized, yet, in a similar way to the ideological contradiction outlined with reference to Conan Doyle's stories, its nature and success resulted from an underlying weakness: "Were the empire as naturally strong and secure as he would have liked his growing number of Scouts to believe, there would have been no need for Scouting to take off on such a grand scale in 1908" (174). Two characters in Kipling's *Plain Tales from the Hills* embody the thrills and pitfalls of conforming to Baden-Powell's conception of the Scout as all-seeing and all-knowing, "so much of his world that his powers of observation cannot themselves be observed" (189). Strickland appears in person or indirectly in a number of stories, as a policeman with complete mastery of native disguises which allow him the kind of control over his colonial surroundings that Sherlock Holmes exercises in the imperial metropolis (interestingly, his goal is "invisibility" (1987b: 24)). He is in the police, thus the institutionalized counterpart of Holmes, and can find out things to which no-one else has access, but the methods he employs to acquire information (Indian disguise, use of local slang, taking part in street life) mean that "people did not understand him" and "said he was a doubtful sort of man" (24). Society's underlying fear is of his crossing of the racial boundaries of Indian society, which involves a loss of identity not only for the individual, but, more threateningly, for the entire colonial structure of government, founded as it is on the preservation of those boundaries. When he wants to become part of the established social system through marriage, Strickland has to give up his forays into native life and resign himself to "departmental routine" (29). Crossing boundaries is at the basis of Green's definition of adventure, and once again, as was the case for Conan Doyle, it carries a destabilizing potential that needs to be neutralized by enticing the adventurer back into the social fold, either in Britain or in British India.

McIntosh Jellaludin in Kipling's "To Be Filed for Reference" is a demonstration of what happens to those who, like Strickland, shift easily between white and native identities, when they are not claimed back by the social order. McIntosh is an Oxford-educated former government official who lives as a Muslim among the natives and is unable or unwilling to cross the social boundary to rejoin the society in which he "enjoyed . . . a position rather higher" than the narrator's (1987d: 236). His present situation is either the cause or the consequence of his comprehensive knowledge of India, which he has collated in a book; at his death the book is the only thing that defines him, as "saving the big bundle of old sheets in the cloth, there was nothing in his room to say who or what he had been" (241). McIntosh has thus achieved the ultimate embodiment of the scouting ideal, losing his very existence except as an all-seeing entity, but in the process he has suffered "damnation" (241), both spiritual and social. It is telling that the story leaves the question of the book's role in McIntosh's degradation unresolved: it is unclear whether the all-consuming knowledge of India the book testifies to could only be achieved at the expense of social and racial identity, or whether it is only the loss of that identity which permits the acquisition of the knowledge set out in the book. Perhaps like the events that led to the Boy's suicide in "Thrown Away" (discussed below), either possibility is too disturbing to contemplate openly, and the impasse is furthered by the fact that McIntosh calls Strickland ignorant, while Strickland claims McIntosh is a liar.

The adventures narrated in John Buchan's "The Grove of Ashtaroth" and "The Green Wildebeest" are embarked upon during surveying expeditions in South Africa, a commercialized version of scouting. Contrary to established tradition, however, the closeness between the scout and the land makes the impossibility of ultimate control of one over the other more apparent. Primitive and unstoppable forces take possession of characters in the two stories, thus revealing the coloniers' own susceptibility to the lure of the primitive, which also has connotations of the mythical and the timeless: the grove of Ashtaroth is "a temple as old as time, and in a land which they say has no history" (1997b: 150). In what is an orgasmic experience in contact with the grove, the narrator discovers "wild knowledge", in contrast with the objective knowledge sought in his professional capacity. The destruction of the grove is inevitable if control over the territory is to be maintained, but the destruction is perceived as sacrilege, "the sin against light which knows no forgiveness" (164). The consequences of such actions are explored in "The Green Wildebeest," where the trespassing of a sacred space haunts the perpetrator into madness, violence, and eventual death.

Whether in India, Africa, or Britain, the instability of identity and of the social order seems inescapable. It is further emphasized by the form in which Holmes's investigations and Kipling's portrait of life in India are presented – the short story. While each investigation is successfully concluded in itself, and therefore by the end of each story Holmes has succeeded in preserving order in the imperial center, the very need for further detection and policing in each story only reiterates the constant threat of disorder emanating from the imperial periphery (detectable in the succession of opium dens, exotic weapons, "dark" strangers that populate the stories) and the

ultimately piecemeal nature of Holmes's investigative feats. As for Kipling's compos-
ite picture of India, it emphasizes the partiality of the white man's experience and
understanding of the country. In an ironic comment on British self-delusion about
their knowledge of what is good for India, "Tod's Amendment" shows that a small
child is more aware of Indian feelings about a proposed piece of legislation than the
British rulers and their advisers. The careful framing of the stories collected in *Plain
Tales from the Hills* stresses possible different versions of the stories, to which the narrator has no access either because of his gender or his race. The impression of a fragmentary understanding is reproduced and enhanced by the extreme briefness of the
stories, whose abrupt beginnings and endings leave the sense of events beyond interpretation. Even when the circumstances surrounding the events are clear to those
involved, they disclose the less palatable aspects of British life in India, so horrific
that they cannot be disclosed and what the story tells is the cover up. "Thrown Away"
illustrates the dangers of believing that the same standards of morality apply in India
as in Britain: a young soldier (only known in the story as "The Boy," as if to stress
the universality of his situation) arriving on colonial duty finds that he cannot live
up to the image of himself and his parents' expectations and shoots himself. The story,
however, does not spell out either the impulses or the actions that led to the boy's
suicide; instead, it centers on the cover-up that the narrator and the boy's Major
engineer to prevent his actions from reaching his parents and fiancée: "It was utterly
impossible to let the letters go Home. They would have broken his father's heart and
killed his mother after killing her belief in her son" (1987a: 21). The narrator's complicity in the cover-up is part of his "profession" (19) as a journalist. Given the pervasiveness of the authorial voice in the *Tales,* and its identification with the narrator,
the story by implication casts doubts on the veracity of the entire volume and raises
the suspicion that much of the reality of India is being wilfully withheld.

Problems of interpretation are even more prominent in Kipling's Boer War stories.
The lack of understanding in "A Sahib's War" is lodged initially with the narrator,
a Sikh soldier who finds himself in a land he does not understand, but goes on to
include the reader, since the Sikh's story has to be glossed by a listener who understands his language, although even he at times is unsure of the accuracy of his interpretation. The story itself is one of colonial adventure, as the Sikh follows his master
(Corbyn, a young British soldier) from Punjab to South Africa in search of glory in
the war, in what appears at first as a staple adventurous situation. However, the
conduct of the war poses further interpretive difficulties to the Sikh, in so far as it
does not conform to the parameters of organized military campaigns. Interestingly,
Corbyn and the Sikh rely for help and a more solid understanding of the strategies
to be used in such unfamiliar territory on Canadian and Australian soldiers, in what
is presented as a show of imperial solidarity, but could also be read as a need for
further mediation of the imperial subject-matter within the story. In spite of the
obvious potential for a conventional adventure plot, the story concludes with the
telling of Corbyn's death, just as, in a conventional scene from adventure fiction, he
is rejoicing from having escaped being shot. What remains of him is an inscription

on a memorial and even then what the commemorative words refer to (a Boer house) has been destroyed by the very men who carved them. "The Comprehension of Private Copper" pursues the implications of a similar gap between events and their textual articulation, as a young working-class soldier gains awareness of the differences between his actual experience of war and what newspapers at home claim that experience to be. Once again the distance from home offers the scope for heroic adventure, but the chance is thwarted by the "mass media . . . governing the representation of the war" (Hagiioannu 2003: 143). In what amounts to a self-defeating disillusion with the reliability of colonial representation, of which he was after all the prime provider commissioned to write about South Africa by the very newspapers whose aims he calls into question, Kipling emphasizes the untrustworthiness of textual renderings of the empire, to the extent that Paula Krebs suggests that while the South African stories "attempt to do *imperial* duty," "they are evidence that imperial stories are impossible" (1999: 169).

The precariousness of this shadowy picture of the empire from inside the imperial metropolis as from its furthest outposts points to the disruptive effect of the short story form on the ostensible ideological self-positioning of colonial adventure tales and signals a clear departure from the broader tradition of the adventure genre. Even though they appeared in instalments, the *B.O.P.*'s tales, like their predecessors already available in book form, rested secure in the breadth of scope, comprehensiveness of subject matter, and coherence of treatment guaranteed by the novel form. The adventurers-protagonists' control over the colonial environment was thus mirrored by the novel form's control over its subject. However, the authors that form the subject of this essay exploit the form of the short story to provide a far less univocal, comprehensive, or optimistic vision of the day-to-day ruling of colonial possessions; the stories are aimed at an adult audience, whose complacent security – born of ideologically blind ignorance of the reality of empire or resulting from the mistaken belief of comprehensive knowledge – they seek to undermine.

Somerset Maugham's stories reprise the tradition of the colonial short story with a degree of self-awareness arguably resulting from the changed attitude towards colonial possessions after World War I, from expansionary goals to administrative retrenchment. The narrator–listener relationship in his Malayan stories frequently involves a policeman or district magistrate, as if to emphasize the institutionalization of the mechanisms of control in the alien territory: the narrative situation thus foregrounds the boundaries of colonial society even as the story itself tells of the breaking of such boundaries. The potential for disruption inherent in adventure is thus more explicitly articulated and more substantially framed than in the earlier authors discussed in this essay. As Philip Holden points out, "binary oppositions" (of race, class, and gender) "anchor the stories" (1996: 47), but those distinctions are ever more difficult to preserve. This seems to be the result of a loss of moral certainties, in turn a consequence of Maugham's (and his characters') heightened awareness that the morality on which colonial behavior was founded was an ideological and textual construct.

"Footprints in the Jungle" is exemplary in its disturbance of the surface of colonial life: the story is told in the club of Tarah Merah, described as the most charming place in Malaya – the charm, as was the case for Stevenson and Conrad, resting in the luscious landscape, while the breaking of the place's tranquility is from within the white community. The story is told by the chief of police, appropriately named Gaze, to a guest: only the latter's transience makes it safe to relate a crime that went unpunished in the past, when Mr Cartwright and his then lover (now wife) planned and executed the murder of the woman's husband. What makes the story interesting is that the murdered husband is the exact reproduction of the heroes of juvenile adventure stories: "He was a great big fellow, very hearty, with a loud voice and a bellowing laugh, beefy, you know, and a fine athlete. There was not very much to him, but he was as straight as a die. He had a red face and red hair. [. . .] He was a handsome chap. He was always fit. He was keen on that. He hadn't much to talk about but rubber and games, tennis, you know, and golf and shooting; and I don't suppose he read a book from year's end to year's end. He was the typical public school boy. He was about thirty-five when I first knew him, but he had the mind of a boy of eighteen" (Maugham 1997b: 470). He and his wife have no children, an implicit comment on the asexuality of the juvenile adventurer, but she does becomes pregnant by the unassuming Mr Cartwright, as if to confirm that the model of the adventurer cannot be reproduced and perpetuated into the future. And yet, in Gaze's judgment, they remain "very nice people" (494); their actions were the result of necessity and do not define their moral qualities. Indeed, consistently, men of strict and unbending certitudes have nefarious effects on their surroundings: Neil MacAdam's straight-laced attitude to sexual desire causes the death of a woman, Cooper in "The Outstation" is outplayed in the management of the colonial post by his suave, morally accommodating rival Warburton, while Mackintosh, confronted by the magnanimity on his deathbed of an old-fashioned colonist he has contributed to killing, cannot live with his conscience and shoots himself. Nor is a modern rational and humanitarian approach to colonial government any more successful: Alban in "The Door of Opportunity" uses reason as an excuse for cowardice, and his wife realizes that his superior class and education are as nothing when confronted with the instinctive bravery of less favored individuals.

If the Malayan stories demonstrate Maugham's awareness of the ideology and textual tradition of adventure and his ambiguous positioning with respect to that tradition, the South Seas tales, reflect on the other aspect of colonial adventure, namely the place of romance and the imagination in the colonial enterprise, and their place vis-à-vis the economic motives for colonial expansion. They also, indirectly, point to a shift in the balance of economic power: the protagonists of the stories are no longer British civil servants but American would-be businessmen. Edward Barnard in the story to which he gives his name is a good example. A young man from Chicago who has to make his fortune in exotic locations after the loss of the family fortune, he reproduces in an American context the hero of numerous British juvenile tales. The heroism required of him is exclusively economic in nature – to make his fortune and return home to his fiancée – but once on island soil he succumbs to the romance of the place and opts out of the quest for money and, as a consequence, also relinquishes the promise of a return within the social order by means of a suitable marriage. The knot of economic, social, and moral imperatives placed on Edward Barnard are made clear by his fiancée's summing up of the situation: " I wouldn't let Edward break our engagement because I thought it would be an incentive to him. [. . .] I thought it anything could enable him to achieve success it was the thought that I loved him. I have done all I could. [. . .] Poor Edward, he's nobody's enemy but his own. He was a dear, nice fellow, but there was something lacking in him" (Maugham 1974c: 102–3). There is no questioning of the link between love and economic success, and any deviation from this model, such as Edward Barnard's, is put down to an inherent personal weakness.

"The Vessel of Wrath" tells an unconventional love story between a woman missionary and a drunk, whom she eventually reforms. The tale is told with a tinge of irony and a degree of self-consciousness apparent from the start, as the story opens with a digression on the power of "four shillings" travel books, however "business-like" and "matter-of-fact," which "cannot dim the poetry that . . . blows with so sweet a fragrance through the printed pages" and gives "mystery and beauty, romance and the glamour of the unknown" (Maugham 1997a: 3–4). The sense is of a discrepancy between the book's price and the richness of its stimuli for the imagination, and it is indeed the imagination that provides the romance, and it is the act of narration that evokes it. The love story "Red" narrates is shattered by the final revelation that the gross, banal man recently arrived on the island is the same person as the handsome young protagonist of Neilson's story: romance is revealed to have purely narrative existence, while in reality it is always threatened by the lure of money. Red is tricked into boarding a ship and is kidnapped, but he then chooses to pursue economic success rather than return to his lover. However, as the disillusioned narrator is perceptive enough to notice, Red and Sally's story maintains its romantic aura precisely because of the intervention of reality in the form of the trading ships: "I think that perhaps they should thank the ruthless fate that separated them when their love seemed still to be at its height. They suffered, but they suffered in beauty" (Maugham 1974d: 134). As was the case in "Youth," the romantic tale is the product of the "exhausted . . . romantic possibility" of the colonies (Holden 1996: 61).

References and Further Reading

Primary Texts

Buchan, J. (1997a). "Fountainblue," in A. Lownie (ed.), *The Complete Short Stories vol. 2*, pp. 25–53. London: Thistle Publishing.

Buchan, J. (1997b). "The Grove of Ashtaroth," in A. Lownie (ed.), *The Complete Short Stories vol. 2*, pp. 145–66. London: Thistle Publishing.

Buchan, J. (1997c). "Basilissa," in A. Lownie (ed.), *The Complete Short Stories vol. 3*, pp. 21–34. London: Thistle Publishing.

Buchan, J. (1997d). "The Green Wildebeest," in A. Lownie (ed.), *The Complete Short Stories vol. 3*, pp. 78–95. London: Thistle Publishing.

Conan Doyle, A. (2001). "The Boscombe Valley Mystery," in *The Adventures and the Memoirs of Sherlock Holmes,* pp. 69–93. London: Penguin.

Conrad, J. (1992a). "The Lagoon," in S. Hynes (ed.), *The Lagoon and Other Stories*, pp. 24–37. London: Pickering.

Conrad, J. (1992b). "An Outpost of Progress," in S. Hynes (ed.), *The Lagoon and Other Stories*, pp. 38–61. London: Pickering.

Conrad, J. (1992c). "Youth," in S. Hynes (ed.), *The Lagoon and Other Stories*, pp. 151–80. London: Pickering.

Joyce, J. (2001) "An Encounter," in *Dubliners*, pp. 11–18. Oxford: Oxford University Press.

Kipling, R. (1987a). "Thrown Away," in *Plain Tales from the Hills*, pp. 16–23. Oxford: Oxford University Press.

Kipling, R. (1987b). "Miss Youghal's Sais," in *Plain Tales from the Hills*, pp. 24–9. Oxford: Oxford University Press.

Kipling, R. (1987c). "Tod's Amendment," in *Plain Tales from the Hills*, pp. 144–9. Oxford: Oxford University Press.

Kipling, R. (1987d). "To be Filed for Reference," in *Plain Tales from the Hills*, pp. 234–41. Oxford: Oxford University Press.

Kipling, R. (1987e). "The Man Who Would be King," in *The Man Who Would be King and Other Stories*, pp. 244–79. Oxford: Oxford University Press.

Kipling, R. (1999a) "A Sahib's War," in *War Stories and Poems*, pp.163–80. Oxford: Oxford University Press

Kipling, R. (1999b) "The Comprehension of Private Copper," in *War Stories and Poems*, pp.183–93. Oxford: Oxford University Press.

Maugham, W.S. (1974a). "The Outstation," in *The Casuarina Tree,* pp. 76–116. London: Heinemann.

Maugham, W.S. (1974b). "Mackintosh," in *The Trembling of a Leaf*, pp. 3–54. London: Heinemann.

Maugham, W.S. (1974c). "The Fall of Edward Barnard," in *The Trembling of a Leaf*, pp. 55–104. London: Heinemann.

Maugham, W.S. (1974d). "Red," in *The Trembling of a Leaf*, pp. 105–37. London: Heinemann.

Maugham, W.S. (1997a). "The Vessel of Wrath," in *Collected Short Stories vol. 2*, pp. 3–44. London: Mandarin.

Maugham, W.S. (1997b). "Footprints in the Jungle," in *Collected Short Stories vol. 2*, pp. 460–95. London: Mandarin.

Maugham, W.S. (1997c). "The Door of Opportunity," in *Collected Short Stories vol. 2*, pp. 495–533. London: Mandarin.

Maugham, W.S. (2000). "Neil MacAdam," in *Far Eastern Tales*, pp. 184–239. London: Vintage.

Stevenson, R.L. (1999a). "The Beach of Falesá," in *South Sea Tales*, pp. 3–71. Oxford: Oxford University Press.

Stevenson, R.L. (1999b). "The Bottle Imp," in *South Sea Tales*, pp. 72–91. Oxford: Oxford University Press.

Critical Works

Boehmer, E. (1995). *Colonial and Post-Colonial Literature: Migrant Metaphors*. Oxford: Oxford University Press.

Bratton, J.S. (1996). "Of England, Home and Duty: The Image of England in Victorian and Edwardian Juvenile Fiction," in J. Mackenzie (ed.), *Imperialism and Popular Culture*, pp. 73–93. Manchester: Manchester University Press.

Bristow, J. (1991). *Empire Boys: Adventures in a Man's World.* London: HarperCollins.

Dawson, G. (1994). *Soldier Heroes: British Adventure, Empire and the Imagining of Masculinities.* London: Routledge.

Dunae, P.A. (1989). "New Grub Street for Boys," in J. Richards (ed.), *Imperialism and Juvenile Literature*, pp. 12–33. Manchester: Manchester University Press.

Green, M. (1980). *Dreams of Adventure, Deeds of Empire: A Wide-Ranging and Provocative Examination of the Great Tradition of the Literature of Adventure.* London: Routledge & Kegan Paul.

Green, M. (1993). *The Adventurous Male: Chapters in the History of the White Male Mind.* University Park: Pennsylvania State University Press.

Hagiioannu, A. (2003). *The Man Who Would Be Kipling: The Colonial Fiction and the Frontiers of Exile.* Basingstoke: Palgrave.

Hanson, C. (ed.) (1989). *Rereading the Short Story.* Basingstoke and London: Macmillan.

Holden, P. (1996). *Orienting Masculinity, Orienting Nation: W. Somerset Maugham's Exotic Fiction.* Westport: Greenwood Press.

Krebs, P.M. (1999). *Gender, Race, and the Writing of Empire: Public Discourse and the Boer War.* Cambridge: Cambridge University Press.

Kruse, J. (1989). *John Buchan (1875–1940) and the Idea of Empire: Popular Literature and Political Ideology (Studies in British History* 7). Lewiston: Edwin Mellen.

Mackenzie, J. (ed.) (1986). *Imperialism and Popular Culture.* Manchester: Manchester University Press.

Mangan, J.A. (1986). "'The Grit of our Forefathers': Invented Traditions, Propaganda and Imperialism," in J. Mackenzie (ed.), *Imperialism and Popular Culture,* pp. 113–39.

Phillips, R. (1997). *Mapping Men & Empire: A Geography of Adventure.* London: Routledge.

Richards, J. (1989). "Introduction," in J. Richards (ed.), *Imperialism and Juvenile Literature,* pp. 1–11. Manchester: Manchester University Press.

Shaw, V. (1983). *The Short Story: A Critical Introduction.* London: Longman.

Turner, E.S. (1975). *Boys Will Be Boys.* London: Michael Joseph.

White, Andrea. (1993). *Joseph Conrad and the Adventure Tradition: Constructing and Deconstructing the Imperial Subject.* Cambridge: Cambridge University Press.

3

Responses to War:
1914–1918 and 1939–1945

Richard Greaves

There is, perhaps, something paradoxical in the idea that the short story can provide a form for responses to such epic events as World Wars I and II. The fact that World War I occurred during the period associated with modernism in the arts, and particularly with literary modernism, may lead us to look in the literary responses to it for formal experimentation, a turn to the representation of subjective consciousness rather than objective events, and the kind of literary impressionism practiced by Ford Madox Ford and that Valerie Shaw finds in the modern short story (Shaw 1983: 13). We might expect in those short stories of the Great War that are still readily available the difficulty of interpretation associated with literary modernism. But Jay Winter cautions against any over-easy linking of the Great War with modernism (Winter 1995: 2–5). It can all too easily be seen as the apocalyptic severing of our own time from what went before, the wall that divides us from the different country that is the past. While a story like Virginia Woolf's "The Mark on the Wall" *does* exhibit experimentation, a concern with inner consciousness, and the obliqueness we expect in a modernist short story, other stories are more straightforward in technique and more direct. Moreover, the opposition between modernism and realism is a false one. Woolf sought to go beyond an outmoded realism into a technique that more closely reflected experience. As Chris Baldick has noted, modernism does not supersede realism but brings it new resources (Baldick 2004: 401).

This essay considers the ways in which experimental and more traditional short stories respond to both wars, and how these responses fit into and help to construct our understanding and perception of both wars, and the differences between them. Both wars differ from their predecessors in their scale and because of the technology available (though we should not forget that the effects of automatic weapons had become evident in wars fought in the previous century). The scale of suffering on the Western Front, brought about by the static trench warfare adopted in response to the weapons available, created its own particular place in the popular imagination. The place of the literature of that war in constructing the popular conception of it has been well documented (Holmes 2005: xvii–xviii). Samuel Hynes claims that the popular conception of the war is colored by the bitterness and disillusionment inflecting what was written about it in the 1920s and 1930s (Hynes 1998: 101–4). Hynes's comment that the Great War changed soldiers' minds – that they went to war believing that the individual could have an effect, but realized eventually that this was not so and they were essentially passive victims – is just. As Hynes indicates, alongside the notion of courage as a matter of spectacular heroic action – of which the Great War certainly has its examples – grows the notion of courage as a matter of stoical endurance (Hynes 1998: 56–8). It is the idea of a mass war suggested here that Lawrence opposes so vehemently in "England, My England."

Although the British army that fought the Great War became a citizen army, increasingly an army of wartime volunteers and conscripts, replacing the "old contemptibles" of the pre-war professional army as they withered under the fire of the modern war machine, one detects in the writing of soldiers who served at the front a sense of us and them, a sense – a certainty for some – that only those who fought could possibly know what the experience of the war was like. David Wilkinson's introduction to *Roads to Glory* points out that this was the case for Richard Aldington (Aldington 1992: xxi). In a story like Richard Aldington's "The Case of Lieutenant Hall," this sense of difference is not without an accompanying resentment, even contempt (Aldington 1992: 227–53). Our conception of the war is undoubtedly constructed, at least in part, by our reading of soldiers like Aldington, who came to feel bitter, betrayed by politicians, their problems on return not understood by those who had not been "there." The writing of those soldiers who fought on the Western Front has a special value as *testimony*; it has authority, the glamor of authenticity. (Hynes 1998: 1–2).

But there is a difference here between World Wars I and II. World War II is more of a total war in its involvement of civilians. There were civilian deaths in World War I, but not on the same scale. The development of aerial bombing, in its infancy in World War I, meant that the war was brought home to the civilian population in a new way. The distinction between combatants and non-combatants was blurred (Hynes 1998: 228). Mark Rawlinson quotes Stephen Spender: "The background to this war, corresponding to the Western Front in the last war, is the bombed city" (Rawlinson 2000: 68). A number of stories deal with the civilian experience of war, especially in the shape of the Blitz.

The stories of Richard Aldington collected in *Roads to Glory*, help to create that picture of desolation and human suffering that is the Western Front in the collective imagination, even today. They also help to construct a view of World War I as a tragedy brought about by incompetent – or even evil – politicians and inflicted on massed armies, innocent volunteers and conscripts, many deluded by patriotism, but soon losing that delusion, many revealing extraordinary heroism, even if only in enduring what seems to us to have been unendurable. Historians such as Richard Holmes and John Keegan now challenge the view of Douglas Haig voiced by one of the young officers in Aldington's story "Sacrifice Post," but it remains a stubborn view in the popular understanding of the war (Holmes 2005: xix–xxii; Keegan 1998: 337–42).

> Ask Haig! Ask my backside . . . It isn't his job to think about such trifles as battalions, let alone individual lives. Why, he thinks in Army Corps, and the smallest unit he worries about is a Division . . . When he loses half a dozen or so he just telephones to Blighty for some more. (Aldington 1992: 174)

John Terraine started the sympathetic revision of Haig with *Douglas Haig: The Educated Soldier* (London: Hutchinson, 1963). Republication of this book by Weidenfeld Military in 2005 perhaps shows how well the rehabilitation of his reputation continues.

Aldington's story "At All Costs" similarly points to the discarding of troops by the British General Staff. The young officers at the heart of the story fully understand that they are being sacrificed. Hanley even shows some resentment of those making the decision – "Held at all costs! All jolly fine and large to write from the safety of Montreuil, but what about those who had to make good such dramatic sacrifices with their lives?" (Aldington 1992: 59). Here Aldington conveys the frustration that is an essential part of the view of the troops on the ground, the frustration that comes from having their lives decided on by those whose perspective is different, focused on strategy and the eventual outcome, bringing home the irresolvable conflict between the absolute value of life and the strategist's need to calculate the relative value of a number of lives. The frustration must have been all the greater on the Western Front, where great sacrifice of lives resulted in only small gains of ground.

The frustration does not lead to mutiny though. Hanley and his comrades, and their troops, obey their orders. Aldington's own bitterness is much clearer in other stories, but this one allows its characters their own voice. The stoicism of the characters is the more touching for this, in the conversation between Williams and others when they have heard the orders, for instance:

> "Well, that's that. Napoo, eh?"
> "Looks like it."
> "What about a drink?"
> "Right-o."
>   (Aldington 1992: 58)

The story is unified in its dealing with a discrete event. Its close focalization through Hanley allows the story to convey something of the texture of life in the trenches, but also something of the psychology of the subaltern in the British army of the Great War. Hanley feels it "easier to carry on" (Aldington 1992: 63) once he has written his final letters home, breaking that last sense of contact with his previous life. The story conveys the agony of the knowledge that one is about to die, especially in the passage where Hanley thinks of his wife, but it also manages to convey the weariness in his existence that fits with, perhaps enables, a resignation to obedience to orders and to death. Hynes quotes an Irish Guardsman from Carroll Carstairs's *A Generation Mourning*:

> In the beginning war is adventure. Then comes war weariness, a period of adjustment. You stick it or give up. The third phase is an acceptance, a resignation, a surrender to faith. The brave man is the man who gets through to the third phase. (Hynes 1998: 33)

Williams volunteers for the post that will be wiped out first, deliberately to "get it over" (Aldington 1992: 63). It is what the characters do not do – no raving, no refusal to obey, no flight – that seems at first remarkable. The achievement of this story is that it gives an intelligible picture of the resigned, stoical minds necessary to the war as it was fought.

Aldington's bitterness is clearer elsewhere. His sense of war as a kind of offence against Nature is conveyed in a technique of opposing natural images to descriptions of human action. In "Sacrifice Post," the very description shows humanity out of kilter with the world.

> That seemingly empty plain was huddled full of men. That peaceful sky hung arched over a desperate death-struggle of the nations. The lovely sun was clotting the blood on men just killed, parching the throats of the wounded, maddening the fever in the blood of men attacked by this new disease . . . (Aldington 1992: 171)

Later in the story, "the night-firing seemed to split the darkness with yellow gashes" (Aldington 1992: 184) shows an active sense of the damage being done to Nature.

All this is in support of something the central character, Davison, thinks but has difficulty articulating, and so jots down in a notebook. There is a difference, he feels, between the true relationship between men of the kind of matey comradeship he shares with fellow officers on a train, and the false comradeship, inculcated by army esprit de corps, that leads to an argument over whether or not the light infantry were "the finest unit in the British Army" (Aldington 1992: 175). Davison's awareness that his thoughts once written down can seem pompous defends Aldington a little from the charge of demagoguery.

There is a sense of despair in Davison's admission that "it was almost impossible for an ordinary uneducated Public School man to think coherently, let alone express his feelings" (Aldington 1992: 177), but also an indication of the ideological control inherent in the social conditioning of the generation to which he belongs. It is hard for Davison to think outside the ideologically constructed envelope of duty, loyalty and patriotism, let alone communicate these thoughts to others. Of course, his notebook is found, his senior officers become cold and unfriendly, in spite of his good record, and he is sent back to the post he had been given a spell away from. As he makes his way there, Aldington's portrayal of ideological forces offers an answer to the question that surely raises itself for many of us: Why didn't more men refuse to go? "The huge mechanical will behind him made him walk on" (Aldington 1992: 185). The story ends with Davison's being killed, and the war in that spot continuing as usual.

Aldington can use Davison as a way of musing, trying to articulate his sense that even in war the better way of humans relating to each other is there for all to see, if only ideological forces did not blind them to it. But Davison also stands for the impossibility of getting such thoughts into a form others will accept and, in his being killed, the inevitable failure of the attempt. The story's passing reference to Shakespeare's *Henry V* reminds us that the rhetoric of war and patriotism has been around for a long time.

Stories like these and Aldington's novel *Death of a Hero*, along with the writings of Siegfried Sassoon, clearly construct the conception of World War I that lasts into today: the feeling of a generation betrayed by its seniors; the feeling that only those who fought on the Western Front could understand its horrors; the feeling that those of the betrayed generation who survived the war continued to be betrayed when they returned; the feeling that some who did not fight profited from the sacrifice of others. The opening of "Meditation on a German Grave" suggests a modernist concern with subjective experience and inner consciousness as its narrator points out that Ronald Cumberland's "recollection of his meditation on a German grave ten years after the event was different from the event itself", though he goes on to say that Cumberland "thought it was the same" (Aldington 1992: 3). But one senses a closeness in the thoughts of the character to Aldington's own feelings that makes the story more declarative than formally experimental.

The story does not detail the experience of the war itself, but rather the experience of the returning soldier. Aldington writes of the officer class; the writers who shaped the popular understanding of the Great War were middle class (Hynes 1998: 33). Here Cumberland returns to a society that has no place for him. He has no work. When he tries to find work in journalism he finds that the jobs are already taken. Even the friend who recommended journalism to him has not been taken back, in spite of a promise that his job would be kept for him. Aldington castigates here the hypocrisy of a nation that wants to celebrate heroism but ignores the heroes, as he has Cumberland recall the words of an editorial in the very paper that can find no job for a previous employee returned from the war: "saved their country, saved civilisation, saved the Liberty of the World, which owes them an imperishable debt of gratitude" (Aldington 1992: 7). Aldington's minimizing of his character's bitterness – "A gust of bitterness blew over Cumberland's spirit, but he scarcely even felt resentful" (Aldington 1992: 7) – suggests the carrying over of the stoical response to what one can do nothing about learned in the trenches. It recruits more of the reader's sympathy for Cumberland and defends the story – at least a little – against becoming too much an embittered diatribe.

Nevertheless, this story is a bitter commentary on the failure of British society to reintegrate its returning soldiers. Through Cumberland's experience, Aldington shows a burning anger at this failure, and at the cash nexus that not only fails to accommodate but even exploits the returners. The increasing of rents as a result of the return of great numbers of soldiers is described by the narrator as "A rich harvest, which was efficiently reaped" (Aldington 1992: 5). The metaphor links the exploitation of the returned soldiers to the earlier exploitation of men on the Western Front by bringing to mind the mowing down of men by the "efficient" automatic weapons of modern warfare.

"Meditation on a German Grave" uses the opposition between natural imagery and the social world to support its criticism of society. Cumberland finds it impossible to keep his thoughts on the beauty of "the little gushing waterfalls" as he convalesces travelling through the Savoy mountains, and thinks instead of "the grim crude laws of human social life" (Aldington 1992: 17). He sees and recognizes the beauty of moonrise over Vesuvius at the same time as he sees and recognizes the exploitation of Neapolitan dock workers. Aldington juxtaposes Cumberland's sense of harmony with the natural landscape with his questioning of the purpose of social existence. This harmony shows as futile not only his experience during the war but also his hard-won success in business afterwards. One can read in Cumberland's discovery that "what was real" about his post-war experience was not the business success but "the relation with Isaacson [his business partner], the friendliness, the comradeship" (Aldington 1992: 26), a symbol for the soldier's perception that in all the suffering of war, the disillusionment with patriotic ideals and his political and military leaders, the comradeship and friendship with his fellow soldiers remains a reality. The point is that the inauthentic social relations that lead to war remain in the post-war world in the exploitation of some people by others for business reasons. The Great War has not brought about a better world. Beyond all this, there *is* the possibility for better – genuine – relations between people. Such relations existed in the comradeship of the trenches and exist between Cumberland and Isaacson. The story expresses Aldington's frustration.

Aldington's setting of a description of the beauty of sunset on the island where Cumberland is continuing his convalescence against one of the desolation of the battlefield would perhaps be sufficient in his building of the sense that human society as it has become, with its commitment – seemingly irrevocable – to finance and commerce, and to war, is diametrically opposed to the nurturing of human relationships as they should be, relationships of friendship and comradeship, possible even in business, as Cumberland's relationship with Isaacson has proved. Criticism of racial divisions is also suggested by Aldington's choice of name for Isaacson. The further comment on the cemeteries that form part of the landscape of the battlefield – "Over them all was the cross, that final, devastatingly ironical hypocrisy. The symbol of the Idealist over the work of the Realists" (Aldington 1992: 28) – can seem offputtingly didactic.

The meditation of the title, where Cumberland, in 1918, addressed a dead German soldier in his grave, may also seem too didactic, too obvious a declaration of admittedly unexceptionable sentiments, too embarrassing a revelation of something keenly felt by Aldington. Recognizing the kinship of humanity, Cumberland mourns his German "enemy" and "brother." Here is an expression of the survivor's guilt that Aldington displaces into a fiction in "The Case of Lieutenant Hall" by having Hall haunted by the memory of shooting four Germans who were trying to surrender. Aldington's disgust at the concept of glory is expressed in the way that Hall becomes a hero for his action, the betrayal of trust involved in shooting a surrendering soldier standing for the betrayal of shared humanity involved in war. In his address to the dead German soldier, Cumberland claims that the dead German will be exploited: "And 'they,' the real enemies, will say you were a hero, they'll say you died for your Fatherland, and that it was sweet and decorous that you should die" (Aldington 1992: 31). One can hear the voice of Aldington himself, deeply affected by the war, in Cumberland's claim to be "a husk from which the life has been ruthlessly smashed by this fratricidal hatred" (Aldington 1992: 32), and in his fear that there will inevitably be another war.

What can seem misogyny in "The Case of Lieutenant Hall" is more an expression through the character of the damage done to soldiers by war that can make them incapable of genuine human relations outside it. When offered the chance of leave in Lille, where brothels are numerous, he reacts violently. "I said that since I had seen so many bodies mangled, suffering and dead, the thought of human flesh was repulsive to me. I said I hated the thought of women" (Aldington 1992: 242). For Hall, women were part of the social machine that forced men into the war. "I don't want your bloody whores! I don't want ever to touch a bloody woman. Didn't they urge us into that hell, and do their best to keep us there?" (Aldington 1992: 242). This can be read as an expression by Aldington of the darker side of the war's effect on him. It can also be read as an indictment of the ideological machine that drove men to war, in which many women were an instrument, helping to enforce the senses of patriotism, duty, and shame that led men to believe they *should* participate. Hall's attitude to women is a condemnation of all that has gone wrong with social relations to make war possible. Hamlet-like, he calls for an end to procreation; but here is more despair at the way human relations have been perverted than misogyny. To marry is to

> condemn some infatuated female to an eternity of drudgery, and get her with kids to come out and be slaughtered in their turn . . . we all ought to submit to castration rather than beget children to be exploited and murdered like the men lying out there. (Aldington 1992: 242–3)

Thinking back to Cumberland's early post-war attempts to earn some money through writing disarms criticism of the too straightforwardly declarative, didactic element of "Meditation on a German Grave." His little sketches based on real events, "trying to give the true 'feel' of the war, the genuine sensations and feelings of soldiers" (Aldington 1992: 10–11) are rejected. His parodies of "comic hero-Tommies" are accepted with enthusiasm. The indignation, bitter irony and despair that burst into Aldington's stories have their own honesty, and cannot always be deflected by the requirement for artistic indirection or for what the reader may want in a story. The story is prophetic too, in its way. To Aldington's despair, there *was* another world war. Perhaps, though, in helping to construct the Great War in the public imagination in the way it was constructed, he helped put an end to the idea that war is a glorious thing. "Nevertheless, in 1939 war could still be justified. What had changed in Western European culture was that the days of its glorification were over" (Winter 1995: 8). World War II had clearer proximate causes and continues to be recognized as a "just" war, at least from the British side (Hynes 1998: 111).

The opposition to World War I expressed by D.H. Lawrence in "England, My England" has the similarity with Aldington's of a conceptual basis – the war is an indication and manifestation of the perversion of human relations. Lawrence's opposition is more abstract though. Lawrence's contention is that mass war is wrong, and un-English. He builds his central character, Egbert – the name presumably carrying some loading of Anglo-Saxon authenticity – as English to the core. But this Englishness is a matter of individuality and freedom: "He had no conception of Imperial England, and Rule Britannia was just a joke to him" (Lawrence 1982: 252). Lawrence shows him resisting a national tide of feeling that he thinks has no claim on him, though his resisting thoughts show that he *feels* some claim: "Shall a man become inferior to his own true knowledge and self, just because the mob expects it of him?" (Lawrence 1982: 252). Propaganda has no effect on him: "As for atrocities, he despised the people who committed them as inferior criminal types. There was nothing national about crime" (Lawrence 1982: 252). Lawrence's opposition to the war is based on his sense that people failed to recognize the feelings of their authentic selves and were duped by nationalism.

Paradoxically, Egbert joins up because when he asks his father-in-law, his father-in-law – "whose soul was quick with the instinct of power" (Lawrence 1982: 253) – tells him he should. Lawrence sets out Egbert's instinctive resistance to joining a mass war in a way that suggests his own support for those instincts; "the giving himself over into the power of the mob-spirit of a democratic army" (Lawrence 1982: 253) is a betrayal of himself, and a betrayal Lawrence's narrator has sufficient distance from the character to show disgust at:

> In the thick, gritty, hideous khaki his subtle physique was extinguished as if he had been killed. In the ugly intimacy of the camp his thoroughbred sensibilities were just degraded. But he had chosen, so he accepted. An ugly little look came on to his face, of a man who has accepted his own degradation. (Lawrence 1982: 254)

The story allows the possibility that Egbert is evading a marriage that has become difficult, and evading the daughter whose permanently injured leg could be attributed to his carelessness. In allowing the decision to be made by someone else, or by circumstances, and in becoming part of a mass war, he betrays the individualism and freedom that seem to form Lawrence's Nietzsche-inflected idea of his essential self. At the end of the story, he is killed.

It is startling to learn from Brian Finney's note that Lawrence based his story on the life of Percy Lucas, who lived on the estate where Viola Meynell lent him a cottage in 1915, whose daughter was lamed by falling over a sickle, and who volunteered for the army. Lawrence wrote the story the month before Lucas was killed at the Battle of the Somme (Lawrence 1982: 531). But in drawing from life, Lawrence seems to find only his own politico-philosophy to express. Egbert is only an instance of the self-betrayal that Lawrence sees around him in an increasingly collective society, and the war only its occasion. Paradoxically, the story only recruits the character into another cause, denying the individuality Lawrence is so insistent on.

Virginia Woolf's "The Mark on the Wall" is modernist in its concern with the inside of consciousness and thought. Its response to the Great War is oblique, the war only mentioned at the close: "Though it's no good buying newspapers . . . Nothing ever happens. Curse this war; God damn this war!" (Woolf 1995: 166). As Trudi Tate points out in the introduction to her anthology of Great War stories, there is certainly a reference to propaganda here, the unreliability of newspapers, and the starving of the public of genuine information that might lead to damage to morale. The reference to the war makes one look back for other responses, however oblique, in the musings of the narrator on her own thoughts. In the first paragraph, the mark on the wall distracts her from "an old fancy" provoked by the fire of a "cavalcade of red knights riding up the side of the black rock" (Woolf 1995: 160). The distraction is welcome because this is an *old* fancy. The Great War has rendered outdated the notion of chivalry.

The narrator muses on life as an affair of loss and arbitrariness: "the mystery of life; the inaccuracy of thought! The ignorance of humanity! . . . what an accidental affair this living is after all our civilization" (Woolf 1995: 161). Civilization gives only an – illusory – air of control. Civilization, built over hundreds of years preceding the Great War was unable to prevent that catastrophe and its losses. The story's reference to the dust that buried Troy reminds us of an earlier civilization, destroyed by war, buried by time.

The target of Woolf's criticism is larger. An earlier, rule-driven society is linked with militarism through the sound of the word "generalization." Growing up brings the possibility of dissent from this rule-bound society, a recognition that the "real things" that symbolized it were "half phantoms," which brings a sense of "illegitimate freedom." What "takes the place of those things" is

> the masculine point of view which governs our lives, which sets the standard, which established Whitaker's Table of Precedency, which has become, I suppose, since the war, half a phantom to many men and women, which soon, one may hope, will be laughed into the dustbin where the phantoms go. (Woolf 1995: 163)

Here is the response to war in this story. Woolf's need is to look beyond the system-building, categorizing attitude that seeks to control the world and that she identifies as masculine, to the possibility of freedom. The war has discredited the masculine point of view, shown the need for it to be superseded. The sense of a need to build a new form of social relations is evident here. Woolf's narrator imagines that laughing away the older form, the form that imprisoned us and led to the war, will leave us with a sense of "illegitimate freedom – if freedom exists" (Woolf 1995: 163). The caution is worth noting. Woolf is aware, as Aldington was, of the difficulties of thinking outside the envelope constructed by ideology. Freedom can be aspired towards, but not understood until the chains of the current mind-set are thoroughly thrown off; freedom can be sensed, but only together with the sense of illegitimacy that comes with testing the ideological shackles to breaking point.

Winifred Holtby's story "So Handy for the Fun Fair" gives the perspective of a woman who did go to France during the war (Holtby 1995). She visits France on a holiday trip fifteen years later and by chance returns to the village where she had been posted during the war and fallen in love with a French farmer. She had been ordered away suddenly and been unable to contact him. Now, on her return, she finds that he had not answered her letters because he had been killed. She does not mention her discovery or the story to anyone else on the trip, believing that the past should stay in the past. Although she enjoyed her experience of the war in France, unlike the soldiers in the trenches, there is a similarity in her separating of her experience from her life afterwards in not talking about the experience. There is, too, the touching stoicism of the narrator's understatement of her reaction to the discovery of the French farmer's death, killed on the very night she had been forced to break a date with him without being able to tell him that she had been ordered away. The story conveys the idea that the war put something in the lives of some people, something that would become part of their past isolated from their other experience, something that people who knew them would not have been able to guess at. It offers, perhaps, an attractive equivalent to what Hynes suggests:

> But for ordinary men – the men who fight our wars – there will probably be only that one time when their lives intersect with history, one opportunity to act in great events. (Hynes 1998: 2)

Somerset Maugham's Ashenden stories are drawn from his experience as an intelligence agent in World War I. They are the stories of a writer who happened to be involved in the war, though, rather than the kind of testimony we have from Aldington. Maugham comments, "Fact . . . is a poor story-teller. the material it offers for stories is scrappy and pointless; the author has himself to make it coherent, dramatic and probable" (Maugham 2002: vii). "The Traitor" concerns Ashenden's winning the confidence of an Englishman with a German wife, who lives in Switzerland and is spying for the Germans (Maugham 2002: 126–68).

It is a more complex story than there is space to demonstrate here, but interesting as a meditation on loyalty, relationships and betrayal. Ashenden is able to manipulate the spy, Caypor, assisted by the fact that Caypor is being put under pressure by his

German controller to produce something useful, into moving from his safe billet in Switzerland to where British agents can capture him. In spite of the reference to a young Spaniard who had been killed by the Germans as a result of the work of Caypor, and his presentation as physically unattractive, one's sympathy is engaged by this character.

His wife is likewise presented as unattractive, and the physical ugliness and lack of intelligence of his bull terrier are dwelt on, but it is through his relationship with these two that the reader finds his/her sympathy most intensely engaged. The end of the story has Caypor's wife, having waited fruitlessly and with increasing anxiety for letters after the departure of her husband, realizing that something awful has happened to him. The reaction of Ashenden himself to news of Caypor's capture focuses on his refusal to dehumanize Caypor as "the enemy," as he recalls an earlier memory to remind the reader that death by firing squad is an horrific event. The building to a moment of crisis of the dog's pining for its master is presented as "a fearful thing" by the narrator: "Fritzi . . . threw back his head and gave a long, long melancholy howl" (Maugham 2002: 168).

The closeness of the relationship between the Caypors, which runs across the international division created by the war, makes the gaining and betraying of Caypor's trust by Ashenden more problematic. Though we accept, as Ashenden does, its necessity as part of war, we are troubled by it, as he is. The psychological damage to the dog, symbol of blind loyalty, further engages our sympathy. There seems something elemental and winning about the relationships between the man and his wife and the man and his dog that throws into doubt any easy feeling that spies deserve to be in their turn betrayed and killed. Certainly, there is the idea that no matter how bad the man, there are those who love him who will be damaged by his loss, but there is also something more. The narrator conveys a laconic and understated quality in Ashenden's thinking and manner, a sense that he thinks rather further than he reveals to us. In this story, one senses Ashenden having to overcome a repugnance at what he does and one is left with the feeling that he has betrayed part of himself.

The Swiss setting of Maugham's story takes it away from those areas of Belgium and Northern France that in the popular British imagination *are* World War I. The Irish settings of Elizabeth Bowen's stories "Sunday Afternoon" and "Summer Night" allow them a slightly distanced perspective on World War II. In "Sunday Afternoon," the war seems a threat distant from but likely to intrude on the characters gathered on an Irish lawn: "The late May Sunday blazed, but was not warm: something less than a wind, a breath of coldness, fretted the edge of things" (Bowen 1980: 616). Henry, returned from London, when asked if the bombing is frightening, answers, "Yes. But as it does not connect with the rest of life, it is difficult, you know, to know what one feels. One's feelings seem to have no language for anything so preposterous" (Bowen 1980: 617). In "Summer Night," the distance of the Irish perspective distorts rather than prevents pain: "In the heart of the neutral Irishman indirect suffering pulled like a crooked knife" (Bowen 1980: 588).

In Bowen's stories set in the London of World War II, she is able to evoke the weird nature of a landscape of damaged and closed-up buildings, and how people respond to the strangeness of their surroundings and the stress of living amid bombing. "Mysterious Kôr," with its lunar landscape, is perhaps the most familiar of these stories (Bowen 1980: 728–40). In "Careless Talk," the characters might seem precious, were it not for what their "bright" conversation strives to conceal.

> "Eric," said Mary, after a minute, "the waiter's trying to tell you there's no more of that wine *en carafe*."
> "Bring it in a bottle then. I wonder how much longer –"
> "Oh, my dear, so do *I*," said Mary. "One daren't think about that. Where we were dining last night they already had several numbers scratched off the wine list." (Bowen 1980: 669)

There is a kind of stoicism in the careless talk. Mary's quick rejoinder cuts off the gaping potential significance of the question, "How much longer . . .?"

Eric reminds us of the change in London society with some of the more well-to-do taking refuge from the bombing elsewhere, and does it with black humour as he fails to be curious about where the Hinckneys are and rather celebrates the absence from London of many of those who have left. The black humour is deflated when Joanna, whom he would like to return, says she cannot because her house has been destroyed. Her comment that in any case she has evacuees to look after is squashed by Mary.

> "But we won't talk about those, will we?" said Mary quickly. "Any more than you would want to hear about the bombs. I think one great rule is never to bore each other." (Bowen 1980: 669)

Bowen's understanding here is of the necessity of denial and evasion, and their part in the stoicism that makes endurance possible.

The stoicism of the servant in "Oh, Madam" is much more obviously close to breaking point, interrupted by the need to give her "nose a good blow" (Bowen 1980: 582). The story takes the form of one side of the conversation between the servant and her mistress, as the servant takes her mistress round the house to inspect bomb-damage. Again one has the sense of a deflection of the most costly side of war as the servant grieves over damage to curtains and comments that "good clothes should be where it's safe" (Bowen 1980: 582). Her fellow servant Johnson is criticized for being nervous and going back to his wife's rather than staying and waiting for "madam." The servant asks permission to go and check on her sister later that day, while acknowledging that her sister's house is where she thinks of as home.

There are clear points to make about subservience and class here, but perhaps more interesting is the evasion involved.

No, I don't know yet, madam; I haven't heard. I didn't care to go asking out on the
street. I expect I'd hear in good time, if – It doesn't do to meet trouble.
(Bowen 1980: 580)

With a similar sense of evasion, she warns her mistress not to look where the
little houses were at the back of the house but rather at the park, since there is
nothing "madam" could do. There does seem a similarity here with the stoic
endurance of the soldiers of the Western Front. Once powerlessness is acknowledged, courage can be shown in enduring. The Blitz spirit is evident in the servant's taking heart from the return of her mistress: "Hitler can't beat you and
me, madam, can he?" (Bowen 1980: 581). Rudyard Kipling's "Mary Postgate" and
Jean Rhys's "I Spy a Stranger" present a rather different, chilling, civilian spirit
in wartime.

Mollie Panter-Downes's fiction-writing technique may be, as Gregory LeStage's
preface claims, "akin to journalism" (Panter-Downes 1999: x), but her treatment of
psychology and emotion is masterly. "Goodbye, My Love" indicates the emotional
stress that is constantly fighting to escape the stoicism with which women strive to
endure the effects of war, in this case Ruth's parting with her husband. Ruth recalls
the French governess who used to be driven to tears by English lack of demonstra-
tiveness. She thinks of all the other women in her position, who – that classic
expression of a certain age and class of Englishness – "don't make a fuss" (Panter-
Downes 1999: 93). The suppressed emotion only breaks through in Ruth when after
their parting, her husband phones to say that after all he has another week of
leave.

In "The Demon Lover," Bowen seems more to use the effects of war to help craft
a ghost story. The relative emptiness of parts of London, many of their residents
having closed up their houses "for the duration", creates the eerie atmosphere of a
kind of limbo. There is an ominous overshadowing of the damaged landscape: "Against
the next batch of clouds, already piling up ink-dark, broken chimneys and parapets
stood out" (Bowen 1980: 661).

Mrs Drover, collecting belongings she needs from her closed-up London house,
is forced to remember the previous war, when her fiancé extracted a promise from
her before leaving for France, where he was subsequently reported missing believed
killed. Besides the understanding Bowen shows of the almost unbearable tension
of the last hours before parting in such circumstances – "this was so near the end
of a leave from France that she could only wish him already gone" (Bowen 1980:
663) – the story conveys a sense of Kathleen Drover's having escaped a potentially
unfortunate relationship with a man of unusual, even sinister, intensity. Between
the wars she marries and has children. This part of her life is presented as of
extreme ordinariness: "the years piled up, her children were born" (Bowen 1980:
664).

But this part of her life drains away when the ghost of her ex-fiancé seems to reach
across time for her:

The desuetude of her former bedroom, her married London home's whole air of being
a cracked cup from which memory, with its reassuring power, had either evaporated or
leaked away, made a crisis – and at just this crisis the letter-writer had, knowledgeably,
struck. (Bowen 1980: 664)

This is a skillful and chilling ghost story. If there *is* a deeper level of meaning, it
is perhaps in the sense of the victim of war reaching across time to claim one of
its survivors. There is a sense of loss being carried forward. There is the sense of a
spirit being released into the limbo of a London damaged by a new war, of that
damage creating the opportunity for the ghost to claim its victim, in the brooding
intention that seems to lie behind the depopulated landscape: "The unoccupied
houses opposite continued to meet her look with their damaged stare" (Bowen
1980: 666).

Rose Macaulay's "Miss Anstruther's Letters" describes a bombing raid in a way
that conveys scale and also the sense of helplessness that must sometimes have overtaken London's people:

A hundred fires, the water given out in some places, engines helpless. Everywhere buildings burning, museums, churches, hospitals, great shops, houses, blocks of flats, north,
south, east, west and centre. (Macaulay 2003: 62)

It is worth noting how buildings are damaged here and we guess at the damage to
human bodies, which is not made explicit. Mark Rawlinson comments on how the
injured human body tends to disappear from the representation of war (Rawlinson
2000: 72–3). In the story, a warden, trying to do his job, but with his thoughts in
another district of London where his family are, reminds us of how we can take flight
into numbers when faced with suffering on a huge scale, and forget that each number
represents an individual human tragedy, as well as indicating the nature of the stress
faced by Londoners whose occupations separated them from their families during
raids. The story's focus on Miss Anstruther's tragedy gives us the intensity of focus
of the personal; the moment of mass-scale description shows us that it must be
multiplied.

One of the ironies of the story is that Miss Anstruther could have saved the letters
from her lover, written over twenty-two years, and the more valuable as he has
recently died, but in the stress of the moment of escaping from the bombed block
of flats where she lives, picks up other things to save instead. She had not been able
even to re-read them, waiting until to do so would not cause unbearable grief. In
a further irony, the one charred remnant she is able to salvage from the destroyed
building holds not one of the phrases that "lit the page like stars" (Macaulay 2003:
63), but a recriminatory "Leave it at that. I know now that you don't care twopence;
if you did you would" (Macaulay 2003: 65), which she is bound to transfer to her
leaving behind of his letters while saving things that meant less to her. The story
presents an instance of the destruction of a life apart from the deaths caused by

bombing, indicating the scope and scale of war. It is a story crafted in response to the multiple individual tragedies brought about by war, a fragment captured in a form that seems to suit the fragmenting nature and effects of war. It presents an embodiment of the regret caused by missed opportunity and the failure to grasp the crucial moment:

> She had failed in caring once, twenty years ago, and failed again now, and the twenty years between were a drift of grey ashes that once were fire, and she a drifting ghost too. She had to leave it at that. (Macaulay 2003: 65)

Alun Lewis's "The Last Inspection" is set in the British Army in England, after Dunkirk. His own comment on the group of stories to which it belongs is:

> Written out of immediate experience, typed up on leave, impelled by a perpetual sense of urgency, they are rather personal observations than detached compositions. (Lewis 1990: 10)

As such, they are testimony. "The Last Inspection" conveys the atmosphere of cynicism and bull that pervades an army in waiting. All that happens of the Brigadier's last inspection is a short journey by rail and lunch, the weather being inclement and lunch not to be hurried. The Brigadier's toast to victory is met with cynicism by a soldier who overhears: "The war's nearly over, Fred . . . We've dug for Victory and saved for Victory. And now they're drinking for it" (Lewis 1990: 22). With brilliant economy, the story ends with a reversal of standard patterns, which brings home the state of limbo of the British Army at this time, but also the way in which World War II blurred the lines between soldier and civilian, widened the scope of war to include civilian populations on a new kind of front line. A telegram awaits the engine driver on his return from the abortive inspection. " 'Oh Christ,' said Fred, turning grey at the thought of his wife and kids in Shoreditch" (Lewis 1990: 22).

Suzanne Ferguson claims:

> the pre-eminence of the short story as a modernist genre grew out of the modern, high-brow audience's acceptance of fragmentation as an accurate model of the world . . . The brevity that marked "minor" to earlier generations became a badge of the short story's superior representational capacity. (Ferguson 1989: 191)

This may be true. But the short story is a form that lends itself to the representation of experience fragmented by war. In the best of these stories, the representation of physical and material damage is extended to include psychological and emotional damage. These stories deal with the response to such damage of strategies of stoicism and evasion. They employ a form whose brevity lends itself to the representation of the intensity of individual experience to emphasize that the humanity of the individual lies in his or her ability to relate to others and in the relationships formed with others. The sense of psychological and emotional damage and loss these stories express brings home the effects of war on that humanity.

References and Further Reading

Aldington, R. (1992). *Roads to Glory*. London: Imperial War Museum, reprinted from the original Chatto and Windus publication of 1930.

Baldick, C. (2004). *1910–1940: The Modern Movement (Oxford English Literary History* 10). Oxford: Oxford University Press.

Boston, A. and Hartley J. (eds) (2003). *Wave Me Goodbye: Stories of the Second World War; Hearts Undefeated: Women's Writing of World War II*. London: Virago.

Bowen, E. (1980). *The Collected Stories of Elizabeth Bowen*. London: Jonathan Cape.

Ferguson, S. (1989). "The Rise of the Short Story in the Hierarchy of Genres," in S. Lohafer and J.E. Clarey (eds), *Short Story Theory at a Crossroads*, pp. 176–92. Baton Rouge and London: Louisiana State University Press.

Holmes, R. (2005). *Tommy: The British Soldier on the Western Front 1914–1918*. London: Harper Perennial.

Holtby, W. (1995). "So Handy for the Fun Fair," in T. Tate (ed.) (1995), *Women, Men and the Great War: An Anthology of Stories*, pp. 52–67. Manchester: Manchester University Press.

Hynes, S. (1998). *The Soldier's Tale: Bearing Witness to Modern War*. London: Pimlico.

Keegan, J. (1998). *The First World War*. London: Hutchinson.

Lawrence, D.H. (1982). *Selected Short Stories*, ed. Brian Finney. London: Penguin.

Lewis, A. (1990). *Collected Stories*, ed. C. Archard. Bridgend: Seren Books.

Lohafer, S. and Clarey J.E. (eds) (1989). *Short Story Theory at a Crossroads*. Baton Rouge and London: Louisiana State University Press.

Macaulay, R. (2003). "Mrs Anstruther's Letters," in A. Boston and J. Hartley (eds), *Wave Me Goodbye: Stories of World War II; Hearts Undefeated: Women's Writing of World War II*, pp. 58–65. London: Virago.

Maugham, W.S. (2002). *Collected Short Stories*, vol. 3. London: Vintage.

Panter-Downes, M. (1999). *Good Evening, Mrs Craven: The Wartime Stories of Mollie Panter-Downes*. London: Persephone Books.

Rawlinson, M. (2000). *British Writing of World War II*. Oxford: Clarendon Press.

Rhys, J. (1987). *The Collected Short Stories*. New York: Norton.

Shaw, V. (1983). *The Short Story: A Critical Introduction*. London and New York: Longman.

Tate, T. (ed.) (1995). *Women, Men and the Great War: An Anthology of Stories* Manchester: Manchester University Press.

Terraine, J. (1963). *Douglas Haig: The Educated Soldier*. London: Hutchinson.

Winter, J. (1995). *Sites of Memory, Sites of Mourning: The Great War in European Cultural History*. Cambridge: Cambridge University Press.

Woolf, V. (1995). "The Mark on the Wall," in T. Tate (ed.), *Women, Men and the Great War*, pp. 160–6. Manchester: Manchester University Press.

4
Irish Short Fiction: 1880–1945

Patrick Lonergan

The period 1880 to 1945 involved a series of unprecedented changes in Irish society and its literature. At the beginning of this era, Ireland was a constituent part of the United Kingdom: much of the writing on Irish subjects was therefore directed towards English audiences, while many of Ireland's most talented authors saw London (and occasionally Paris) as the metropolitan center of creativity towards which they should move. Within forty years, Ireland had experienced the celebrated literary revival (*c.*1898–1926), which brought the works of Synge, Yeats, Joyce, and countless others to international prominence; and it had undergone rebellion, a war of independence, a civil war, and the division of the island into the Irish Free State and Northern Ireland. By the end of World War II, the Irish Free State was firmly established but isolated and culturally stagnant: many of its best writers had emigrated, while those who remained at home were stifled by a conservative legislature that was hostile towards many forms of literature. Irish society did not so much *develop* during this sixty-five-year period, as experience a series of radical shifts, each of them to some extent representing a break from the immediate past. Accordingly, a history of literary production in Ireland during this period cannot easily be presented in a linear narrative. Instead, what is required is a tracing of writers' differing responses to a series of cultural and political ruptures.

This difficulty is compounded by the divided nature of Irish society throughout this period. In 1880, Irish society was stratified in many ways – in terms of religion, language, class, land ownership, and politics. Much of the writing before Irish independence in 1922 reveals individual authors' responses to such divisions: just as there was a jostling in Irish society for the dominance of different political views, it is similarly possible to see the development of Irish fiction during this time as offering contesting views about what "Irish fiction" could or should be. And just as the independence of Ireland in 1922 involved victory for one particular political outlook, we also see the emergence from this time onwards of an exclusivist conception of what a genuinely "Irish" fiction should be. Writers who did not conform to that conception were regarded as "un-Irish": their works were often banned in the country, and many of them felt that they had no alternative but to live abroad. Furthermore, a rewriting of Irish literary history took place, where many writers from the pre-independence period were omitted from the canon because they too were seen as "un-Irish." So the development of Irish short fiction from 1880 to 1945 can be seen as a clash between various short *fictions*, each of them offering contrasting notions of Irish identity itself.

By 1880, a tradition of short fiction had been well established in Ireland by such writers as William Carleton, Joseph Sheridan Le Fanu, and Anthony Trollope – but difficulties arise in characterizing it due to authors' attempts to blend Irish subject matter with the formal and thematic conventions of British writing.

Writers who chose to present Irish subjects for a largely English readership during the nineteenth century faced a number of difficulties. The conventions of British fiction were dependent on a sense of shared values between reader and author: there was the notion that truths could be "universally acknowledged" (even ironically), and a belief in a sense of "realism" that was dependent on those values. Such conventions simply could not be made to fit to Ireland: the country lacked any of the stable bases that writers in more industrialized countries had depended on. Language in Ireland was in a difficult state: Gaelic was in decline, yet there was no standardized version of Hiberno-English capable of being taught or learned. The form of speech used by Irish characters in short fiction was thus represented not as a language or idiom in its own right, but instead as a deviation from Standard English: the majority of Irish characters speak a language requiring annotation and explanation, and so are perpetually marked out as different. Ireland also lacked the industrialized urban areas that could stimulate a psychological novel such as *Great Expectations* (1861), *Les Misérables* (1862), or *Crime and Punishment* (1866); most Irish stories therefore are set not in a recognizable urban environment, but against a usually nameless landscape. And of course the problem with Ireland then as now was that few truths could be acknowledged universally.

Accordingly, much Irish fiction before 1880 can be seen as an attempt to blend incompatible elements: to use formal and thematic conventions appropriate to British society to describe a place that was in many ways very different to Britain. Such writing can be characterized as "regional" because it establishes Irish life in a marginal relationship with the dominant mores and values of British society. This means that much short Irish fiction in the nineteenth century had to operate on two levels, with a central "Irish" narrative – sometimes of a mythic, symbolic, or romantic kind – framed by a more conventional narrative that provides for the metropolitan reader some kind of interpretative and moral anchor. The classic example of this phenomenon is Maria Edgeworth's novella *Castle Rackrent* (1800), which includes an editorial and glossary that attempt to sanitize and explain the narrative of the central Irish character, Thady Quirke. Countless other examples exist: the recognizable Standard English voice of the narrator of many of William Carleton's *Traits and Stories of the Irish Peasantry* (1830–74), or the use of English heroes who can interpret the action for an

English audience, such as Henry Lowe in Charles Kickham's *Knocknagow* (1879). At its best (as in Edgeworth), such fiction places the Irish and British elements into dialog with each other so that, although Irish characters' apparent deviation from British norms is a subject of laughter and (occasionally) condescension, an air of mockery is also used to describe English characters' (and, by extension, English readers') unwillingness to see Irish life as culturally different rather than an inferior version of their own society.

By the end of the nineteenth century, this mode of fiction was disappearing, but one important example of it can be considered: the *Irish R.M.* stories of "Somerville and Ross," the *noms de plume* of Edith Somerville (1858–1949) and Violet Martin (1862–1915), two members of the Anglo-Irish ascendancy who wrote collaboratively over a number of years. Both occupied political and social positions that were slowly being destabilized: they were in favor of maintaining the union between Britain and Ireland at a time when the latter country was moving towards Home Rule; they were committed to maintaining the social structures in Ireland at that time, which situated the landowning Protestant aristocracy (their own class, in other words) as the dominant force within the country. However, their works are in no way partisan, instead showing a genuine affection for all aspects of Irish life, especially those which were in the process of slipping away.

Originally published in the English magazine *Badminton*, *The Irish R.M* stories first appeared in 1898, and focus on Major Yeates, a "regional magistrate" working in rural Ireland, who describes himself as being of Irish ancestry but is entirely English in upbringing and outlook. He encounters various forms of delinquency in his courtroom – most of them involving the stereotypical Irish traits of drunkenness and brawling – and is frequently confounded by local attitudes towards the law: Irish characters make use of the legal system for their own benefit, but tend not to cooperate when a crime has been committed against British rule. Much of the energy of the stories arises not from its treatment of Irish law, however, but instead from their authors' loving recreation in such stories as "Philipa's Fox Hunt" of the traditions of hunting that were so much a part of rural Irish life at the close of the nineteenth century. The stories may therefore be seen as offering something of a "tourist's gaze" upon Ireland, presenting those aspects of the country most likely to be of interest to English readers. It is worth noting in this context that Somerville and Ross later achieved great success by writing travelogues of visits to Europe and Britain.

The lasting value of the stories arises from their presentation of Ireland at a transitional period. In her Preface to the collected edition of the thirty-four *R.M.* stories, Somerville wrote in a tone of regret that "the arduous post of Resident Magistrate in Ireland exists no more. It has been extinguished, like many other features of an earlier regime" (1928: 1). Yeates represents the values of the British government and the Anglo-Irish ascendancy and, although his encounters with a devious Irish peasantry and a cunning Irish middle class give rise to much of the stories' humor, his inability to stamp control firmly on his environment – or to enter fully into the country's life – may be seen as evidence of a gradual erosion of the authority that he represents.

One of the central relationships in the stories is between Yeates and the upwardly mobile Flurry Knox, described by the authors as "a stableboy among gentlemen and a gentleman among stableboys" (10). By the time these stories appeared in collected form in 1928, people like Flurry had become dominant in Ireland; the British government had relinquished control of the country; and the Anglo-Irish ascendancy had largely disappeared, due to bankruptcy, emigration, or political violence. *The Irish R.M. Stories* therefore offer a warmly humorous presentation of a mode of Irish life that was passing away. Later collections such as *All on the Irish Shore* (1903) and *Some Irish Yesterdays* (1906) are similarly nostalgic and at times elegiac; what gives them depth, however, is their authors' willingness to engage with their subjects with open-mindedness and objectivity.

The writings of Somerville and Ross have not received their due attention, perhaps because they were overshadowed by a significant contemporary development: the early period of the Irish literary renaissance, which emerged in the late 1890s in response to the political stagnation caused by the death of Irish leader Charles Parnell. The renaissance was not (as is sometimes thought) a unified grouping of nationalist artists who aimed to make the case for Irish independence through literature. Rather, it involved large numbers of writers from different traditions and backgrounds, who used their fictions to present arguments about the appropriate subjects of Irish literature – about whether it should be written in Irish or English, whether it should focus on rural Irish life or on the city, whether it should identify itself in relation to Britain or Europe, and so on. The short fiction of this time can thus be seen as a conversation – and sometimes as an argument, bitterly conducted – amongst various writers about the future of Ireland, in which two key features can be identified: an emphasis on rural life, and the use of folklore and oral storytelling.

Whereas many writers of Irish fiction in the nineteenth century had looked to such British writers as Walter Scott, Jane Austen, or Charles Dickens for inspiration, authors of the short fiction of the Irish revival tended to look further east, particularly towards Russia. Many of the short stories that emerged in Ireland in the early years of the twentieth century are strongly indebted to Turgenev, who wrote about Russian serfdom with a combination of artistic distance and deep-seated sympathy, a perspective that countless Irish writers would attempt to adopt.

This is particularly true of George Moore, who returned to Dublin from Paris to participate in the emerging literary movements. He was inspired by the suggestion of his friend W.K. Magee that he become "Dublin's Turgenev" – an idea that "appealed to Moore's taste and vanity," according to Adrian Frazier (2000: 306). Accordingly, from September 1901, Moore began to write a series of short stories of rural Irish life, focusing on Catholicism ("Patchwork," "The Window"), emigration ("The Wedding Feast"), and on artist-figures whose relationship with Ireland is marked by disillusionment ("In the Clay"). When these stories appeared in collected form as *The Untilled Field* (1903), Moore had clarified his volume's thesis: that "Catholicism and nationhood are incompatible" (qtd by Frazier 2000: 308). Moore may have begun by attempting to revitalize his country's culture by looking to the past, yet his collection ultimately aimed to determine the nation's future. As such, *The Untilled Field* offers a useful example of how the works of the early Irish Literary Revival attempted to strike a difficult balance between forging national self-confidence and drawing attention to the country's problems.

The influence of Turgenev and other Russians is apparent in other stories, such as Seamus O'Kelly's "The Weaver's Rest" (1913), a fine example of storytelling focused on rural Irish life. But this influence may perhaps best be seen in short fiction written in Irish at this time. Although most scholars regard it as a novel, Peadar Ó Laoghaire's *Séadna* is perhaps the most influential text in this regard. Serialized in *Irisleabhar na Gaedhlige* during 1894–7, *Séadna* presents a series of short episodes in the life of the eponymous hero, a shoemaker who sells his soul to the devil. Combining colloquial idiom with vivid descriptions of Irish life, Ó Laoghaire's text provided an important model for later writers in Irish of how short fiction might combine incident and observation within a tight narrative framework.

The most important of these writers is Padraic Ó Conaire, who produced stories of rural Irish life that present individuals in isolated settings, alienated from those around them as well as their immediate surroundings. Anticipating many of the strategies that would later be employed by modernist writers of short fiction, his stories offer bleak and uncompromising presentations of human life. "We live in a . . . complex world and new methods and a new metaphysic are needed to explore and express it" wrote Ó Conaire in 1908, the year before the appearance of his first collection *Nora Mharcus Bhig agus Sgéalta Eile* ("Marcus Big's Daughter Nora and Other Stories"; qtd by Ó hAnluain 1991: 845). The title story of that collection, written when Ó Conaire lived in London, describes a Connemara father's rejection of his daughter when he comes to believe that she has lived a "corrupt" life in London. Placing the contrast between idealized versions of city and rural life at its center, Ó Conaire's story is a fascinating development of a theme that would soon dominate much Irish fiction: the clash between appearance and reality.

This clash was one of the key themes of the Irish literary revival, receiving its fullest expression on the stage of the Abbey Theatre, Dublin – notably in the plays of John Millington Synge which, by considering the difference between the ideal and the real, offered an important corrective to some of the currents in Irish nationalism, which idealized Ireland in a way that ignored some of the most pressing social problems in the country. This theme can also be seen in some Irish short fiction during the period, particularly that which aimed to represent Irish myth and folklore in the form of the short story.

Irish myth and folklore had been gathered in Ireland since the mid-nineteenth century, much of it in the form of anthropology rather than fiction. The person most responsible for integrating myth into modern modes of narrative is Lady Augusta Gregory, whose volumes *A Book of Saints and Wonders* (1906) and *The Kiltartan History Book* (1909, 1926) make excellent use of the short story to bring ancient Irish myths into a form that contemporary audiences could identify with. Gregory, like many writers during this period, reveals that the short story is a form ideally suited to the traditions of Irish storytelling, which are oracular, rooted in colloquial speech, and episodic in character. She claimed to have taken the stories directly from the people who lived in Kiltartan, the Galway district where she lived – "from beggars, pipers, travelling men, at my own door or in the Workhouse"; the stories, she claimed, could be seen as "myths in the making" (Gregory 1995: 528).

Another important re-teller of Irish folk stories is James Stephens, whose collections include *Here Are Ladies* (1913) and *Irish Fairy Tales* (1920). Whereas Gregory presented herself as a mediator or editor of the Irish people's stories (characteristically disguising her own role in the creative process), Stephens's stories on Irish subjects give full rein to his imagination, adopting a style that would later influence the reception of such writers as Flann O'Brien. Similarly, the writer Padraic Colum – who is best known for his poetry and a biography of James Joyce – achieved success with his re-telling of ancient Irish myths in *The King of Ireland's Son* (1916). Like Gregory, he claimed to have heard many of these stories from someone else – in this case, from his grandmother – but there is again much evidence of his own creative powers. Colum's work was ostensibly written for children but, as John Wilson Foster observes, it is a "structural masterwork" (2006: 139) that reveals, interrogates, and decodes many of the dominant tropes of the Irish revival, such as the notion that the Irish peasantry are a usurped nobility. Foster further suggests that the freedom of form offered by folktale becomes in Colum's work a metaphor for the creation of "a new national self" (2006: 139). The folktales told by Gregory, Stephens, and Colum thus involve a tension between the imagined Ireland they describe and the real Ireland in which their books were sold – though that contrast does not aim to denigrate the real, but to use the ideal to inspire transformation.

Taken in their entirety, the stories of such writers as Moore, Ó Laoghaire, Ó Conaire, Gregory, Colum, and Stephens show that there are as many similarities as differences between the writers of the Irish revival. All use the culture of rural Ireland as a launching point for their own works. Some, like Gregory and Colum, celebrate ancient Irish culture; others, like Moore and Ó Conaire, take a dimmer view on Irish life. Also notable is the variety of linguistic registers employed: Gregory attempts to present rural Irish speech in Anglicized form; Ó Conaire and Ó Laoighre attempt to regenerate Gaelic; while Moore and Stephens adopt a tone that is for the most part Standard English. These early works of the Irish revival can therefore be seen as offering a range of possibilities – can be seen, that is, as experiments in form. As is discussed below, many of these writers' innovations would be taken up by other authors; but what is most noticeable about this period is that writers' belief that they were effectively inventing a new form lent their works an air of excitement and innovation.

A further notable feature of these writers' careers is that many of them wrote their best work about Ireland abroad: Stephens and Moore in Paris, O Conaire in London. In doing so, they tapped into an important tradition, of Irish writers who might best be described as "cosmopolitan": that is, their work was not limited to national boundaries or preoccupations, but instead ranged freely across a global culture, which their authors saw as transcending national and ideological borders.

Among the best of such writers is Oscar Wilde, whose short stories are among his finest achievements. "The Sphinx Without A Secret" (1891) is a classic example of Wilde's ability to blend different literary styles. In it, he presents a dialog between two men about a mysterious woman, whose secret (the characters suggest) is that she deliberately cultivates an air of mystery in order to disguise her lack of depth. Drawing from classical literature and the European visual arts, and moving freely from London to Paris, Wilde's story is also a polite mockery of the British mystery story, then fashionable in Britain thanks to Arthur Conan Doyle (whose Sherlock Holmes first appeared in 1886). Like many of Wilde's other writings, "The Sphinx Without A Secret" might be seen as involving a victory of style over substance; it is however more subtle in form and more ambivalent in outcome than it first appears. Wilde ultimately presents a cautionary tale about the dangers of idealization – something that would be echoed some years later by Synge and other Irish writers.

Wilde's stories for children are much loved, but not given much serious scholarly attention. This is unfortunate: the stories are delightful fables that make use of many of the archetypal traits and themes found in the folk stories of Ireland and other European countries. In particular, such stories as "The Happy Prince" emphasize the nobility of self-sacrifice – a feature that is seen (probably correctly) by many commentators as Wilde's expression of his feelings about Christianity. It should be noted, however, that such stories also display similarities to ancient Irish myths about saints and tribal leaders – stories that Wilde's mother had gathered for publication under the pseudonym "Speranza" as *Ancient Legends, Mystic Charms, and Superstitions* (1887, two vols). Wilde's short fiction is therefore an excellent example of a mode of writing that fits comfortably within an Irish context, but which can be located with ease in other contexts and settings.

A further example of this "cosmopolitan" mode of Irish short fiction is the gothic short story, a genre that had enjoyed its strongest period in Ireland from Charles Maturin's *Melmoth the Wanderer* (1820) to Sheridan Le Fanu's *In A Glass Darkly* (1872). The form experienced a minor renaissance towards the end of the century, however, following the publication of Bram Stoker's *Dracula* (1897). Stoker himself produced many short stories in the style of *Dracula*, which were collected after his death as *Dracula's Guest and Other Weird Stories* (1914). Like *Dracula*, these stories have little artistic merit, but feature literary creations so imaginative that they manage to escape the confines of Stoker's dreadful prose. The stories also draw on themes and tropes present throughout Irish gothic (and also evident in much Irish short fiction): the superstition of Catholic peasantry, the appealing yet alienating quality of rural landscapes, and the mysterious behavior of people on the social margins, such as gypsies and poor farmers. Whether Stoker draws these people from his experience of Irish life or from other sources remains a moot point: his work is, in any case, an interesting example of the persistence of a tradition of Irish storytelling that remains popular even at present (as shown by the success of Conor McPherson's ghostly 1997 play *The Weir*).

The novelist Rosa Mulholland also shows a familiarity with the gothic throughout her short fiction. Her story "The Hungry Death" (1890), for example, uses the gothic form to describe the impoverished conditions of a group of islanders living off the coast of Ireland. Her strategy of using gothic techniques to describe the real horrors of Irish life is generally effective, recalling William Carleton's classic short story "Wildgoose Lodge" (1830), while anticipating the use by twentieth-century writers of gothic modes to describe real political violence in Northern Ireland.

A number of explanations have been offered for the fact that so many Irish Protestant writers during this period chose to write in the gothic style. Roy Foster sees it as related to fear of the "threat of a takeover by the Catholic middle classes" (1993: 220), for example; many other critics have suggested that some forms of Irish gothic should be seen in relation to the colonization by Britain of Ireland. Such views may be accurate, but it is also possible to see the existence of the genre simply as evidence of Irish writers' willingness to write in modes that transcend national boundaries, allowing their works to be interpreted in multiple ways by audiences internationally.

As political events in Ireland turned towards insurrection – and as European society came to terms with the technological horrors unleashed during World War I – Irish writing underwent a dramatic shift, as writers adjusted not only to the new political realities within Ireland itself, but (in common with writers throughout the world) attempted to find aesthetic modes that could account for the collapse of Victorian certainties after 1918.

Perhaps the first sign of this shift was the publication in 1914 of James Joyce's masterpiece *Dubliners*. Mostly written between 1904 and 1907, the fifteen stories collected by Joyce draw on much of the writing that had come before, and offer glimpses of much that followed. Joyce's objective – which became crystallized as he spent years defending his stories against accusations of defamation and obscenity – was not so much nationalist as patriotic: he wished to reveal what he saw as the truth about Ireland and, in so doing, to "civilize" it, to rescue Dublin from what he saw as "the soul of that . . . paralysis which many consider a city" (*Letters* 1957: 55).

He did so by arranging his stories into four sections, each of them representing a phase of human existence: childhood, adolescence, maturity, and public life. In each case, we see characters experiencing various forms of paralysis. These include a young boy in the opening story "The Sisters," whose friendship with a priest leads his family to believe he is himself destined for the priesthood. The termination of this relationship by the paralysis and subsequent death of the priest comes as both a literal and imaginative liberation for the boy, who is free to determine the direction of his own life. Other forms of entrapment – and other possibilities of freedom – are explored throughout the book. There is, for example, the entrapment caused by inherited notions of romantic love and interpersonal relationships, as experienced by women in "Eveline" and "A Painful Case." There is the restrictive lifestyle of Dublin's young men, feckless and directionless, who find themselves in loveless relationships ("The Boarding House"), abusing alcohol ("Grace"), or, quite literally, spending their time going around in circles ("Two Gallants"). The volume's final story, the magnificent "The Dead," both clarifies and expands upon the theme of paralysis, presenting a vision of Dublin that locates it in relation to the rest of the world – in terms of London, Europe, and the imaginative space of the west of Ireland – to suggest that life in Dublin is a form of banishment from these other, more desirable, places. This presentation of Ireland's capital means that Joyce's collection is at once regional, national, and cosmopolitan: it is a description of a single place which is judged unfavorably in comparison to greater cities, it is an imaginative account of what Ireland ought to become and, in its allusions to the works of Homer and Dante, is firmly European. Each of these strands would be taken up in different ways by many of the writers that followed.

Despite Joyce's attempt to persuade Ireland of its paralysis, post-independence Ireland became more stultified, due to a variety of factors. International isolation after a trade war with England was intensified by neutrality during World War II. The Catholic Church had increasing influence on Irish politics and society, with frequently (though not universally) negative effects. The country experienced economic stagnation and high rates of emigration. And, like many countries in Europe, the new Irish State adopted an enthusiastic approach towards literary censorship, with most of the great Irish writers (and many of the mediocre ones) being banned in their own country. Such social developments were matched by the emergence of an increasingly rigid definition of what Irish writing could be.

The most influential text in this respect is a critical work by the short-story writer Daniel Corkery, whose *Synge and Anglo-Irish Literature* (1931) aimed to define the future of Irish writing, while redefining its past. He writes in a dismissive tone of many of his predecessors (not to mention almost all of his rivals), whom he sees as "Irishmen who neither live at home nor write primarily for their own people" (6). He defines the exile (voluntary or otherwise) of such short-fiction writers as Wilde, Moore, and Joyce as an example of a "chronic disease" within Irish letters (7). He is even more dismissive of such writers as Edgeworth and Somerville and Ross, authors of what he terms "Colonial Literature" which was presented not for an Irish readership but for England by people Corkery saw as "spiritual exiles" (10). The true subject of a genuinely "Irish" literature, Corkery argued, was threefold: the land, nationalism, and religion.

Corkery's view of Irish writing is an extreme example of a tendency in post-independence Irish culture to devise essentialized notions of Irish identity and literature. Many writers attacked Corkery's views yet, if his tone is objectionable, his observations are not entirely inaccurate. From 1922 onwards, much of the short fiction produced in Ireland was narrowly focused on the three areas to which Corkery had alluded. Likewise, such "expatriate" writers as Joyce and (later) Samuel Beckett and Elizabeth Bowen remained largely unread and undervalued in their home country, while the reputation of the so-called "Colonial" writers steadily declined – the works of Somerville and Ross, for example, were almost entirely out of print by the 1930s.

Yet despite this narrowing of the themes of Irish literature, the period after 1922 is noted for the appearance of some of the greatest works of short fiction in Irish (and indeed Anglophone) literary history. Corkery's own short fiction lays the ground for some of the best subsequent work: *A Munster Twilight* (1916) offers a portrait of the culture of Corkery's native county Cork, which displays a clear-headed awareness of the stratification of small Irish communities, as well as a keen sense of the dramatic possibilities of colloquial speech. His interest in the people of urban Cork communities is an important development in Irish writing, creating an imaginative space that would later be occupied by such writers as Sean O'Casey. Subsequent volumes such as *The Hounds of Banba* (1920) and *Earth out of Earth* (1939) build on some of these achievements.

However, the greatest achievements in short fiction during this time were not by Corkery, but by two other Cork writers, Frank O'Connor and Seán O'Faoláin. O'Faoláin was a one-time protégé of Corkery, but later turned against him: having studied at Harvard and taught in London, O'Faoláin had developed a strong sense of the value of an international perspective on Irish writing, which lends his work an air of dispassion that is sometimes absent from Corkery's fiction. His first collection, *Midsummer Night Madness*, appeared in 1932; his second, *A Purse of Coppers*, appeared five years later. He continued to publish short stories throughout his life, many of them in *The Bell*, the influential journal which he edited from 1940. As with many other Irish writers, he deals with themes of sexual jealousy and betrayal with a combination of wit and compassion (as in "Lovers of the Lake" and "The Faithless Wife"). However, the most outstanding quality of his writing – in such stories as "Midsummer Night Madness" and "The Man Who Invented Sin" – is his willingness to infuse accurate observation of Irish life with symbolical and metaphysical elements. This combination brings a thematic richness and formal complexity to the Irish short fiction of this period.

O'Faoláin was also one of the first writers to explore the consequences for Ireland of national independence – something for which he himself had fought. His story "Liliput" (1926), for example, invokes Swift's land of tiny people as a metaphor for the new Ireland – a brave gesture, given that the state was then only four years old. O'Faoláin continued to write short fiction after World War II; he also wrote an important critical work called *The Short Story* (1948), which is a useful aid for the understanding of his works, as well as a fine piece of criticism.

Frank O'Connor (another of Corkery's former students) is regarded by many as the master of the Irish short story. Whereas O'Faoláin's works create their impact through the author's sense of detachment and playfulness, the power of O'Connor's fiction lies in his ability to provide an intensely moving and intimate perspective on a variety of people living in Ireland.

"Guests of the Nation" (1931) is a classic of its kind. It describes a group of Irish guerrilla fighters during the Anglo-Irish war (1919–21), who are holding two

English soldiers captive (hence the ironical title). Prisoners and captors form a strong bond, realizing that they share a compatible view of the demands of military life, work, and relationships. Their camaraderie is disrupted, however, by duty: the Irish soldiers are ordered to execute the English in reprisal for a British military action.

It is a sign of O'Connor's ability to present characters convincingly that he demands that his Irish readers sympathize with two soldiers who, only ten years previously, would have been regarded as members of a brutal occupying army. Not only does he take the courageous step of humanizing this enemy, he also proposes that there is no fundamental difference between Irish and English soldiers – all of whom are presented as sharing a common sense of humanity, their military actions determined by loyalty to an abstract sense of duty that none of them fully recognizes. The story's conclusion (which deliberately echoes Joyce's "The Dead") proposes that the conflict against England was not a heroic war of liberation, but a debasement of its participants' humanity. As the English soldiers lie dying in the Irish wilderness, the narrator comments that:

> It was as if the patch of bog where the Englishmen were was a million miles away . . . and the birds and the bloody stars were all far away, and I was somehow very lost and lonely like a child astray in the snow. (Trevor 1989: 353)

For O'Faoláin, post-independence Ireland was a Liliput; for O'Connor its independence was achieved by a similar shrinking of its inhabitants' sense of humanity.

O'Connor wrote brilliantly about the Irish war of independence and Civil War, but he also wrote about other important themes. His "The Majesty of the Law" (1935), for instance, presents a light-hearted exchange between an Irish farmer and a policeman that shows how both have a skewed sense of their legal responsibilities – making the story a neatly observed episode that recalls (probably unintentionally) *The Irish R.M.*. And he showed a keen sense of imaginative perspective in his treatment of childhood and sexuality – issues that would become more prominent in his later fiction.

The immediate period after independence saw the emergence of many other important writers. Of these, Liam O'Flaherty (who also wrote in Irish as Liam O Flaithearta) is probably the most notable, although his works are no longer widely read. Just as Moore and others had been influenced by Turgenev, O'Flaherty drew inspiration from Dostoevsky and Gogol. Many of his works are uncompromisingly realistic portraits of rural and urban Ireland; his 1929 "The Tavern," for example, offers a disturbingly objective account of a Civil War ambush. His work has dated rather badly, however, probably due to his use of outmoded symbolism, notably in his portrayal of women, who are often presented as idealized and sexless figures. His reputation for writing in Irish has remained relatively strong, however, due to the success of *Dúil*, his 1953 collection of short stories (almost all of which were published before 1945). Of these, the most successful is "An Chulaith Nua" ("The New Suit"), which uses the simple act of the weaving of a new suit to present a meditation on the deeper meanings of everyday activities.

As World War II drew to a conclusion, the sense of provincialism and isolation that had dominated Irish life since 1922 was beginning to lift, as many writers began to travel to – and seek inspiration from – the United States. This development had been anticipated some years earlier, with the appearance in 1935 of Maurice Walsh's short story, "The Quiet Man" in the volume *Green Rushes*. Subsequently adapted for a 1952 John Ford film starring John Wayne and Maureen O'Hara, "The Quiet Man" provides evidence of a gradual shift in the relationship between Ireland and the rest of the world. Whereas the fiction of Ó Conaire and Moore had presented characters who returned to an Ireland that was inhospitable, Walsh's story complicates that theme, showing that the exile's sense of nostalgia has a corollary: the desire in those who remain at home to escape to a better life, represented in this case by the United States. As well as having historical interest, Walsh's story marks the intensification of Irish writers' engagement with America, both as an ideal and as a source of work. In subsequent years, much of the best Irish writing would appear not at home but in the pages of *The New Yorker*, where established writers such as Frank O'Connor would appear alongside an emerging generation, including Mary Lavin (whose first collection of stories *Tales from Bective Bridge* was published in 1942), Maeve Brennan, and Brian Friel.

During the post-independence period, many Irish writers made their homes outside of the country, sometimes addressing Irish themes directly and, more frequently, writing works set in other countries and considering themes of universal rather than rigidly national importance. Of these writers, the two most significant are Elizabeth Bowen and Samuel Beckett.

Beckett's only short fiction before World War II is his 1934 *More Pricks than Kicks*, a collection that was positively reviewed upon publication but sold very poorly; it was also banned in Ireland (much to the consternation of Beckett's mother). Displaying the influence of Joyce, the stories focus principally on a character named Belacqua. Full of literary allusion, *More Pricks* adopts an absurdist approach to storytelling in an Irish milieu – a technique that would later be perfected by Flann O'Brien in such works as *At-Swim-Two-Birds* (1939). The stories in the collection are not without merit, but Beckett's approach to short fiction would change substantially in later years.

Elizabeth Bowen's first collection of short fiction appeared in 1923; she went on to produce five further collections before 1945. As with the rest of Bowen's literary output, these stories move easily from Ireland to England, and employ a variety of narrative modes and styles. As a result, her work has proven difficult to categorize: Bowen is as likely to appear in histories of English as Irish literature, but fits comfortably into neither. Some of her stories explicitly position themselves in relation to Irish literary traditions: *The Demon Lover* (1945) in particular can be seen in relation to the Irish gothic, while other stories draw on the tradition of "Big House" literature, which focuses on the Anglo-Irish landed ascendancy – making Bowen's work relevant to that of Somerville and Ross, among others. Perhaps, however, Bowen might best be seen as an Irish writer like Wilde or Beckett – someone who wrote not as a citizen of a nation, but as an inhabitant of the world. It is scarcely surprising that recent attempts within Ireland to reconsider the importance of Bowen coincide with a period of increased multiculturalism and globalization in the country: her fiction is rooted in an Ireland that is seen from multiple perspectives, and which occupies just one part of her imagination.

This essay began with an exploration of the period 1880 to 1921, suggesting that the development of Irish short fiction could be considered from three interlinking perspectives. The works of Somerville and Ross and others can be seen as "regional": insofar as they address a metropolitan audience and locate Ireland as a marginal but essential element of the United Kingdom. A second mode of writing evident at this time might be described as "nativist" or nationalist – writings addressed directly towards Irish audiences, which attempt to promote the notion that the country is not only worthy of political independence but also deserving of its own distinctly "national" literature. Finally, there is also a "cosmopolitan" mode of short fiction; that is, works by Irish writers who see the subject of their literature as transcending national boundaries, while also crossing the boundaries of realism into the fantastic and mythological.

A similar three-part perspective could be used to chart the development of Irish writing from independence to the end of World War II. Where before there was a regional fiction, post-independence Ireland saw the emergence of "localized" writing, involving the description in intimate detail of specific places within rural Ireland, such as Corkery's Cork, or the rural villages of Frank O'Connor. And, just as the pre-independence period saw the development of a nationalist fiction, Ireland after 1922 witnessed the emergence of a "national" approach to the production and reception of short fiction, which promoted essentialized versions of Irish identity: a particular set of traits and characteristics were presented as distinctly Irish, which led to the exclusion of much that was valuable from the country's sense of its literary heritage. To counteract that development, it is useful to observe in the works of Beckett and Bowen an "international" approach to short fiction, whereby Irish writers enter into a dialogic relationship with the national space: they draw on other national literary traditions or write from other countries, but do so with an awareness of traditions in their home country.

These perspectives on Irish short fiction before and after independence are of course schematic – and necessarily so. Many Irish writers moved from one kind of writing to the other; few if any of them were conscious of themselves as operating within a particular tradition; and only a minority – perhaps less than half – of the writers discussed above saw their work as being exclusively or narrowly "Irish." Rather, these perspectives are offered in order to show the many different trajectories explored by Irish writers during this period – journeys that were an attempt not only to chart the development of an important literary form, but which might also be seen in other important ways: as explorations of the writer's place in the world, as statements about the future direction of Ireland itself, and as attempts to answer that most challenging questions: what does it mean to be Irish?

REFERENCES AND FURTHER READING

Bowen, E. (1945). *The Demon Lover*. London: Cape.

Corkery, D. (1931). *Synge and Anglo-Irish Literature*. Dublin: Gill and Macmillan.

Foster, J.W. (2006). "The Irish Renaissance, 1890–1940: Prose in English," in M. Kelleher and P. O'Leary (eds), *The Cambridge History of Irish Literature* vol. 2, pp. 113–80. Cambridge: Cambridge University Press.

Foster, R. (1993). *Paddy and Mr Punch*. Harmondsworth: Penguin.

Frazier, A. (2000). *George Moore: A Life*. New Haven and London: Yale.

Gregory, A. (1995). *Selected Writings*. Harmondsworth: Penguin.

Joyce, J. (1957). *Letters*, vol. 1, ed. S. Gilbert. New York: Viking.

Lavin, M. (1942). *Tales from Bective Bridge*. Boston: Little, Brown; UK edn, London: Joseph, 1943.

O'Faolain, S. (1948). *The Short Story*. London: Collins.

Ó hAnluain, E. (1991). "Irish Writing: Prose Fiction and Poetry 1900–1988," in S. Deane (ed.), *The Field Day Anthology of Irish Literature*, vol. 2, pp. 814–16. Derry: Field Day.

Somerville, E. and Ross, M. (1928). *The Irish RM Complete*. London: Faber.

Tóibín, C. (ed.) (1999). *The Penguin Book of Irish Fiction*. Harmondsworth: Penguin.

Trevor, W. (ed.) (1989). *The Oxford Book of Irish Short Stories*. Oxford: Oxford University Press.

5
The Detective and Crime Story: 1880–1945

Jopi Nyman

While crime stories are as old as humanity, the roots of the modern detective story are in the writings of Edgar Allan Poe and in particular in his stories featuring the cerebral Paris detective Dupin. Owing to Poe's influence the new form transformed the existing forms of popular crime narrative in nineteenth-century Britain. In connection with the professionalization of the police force as seen in the formation of the London metropolitan police force in 1828, the new image of the detective replaced the formerly dominant form of crime writing, the popular criminal biography, which told the public of the hideous crimes of criminals and their punishment. Most prominently present as the *Newgate Calendar* and Newgate novels, this form was gradually replaced, partially because of moral pressure, with new forms of popular narrative where the potentially subversive figure of the criminal is present only at the end of the story, not with his name, picture and final words as was the case in the broadsheets (Woods 1990: 16–17). Thus the emergence of the detective story as a popular form tells how the focus of the crime narrative changes from the criminal to the maintenance of law, order and respectability.

Aiming at the preservation of the status quo, detective fiction has often been seen as a conservative genre where criminals are punished for transgressing legal and social boundaries: as soon as the upper-class detective has discovered that the murder in the country house has been committed by the butler, the local constabulary restores order and eliminates the source of disturbance. While this view holds in particular for British detective fiction published in the golden age of the detective story between the two world wars, recent criticism of the genre has revealed a variety of issues suppressed in earlier critical responses and connected British detective fiction to such larger questions as those of empire, gender, and Englishness. These concerns are present in the development of the short story in the period 1880–1945: in this period the detective story formula fully emerges in the work of Arthur Conan Doyle and becomes a regulated form in the "whodunits" and "clue-puzzles" of the inter-war golden age writers Agatha Christie, Dorothy L. Sayers, and Margery

Allingham. While the short story was the dominant form in detective fiction in the late nineteenth century, changes in general reading practices made the novel gradually more important. The short story, however, has played an important role in the development of detective fiction, and some critics, most notably Jacques Barzun, have argued that it is aesthetically the most pleasing form of detective fiction (1981: 146).

Arthur Conan Doyle and Sherlock Holmes

While a set of moral issues involving right and wrong can be located at the core of the detective story, its development in the nineteenth century is intricately linked with modernity and its emphasis on rationality, social control, and science, all exemplified in Poe's detective Dupin, whose reasoning helps him to see through the chaotic and mysterious. Therefore, while the roots of detective story are also in the fantasies of the sensation novel of the 1860s, and in the work of William "Wilkie" Collins in particular, the figure of the detective as someone who gains knowledge by using scientific methods is a clear marker of the modern attitude. The new detective, epitomized in Britain in the figure of Sherlock Holmes, is an expert on poisons, anatomy and fingerprints, i.e., in "the science of deduction."

A Study in Scarlet, the first narrative telling of the adventures of Sherlock Holmes, was published in 1887. While the publications of Arthur Conan Doyle (1859–1930) range from science fiction and historical novels to plays and history books, his main contribution to the detective story is the character of Sherlock Holmes, whose alleged rooms in 221B Baker Street have become a tourist attraction in London. Between the years 1887 and 1927, Conan Doyle's eccentric detective with his assistant Dr John Watson, a former army doctor and the narrator of the stories, plays a major role in sixty stories. These include four novellas – *A Study in Scarlet* (1887), *The Sign of Four* (1890), *The Hound of the Baskervilles* (1902), *The Valley of Fear* (1915) – and five collections of short stories: *The Adventures of Sherlock Holmes* (1892), *The Memoirs of Sherlock Holmes* (1894), *The Return of Sherlock Holmes* (1905), *His Last Bow* (1917), and *The Case-Book of Sherlock Holmes* (1927). In addition to these stories, the reputation of Holmes has been supported with a great number of film and television adaptations, fan clubs, internet sites, and novels featuring the character created by Conan Doyle.

Doyle's early writing was influenced by earlier detective fiction such as that of by Poe and the French writer Emile Gaboriau – who are referred to explicitly as characters in *A Study in Scarlet* – and also by the writing of Robert Louis Stevenson (Knight 1980: 68–9). The first two novellas pave the way for the Holmes phenomenon by developing the characters and Holmes's method, and sought to create exciting narratives around mysterious incidents (Knight 1980: 69). Regardless of their presentation of the central tenets of the Holmes story, the formula becomes successful only in the short stories with their publication in the popular magazine *The Strand*, whose

Canadian editor George Newnes commissioned Doyle to write initially six stories (Knight 2004: 58).

The Holmes stories were later published as collections. The first two of them, containing in all twenty-three stories, tend to be considered his best, partially because "The Final Problem," the concluding story in *The Memoirs of Sherlock Holmes*, was supposed to be the final Holmes story. This story shows the death of the detective together with that of his arch-enemy Professor Moriarty, "The Napoleon of crime" (n.d.: 471), in the falls of Reichenbach in Switzerland. Due to public demand, Doyle was forced to awake Holmes from dead and publish further stories for his fans. Many of the later stories, reported by Watson as cases from the early career of Holmes, are set in the 1890s rather than in the twentieth century.

The Holmes stories, with an average length of 12,000 words and a lot of plot (Knight 2004: 58), fit easily into the period's world view, emphasizing individualism and materialism, as propagated in *The Strand* and created a new type of expert hero. Indeed, as Watson mentions, Holmes, while knowing "nil" about literature, philosophy, and astronomy, has "profound" knowledge of chemistry and his knowledge of sensational literature is "immense" (n.d.: 22–3). His knowledge, in other words, is of matters that help him to solve crimes that the institutional police find puzzling. Unlike the thinking and analytical Dupin, Holmes is involved in action, moving around the city of London in disguise if necessary. On such occasions, his ability to perform as someone never ceases to surprise Watson. This can be seen in the incident set in an opium den east of the City of London in the story "The Man with the Twisted Lip" where Holmes performs the role of an old opium addict.

In addition to constructing an imaginary geography of London, the narratives map those places in terms of class, placing the den beyond the reach of the respectable middle class. Class, however, plays another interesting role in many Holmes stories, including "A Scandal in Bohemia" and "The Adventure of the Noble Bachelor," which show how the aristocracy is unable to solve their problems but need to hire the services of a middle-class professional. While the former story, indeed, shows how the King of Bohemia enters the rooms of Holmes in a disguise and hires him to restore a set of intimate letters held by the American opera singer Irene Adler, the latter's focus on the marriage of Lord St Simon to a suddenly vanishing lady reveals that for the Lord worse than loss of a loved one is a public loss of face. "What will the Duke say [. . .] when he hears that one of the family has been subjected to such humiliation?" (n.d.: 297). Both clients emphasize the need for discretion, but Holmes – and also the middle-class reader – is aware of their faults and inability to control their urges. Women, and a female sexuality which seeks to go beyond the possibilities of representation in these Victorian realist texts, can only be portrayed as mysterious and shadow-like, as Catherine Belsey's famous reading of Conan Doyle claims (1980: 109–17).

Some other aspects of gender emphasized in the stories are linked to masculinity. Holmes's detective work in the city has been connected to scouting, and Baden-Powell indeed suggested that boys read Holmes's narratives (Kestner 1997: 2). This role of Holmes as a scout and a spy able to gain information unavailable to the others further underlines his special status and masculinity. Many of the Holmes stories are indeed dependent on issues of masculinity and maleness, ranging from the homosocial relationship between Holmes and Watson to the latter's military career in Afghanistan. In his study of masculinity in Conan Doyle's fiction, Joseph Kestner (1997: 7) suggests that the stories can be read in the framework of the late-nineteenth-century concerns about gender and masculinity in particular. While this crisis was seen, for instance, in the Wilde trial and the attacks on patriarchal values by early feminists, traditional forms of imperial and military masculinity were sought to reconstruct in the period's adventure narratives and other forms of popular culture, of which the Holmes stories are also examples. A particularly striking example of this is the story "The Engineer's Thumb," which connects the discourses of masculinity and nation. It tells the story of the young engineer Victor Hatherley who is taken outside London to repair some machinery by Colonel Lysander Stark, a man speaking with a German accent. In the course of the story Hatherley, while saved from death at the hands of a group of Germans (with a British traitor) occupying a house with mysterious and gigantic hydraulic machines in the village of Eyford near Reading, loses his thumb. This story, voicing the nation's fear of the emerging military rivalry with Germany, has been interpreted as a narrative of masculine anxiety (Kestner 1997: 79). Framed in a narrative of nation, the loss of a digit becomes symbolic act of castrating an Englishman and thus reveals an explicit concern for the need to maintain a strong sense of national identity peculiar to the period (see Nyman 2000: 1–40). Englishness, indeed, is constructed in the stories as Holmes's brave and active masculinity located in the metonymic space of the metropolis. While Watson represents the modern everyman, honest and loyal, it is Holmes who saves the nation through action and intelligence.

G.K. Chesterton's Father Brown and
Early Twentieth-Century Detection

One of the most peculiar and unlikely detective heroes in the early twentieth century is Gilbert Keith Chesterton's (1874–1936) metaphysical protagonist Father Brown, a harmless- looking Catholic priest – the opposite of Holmes in many ways – from Essex. Chesterton, a well-known Edwardian author and public figure who worked in several genres, published five collections of short stories: *The Innocence of Father Brown* (1911), *The Wisdom of Father Brown* (1914), *The Incredulity of Father Brown* (1926), *The Secret of Father Brown* (1927), and *The Scandal of Father Brown* (1935). This output has been particularly attractive to readers preferring serious detective fiction, and Martin Kayman describes it as an "attempt to raise the genre into something that is simultaneously entertaining and ideologically influential" (2003: 55). By combining the detective story with a critique of contemporary culture, the Father Brown stories seek to criticize the materialist tendencies in modern society, suggesting that reason alone is not enough. The classical example of this attitude can be found in the early story "The Blue Cross," where Father Brown reveals to the French master criminal Flambeau how he recognized that the latter was merely masquerading as a priest: "You attacked reason [. . .] It's bad theology" (Chesterton 1981: 23).

While Chesterton originally argued for the metropolis as the space of the modern in his 1902 essay claiming that the detective story is the romance of the modern city (1976: 3–6), his stories offer fewer visions of the exotica offered by the urban space than do those of Conan Doyle. While "The Blue Cross" follows Flambeau and Father Brown walking towards Hampstead, and "The Queer Feet" is set in an exquisite Hotel in Belgravia, the atmosphere of the city remains secondary to the overwhelming sense of mystery, suggesting perhaps that there is something wrong with the city, its values, and lifestyle with mysterious religious cults as presented in "The Eye of Apollo." Similarly, the impact of imported modernity also affects the countryside: as it transforms the harmonious values attached an imagined England into "strange things," what we hear is "a tragic tale" (Chesterton 1981: 89). "The Wrong Shape" is set in such a space, by "certain of the great roads going north out of London" in an Anglo-Indian house looking like it had been "built chiefly for the hot weather" (89). Indeed, its owner the poet Leonard Quinton, a writer of "erotic verses on vellum" (91), is dealing with issues out of place in England:

There is an undercurrent in Chesterton's stories that can best be described as a form of anti-modernism where an imagined English tradition is pitted against the values of imported modernity and the foreign, including orientalism, American religious movements, and decayed European aristocrats (see Nyman 2000: 31–5). For Chesterton, their presence even in remote villages in the English country creates problems for the maintenance of community and harmony. Whereas "God of the Gongs" introduces a voodoo conspiracy involving "octoroons and African half-bloods of various shades" (1981: 281) passing for Italian waiters in an East Anglian seaside resort out of season, and thus creating an invisible danger, "The Sins of Prince Saradine" places an Italian vendetta in Norfolk. Yet, as the ending of the story puts it clearly, there are still "happier" and untouched places in the English countryside with "[a] smell of hawthorn and of orchards" (1981: 118).

In addition to privileging rural England, the stories contribute to the making of Englishness by championing the notion of common sense: Father Brown is constantly shown to be able to see through smokescreens and find a simple explanation for every event. What makes this idea of common sense particularly interesting in the context of Englishness is that it is a form English empiricism, preferring the concrete to the abstract, and the objective to the subjective (Easthope 1999: 90). In the stories this moment is repeatedly narrated as a form of revelation when Father Brown suddenly realizes the meaning of the paradox and rules out supernatural explanations of earthly crimes: "Then I thought for a minute and a half more. And I believe I saw the manner of the crime, as clearly as if I were going to commit it" (1981: 51). Thus the Father Brown stories are located in a framework of Englishness and promote common sense and reason. They also wish to combine them with a moral view deemed lacking in contemporary society based on the privileging of technology and machinery.

Following the success of Sherlock Holmes, the detective became a popular hero as seen in the numerous detective stories published in the period. Stephen Knight (2004: 68–80) divides the early twentieth-century detective stories into the following categories: scientific detectives, e.g., Jacques Futrelle's Professor S.F.X. Van Dusen, aka "The Thinking Machine" (*The Thinking Machine* (1907)), and R. Austin Freeman's Dr Thorndyke (*John Thorndyke's Cases* (1907)); ironic anti-heroes, e.g., E.W. Hornung's gentleman-cum-criminal Raffles (*The Amateur Cracksman* (1899)); low-level detection, e.g., Arthur Morrison's Martin Hewitt stories and Chesterton's Father Brown; women detectives, e.g., George Sims's *Dorcas Dene, Detective: Her Adventures* (1897), and Baroness Emmuska Orczy's *Lady Molly of Scotland Yard* (1910).

As the list shows, detective fiction was for some writers only one of the genres to utilize; Baroness Orczy is better known as a romance writer. Another productive author worth mentioning is Edgar Wallace. In addition to his numerous thrillers and colonial adventure stories, Wallace's contribution to the short story includes the collection *The Mind of Mr. J.G. Reeder*. These stories feature Mr Reeder, a curious Scotland Yard detective officer, who is able to solves puzzles because, to use his own words, "'I – I see wrong in everything. That's my curious perversion – I have a criminal mind!'" (1977: 8).

The Golden Age

The period between the two world wars is generally seen as the golden age of detective fiction when the development of the clue-puzzle is enhanced with the introduction of the codification of the genre and its general rules. The term is somewhat problematic as it seems to suggest a homogenous literary form and even to romanticize the period as an idyll (Knight 2004: 85–6). In addition to the fact that the detective novel becomes the dominant form, partly because of lending libraries, changes in modes of urban travel and the increase in middle-class women readers (Symons 1992: 86–7), the dominant mode of the detective story is the clue-puzzle. This form, associated perhaps most strongly with the work of Agatha Christie Mallowan (1890–1976) in Britain and S.S. Van Dine (1887–1939) in the United States has such structural uniformity, lacking from earlier detective narratives, that it can be seen as a separate subgenre. Stephen Knight (2004: 87–9) suggests that it is based on the following five features. First, it deals with murder taking place amongst the upper-middle class staying at a country house. Second, it also tends not to include proper criminals and working-class characters and deny the existence of social conflicts. Third, the victim is someone with authority and money and who is generally envied and hated by a larger group of relatives, visitors, or other subjects suspected of the crime. Fourth, the detective work is based on a rational attempt to solve the puzzle. Fifth, the clue-puzzle usually avoids humour and romantic plots in order to intellectualize the reading – the reader is supposed to work actively with the clues as well as the detective in order to solve the crime.

The codification of the conventions is evident in two well-known sets of rules, those presented by Ronald A. Knox in "A Detective Story Decalogue" (1929) and S.S. Van Dine in "Twenty Rules for Writing Detective Stories" (1929). These sets of rules construct the detective story as a game that should be played fairly by both writers and readers – to use the words of Van Dine, "The reader must have equal opportunity with the detective for solving the mystery" (1976: 189). According to these rules, any event in the detective story should provide a clue for the reader, who – like the detective – should be able to arrive at the correct interpretation. The emphasis on fair play is evident in Knox's "Decalogue," where the first rule says that "The criminal must be someone mentioned in the early part of the story, but must not be anyone whose thoughts the reader has been allowed to follow (1981: 200). Similarly, Knox forbids the use of "more than one secret room or passage" (1981: 200) and says that "No Chinaman must figure in the story" (1981: 201). In sum, the sets of rules seek to elevate the genre into a chess-like intellectual pastime. At the same time, the content of the stories and their representations of class and gender are rendered secondary.

Such clue-puzzles were created by the three major writers of the period, including those to be examined in more detail below: Agatha Christie, Dorothy L. Sayers (1893–1957), and Margery Allingham (1904–66); other writers of the period include Anthony Berkeley Cox, Ngaio Marsh, Patricia Wentworth, and Patrick Hamilton. As the genre becomes increasingly dominated by women writers, there are also shifts in the stories' representation of gender and nation. It can be argued that the inter-war detective story replaces the jingoistic and patriotic narrative of Englishness with a more domestic and inward-turning story: this England is a nation replete with images of country houses, gardens, and small villages. Alison Light's important study of Agatha Christie in the context of the period's changing attitude to the national idea paves way for an understanding of golden age detective fiction more generally:

[T]he 1920s and '30s saw a move away from formerly heroic and officially masculine public rhetorics of national destiny and from a dynamic and missionary view of the Victorian and Edwardian middle class in "Great Britain" to an Englishness at once less imperial and more inward-looking, more domestic and private – and, in terms of pre-war standards, more "feminine." (1991: 8)

Agatha Christie

Agatha Christie is undoubtedly one of the world's best-known authors, whose literature output includes more 120 books and several plays over a period of more than fifty-five years. Christie, indeed, continued to write detective stories well beyond World War II into the 1970s. Between the publication of her first novel in 1920 and 1945, she created her famous detectives, the Belgian private detective Hercule Poirot and Miss Jane Marple, both of whom show how the image of the detective changes from the great masculine hero to a more domestic and feminine actor. In addition to these protagonists, she wrote several stories about other detectives, including the private investigator Parker Pyne and the light-hearted 1920s couple Tommy and Tuppence. She also published several collections of short mystery stories with gothic elements.

The character of Hercule Poirot is an example of the change in the detective hero and his official Englishness. The retired Belgian policeman is nearly a parody of established conventions. Unlike the tall Englishman Holmes, Poirot is a small and fussy foreigner, "a funny little man with [an] egg-shaped head and the enormous moustaches" (Christie 1955: 1) and almost effeminate in his behavior. While Poirot made his first appearance in Christie's first novel, the first collection of short stories *Poirot Investigates* (1924) presents eleven cases; some other stories written in the period were collected in *The Under Dog and Other Mysteries* (1951), *Murder in the Mews and Three Other Poirot Cases* (1927), and *The Regatta Mystery and Other Stories* (1939), the last featuring stories about Poirot, Marple, and Parker Pyne. The early Poirot stories are based on the Doylean model, opening often with a scene where Poirot is in his rooms with his friend and assistant Captain Hastings and waits for clients, and constructing Hastings as a storyteller and writer of Poirot's casebook. Poirot's methods, based on psychology and his "little gray cells," are explicitly contrasted with those of the Inspector Japp from Scotland Yard, Poirot's friend and a regular minor character in the stories (Christie 1955: 67).

The stories in *Poirot Investigates* send Poirot to the English countryside, fashionable areas of London, and as far as Egypt, to solve murders and to locate missing persons (including a kidnapped prime minister) and official documents. Poirot's success in solving the cases reinforces the change in the detective story and its feminization. In solving the cases, Poirot often reinterprets clues and events by using his knowledge of gendered psychology inaccessible to many other male characters in the stories accustomed to traditional patterns. In other words, it is his marginality in British society that allows him to think differently. For instance, the explanation in the "The Adventure of 'The Western Star'" shows how Poirot's knowledge of women's behavior surpasses that of Hastings: "'*Si, si mon ami*, it is a pity that you study not the psychology. She told you that the letters were destroyed? Oh, *la la, never* does a woman destroy a letter if she can avoid it! Not even if it would be more prudent to do so!'" (Christie 2001: 40; italics original). Furthermore, he also shows that the apparent suicide of the elderly Mr Maltravers in "The Tragedy at Marsdon Manor" is a result of careful planning by his young and scheming wife.

In the view of Plain (2001: 41), the attraction of death in inter-war detective fiction is linked to cultural ambiguity related to death in the period: a more general human obsession with death conflicts with the post-war attempt to escape its presence. As

Plain concludes, "detective fiction thus become[s], paradoxically an integral part of both those rituals of remembrance and the self-preserving necessity of forgetting" (2001: 41). The detective story, by providing a coherent explanation to the mystery of death, is "a narrative of reassurance" (Plain 2001: 41). While Poirot's success provides such reassurance within the narrative, Christie's stories do not promote a nostalgic vision of pre-war England as a site of harmony and an acceptance of its social order – such an understanding of Christie may have been promoted by late-twentieth-century television adaptations of her work. Rather, the Poirot stories set amongst the upper classes show that the traditional pillars of society are not morally intact and many of them cannot be trusted. For instance, "The Million Dollar Bond Robbery" shows that the respectable general manager of the London and Scottish Bank is willing to blame his partner's nephew for committing a theft of valuable Liberty Bonds that he is guilty of himself. Similarly, "The Incredible Theft" shows that the respectable Lord Mayfield is guilty of treason. Thus the golden age mystery is not a mere narrative of idealized community but it – and Christie's work in particular – rests on issues of personal uncertainty and the ever-present threat of danger and betrayal in that community (Knight 2004: 92–3).

Another detective created by Christie seeking to isolate the dangers behind respectable facades is Miss Jane Marple, an elderly unmarried woman from the village of St Mary Mead, introduced in the collection *The Thirteen Problems* (1932), in addition to numerous novels. The collection is structured as a series of mystery stories told by the members of "The Tuesday Night Club," meeting weekly to talk about mysterious events. Gradually its participants, including, among others, Marple's nephew the writer Raymond West and Sir Henry Clithering from Scotland Yard, learn about Jane Marple's ability to solve crimes on the basis of various village incidents: they "throw [. . .] considerable light on human nature" (Christie 1993: 147). Able to explain incidents that have troubled other members of the party for a long time, she surpasses the patronizing expectations of the younger and male participants (1993: 52).

The everyday tragedies of St Mary Mead have provided Marple with a deep understanding of the workings of the human mind, which shows how futile life has become in interwar Britain. The fact that Christie's stories are not beyond the impact of modernity is also seen in the modern lifestyle of the detective couple Tommy and Tuppence Beresford featured in the collection *Partners in Crime* (1929). Tuppence, in particular, is shown as a representative of urban modernity, speaking its language, shopping for endless hats and luxury items such as silver cigarette cases, and talking about nightclubs and affairs. Consisting of the interlinked cases of Blunt's Brilliant Detectives, this collection positions the young couple in a series of parodic detective adventures. A good example is "The Man in the Mist" which finds them in the cocktail bar of the Grand Adlington Hotel as they have just failed to find a stolen pearl necklace regardless of their best attempts (Christie 1995: 96).

Amongst other short fiction by Christie in the period, the short stories collected in *Parker Pyne Investigates* (1932) are worth mentioning. These stories feature Parker

Pyne, a retired government official whose career has been spent compiling statistics. Pyne advertises daily in *The Times* with an inviting text: "ARE YOU HAPPY? IF NOT, CONSULT MR. PARKER PYNE" (1982: 7; capitals original). Pyne, however, is not primarily involved in solving crimes: rather, his interest is in reconstructing the problems – and lives – of his clients. Many of the people coming to see Pyne suffer from what he calls "human troubles." In "The Case of the Discontented Husband" we learn: " 'There is ill health. There is boredom. There are wives who are in trouble over their husbands. There are husbands' – he paused – 'who are in trouble over their wives'" (1982: 46).

The rest of Christie's short stories in the period tend be generic mixtures, combining elements from the gothic, romance fiction, and mystery stories. The stories about Harley Quin in *The Mysterious Mr. Quin* introduce an unknown and secretive man who turns up in places where a crime has been committed, leading to an uncovering of the event. Other examples include, for instance, "Philomel Cottage" in *The Listerdale Mystery and Other Stories* (1934), a story that tells how Alix Martin marries a man whom she has known for a short period of time and who, as she gradually discovers, is planning to murder her. Elements of mysticism and occult abound in many of these stories: "The Strange Case of Sir Arthur Carmichael" in *The Hound of Death and Other Stories* (1933) suggests that Lady Carmichael, with "Asiatic blood," has used her secret powers to metamorphose her husband's son into a cat.

Dorothy L. Sayers

Sayers's detective fiction, consisting of about twelve novels and approximately two dozen short stories, was mainly published in the period 1923–37. After having established financial independence for herself, in addition to a reputation as one of the major authors in the genre, Sayers turned to what she considered more serious writing, i.e., essays and the translation of Dante's *Divina Commedia*. Considered a master of the form and the creator of one of its most eccentric detectives, Lord Peter Wimsey, Sayers's reception has been slightly ambiguous. While she has been dismissed by critics of the genre such as Julian Symons (1992: 99–101), mainly because of the snobbishness of her main detective, her stylishness and literariness are praised by many. More recently some more extensive readings have been presented. As an example, Gill Plain (1996: 45–67) has presented an important reading of Wimsey and his behavior in the context of war trauma and the reconstruction of identity. In addition to the Wimsey stories, Sayers also wrote several short stories about the traveling salesman Montagu Egg, who solves crimes quoting his salesman's handbook.

The short stories about Lord Peter Wimsey are less elaborate than the novels in their treatment of the main character. What is often seen as an important development in the Wimsey novels – the developing relationship between the detective and Harriet Vane, a writer of detective fiction – is not present in the short stories published in Sayers's lifetime. Wimsey, "belonging to one of the oldest ducal families in England"

(Sayers 1969: 147), is a representative of an upper-class Englishness replete with clubs, country houses, and movement in appropriate social circles. Wimsey's companion is his reliable manservant Bunter. Yet Charles Rzepka (2005: 162) claims that the stereotype of the aristocratic playboy is one of the many roles he is able to use: by solving crimes Wimsey tries to make himself useful and negotiate the guilt has for sending his men to death during World War I.

While the key collection of Wimsey stories is *Lord Peter Views the Body* (1928), the collections *Hangman's Holiday* (1933) and *In the Teeth of Evidence* (1939) include several Wimsey and Montagu Egg stories. The posthumously published collection *Striding Folly* (1973) contains three Wimsey stories and publishes the final Wimsey story "Talboys" for the first time. The twelve case stories in the first collection locate Wimsey in a particular social class and show his preference for its values. What they create is a particularly exquisite, even snobbish atmosphere. For instance, "The Fascinating Problem of Uncle Meleager's Will" shows how the amateur detective spends his morning in "mauve silk legs" before bathing in "verbena-scented water" (1969: 36). The mode of discourse applied is appropriate to the class and period. The opening of the short story "In the Teeth of Evidence" shows Wimsey relying on his usual banter – which resembles the writing of P.G. Wodehouse – even when visiting his dentist (2003: 1). In these social circles evenings are spent at dinner parties and clubs. The description of the Soviet club where his sister takes him in an early story develops Wimsey's snobbishness: the level of its cooking is "beastly, the men don't shave, and the conversation gets [his] goat" (1969: 37). Yet the description of its atmosphere reveals an attitude towards the period's fashionable flirting with socialism and radicalism amongst the intelligentsia, discussing "[e]thics and sociology, the latest vortices of the Whirligig school of verse" (1969: 39).

Sayers's amateur hero is constructed in an intellectual context, which is developed in the stories through Wimsey's character. While Sherlock Holmes's knowledge of literature and philosophy was nil, Wimsey quotes Dickens fluently, is a collector of classic literature and even bases his judgment of character on people's aesthetic views – and the stories abound with references to English proverbs and literary texts. "The Undignified Melodrama of the Bone of Contention" is set in the library of the deceased Mr Burdock, an abandoned and damp room with "[t]he curious and musty odour of decayed leather and damp paper add[ing] to the general cheerlessness of the atmosphere" (1969: 113). To add to neglect of the tradition of learning, symbolizing loss of respect for the values of the imaginary England of the past, the younger son Havilland showing the library to Wimsey is a City businessman with mundane opinions on literature (1969: 14). As this shows, the crime in some of Sayers's fiction is not only the literal murder committed but it is a crime against what Susan Rowland considers the nationalist dream in Sayers: "an imagined England of whole, sufficient, cultural peace" (2001: 70).

In the context of gender, Wimsey's intellectualism, love of the arts, and knowledge of good cooking and fine wines make his masculinity somewhat feminized – especially if contrasted with the images of hard-boiled males emerging in the works of American detective fiction writers Dashiell Hammett and Raymond Chandler in the same period. Some critics have suggested that, as such a representation of intellectualism, Wimsey appealed particularly well to middle-class women readers (Knight 2004: 99). Yet, it should be noted, Wimsey is also represented as a military hero and an English gentleman fond of riding and life in the countryside. To emphasize her hero's allegiance to causes of national importance, some stories weave political aspects into their narrative. While "The Adventurous Exploit of the Cave of Ali Baba" shows Wimsey faking his own death in order to infiltrate an increasingly powerful secret society, "The Bibulous Business of a Matter of Taste" takes Wimsey to France to purchase the formula a new poison gas for the British government. Upon reaching the house of its inventor he meets there two agents, both of whom claim to be the real Peter Wimsey. To pinpoint the role of class, the story culminates in a blind-tasting of fine wines over the dinner and shows that the original Wimsey, because of his expert knowledge and manners, cannot be beaten by treacherous Englishmen (Sayers 1969: 155).

As the above discussion of the Wimsey stories has shown, they are not mere clue-puzzles to be followed by the reader. Sayers, indeed, often sought to exceed the conventions of the genre. Yet its elements are central in many stories and particularly so in such stories as "The Fascinating Problem of Uncle Meleager's Will," where the detective and his party try to find the will by answering the clues which are presented in the form of a crossword puzzle. Similarly, "The Vindictive Story of the Footsteps That Run," in which Mrs Brotherton is murdered in her kitchen when preparing a roast chicken meal, is based on the absence of the murder weapon. Indeed, the skewer used has been stuck into the chicken which her husband has put into the oven after the murder – fortunately Wimsey takes the dish out before it is too well-done and the laboratory finds enough of the victim's blood in the weapon. Strange events and medical conditions, often found characteristic of Sayers, figure in "The Incredible Elopement of Lord Peter Wimsey," where the jealous American husband of a beautiful woman keeps her in isolation in a village in the north of Spain and, by refusing to give her medication for her thyroid condition, keeps her in a demented state of mind.

While the short stories map shorter episodes in Wimsey's life than the novels, the posthumously published "Talboys" deserves a mention because it shows the later life of Lord Peter Wimsey, now married to Harriet Vine and a father of three boys. With a narrative of family problems and child psychology, the domestication of the detective appears complete. Here the detective-cum-father also regains the possibility of social responsibility and illustrates the words of Rzepka: "Sayers's aim in creating Wimsey was, in part, to rehabilitate the idea of social responsibility for her own 'lost generation' by embodying it in a member of England's ostensibly least responsible and currently most superfluous class" (2005: 165).

The rest of Sayers's short stories deal with the traveling salesman Montagu Egg or they are general mystery stories. While a word-guessing game played in

"Nebuchadnezzar" leads a guilty man to confess his wife's murder, "The Leopard Lady" imagines a removal firm removing unwanted people, including the story's protagonist's protégé Cyril. The Montagu Egg stories are set in a lower middle-class world of ill-kept hotels and their bars, where men meet and discuss their trade. As a representative of Plummet & Rose, Wines and Spirits, Piccadilly, Egg, however, enjoys access to the houses of the upper class. The stories are a curious mixture of old and new. At one level, they satirize the US-imported rhetoric of business, as they show Egg constantly quoting his written guidelines: "He smiled pleasantly, bearing in mind Maxim Number Ten of the Salesman's handbook, 'The Goodwill of the maid in nine-tenths of the trade'" (Sayers 1974: 91). A particular crime that Egg meets on the road concerns poisoning: while in "The Poisoned Dow '08" Lord Borrodale's butler has cleverly poisoned his master's port wine as an act of revenge, in "Bitter Almonds" the cause of Mr Whipley's death is the poisonous oil in the liqueur bottle which has remained unopened too long and risen to the top. Compared to the Wimsey stories, the Egg stories are less literary and aim at a more immediate humorous effect.

Margery Allingham

Margery Allingham, the third significant female crime writer of the golden age, is less frequently studied than Christie and Sayers, although her writing is humorous, characters lively, and her fiction provides interesting viewpoints on life in Britain in the period. While Allingham's first novel *The White Cottage Mystery* (1927) was originally serialized, she also wrote a several short stories featuring her amateur detective Albert Campion, one of the period's apparently foolish and mannered investigators. Several of the stories she wrote for the *Strand Magazine* in the 1930s were published in the collection *Mr. Campion and Others* (1939). This collection partially overlaps with the US-published collection *Mr. Campion: Criminologist* (1937), which, however, presents each story as a part of "Albert Campion's Casebook" and precedes them with the detective's "Private Notes." Allingham continued her writing career to the 1960s, publishing more novels and stories, all of which were not detective fiction.

In the case of Allingham, the short stories tend to present further episodes in the career of the detective than to open up entirely new perspectives on to him. As the first Campion novel was published in 1928, he was already known to the readers when the stories were published. Like Wimsey, Campion, a bachelor and an owner of a flat in Piccadilly, is a member of the upper classes who frequents the most expensive and fashionable restaurants in town, such as the Gillyflower in "The Hat-Trick" (Allingham 1991: 51). The crimes that Campion solves are particularly suitable for his social circles where class, marriage and a leisured lifestyle are important: these people are concerned with stolen jewels, kidnappings, and murders at gentlemen's clubs. Allingham's plotting is careful and the short stories contain elements of surprise. For instance, in "The Case of the White Elephant" Campion follows closely the odd behavior of Miss Margot Matisse, a visiting manicurist and a partner of a well-known burglar. Miss Matisse, while having tea at one of the most expensive restaurants and listening to a performing balalaika ensemble, suddenly shouts out aloud "Mrs. Gregory! Mrs. Gregory!" (Allingham 1963: 96), and claims to have mistaken somebody for her friend; later the police tailing her witness a similar scene at the luncheon program of the Venetian cinema when she shouts for "Mattie," again in vain, for nobody comes. Campion discovers that the criminals are using code.

Allingham's stories are particularly rich in their representations of Englishness and show that a sense of true national identity is constructed in opposition to national (and other) Others such as French criminals. In addition to "The Case of the White Elephant," the link between foreignness and crime is made in "The Frenchman's Gloves," in which a gang with French members kidnaps a French businessman visiting Britain. Susan Rowland has suggested that Allingham's early fiction contrasts an English tradition and a foreign one, conflating the latter also with "corporatism, big business and urban modernity" (2001: 68). Urban modernity remains ambiguous in Allingham, which is also the case with Doyle and Chesterton. While modern urban spaces enable Campion and his friends to benefit from a consumer culture with good restaurants, not to mention new fast cars and jewelry, they are also sites where criminals threaten the maintenance of such a lifestyle. Indeed, Soho is represented as a "dark, shabby" place avoided by the police in the night-time (Allingham 1991: 144), and the danger posed by the lower classes is evident in the casual way in which the pickpocket Cassy Wild moves around the Pantheon Hall of Varieties, one of the remaining music halls in "The Meaning of the Act," a story collected in *Mr. Campion and Others*.

The crisis of traditional Englishness is taken further in such stories where the representatives of the upper class enter the ranks of the criminals. This distrust in tradition is nearly imagined as a narrative of decay in "Safe as Houses" where Second Cousin Monmouth, "a sad and fantastic figure [. . .] with a depressed gaze" (1991: 171) tries to raise money by claiming that Aunt Charlotte's house in Kent is available for rent in Sussex. Similarly, the jewel thief Rocks Denver is able to pose as member of a house party because of his background – "He's one of the lads who let his school down" (1991: 39) – thus making him a traitor to class, gender and nation, a traitor more dangerous because of his ability to pass as one of "us" (1991: 43).

The development of the English detective story is embedded in the ways of imagining Britain from the days of empire to the more inward-turned Englishness between the world wars. In addition to offering exotica, adventure, and a sense of mystery to their readers, these narratives show a concern for law and social order and their maintenance. Rather than mere puzzles with no social meanings, these stories shed light on the transformation of values and ideologies in a modernizing Britain by presenting both overtly masculine detectives basing their work on science and rationality and more feminized ones relying on soft values and psychology.

REFERENCES AND FURTHER READING

The most up-to-date essay collection dealing with detective fiction is Priestman (2003). Herbert (1999) is a standard reference work, and classic essays in the field can be found in Haycraft (1976) and Winks (1981).

Allingham, M. (1963). *Mr. Campion: Criminologist.* New York: Macfadden (original work published 1937).

Allingham, M. (1991). *Mr. Campion and Others.* New York: Avon (original work published 1939).

Barzun, J. (1981). "Detection and the Literary Art," in R. Winks (ed.), *Detective Fiction: A Collection of Critical Essays*, pp. 144–54. Englewood Cliffs: Prentice-Hall (original work published 1976).

Belsey, C. (1980). *Critical Practice.* London: Routledge.

Cawelti, J.G. (1976). *Adventure, Mystery and Romance: Formula Stories as Art and Popular Culture.* Chicago: University of Chicago Press.

Chesterton, G.K. (1976). "A Defence of Detective Stories," in H. Haycraft (ed.), *The Art of the Mystery Story: A Collection of Critical Essays*, pp. 3–6. New York: Biblo and Tannen (original work published 1946).

Chesterton, G.K. (1981). *The Complete Father Brown.* London: Penguin.

Christie, A. (n.d.). *The Listerdale Mystery and Other Stories.* London: Collins (original work published 1934).

Christie, A. (1955). *The Under Dog and Other Mysteries.* New York: Pocket Books (original work published 1951).

Christie, A. (1967). *Murder in the Mews and Three Other Poirot Cases.* London: Fontana (original work published 1927).

Christie, A. (1971). *The Mysterious Mr. Quin.* London: Fontana (original work published 1930).

Christie, A. (1981). *The Hound of Death.* London: Collins (original work published 1933).

Christie, A. (1982). *Parker Pyne Investigates.* London: Fontana (original work published 1934).

Christie, A. (1984). *The Regatta Mystery and Other Stories.* New York: Berkley Books (original work published 1939).

Christie, A. (1993). *The Thirteen Problems.* London: HarperCollinsPublishers (original work published 1932).

Christie, A. (1995). *Partners in Crime.* London: HarperCollinsPublishers (original work published 1929).

Christie, A. (2001). *Poirot Investigates.* London: HarperCollinsPublishers (original work published 1924).

Doyle, A.C. (n.d.). *The Complete Sherlock Holmes.* Leicester: Blitz.

Easthope, A. (1999). *Englishness and National Culture.* London: Routledge.

Haycraft, H. (ed.) (1976). *The Art of the Mystery Story: A Collection of Critical Essays.* New York: Biblo and Tannen (original work published 1946).

Herbert, R. (ed.) (1999). *Oxford Companion to Crime and Mystery Writing.* Oxford: Oxford University Press.

Kayman, M.A. (2003). "The Short Story from Poe to Chesterton," in M. Priestman (ed.), *The Cambridge Companion to Crime Fiction*, pp. 41–58. Cambridge: Cambridge University Press.

Kestner, J.A. (1997). *Sherlock's Men: Masculinity, Conan Doyle, and Cultural History.* Aldershot: Ashgate.

Knight, S. (1980). *Form and Ideology in Crime Fiction.* London: Macmillan.

Knight, S. (2004). *Crime Fiction 1800–2000: Detection, Death, Diversity.* Houndmills: Palgrave Macmillan.

Knox, R.A. (1981). "A Detective Story Decalogue," in R. Winks (ed.), *Detective Fiction: A Collection of Critical Essays*, pp. 200–2. Englewood Cliffs: Prentice Hall (original work published 1929).

Light, A. (1991). *Forever England: Femininity, Literature and Conservatism between the Wars.* London: Routledge.

McCracken, S. (1998). *Pulp: Reading Popular Fiction.* Manchester: Manchester University Press.

Nyman, J. (2000). *Under English Eyes: Constructions of Europe in Early Twentieth-Century British Fiction.* Amsterdam: Rodopi.

Plain, G. (1996). *Women's Fiction of the Second World War: Gender, Power and Resistance*. Edinburgh: Edinburgh University Press.

Plain, G. (2001). *Twentieth-Century Crime Fiction: Gender, Sexuality and the Body*. Edinburgh: Edinburgh University Press.

Porter, D. (1981). *The Pursuit of Crime: Art and Ideology in Detective Fiction*. New Haven: Yale University Press.

Priestman, M. (ed.) (2003). *The Cambridge Companion to Crime Fiction*. Cambridge: Cambridge University Press.

Rowland, S. (2001). *From Agatha Christie to Ruth Rendell*. Houndmills: Palgrave Macmillan.

Rzepka, C. (2005). *Detective Fiction*. Cambridge: Polity.

Sayers, D.L. (1969). *Lord Peter Views the Body*. New York: Avon (original work published 1928).

Sayers, D.L. (1974). *Hangman's Holiday*. London: New English Library (original work published 1933).

Sayers, D.L. (1980). *Striding Folly*. London: New English Library (original work published 1973).

Sayers, D.L. (2003). *In the Teeth of Evidence*. London: Hodder and Stoughton (original work published 1939).

Symons, J. (1992). *Bloody Murder: From the Detective Story to the Crime Novel: A History*. London: Pan Macmillan.

Thompson, J. (1994). *Fiction, Crime, and Empire: Clues to Modernity and Postmodernism*. Urbana: University of Illinois Press.

Van Dine, S.S. (1976). "Twenty Rules for Writing Detective Stories," in H. Haycraft (ed.), *The Art of the Mystery Story: A Collection of Critical Essays*, pp. 189–93. New York: Biblo and Tannen (original work published 1946).

Wallace, E. (1977). *The Mind of Mr. J. G. Reeder*. Bath: Lythway Press (original work published 1929).

Winks, R. (ed.) (1981). *Detective Fiction: A Collection of Critical Essays*. Englewood Cliffs: Prentice-Hall.

Woods, R. (1990). "'His Appearance is Against Him': The Emergence of the Detective," in R.G. Walker and J.M. Frazer (eds), *The Cunning Craft: Original Essays on Detective Fiction and Contemporary Literary Theory*, pp. 15–44. Macomb, Illinois: Western Illinois University.

6

The British and Irish Ghost Story and Tale of the Supernatural: 1880–1945

Becky DiBiasio

The Roots of the Ghost Story

In the middle of the isolation of war-time a number of the English Strand Magazine fell into my hands; and, among other somewhat redundant matter, I read a story about a young married couple who move into a furnished house in which there is a curiously shaped table with carvings of crocodiles on it. Towards evening an intolerable and very specific smell begins to pervade the house; they stumble over something in the dark; they seem to see a vague form gliding over the stairs – in short, we are given to understand that the presence of the table causes ghostly crocodiles to haunt the place, or that the wooden monsters come to life in the dark, or something of the sort. It was a naïve enough story, but the uncanny feeling it produced was quite remarkable. (Freud 1955: 244–5)

This anecdote from Sigmund Freud's 1919 essay on "The Uncanny" ("Das Unheimliche"), which remains one of the clearest statements about the power of literary fantasy, illustrates several characteristics of the English ghost story: the story occurs in a familiar, safe British setting and the narrative gradually develops an atmosphere of discomfort and tension; a small group of characters are isolated and threatened by a representative of the dead; they are not directly or necessarily linked to the object which contains a malignant spirit; and the experience for the characters is sensory as they smell, touch, and possibly see something that is both alien and localized. The story lacks a stated rationale for the appearance of the supernatural, but there is an element of dark humor – presumably they are renting the malignant spirit as well as the house. The table that houses the spirit is alien, a souvenir of empire and colonialism, and it haunts the home and therefore the couple just as the repercussions of empire building haunted the British at the turn of the century.

Freud does not bother to give us the resolution of the story. For his purpose in the essay, closure is unimportant; his focus is on the shared moment of dislocation and unease experienced by the reader as well as by the characters when the table comes to life. That focus on the temporary displacement of both reader and characters is also typical; a rationale for the appearance of a ghost or alien is replaced by tension through the implication and creeping fear that the world is not what we think it is.

Freud does stress that there is a difference, primarily aesthetic, between the literary uncanny and any real-world experience of the uncanny. Readers of fiction experience the uncanny only if an author creates the proper mood and the setting is real but the characters or events are supernatural, or if they empathize with the emotional state of a character. For example, in Walter de la Mare's supernatural tale, "Seaton's Aunt," which first appeared in the April 1922 issue of *The London Mercury*, the narrator slowly comes to the realization that both the guardian and the shadowy inhabitants of the ancestral home of a schoolfriend are repulsive vampiric beings and that no one can save Seaton from being slowly destroyed by them. The narrator cannot even imagine a way to describe to the police or other adults what he senses. Who would believe him? The story is effective, in part, because the reader can sympathize with the fear and frustration of a boy who knows that he will not be believed – he can only observe and be horrified by what he sees.

Freud creates another link to the British ghost story when he points out that many languages do not have any words that are equivalent to the German "unheimlich" (uncanny), but English has several, including: "Uncomfortable, uneasy, gloomy, dismal, uncanny, ghastly; (of a house) haunted; (of a man) a repulsive fellow" (Freud 1955: 221). Speakers of English are, in a sense, linguistically predisposed to be attracted to ghost stories.

In the eighteenth century, "fantasy" was a term used to describe any use of imagination, but became associated particularly with literary tales of the supernatural. The literary fairy tales of German romanticism such as Johann Ludwig Tieck's "The Elves" and E.T.A. Hoffmann's "The Sandman" (which is the primary text that Freud analyzes in his essay) reflect themes of doppelgängers, alienation, madness, and isolation that were adapted by writers of gothic fiction.

Gothic tales were particularly popular in Britain from 1764 to 1820: stories about innocent characters who were powerless and at risk of physical, sexual, and mental violation by patriarchal villains. Medieval castles and abbeys, exotic locales, and the ruins of religious houses provided the settings. These stories of evil patriarchs and terrorized but resourceful young heroes and heroines caught the interest of a variety of readers, many of whom were marginalized by class and/or gender, were literate, and had to cope with political, social, and economic revolutions in their own lives.

Celebrated gothic novels include Horace Walpole's *The Castle of Otronto* (1764), in which the supernatural is an important element of the plot and action, Ann Radcliffe's *Mysteries of Udolfo* (1794), in which seemingly supernatural elements are rationalized, Matthew Lewis's lurid *The Monk* (1796), which focuses on sexual, moral, and religious transgressions, and Mary Shelley's *Frankenstein* (1818), which contrasts the ideals of the Enlightenment with those of romanticism. These stories caught the attention of readers of all classes and reflect subversive reactions to the political repercussions of the Enlightenment, the rise of the middle class, the geographic redistribution of population, and an economic redistribution caused by the Industrial Revolution.

Gothic fiction influenced the development of several subgenres of popular fiction in the nineteenth century, including: the ghost story, the sensation novel, the uncanny or weird adventure tale, the detective story, and supernatural horror tales. We are still familiar with the conventions of most of these subgenres, but sensation fiction is a particularly Victorian staple of inexpensive books and magazines that foregrounds the lack of options for unhappily married women. *Lady Audley's Secret* (1862), by Mary Elizabeth Braddon, was one of the earliest and most notorious sensation novels. The title character, a young wife, becomes an adulteress and, ultimately, a murderess as well. Even more popular was *East Lynne* (1861), by Mrs Henry Wood, which combined a lurid domestic crime with realistic settings and real current events. Sensation novels revealed the rot at the heart of Victorian middle-class values by focusing on the fragmentation of life for middle-class women who had no legal rights and very few opportunities to voice their discontent. Both Wood and Braddon were well-known literary figures in London who also wrote ghost stories, supernatural tales, and political essays; in addition they were both editors of influential magazines and published many ghost stories.

Ghost Stories

The British ghost story tends to reduce or limit setting and action to a domestic, realistic setting in which the dead return and interact with the living, or a spirit representative of the past will not stay in the past. Usually, both the returning dead and representatives of the past are associated with a specific object, an event, a structure, or a person and any attempt to restore order is reliant on the appeasement of the spirit or ghost. Revenge and a need to be acknowledged are dominant themes. Very few ghost stories address any aspect of religious belief, relying instead on fear and terror to activate belief in the power of revenants.

Sir Walter Scott wrote a very early gothic ghost story, "Wandering Willie's Tale," as a chapter in his novel *Redgauntlet* (1824), and another that has a recognizably English setting, "The Tapestried Chamber" (1828), but Charles Dickens published the first British ghost story, distinct from the gothic tale, in which the ghosts are essential to the theme as well as the plot of the story, in "The Goblins Who Stole a Sexton," in *The Pickwick Papers* (1836–7). This ghost story, told on Christmas Eve by Mr Wardle, initiated a tradition of ghost stories being associated with Christmas.

Mr Wardle's tale concerns Gabriel Grub, a mean-spirited soul, who sets out to dig a grave on Christmas Eve. Goblins rise from the gravestones and drag him back down below the graveyard where they show him the past, the future, and the error of his ways. It certainly prefigures *A Christmas Carol* and it is accompanied by illustrations by "Phiz" (Hablot Knight Browne). Dickens also began to publish several ghost stories in each of the Christmas numbers of his magazines, *Household Words* (1850–9) and *All the Year Round* (1859–70). These Christmas issues sold several times the circulation of the magazines during the rest of the year.

Joseph Sheridan LeFanu was another early influence on the development of the ghost story. He was an Irish scholar, the editor and publisher of *Dublin Univeristy Magazine*, a sensation novelist, and writer of ghost stories. His best collection of supernatural stories, *In a Glass Darkly* (1872), garnered some attention, but he was better known during his lifetime for his novels and as a publisher. Several of his stories, macabre and often grotesque, had a great impact on twentieth-century writers, after M.R. James published a collection of LeFanu's ghost stories in *Madam Crowl's Ghost and Other Tales of Mystery* (1923). Two of his best-known tales are "The Ghost and the Bonesetter" (1838) and "An Account of Some Strange Disturbances in Aungier Street" (1853).

Le Fanu was also an early minor figure in the literary Irish revival in which many writers evinced a renewed interest in Irish myths and legends, Arthurian romances, and fairy tales, which led to popular interest in an idealized, anti-industrial medieval culture. Yeats, Lady Gregory, Lady Wilde, and Lord Dunsany used Celtic myth, legend, and folklore to create new fantasies of national identity. Early in the twentieth century these stories combined Irish myths and legends with modern characters whose experiences with modern manifestations of Celtic heroes and villains were sometimes whimsical, or melancholy, but more often were mordant, witty, and ironic. They often ended badly for the modern man or woman, as in Lord Dunsany's "Two Bottles of Relish" or Charlotte Riddell's "Hertford O'Donnell's Warning." Most of these writers, including James Stephens, Douglas Hyde, and Joseph O'Neill, also experimented with tales that were much darker than fairy tales, focusing on the individual and alienation, loss, madness, or physical and mental isolation.

Most British ghost stories have settings that are carefully described, well developed, realistic and ordinary. This tendency to set stories in familiar, easily imagined settings that slowly become disturbingly unfamiliar distinguishes the ghost story from the gothic tale; the narrators of the British ghost story sometimes tell tales based in outposts of imperialism, but the tales are told in decidedly British settings. Many later writers, born in the last quarter of the nineteenth century, including A.E. Coppard (1878–1957) in witty and comic tales such as "Ahoy, Sailor Boy!" (1933), and "The Kisstruck Bogie" (1923); Walter de la Mare (1873–1956), who wrote weird tales and ghost stories such as "The Promise" (1919); and the Anglo-Irish writer Elizabeth Bowen (1899–1973), in her collection of ghost stories, *The Demon Lover* (1945), lived through World War II and experienced the bitter aftermath of the end of empire.

Their stories often contrast formerly bucolic English towns or countryside with industrialized or urban settings.

Several colonial and postcolonial writers, such as the Australian Christina Stead in "The English Gentleman's Tale – The Gold Bride" (1934), Alice Perrin (an Anglo-Indian writer) in "Caulfield's Crime" (1901) and "The Bead Necklace", Saki (pseudonym of H.H. Munro; Anglo-Burmese in background) in "The Soul of Laploshka" (1910), and Katherine Mansfield (New Zealand) in "A Suburban Fairy Tale" (1917), use the supernatural to subversive effects. Others, such as Fiona Macleod (pseudonym of Scottish writer William Sharp) in "The Sin-Eater," Kenneth Morris (Welsh) in "The Secret Mountain," and Arthur Machen (Welsh) in his collection *The House of Souls* (1906), turned to Celtic myth and fantasy in a search for a distinctive national identity.

Other writers, including Lord Dunsany (Anglo-Irish) in his collection *The Sword of Welleran and Other Stories* (1908), and John Buchan (Scottish) in *The Moon Endureth: Tales and Fancies*, used the supernatural short story to defend imperialism. Rudyard Kipling is often thought of as defending the empire in his ghost stories, but close readings of his ghost stories and supernatural tales, especially, "The Mark of the Beast," reveal an ambiguous attitude toward his fellow countrymen and empire building.

By the final decades of the nineteenth century, ghost stories and weird or uncanny tales of the supernatural began to reflect the alienation experienced not only by women, the working class and the poor, but also by British military and merchants in the colonies. Irish writers, especially those involved in the Irish revival, were particularly prolific and successful in writing such stories. B.M. Croker's ghost story, "To Let" (1890), is typical of this type. Bithia Mary Croker was raised in Ireland, but spent most of her adult life in Burma and India with her husband, a military officer stationed in a variety of outposts. She published some stories in English-language Indian journals, but sent most of her ghost stories to editors in England. Many of her stories focus on women like herself, military wives and daughters who are sensitive to the resentment and the folklore of the people they are there to govern. In "To Let," women left in a local village in India see, hear, and then feel the effects of the violent death of a British soldier as they attempt to recreate England by following rigid social schedules of visits and outings, but only become more alienated from their surroundings in the process. The soldier's ghost haunts one bungalow and repeatedly acts out the gruesome pantomime of his death. The only way the women can survive is to retreat – to abandon the bungalow and hide behind the walls and habits of empire.

World War I became the focus of many British ghost stories. Among the eeriest is Herbert de Hamel's "The House of Dust" (1934), in which a German officer in Belgium loses his mind after a sexual encounter with the ghost of a woman who was murdered during the war. Many stories written in the aftermath of the war refer to it indirectly. Virgina Woolf's 1921 short story "A Haunted House" presents a narrator who longs for the safety of the past. Arthur Machen's "The Soldiers' Rest" and "The Bowmen," from his collection *The Angels of Mons* (1915), present fantasies in which the ghosts of medieval British warriors appear to help their modern counterparts in the war. By 1918, however, few writers besides John Buchan glorified the war; a few who examined the horrors of war and its effects on Britain and the British include H.G. Wells, Rudyard Kipling, Mary O'Malley, and Elizabeth Bowen.

I.A. Ireland is remembered primarily for *A Brief History of Nightmares* (1899). His one ghost story, "Climax for a Ghost Story" (1919), is, like many eighteenth-century gothic tales, in the form of a fragment. Unlike those gothic fragments, however, Ireland's ghost story has a dry, ironic tone that hints at the very real disruption of life in Britain that continued long after the Armistice:

> "How eerie!" said the girl, advancing cautiously, "– And what a heavy door!" She touched it as she spoke and it suddenly swung to with a click.
>
> "Good Lord!" said the man, "I don't believe there's a handle inside. Why, you've locked us both in!"
>
> "Not both of us. Only one of us," said the girl, and before his eyes she passed straight through the door, and vanished. (Sandner 2001: 734)

Ireland's story, brief as it is, exhibits the conventions Michael Cox and R.A. Gilbert use to define the traditional English ghost story in the introduction to their definitive collection, *The Oxford Book of English Ghost Stories*:

> each story should reveal to the reader a spectacle of the returning dead, or their agents, and their actions; there must be a dramatic interaction between the living and the dead, more often than not with the intention of frightening or unsettling the reader; the story must exhibit clear literary quality . . . ; there must be a definable Englishness about the story . . . English characters and institutions, and qualities (both stylistic and thematic) representative of the English ghost-story tradition as a whole; and finally . . . the story must be relatively short. (Cox and Gilbert 1986: xvi)

And Ireland's story has a narrative detachment that is also typical of the British ghost story.

Montague Rhodes James (1862–1936), a highly respected medievalist and provost of King's College, Cambridge, and, later, Eton, re-established general interest in the British ghost story: first, by editing and re-publishing the ghost stories of the Irish writer Joseph Sheridan Le Fanu; then by writing a number of excellent ghost stories, including a vampire tale, "Count Magnus," a horror story of a witch's monstrous haunting in "The Ash-tree," and a mingling of eerie Celtic legends in "Casting the Runes." He published *Ghost Stories of an Antiquary* (1904), and three other collections of his own ghost stories, most of which begin in common daily activities into which the unfamiliar, ghastly, or seemingly alien events and creatures creep slowly. His stories are set in a familiar world of universities and the English countryside; the narrator's voice is dry, ironic, and occasionally amused, as the narrators attempt to find a way not only to describe, but to accept the eruption of the supernatural in their daily activities. One narrator's detachment serves to foreground the structure of the twentieth-century British ghost story, in "A School Story," as he recites a kind of catechism of ghost story conventions:

> "Let's see. I wonder if I can remember the staple ones that I was told. First, there was the house with a room in which a series of people insisted on passing a night; and each of them in the morning was found kneeling in a corner, and had just time to say, 'I've seen it,' and died."
> "Wasn't that the house in Berkeley Square?"
> "I dare say it was. Then there was the man who heard a noise in the passage at night, opened his door, and saw someone crawling towards him on all fours with his eye hanging out on his cheek. There was besides, let me think –." (James 1992: 98)

Some of those "characters, institutions and qualities" frequently include: a first-person narrator who expresses doubt or disbelief about the tale he or she hears or tells; a self-reflexive or ironic narrator; or a framing device of a small group of like-minded people who tell ghost stories to pass the time. For instance, in F. Marion Crawford's "The Upper Berth" (1886), the frame narrator is a bored club member who has had too many cigars, drunk too much wine, and heard too many stories, when one of his companions claims to have seen a ghost:

> A chorus of exclamations greeted Brisbane's remarkable statement. Everybody called for cigars, and Stubbs, the butler, suddenly appeared from the depths of nowhere with a fresh bottle of dry champagne. The situation was saved; Brisbane was going to tell a story. (Cox and Gilbert 1986: 70)

The previous sentence could have been the signal for the comedy of a P.G. Wodehouse story; instead, the irony is deliberate. The story that follows is developed slowly, building to a frightening climax, yet the club members and the reader are left in doubt by Brisbane's dry conclusion, "That is how I saw a ghost – if it was a ghost. It was dead, anyhow." His statement pulls us out of the ghost story and back into the smoke-filled clubroom, but his hesitation in defining the thing that he saw serves to stress the dread of the unknown and the indefinable. It also highlights the randomness of the haunting – there is no clear link between the revenant and the narrator.

Weird Tales

The weird tale is also an offshoot of the gothic that stresses encounters between humans and the alien, ancient, or mythic. The writers use elaborate and lapidary phrasing in an assault on the senses of characters and readers alike. H.P. Lovecraft, the American writer of weird tales and horror stories, defines this form of fiction, and provides an example of the language and phrasing of the stories, in a long essay "Supernatural Horror in Literature":

> The true weird tale has something more than secret murder, bloody bones, or a sheeted form clanking chains according to rule. A certain atmosphere of breathless and unexplainable dread of outer, unknown forces must be present; and there must be a hint, expressed with a seriousness and portentousness becoming its subject, of that most terrible conception of the human brain – a malign and particular suspension or defeat of those fixed laws of Nature which are our only safeguard against the assaults of chaos and the daemons of unplumbed space. (Lovecraft 1973: 15)

Lovecraft goes on to claim that it is more important for a weird tale to create an atmosphere of dread, a sensory recognition and contact with the unknown than to have a fully realized plot (1973: 16). The weird tale developed in tandem with the art and fiction of the decadents and the symbolists, displaying a fascination with death, horror, and the grotesque. The plots of these stories often revolve around the chaos that erupts from an ancient site or artifact when humans tamper with the past. M.R. James's vampire tale "Count Magnus" and the description of the appearance of an ancient and evil spirit in "Oh Whistle, and I'll Come to You, My Lad" are examples of stories that revitalized the supernatural short story.

Grant Allen, who wrote non-fiction essays on prehistoric barrow mounds and other British archaeological sites, also wrote weird tales; one of his best was based on his own research. "Pallinghurst Barrow" is a spare story in which the narrator goes to a country house party where only he and a lonely young girl can feel the terror and see the rites and celebrations of the spirits of the barrows.

Vernon Lee's (pseudonym of Violet Paget) "Dionea," in which a young girl is an avatar of a goddess who wrecks havoc in a Greek fishing village, and Arthur Machen's great tale of terror, "The Great God Pan," show the horror that is unleashed by the tampering of a well-meaning man with forces that are not just old, but malign. The exotic, the deviant, and the perverse were associated with the return of the ancient past and themes often dealt with the impact of a god interacting with humans, or a human encountering a doppelgänger or nemesis.

Algernon Blackwood, a prolific writer of weird tales, was also an active participant in the spiritualist movement and lectured on radio and, much later, on television about ghost sightings and paranormal events. "The Willows" is an effective tale about two Englishmen who camp in Eastern Europe. Their arrogance and sense of entitlement are destroyed by their encounter with alien beings who have invaded the area. Some of Blackwood's best weird tales are collected in *The Listener* (1907) and *Pan's Garden* (1913). Robert Louis Stevenson, Arthur Conan Doyle, Walter de la Mare, H. Rider Haggard, James Stephens, H.G. Wells, Barry Pain, and Violet Hunt also wrote weird tales that were published in several magazines, especially

The Yellow Book in the 1890s, *The Strand* and *The Pall Mall Gazette*, and the American magazines *The New Yorker*, the *Saturday Review*, and *Weird Tales* through to the 1940s.

"The New Mother" (1888) by Lucy Clifford is a very early example of the weird tale. A young mother is left with an infant and two children, Turkey and Blue Eyes, who explore the local woods and the nearby town. They meet a gypsy girl who encourages them to misbehave and as they become more independent and more uncontrollable, their mother warns them that if they do not behave she will leave them with a new mother. One day the mother takes the infant and leaves the house; she is replaced by a monstrous "mother," with eyes that flash and whirl and a tail that clacks against the floor. The children's bid for independence brings horrible consequences.

These tales are marked by realistic settings in a modern world and characters who are linked to an ancient or alien supernatural being or artifact and are altered or destroyed by it. A hallmark of the weird tale is the atmosphere – uncanny, strange, or horrible. Arthur Conan Doyle's story "Lot 249" has a familiar university setting in which two students are destroyed by a mummy they have purchased. Their loss of control and destruction is gradual and becomes more horrific as time passes. Quests such as theirs often end in the emotional, physical, or mental destruction of the seekers.

Many weird tales are set in ancient times or on other planets and reflect popular interest and discoveries in archaeology, biology, physics, astronomy, and new technology. Certainly, the writings of Darwin, and pseudoscientific theories, such as those contained in Max Nordau's *Degeneration* and Richard Krafft-Ebbing's *Psychopathia Sexualis*, provided grist for stories of strange rituals and behaviors such as Charlotte Mews's "White Night," in which three travelers witness a ritual and appalling human sacrifice. Two of the travelers are horrified by the events, but one is exhilarated and titillated.

The popularity of supernatural tales coincided with the invention and popularity of photography and photographs were often published in the same magazines. People associated photography with death and with war. Photographers were often called upon to create memorial photographs of the dead in their coffins. In 1854 and 1855, photographs of the Crimean War appeared in the newspapers and magazines. Due to the amount of equipment necessary for the photographers and to the long exposure time necessary for clear photos, the only subjects were the dead left on the battlefields and formal portraits of officers who could pay for their photos. Some photographs of the horrible conditions in which ordinary soldiers lived were published and led to a public outcry against the military. Later, after military censors reviewed all commercial photographs during World War I, periodicals such as the *Illustrated London News* dedicated several pages in each issue to portrait photos of officers killed in World War I. Photographs provided permanent images and encouraged people to seek contact with the spirits of the dead. The activities of the American and British Societies for Psychical Research, supported by respected social scientists such as William James, also added unintentionally to the popularity of both ghost stories and weird tales, while the development of museums raised general public awareness of, and interest in, the distant past. A growing interest in spiritualism, mesmerism, and psychical research that began just after the Crimean War and peaked in the years just before and following World War I, gave credibility to the search for life after death that cut across the boundaries of social class.

Several stories written after 1914 focused on the emotions and mental states of those who had survived the random, chaotic pointlessness of the horrific experiences of the young men who became fodder for the battlegrounds of the Crimea and the trenches of France, orchestrated by a misguided military aristocracy. By 1918, everyone was haunted by those who had died in the trenches or had survived physically but not mentally or emotionally. Weird tales stress that we are not in control, no matter how fast our locomotives and steamboats, how bright our gaslights, or how much we manufacture.

Magazines, Women, and War

By 1840, a literate population, cheaper paper and printing processes, and an efficient and inexpensive postal system led to a proliferation of quarterly, weekly and monthly journals, magazines, and newspapers that provided short fiction in large amounts. Everyone read magazines that combined serialized novels and showcased short stories, essays, debates on science, politics, and theology, As shown above, even Freud read British magazines. The ghost story was a staple of the magazines, particularly in the Christmas numbers from the 1840s through the 1890s.

The *Strand Magazine* (1890–1950) was founded by George Newnes and edited by H. Greenough Smith from 1891 to 1930. Taking advantage of a new, inexpensive three-color printing process, the magazine also contained illustrations that attracted advertisers as well as readers. The additional income from advertisers allowed Smith to pay higher prices than competitors could for fiction from popular authors. Arthur Conan Doyle, a friend of both Smith and Newnes, was one of the star writers for the magazine, which published all of his Sherlock Holmes stories and several of his ghost stories and supernatural fiction. Many of his stories were illustrated by Sidney Paget, whose drawings became identified with Doyle's stories. The *Strand* also regularly published ghost stories and supernatural tales such as "An Inexperienced Ghost" (1902) by H.G. Wells and "The Toll-House" (1907) by W.W. Jacobs.

The magazines catered to broad general audiences and they needed a steady weekly, fortnightly, or monthly supply of short stories. The *London Journal* (1845–1912) was a weekly that catered to a working-class audience with gothic tales, ghost stories, sensation fiction, historical and sentimental romances, and horror. *Argosy* was a monthly magazine with two illustrations in each issue. It was edited by Mrs Henry

Wood and published her own ghost stories as well as stories by Rhoda Broughton, M.E. Braddon, Robert Louis Stevenson, Wilkie Collins, and Amelia B. Edwards. Braddon and Edwards also published often in Dickens's *All the Year Round.* Several magazines were edited by women who wrote ghost stories and supernatural tales and who purchased large numbers of ghost stories. Mary Elizabeth Braddon edited *Temple Bar* and, in addition to stories by Rhoda Broughton, published Arthur Conan Doyle's "The Captain of the 'Pole-Star' " in 1883, and E. Nesbit's "John Charington's Wedding" in 1891.

Pall Mall Magazine (1893–1914) competed with the *Strand* for both ghost stories and weird tales. *Pall Mall* published Robert Louis Stevenson's "The Body Snatcher" in the 1884 Christmas number, M.R. James's chilling tale of the revenge of murdered children, "Lost Hearts," in 1895, and Algernon Blackwood's "A Case of Eavesdropping" in the Christmas number, 1900, and "The Kit-bag" in the Christmas number, 1908.

While we tend to think of Victorian fiction as emphasizing social realism, women writers were able to explore controversial and taboo topics and themes through fantasy in magazines, particularly through ghost stories. Charlotte Riddell, M.E. Braddon, E. Nesbit, Virginia Woolf, Vernon Lee, Sylvia Townsend Warner, Elizabeth Bowen, and Edith Wharton all took advantage of the subversive properties of fantasy to explore themes of physical and psychological alienation as well as national and temporal isolation.

At the same time, the works of Freud and Jung were influential in legitimizing or establishing dream states, doppelgängers, doubles, vampires, case studies of conflicted sexual identity, and the unconscious, as thematic material. Many of the women writers mentioned above also wrote children's literature, romances, social realist fiction, and were journalists and editors. This psychological focus carried over into the early twentieth century, in the wake of World War I, in the stories of Charlotte Mew, May Sinclair, Florence Marryat, and E. Nesbit.

Women writers were, certainly, influential in expanding the themes of the ghost story from stories of gothic dread to stories that focused on the psychology of characters caught up in or by the past through isolation and alienation. One of E. Nesbit's most effective ghost stories, "Man-Size in Marble" (*Grim Tales*, 1893), is in the gothic tradition but makes the malign and random acts of the ghosts, who inhabit marble tomb effigies of medieval knights, and the desperation and hopelessness of the narrator who survives their visitation, the central focus of the tale:

Although every word of this story is as true as despair, I do not expect people to believe it. Nowadays a "rational explanation" is required before belief is possible. Let me then, at once, offer the "rational explanation" which finds most favour among those who have heard the tale of my life's tragedy. It is held that we were "under a delusion," Laura and I, on that 31st of October; and that this supposition places the whole matter on a satisfactory and believable basis. The reader can judge, when he, too, has heard my story, how far this is an "explanation" and in what sense it is "rational." There were three who

took part in this: Laura and I and another man. The other man still lives, and can speak
to the truth of the least credible part of my story. (Cox and Gilbert 1986: 125)

Edith Wharton, though an American by birth, wrote a number of ghost stories
before and after World War I that chart the alienation of women by the ghosts of
a world and way of life that ended in the trenches of France. "Afterward" (1909),
"Kerfol" (1916), and "Pomegranate Seed" (1928), point to the increasing isolation
of the women left behind. That loss of a generation of young men and the attendant
despair of the women left behind, coupled with the fragmentation of Europe and
permanent changes in the class system, could be charted through her ghost
stories.

The magazine market changed after the war and so did readers' interests. The real
world had done far more than fiction could to illustrate for readers a shattered world.
Edith Wharton blamed the invention of the wireless and the cinema for the lack of
interest in short-story fantasy fiction, but Kipling's "Wireless," Barry Pain's "The
Case of Vincent Pyrwhit," and M.R. James's "Casting the Runes" cleverly adapted
new technology to their ghost stories.

Between the wars, the short ghost story and the weird tale began to give
way to supernatural horror or adventure tales of aliens and lost worlds. The
heyday of quarterly or monthly illustrated magazines full of short fiction that
appealed to a general public was over; monthly or weekly publications full of
weird tales and pulp sensational fiction were targeted to narrow, specific markets.
W.H. Smith and others began to publish texts in pocket size to appeal to the
riders on commuter trains. The readers of supernatural fiction, especially of the
weird tale and science fiction stories, could buy collections of short stories for
pennies.

The war years 1939–45 provided, *sans* the printed page, the quite real horrors of
the unimaginable that exceeded all fictional horrors. War brought about a breakdown
of cultural identities and barriers; we became the monsters and the ghosts. The war
changed maps and countries literally, too. Science fiction began to absorb the conventions of the supernatural tale, while the uncanny or weird gave way to pure horror.
The technology of mass destruction had a lasting impact on the supernatural tale,
while the ghost story began to incorporate elements of spiritualism, naturalism, and
the psychological portrait in short stories by writers as disparate as H.G. Wells,
A. Conan Doyle, Virginia Woolf, Katherine Mansfield, Elizabeth Bowen, and
R.L. Stevenson.

Conclusion

While ghost stories and supernatural tales after World War I often dealt with the
loss of a way of life as well as personal losses, the ghost story during World War II
frequently refers back to the first war as a source of ghosts and horror. Elizabeth

Bowen's ghost stories are good examples of this. Bowen (1899–1973) was an Anglo-Irish writer who combined an ability to succinctly describe rural life and settings with an acute understanding of the psychology of characters who, in the midst of familiar, daily activities and locales, must deal with the unexpected.

She wrote several novels, including *In the Heat of the Day*, but her short stories set during and immediately after the blitz in London may be the apex of her work. "Mysterious Kôr" presents London, itself, as a ghost. In "Pink May," a woman in wartime blames the failure of her marriage on a ghost in a furnished house, but she is haunting her own life. "The Demon Lover" is one of Bowen's best-known short stories; in it, a married woman goes to retrieve some things from her blitzed London home. Once there, she finds and rereads a letter from an old lover who was lost in World War I, gathers her personal items, enters a taxi, and disappears into the horrors of both wars, with her dead lover at the wheel of the cab.

The power of the story depends in part on the lack of rationale and in part on the chaos of the Blitz and the woman's horrified recognition of the revenant of her youth. "The Demon Lover" takes an old plot element of the nineteenth-century ghost story – a corpse claiming his bride – familiar in stories such as E. Nesbit's "John Charrington's Wedding," retains the brevity and economy of the traditional ghost story, adds a third-person narrator and only as much detail as is necessary for the reader to follow the character through the rubble of her home into pure horror.

Bowen wrote many other ghost stories, ranging from an early tale, "The Shadowy Third," in which a malevolent ghost haunts the home of her husband and his new wife, to "Hand in Glove," an often anthologized story from the 1950s, in which a dry narrator adds an ironic twist to the story of two sisters who inherit a trunk from India that harbors a deadly gift. "Hand in Glove" also refers back to an earlier tale, Henry James's "The Romance of Certain Old Clothes."

Several of Bowen's ghost stories evoke horror, but she shares with M.R. James a concern with the acceptance of ghosts as simply another hazard of British life – one more thing to deal with in the course of a day. Bowen is so detailed in creating the ordinary, familiar landscape and activities of daily life in London and in the Irish and English countryside, that the reader, as well as the characters, is often astonished by the disruption caused by ghostly encounters.

Margery Lawrence (1889–1969) is much less well known today than Elizabeth Bowen, but she excels at conveying to the reader a postmodern sense that we, as well as her characters, may be unwelcome in a world in which so much is hidden that we are never fully aware of an alien threat until it is made manifest. Her fiction is representative of the shift from the traditional ghost story and the weird tale to postmodern horror and science fiction. Lawrence, like May Sinclair, became interested in the occult and attended séances and activities of the Society for Psychical Research during World War I and later published several supernatural stories in which artifacts of the past overpower people in the present. Her fiction shows the influences of

Vernon Lee and Arthur Machen as well as, rather improbably, H. Rider Haggard and Bulwer-Lytton.

One of her most successful supernatural tales, "Robin's Rath" (1926), begins with a frame, tone, and atmosphere much like Crawford's "The Upper Berth," as club members tell after-dinner stories and, again as in Crawford's story, the narrator is something of a cynic. The protagonist, a spoiled, social-climbing American heiress, has purchased a country house as part of her campaign to marry an English aristocrat, and is guilty of hubris. The narrator describes her as "Not the daughter of a hundred earls, but of one immensely wealthy pork-packer who could deny her nothing, even to the purchase of Ghyll Hall" (Dalby 1995: 369). The purchase includes a stand of old-growth forest that blocks the American's path to the local golf course. When she decides to cut through it to make a road, the locals try to dissuade her, but are unsuccessful. For her presumption, she is seduced by Robin, the green man of the forest; her punishment is that instead of being impregnated by the avatar of the Green Man she has been emptied and returned to New York, where "an anxious father goes from specialist to specialist with a lovely dark-eyed girl, once bright, alert, vivacious, now blank and dull, half-witted almost, with the springs of her vivid womanhood dried up and dead within her" (386). The narrator lacks sympathy for the girl and the story provides a brief and pithy comment on the arrogance of colonials and the green world's response.

Lawrence wrote several stories and novels in which young women are put in danger, not by their own actions, but by a husband's or father's fascination with artifacts of colonialism. "The Mask of Sacrifice" (1936) is one of her shortest and best supernatural tales in which a young bride is repulsed by an ancient sacrificial mask that her husband refuses to part with. Finally, his thoughts and actions are completely dictated by the mask until he accidentally destroys it. Throughout the story, Lawrence focuses on oppositions in gender, marriage, friendship and in sensitivity to the supernatural – experience and recognition of the uncanny and respect for the power of intuition are the keys to survival. That hesitation between the possible and impossible, or the imaginable and the unimaginable, has remained a key element of postmodern ghost and supernatural tales as well.

References and Further Reading

Cox, M. and Gilbert R.A. (eds) (1984). *The Penguin Book of Horror Stories*. New York: Penguin Putnam.

Cox, M. and Gilbert R.A. (eds) (1986). *The Oxford Book of English Ghost Stories*. New York: Oxford University Press.

Cox, M. and Gilbert R.A. (eds) (1992). *Victorian Ghost Stories: An Oxford Anthology*. Oxford: Oxford University Press.

Dalby, R. (ed.) (1995). *The Mammoth Book of Victorian and Edwardian Ghost Stories*. New York: Carroll and Graf.

Dalby, R. (ed.) (1998). *Twelve Gothic Tales*. New York: Oxford University Press.

Dalby, R. (ed.) (2006). *The World's Greatest Ghost Stories*. New York: Constable and Robinson.

Freud, S. (1955). "The Uncanny," in J. Strachey (ed.), *The Standard Edition of the Complete*

Psychological Works of Sigmund Freud, vol. XVII. London: Hogarth Press (original work published 1919).

James, M.R. (1992). *Collected Ghost Stories*. Ware: Wordsworth Editions.

Lovecraft, H.P. (1973). *Supernatural Horror in Literature*. New York: Dover.

Sandner, D. and Weisman, J. (eds) (2001). *The Treasury of the Fantastic: Romanticism to Early Twentieth Century Literature*. Berkeley: Frog.

Williams, Susan A.(ed.) (1992). *The Lifted Veil: The Book of Fantastic Literature by Women*. New York: Carroll and Graf.

7
Finding a Voice: Women Writing the Short Story (to 1945)

Sabine Coelsch-Foisner

The modernist foregrounding of moment-by-moment experience was both conducive to the development of the short story and indebted to the formal economy which the latter required. It also seems to be especially connected with an image of the writer emerging in the late nineteenth century and coming to maturity during the first half of the twentieth century: that of the autonomous woman writer. It is a striking feature of English modernism that among its major representatives are some of the most outstanding women short-story writers: Virginia Woolf (1882–1941), Katherine Mansfield (1888–1923), Sylvia Townsend Warner (1893–1978), Jean Rhys (1890–1979), Frances Bellerby (1899–1975), and Elizabeth Bowen (1899–1973). While this nexus may serve as a starting point for exploring the work of these writers, it is equally apt to disrupt common notions of a modernist feminine aesthetics. Their different origins, life stories, and careers suggest that the history of the short story until 1945 is not limited to Bloomsbury, nor is it wholly the result of its androgynous construction of womanhood and the independent lifestyle of the New Woman. The struggle for independence, in various fields, threatened to outweigh its triumphs.

Both Katherine Mansfield (née Beauchamp) and Jean Rhys were born in outlying parts of the British Empire: Mansfield in New Zealand, and Rhys in Roseau, Dominica, in the West Indies. Both came to London to fulfill their dreams – Mansfield to become a writer, and Rhys to become an actress – and experienced the difficult struggle for acceptance in an alien culture. Divided about their identity, they traveled restlessly without ever abandoning their emotional ties with the past. Rhys spent the years after World War I in Paris and after 1928 in England; Mansfield became a famous London literary figure, married to the critic John Middleton Murry and befriended by D.H. Lawrence and Virginia Woolf. Elizabeth Bowen, too, was an expatriate, torn between her family's estate, Bowen's Court in County Cork, where she was born, and England, where she was sent at the age of five and where she lived for most of her formative years.

Sylvia Townsend Warner lacked such multicultural experience herself, but her literary imagination drew on her mother's recollections of southern India, where she was born. Townsend Warner had many friends in London, among them David Garnett, and like Mansfield, who was drawn to Ida Constance Baker, led a bohemian life, the writer Valentine Ackland being her partner for forty years. World War I was a particularly painful experience for both Mansfield and Frances Bellerby: their brothers were killed in battle, and both express in their stories a recurrent effort to revisit the past. Ill health provides a further link between them. Mansfield suffered from tuberculosis and died young, and Bellerby's life was marked by a terrible record of severe illnesses, which drove her into isolation.

Women's short fiction of the first half of the twentieth century is the history of both the center and the margin. Experiences shared by individual writers, such as cultural migration and expatriation, homosexuality and literary friendships, are pertinent to understanding the modernist literary scene, with its institutions and channels of distribution, its cultivated elitism and literary circles and coteries. However, apart from suggesting a predilection for certain themes, such as childhood, war, bereavement, and alienation, such biographical correspondences reveal little about the individual uses of the short story, the choice and function of the form within a writer's oeuvre. It is therefore also problematic to attribute the great achievements in women's short fiction to a phase in the history of women's literature. For Mansfield, the short story was the dominant form. It suited her interest in lonely women living on the margins of society. Jean Rhys was equally concerned with deserted and alienated women, and explored their destinies in short as well as long forms of fiction, both experimental in technique: *Postures* (1928), retitled *Quartet* (1929), *Good Morning, Midnight* (1939), and *Wide Sargasso Sea* (1966). Bellerby, by contrast, abandoned the short story in mid-life in favor of poetry, and both forms play a vital role in her lifelong effort to recover the past, especially since her attempt to write an autobiography failed. For Bowen, who wanted to become a painter, the short story served as a means of going beyond the familiar horizons of experience. Townsend Warner wanted to become a composer and showed great versatility as to the forms she employed and blended: long and short fiction, poetry, and biography. She published ten volumes of short stories between 1932 and 1977, with 144 stories printed in *The New Yorker* from 1936 onwards, whereas her poetry had to wait for a posthumous collection to reach a wider audience. Virginia Woolf's experimental zeal and audacious technical innovations mark her out as a pioneer of modernist fiction. In several instances, her short stories interlink with her novels, like the stories clustering around *Mrs Dalloway* (1925). This has not only made it difficult to distinguish differences of style and method between these two forms, but led critics to deny her stories independent generic status. Her own emphasis on emotions rather than a visible surface structure when discussing the "form" of fiction in "On Re-reading Novels" has added to this difficulty (Woolf 1966: 2.122–30).

"Finding a voice," naturally, has different meanings for each of these writers, and to define their voices in terms of a feminine or feminist struggle for creative expression would delimit both the thematic and formal-aesthetic range of their work. Still, what is shared by these women writers, born in the late nineteenth century and reaching maturity in the first half of the twentieth century, is a climate of ideas and a literary horizon that encouraged experiment and innovation, both of which shaped the perception of the short story as a distinct and important form. Woolf, Mansfield, Bellerby, Bowen, Townsend Warner, and Rhys contributed significantly to this perception and to the leading role of the short story for women writers in the postmodern era. It is in connection with what the aesthetics of the short story, with its brevity and inherent economy along with the modernist call for originality, meant for these widely heterogeneous voices, that their oeuvre may be explored in terms of "finding a voice." They expressed realms of experience hitherto unnoticed and unexpressed, experimented with modes of perception and style, and opened up disruptive and alternative perspectives on life.

Katherine Mansfield started publishing stories in A.R. Orage's *New Age*. Her first volume, *In a German Pension* (1911), gives a foretaste of the collisions between reality and dream which she considered essential in women's experience, and exploited with psychological acuity in her mature stories written during the last years of her life. While her obsessive preoccupation with childbirth and death, the hardships of women's lives in patriarchal culture, and their ambivalent relations with both men and women in these early sketches is more directly connected with distressing events in her life (Nathan 1993), the stories from *Bliss* (1920) and *The Garden-Party* (1922) reflect a more withdrawn stance. Composed over a short period of time, they capture Mansfield's favorite themes of isolation, self-delusion, and homelessness, coupled with a deep interest in life. In a letter to her husband, John Middleton Murry, of February 3, 1918, she explains the two motives underlying her work: "real joy" and "an *extremely* deep sense of hopelessness – of everything doomed to disaster – almost wilfully, stupidly [. . .] *a cry against corruption*" (Mansfield 2006: 323). One of the hallmarks of Mansfield's work is the dramatic immediacy with which this conflict is brought home. When her stories concentrate on social outcasts, very much in the tradition of Romantic humanitarianism (Dunbar 1997), the causes of their isolation are diagnosed with an impersonality of tone (Head 1992) and the empirical focus on experience characteristic of modernist writing.

Life tends to be harsh for Mansfield's heroines: the pressures of marriage and motherhood bear on them ("The Prelude," "Honeymoon"); relationships are experienced as hostile or destructive ("The Tiredness of Rosabel"), and the body is commonly a site of unease and appropriation. Both Miss Ada Moss, the impoverished singer in "Pictures" (1919), and "Miss Brill" (1920) offer piercing glimpses of ageing women reduced to indigence. Miss Moss queues in vain for a film appointment; Miss Brill, a former actress, indulges in idle rituals that make her immune to reality. The frustration lurking underneath the jaunty surface of their lives is laid bare in singular moments of epiphanic intensity. Characterization in Mansfield's stories is typically the result of alternating focalization and dramatic objectification: while the introspective narrator superbly arrests Miss Brill's self-delusion in the mannered description of "the blue sky powdered with gold and great spots of light like white wine splashed over the Jardins Publiques" (Mansfield 2006: 204), the revelation is a matter of showing rather than telling. As every Sunday, Miss Brill attends the concerts, wearing her fur, to which she clings like a fetish. When two young lovers pass by, they make a degrading comment about her age and declining looks. The woman's complicity with the male sex in humiliating women, a recurrent topic in Mansfield's treatment of gender relations, gives full force to the dramatic irony of the scene: what is revealed to the reader is deliberately held at bay by the protagonist. When Miss Brill returns home and puts her fur back into the box, "she thought she heard something crying" (Mansfield 2006: 208). The climactic revelation towards which the story moves is symbolically stowed away in a box. Only the reader has realized Miss Brill's despair.

Miss Moss's derelict state is equally brought to view via her intercourse with other people: the taxi driver calling after her, the sneering glances of competing applicants for the job, and the fat old gentleman with whom she eventually leaves the Café de Madrid. Mansfield's lonely women – young girls, spinsters, and elderly women – are subject to close scrutiny from outside. An incidental encounter or the fragment of a conversation are apt to reveal their dire situation. Such epiphanic glimpses and reversals of action afford the reader insights into the sheer theatricality of their lives. Miss Brill literally plays a role: "They weren't only the audience, not only looking on; they were acting. Even she had a part and came every Sunday" (Mansfield 2006: 206). Her performance is still enhanced by a mass of objects crowding like props on a stage and encapsulating her inner crisis: cupboard, red eiderdown, necklet, box, and fur. As these fail to become objective correlatives – fully realized expressions of internal states of mind – for the characters themselves, they preserve their dialogic potential and serve both the impressionist quality of Mansfield's style and the Romantic hiatus between dream and reality.

Even the self-conscious first-person account of the writer Raoul Duquette, in "Je ne parle pas français" (1918), is marked by this tension and betrays his role-play. By addressing an imaginary interlocutor as he describes his body and gestures beheld in a mirror, Duquette flaunts his role as a writer while objectifying his parasitic interest in real life. "Suddenly I realized that quite apart from myself, I was smiling. Slowly I raised my head and saw myself in the mirror opposite. Yes, there I sat, leaning on the table, smiling my deep, sly smile, the glass of coffee with its vague plume of steam before me and beside it the ring of white saucer with two pieces of sugar" (Mansfield 2006: 123).

Identity is never fixed in Mansfield's stories, which reflects her own obsessive need to stay mobile and to act and put on masks. Her protagonists are commonly at odds with themselves, whether they enact their false personalities in a stage-like scenario or in an inward struggle for identity, as in the "Prelude" (1917), where Beryl doubts whether she is ever her "real self" and imagines a double: "It was her other self who had written that letter" (Mansfield 2006: 113).

Exiles in a mundane society, Mansfield's characters embody the instabilities of modern life and the modernist effort to seize its dazzling complexity and fluidity. Childhood is a prime site for facing the unknown, which she believed to be far greater than the known, and for exploring conflicting experiences. Just as women are victimized by exploitative sexual politics, children are exposed to the vicissitudes of adult life, as in "Sun and Moon," a typical initiation story, where the innocent excitement over a party yields to a feeling of staleness and corruption when the children see the violated delicacies left over by the guests. The innate dilemma of growing up is aggravated by the social chasms dawning on Laura in "The Garden-Party" (1921). Slowly, she begins to see the condescension and unfeeling attitudes of her family towards the working classes, when in the midst of the preparations for a party a man is reported to have died in an accident. Nothing stops their laughing and dancing; only Laura carries a basket of food to the man's house. When asked into the room with the laid out body, she is seized by a deep-felt truth and revolts against the socially insulated life and numbing pleasures of the upper class. The dead body, which strikes her as perfectly calm and happy, does not only correct the artificiality of Laura's upbringing, but more profoundly conjoins the opposites of horror and beauty. Laura's confrontation with death is coextensive with her discovery of life. As in Miss Brill, the unspeakable seals the moment of total awareness, which Laura fails to express in words: "'Isn't life,' she stammered, 'isn't life –'. But what life was she couldn't explain" (Mansfield 2006: 298).

When describing the dead body, Mansfield's narrator steps out of Laura's perspective and arrests the real world in one of those rare flashes of understanding that form the climax of her stories: "There lay a young man, fast asleep – sleeping so soundly, so deeply, that he was far, far away from them both. Oh, so remote, so peaceful. He was dreaming. Never wake him up again" (Mansfield 2006: 298). Death is not normally accessible to consciousness and for this reason holds a particular interest, technical rather than philosophical, in modernist writing, as Virginia Woolf's story "Sympathy" (1919) illustrates. The first-person narrator learns from an obituary that Humphry Hammond has died. This triggers a wave of memories, an imaginative vision of his deathbed, and a complete change in her perception of real things. Past moments shared with Hammond's wife, Celia, and precise images such as the "one bee humming through the room and out again" (Woolf 2003: 105) swarm in her mind, mingling with thoughts about death, until she receives an invitation by Celia and is informed that the obituary refers to the latter's father-in-law, not to her husband. The "fancy," so vividly called forth by the event while totally disconnected from it, locates the process of creation in the inner operations of the mind – a quintessential presupposition in Woolf's fiction.

As in Mansfield's impressionistic sketches, the separateness of a world outside consciousness is only patchily realized by Woolf's protagonists. A tiny mark on the wall bestows a "satisfying sense of reality" (Woolf 2003: 82), while carrying the narrator's thoughts away from wartime. The seemingly uncontrolled flow of consciousness is interspersed with meta-narrative remarks foregrounding the aesthetic experience: "And the novelists in future will realise more and more the importance of these reflections" (Woolf 2003: 79).

Both Mansfield and Woolf felt an urgent need to reform literature, and both were anxious to perfect their styles and methods – Mansfield by employing epiphanies and symbols for characterization; Woolf by switching perspectives to the point of disowning any narrative presence and exploiting the suggestive power of colors, sounds, and rhythms. "The String Quartet" and "Blue & Green" (both 1921) are richly evocative exercises in word-painting and sound-music, connecting modernist intermediality with the aestheticist *Anderstreben* of the arts in a perfect harmony of form and meaning. The short story offered Woolf a site for testing the emotional implications of an aesthetic predicated on the incompleteness and illogicality of experience. Although she wrote short stories all her life, only one collection, *Monday or Tuesday* (1921), appeared during her lifetime, crowning her most productive years between 1917 and 1925. After destabilizing in her early stories the traditional male viewpoint in favor of women's intimate histories, as in "Phyllis and Rosamond," written in 1906, Woolf embarked on a phase of daring experiment, blending a character's perceptions with the physical setting, displacing all outer action into streams of consciousness, and applying photographic as well as cinematographic devices to the art of fiction. Woolf's late stories are more conventional in their handling of plot and character presentation, but the feminist concerns voiced in them connect them with the early stories.

"The Legacy" (1940) is about a widower learning from his wife's diary that she had an affair with her maid's brother and that both committed suicide. Promoting a deeper understanding of Angela's true history, the voice of the diary ironically defeats Gilbert Clandon's self-centered point of view. As he imaginatively recreates his married life, central issues of Woolf's feminism are brought to the fore: the social division of the sexes into private and public spheres, class status, and women's shadowy role in history. Angela's name carries overt echoes of the Victorian Angel in the House, whom Woolf had declared the foe of women's liberation. The story's obvious autobiographical and critical implications point to the wealth of documentary material contained in Woolf's own diaries.

"A Haunted House" (1921), by contrast, marks an early experiment with language. The voice of the story magically captures the beating pulse of the house, as it wanders swiftly from the mind of a sleeping woman who feels the presence of a ghostly couple to the latter's hushed conversation as they search for a treasure, following their airy flight into the garden and merging with the wind and moonbeams. "A Haunted House" recreates in audaciously compressed images the stream of the unconscious, with rapid transitions of vantage point emulating the feverish pace of a dream, with its unfixed perspectives and instances of self-mirroring.

A similar intensity is achieved in "Kew Gardens" (1919), where the stationary position of a snail in a flower bed yields an imagistic train of scenes both within and outside its sphere of vision. The periodic patterning of the text recalls the cinematographic technique of montage and enables the narrative voice to enter several consciousnesses, rapidly shifting its focus of attention – not like a persona, but like a disengaged camera zooming in on minute details and producing such sensuous close-ups as "the flesh of a leaf, revealing the branching thread of fibre beneath the surface" (Woolf 2003: 84). The next moment it adopts the eye-level of a passer-by: "Here he seemed to have caught sight of a woman's dress in the distance" (Woolf 2003: 86). The camera's lens is not tied to one mind: buried in the flower beds, soaring high, or hovering above ground, it alternately produces myopic and telescopic shots. Such a view without a center makes possible metamorphic shifts between past and present, and is apt to cross the borders between animal and human, man and woman, waking mind and daydream.

Shrugging off conventions of plot, incident, or unifying theme (Skrbic 2004), many of Woolf's stories are self-conscious exercises in storytelling, such as "In the Orchard" (1923), where the same scene is told in three different ways, first, by exploring the poetic potential of an external view of events: Miranda lying asleep under an apple tree, the voices of school children and the ringing of church bells; second, by slipping into Miranda's consciousness and narrating how her inner world transforms these incidents and gives them fresh coherence; and, third, by imitating the anonymous stance from nowhere and attempting a positivist account of the scene in the manner of Wittgenstein's *Tractatus Logico-Philosophicus*: "1 The world is all that is the case. 1.1 The world is the totality of facts, not of things" (Wittgenstein 1961: 3). Impartially documenting the raw data of experience, the last view records the failure of the imagination, while, in the context of the two preceding versions, it completes the range of the writer's vision and stresses the shaping power of narrative.

Woolf's imagistic sketches abound in meta-narrative signposts resolving the tension between life and art. Written in 1929, "Three Pictures" is both a painterly text and a self-begetting story in which the narrator's mind, reminiscent of the unifying method of metaphysical poetry (Baldwin 1989), develops and contextualizes three apparently separate pictures: a happy sailor and his wife, an atrocious cry in the night, and a gravedigger, until they make sense together. This method has pragmatic implications for the reader, who must actively engage with the component parts of a story, and, as in poetry, uncover their hidden meanings – uncanny currents and lesbian subtexts, biographical implications, and intertextual allusions, such as the Shakespearean overtones in "Lappin and Lapinova" (1939).

Woolf unfolds the most intricate visions of wholeness out of discrete moments of being. Even the least conspicuous fragment of an object can haunt the mind, like the polished piece of glass which John in "Solid Objects" (1920) is seen to pick up on the beach. Initially glimpsed from a neutral camera position, the scene is progressively evolved into a story about his life. The object functions both as a catalyst prompting the narrative and as an objective correlative vital to John's life as it isolates him in the manner of its own solitary being: "Looked at again and again half consciously by a mind thinking of something else, any object mixes itself so profoundly with the stuff of thought that it loses its actual form and recomposes itself a little differently in an ideal shape which haunts the brain when we least expect it" (Woolf 2003: 98). The shift from an objective to a subjective stance is but one instance of Woolf's ingenious handling of the short story which she turned into a site of daring generic transformations, mixing it with other forms (essay, sketch, lyrical meditation) as well as deconstructing it by suggesting the impossibility of telling complete stories.

Incompleteness is also the hallmark of Frances Bellerby's short stories. Unlike Woolf, however, Bellerby was not interested in experiment as such. The obsessive dashes and dots rupturing her narratives and creating an impression of things hidden, unsaid, or unfathomable result from an effort to cope with the turning points in her life. Bellerby is interesting for the debate about women's short fiction, because her handling of the genre reflects an ambivalent desire to tell and to withhold stories. The boundary between confession and inarticulacy is strikingly thin in her work. Springing from her own tragic life, Bellerby's stories focus on exceptional experiences and events too large or formidable to understand: the traumas of war, pain, and bereavement. In 1930 Bellerby injured her spine in an accident and remained a cripple for the rest of her life. This was the beginning of an almost unbroken series of illnesses, aggravating the first two shattering blows of her life: her brother's death in action in the Great War and her mother's suicide. Gaps and stoppages are symptomatic of Bellerby's work. Both her poetry and her short stories were written during and after World War II – *Come to an End* (1939), *The Acorn and the Cup* (1948), *A Breathless Child* (1952) – when she already felt excluded from all that meant happiness to her: the cherished company of her family, an athletic body, and life without pain. Bellerby's creative work was motivated by the desire to restore childhood and to overcome her vulnerable time-bound self. Not surprisingly, in 1957 she began to write an autobiography, which proved excruciating and was given up more than fifteen years later.

Obsessively reworking biographical material (the sibling situation, parental suicide, illness, and medical treatment), her stories mark an important stage in this effort. The progress from stories displacing painful episodes into the lives of others, via internal dramatizations by a poetic voice, to an attempt at autobiography suggests an increasingly personal mode. Given her abandonment of the latter genre, however, short forms seem to have conformed better to Bellerby's autobiographical quest, with narrative strategies of scenic presentation through dialog and direct speech, inner monologue and stream-of-consciousness being better suited to the temperament of a writer anxious to reconcile her present self to her past self while extremely reticent about her personal life.

Addressing critical moments when worlds are shattered or life is transfigured, rather than tracing the epiphanic potential of small incidents in the manner of

Mansfield, Bellerby's stories typically convey a halt in the continuum of life and verge on the unspeakable. "The Doctor" deals with a woman who has to undergo an operation and is afraid of a dream of unbearable pain which she feels could be borne if only it could be expressed in words. Yet, language fails: "I cry out, I cry out in a perfect ecstasy, all brilliant with relief and amazement: 'Well, then, everything *is* bearable, because . . .' I can't finish the sentence" (Bellerby 1986: 31). A similar crisis is encapsulated in "Come to an End," the title story of Bellerby's first collection, which is all about a father's inability to tell his son that his little sister has died in an accident. The inadequacy of language to meet the immensity of the event is symbolically enshrined in recurrent images of closure: shut doors, locked rooms, drawn curtains, gates, and decayed houses point to realms inaccessible to her protagonists and beyond the reach of words.

The action of Bellerby's stories often sets in when a fundamental change in a character's life has occurred. In "The Cut Finger" a family's move to the seaside in order to improve the father's ill health proves disastrous for the little girl. Her world is shattered when she beholds her mother crying. The child compulsively begins to arrange pebbles in the garden, instinctively trying to compensate for the loss of continuity. Visibility is crucial in these childhood memories. The two children in "Pre-War" literally step out of space and time when they climb to the top of a house: "Down there all was just as usual, but up here nothing was as usual, nothing at all –" (Bellerby 1986: 20). When Roger endeavors to fix a toy soldier on to the highest point of the roof, Anne has a sudden vision of her brother's absence. The reader does not know whether this indicates an emotional failure or the boy's actual fall.

Bellerby's stories abound in such moments suspended between life and death. In "The Carol", an eerie story about a soldier's homecoming, the primary text-world is transgressed in a fantastic shift of perspective. When the young man enters his room, he remembers a carol from his childhood and begins to whistle it. All of a sudden he perceives a photograph of himself bearing the inscription: "'Killed in Action at Givenchy, Aged 18, August 8th, 1915.' This gave him a tremendous shock –" (Bellerby 1986: 24). The sight explodes both the time frame of the story and its realist tenor, because the soldier's vantage point is that of a ghost. Playing against conventions of narrative coherence, logic, and mimetic reference, the reiterated suggestions of life, warmth, and vitality (the dog, the tune) turn out to be dead images of art. Yet these, like the photograph, provide the only link between the past and the present. The last sentence is set apart by an extra space and confirms this invisible subworld from the mother's point of view: "So when his mother, hearing, as she often did, the softly whistled carol, ran upstairs and opened the door to look in, the room was, as usual, empty" (Bellerby 1986: 24). The crisis, as so often in Bellerby's stories, lies hidden in the interstices or silences of the text, suggesting the insurmountable gap between life and language.

Pointing to the aesthetic rationale of Bellerby's inconclusive stories, such absences harbor intriguing possibilities within the vast field of autobiographical writing, with which subsequent generations of women writers have fruitfully experimented. The mysterious dimension in Bellerby's stories provides a further link with her own generation of short-story writers, especially with Elizabeth Bowen and Sylvia Townsend Warner, who both explored in their stories realms of the fantastic.

Bowen's stories are haunted by the supernatural, which she herself considered inseparable from her "sense of life" (Bowen 1975: 7). Ghosts and eerie presences create a shadow world that has its roots in her childhood and her Irish heredity. Bowen shuttled most of her life back and forth between Bowen's Court and England, where she was encouraged to publish by Rose Macauley and matured as a writer. Her imagination remained anchored to her ancestral home. Even though the stories actually set in Ireland – "Sunday Afternoon," "Her Table Spread," "Summer Night," "The Happy Autumn Fields," and "Hand in Glove" – are surprisingly few in number and were all composed during and after World War II, the interrelationship between people and places and the value attached by the Irish ascendancy class to the big house are traceable throughout her work, ranging from *Encounters* (1923) and *Ann Lee's* (1926), via *Joining Charles* (1929) and *The Cat Jumps* (1934), to her wartime volumes *Look at All those Roses* (1941) and *The Demon Lover* (1945). Villas, mansions, hotels, and flats abound in Bowen's stories and are linked with her preferred themes of loneliness, the longing for love, and alienation. Often hollow, dilapidated, or abandoned, houses are sites of conflict and, especially for women, potentially destructive, the haunted house being a prime trope.

The empty seaside hotel in "Love" (1939) becomes a trap for two girls who are lured into a gothic nightmare world: they are greeted by a row of mackintoshes looking like "corpses"; a mad bejewelled lady bars their entrance, and the surly hotelkeeper who refuses to serve tea reveals himself to be a presumed murderer. As if under a spell, this gloomy place resonates with images of a glorious past. As in Bellerby's stories, memories are like ghosts that challenge characters to re-experience lived moments, whereas the present is but an intrusion, as the narrator in "Coming Home" (1923) explains: "An actual occurrence was nothing but the blankness of a shock, then the knowledge that something had happened; afterwards one could creep back and look into one's mind and find new things in it, clear and solid" (Bowen 1982: 94). This shift from occurrence to response is essentially a literary process – consequently literature "drains away some of the shockingness out of life" (Bowen 1982: 780) – and involves various kinds of tension: between past and present, inside and outside, light and dark (blindness, paranoia, crime), the tangible and the intangible.

Child characters are particularly vulnerable to this shock, often related to sexuality and experienced on the threshold of adulthood, as in "A Day in the Dark" (1956), where the young girl living with her uncle is cheated by the "oversized" Miss Banderry. The encounter between the middle-aged Mr Barlow and the flirtatious Contessina proves equally disastrous for the sixteen-year-old girl, as she hurts her palms in a little boating accident. Male sexual desire proves incompatible

with feminine romance. Dramatizing the imbalance of the sexes, Bowen's stories
abound in selfish or vengeful lovers, criminals, and malevolent intruders. Women
are reduced to passive waiting ("Human Habitation," 1926) or threatened by
destructive males, such as the demon lover in the story bearing the same title.
Upon returning to her damaged London house, Mrs Drover finds a letter written
by her former fiancé and feels oppressed by his invisible presence, with images
of death and entrapment presaging her doom. When she enters a taxi, deeming
herself safe, she recognizes her demon lover in the taxi driver. The pitch of her
fear is superbly understated in the vivid account of the scene imitating time-lapse
photography:

> The driver braked to what was almost a stop, turned round and slid the glass panel
> back: the jolt of this flung Mrs Drover forward till her face was almost into the glass.
> Through the aperture driver and passenger, not six inches between them, remained for
> an eternity eye to eye. Mrs Drover's mouth hung open for some seconds before she could
> issue her first scream. After that she continued to scream freely and to beat with her
> gloved hands on the glass all round as the taxi, accelerating without mercy, made off
> with her into the hinterland of deserted streets. (Bowen 1982: 666)

The narrator's detached stance cruelly delivers the victim into the hands of her
tormentor, remolding the perennial story of women's subjection by male force into a
breathtaking tale of gothic terror. Bowen's deep insight into human psychology adds
to the creation of suspense and is often resolved in comic and satirical tones. Ethel,
in "Hand in Glove" (1952), feels the ghostly gaze of her deceased aunt when searching
her trunks in the attic for a pair of gloves. All of a sudden she is physically attacked
by a glove that magically fills out.

Bowen's characters are inseparably tied to their settings, not only in the sense of
gaining emotional continuity through them, but because they are defined by them.
Valeria Cuffe, in "Her Table Spread" (1930), is heiress to an Irish castle and subdued
by her stultifying aristocratic heritage. Henry Russell's bombed London flat in
"Sunday Afternoon" (1941) foreshadows the loss of identity awaiting Maria when she
will leave her Irish mansion. She does not yet know that she owes her self to her
home. Riveting the reader's attention to keenly observed locales, Bowen's characters
are sketched with a few skilled touches. Ann Lee's shop vibrates with excitement
when Mrs Dick Logan and Miss Ames enter it to buy a hat, and neither the customers' lack of style nor Ann Lee's condescending attitude toward them escapes the narrator's shrewd eye: "If Mrs Logan and her friend Miss Ames had had either eyes,
minds, or taste for the comparison, they might have said that she seemed to grow
from the floor like a lily" (Bowen 1982: 106). Bowen's narrator is characteristically
aloof, but rarely as self-effacing as the lens of a camera. Her point of view suggests
a deep familiarity with sophisticated London society and a penchant for both satire
and extravagant metaphors. Thus when a fatal-seeming stranger enters Ann Lee's
shop and disturbs the feminine intimacy, the crisis is displaced in violent phallic

metaphors. When a stranger later crosses the customers' path, his identity is established via these sexual metaphors (metal, sword, stab, cold air), which give him a palpable physical reality and pitch the intense terror of recognition against the cruelly understated drama: "It was by his breath that they knew how terrible it had been – terrible" (Bowen 1982: 111).

Bowen's wartime collections, *Look at All those Roses* (1941) and *The Demon Lover* (1945), combine such strange encounters with the alienating atmosphere of war and its traumatic displacements. War has come to represent that haunting "zone of death" (Bowen 1982: 621) previously expressed through disembodied sounds and voices. Henry Russell's visit to the Irish mansion shows how precarious the elegant view of life inside the gate has become in the light of "the new catastrophic *outward* order of life" (Bowen 1982: 620). "Mysterious Kôr" (1944) is a haunting story about two homeless lovers strolling through the empty streets of London and dreaming about the forsaken city of Kôr. Kôr is more than a hallucination: it crystallizes the story's pervasive erotic loneliness, the unlived years, and wasted lives into a potent metaphor of home when London itself has become as surreal as "the moon's capital – shallow, cratered, extinct" (Bowen 1982: 728).

Such comparisons are memorable and often create great poetic beauty. Blending impressionistic views, reminiscent of Woolf's cinematographic method, with satirical observation, Bowen manages to bring intensely dramatic scenes within a visual compass and delineate the atmosphere of a place or the essence of a character with utmost economy. An observation like "Mr. Barlow's hand, arm, shoulder, and flushed bent neck came within her field of vision" (Bowen 1982: 139) enforces the camera lens's limited scope while bringing home the uneasy sexual undertones of the scene; the Contessina's coquettish nature is embodied in her parasol which "unfurled magically as though it had been wings" (Bowen 1982: 136); and a tiny detail in the farewell scene between Maria and Henry in "Sunday Afternoon" throws up a glow of passion amidst the debris of war: "Faded dark-pink stamen from the flowers above them had moulted down on to her hair" (Bowen 1982: 621).

Sylvia Townsend Warner's short stories share significant traits with Bowen's: an interest in the supernatural, minimal plots, a superbly controlled style, witty, even cynical tones that merge with impressionistic descriptions, and a profound interest in place, as she explains in a letter to William Maxwell dated January 7, 1961: "It may amuse you to know that the whole of this story sprang from a house that happened to catch my eye as I was travelling from Lewes to Worthing" (Maxwell 1982: 189). This process is traced in the title story of her posthumous volume *Scenes of Childhood* (1981). It tells of an enchanted garden, described with minute attention to detail and a sense of suppressed wonder. As the first-person narrator remembers treading on the peasticks on a rubbish heap, the sensations of touch and sound give her a feeling of being surrounded by an ocean. The moment she is carried away, the perspective switches again from direct involvement to memory. Written from a distance and dramatizing the act of remembering rather than attempting to re-enter the past,

Townsend Warner's stories about childhood never achieve the spontaneity of Bowen's.

Like the latter preoccupied with the transition from innocence to experience, Townsend Warner tones down the epiphanic effect of such transitions in favor of their subversive potential. For scandals are legion in her stories, highlighting the gap between social decorum and transgressive impulses, and frequently resulting from an overthrow of heterosexual relationships in favor of a character's suggested incestuous, lesbian, paedophile, or even sodomitic inclinations. The simple-minded Silas Honey in "How to Succeed in Life," from *A Moral Ending* (1931), experiences an infantile joy when drinking from a cow's teats and subsequently develops a strange attachment to the animal, treating it as his life companion; when Major Beldam in "Scenes of Childhood" calls one morning to play games with the girl in the garden, he shows her the varicose ulcer on his leg, which arouses the neighbors' curiosity. But no explicit comment is made. A similar silence shrouds the incestuous love affair between siblings in the war story "A Love Match" (1947). While their illicit pleasure and their efforts to conceal it are disclosed to the reader, the town where they live remains ignorant. When the house is bombed, a search troop discovers the loving couple embracing in bed. Far from trumpeting their shame, the rescue workers divulge a harmless hypothesis which is accepted as the truth: "He must have come in to comfort her. That's my opinion" (Townsend Warner 1988: 20).

Such dramatic ironies are characteristic of Townsend Warner's unorthodox visions. Intimating a secret to the reader which remains hidden from her characters, her narrative voice characteristically flickers between privacy and open revelation, as in the conversation between a woman seeking a divorce and her lawyer in "A Pigeon," from *The Museum of Cheats* (1947), or in the scene when the curious Mrs Colley in "The Nosegay," from *More Joy in Heaven* (1935), overhears the slighting remarks of two young ladies about the Victorian posies prepared for them by the plain Mary Matlask. Though mostly dry and sardonic, Townsend Warner's voice is the result of a plotting consciousness, most clearly traceable in a wealth of highly idiosyncratic, even eccentric metaphors that remotely echo the metaphysical conceit. Thus, while giving prevalence to the external physical space, the narrator of the title story of *Winter in the Air* (1955) vividly captures its atmosphere through a coherent register of bodily images:

> The furniture, assembled once more under the high ceiling of a London room, seemed to be wearing a look of satisfaction, as though, slightly shrugging their polished shoulders, the desk had remarked to the bookcase, the Regency armchair to the Chippendale mirror, "Well, here we are again." And then, after a creak or two, silence had fallen on the dustless room. (Townsend Warner 1988: 21)

Concentrating on the minutiae of everyday life, such as the charwoman's manner of putting sofa cushions cornerwise, Townsend Warner subjects a disenchanted world to a charmed view. Her handling of imagery creates the impression of a catalyst consciousness in accordance with Eliot's notion of the artist's mind forming ever new wholes out of disparate parts. Pivotal images as in "A Pigeon," "The Cheese," or "The Golden Rose" vary with richly poetic and compound similes and metaphors drawn from the most heterogeneous realms: the charwoman's manner is described as "sterile as the wind of the desert"; the rose-wood table is "darkened here and there with old ink-stains like sea-leopard skin"; the tree is seen as a "sparrow-rack"; and recovering from a broken relationship is like wringing "the sea-water of shipwreck out of one's hair" (Townsend Warner 1988: 21–4). The narrator's unconventional angle makes a disjointed world cohere again, with intertexts aiding this unifying process. Hermione's trial from *The Winter's Tale* provides a powerful subtext to Barbara's loneliness after a failed relationship, underpinning her feeling of being rejected and her ineffectual revolt against male injustice.

Townsend Warner was both a highly prolific and versatile writer. Her *Selected Stories*, edited by her executors in 1988, offers a concentrated insight into the diversity of her themes, characters, and styles. Delighting in technical experiment, her short fiction ranges from brief, almost plotless sketches and anecdotes to novella-length studies, and from allegorical fantasies to satirical character portraits. Mainly interested in women characters, she covers a broader social range than her peers, dedicating herself to the working classes in *A Moral Ending* (1931) and *The Salutation* (1932) and satirizing members of the upper class in *More Joy in Heaven* (1935). Townsend Warner's short stories also evince a rare interest in the political situation. In her wartime collections she attacked England's non-interventionist policy vis-à-vis the Spanish Civil War and exposed the country's failure to confront the threat of Nazism. The effects of the war still echo in *The Museum of Cheats* (1947) and *Winter in the Air* (1955), while her late volume, *The Kingdom of Elfin* (1977), brings together tales about a terrible society of werewolves, fairies, and elves, with fantastic names, settings, and odd manners giving a new dimension to her biting social criticism. These late stories combine many of the chief traits of her earlier work: terse comment and satirical observation, sharp images and metaphors, and her attention to the everyday with its hidden disasters, defying moral outrage even when at the court of Brocéliande cockfights are replaced by a spurred fight between a pair of eunuchs. Eventually, the wanton Queen Melior agrees to have the two cripples deported to the Island of Repose. These mordant allegories once more prove Townsend Warner's original handling of the short story, counterbalancing the modernist idea of the self-sufficient poetic image by a profound interest in social life, and society's masculinity by subversive feminist currents, thematizing failed and unsatisfactory relationships between men and women, and skillfully shifting between a public and a private view.

Feminine experience reached a different scale of vulnerability in the work of Jean Rhys. Sharing Mansfield's concern with social outcasts and equally drawing inspiration from Paris, Rhys started writing much later in her life, and her stories dealing with sad women strike a harsher note of abuse than Mansfield's. The sense of defeat is not limited to female experience and is frequently reflected in places indicating confinement, as in "At the Villa D'Or," "The Sidi," and "From a French Prison." Primarily concerned with what happens, Rhys concentrates on the quotidian. Scenes in a park, in a café, and in a prison are observed with striking detachment, commonly setting into relief an individual's perception against the ordinary course of events. The first-person narrator of "Rapunzel, Rapunzel" feels a hostile presence among the inmates of a convalescent home, until her unease crystallizes in the shape of a barber who cuts an old patient's long hair short instead of trimming it. What seems a trifling act is tragic in this vulnerable situation: the woman dies.

Rhys's attention to crowds is reminiscent of the satirical vein of one of the great miniaturists of low life: William Hogarth. Just as the latter's modern morality genre had introduced into painting scenes from all areas of life, Rhys creates in her stories her specific cast of characters, often reduced to one feature effectively conveyed in a simile, such as the old chuckling, rat-like woman, the warden looking "like a huge spider – a bloated, hairy insect born of the darkness and of the dank smell," and women "whipped into a becoming meekness" (Rhys 1987: 11). These social types provide the foil against which the narrator in "From a French Prison" perceives the sorrow of an elderly foreigner repeatedly refused access. Significantly, the twelve mannequins at Jeanne Veron's are referred to as "types," each performing her fixed role and style ("Mannequin"), while the buyers embody national stereotypes: a "stout Dutch lady," a "silver-haired American gentleman," and a "hook-nosed, odd English lady of title" (Rhys 1987: 25). Anna, the new mannequin is trapped in the salon, and her fatigue is absorbed in the daily routine of her job. Apart from the mannequins' shared lot – when the girls emerge from the shops, "the Paris night swallowed them up" (Rhys 1987: 26) – there is little room for either individual action or social integration. Rhys's emphasis on anonymous crowds strengthens her characters' loneliness and their failure to belong anywhere. Exclusion commonly results from social, sexual, and racial prejudice. Selina Davis, the West Indian immigrant from "Let Them Call It Jazz," is a prototypical outsider, turned homeless, ignored and maligned by the English, whom she implicitly criticizes when recounting her experiences in her non-standard English. First-person narration proves a powerful means for exposing the yawning cultural gulf between Rhys's defenceless solitary figures and their hostile surroundings. By fabricating a story about a West Indian shooting party, the narrator from "On Not Shooting Sitting Birds" unwittingly provokes her own rejection by her male English interlocutor.

Favoring cosmopolitan settings, Rhys's stories draw on a wide range of interiors and enclosed spaces: studios, cafés, and city streets, her preferred topographies being the West Indies, Paris, and London during the war. Relevant as these places are to a character's experience, they are frequently sketched in a few telegram-like phrases as in "Mannequin" – "Twelve o'clock. *Déjeuner chez* Jeanne Veron, Place Vendôme" (Rhys 1987: 20) – and of little importance in themselves, as Ford Madox Ford had noted appreciatively in his preface to the first edition of *The Left Bank* (1927), suggesting that Rhys's major concerns are "passion, hardship, emotions" (Rhys 1979: 26).

The *Rive Gauche* of Paris held a deep attraction for Rhys and, given the mournful aspects of life suggested by the epithet "left," provided her with the moods and lifestyles to which she creatively responded. The influence of French syntax and lexis accounts for much of the authenticity of her style, and there is often an air of melancholy and subdued debauchery in the locales she preferred. Telling the story of women's sexual exploitation, the tenor's song "Les Grues de Paris!" perfectly captures the story's disillusioned undertones ("In a Café"). Rhys's stories evince a profound sense of futility and resignation. Showing little zest or joy in life, and often lacking any purpose, her heroes and heroines simply go on. They are capable of experiencing deeply, but are completely at the mercy of external forces. This feeling of exposure is reinforced by the penetration of narrators' and characters' texts by the texts of others, as in "Fishy Waters" or "The Insect World" (Malcolm and Malcolm 1996), and corresponds to Rhys's observation: "You're picked up like a pen, and when you're used up you're thrown away, ruthlessly, and someone else is picked up" (Plante 1983: 111–12). To render intense subjective experience, Rhys experimented widely with style and technique. The broken monologue of a former mannequin in "Hunger" vividly transcribes the speaker's feeling through excessive dots and pauses, repetitions and exclamations, while the rapid shifts of focus in "Mannequin," by contrast, express the mixed feelings of luxury and boredom and adequately capture the gap between the protagonist's inner revulsion and her outer passivity.

By voicing women's social and sexual marginalization, their exposure to male power, and their ambivalent strategies of submitting to or deconstructing assigned identities, often from an exiled position, early twentieth-century women short-story writers broke new ground. At the same time they continued a tradition of women's writing foregrounding the sensibilities of female characters, as exemplified in the novels of Jane Austen, George Eliot, and Elizabeth Gaskell. Drawing on their own lives, Rhys, Townsend Warner, Bellerby, Woolf, Bowen, and Mansfield translated the tensions between social convention and independence, between reality and fancy, and between subordination and revolt into the terms of early-twentieth-century experience and, to meet its complexity, searched for new modes of expression. Women's short fiction of the first half of the twentieth century shows an experimental vigor hitherto unknown. Encouraged by modernist poetics and developments of the form, such as Chekhov's short sketches which were popular in the 1920s and 1930s (Baldwin 1989), their innovative energies produced a unique blend of theme and form, giving women's varied, even contradictory, experiences a degree of authenticity inconceivable without the daring shifts of viewpoint, modulations of tone and style, and devices imported from the other arts characteristic of their work. What experience means in the individual writers' work (thrilling plots, internal crises, psychological insights into other characters, autobiographical self-inspection, fantastic flights, dramatic involvement, or satirical detachment) is itself an index of the realization of women's complex situation in the first half of the twentieth century and of the challenges it harbored for the writer.

The women writers discussed in this chapter have variously taken up this challenge. Commenting on the "limited" material out of which Mansfield developed moments of revelation, Eliot described the skillful handling of such minimal experience as "feminine" (Mansfield 2006: 343). If this claim applies to miniature sketches and stories favoring the narrow compass of things, the force of imagination, even brought to small worlds, and the wealth of hybrid forms, incorporating into the short story elements of the essay, review, and (auto)biography, suggest that modernist and late-modernist women writers not only found a voice within this "minimal" sphere, but effectively struggled against it and, in so doing, significantly expanded the generic boundaries of the short story and enriched its experiential range.

References and Further Reading

Athill, D. (ed.) (1987). *Jean Rhys: The Collected Short Stories*. New York and London: Norton.

Baldwin, D.R. (1989). *Virginia Woolf: A Study of the Short Fiction*. Boston: Twayne Publishers.

Bell, A.O. (ed.) (1979). *The Diary of Virginia Woolf*, 5 vols. Hardmonsworth: Penguin.

Benzel, K.N. and Hoberman, R. (eds) (2004). *Trespassing Boundaries: Virginia Woolf's Short Fiction*. New York: Palgrave; Basingstoke: Macmillan.

Bowen, E. (1975). *Pictures and Conversations*. London: Allen Lane.

Bowen, E. (1982). *The Collected Stories of Elizabeth Bowen*. New York: Vintage Books.

Dick, S. (ed.) (2003). *Virgina Woolf. A Haunted House: The Complete Shorter Fiction*. London: Vintage.

Dunbar, P. (1997). *Radical Mansfield: Double Discourse in Katherine Mansfield's Short Stories*. Basingstoke: Macmillan.

Freedman, R. (ed.) (1980). *Virgina Woolf: Revaluation and Continuity*. Berkeley/Los Angeles/London: University of California Press.

Friies A. (1946). *Katherine Mansfield: Life and Stories*. Copenhagen: Munksgaard.

Glendenning, V. (1979). *Elizabeth Bowen: A Biography*. New York: Avon Books.

Head, D. (1992). *The Modernist Short Story: A Study in Theory and Practice*. Cambridge: Cambridge University Press.

Hooker, J. (ed.) (1986). *Selected Stories by Frances Bellerby*. London: Enitharmon.

Kobler, J.F. (1990). *Katherine Mansfield: A Study of the Short Fiction*. Boston: Twayne Publishers.

Lassner, Phyllis (1991). *Elizabeth Bowen: A Study of the Short Fiction*. New York: Twayne Publishers.

Malcolm, C.A. and Malcolm, D. (1996). *Jean Rhys: A Study of the Short Fiction*. New York: Twayne Publishers.

Mansfield, K. (2006). *The Collected Stories*. Ware, Hertfordshire: Wordsworth Editions.

Maxwell, W. (ed.) (1982). *Sylvia Townsend Warner: Letters*. London: Chatto & Windus.

Nathan, R.B. (ed.) (1993). *Critical Essays on Katherine Mansfield*. NewYork/Toronto: Hall/Macmillan.

O'Sullivan, V. (ed.) (2006). *Katherine Mansfield's Selected Stories*. New York/London: Norton.

Plante, D. (1983). *Difficult Women: A Memoir of Three*. London: Victor Gollancz.

Rhys, J. (1979). *The Left Bank*. New York: Arno Press (original work published 1927).

Rhys, J. (1987). *The Collected Short Stories*. New York and London: Norton.

Robinson, R. (ed.) (1994). *Katherine Mansfield: In from the Margin*. Baton Rouge and London: Louisiana State University Press.

Skrbic, N. (2004). *Wild Outbursts of Freedom: Reading Virginia Woolf's Short Fiction*. Westport: Praeger.

Smith, A. (1999). *Katherine Mansfield and Virgina Woolf: A Public of Two*. Oxford: Clarendon Press.

Townsend Warner, S. (1988). *Selected Stories*. London: Chatto & Windus.

Wittgenstein, L. (1961). *Tractatus Logico-Philosophicus*, trans. D.F. Pears and B.F. MacGuinness. London: Routledge (original work published 1921).

Woolf, V. (1966–7). *The Collected Essays*, 4 vols. London: Hogarth Press.

Woolf, V. (2003). *The Haunted House and Other Stories: The Complete Shorter Fiction of Virginia Woolf*. London: Vintage.

8
Rudyard Kipling's Art of the Short Story

David Malcolm

Kipling dedicated himself to the short story like few other canonical British authors. Only H.G. Wells, Walter de la Mare, V.S. Pritchett, and Somerset Maugham show a comparable interest in short fiction. Depending on how one calculates it, Kipling published some seventeen collections of short stories between 1888 and 1932. The number of his short stories runs to over 250. This is a substantial output of short fiction, and it is difficult to discuss it as a whole in a way that does justice to the entirety and to individual texts. This essay approaches Kipling's short fiction from two directions. First, it offers a discussion of some major aspects of the work as a whole: genre, narration, character relations, and setting. Second, it analyzes three central Kipling short stories: "On the City Wall" (1888), "Mary Postgate" (1917), and "The Bull That Thought" (1926). The aim is to provide a sense of Kipling's art of the short story.

1

Critics have noted the genre range and variety of Kipling's short fiction. T.S. Eliot commented on his "versatility" and found it suspicious (qtd in Harrison 1982: 103). It is also noted by Gerhard Stilz (1980: 154–76), James Harrison (1982: 149–51), and is related by Clare Hanson to modernist experimentation (1985: 35).

The genre multifariousness of Kipling's short fiction is, indeed, striking – at least on the surface. The largest group of stories in his output belongs in terms of genre to the conventions of social-psychological fiction that dominate British fiction in the nineteenth and twentieth centuries. These include an interest in psychological states, in the placing of characters within social and political contexts, an avoidance of fantastic elements, and an occlusion of the fictive nature of the text. Throughout his career, Kipling writes – *mutatis mutandis* – mini versions of *Middlemarch*. Most of the stories in his first collection, *Plain Tales from the Hills* (1888), are such, and almost half of the stories in his last, *Limits and Renewals* (1932), are too. There is a genre continuity that runs from "Venus Annodomini" to "The Tender Achilles," and social-psychological fiction recurs throughout Kipling's output from "The Finest Story in the World" and "The Record of Badalia Herodsfoot" in *Many Inventions* (1893), through "An Habitation Enforced" in *Actions and Reactions* (1909), to "The Janeites" in *Debits and Credits* (1926). Even fiction that contains the markers of other genres, such as a supernatural story like "The Brushwood Boy" (*The Day's Work* (1898)) or war fiction like "A Madonna of the Trenches" (*Debits and Credits*), also contains clear signals of social-psychological fiction.

What distinguishes Kipling's social-psychological stories is, above all, a matter of setting and character. *Plain Tales from the Hills* offers stories with Indian settings and, indeed, Indian characters, which is not typical of late nineteenth-century social-psychological fiction. Indeed, Indian characters predominate in *In Black and White* (1888). Kipling's deployment of working-class characters, especially in the stories involving his trio of British soldiers, Mulvaney, Ortheris, and Learoyd, is actually quite typical of the short fiction of the last years of the nineteenth century (compare, for example, stories by Arthur Morrison and Hubert Crackanthorpe), even in the extensive use of working-class and regional dialect. Kipling has two short stories that focus on children's psychological experience, the autobiographical "Baa Baa, Black Sheep" and "His Majesty the King" (both from *Wee Willie Winkie* (1888)), but these are rather unusual in his short fiction, which is predominantly concerned with adult mental and social experience. Some stories clearly have a socially satiric purpose; indeed, many of the pieces in *Plain Tales from the Hills* are surprisingly cynical studies of Simla society, for example, "Consequences" and "The Rescue of Pluffles."

Kipling also produced substantial quantities of war fiction, from "The Taking of Lungtungpen" in *Plain Tales from the Hills*, "The Drums of the Fore and Aft" in *Wee Willie Winkie*, through "The Captive" and "A Sahibs' War" in *Traffics and Discoveries* (1904), to the many such texts in *A Diversity of Creatures* (1917) and *Debits and Credits* (1926). With regard to these last two volumes, it should be noted that most of the war stories have a psychological focus, and are very often set at a considerable physical distance from the Great War itself. "Mary Postgate" (1917) and "The Gardener" (1926), with their female protagonists, are typical of this aspect of Kipling's engagement with the war of 1914–18.

Historical fiction runs through Kipling's output of short stories. *Puck of Pook's Hill* (1906) and *Rewards and Fairies* (1910) are collections of historical pieces, with all the markers of the genre of historical fiction (past setting, a mixture of documented and undocumented characters and events, an attempt to reconstruct a past mentality, experience and environment, and, indeed, a clear contemporary relevance). "The Eye of Allah" in *Debits and Credits*, and "The Church That Was at Antioch" and "The Manner of Men" in *Limits and Renewals* are later examples of Kipling's historical short fiction. With regard to his deployment of this genre, one should note, however, that it overlaps with supernatural fiction, for Puck, a supernatural figure, magically conjures up figures from the past for Dan and Una. One should also note that in many historical stories the focus is again on psychological experience, rather than on great historical events. "The Knife and the Naked Chalk" from *Rewards and Fairies* is a good example. It is fundamentally a universal story of self-sacrifice and loss rather than an attempt to reconstruct a particular milieu.

All these genres – social-psychological fiction, war fiction and historical fiction – are quite close to each other in genre conventions, as, indeed, are the school stories in *Stalky & Co.* (1899), and those that turn up in *A Diversity of Creatures* (1917) ("Regulus") and in *Debits and Credits* ("The United Idolaters" and "The Propagation of Knowledge"). A different set of conventions is employed, however, in the adventure stories that form a substantial part of Kipling's work. Here exotic locales and violent and colorful action and figures dominate. Uninflected adventure stories occur in *Many Inventions* ("A Matter of Fact") and *The Day's Work* ("The Devil and the Deep Sea"), but most of Kipling's work in the genre are examples of the story of imperial adventure. Such stories run throughout his fiction, from "The Judgement of Dungara" in *In Black and White*, through many of the texts in *Life's Handicap* ("The Head of the District" and "Namgay Doola," for example), to "In the Rukh" and "Judson and the Empire" in *Many Inventions*, and to "The Bridge-Builders" in *The Day's Work* and "A Deal in Cotton" and "Little Foxes" in *Actions and Reactions*. Stories within this genre either illustrate European control over (largely) Indian peoples and situations ("William the Conqueror" from *The Day's Work* demonstrates this clearly), or else a threat to and the breakdown of that control. "The Strange Ride of Morrowbie Jukes" (*Wee Willie Winkie*) and "The Bridge Builders" (*The Day's Work*) exemplify the latter. Some tales of imperial adventure cross into the travel sketch – "The City of Dreadful Night" in *Life's Handicap*, for example, which is barely a narrative text at all, and certainly not a story. A late example of the genre, "The Debt" in *Limits and Renewals*, is a highly deviant one, in which setting and character are appropriate to the genre, but action (George V's advising an officer to wear a coat) is not. One text, "One View of the Question" (*Many Inventions*), is an inverted example of the genre, in that it presents an Indian nationalist's (of a sort) views on a corrupt and decadent Britain.

Kipling did very little work in two genres, the detective story and the espionage story, that are historically related to the adventure story, and which emerged as discrete and powerful genres in the late nineteenth and early twentieth centuries – "The Return of Imray" in *Life's Handicap* and "Fairy-Kist" in *Limits and Renewals* are examples of the former, and "The Edge of the Evening" in *A Diversity of Creatures* of the latter. However, his work shows an interest in non-mimetic genres, in which the conventions of all the genres discussed so far are breached. These are supernatural fiction, legend, and fable, and (to a much lesser degree) scientific romance and utopia/dystopia. Despite the frequent appearance of supernatural stories in anthologies of Kipling's work, these are, in fact, not very numerous. "The Bisara of Poree" is the only example in *Plain Tales from the Hills*; others are "The Phantom Rickshaw" in *The Phantom Rickshaw* (1888), "The Mark of the Beast" in *Life's Handicap*, "The

Finest Story in the World" and "The Lost Legion" in *Many Inventions*, "The Brush-wood Boy" in *The Day's Work*, "Wireless" and "They" in *Traffics and Discoveries*, the frames and some of the action in the stories in *Puck of Pook's Hill* and *Rewards and Fairies*, "The House Surgeon" in *Actions and Reactions*, "The Wish House" and (prob-ably in the end) "The Gardener" in *Debits and Credits*, and "Unprofessional" in *Limits and Renewals* (although this story is also marked by signs of scientific romance).

Kipling produced a large number of fables, especially beast fables, with talking, anthropomorphic animals, and a moral *pointe*. Many of the texts in *Just So Stories* are of this kind ("The Elephant's Child," for example), but Kipling also returns to them in *The Day's Work* ("A Walking Delegate," "The Maltese Cat"), *Traffics and Discoveries* ("Below the Mill Dam"), and *Actions and Reactions* ("The Mother Hive"). Kipling, indeed, produces variants of the beast fable, with talking machines rather than animals in "The Ship That Found Herself" and ".007" (*The Day's Work*) and "Below the Mill Dam." Most of the stories in both *Jungle Books* are beast fables of a sort (although not all, for example "Toomai of the Elephants," "The Miracle of Purun Bhagat" and "Quiquern"). But even those that are beast fables, especially the Mowgli stories, show a clear tendency toward psychological and even social interests, and while they make moral points, these are by no means simple ones. Kipling's output also contains texts that are pseudo-legends or pseudo-myths, with supernatural beings of overt metaphorical/symbolic constitution, aiming to illustrate some cosmic truth: "The Children of the Zodiac" in *Many Inventions*, "The Enemies to Each Other" and "On the Gate" in *Debits and Credits*, and "Uncovenanted Mercies" in *Limits and Renew-als*. There are very few examples of other non-mimetic genres in Kipling's short fiction. Scientific romance is limited to "With the Night Mail" (*Actions and Reactions*) and "As Easy as A.B.C." (*A Diversity of Creatures*). The latter story also shows strong markers of the utopia, as does "The Army of a Dream" in *Traffics and Discoveries*. Surprisingly, given his well-documented political views, Kipling's only dystopia is the vision of the future of the USA in "The Prophet and the Country" in *Debits and Credits*.

In addition, Kipling produces some texts that are very peculiar in terms of genre. *Wee Willie Winkie* contains two dramatic texts – "The Hill of Illusion" and "Mrs Hawksbee Sits Out" – which is unusual in a collection of narrative prose. Most pecu-liar of all are what can only be described as anecdotes of low and high life. These operate within the conventions of social-psychological fiction, but have story materials that are unusual for that kind of fiction. They are all comic and involve actions that are fundamentally trivial in comparison with those of traditional social-psychological texts. They usually involve elaborate tricks and practical jokes played on others. "Brugglesmith" in *Many Inventions*, "My Sunday at Home" in *The Day's Work*, "A Naval Mutiny," and "Aunt Ellen" and "Beauty Spots" in *Limits and Renewals* are examples of this kind of text, which seems to be peculiarly Kiplingian. Equally unusual, in the field of prose short fiction, is Kipling's use of verse throughout his collections. Poems sometimes preface, and, more frequently, conclude stories. One is compelled to say that with some exceptions (the poems in *The Jungle Books*, and the poem that concludes "Mary Postgate") most of the verse seems a distraction from the stories, at best classed, as by Edmund Wilson, as "synthetic verse" (1961: 153). But the poetry does indicate Kipling's genre restlessness, with his constant innovation in the field of genre and kind.

What conclusions can be drawn from this picture of genre diversity in Kipling's work? First, there clearly is a considerable amount of genre variety within his short fiction. Second, many texts are mixed in terms of genre, and are pulled in different directions by, for example, social-psychological and supernatural motifs. Third, there are texts – the anecdotes discussed above – that are most peculiar in terms of genre. Fourth, within particular volumes the clash of genres gives the collection a particular energy and vibrance. For example, *Debits and Credits* moves from pseudo-legend to war fiction through psychological story to dystopia, beast fable, school story, historical fiction, and supernatural story – all within the space of fourteen stories. Finally, however, it must be noted that Kipling actually stays predominantly within the conventions of realist short fiction. Historical stories, war fiction and social-psychological fiction are his favored genres, despite the presence of supernatural texts within his output. Even where there are obvious supernatural motifs – "The Brushwood Boy," "The Wish House," and "The Gardener" – the stories' fundamental focus is on characters' psychological states. This is, finally, true even of Kipling's greatest supernatural story, "They," with its presentation of the narrator's and the blind lady's sense of loss.

2

The critical discussion of narration in Kipling's short fiction focuses on three main, ultimately connected, topics: the knowingness of the narrator (especially in the early stories); the degree of distance toward narrators generated by particular stories, and, thus, the reliability of some narrators; and the presence of ellipses and ambiguities in narrators' accounts of events. Thus Harrison refers to the "knowing, dogmatic tone" of the narrator in Kipling's Anglo-Indian stories (1982: 27). Martin Seymour-Smith writes of *Plain Tales from the Hills* that they are "often over redolent of worldly wisdom" (1989: 69), a sentiment shared by Hanson (1985: 35) and Harold Orel (1986: 152). Andrew Hagiioannu calls him a "firm, bullish narrator" (2003: 7). Yet critics also point to the way in which, and not just in Kipling's later work, texts ask readers to look at narrators with some degree of distance, and even to question their reliability. Philip Mallett sees this narrational strategy even in *Plain Tales from the Hills*. "The assumed authority of the narrative voice is repeatedly undermined," he notes, "by the shifts and uncertainties within the stories, and the incompleteness of the explanations they offer" (2003: 31). This is echoed by Stilz (1980: 150), and B.J. Moore-Gilbert insists that "Many of Kipling's narrator figures not only parade their limited authority, but also work explicitly to undermine any sense of complacent alliance with the reader" (1986: 181). However, some critics question this view. Wilson is certain that Kipling after the Boer War becomes a propagandist for British Imperialism (1961: 133), and Andrew Lycett insists that "for all his command of irony, he [Kipling] actually believed in his imperialism" (1999: 590). The great Indian writer Nirad C. Chaudhuri strikes a suitably ambiguous note. "Kipling the writer is always able to rise above Kipling the political man," he writes; however, Chaudhuri records that he refused to read anything by Kipling except *The Jungle Book* until after Indian and Pakistani independence in 1947 (1972: 29, 28).

The question of ellipses and ambiguities within narrators' accounts is a central issue in discussions of Kipling's narrators. Valerie Shaw writes that "as his [Kipling's] career went on, narration came more and more to consist of fragments which it was the reader's job to piece together with little or no help from the author" (1983: 103). Such a view is endorsed by Helen Pike Bauer who writes of Kipling's creation of narrational ambiguity (1994: xv–xvi), and Sandra Kemp argues that Kipling's stories "encourage suggestion and allusion" and "resist interpretation and integration" (1988: 7–8). Both Mallett (2003: 150) and Kemp (1988: 1) see such a narrational strategy as part of Kipling's experimentalism and his covert relation to Modernism, a position endorsed by Andrew Rutherford (1971: 10).

As with regard to genre, the range of Kipling's narrators is noteworthy. They are varied socially and ethnically, although it needs to be stressed that working-class narrators are always contained within frames set up by middle-class narrators, and Indian narrators are also, except in four stories in *In Black and White* and one ("One View of the Question") in *Many Inventions*. Linguistic variety is also present in the narratives of Mulvaney (for example, "The Courting of Dinah Shadd") and Pyecroft (for example, "The Horse Marines"), in which working-class informal speech contrasts with the frame narrator's more formal standard language. Throughout his short fiction, Kipling also presents what is by convention to be understood as an 'Englishing' of Indian subcontinent languages. One finds this in *In Black and White*, but also in a late story, "The Debt," from *Limits and Renewals*. This volume also contains, in "The Miracle of Saint Jubanus," one of Kipling's attempts to give the impression of a character speaking French. His pseudo-legends, "The Enemies to Each Other" and "The Children of the Zodiac," deploy an appropriately formal language.

Kipling also runs through a wide range of narrational strategies – third-person omniscient narrators, first-person major and minor characters, and narrations within frames. Many Kipling stories are narrated principally through dialog. This is true, above all, of framed narrations, like "The Three Musketeers," but also of texts such as "On Greenhow Hill" and "The Wish House." In his short fiction, it is impossible to say that he favors one narrational strategy over another. Predominantly, however, one is confronted with highly authoritative narrators. First-person or third-person narrators, from *Plain Tales from the Hills* to *Limits and Renewals*, are ultimately knowing ones, confident in their perceptions and judgments. These are at times complex, but it is hard to find a self-doubting narrator in Kipling's work. (Surprisingly, the utopian "The Army of a Dream" (*Traffics and Discoveries*) offers one, at least in its second last paragraph.)

The issue of narrational reliability and ellipsis and ambiguity is a complex one. There is a critical consensus that Kipling's narrators are not fully reliable and that stories are at times obscure. One wonders if this is actually so. Inevitably frame narrations raise the issue of unreliability, because the reader is made aware of the process by which an account is made. A frame can, however, also work as an authentication device. Which stories are really marked by narrational unreliability? "The Strange Ride of Morrowbie Jukes," in which the reader is told that the manuscript has been tampered with? "The Mark of the Beast" in which the narrator refuses to tell the reader what he and Strickland did to the leper? Even here, there is no real question of unreliability. Jukes's manuscript has only been "touched . . . up in places," and, in fact, the frame narrator insists on the veracity of what he writes. In "The Mark of the Beast" it is, in fact, extremely clear what the narrator and Strickland do to the leper (they torture him). The same is true of elliptical stories like "Friendly Brook" and, really, despite one obscurity (the second corpse) of "Mrs Bathurst." The latter is a powerful, but far from obscure, study of Vickery's self-destructive obsession and madness narrated by figures on the margins of the action, and not the opaque enigma it is sometimes seen to be. Kipling's short stories are complex, but the content of ellipses is usually quite clear, and narrators are not unreliable, as Marlow is in Conrad's "Heart of Darkness," or the governess is in James's *The Turn of the Screw*.

3

The issues of character relations and special/temporal settings are best dealt with briefly in general terms. The discussions of particular short stories that follow will illustrate patterns of both in a more concrete fashion.

Despite the wide range of characters in Kipling's short stories – human, animal, metaphysical, mechanical, European, Indian, North American, male, female – certain common relations hold among them. These are threefold: hostility and cruelty; aid and support; secrecy and initiation. They overlap to some extent, but can be distinguished. Examples of hostility and cruelty run throughout the fiction. Kipling's characters are good abusers and good haters. The jocular friction among the four British colonial officers in "At the End of the Passage" (*Life's Handicap*) is typical in this respect, as is the gentlemanly animosity towards the Russian officer in "The Man Who Was" and the ritualized cursing in "The Courting of Dinah Shadd" (*Life's Handicap*). Bees snap at each other in "The Mother Hive" and dirigible pilots and engineers curse and josh each other abrasively in "With the Night Mail" (*Actions and Reactions*). "My Sunday at Home" (*The Day's Work*) and "Sea Constables" (*Debits and Credits*) present varieties of aggression towards others, while an ability to curse others is highly valued in Mowgli's jungle ("There is no speech in the world so rancorous and so stinging as the language the Jungle People use to show scorn and contempt" ("Red Dog")). *Stalky & Co.* is all about malicious pranks on others, and Manallace pursues Castorley with unremitting malice throughout "Dayspring Mishandled" (*Limits and Renewals*).

Yet aid and support also mark relations among characters in Kipling's short fiction. Mowgli learns words of politeness as well as scorn in the jungle, and ways to avoid its aggression (for example, the very useful "what to say to Mang the Bat when he disturbed him in the branches at midday" ("Kaa's Hunting")).The locomotives in ".007" may snap at each other harshly, but in the end they work together (*The Day's Work*). The bristly masons in "In the Interests of the Brethren" offer solace to the war damaged (*Debits and Credits*); the professional wrangling and trickery of "The Tender Achilles" redeem Wilkie (*Limits and Renewals*). This last story, like so many of Kipling's trick or practical joke stories, illustrates a further persistent pattern in his short fiction – one in which characters have superior knowledge to others. "Thrown Away" (*Plain Tales from the Hills*), in which the narrator and his accomplice conceal "the Boy's" suicide, is typical in this respect. The same motif occurs in "They" and "The Wish House," and in most of the Masonic stories, like "In the Interests of the Brethren" and "Wireless." "Dayspring Mishandled" is about the uses of secrecy and superior knowledge, while Puck inducts Dan and Una into the hidden life of English history, and Baloo imparts jungle lore to Mowgli. Running throughout Kipling's fiction, there are hidden stories, known to some and not to others. "Friendly Brook," with its covert but clear murder story, exemplifies this motif.

In general terms, time and space in Kipling's short fiction can be dealt with succinctly. Both are marked by considerable range – stories of contemporary urban life jostle with ones set in a legendary, historical, or pre-historical past; Indian stories lie next to ones set in France and next to others set in Southern Africa; metaphysical worlds interweave with closely realized material settings; the reader encounters bee hives, country houses, jungles, oceans, and the command deck of a dirigible; the past penetrates the present; one can leave polite Simla for the Gate of a Hundred Sorrows and McIntosh Jellaludin's sordid quarters. Analyses of individual stories, however, reveal better than generalizations typical features of character relations and setting in Kipling's created worlds.

4

"On the City Wall" was first published in 1888 in the Indian edition of *In Black and White*. It had not previously been published, as had the rest of the stories in that volume, in the weekly supplement to the Allahabad *Pioneer*. It concludes a collection of eight texts which deal with trickery ("The Judgment of Dungara," "At Howli Thana," "Gemini," and "The Sending of Dana Da"), vengeance ("Dray Wara Yow

Dee" and "At Twenty-Two"), and passion (the previous two stories and "In Flood
Time"). The collection is remarkable because most of the stories are given in the voices
of Indians (the exceptions are "At Twenty-Two," "The Sending of Dana Da," and "On
the City Wall"), and even when the narrator is not an Indian, the point of view, as
in "At Twenty-Two," is principally that of one. This context suggests certain interpretative possibilities.

"On the City Wall" tells a story of trickery, passion, and vengeance of various
kinds. Narrated by an anonymous Englishman, very similar to the recurrent English
journalist-narrator of many of Kipling's Indian stories, it recounts a plot to smuggle
an aged Indian nationalist, Khem Singh, from imprisonment in the British-controlled
fort of an unnamed northern Indian city, a plot hatched by Lalun, a high-class prostitute, and Wali Dad, a Western-educated young Indian Muslim. The English narrator is duped and charmed into helping the escape of the nationalist. A background
to the latter stages of the story material is formed by a sectarian riot, Hindus against
Muslims, which the British authorities put down by force. During it, the highly
Westernized Wali Dad becomes violently emotional and identifies himself with his
co-religionists. The story ends with the narrator's realizing that he has been used by
Lalun, and Khem Singh's return to imprisonment, he having realized that his days as
a rebel are past.

The narrator recounts events in a linear, chronological manner, and is the kind of
knowledgeable and confident narrator that manages so many of Kipling's stories.
Throughout the story, the reader is made aware of his competence and understanding.
For example, he introduces Lalun, and gives details of the position of a high-class
prostitute. The narrator gives a detailed account of Wali Dad's past and present
(1937a: 344). He explains, again in detail, how the Indian government ("the Supreme
Government") operates (345–7) and the background to communal tensions and rioting
in the city (360–1).

Yet the narrator is a more ambiguous figure than he seems at first glance. First,
and most importantly, he is deceived by Lalun. "I was not so clever," he ruefully notes
towards the end of the story (372). "But I was thinking how I had become Lalun's
Vizier after all" is the text's final sentence (374). Second and subsequent readings of
the story show how he is manipulated by Lalun, how his attention is diverted from
the old Sikh rebel in the fort (357), how he is charmed by her (359), and finally how
he is made the agent of the old nationalist's escape (368). Second, the narrator clearly
inhabits a peculiar position in the racial situation in the city. He spends time in
Lalun's *salon*, among its very heterogeneous Indian company, and also at the British
Club. On the street during the riot he is with the old Sikh (in disguise) and is also
recognized and talked to by British police officials (364–5). He clearly moves between
two worlds, to a degree unplaced. Indeed, he has a subversive imagination, for once
he "dreamed that Wali Dad had sacked the City and I was made Vizier, with Lalun's
silver pipe for mark of office" (361).

Place is, however, very important in "On the City Wall" (as it is in so many Kipling
stories). The very title indicates its importance. The city wall divides and cuts off,

but also provides a vantage point and a point of contact between two spaces. It is a historic Indian wall, now marking British control and authority. Lalun's house on the city wall, and thus liminal and mediating, is in contrast with "the blackened wall" of the ancient fort that dominates the city (1937a: 352). Fort Amara itself is associated with time, and in this respect the story involves a considerable range. "Three kings built it hundreds of years ago," the narrator informs the reader. "It is peopled with many ghosts" (352). The story's climax occurs at the festival of Mohurrum, on a date which commemorates a past event, and the past is present throughout the story from "the red tombs of dead Emperors beyond the river" (344) to Khem Singh's stories of Fort Amara's past (356). The past is also connected with Khem Singh himself, who, the reader is told, fought the British on three occasions in the past, in 1846, 1857, and 1871 (352, 356). Thus, the story brings together the present of British India (the months of the year are given on two occasions (349, 357)), and a distant and more recent Indian historical past.

There is a similar range in terms of character. The company in Lalun's house is notably mixed (349), and the crowd during the riot is made up of many different inhabitants of the city, as well as police and Indian and British troops. However, the text clearly marks the division between Indian and British. On the one hand, there are the officers of the British government, their troops and police, and gentlemen from the British Club. On the other, the story presents, among a host of nameless Indian characters, Lalun, Khem Singh, and Wali Dad. It is striking that the Indian characters are much more prominent than the British ones, and the narrator spends much more time with them. Lalun is largely a stock character, an Eastern charmer and temptress (although the narrator clearly does feel her charm (368)). Khem Singh is allowed to speak very clearly of his hatred for the British and his desire to fight them again (355–6). Wali Dad is made quite a complex figure, free-thinking, anti-British yet disdaining his own people, and in the end identifying himself with his co-religionists whom he has previously mocked.

Certain motifs run throughout the text. Among the principal ones are knowledge and secrecy. The narrator seems knowing, but there are secrets kept from him. The Supreme Government of India deals with subversives with effective stealth. "There is no outward sign of excitement; there is no confusion; there is no knowledge" when troublemakers are exiled (347). The world of the story is also marked by motifs of division and mixture. British are separate from Indians, as in the "Commissioner's tennis-parties" that Wali Dad mocks (359). Muslim battles Hindu in the Mohurrum riot. The city is a divided one. Yet, the narrator does mix with Indians at Lalun's, and is part of the rioting crowd. Wali Dad stands apart from his co-religionists, yet, in the end, identifies himself with them. He does so at a point when inter-communal violence breaks out, and, indeed, the motif of violence runs throughout the text. Newspapers are silent about government actions out of fear (347); Khem Singh has dreams of bloody revenge (355–6); the Subaltern knows his guns can "pound the City to powder" (356). The story ends with a riot and with violence on all sides. "Everywhere men struck aimlessly with sticks, grasping each other by the throat, howling

and foaming with rage, or beat with their bare hands on the doors of the houses"
(366). "Then followed the ringing of rifle-butts and shrieks of pain. The troops were
banging the bare toes of the mob with their gun-butts" (369). Violence transcends
race. The Indians of the city seek violence; so, too, do the British troops ("I am sorry
to say they were all pleased, unholily pleased, at the chance of what they called 'a
little fun'" (367)).

"On the City Wall" is a complex story. On the one hand, it is about the assertion of British power over a subversive Sikh and a rioting mob. It offers some traditional stereotypes of Eastern characters – the temptress Lalun, and the educated
Wali Dad who reverts to an uncivilized level under pressure. It has a knowing and
confident British narrator. But, on the other hand, the Indian characters are central
to the story, and are more complex and charming than most of the British ones.
(One should note that Lalun echoes Rahab in Joshua 2.15, a positive figure.) British
superiority is queried continually in the text. British soldiers like a little violence,
as much as an Indian mob does. An Indian past (the Emperors' tombs, the old Sikh's
memories) is brought into close relation with a British present. In addition, the
clever British narrator occupies a very strange position between rulers and subject,
himself entertains subversive imaginings, and finally is shown not to be nearly as
clever as he thought. He is at home in Lalun's crowded *salon* and in the narrow
streets. The story is of further interest because it shows several recurrent features of
Kipling's work: the broad sense of time; the wide range of characters; the motifs
of secrecy and knowledge; and, always, between characters, violence and the threat
of violence.

5

"Mary Postgate" is a story about violence, cruelty perpetrated by an unlikely figure.
Oliver Baldwin called this "the most wicked story ever written" (qtd in Mallett 2003:
168). It is certainly intended to be disturbing. It concludes *A Diversity of Creatures*, a
collection that is certainly full of stories of redemption and healing, like "My Son's
Wife," but that also contains stories of violence and revenge ("As Easy as A.B.C.,"
"Friendly Brook," and "The Edge of the Evening"). "Mary Postgate" is preceded by
a piece of anti-German war propaganda ("Swept and Garnished"), that imagines the
mental torment of a dying German civilian, assailed by the ghosts of those killed in
German war crimes.

The central figure of "Mary Postgate" is a lady's companion, the eponymous
heroine, who becomes devoted to her employer Miss Fowler's nephew, Wynn. At the
outbreak of the Great War, the young man joins the Flying Corps, only to die, falling
from his airplane, during training. Mary and Miss Fowler respond to his death with
self-control. They decide to burn Wynn's effects. While buying paraffin in a nearby
village, Mary witnesses the death of a child in a German bombing raid. Later, as she
burns her beloved Wynn's toys, books, and clothes, she sees the body of a German

airman lying under a tree. She assumes he has, like Wynn, fallen from his plane, in this case the one that dropped a bomb on the village. He is dying and appeals for help, which she refuses, and she lets him die, taking deep pleasure in his suffering. The appendix to the story is a poem which has as its refrain "When the English began to hate."

The proportions of the story material in this text are striking. Two thirds of the story are taken up with the few days following Wynn's death. The pre-war years are dealt with succinctly, and the story's emphasis is clearly on death and Mary's and Miss Fowler's response to it. Over half the text is taken up with the events of the day Mary burns Wynn's effects. This focus on civilian reaction to the war is emphasized by spatial settings: they are far from France and are predominantly domestic, rooms and a garden. The narrator's voice also seems peculiar in a story about war published in 1917. It is usually detached and objective, for example, in the account of Wynn's funeral (1937b: 428), or in the passage reporting Mary's watching Wynn's plane fly overhead and her learning of his death (426–7). The narrator, however, occasionally uses an elevated lexis of the central figures. Wynn's airplane is a "flying chariot" (426); the paraffin that Mary uses to burn Wynn's things is a "sacrificial oil" (436); the dreary corner of the garden where this takes place is "the sanctuary" and the incinerator is a "pyre" (436). Domesticity is given a heroic grandeur and the particular elevated to something more general.

Frequently, especially in the latter stages of the text, the narrator adopts Mary's point of view, and she is clearly the central figure in the story. Her lack of physical attractiveness is emphasized throughout: her colorless hair, her gaping mouth, her ungainliness. She is almost a non-entity, without any qualities, save efficiency and kindliness to children (421–2, 431). "Would you *ever* have been anything except a companion?" Miss Fowler asks her (426). She is, however, clearly devoted to Wynn. The passage in which she "lifted her lean arms" to Wynn's airplane illustrates this well (426–7). The story is about her response to Wynn's death. This reaction is marked by reserve: not for her (or for Miss Fowler) the public tears of another bereaved woman (427). It is also marked by anger. "It only makes me angry with the Germans," she says (429). "Bloody pagans!" she exclaims to herself after the bombing (435). There is also a violence in her response. "It's a great pity he didn't die in action after he had killed somebody," she remarks immediately after Wynn's death (427). She relishes the dying agony of the German airman (whom she sees as "It") (440–1). The sexual overtones of this passage cannot be missed; the phallic revolver and poker in her hand, her "increasing rapture" (440–1) all point to it, as do Mary's hot bath and her improved appearance after the burning and the airman's death (441). This ruthless cruelty towards the enemy, she reflects, is a woman's work, and one that can be stimulating (440–1).

"Mary Postgate" is a study of an extreme psychological state, and a comment on the Great War. The English will "begin to hate," especially the women, and the world had better look out. Yet the text is more complex than this. First, the Great War is reduced to something deeply unheroic in any traditional sense — a spinster lets a wounded airman die. Second, some of Mary's perceptions may be delusions. She declares that the child dies in a bombing; the doctor denies it (434–6). Only she sees the dying German airman, and that in the dark by the uncertain light of the incinerator. The German's death parallels Wynn's very closely. Are the bombing and the dying airman projections of Mary's disturbed psyche? The reader cannot tell, for the narrator is enigmatic on this matter. But the story remains a complex study of the effects of death, violence, and violent feelings on an unremarkable protagonist, who herself reveals depths of cruelty that are unexpected, whether they have real objects or not.

6

"On the City Wall" and "Mary Postgate" are the kind of complex social-psychological studies that predominate in Kipling's output. "The Bull That Thought," while not exactly a non-mimetic beast fable, is a different kind of text, nearer to fable and legend. It is placed in one of Kipling's most diverse volumes in terms of genre, *Debits and Credits*. It is surrounded by stories that present emotional and physical desolation, like "The Wish House" and "The Gardener," violence, like "Sea Constables: A Tale of '15," a modicum of healing ("In the Interests of the Brethren"), and stories that focus on the role of art and the exceptional artist in human affairs ("The Janeites," "The United Idolaters").

"The Bull That Thought" tells the story of an intelligent bull, Apis, that can out-think the humans who surround him. The climax to the story takes place in a bullring where Apis defeats all the humans sent against him, only finally to put on a show for the audience with a second-rate bullfighter called Chisto. So superb, and so comic, is their performance that the bull is not killed and he and his co-performer leave the ring in glory. The text is one of Kipling's frame narratives. An unnamed Englishman in southwest France meets M. Voiron, a local businessman, who tells him the story of Apis. Thus the far-fetched story is contained within a frame that at once endorses and questions its veracity. Both the unnamed narrator and Voiron present themselves as credible and knowledgeable figures. Voiron, further, pushes his tale in the direction of allegory, by relating Apis's actions to the war and even to French politics (1937c: 184–5). His constant references to art reinforce the reader's sense that this is a loosely allegorical text.

The text's frame is set sometime after the Great War, but Voiron's story is time-less, as befits a fable, although the "inconceivable" nature of the bull is seen as part of the post-war world (174). The story is set in France and Spain, not typical settings for Kipling's work, and indicative of his geographical range. The topography of the created world, as always with Kipling, is carefully organized. The open road along which the two narrators speed at the story's start contrasts with the enclosed spaces of the darkened hotel dining room where Voiron tells his story and the more open, but still enclosed bullring where Apis and Chisto perform, and out of which they depart at the story's close. The two central figures are both anthropomorphic: the bull Apis and the narrator's car, which has a name, Esmeralda. Both are figures of power. The car achieves an impressive speed (172). It is the bull, however, that dominates the text.

Apis is the focus of all the major motifs of the story: violence, humor, art, and ecstasy. The bull is an extremely violent creature. This is emphasized throughout the text, but is particularly clear in his slaughter of the various men and horses sent against him in the ring (183–5). His cruelty is coupled with humor: "and he was a humorist also," Voiron remarks, "like so many natural murderers" (177). He is called a "pure *farceur*" (179), and the end of his and Chisto's performance in the ring is a comic *"détente"* (190). The bull, too, is the center of motifs of art and artistry. Even when young, he is a "true artist" (178), and the action in the bullring is constantly compared to a play with its participants seen as actors (182–91). The second-rate Chisto is "at heart an artist," alone able to rise to the occasion offered by Apis (188). The text's ending is one of ecstasy. The final performance exceeds the bounds of the normal. Apis excels even by his own standards; Chisto is transformed and for him "a miraculous hour of dawn returned to gild the sunset" (190); the audience is held to an "unbearable" degree; and, in the end, bull and man defy all rules, comically collaborate, and leave the ring by the gate through which no bull has ever left before (190–1). The story's end (open, one must note) parallels the narrator's car's run on a perfect night at the text's beginning (171–2), and the glorious wine which Voiron supplies, "composed of the whispers of angel's wings, the breath of Eden and the foam and pulse of Youth renewed" (173). The story becomes a meditation on the connection of cruelty and humor, the role and potential of art, and the possibility of escape from mundane confines. It illustrates particularly well the craft, the range, and the complexity of Kipling's art of the short story.

REFERENCES AND FURTHER READING

Bauer, H.P. (1994). *Rudyard Kipling: A Study of the Short Fiction*. New York: Twayne.

Chaudhuri, N.C. (1972). "The Finest Story about India – in English," in J. Gross (ed.), *Rudyard Kipling: The Man, His Work and His World*, pp. 27–35. London: Weidenfeld and Nicholson.

Hagiioannu, A. (2003). *The Man Who Would Be Kipling: The Colonial Fiction and the Frontiers of Exile*. Basingstoke and New York: Palgrave Macmillan.

Hanson, C. (1985). *Short Stories and Short Fictions, 1880–1980*. London and Basingstoke: Macmillan.

Harrison, J. (1982). *Rudyard Kipling*. Boston: Twayne.

Kemp, S. (1988). *Kipling's Hidden Narratives*. Oxford: Blackwell.

Kipling, R. (1937a). "On the City Wall," in *Soldiers Three and Other Stories. The Sussex Edition of the Complete Works in Prose and Verse of Rudyard Kipling*. London: Macmillan (original work published 1888).

Kipling, R. (1937b). "Mary Postgate," in *A Diversity of Creatures. The Sussex Edition of the Complete Works in Prose and Verse of Rudyard Kipling*. London: Macmillan (original work published 1917).

Kipling, R. (1937c). "The Bull That Thought," in *Debits and Credits. The Sussex Edition of the Complete Works in Prose and Verse of Rudyard Kipling*. London: Macmillan (original work published 1926).

Lycett, A. (1999). *Rudyard Kipling*. London: Weidenfeld and Nicholson.

Mallet, P. (2003). *Rudyard Kipling: A Literary Life*. Basingstoke and New York: Palgrave.

Moore-Gilbert, B.J. (1986). *Kipling and "Orientalism."* London and Sydney: Croom Helm.

Orel, H. (1986). *The Victorian Short Story: Development and Triumph of a Literary Genre*. Cambridge: Cambridge University Press.

Rutherford, A. (1971). "Introduction," in R. Kipling, *Short Stories: Volume 1*. Harmondsworth: Penguin.

Seymour-Smith, M. (1989). *Rudyard Kipling*. London: Queen Anne Press/Macdonald.

Shaw, V. (1983). *The Short Story: A Critical Introduction*. London and New York: Longman.

Stilz, G. (1980). *Die Anglo-Indische Short Story: Geschichte einer Kolonialliteratur*. Tübingen: Max Niemeyer Verlag.

Wilson, E. (1941; 1961). *The Wound and the Bow*. London: Methuen.

Reading Individual
Authors and Texts

9
Robert Louis Stevenson: "The Bottle Imp," "The Beach of Falesá," and "Markheim"

Michael Meyer

Robert Louis Stevenson's (1850–94) short fiction often takes the shape of: (1) a tale with a central element of the supernatural in the tradition of the romance and the folktale; (2) a novella with its oral quality of telling a story about an intense experience of danger unheard of before (Good 1994: 160–3); and (3) a modern condensed short story, recording the impressions of a decisive moment in life. "The Bottle Imp" (1892/93) takes up the motif of the Faustian pact from European fairy tales, "The Beach of Falesá" (1892/93) unfolds the deadly struggle between two colonial traders on an exotic island, and "Markheim" (1887) concentrates on a murderer's psyche immediately after his crime.

Stevenson's publishers urged the author to combine "The Bottle Imp" and "The Beach of Falesá", which share the topic of ethics in an exotic setting but differ in scope and effect, in one volume called *Island Night's Entertainments* in 1892/93 (Menikoff 1984: 20–7). "The Bottle Imp" locates the European motif of the pact with the devil, risking eternal pain in hell in return for temporary pleasure in worldly life, on Hawaii. The imp in the magic bottle fulfills all of his present owner's desires except for bestowing eternal life. However, the bottle has to be sold for less than its previous price in coins before its owner's death, otherwise his or her soul is lost to the devil forever. The suspense of the story hinges upon the fact that the bottle becomes less and less expensive but more difficult to sell while changing hands. People either do not believe in its power at such a low material price or are appalled at the spiritual price they would have to pay. Since the bottle has to be paid for in coins, the buyer who acquires it for the coin of the least value forfeits his soul. The buyer's happiness is qualified because, first, it turns out that the evil power takes devious ways to fulfill one's wishes: the protagonist Keawe wishes for a beautiful mansion on Hawaii, and it turns out that his uncle and his cousin die so that he inherits a rich legacy, which exactly covers the cost of the extravagant home. Keawe takes the moral test lightly, being prepared to reap the full benefit at his risk: "Little as I like the way it comes

to me, I am in for it now, and I may as well take the good along with the evil"
(Stevenson 1994: 284). Second, the fear of punishment foils the pleasure of enjoying life in luxury. Third, it seems that after the owner sells the bottle, he or she
is beset by bad luck, as if being punished for the illegitimate deal. Keawe, who
falls in love with the beautiful and clever Kokua, is infected with leprosy just
before marriage and cancels it out of a sense of responsibility toward his beloved.
He buys the bottle back in order to cure his disease and marry the love of his
life. However, having sacrificed his soul for his health and his love, he cannot be
happy with Kokua, who despairs in turn when she secretly buys the bottle in
order to sacrifice her soul for him. In this way, the acquisition of the bottle
becomes an ordeal. Both of them pass the test of true love and are finally
rewarded because a reckless boatswain buys the bottle for good, because he claims
to be beyond redemption anyway. Poetic justice seems to rule in the end: Keawe
gave in to temptation, but the ordeal of the lovers, sacrificing their souls for each
other in spite of their great suffering from fear of damnation, warrants their happy
and prosperous life ever after. However, the ending cannot override the facts that
the lovers' wealth and happiness are based on the deaths of Keawe's relatives,
and on saving themselves by passing the buck on to someone else who yields to
temptation.

The novella "The Beach of Falesá" (1892) is more complex and sinister than "The
Bottle Imp." While the tale asserts a moral order ultimately guaranteed by supernatural forces, the novella castigates immorality and the manipulation of superstition for
mercenary ends. The novella "deliberately sets out to undercut any Treasure Island
expectations of island adventure" (Hanson 1985: 26) and subverts "the ethos of imperial England" (Menikoff 1984: 5). The South Sea island is a "moral frontier" (Hillier
1989: 197), which puts faith and ethics to the test. The use or abuse of religion can
hinder or further sexual, racial, and economic exploitation. The remotest part of the
world becomes the stage for realizing – in both senses of the word – the worst of
capitalist Western culture.

The narrative about the rivalry between white traders and the corruption of a
Polynesian island is ironically mediated by the mediocre agent Wiltshire. His use
of language reveals the underdog's take on colonial ideology: "the language of the
sailor, Polynesian, and trader, however violent and crude, was an integral part of
the novel's themes of racism, colonialism, sexism, and cultural disintegration"
(Menikoff 1984: 58). Wiltshire's "bastard idiom" (Menikoff 1984: 62) is lower-class
colloquial, peppered with mistakes in grammar and incongruous metaphors that
inadvertently create comic effects, inviting the reader's critical distance. The first-
person narrator, Wiltshire, is unreliable because of his inconsistency and contradictions. In spite of registering with a certain detachment his slowly growing insight,
he retains most of his former prejudices and blind spots. Wiltshire gradually realizes
that he is a pawn in the game of the Machiavellian mastermind Case, who is a
perfect actor and the director of the devious play that dominates life on the island.
Case manipulates others to play roles but keeps them ignorant of his plotting. Time

and again, Wiltshire, who stresses his experience as a trader with South Sea island-ers, feels like an ignorant "fool" and a "stranger" on a "strange" island, who becomes a spectacle staged for the natives and an object of their fear and laughter. He is a no-nonsense man of action rather than reflection, who is proud to solve conflicts with his fists rather than his tongue and reluctantly admits to having repeatedly lost control of himself, puzzled by "queer" characters and afraid of "queer" phenom-ena. He is full of "shame" for his ignorance, his fear, and his complicity in a fraudu-lent marriage.

Wiltshire's yarn invokes and debunks the romantic image of the exotic island, and the idealistic conception of colonialism as a civilizing mission in conjunction with a substantial return upon investment. At first, the most easterly populated South Sea island, Falesá, appears to be enchanting and its trading post the "best station in the South Pacific" (Stevenson 1994: 308). Wiltshire looks forward to white company but is confused by mysterious stories of his predecessors' sudden decampments or deaths.

In spite of having been warned of the other traders' "gallows bad reputation" (309), Wiltshire initially trusts the versatile, clever, and eloquent Mr Case, who pretends to initiate him into the culture and the trade on the island. Case turns out to be treacherous, ruthless, and cruel, using all his ingenuity to advance his profit at any cost whatever: he has scared one rival away, poisoned another, and buried a third one alive. Case, who speaks English well but is of unknown descent, represents the epitome of white colonial hypocrisy and rapacity. He and his companion, the African Jack, manage and plunder the trading station of old Captain Randall, who has gone native and forms a warning example of degenera-tion, being continually half-naked, dirty, drunk, and violent. Wiltshire realizes that his own copra has been stolen while Case left him drinking with Randall, whose stock increased by the same amount overnight. Case sets up Wiltshire with a young woman he desires in a degrading and fraudulent marriage ceremony, which turns out to be a trap because Case has manipulated the islanders to taboo the outsider Uma, who had snubbed him before, and they consequently shun the new trader associated with her. Instead of separating from her in order to start his business, Wiltshire decides to become regularly married to Uma, whose love and devotion touch him deeply. However, his soft spot neither eclipses his con-descension towards the object of his desire and to other natives, nor his ultimate interest in trade.

In defiance of the taboo imposed upon him, the poor white trader Wiltshire expresses his arrogant self-esteem and pretensions to missionary zeal:

> I'm a white man, and a British Subject, and no end of a big chief at home; and I've come here to do them good and bring them civilisation; and no sooner have I got my trade sorted out, than they go and taboo me and no one dare come near my place! [. . .] if they think they're going to come any of their native ideas over me, they'll find them-selves mistaken. [. . .] I know how to deal with kanakas. (327–8)

In spite of his ignorance of the indigenous language and culture, he denies that the islanders have a real government and a legal system, but even if so, "it would be a good joke if it was to apply to a white man. It would be a strange thing if we came all this way and couldn't do what we pleased" (328). Ironically, the South Sea Island turns out to be the site of a cut-throat competition for profit between traders, because the white men Wiltshire identifies with lay claim to the same liberty. Robert Kiely argues that Wiltshire's racism expresses the "civilized myopia of a benevolent British colonial" (1964: 171), which the story endorses because the natives are childish and passive (qtd in Gilmour 1983: 192). It is true that many islanders are taken in by Case, but not all the islanders fear or shun the tabooed trader: Wiltshire learns that individual natives who meet him in private rather think him to be a fool than a devil (348), and one important chief decides to trade with Case in spite of the taboo. In addition, the natives counter the traders' cheating by watering their copra. Wiltshire considers Uma to be like a child but he is unable to hold his ground in discussions with her, because she is not only beautiful but also clever (Hillier 1989: 174).

In order to defy Case, to legalize his bond with Uma, and to learn more about the native culture, the trader reluctantly resorts to help from missionaries. Wiltshire has a warped sense of ethics and plainly regards the Christian religion as an impediment to the fulfillment of his sexual and economic desires. He feels shame at the grotesque parody of a Christian wedding but attributes the blame for the fraud to the missionaries: "If they had let the natives be, I had never needed this deception, but taken all the wives I wished, and left them when I pleased, with a clear conscience" (316). He introduces himself to the missionary Tarleton as a hard-boiled trader: "I'm no missionary nor missionary lover; I'm no kanaka nor favourer of kanakas: I'm just a trader, I'm just a common, low, god-damned white man and British subject" (337). In the face of a moral authority, the claim to his profession, race, and nationality sounds aggressive but belies his previous self-aggrandizement.

The encounter of Western Christianity and Eastern religions fosters hybridity, and the boundaries between Protestant denominations, Catholicism, and "superstition" dissolve for most of the white men and the islanders. The Baptist Captain Randall and the Protestant convert and native missionary Namu use the Catholic sign of the cross against "evil." Tarleton and Wiltshire fail to convince natives of the non-existence of devils on the island. Wiltshire himself, who resents Uma's critical questions about his neglect of prayer and who haughtily dismisses Uma's stories about devils, temporarily succumbs to fears from evil apparitions in the sombre jungle, and even thinks that he "might as well take the off-chance of a prayer being any good" (354). His excuse that even "splendidly educated white men" (353) take up native superstitions generalizes the weakness of Western culture and rationality in the face of the unknown.

Christian religion reveals its potential for corruption and abuse as an instrument of power and revenge rather than being a means of promoting moral and spiritual elevation. Case, who merges missionary teaching and the native folk tradition, turns "the metaphysical contact zone" (Harris 2003: 384) to his advantage, establishing himself as a sort of mediator between the power of Christianity and that of native devils. Like a puppet master, Case sets up a show of devils in the jungle with the help of luminously painted masks and aeolian – or, in the words of the narrator, Tyrolean – harps. He purports to converse with the devils, using the timeworn imperialist strategy to control "economic markets by establishing the signs of supernatural authority" (Harris 2003: 385). He slanders his white rivals and manipulates the islanders to fear both his fabricated local devils and the foreign devils, his rivals, who have to be eliminated.

The resolution to the conflict sums up, but does not solve, the key problems of ethics, trade, racism and sexism. The lethal showdown between Wiltshire and Case in the dark jungle symbolizes the protagonist's encounter with his own heart of darkness. Having voluntarily married an outsider and having been temporarily reduced to laboring at his own copra, Wiltshire feels "empowered through his self-righteous martyrdom" (Kucich 2001: 385), and manages to kill Case in a bout of furious violence. As Wiltshire feels Case's blood on his hands, he faints and his head falls on his dead antagonist's mouth, as if receiving a kiss from his alter ego. In the end, Wiltshire fulfills Case's dream because he is the only trader left (Kucich 2001: 385).

The two fratricidal traders are very closely related by their egoism, imperialist rivalry, and fraudulent means of conducting their affairs (Hammond 1984: 89; cp. Hillier 1989: 172; Linehan 1990: 420). Case "represents a hard-boiled version of Wiltshire's worst tendencies," whereas Wiltshire displays a "capacity for conscience and self-doubt" (Linehan 1990: 417). However, economic self-interest warps Wiltshire's moral sense; he knows which side his bread is buttered on and does not always follow the promptings of his conscience. Tarleton, having re-established the trader's acceptance with the islanders in return for the promise of a fair deal, asks him to honor the missionary's pledge. Wiltshire considers the promise "a meanish kind of a revenge" (370) and justifies his dishonesty: "We all have queerish balances, and the natives all know it and water their copra in proportion; so that it's fair all round" (370). He finally moves on to a different island, speciously arguing that the pledge to deal fairly is not valid on other islands.

Wiltshire does not achieve his objective to pocket a great profit and return to England. He is "stuck" (371) on the Pacific islands because of his mixed-race children, who would be worse off "in a white man's country" (371). His typically flawed and contradictory argument reveals the discriminations of race and gender. Whereas he sends his son to get a good education in New Zealand, he is worried about his "half caste" daughters' status and future in spite of the fact that their mother, whom he has just praised as "an A one wife" (371), is also the daughter of a white trader and a Polynesian woman: "there's nobody thinks less of half castes than I do; but they're mine, and about all I've got; I can't reconcile my mind to their taking up with kanakas, and I'd like to know where I'm to find them whites" (371). Wiltshire's conclusion flies in the face of his disillusioning experience of white men in the South Seas, but his ingrained ethnic prejudice cannot be assailed by evidence to the contrary. The foolish narrator-protagonist turns the story into "at once a critique and an enactment of racism and sexism" (Linehan 1990: 408; Niederhoff 1994: 144–5).

The story is neither evasive and escapist, as Gilmour argues (1983: 193), nor particularly optimistic, as Hillier (1989: 193) and Niederhoff claim (1994: 141), but profoundly ironic and ambiguous. The fusion of faith and superstition and the escalation of ruthless violence among the traders erase the difference between civilization and barbarism. The conclusion suggests that there is no end to sexual, racial, and economic discrimination. However, it seems that the colonial endeavor, which should have been a springboard for social rise, turns out to be a dead end. Wiltshire and Uma are neither markedly changed by experience nor assimilated in the particular island culture, as Hillier would have it (1989: 193): the white trader and the half-caste out-islander are exiled and caught in between cultures, repeating the story of Uma's parents. The symbolic shady atmosphere, the moral ambivalence, and the ideological contradictions of the narrative form a worthy predecessor of Joseph Conrad's "Heart of Darkness."

Stevenson used the idea of the alter ego or the doppelgänger as an expression of desire and fear in his colonial narrative and in his gothic fiction. In Stevenson's short novel or "longish short story" (Orel 1986: 124), *The Strange Case of Dr. Jekyll and Mr. Hyde* (1886), the doppelgänger is a deformed and atavistic mutation of a sophisticated and civil middle-class gentleman, who commits suicide because he can no longer control his evil self. "Markheim" (1887), however, is a member of the lower class, whose doppelgänger is a figment of his frenzied imagination after the murder of his treacherous opponent, his external alter ego. The choice of the third-person narrative, mostly focusing on Markheim's point of view, seems to render a direct insight into a criminal mind: "Rarely has a writer depicted so forcefully the combination of guilt and terror which afflict a criminal in the immediate aftermath of his deed" (Hammond 1984: 81).

The central horrifying encounter takes place in a pawnshop "with the mingled shine and darkness" (Stevenson 1994: 86) of candlelight on a Christmas day, evoking the ideas of profiting from the poverty of others and the chance of a moral turn towards charity. The pawnbroker and his customer are like-minded individuals, who distrust each other's penchant for trickery. They represent a society that is driven by profit and regards fellow human beings primarily as means to an end. The cynical dealer summarizes this egoistic and materialistic position at the very beginning of the story: "'our windfalls are of various kinds. Some customers are ignorant, and then I touch a dividend on my superior knowledge. Some are dishonest,' and here he held up the candle, so that the light fell strongly on his visitor, 'and in that case,' he continued, 'I profit by my virtue'" (86). Both men are single and isolated from human company. The dealer would balance his books at Christmas; the customer pretends to be interested in a gift for a lady with the prospect of a rich marriage, a very unlikely event given his admitted neglect of shopping until the very last moment. Markheim invites the dealer's confidence, suggesting that they drop their masks and talk openly to each other, but he has brought a knife and is prepared to murder the other man. His advance betrays the dire need of, but little hope for, friendship. He rather seems to tease the dealer or to put him to a test in order to find out whether his preconceived notions of the other man are true: "Not charitable; not pious; not scrupulous; unloving, unbeloved; a hand to get money, a safe to keep it. Is that all? Dear God, man, is that all?" (88). Markheim's enumeration of Victorian values in the negative reveals a sense of urgency, disgust, and despair, and forms an indirect characterization of himself in the other, except for the tainted talent of accumulating capital. His murder of that other is motivated by his hate for the exploitive trader and his own paltry existence as seen reflected in his alter ego rather than only his need for money.

The dealer's lamp and the mirror he offers to his customer become leitmotifs in the search for truth. Markheim shies away from the light and is infuriated by the idea of giving a mirror as a present because it reveals the ageing and corruption to its owner. Stevenson captures the high-strung murderer's distorted perceptions: the flickering candlelight in the sombre shop animates gloomy shadows, and numerous mirrors reflect many-faceted images of the murderer, representing his conscience and his growing – if inconsistent and partial – insight into himself. Being terrified by the fear of detection, Markheim develops a frenzied sense of time, marked by the loud and maddening ticking of the clocks in the shop and his hallucination of an ominous presence, "simply a figment of Markheim's disordered imagination" (Hammond 1984: 81). The apparition takes over the form and the function of the light and the mirrors: "the outlines of the newcomer seemed to change and waver like those of the idols in the wavering candle-light of the shop; and at times he thought he knew him; and at times he thought he bore a likeness to himself" (96). The alter ego cannot only be pinned down to the role of the externalized conscience because it also plays the tempter, intensifying Markheim's turmoil of opposite emotions and contradictory reflections.

The perpetrator is torn between the desire to escape immediately and to find the money. He proves to be callous in the face of his victim but waxes sentimental at recalling images of famous crimes in his childhood and the sound of hymns sung by a choir in the neighborhood. He is not appalled by his crime but rather by the chance of not profiting from it if he does not come away with the money: he feels "penitence, no, not a tremor" (93). In a self-righteous way, he feels that God is on his side: "his act was doubtless exceptional, but so were his excuses, which God knew" (94). The murderer is not afraid of God but of being detected and brought to human justice. The interaction with the alter ego is a moral discussion about good and evil in the shape of a bout of psychomachia: "Evil and good run strong in me, haling me both ways. I do not love the one thing, I love all" (99). The murderer initially denies any responsibility because he was "a bond-slave to poverty" (99), but then he admits that he could not resist any temptation to indulge in pleasure. Being confronted with the perspective of a criminal career that inexorably seems to point downward, the thirty-six-year-old culprit claims the force of free will, musters the courage and dignity to resist the temptation to escape and commit more crimes. He confesses his murder to the maid and submits to the authorities "with something like a smile" (101), revealing fortitude and relief.

The evil protagonist's moral turn upon the confrontation with an apparition at Christmas recalls Charles Dickens's "A Christmas Carol" (1843), but is less sentimental and more sinister. The mid-Victorian miser's conversion to charity and generosity suggests a moral and social solution to economic inequality by those who continue to profit from the system of exploitation. The late Victorian proletarian Markheim has nothing to lose but his dignity and his life in the absence of money, a job, moral bearings, and a social network. In Stevenson's story, it takes a murder to trigger a process of moral reflection, which does not result in a turn to goodness but in a restraint from evil, which recovers the poor man's dignity but will neither ameliorate his alienation and misery nor save his life when being brought to justice.

The three stories under discussion negotiate a kind of moral economy, a conflict between material interests and moral values. In a patriarchal world marked by competition, distrust, and transgression, female characters form a positive but marginalized presence. The protagonists are lower-class male characters, who face ethical and cognitive challenges as they aim to improve their economic situations. They are muddling through and seem to be driven by impulses and circumstances, but in the end they achieve limited insight and partial control. These late Victorian stories present mixed lower-class characters, moral and epistemic ambiguities and ambivalent resolutions, which reveal that victories are tainted and the restorations of order compromised.

REFERENCES AND FURTHER READING

Gilmour, P. (1983). "Robert Louis Stevenson: Forms of Evasion," in A. Noble (ed.), *Robert Louis Stevenson*, pp. 188–201. London and Totowa: Vision and Barnes & Noble.

Good, G. (1994). "Notes on the Novella," in C.E. May (ed.), *The New Short Story Theories*, pp. 147–64. Athens: Ohio University Press.

Hammond, J.R. (1984). *A Robert Louis Stevenson Companion: A Guide to the Novels, Essays and Short Stories*. London and Basingstoke: Macmillan.

Hanson, Clare (1985). *Short Stories and Short Fictions, 1880–1980*. London: Macmillan.

Harris, Jason Marc (2003). "Robert Louis Stevenson: Folklore and Imperialism," *English Literature in Transition (1880–1920)* 46/4: 382–99.

Hillier, R.I. (1989). *The South Seas Fiction of Robert Louis Stevenson*. New York: Lang.

Kiely, R. (1964). *Robert Louis Stevenson and the Fiction of Adventure*. Cambridge, Mass.: Harvard University Press.

Kucich, J. (2001). "Melancholic Magic: Masochism, Stevenson, Anti-imperialism," *Nineteenth-Century Literature* 56/3: 364–400.

Linehan, K.B. (1990). "Taking up with Kanakas: Stevenson's Complex Social Criticism in 'The

Beach of Falesá'," *English Literature in Transition (1880–1920)* 33/4: 407–22.

Menikoff, B. (1984). *Robert Louis Stevenson and "The Beach of Falesá": A Study in Victorian Publishing.* Stanford: Stanford University Press.

Niederhoff, B. (1994). *Erzähler und Perspektive bei Robert Louis Stevenson.* Würzburg: Könighausen & Neumann.

Orel, H. (1986). *The Victorian Short Story: Development and Triumph of a Literary Genre.* Cambridge: Cambridge University Press.

Stevenson, R.L. (1994). In I. Bell (ed.), *The Complete Short Stories*, the Centenary Edition, 2 vols. New York: Holt.

10
Thomas Hardy: *Wessex Tales*

David Grylls

1

Compared with his novels, Thomas Hardy's short stories have received little critical attention. Most critics have regarded them as obviously inferior: among the hundreds of books on Hardy, only two have been devoted to them (Brady 1982; Ray 1997). Yet Hardy was always a versatile author, and his short stories frequently exhibit qualities – symbolic intensity, narrative reversal, vivid evocation of atmosphere – that typify the strengths of the genre.

Wessex Tales (1888) was the earliest of Hardy's four collections of short fiction. Originally it contained only five stories ("The Three Strangers," "The Withered Arm," "Fellow-Townsmen," "Interlopers at the Knap," and "The Distracted Preacher"), all published first in periodicals. For the 1896 reprinting, Hardy added "An Imaginative Woman," but in 1912 moved this to another collection, *Life's Little Ironies*, while simultaneously transferring two stories – "A Tradition of Eighteen Hundred and Four" and "The Melancholy Hussar of the German Legion" – from *Life's Little Ironies* to *Wessex Tales*.

Why this tinkering around with the groupings? The most plausible answer highlights the periods that characterize the collections. Most of the stories in *Wessex Tales* are set in the early nineteenth century: they therefore differ from Hardy's novels, most of which have settings from the 1840s onwards. They differ, too, from those in *Life's Little Ironies*, which are largely contemporary in focus. Given this distinction, "An Imaginative Woman," a satire on late Victorian values, clearly fitted better in the later collection, while "A Tradition" and "The Melancholy Hussar," set in the Napoleonic era, were appropriate for *Wessex Tales*.

The collection is, then, united temporally, being set largely in the decades immediately preceding Hardy's birth. But it is also, as its title implies, united geographically. The first of Hardy's works to have "Wessex" in its title, it concentrates on an area of western England roughly coterminous with Dorset. As is well known, Hardy revived the name of an ancient Saxon kingdom to define the provenance of his fiction. Thinly disguising real place names under fanciful designations (Casterbridge for Dorchester, etc.), he created a "partly real, partly dream-country" that supplied a memorable matrix for his writings. Deeply familiar with his native county, Hardy naturally wrote about Dorset; yet in "Wessex" he was also creating a brand. One of the stories in *Wessex Tales*, "A Tradition of Eighteen Hundred and Four," was originally set in Sussex. Adapting its details to suit Dorset, Hardy made the tale more attractive to readers devoted to his fictional world.

The ambiguous status of the Wessex locations – fictional, yet grounded in reality – is paralleled by the tales' use of history and tradition. Repeatedly, in letters and prefaces, Hardy stressed the factual basis of his stories. Of "The Withered Arm," he noted that "its cardinal incidents are true, both the women who figure in the story having been known to me." Recommending a different ending to "The Distracted Preacher," he wrote: "Moreover it corresponds more closely with the true incidents of which the tale is a vague and flickering shadow." Of the burial register quoted in "The Melancholy Hussar," he observed that it was "literal, to be read any day in the original by the curious who recognize the village." Yet despite the accumulation of such claims, he concluded his 1896 Preface to the *Tales* with the disclaimer, "However, the stories are but dreams, and not records" (Hardy 1991: xv, 233, 223). It was characteristic of Hardy to present his work as both factual and purely invented.

A similar slipperiness attends his use of local legend and oral tradition. "The Three Strangers" and "The Melancholy Hussar" both conclude by referring to the survival of the story among the local populace. The latter tale includes the lines: "Phyllis told me the story with her own lips. She was then an old lady of seventy-five." "A Tradition" is narrated by "old Solomon Selby," whose compelling yarn was known, he says, to "no maker of newspapers or printer of books" and so has been dismissed by those "who only believe what they see in printed lines." In fact, for this story Hardy drew on an article in the *True Briton* of November 1803, just as he incorporated into "The Melancholy Hussar" details taken from the *Morning Chronicle* (Hardy 1991: 229, 233). This is not to deny that Hardy was committed to the fictional use of local legend. However, explicit allusions to tradition should be read as literary conventions (enhancing the dignity of the unlettered and supplying narrative framing devices) rather than factual acknowledgments.

How do Hardy's short stories work and what are their typical ingredients? The best way of answering such questions might be to analyze a couple in detail, and this is attempted below. First, though, it is worth observing that their concerns overlap with those of Hardy's other writings. Like the novels, they are keen to memorialize the customs and practices of rural communities – what Hardy called the "vast mass of unwritten folk-lore, local chronicle, local topography, and nomenclature" (Hardy 1928: 313). In "Interlopers at the Knap," for example, when the bereaved Mrs Hall taps tearfully at her beehives, the narrator comments: "It was the universal custom thereabout to wake the bees by tapping at their hives whenever a death occurred in the household, under the belief that if this were not done the bees themselves would pine away and perish during the ensuing year." Both stories and novels retail local superstitions, often suggesting they are not merely that. Like the novels, too, the stories make use of dialect, occasionally glossing regional idioms for the benefit of the uninitiated.

As a writer of popular Victorian novels, Hardy had to comply with the requirement for conventional romantic plots, and the same is largely true of his short stories. Courtship and romance provide the momentum, but not necessarily the main focus, in several of the *Wessex Tales*. Typically of Hardy, love tends to be unsatisfying (as in "The Withered Arm") or unfulfilled (as in "The Melancholy Hussar," "Fellow-Townsmen," and "Interlopers at the Knap"). Only one story, "The Distracted Preacher," culminates in a happy marriage, for which Hardy apologized later. The note he added is remarkably similar to the one attached to *The Return of the Native*, disavowing the marriage of Thomasin and Venn. In both cases the demands of magazine publication are blamed for the lapse into happiness.

The gothic elements in Hardy's imagination are amply evident in his fiction and especially his poetry, which often evokes graveyards, coffins and corpses, headstones, ghosts, and shrouds. Some of Hardy's stories are also gothic, for example his repulsive shocker "Barbara of the House of Grebe" (in *A Group of Noble Dames*, 1891). In *Wessex Tales*, however, this aspect of his writing is relatively muted. Admittedly, three stories deal with executions, a "neglect of contrast" excused by Hardy on the grounds that "hanging matters used to form a large proportion of the local tradition" (Hardy 1991: 3). But only one, "The Withered Arm," has supernatural implications, and even these are ambiguous. Churchyards and tombstones figure frequently, but it is typical of the collection's lighter touch that in "The Distracted Preacher" a family vault is used to farcical effect, when customs men pile tubs upon it. Sly humor, in fact, infiltrates the tales, often arising from romantic inconsistencies (as with Stockdale in "The Distracted Preacher") or naiveties of speech ("The boy said she was a widow-woman, who had got no husband, because he was dead"). There is also a streak of social satire, though this is less marked than in *Life's Little Ironies* (for example, in "The Son's Veto," which Hardy regarded as his best short story) or novels like *The Hand of Ethelberta*. Perhaps the most prominent target here of Hardy's social mockery is Barnet's patrician wife in "Fellow-Townsmen."

The first edition of *Wessex Tales* included the subtitle, "Strange, Lively, and Commonplace." Providing a clue to the range of qualities – weirdness, humor, and everyday detail – that Hardy saw the collection encompassing, the epithets are nevertheless paradoxical. These "lively" stories often treat of death; and "strange" and "commonplace" are opposites. There is evidence, though, that paradox was central to Hardy's conception of fiction. In July 1881 he wrote:

> The writer's problem is, how to strike the balance between the uncommon and the ordinary so as on the one hand to give interest, on the other to give reality.
>
> In working out this problem, human nature must never be made abnormal, which is introducing incredibility. The uncommonness must be in the events, not in the characters; and the writer's art lies in shaping that uncommonness while disguising its unlikelihood. (Hardy 1928: 150)

In the light of these remarks, the subtitle of *Wessex Tales* reads rather like a capsule manifesto. Hardy, it seems, was deliberately attempting to reconcile discrepant literary effects. How successfully he did so may be estimated by analyzing two stories that amalgamate the strange and the commonplace.

2

"The Three Strangers" opens with a paragraph evoking Hardy's characteristic world: an isolated, sparsely populated area that has changed little over the centuries. It provides a neat contrast with what follows: a story with a large cast of characters, the arrival of several outsiders, and a sequence of startling events. In outline the story is simple. Shepherd Fennel and his wife are holding a party to celebrate the christening of their daughter. A bedraggled stranger arrives at their cottage, is welcomed, and warms himself by the chimney corner. Soon after, another stranger turns up, older, more expansive, and dressed in cinder-grey. He too is admitted – "a trifle less heartily." Seated at the table near the chimney, he downs a whole mug of the best mead, while declining to reveal his identity. Gradually, through the words of a song, he reveals he is a hangman, making his way to Casterbridge, where a sheep-stealer is to be hanged the next morning. Only the first stranger remains affable: the guests are increasingly appalled. Their consternation is heightened by the arrival, just before the song's climax, of a third stranger, who stares at the singer in terror before fleeing from the room. When a distant gun announces that a convict has escaped from Casterbridge gaol, the suspicious third stranger is pursued and arrested, only to reveal he is the convict's brother. The real fugitive was the first stranger, who after hobnobbing with the hangman has successfully escaped.

The events are, in Hardy's term, "uncommon," but their unlikelihood is skillfully disguised. The tale is dense with details of Dorset life in the early nineteenth century – the mead brewed from maiden honey, the utensils laid out to catch rainfall, the hedge-carpenter with his fingers full of thorns. Psychologically, too, the story is convincing, especially in its contrast between the reckless hospitality of the shepherd and the growing alarm of his wife. Given the crowdedness of their cottage, and the intrusiveness of their visitors, the arrival of three uninvited guests puts a severe strain on their composure, creating a pattern of black comedy: the first stranger is greeted heartily, the second rather more dutifully, and the third with stunned dismay.

Constructing a fictional microcosm, a consistent social and emotional world, is frequently a function of the good short story, but what makes this one particularly impressive is its masterly handling of structure. The successive arrival of the three strangers, providing amazement and then enlightenment, is paralleled by the three stanzas, at first perplexing and then revealing, of the hangman's song. Moreover, the whole story falls into three phases, each with its prevailing literary mode. The first phase, up to the entry of the fugitive, sets the scene for the main action and is written as domestic realism. The second phase, the impact of the visitors, creating puzzlement and providing clues, is rather like a mystery novel (by, for example, Wilkie Collins). But this part also has sinister comedy, an effect expanded in the final phase, a broad comic coda in the mode of farce – or perhaps of Shakespearean comedy. The quavering constable's maladroit phrases hark back to Dogberry in *Much Ado About Nothing*, while his comic complaint that the prisoner has not remained in gaol "in a decent proper manner to be hung to-morrow morning" recalls Pompey in *Measure for Measure* ("You must be so good, sir, to rise and be put to death": IV. iii. 27–8). For the reader the story moves from calm contemplation through tension to cathartic laughter.

What is most satisfying about the structure is the artful control of information, its nature, salience, and sequencing. Certain facts are made misleadingly prominent while others are cunningly recessed. As with detective fiction, the significance of some details only comes out when the story is re-read. This applies particularly to the fugitive, who, we then notice, is walking away from "the distant town" (only later identified as Casterbridge), "through the rain without a pause," taking a "little-worn path." When, upon hearing the second stranger knocking, he "took up the poker and began stirring the brands as if doing it thoroughly were the one aim of his existence," is he merely diverting attention from himself or also grabbing a potential weapon? He is keen, of course, not to be noticed or identified: he quickly deflects the supposition that he comes from the shepherdess's neighborhood and conceals his hands after claiming to be a wheelwright. But he is also keen not to offend. His "testimony to the youthfulness of his hostess" is echoed by his "testimony" to the hangman's humor. His conversation consists largely of assenting repetition. Just as he joins in the hangman's chorus (despite the painful nature of the lyrics), so he politely seconds his sentiments in their final conversation. When, though, he sums up the evidence against the terrified third stranger, he is not simply making himself agreeable but reinforcing a false trail – safe in the knowledge that the suspect, his brother, will easily prove his innocence.

All this becomes apparent upon a second reading, but a signal merit of "The Three Strangers" is that certain questions remain unresolved. When does the convict identify the hangman? Certainly before the other guests, but we cannot say for sure. And what about the moment when his brother enters? We are informed that the third visitor becomes terrified when "his eyes lighted on the stranger in cinder-grey," but this turns out to be a cunning use by Hardy of the device of free indirect discourse, the information not being objectively true but reflecting the inference of observers. The frightened man explains that he first saw his brother, and then the hangman, whom he identified from his song. He adds: "My brother threw a glance of agony at me, and I knew he meant 'Don't reveal what you see – my life depends on it'." Flicking back to that moment, we discover that the convict was repeating the final refrain of the song: "And on his soul may God ha' merc-y!" Despite the fact that he was "waving cups with the singer," did the words accompany his "glance of agony," thus gaining a poignant additional meaning? If so, they would join other words in the story (such as the inscription on the mug of mead, "THERE iS NO FUN/UNTiLL i COME") which are powerfully ironic in context.

Circumstantial irony runs through many of Hardy's stories, and "The Three Strangers" – with hangman and convict sitting together, clinking mugs and shaking hands – is hallmarked by this device. So too is "The Withered Arm," though this tale, in which hanging is not averted, is darker as well as weirder.

Faded Rhoda Brook, a poor milkmaid, is Farmer Lodge's former lover; youthful Gertrude, his beautiful new wife. Lodge has had a child by Rhoda but acknowledges neither her nor the boy, now twelve. Rhoda gets her son to report the wife's appearance, then vividly dreams of her, grandly dressed but horribly aged, scornfully flashing her wedding ring. Gasping, she whirls the specter backward by its arm. The next day, she receives a friendly visit from Gertrude, who confides that she has a painful arm, with discolorations like fingermarks. Alarmed to see the blight steadily worsen, Rhoda helps Gertrude consult Conjuror Trendle, who diagnoses "the work of an enemy," obliquely revealed to be Rhoda. Years pass and Gertrude's affliction worsens; her marriage suffers in consequence. Eventually, on Trendle's advice, she seeks a remedy by touching the neck of a hanged man. Doing so, she discovers that the victim was Rhoda's son: both parents have come to collect the corpse. Doubly shocked, Gertrude dies, followed by Lodge two years later. Rhoda toils on at the dairy.

Melodramatic in summary, "The Withered Arm" might seem to sacrifice plausibility to strangeness. Seemingly the story of an occult curse, it depends on supernatural effects. The onset of Gertrude's obscure affliction coincides exactly with Rhoda's trance, while the marks on her arm are imprinted precisely in the shape of Rhoda's clutch. Gertrude, helped by the "white wizard," identifies Rhoda as the cause, even though at this point she knows nothing of her husband's former affair.

Despite this concurrence of spooky detail, the story also raises doubts about the supernatural. It harbors phrases such as "what was revealed to her, or she thought was revealed to her." Revising the serial for volume editions, Hardy increased the incidence of such phrases: before Rhoda's identification of the fingermarks, he added, "she fancied that"; what Rhoda had "seen" became what she had "dreamt of" (Ray 1997: 38, 40). The result is that verbally the tale is situated on a cusp between sorcery and delusion: what is perceived as potently phantasmal might also seem merely fantastic.

The possibility of alternative readings is raised in the text when Gertrude muses: "the words of the conjuror, 'It will turn your blood,' were seen to be capable of a scientific no less than a ghastly interpretation." Although it is not clear to a modern reader what scientific sense the words might bear, the remark recalls Victorian attempts to apply science to supernatural phenomena. Hardy once said he would give ten years of his life to see "an authentic, indubitable spectre" (Archer 1901: 313). Like many Victorians, he was committed to science while remaining enthralled by the occult.

Whatever its contemporary resonances, Gertrude's distinction might encourage us to seek a rational, rather than mystical, explanation of the tale. This could take off from its oddest feature – that Rhoda never consciously utters a curse. She dreams, or has a vision, and the blight just happens. When she actually meets Gertrude, she almost feels affection. As Gertrude's condition deteriorates, she feels alarm and even dread. Nevertheless, at a deeper level, she clearly resents the younger woman, who is prettier and socially superior. Through her "unconscious usurpation" Gertrude has rendered it impossible for Lodge to make reparation to Rhoda. As a "fallen" woman, Rhoda is stigmatized as a sorceress: hardly surprising that she should take a quiet pride in the power this appears to give her. Jealously visualizing Gertrude, she "sees" her in the costume described by the boy, yet withered as Rhoda would wish her. Even after meeting her, Rhoda is ambivalent about the blight and its possible cause: "In her secret heart Rhoda did not altogether object to a slight diminution of her successor's beauty"; likewise "she did not altogether" regret that Gertrude should identify her agency. Her "gruesome fascination" with her stricken rival is matched by a "horrid fascination" with the occult. Part of her wishes to blast Gertrude's beauty and hence to alienate her husband (for, as she grimly acknowledges, she knows how he values appearance). The assurance that "everything like resentment" has "quite passed away" from Rhoda's mind is contradicted by her shrill reproach ("Hussy – to come between us and our child now!") at the climax of the action.

Interpreted psychoanalytically, the story describes the fulfillment of a destructive but unacknowledged wish. This reading is rendered more persuasive by a startling parallel between Rhoda and Gertrude. Just as Rhoda is amazed and shocked by the manifestation of her subconscious desires, so too is Gertrude at the end of the story. Obsessed with Trendle's proposed remedy, she "wellnigh longed for the death of a fellow creature. Instead of her formal prayers each night, her unconscious prayer was, 'O Lord, hang some guilty or innocent person soon!'" Confronted with the corpse of Rhoda's son, she is cursed with the fulfillment of her prayer. In a sense she has willed the death of the boy for whom she once felt compassion.

A psychoanalytical reading of the tale fits Freud's definition of projection: "the ego thrusts forth upon the external world whatever within itself gives rise to pain" (Freud 1959). However, even if we invoke this concept, the objective injury to Gertrude receives no further explanation than the phrase "the freaks of coincidence." The tale can certainly be read symbolically, but uncanny occurrences remain. Whether we favor a supernatural or a psychological interpretation, the story supports divergent readings. This is true even of small details – for example, the graphic phrase describing Rhoda's cottage: "here and there in the thatch above a rafter showed like a bone protruding through the skin." A hint of Rhoda's poverty and emaciation? An image of injury marring a smooth surface (thus anticipating the main story)? Or an apt suggestion of harsh reality breaking through a thin facade? Each of these interpretations – social, structural, thematic – is consistent with the text.

Harold Orel has argued that "*Wessex Tales* stresses the violent and the extraordinary more than any of [Hardy's] subsequent three collections" (Orel 1986: 106). Indeed, but extravagant events are subsumed within quotidian rhythms. "The Withered Arm," for instance, begins and ends with Rhoda monotonously milking. The pastoral location of the stories roots them in rural reality; their historical perspective presents the outré as part of local folklore. Since Hardy's fictional aesthetic committed him to "uncommon" events, the stories spring many surprises – abrupt reversals, mysterious actions, intrusions into settled routines. But since it also pledged him to credibility, the reversals are carefully prepared for, characters have recognizable motives, and social and economic details are plausibly established. In this collection Hardy's attachment to irony does not result in outright fatalism. Although some characters, such as the melancholy hussar, appear to be puppets of circumstance, others are masters of their destiny. In "The Three Strangers" the convict's ingenuity allows him to elude the hangman. Even characters who are disappointed (such as Barnet in "Fellow-Townsmen" or Darton in "Interlopers at the Knap") are largely responsible for their failures. A striking feature of *Wessex Tales*, as of many of Hardy's novels, is the admiring portrayal of independent women – the spirited Lizzie in "The Distracted Preacher," reluctant to renounce the thrills of smuggling, or the resolute Sally in "Interlopers," who cheerfully remains single. Just as it reconciles oral tradition with sophisticated fictional skills, so *Wessex Tales* unites homage to the past with surprisingly modern values.

REFERENCES AND FURTHER READING

Archer, W. (1901). "Real Conversations," *The Critic* 38: 309–18.

Brady, K. (1982). *The Short Stories of Thomas Hardy*. London: Macmillan Press.

Freud, S. (1959). "Instincts and Their Vicissitudes," in A. Freud, E. Jones, J. Riviere, and A. Strachey (eds), *The Collected Papers of Sigmund Freud* (4: 60–83). New York:

Basic   Books   (original   work   published
    1915).
Hardy, F.E. (1928). *The Life of Thomas Hardy
    1840–1928*. London: Macmillan, 1962.
Hardy, T. (1980). *The Collected Letters of Thomas
    Hardy*, ed. R.L. Purdy and M. Millgate. Oxford:
    Clarendon Press.
Hardy, T. (1991). *Wessex Tales*, ed. K.R. King.
    Oxford: Oxford University Press.
Hardy, T. (1996). *The Complete Stories*, ed. N. Page.
    London: Dent.

Millgate, M. (1982). *Thomas Hardy: A Biography*.
    Oxford: Oxford University Press.
Orel, H. (1966). *Thomas Hardy's Personal
    Writings*. Lawrence: University of Kansas
    Press.
Orel, H. (1986). *The Victorian Short Story: The
    Triumph of a Genre*. Cambridge and New York:
    Cambridge University Press.
Ray, M. (1997). *Thomas Hardy: A Textual Study of
    the Short Stories*. Aldershot: Ashgate.

11

Joseph Conrad: "The Secret Sharer" and "An Outpost of Progress"

Christopher Thomas Cairney

It is hard to think of anything as dissimilar in Conrad as "An Outpost of Progress" and "The Secret Sharer." "An Outpost of Progress" employs an anonymous omniscient narrator; "The Secret Sharer" employs a first-person one. Indeed, "An Outpost of Progress" relies heavily for its effect on its detached narrator's ability to provide ironic distance as well as commentary on the action of the story; "The Secret Sharer" on the other hand depends for its effect on the author's ability to create a situation where there is no such detachment: as readers we seem, in an uncanny way, to enter the consciousness of the narrator and to be held entirely within that consciousness for the entire story, and our perspective is largely controlled by the narrator's point of view. If we wish to consider techniques of fiction which contribute to the writing of "a good short story," then leading to the success and appeal of "An Outpost of Progress" is its unity of effect and stringent economy which allows for no digression; "The Secret Sharer" on the other hand seems to meander psychologically in all kinds of mysterious directions. "An Outpost of Progress" remains fairly close to the surface throughout, while in "The Secret Sharer" one must delve deeper to find the real story. Both stories rely on irony, but "An Outpost of Progress" more so: irony is central to the overall effect of "An Outpost of Progress," which can be called an ironic story. Lothe writes about the effectiveness of Conrad's use of sustained irony and narrative distance in the omniscient perspective (1989: 45–6). Hawthorn sees "An Outpost of Progress" as:

> the work in which Conrad first achieves a full maturity of vision and execution which is both technical and intellectual, a work in which a reader feels in the company of a major talent. (1990: 159)

Interpretation is also a different challenge in the two stories: while "An Outpost of Progress" is largely *told*, "The Secret Sharer" is, to the same degree, *shown*, and the reader is left with much more responsibility and much more leeway in "The Secret Sharer" for extracting the meaning. And while "The Secret Sharer" is arguably

Conrad's most popular short story with publishers (and still, today, his work of short fiction most likely to be in print), "An Outpost of Progress" was Conrad's own favorite (Najder 1978: 83). "The Secret Sharer" (1909; 15,000 words) is also longer and later in composition than "An Outpost of Progress" (1896; 10,000 words). "An Outpost of Progress" involves the issue of self-knowledge as a dark epiphany; "The Secret Sharer" deals with the same issue in a more positive way. "An Outpost of Progress" deals with determinism in fate, hypocrisy in colonialism and seems to be, in part, Conrad's act of reprisal toward the Belgians for humanistic and cultural disagreements; "The Secret Sharer" deals with the old age of sail, initiation, choices in fate, and the psychology of command.

Both stories are sourced from Conrad's rich and varied personal experiences; neither story employs the kind of frame narrative famously used in "Heart of Darkness," and both stories deal with subjects "outside the general run of everyday experience" (Conrad 1950b: vii). In both stories the diction and the lush yet precise descriptions are deliciously Conradian. Both stories are also "warm-ups" for later and longer masterpieces that more fully develop their themes: "An Outpost of Progress" is thus linked with "Heart of Darkness" (1899) and "The Secret Sharer" with *The Shadow Line* (1917). Both stories employ an essential conflict of opposites: though it is Africa that is victimized in "An Outpost of Progress," it shows a struggle not of the European against the African so much as of the European against "himself," and he defeats himself. And the question is, is it philanthropy or robbery? Is it "progress" or just another vile theft of resources? Similarly, in "The Secret Sharer," the essential juxtaposition is really the captain in dialog with Leggatt, an extension of himself, rather than the captain in conflict with his crew; that is just a frame. Through Leggatt, the reader observes a conflict between two types of skipper (one traditional and romantic, the other mechanically "arch bold"), and a struggle inside the captain to realize internally the kind of skipper who can reject what Archbold represents. The conflict is between "the soul of command" (timeless) versus "the letter of the law" (culturally and temporally relative), and the point made by the captain in "The Secret Sharer" applies equally to Jim's "ideal of conduct" in *Lord Jim* (Conrad 1926: 121, 415):

> I wondered how far I should turn out faithful to that ideal conception of one's own personality every man sets up for himself secretly. (Conrad 1947b: 94)

Both stories also involve a confusion of identities and insanity or near insanity: in "The Secret Sharer" the confusion between the captain and Leggatt is central to the story ("It was very much like being mad") (1947b: 113–14). In "An Outpost of Progress" Kayerts and Carlier are both conventional, out of place, unhappy and incompetent in Africa, and also so totally dependent on each other that Carlier loses his sanity while *watching* the other:

> Then he tried to imagine himself dead, and Carlier sitting in his chair watching him; and his attempt met with such unexpected success, that in a very few moments he

became not at all sure who was dead and who was alive. This extraordinary achievement of his fancy startled him, however, and by a clever and timely effort of mind he saved himself just in time from becoming Carlier. (Conrad 1947a: 111)

This confounding of identity between Kayerts and Carlier at the end of "An Outpost of Progress" may foreshadow the more complex process of confounding identity between Kurtz and Marlow in "Heart of Darkness," where Marlow, fascinated with Kurtz to the point of becoming his alter ego, even comes to resemble Kurtz physically.

Though all of Conrad's work is against a harsh background – perhaps best summed up by Arthur Symons's epigraph to *'Twixt Land and Sea*: "Life is a tragic folly" ("old Symons," "the big one with the beard" in *Lord Jim* recalls Mahon in "Youth" and anticipates "whiskers" in "The Secret Sharer") – "The Secret Sharer" and "An Outpost of Progress" can nevertheless be differentiated on the basis of "The hope of youth" (the characters' process of proving worthy and "finding themselves" goes right) as opposed to "the danger of youth" (proving worth and the process of finding themselves goes tragically and fatally wrong). "Youth," "The Secret Sharer," and *The Shadow Line* are based on action and turn out fairly well, while "An Outpost of Progress," *Lord Jim*, and "Heart of Darkness" are based on inaction; they involve passively watching and examining, like the slow development of a theory. In the end, it is a matter of successful endeavor and life as opposed to failure and death.

The earlier work, "An Outpost of Progress," examines – with palpable contempt – a type of bourgeois European who "knows nothing real beyond the words" (1947a: 105): Kayerts and Carlier are thoughtlessly creatures of comfort in that they depend on the supports of city life like insentient drones, eating and functioning mechanically, but they are helpless and ineffectual outside that civilization. The narrator documents, in almost textbook fashion, their slow slide into corruption, hastened by a lack of foresight, ultimately caused by their tragic lack of self-knowledge. True and almost comic fools, they are willing conspirators in each other's self-deception, encouraging each other in their lack of industry and in their smug willingness to believe the vague notion of "progress," even in the face of all they have been witness to (Hawthorn 2005: 213). Intellectually and functionally dependent creatures, they need civilization but when given the chance to build an "outpost" of their society – miles from the structures and people they depend upon – they fail pathetically. On the other hand, sailors must recreate their society each time they sail into the void, or face disaster, and so in "An Outpost of Progress," Kayerts and Carlier receive a sea captain's contempt if one locates Conrad the man behind the omniscient narrator. At least Makola – Henry Price – "did something" (Conrad 1923: 119). Kayerts and Carlier do nothing, and the indictment of the European colonial goes deeper still, for neither does the arrogant and disdainful "director" do anything to help Kayerts, his agent. His ironic arrival at the end is too late, and for all his arrogance, he himself is as useless as the agents he so despises. The director ensures, in almost scientific fashion, that what aid they require is withheld. His own arrogance and greed prevents him from being a successful director of the company.

The great success of "The Secret Sharer" with publishers in the years since it first appeared in print (1910) may account for the large critical response to it; or one may attribute the volume of criticism the story has generated to its being perhaps Conrad's most ambiguous story. On the surface, it seems to be about a ship captain's dilemma as to whether to follow the law or personal feeling by either detaining or, alternatively, abetting, a fugitive from another ship, a man by the name of "Leggatt." Ambiguous by design, the story has sometimes been taken literally, but perhaps more often symbolically, by critics. This situation renders criticism and interpretation of the story less than satisfying, for if the story is read somewhat literally, then there *is* a "Leggatt" as a fully realized other person opposite the captain, but if it is read symbolically, then one must question whether Leggatt exists at all outside the captain's imagination – or psychosis. The two positions are not reconcilable, for readings that follow from the first position, that Leggatt exists, should find difficulty in including criticism and assessments of meaning that follow from the assumption that Leggatt is a mental creation of the captain with no separate existence of his own in actuality, and vice versa.

Among the critics, Moser considers the story a warm up to a longer work, *The Shadow Line; A Confession* (1917) (1957: 2), itself a story of initiation pertaining specifically to the stresses of a captain's first command. This idea would strengthen the interpretation of the "The Secret Sharer" as being less about a moral dilemma (Leggatt is real) and more about how a captain might successfully pass the initiation test occasioned by his first command. (Leggatt, on board the captain's ship at least, is a creation of the captain's mind while the captain is under considerable professional stress.) One might ask which is the more important topic for Conrad in this story and in the context of his work as a whole. Morality is somewhat ancillary in Conrad's work and is often dealt with in an ambiguous and even ironic manner, while "initiation" is a central Conradian theme and is fairly straightforward: it is about having "the right stuff." About this Conrad does not waffle. Guerard calls "The Secret Sharer" and *The Shadow Line* "among the first and best . . . symbolist masterpieces in English fiction" (1958: 14). He sees the captain's encounter with Leggatt, in Jungian terms, as a productive encounter between two sides of the captain's own psyche. For Guerard, Leggatt represents a secret darker side of the self. Johnson and Garber discuss psychoanalytic readings of the story that have to do with "the pathology of the author" or "the pathology of the protagonist," in terms of unconscious conflicts rather than conscious attitudes (1987: 631). If Leggatt does not actually exist, the psychology behind this makes the captain an unreliable narrator, or at least a very ambiguous or a very tricky one. A "real" Leggatt, on the other hand, would have noticeable similarities with the protagonist of *Lord Jim* (1900), being legally and perhaps emotionally on the lam; but then the captain's "other" – or hidden self – could also feel emotionally an outcast or wanderer.

Leggatt, the fugitive, is mysteriously described by the captain as "my double" (Conrad 1947b: 100, 104, 109, 112, 128), or else as "myself" (1947b: 138), "my other self" (1947b: 111, 128, 138, 142), "my second self" (1947b: 115, 117, 129, 136, 141), "my very own self" (1947b: 137), or "my secret self" (1947b: 114). This double, Leggatt, has been seen by the critics as *metaphorically* a mirror image, in that he is both similar to and different from the captain, both allegorically and psychologically (Watts 1977; Steiner 1980). But, in the story, he is also described *literally* as like "my own reflection . . . in an immense mirror" (Conrad 1947b: 101). Though ambiguity is carefully and perhaps playfully maintained, the effect is cumulative and the hints are actually quite strong that the captain, and perhaps the author as well, is musing rather darkly while looking in a mirror, perhaps a mirror hanging on the back of the door to his cabin: "He had turned about meantime; and we, the two strangers in the ship, faced each other in identical attitudes" (1947b: 110). The trick of this technique is to treat the mirror image *as if it was another person,* and then to be consistent with that and with a scrupulously maintained ambiguity that never totally violates the reality of reflection. In this connection we can note that the two, Leggatt and the captain, both go barefoot (1947b: 100) and also wear the same clothes: a "sleeping suit" (100, 102, 104, 135). The prolonged wearing of the sleeping suit by both Leggatt and the captain tends to reinforce the "dream" quality of Leggatt's comings and goings. This together with the fact that they are both Conway boys (1947b: 101) – from the famous training ship also alluded to in *Lord Jim* (like Leggatt, Jim is a parson's son) – these are all strong hints that Leggatt is, first, literally, and, then, figuratively, a mirror image of the captain: being a "Conway boy" means that he must live up to the *image* of a Conway boy, and to all the competence and tradition that image implies. Conrad, "the double captain" (1947b: 138), is talking to himself in the mirror both about and because of the loneliness of command. The ambiguity is simply his toying with the mirror idea to make a deeper impression about the private and potentially embarrassing aspect of a lonely captain's resorting to this kind of self-dialog.

In this loneliness there is not so much a moral judgment as a sharing, a confession of his common humanity and frailty, a frailty he must conquer for the good of his ship and crew. So, like *The Shadow Line* with its subtitle, "a confession," "The Secret Sharer" also seems to be confessional, albeit a confession thinly veiled by the playful ambiguity of the mirror. A look at *The Shadow Line* is certainly revealing in this regard about a captain's use of his private spaces and private times away from the crew:

> The mahogany table under the skylight shone in the twilight like a dark pool of water. The sideboard, surmounted by a wide looking-glass in an ormulu frame, had a marble top . . . I sat down in the armchair at the head of the table – the captain's chair . . . A succession of men had sat in that chair. I became aware of that thought suddenly, vividly, as though each had left a little of himself between the four walls of these ornate bulkheads; as if a sort of composite soul, the soul of command, had whispered suddenly to mine of long days at sea and of anxious moments. (Conrad 1917: 75)

Like the Captain in "The Secret Sharer," who admits to "constantly watching myself" (Conrad 1947b: 113), the narrator in *The Shadow Line* examines himself in the mirror:

> It struck me that this quietly staring man whom I was watching, both as if he were myself and somebody else, was not exactly a lonely figure. He had his place in a line of men whom he did not know, of whom he had never heard; but who were fashioned by the same influences, whose souls in relation to their humble life's work had no secrets for him. (1917: 77)

He also discusses the "searching intimacy with your own self" (1917: 76) one gets from thus looking in the mirror:

> Deep within the tarnished ormulu frame, in the hot half-light sifted through the awning, I saw my own face propped between my hands. And I stared back at myself with the perfect detachment of distance, rather with curiosity than with any other feeling. (1917: 75–6)

For the captain in "The Secret Sharer" it might indeed have seemed "like being haunted" (1947b: 130), for as *he* looks at Leggatt "as though . . . in . . . an immense mirror," his double, of course, behaves and looks a lot like himself: "The shadowy, dark head, like mine, seemed to nod imperceptibly above the ghostly gray of my sleeping suit" (1947b: 101).

The captain's cabin, where Leggatt is consulted on a regular basis throughout the story, is "L" shaped, and the fact that the narrator goes to such pains to point this out (1947b: 104) has led some critics to suggest the obvious, that "L" stands for "Leggatt," a homophone for "legate" or "messenger": in this case clearly a messenger from the souls of captains now and in the past. So in this sense it is the L-shaped room itself which is "Leggatt": this is where the captain encounters the "soul of command" communicated though a looking glass, a mirror/window both into himself and into the soul of like-minded spirits alone on the sea; a room which is haunted with ghosts of captains only a fellow captain can *see* or *feel*. And there are Conradian hints that it is the sea itself that tests a man, or a line of men, sea captains, and so the real mirror is perhaps "the mirror of the sea," the title of Conrad's autobiographical work of 1906, a text described by Conrad himself as "Essays – impressions, descriptions, reminiscences [,] anecdotes and typical traits – of the old sailing fleet which passes away for good with the last century" (Karl and Davies 1983: 114). Conrad adds in an author's note that *The Mirror of the Sea* offers "a very intimate revelation" and "a true confession" of "the inner truth of almost a lifetime" (Conrad 1950a: ix–x). Yet more so even than in *The Mirror of the Sea*, that "true confession" may well come in "The Secret Sharer":

> Walking to the taffrail, I was in time to make out, on the very edge of a darkness thrown by a towering black mass like the very gateway of Erebus – yes, I was in time to catch

an evanescent glimpse of my white hat left behind to mark the spot where the secret sharer of my cabin and of my thoughts, as though he were my second self, had lowered himself into the water to take his punishment: a free man, a proud swimmer striking out for a new destiny. (Conrad 1947b: 143)

In this quote, the ambiguous coda of "The Secret Sharer," the white hat is an allusion to "Old White Hat," the owner of the *Cutty Sark*, the fateful 1880 voyage of which was one of the sources Conrad used for the story (Lubbock, 1960: 143). There are also links here to the coda of "The Planter of Malata" (1914), and to the motif of suicide in general -but it is an unrepentant, almost heroic act: "I didn't mean to drown myself, I meant to swim till I sank – but that's not the same thing" (Conrad 1947b: 108). In the spirit of the *Übermensch*, this "Byronic" suicide involves swimming – not "jumping overboard" like Captain Brierly in *Lord Jim* (based upon the suicide of Captain Wallace, the real skipper of the *Cutty Sark* in 1880):

But I hardly thought of my other self, now gone from the ship, to be hidden forever from all friendly faces, to be a fugitive and a vagabond on the earth, with no brand of the curse on his sane forehead to stay a slaying hand . . . too proud to explain. (1947b: 142)

Jim's own "suicide" is related, as is that of the real-life "Conway boy," Captain Matthew Webb, whose famous portrait matches the description of Leggatt in "The Secret Sharer" (1947b: 100). Decoud in *Nostromo* also goes overboard, after shooting himself, and this shooting links the motif back to Kayerts's suicide in "An Outpost of Progress" – and to Conrad's rash attempt on his own life as a young man in Marseilles.

The negative and the positive are not exactly alternative spheres in Conrad's art, but spheres that interfuse each other and commix in the individual soul: each of us is a "captain" with choices and frailties as well as strengths, fears of failure, as well as feelings of youthful indomitability. Whether lucky or wise, or fatally flawed, an old man is a youth grown weary. For Conrad, the tragedy of the human condition is mutability: mutability of choices – the ones we make and the ones we are given – and mutability in life. The windmill Conrad tilts at is a paradox, an attempt to capture this mutability in a text, to render the changeable changeless: in the end, a task doomed to failure. For like his work in *The Mirror of the Sea*, an elegy for the age of sail, all ships, kept afloat by a succession of heroic and facile captains and crews, are doomed inevitably to sink. While "An Outpost of Progress" displays an Olympian deterministic note of fatality and perhaps futility, as well as writerly discipline, economy, and unity of effect, all is united in a tale like "The Secret Sharer": links to the dark and to the light, the pessimism and the acceptance, the heroic struggle and the simple assertion of professional competence. You can see these traits exhibited on ships like the *Sephora* in "The Secret Sharer," you can see them in the tragic and feckless incompetence of Kayerts and Carlier in "An Outpost of Progress," and you, the empathetic reader, can see them when you look soberly and in solitude at your own reflection in a mirror.

REFERENCES AND FURTHER READING

Conrad, J. (1917). *The Shadow Line.* London: J.M. Dent.

Conrad, J. (1923). "Heart of Darkness," in *Youth and Other Stories.* London: J.M. Dent (original work published 1899/1902).

Conrad, J. (1926). *Lord Jim.* London: Dent.

Conrad, J. (1947a). "An Outpost of Progress," in *Almayer's Folly and Tales of Unrest.* London: J.M. Dent (original work published 1896).

Conrad, J. (1947b). "The Secret Sharer," in *'Twixt Land and Sea.* London: J.M. Dent.

Conrad, J. (1950a). *The Mirror of the Sea and A Personal Record.* London: J.M. Dent.

Conrad, J. (1950b). *Within the Tides.* London: J.M. Dent.

Guerard, A.J. (1958). *Conrad the Novelist.* Cambridge, Mass.: Harvard University Press.

Hawthorn, J. (1990). *Joseph Conrad: Narrative Technique and Ideological Commitment.* New York: Edward Arnold.

Hawthorn, J. (2005). "Artful Dodges in Mental Territory: Self-deception in Conrad's Fiction," *Conradiana* 37/3 (fall): 205–31.

Johnson, B. and Garber, M. (1987). "Secret Sharing: Reading Conrad Psychoanalytically," *College English* 49/6 (Oct.): 628–40.

Karl, F.R. and Davies, L. (eds) (1983). *The Collected Letters of Joseph Conrad.* Cambridge: Cambridge University Press.

Lothe, J. (1989). *Conrad's Narrative Method.* Oxford: Clarendon Press.

Lubbock, B. (1960). *The Log of the Cutty Sark.* Glasgow: Brown, Son and Ferguson.

Moser, T.C. (1957). *Joseph Conrad: Achievement and Decline.* Cambridge, Mass.: Harvard University Press.

Najder, Z. (ed.) (1978). *Congo Diary and Other Uncollected Pieces.* New York: Doubleday, 1978.

Steiner, J.E. (1980). "Complexities of the Doubling Relationship," *Conradiana* 12: 173–86.

Watts, C. (1977). "The Mirror-tale: An Ethico-structural Analysis of Conrad's 'The Secret Sharer'," *Critical Quarterly* 19/3: 25–37.

12

The Short Stories of
Hector Hugh Munro ("Saki")

Sandie Byrne

Hector Hugh Munro was born in 1870, to Charles Augustus Munro, then a major in the Burma police, and Mary Frances Mercer, daughter of a Rear Admiral. Charles Hector was born in Akyab, Burma, following an older sister, Ethel Mary, and brother, Charles Arthur (Charlie). Mary Mercer returned to England during a difficult fourth pregnancy, and was killed (family tradition says by a runaway cow) when Hector was two years old, and the three children were sent to Devon to be brought up by their grandmother and aunts. The aunts, Augusta and Charlotte (known as Aunt Tom), were strong characters who dominated the children's lives, particularly after the death of their milder mother, and whose perpetual state of feud, with its opportunities for playing one off against the other, provided the children's only respite from a strict and circumscribed regime. Playing with other children was not allowed, other than at one annual party, and diversions mostly consisted of drawing, reading, and church-going. Hector was not strong but seems to have been both highly strung and energetic. His imagination was clearly colored by the number of Old Testament fire-and-brimstone and eye-for-an-eye sermons the children were forced to listen to, and his sense of language by the collects and hymns they were required to learn. One of Ethel Munro's earliest memories of him was of Hector running around the nursery with a blazing hearthbrush shouting, "I'm God I'm going to destroy the world" (reported in Ethel Munro's memoir of her brother, published in *The Square Egg and Other Stories* [Munro 1924: 3]).

After a short time at an Exmouth prep school, Hector was sent to Bedford School, but remained there less than two years. The retirement of their father, now Colonel Munro, and his return to England liberated him and his sister, though it was rather late for Charlie, who was destined for a crammer and, since poor eyesight kept him out of the army, Burma and the military police. Hector, Ethel, and their father embarked on a protracted continental tour, taking in parts of Germany, Poland, Switzerland, and France, before settling in South Devon. After two more years of family life, and five years after the Colonel's return, Munro entered into his first paid employment; his father arranged for him to join Charlie in the Burma military police.

Munro's time as a military officer lasted thirteen months and seven bouts of fever before he was sent home, probably under the assumption that it was to die. He survived, however, recuperated at home in South Devon, and then left for London to pursue a more congenial occupation. For three years, presumably supported by his father, Munro researched in the British Museum. The fruit of his work, published in 1900, the year he became thirty, *The Rise of the Russian Empire*, was written from an interest in Russian history, language and culture, but before he had visited the country. It was not his first publication. In 1899, *St Paul's* magazine took a short story, "Dogged," signed "H.H.M.," which seems to be the first published piece of Sakian fiction. At around this time, Munro was introduced to the political cartoonist Francis Carruthers Gould, and a different outlet for his writing talents. In 1900, Gould was working for the *Westminster Gazette*, and persuaded the paper's editor to commission a series of political sketches by himself and a new collaborator. The "Alice in Westminster" satires, based on Lewis Carroll's *Alice* stories, were later published in book form by *Westminster Gazette's* press. The series was a success, and was followed by satires based on Omar Khayyam and a longer run of skits based on Kipling, called "The Political Junglebook," and later (from the "Just-So Stories") the "Not-So Stories."

During his collaboration with Gould, the *Westminster Gazette* also began to take Saki's fiction, publishing "The Blood-feud of Toad-Water" early in 1901, and in September of that year the first of the "Reginald" stories, which were to comprise Saki's first collection. Nonetheless, Munro changed allegiance, taking employment with the *Morning Post*, whose high Toryism was more suited to his political inclinations than those of the Liberal *Westminster Gazette*. He did not simply transfer his political columns from one paper to another, however. For the *Morning Post*, he became a foreign correspondent, and in 1902 left England for Macedonia.

Between 1902 and 1907, Munro reported from Vuchitrn, Belgrade, Sofia, Uskub, Salonica, Warsaw, and St Petersburg. He sent back dispatches on uprisings, battles, explosions, murders, massacres, and the recent (and not-so recent) political history of the troubled regions, was almost shot as a spy, and witnessed the bloody events in St Petersburg of early 1905. While he was away, Methuen published his first collection of stories, *Reginald*. It was more than five years before they brought out his second, *Reginald in Russia*, in 1910, and, at least in part because of Methuen's desultory marketing, neither attracted many reviews or achieved good sales.

After a stint in Paris, in 1907 Munro moved back to London, and took a cottage in Caterham, where he installed his sister. He began a long association with John Lane, proprietor of The Bodley Head, who was to publish all of his remaining books: *The Chronicles of Clovis, Beasts and Super-Beasts* (the last collection of stories to be published in Munro's lifetime), and the two novels *The Unbearable Bassington* and *When William Came*, as well as the posthumous collections *The Toys of Peace* and *The Square Egg*. The later Bodley Head uniform series also included Munro's plays. In addition to the stories, Munro continued to produce political and other journalism, including occasional "Potted Parliament" pieces for periodicals such as *Outlook*.

In 1976, Doubleday published a collected edition of Saki's writing, which was published in paperback by Penguin in 1982, with an introduction by Noël Coward, a long-term fan of Saki's. It is from this edition that quotations in this essay are taken.

When war was declared, in September 1914, Munro lied about his age in order to enlist. He joined the King Edward's Own Cavalry but found the life too strenuous, and transferred to the 22nd Regiment of the Royal Fusiliers. His company was sent to France in 1915 and he was killed by a shot to the head in November 1916. His last recorded words were: "Put that bloody cigarette out."

Munro's characteristic style is deadpan, formal, and blackly humorous. The narratives can get away with the terrible fates they inflict upon less favored characters because the reader is never invited to make any emotional investment in them. Although the characters engage and amuse, they are not three-dimensional enough to encourage identification or empathy. The first Reginald story is a monologue by an anonymous narrator about Reginald, Saki's first dandy-youth. The subsequent stories in the collection are told in the third person but are the reported monologues or near-monologues of Reginald. Although the main point is Reginald's wit, the stories are also used as the vehicles for some social satire. The early stories are short, often taking up only a couple of newspaper columns or pages of the Methuen volume, and are mostly concerned with exhibiting the character of Reginald: utterly self-centered, vain, hedonistic, and blasé.

Reginald is given some wonderful epigrams:

"To have reached thirty," said Reginald, "is to have failed in life." ("Reginald on the Academy," Munro 1982: 12)

He also caps other people's beautifully:

"Youth," said the Other, "should suggest innocence."
   "But never act on the suggestion." ("The Innocence of Reginald," Munro 1982: 38)
   "When I was younger, boys of your age used to be nice and innocent."
   "Now we are only nice. One must specialize in these days." ("Reginald at the Theatre," Munro 1982: 14)

"You really are indecently vain of your appearance. A good life is infinitely preferable to good looks."
   "You agree with me that the two are incompatible. I always say beauty is only sin deep." ("Reginald's Choir Treat," Munro 1982: 17)

Reginald appears only once in Saki's second collection, *Reginald in Russia*, in the title story. Some of the stories are more fleshed out than the earliest episodes, and the themes are more diverse, but a few, such as "A Young Turkish Catastrophe" and "The Soul of Laploshka," are thin and uninspiring. They include, however the first Sakian metamorphosizing character – the beautiful youth who is revealed as a werewolf in the fully realized and polished story "Gabriel Ernest."

The eponymous hero of *The Chronicles of Clovis* is as witty as Reginald:

> "All decent people live beyond their incomes nowadays, and those who aren't respectable live beyond other people's. A few gifted individuals do both." ("The Match-Maker," Munro 1982: 107)

He is equally vain and hedonistic, but more adept at planning and carrying out the elaborate hoaxes which are the foundation of several Saki plots. It is in this collection that Saki introduces the supernatural and macabre often associated with his writing. The stories include a talking cat, a stag incited to kill by a young Pan, and a giant polecat-ferret with a taste for justice, and human flesh.

Beasts and Super-Beasts contains more Saki transformations: a (fake) woman-to-wolf spell; a (probably real) woman-to-otter reincarnation; and a (pretend) ghost dog; however, a number of the beasts are simply real, but put to good use: a pig provides an enterprising young girl with an opportunity to make some money; an ox in a drawing-room reinvigorates an artistic career. Some are kept off-stage but provide the matter of the plot: an elk with a habit of tossing female aspirants to the hand of a wealthy young man; an imaginary pullet saved from the hypnotic stare of a snake by its feathery forelock; a horse whose sale to an eligible bachelor almost obstructs an advantageous marriage.

The two posthumous collections, *The Toys of Peace* and *The Square Egg*, are made up of uncollected and unpublished writing. They include some stories and journalism written from the trenches between 1915 and 1916, such as "For the Duration of the War" in *The Toys of Peace*, and the title story and "Birds on the Western Front" in *The Square Egg*.

Saki reserves his worst fates for adults, particularly women, who are cruel or cold to children. The guardian of the boy hero of "Sredni Vashtar," Mrs De Ropp, is both cruel and cold. She is also a hypocrite, unable to confront her own dislike of the boy, which is contrasted with the child's clear-sighted and honestly acknowledged hatred.

Conradin, whom we are told in the first sentence of the story is not expected to live to the age of fifteen, has no warmth in his life, and expends all his affection on two pets, a ragged houdan hen and a polecat-ferret he has secreted in a garden shed. The ferret has become more than a pet to him. Its sleekness, strength, killer instinct, and the perfection of its design as a predator is the antithesis of the trammeled, sickly, disempowered boy, and he both loves and fears it. It is:

> a secret and fearful joy, to be kept scrupulously from the knowledge of the Woman, as he privately dubbed his cousin. And one day, out of Heaven knows what material, he

spun the beast a wonderful name, and from that moment it grew into a god and a religion. . . . [I]n the dim and musty silence of the tool-shed, he worshipped with mystic and elaborate ceremonial before the wooden hutch where dwelt Sredni Vashtar, the great ferret. ("Sredni Vashtar," Munro 1982: 137)

Mrs De Ropp has the hen taken away and, suspecting that Conradin has something else hidden, begins to search for it. When she finds the ferret, Conradin knows that she will have won, life will hold nothing of warmth or affection or interest for him, and he will indeed die.

He knew that the Woman would come out presently with that pursed smile he loathed so well on her face, and that in an hour or two the gardener would carry away his wonderful god, a god no longer, but a simple brown ferret in a hutch. And he knew that the Woman would triumph always as she triumphed now, and that he would grow ever more sickly under her pestering and domineering and superior wisdom, and the doctor would be proved right. And in the sting and misery of his defeat, he began to chant loudly and defiantly the hymn of his threatened idol:

Sredni Vashtar went forth,
His thoughts were red thoughts and his teeth were white.
His enemies called for peace, but he brought them death.
Sredni Vashtar the Beautiful.
(Munro 1982: 139)

Conradin's prayer is answered. Instead of The Woman, what emerges from the shed is a huge, sleek beast with blood on its jaw and throat. The story is appropriately named, since the beautiful deadly beast is at its center, taking the place of the beautiful, sometimes feral, youths who are the objects of aesthetic or erotic attention in other stories.

Reginald and Clovis can orchestrate their own revenge on those who cross them, and the other hoaxers can mete out the sentences they deem appropriate for those they accuse of crimes, ranging from dullness to interference with youthful pleasures. Younger boys such as Conradin, however, are at the mercy of the powerful forces of aunts and guardians who keep them repressed and powerless; so on the boys' behalf the author calls up something powerful, ruthless, and single-minded to act as Nemesis. Conradin responds to the death of his guardian with great *sangfroid*, giving himself the rare pleasure of slowly buttering himself a second slice of toast. Already he is stronger, making choices for himself, enjoying simple but sensual pleasures, and entering into the life his guardian denied him. It is possible that one or both of Munro's aunts provided the model for Mrs De Ropp. Ethel Munro, in the memoir of her brother included in the posthumous collection *The Square Egg*, records that as a child one of the few pets her brother was allowed was a houdan hen, and that when it became ill his aunt refused to have it taken to a vet, so that it had to be destroyed (Munro 1924: 10).

The genius of "Sredni Vashtar" is its compression, economy, and exactness. The prognosis of Conradin's early death is followed by: "The doctor was silky and effete, and counted for little, but his opinion was endorsed by Mrs De Ropp, who counted for nearly everything" (Munro 1982: 136). Saki uses to excellent effect both antithesis and the opposition of near-identical things whose slight differences become highly significant: The joylessness of the regime imposed by The Woman is opposed to the "secret and fearful joy" Conradin has in Sredni Vashtar. Mrs De Ropp is "dimly aware" that she does not find thwarting Conradin "particularly irksome"; Conradin hates her with a "desperate sincerity" he is "perfectly able to mask." The phrasing may some- times seem almost arch: Conradin's imagination is "rampant under the spur of loneli- ness"; in the tool shed, he finds something that "took on the varying aspects of a playroom and a cathedral" which he "had peopled with a legion of familiar phantoms" (Munro 1982: 136–7), but each adjective, each noun, and each sparingly used meta- phor is appropriate and evocative. Fruit trees in the garden are set "jealously apart" from Conradin's plucking. The narrative voice is not neutral or equivocal; though deadpan, it nonetheless manages to demand outrage. It comments on the setting aside of the fruit trees "as though they were rare specimens of their kind blooming in an arid waste; it would probably have been difficult to find a market-gardener who would have offered ten shillings for their entirely yearly produce" (Munro 1982: 137).

"The Open Window" contains many of the elements of an archetypal Saki story: the (pretend) supernatural; a young person with a vivid imagination; a storyteller; a practical joker; and a character who takes it upon his or herself to act as Nemesis; often, as here, the same character. Structurally, it has much in common with other stories, such as "The Unrest-Cure." Both involve a lively young person's shaking up the life of a dull one by an elaborate hoax, in "The Unrest-Cure" by the pretence that a country house is about to be the stage for a massacre, and in "The Open Window" by the pretence that the country house is haunted by the victims of a tragedy. Both involve imagined violent death intruding upon a domestic scene, and both require a credulous audience/victim, though, surprisingly, the story of four ghosts, including a dog, appearing through an open window requires less credulity and seems less implausible than the tales spun by Clovis for the benefit of his victims in stories such as "The Unrest-Cure," "The Hen," and "Shock Tactics."

"The Unrest-Cure" gives unmissable clues to the identity of the hoaxer, whom the reader meets at the beginning of the story as Clovis, before encountering him again as "Stanislaus." In "The Open Window," however, the reader is not in on the hoax from the beginning, but is placed in the position of the victim, Framton Nuttel, a stodgy young man on a "nerve cure." Nuttel, and, by extension, the reader, accepts the tale spun by the hoaxer, Vera, "a very self-possessed young lady of fifteen" ("The Open Window," Munro 1982: 259). Vera appears to offer as the unvarnished truth, and so Nuttel accepts it, that her aunt believes that her dead husband and brothers (and their dog) will return through the open window. Vera makes it clear that her aunt's belief is a delusion she does not share, and Nuttel receives it as such, but she is unable to suppress a slight tremor as she looks at the open window, and he is unable to suppress a slight frisson and sideways glance at the news that this very day is the anniversary of the tragedy.

At this stage, the reader's sympathies, like those of the victim, are with Vera, the healthy young girl who has to live with her aunt's morbid imaginings. When the figures do appear in the gathering dust, the husband carrying a white waterproof coat over his arm, the younger brother, singing "Bertie, why do you bound?", and the brown spaniel at their heels, just as in Vera's description of their departure before the tragic accident, the reader is clearly expected, for one moment, to see them as supernatural apparitions. That Vera does not at this point overreact or even call Framton's attention to the apparitions, but only stares, "through the open window with dazed horror in her eyes" (Munro 1982: 261), is masterly. The victim rushes from the room, and without giving the reader any more details that could be analyzed, or time to become skeptical, the story cuts to the "ghost" husband's prosaically remarking that he and his brothers-in-law are fairly muddy, but that most of the mud is dry. It is at that point that we realize we have been listening to an entirely made-up story; we are spectators of a hoax. It is swiftly followed by another, produced to account for the guest's rapid departure. This, involving a cemetery, a newly dug grave, and a pack of pariah dogs, is even more lurid than the first. The narrative voice then breaks frame, directly addressing the reader to remark that "Romance at short notice was her [Vera's] speciality" (Munro 1982: 262).

Vera is of course ironically named, since her name derives from the Latin for truth. Her hoax, like many others in Saki's writing, depends for its success on the victim's gullibility and unwillingness to blunder into a social solecism, such as touching on a delicate or painful topic. In "The Hen," Jane Martlet would have unmasked Clovis as a liar if she could have brought herself to ignore his assertion that she cannot enquire about her hostess's butler's alleged homicidal tendencies because: "My mother mustn't hear a word about it [. . .] it would upset her dreadfully. She relies on Sturridge for everything" ("The Hen," Munro 1982: 258). Similarly, Nuttel could have tumbled Vera's pack of lies if he had made some allusion to the alleged tragedy when, as he believes, he is the audience to her aunt's playing out of her delusions.

> "I hope you don't mind the open window," said Mrs Sappleton briskly; "my husband and brothers will be home directly from shooting [. . .]"
>   She rattled on cheerfully about the shooting and scarcity of birds, and the prospects for duck in the winter. To Framton, it was all purely horrible. He made a desperate but only partially successful effort to turn the talk on to a less ghastly topic [. . .]. (Munro 1982: 261)

Both Vera and Conradin are storytellers; the difference is that Conradin's stories are for himself alone. His imagination has been all that has sustained him during a long and lonely imprisonment.

> One of these days Conradin supposed he would succumb to the mastering pressure of wearisome necessary things – such as illnesses and coddling restrictions and drawn-out

dullness. Without his imagination, which was rampant under the spur of loneliness, he would have succumbed long ago. ("Sredni Vashtar," Munro 1982: 136)

Imagination in Saki's fiction is almost entirely the preserve of males and pre-pubescent girls. There are a few girl "romancers," such as Vera, and, in "The Boar-Pig," Matilda (whose name might remind us of Belloc's Matilda, who "told such dreadful lies/ It made one gasp and stretch one's eyes"), but most older women are represented as narrow-minded, dull, and materialistic: the enemy. Conradin locks his guardian out "from the realm of his imagination" as "an unclean thing which should find no entrance" ("Sredni Vashtar," Munro 1982: 137). To allow The Woman to penetrate his imagination would be a horrific, unbearably intrusive intimacy. Two words used to describe Mrs De Ropp, "pestering" and "domineering," could be applied to many of the women (with a few exceptions) in the stories, and Saki's narrators could be accused of misogyny as well as anti-Semitism, imperialism, and jingoism.

The weakest of Saki's stories depend upon a punchline or last paragraph reversal. The strongest combine instant characterization, wit, tension, shock, great humor, and pathos.

References and Further Reading

Byrne, S. (2007). *Saki*. Oxford: Oxford University Press.

Gillen, C.H. (1963). *H.H. Munro (Saki)*. New York: Twayne.

Langguth, A.J. (1981). *Saki: A Life of Hector Hugh Munro, with Six Stories Never Before Collected*. London: Hamish Hamilton; New York: Simon and Schuster.

Saki (H.H. Munro) (1902). *The Westminster Alice*. London: The Westminster Gazette.

Saki (H.H. Munro) (1904). *Reginald*. London: Methuen

Saki (H.H. Munro) (1910). *Reginald in Russia*. London: Methuen.

Saki (H.H. Munro) (1911). *The Chronicles of Clovis*. London: John Lane, The Bodley Head.

Saki (H.H. Munro) (1912). *The Unbearable Bassington*. London: John Lane, The Bodley Head.

Saki (H.H. Munro) (1913). *When William Came*. London: John Lane, The Bodley Head.

Saki (H.H. Munro) (1914). *Beasts and Super-Beasts*. London: John Lane, The Bodley Head.

Saki (H.H. Munro) (1919). *The Toys of Peace*. London: John Lane, The Bodley Head.

Saki (H.H. Munro) (1924). *The Square Egg and Other Sketches*. London: John Lane, The Bodley Head.

Saki (H.H. Munro) (1930). *The Short Stories of Saki*. London: John Lane, The Bodley Head.

Saki (H.H. Munro) (1933). *The Complete Novels and Plays of Saki*. London: John Lane, The Bodley Head.

Saki (H.H. Munro) (1963). *The Bodley Head Saki*. London: John Lane, The Bodley Head.

Saki (H.H. Munro) (1982). *The Complete Saki*. Harmondsworth: Penguin.

Spears, G.J. (1963). *The Satire of Saki: A Study of the Satiric Art of H.H. Munro*. New York: Exposition Press.

13
Paralysis Re-considered:
James Joyce's *Dubliners*

Richard Greaves

In what seems to have been the standard approach to *Dubliners*, one seeks the epiphany of a story, that moment where some kind of revelation takes place. The revelation will be associated with a view of the city of Dublin that the collection as a whole affords us. This view is of a paralyzed city, following Joyce's hint in his letter to the publisher, Grant Richards (Joyce 2000: xxxi). The moral impetus of the collection is to impart this view.

Criticism of *Dubliners* has its revisionists. The complexity of Joyce's use of point of view renders problematic the attempt to arrive at a definite interpretation via a story's epiphany. The paralysis approach, as Dominic Head persuasively argues, has been used in an oversimplified way that in turn oversimplifies the stories (Head 1992: 39–78). Moreover, critics have tended to rely uncritically on what Joyce himself wrote about the stories, treating his pronouncements as a guide to how to read instead of part of a vexed dialog with his publisher, who was nervous of publishing material likely to be seen as immoral. Joyce's claims to a moral purpose for his stories should be evaluated in the light of the context of those claims. Head perhaps overstates his case, though:

> The strident emphasis on a moral programme implies that the text itself contains clear evidence of an authorial stance of disapprobation, and this implication glosses over the element of narrative ambiguity in the book. (Head 1992: 41)

Head's complaint about oversimplification is justified. But "programme" strays towards exaggeration for the sake of argument here. Finding a moral purpose in *Dubliners* does not require us to reduce the complexity of the text by finding it displaying such "clear evidence." Terence Brown's view is convincing:

> For Joyce the symbolic power of writing lay in its capacity, as if it were a kind of revelation or manifestation, to suggest mood, psychology, the moral significance of an

occasion, without . . . obtrusive authorial presence or palpable design upon a reader. (Joyce 2000: xxxiii)

The words "obtrusive" and "palpable" should not be overlooked here. And there is no need to discard Joyce's comments on the book completely. The moral purpose Joyce claimed in a letter to Grant Richards quoted by Brown, was to hold up a mirror to Dublin society (Joyce 2000: xv). This is Joyce's view of the moral stance of the artist, specifically not didactic or programmatic. Narrative ambiguities, ellipses, skillful use of point of view and free indirect style contribute to the withdrawal of the author, according to Flaubertian principle.

L'artiste doit être dans son oeuvre comme Dieu dans la création, invisible et tout-puissant; qu'on le sent partout, mais qu'on ne le voie pas. (Flaubert 1980: 219)

(The artist must be in his work like God is in creation, invisible and all-powerful; so that one is aware of him everywhere, but doesn't see him.)

Understanding of the stories grows as the reader absorbs the atmosphere Joyce creates in them. The paralysis he wrote of is clear in the seedy environment and impoverished (in different ways) lives of Dublin's inhabitants. The relationship between people and environment is explored in these stories in a way that suggests its dialectical nature: it is not just that people are constructed by their society, their economic position, and their moment in history, though to deny the impact of these forces would be foolish; it is also that the people so constructed contribute to the environment that constructs them. Through his representative characters and carefully crafted environment, Joyce illuminates the forces that determine, but in such a way that we can see those forces as imprisoning, binding, paralyzing. The atmosphere of *Dubliners*, and the characters' experience of isolation, relationship and its betrayal, domestic imprisonment, humiliation, and disillusionment, form the focus of the consideration of the stories that follows.

Even if we set aside Joyce's pronouncements for the moment, the first story in *Dubliners*, "The Sisters," sets up the shadow of Father Flynn, paralyzed priest, to loom over the rest of the collection. The story's young narrator adds resonance to the image with his repetition of the word on the first page:

it sounded to me like the name of some maleficent and sinful being. It filled me with fear, and yet I longed to be nearer to it and to look upon its deadly work. (Joyce 2000: 1)

The story introduces us to Joyce's method of creating uncertainty through the use of a point of view with limited understanding. Old Cotter cannot say in detail in the child narrator's presence, even if he knows, why precisely he would not want his own child to have associated with Father Flynn or, as he puts it even more damningly, "a man like that" (Joyce 2000: 2). Old Cotter says nothing of which the boy narrator can interpret the significance, but says it with apparent dark meaning. The first layer of an atmosphere of paralysis is laid down here by the literalization of metaphor, as is that of an atmosphere of immorality, and both are associated with the Church. Incomprehension of and fascination with these elements of atmosphere are conveyed through the restricted point of view of the boy narrator.

The book falls into sections of childhood, adolescence, maturity, and public life (Joyce 2000: xxxi). "Araby" is another story of childhood. The central character is a boy who has promised to bring from the bazaar a present for his friend's sister, on whom he has a "crush." The choice of her surname, Mangan, carries into the story an association of romantic, poetic love, through the allusion to the poet, James Clarence Mangan, also a Dubliner. It is a first-person narration, but seems to be told somewhat later, the narrator seeming older than the boy in the story.

Tension builds through the evening on which the boy is to visit the bazaar, Araby, as he waits for his uncle to return and give him the requisite money. In an indication of that lesson of growing up, that one's own concerns are not always important to others, the uncle has forgotten about the expedition. In one of those small textural knittings of the stories together that helps the atmosphere of *Dubliners* to be pervasive and cumulative, the garrulous Mrs Mercer provides "Araby" with an adult irritant equivalent to old Cotter in "The Sisters."

This tension of delay mirrors the sexual tension that the boy feels and does not understand, or sublimates into romantic notions. Joyce undercuts the romance early by the boy's furtive not-quite voyeurism in his peeping under the blind to observe the departure of Mangan's sister in the mornings so that he can follow her on his way to school. His feeling of superiority to the people around him, in those "places the most hostile to romance" (Joyce 2000: 22) where he accompanies his aunt shopping, is similar to the fastidiousness about contact with their fellow humans of Chandler in "A Little Cloud" and Duffy in "A Painful Case." In "I imagined that I bore my chalice safely through a throng of foes" (Joyce 2000: 23) the boy distinguishes himself, in another of those knittings of cohesiveness, from Father Flynn in "The Sisters," whose troubles are traced back by one of his sisters to his breaking of a chalice. Conclusions on what the safe bearing or breaking of a chalice might symbolize, and to whom, and whether there is a symbolic connection between the two stories as well as a structural one are left to the reader.

In imagining himself bearing his chalice, the boy also paints himself into the romantic figure of the pure knight, by association with, as Brown suggests, "the quest romance tale of the Holy Grail" (Joyce 2000: 252n14). Or the narrator so paints him, with ironic amusement at his younger self. The consciousness that shortly afterwards comments on the boy's "confused adoration" seems an older, more knowing one. In the moment of pseudo-climax that follows, the descriptive language is that of an older consciousness too, one self-conscious in its use of language: "Through one of the broken panes I heard the rain impinge upon the earth, the fine incessant needles of water playing in the sodden beds" (Joyce 2000: 23).

Whose consciousness is responsible for the further undercutting of boyish romance in the image of Mangan's sister at the railings?

> While she spoke she turned a silver bracelet round and round her wrist . . . I was alone at the railings. She held one of the spikes, bowing her head towards me. The light from the lamp opposite our door caught the white curve of her neck, lit up her hair that rested there and, falling, lit up the hand upon the railing. (Joyce 2000: 23–4)

This importing into the story of an overt sexuality different from the boy's consciousness of his feelings could be the work of the narrator as older version of the boy. It could be a later recognition of the sexual impulse that underlay his feelings for the girl even though he would not have thought of it as such at the time. But if this seems too much of a jeer at a younger self, then it could hint at the presence of a consciousness beyond that of the narrator, which has interesting consequences for the end of the story, the epiphany that, according to the orthodox approach to *Dubliners*, is the story's "point."

When the boy reaches Araby, that place of exotic Eastern promise, he finds it in the act of closing. The stall where he attempts to buy his present for Mangan's sister is staffed by a young woman more interested in flirting with two young men than attending to him. The two young men have English accents. Whether this is a mark of their being more important to the young woman than the boy, or a throwaway sign of the cultural hegemony of the metropolitan power, the boy is effectively dismissed. In simple terms, this is a story where the boy learns of his insignificance to others: that his uncle can forget about a trip of which he had been reminded; that a salesgirl can be uninterested in him. It is a story of childish disappointment: the bazaar is over when he gets there; the one moment of conversation he manages with the girl of his dreams leads to his failure to fulfill a promise to bring her a gift.

Susan Bazargan points out that "Araby" "is dominated by a narrative voice intent on calling attention to his *writing* and linguistic prowess as much as to the mere telling of the story" and asks, pertinently, to whom the story's final realization belongs (Bazargan 2004: 50–1). Head's interesting account of the story points out that at the conclusion, "the tone of mature reflection jars with the scene of adolescent humiliation," but also that, in the comparison of the hall with a church after a service, "the ironic religious allusion reveals a stance beyond the narrator, and this is typical of the complexity of the voice that pervades *Dubliners*" (Head 1992: 50–1).

It is in the nature of the stories of *Dubliners* to provoke questions about the narrative voice and what the author thinks of what it is saying. In stories like "Eveline" and "Little Chandler" one is aware of the use of free indirect style and how it enables variation of the distance between the narrative voice and the consciousness of the character, sometimes moving right into the thoughts of the character. The variability of this distance leads to an element of interpretive instability. When is there irony at the character's expense, and to what extent?

"Gazing up into the darkness I saw myself as a creature driven and derided by vanity; and my eyes burned with anguish and anger" (Joyce 2000: 28). The balanced alliteration of "driven and derided" and "anguish and anger" is enough to call our attention to the importance of how this sentence sounds to . . . someone. It is tempting to say that there is enough, at the level of content, from what happens in the story – let alone its evocation of the childish "crush" – for the story to give a satisfying image of disappointment, humiliation, unjustified shame, and frustrated anger, feelings that are part of growing up. The last sentence could be the narrator's vanity, putting the realistically evoked feelings into fine words. They could be the distortion of these feelings in the attempt to remember and represent them. They could be the result of the consciousness that lies outside that of the narrator and is able to exhibit with irony the mildly pathetic attempt of fine language to convey a sensation that would have been much more real to the consciousness of the boy who experienced it. Clearly, the simpler way to read the story is to see the big build-up to the moment of epiphany, the self-realization in the boy's final description of himself. But it is an anti-climactic realization of anti-climax. Putting it in play with other readings suggested by the stance of narrator to boy and of the implied further consciousness to the narrator creates a more suggestive instability.

In the next story, the technique of knitting in cohesion is evident in Eveline's leaning against the curtains as the boy in "Araby" leans his head against the cool glass of the front window. She is subject, too, to romantic notions, seeing in Frank the figure of the rescuing hero who will take her away to a better life. The use of free indirect style taking the narrative voice into the thoughts of the central character is clear in, for instance, "Ernest, however, never played: he was too grown up" (Joyce 2000: 29). "He was awfully fond of music and sang a little" (Joyce 2000: 32) gives part of her view of Frank in her words. The technique helps us to share her feelings but allows enough distance for us to be more likely to share her father's distrust of Frank.

We are taken through Eveline's thoughts about her violent, potentially abusive father, but also allowed her point of view on the security of the familiar and of home. The homely dust of the curtain she inhales in the opening of the story stands for the pervasive comfort of the familiar, and perhaps its deadening, paralyzing quality. Her "watching the evening invade the avenue" points to her perception of what comes from outside as threatening. We should not be too surprised, then, when she does not go with Frank: "All the seas of the world tumbled about her heart. He was drawing her into them: he would drown her" (Joyce 2000: 34). Her final stance, though passive, is obdurate.

We could see this story as showing the way in which women are oppressed by a sense of domestic duty: Eveline promised her now dead mother that she would look after the family. Joyce's letter to Nora Barnacle, which Brown quotes in his introduction to *Dubliners*, suggests that we could make the comparison with how Joyce saw his own mother, sacrificed to a brutal system (Joyce 2000: ix). We could also see the reflection in the story of how the paralyzed city renders its citizens paralyzed as individuals: they are unable to act to free themselves; they are weak and cling to what is familiar rather than striking out for what might be freedom and a better life. But without getting into excessive clue-hunting, we should allow the voice of Eveline's father to give us pause – "I know these sailor chaps" (Joyce 2000: 32) – and consider that although her view is deliberately presented to us as immature, she still, maybe, has the sense not to go with Frank, rather than lacking the initiative, desire for freedom, or courage to leave.

If the dangers are not clear from the narrative, there are other clues. Frank's name may be ironic; Eveline's idea of "open-hearted" may not be our idea of honest. Eveline is Eveline Hill; Fanny Hill in Cleland's novel *Memoirs of a Woman of Pleasure* is led into prostitution. Frank is to take Eveline to Buenos Aires; the phrase "Going to Buenos Aires" was slang for becoming a prostitute (Joyce 2000: 254–5n9). Katherine Mullins's contribution to Attridge and Howes's *Semicolonial Joyce* gives fascinating detail on Irish emigration to Argentina, "Eveline," and *The Irish Homestead*, for which the story was written (Attridge and Howes 2000). Readings that see Eveline as the victim of a social system oppressive to women are obviously still available. Those open to the spirit of romance, or desperate enough to escape domestic drudgery to hear its voice in the mercenary seducer, or desperate and naive enough to project the forms of romantic imagination on to the superficially likely lad, are vulnerable and likely to escape to worse. The story offers a critical view of what is available for Dublin's women. It deals with domestic imprisonment, paralysis, and the dangers of the false hope offered by romantic imagination.

"A Little Cloud" takes up the theme of domestic imprisonment from a different angle. Chandler envies the freedom of the life abroad that his friend Gallaher seems to enjoy. Free indirect style shows us the admiration Chandler feels for Gallaher: "It was something to have a friend like that" (Joyce 2000: 65). His description as slightly effeminate and fastidious about his appearance contrasts with the coarser Gallaher, with his "large closely cropped head" (Joyce 2000: 69–70). At their meeting, Chandler shifts from admiration to some resentment. His envy of his friend's freedom and access to excitement in comparison to his own situation will gnaw at him more when he returns home.

The agonistic element in male friendship is brought home by Chandler's determination to discomfort Gallaher by insisting that one day he too will marry, "put your head in the sack" (Joyce 2000: 76). Gallaher's bravado and the suggestion of the mercenary degradation of relationship and marriage, evident also in "Two Gallants" and "The Boarding House," are not enough to convince us that he has shrugged off Chandler's moment of self-assertion. He in his turn is subject to at least a moment's anxiety that he may be missing something that his friend has. His introduction of the topic of Chandler's marriage – "tasted the joys of connubial bliss" (Joyce 2000: 74) – suggests bantering irony as well as the use of conventional language, but there follows an acknowledgment of Chandler's having proved his manhood in the fathering of a son. Any sexism here is Gallaher's; Chandler says, "*We* have one child."

There is something of the Yeatsian opposition of poet and journalist in this story, but Joyce makes clear his contempt for the style of poetry designed to supply an English taste for green-tinged sentimentality in Chandler's imagining of the notices his verse might receive if he could write and publish it: "*A wistful sadness pervades these poems . . . The Celtic note*" (Joyce 2000: 69). His self-consciousness – "Melancholy was the dominant note of his temperament, he thought, but it was a melancholy tempered by recurrences of faith and resignation and simple joy" (Joyce 2000: 68) – leads us to mistrust the authenticity of his feelings. The image of the autumn sunset "cast[ing] a shower of kindly golden dust" (Joyce 2000: 65) seems one of those uses of free indirect speech that allow Joyce's narrator to enter the linguistic style of a character for ironic effect. Chandler is cast as a poor aspirant to poetry. The dust's being cast on "untidy nurses and decrepit old men" may show the flexibility of this kind of narration, with Chandler's tired "poetic" image failing to cover the real presentation of real, human Dublin people. The closeness in the text of "his tiresome writing" (Chandler is a clerk) may be a little joke from the narrator at his expense. "He felt how useless it was to struggle against fortune, this being the burden of wisdom which the ages had bequeathed to him" (Joyce 2000: 66) seems both a statement of the character's sense of imprisonment and paralysis and of that character's inability to express it through anything other than the tired sentimental stoicism that is his proper idiom.

The way Chandler "pick[s] his way deftly through all that minute vermin-like life" of the children of the city, giving them "no thought" (Joyce 2000: 66), shows a kind of fastidiousness, a keeping of oneself untouched and apart that reminds the reader of the boy bearing his chalice in "Araby" and of James Duffy in "A Painful Case." In Chandler's case, his deftness is ironically returned when later his wife "put the sleeping child deftly in his arms" (Joyce 2000: 77). His reaction to Gallaher's talk is to resent that he has missed the passion he thinks should be a part of his life. That he feels his home is a prison is emphasized in the sounds of "prim" and "pretty," the words used to describe his wife and the furniture she has chosen. His life does not match his aspirations, but the language used to describe the frustration of his situation and his feelings – "the melancholy of his soul," "He was a prisoner for life" (Joyce 2000: 79–80) – seems in excess of the character. It is Chandler's view of his own situation that is melodramatic and sentimentally self-pitying. The return of his wife and her uncannily accurate accusation – "What have you done to him?" – complete his humiliation and sense of inadequacy.

As the character's realization of inadequacy, though, the epiphany does not offer stability for the interpreter, who is unlikely to trust Chandler's judgment, and may think of the likely temporary nature of the influence that provoked the breaking of the power of his habitually cultivated sentimental stoicism to console him for the shortcomings of his life. Our response to Chandler's sense of his predicament may be influenced by the more obvious entrapment of Doran in the preceding story, "The Boarding House." If Gallaher's bravado leads us to think of the tawdrily immoral Dublin reflected in "Two Gallants," "The Boarding House" makes us think of the mercenary exploitation of bourgeois morality, as Doran's fear over the possible loss of his job if he is reported to have behaved immorally is used to lever him into marriage. Mrs Mooney's passive connivance in allowing the opportunity for immorality shows her worse than those who merely break the rules. This story offers a fierce critique of a society in thrall to a hypocritical morality. Any contempt we feel for Chandler should be tempered by Farrington's beating of his son in response to his own humiliation in the story that follows "A Little Cloud," "Counterparts."

In "A Painful Case," the Nietzsche-reading central character, James Duffy, fancies that he has detached himself from convention, but his reaction to Mrs Sinico's physical reaching out to him and to the report of her death show him as all too heavily in thrall to bourgeois morality. He is so far imprisoned that he feels pain and humiliation at the thought of having spoken of things he holds sacred to a woman who later degraded herself through drink. It is possible to see Duffy as damaged by the morality he has internalized, as it has led him to repress his homo-sexuality. This would explain his retreat from the advances of Mrs Sinico once they become interpretable as sexual, and his note that "Love between man and man is impossible because there must not be sexual intercourse and friendship between man and woman is impossible because there must be sexual intercourse" (Joyce 2000: 108).

It is also possible to see Duffy as the victim of a paralyzing self-consciousness (evi-denced by his habit of self-commentary). It would be easy to find no sympathy with such a remote character. He has too little understanding of others to realize how Mrs Sinico will interpret his discourses on "the soul's incurable loneliness," and his disap-pointment seems to stem from the loss of what she as a companion could give to him, without thought of her feelings. His abandonment of her on their last meeting, "fearing another collapse on her part" (Joyce 2000: 108), could be the final blow to the reader's sympathy for him.

But the moral tone of his response to reading the report of her death – "He had no difficulty now in approving of the course he had taken" (Joyce 2000: 112) – indi-cates Duffy's own imprisonment by the judgmental morality that, as Patrick Bixby suggests, he has internalized (Bixby 2004: 112–21), perhaps the paralyzing effect of Dublin society on him and what might have been his humanity. His moment of self-realization is given an afterthought that is either a further chilling diminishment of his earlier self-importance or strikes a note of sardonic mockery: "His life would be lonely too until he, too, died, ceased to exist, became a memory – if anyone remem-bered him" (Joyce 2000: 113). It is a moment of thought for Mrs Sinico that shatters his moral certainty: "Why had he withheld life from her? Why had he sentenced her to death? He felt his moral nature falling to pieces." This perhaps exposes the selfish-ness of his moral nature; it cannot stand up to this forced consideration of another. There is also the possibility of reading here, though, his continuing self-absorption and self-centeredness in his attribution of her decline and death to his rebuff. The "rectitude of his life," left to him to gnaw, having been "outcast from life's feast" (Joyce 2000: 113), has become unsatisfying. In the story's final moment, just as he fears not being remembered, he finds that his memory of Mrs Sinico is lost. He is alone.

His looking at a Dublin, whose lights "burned redly and hospitably in the cold night" (Joyce 2000: 113), shows us, when we consider his choice to live as far away from Dublin as he can, the element of self-imposition in his solitude. The fact that in his talks with Mrs Sinico he hears a "strange impersonal voice which he recognised as his own" (Joyce 2000: 107) shows a deliberate self-distancing from life, and a deliberate reserving to himself of some part of himself. The story can be read as an indication of the imprisoning nature of social codes when they so tightly construct an individual or when he so rigidly internalizes them, perhaps especially when they are at odds with some part of himself that he is thereby forced to repress. It can also be read as an indication of the danger of withholding oneself from emotional life and of intellectualizing rather than experiencing emotion.

The stories of *Dubliners* generate a texture in the relationship between characters and environment through the cumulative evocation of atmosphere. Characters are shown as part of that atmosphere, not just as subject to it. Joyce's technique, throwing into doubt to whom thoughts, values, or uses of language can be attributed, leads to instability in interpretation: one is aware both of the determining forces of environment on the individual, and of the individual's moments of potential freedom.

REFERENCES AND FURTHER READING

Attridge, D. and Howes, M. (eds) (2000). *Semicolonial Joyce*. Cambridge: Cambridge University Press.

Bazargan, S. (2004). "Epiphany as Scene of Performance," in O. Frawley (ed.), *A New and Complex Sensation: Essays on Joyce's Dubliners*, pp. 44–54. Dublin: Lilliput.

Bixby, P. (2004). "Perversion and the Press: Victorian Self-fashioning in 'A Painful Case'," in O. Frawley (ed.), *A New and Complex Sensation: Essays on Joyce's Dubliners*, pp. 112–21. Dublin: Lilliput Press.

Flaubert, G. (1980). *Correspondance*, vol. 2, ed. J. Bruneau. Paris: Gallimard.

Frawley, O. (ed.) (2004). *A New and Complex Sensation: Essays on Joyce's Dubliners*. Dublin: Lilliput Press.

Head, D. (1992). *The Modernist Short Story: A Study in Theory and Practice*. Cambridge: Cambridge University Press.

Joyce, J. (1988). *A Portrait of the Artist as a Young Man*. London: Paladin (original work published 1916).

Joyce, J. (2000). *Dubliners*, ed. Terence Brown. London: Penguin (original work published 1914).

14

H.G. Wells's Short Stories: "The Country of the Blind" and "The Door in the Wall"

Sabine Coelsch-Foisner

H.G. Wells's short stories, most of them published between 1894 and 1906, constitute an important corpus in his *oeuvre*, both as regards their immense popularity and their imaginative scope. Given Wells's commercial success and the periodicals' general readiness to print short stories, among them *The National Observer, The New Review, The Fortnightly Review, Longman's Magazine*, and *The Yellow Book*, Wells was convinced that the 1890s was "a good and stimulating period for a short-story writer" (Wells 1911: 8), yielding far more and better stories as well as higher standards of criticism than the commencing twentieth century. Still, the generic status of these stories is difficult to define, partly because they were written at the same time as the scientific romances and, together with these and the early journalistic work, bear testimony to the extraordinary inventive power of Wells's mind; partly because the more systematic body of ideas shaping his increasingly committed writings after he had joined the London Fabian Society in 1903 has tended to overshadow his early speculative work.

Wells's own comments on his short fiction complicate the question of genre. In his introduction to the thirty-three stories he wished to preserve in *The Country of the Blind* (1911), – a selection from his four preceding collections, *The Stolen Bacillus and Other Incidents* (1895), *The Plattner Story and Others* (1897), *Tales of Space and Time* (1899), and *Twelve Stories and a Dream* (1903), together with some uncollected work – he stresses the variety of topics and moods ("it may be horrible or pathetic or funny or beautiful or profoundly illuminating") and suggests that the stories should be received in a "spirit of miscellaneous expectation," each being "a thing by itself." Wells was reluctant to define the form except in terms of length ("having only this essential, that it should take from fifteen to fifty minutes to read aloud"; Wells 1911: 10) and warned critics against treating "the short story as though it was as definable a form as the sonnet" (9). However, when in the same compilation he tries to account for his "diversion of attention to more sustained and more exacting forms" (7), he implicitly suggests aesthetic criteria for the short story, calling it a "compact, amusing form" and associating it with a sense of "ease and happiness in the garden of one's fancies" (9). Brevity, an essential criterion for publication, proved conducive to Wells's fertile imagination: "I became quite dextrous in evolving situations and anecdotes from little possibilities of a scientific or quasi-scientific sort" (Wells 1934: 433). In 1911, he could not foresee the impact of exploring such "little possibilities" within the framework of the "single sitting story" on twentieth-century concepts of the short story. To demonstrate how Wells's restless desire to invent and invert life is rooted in late Victorian and early Edwardian culture, while expanding the experiential horizon of this generic framework, two of his best-known stories will be examined: "The Country of the Blind" (1904) and "The Door in the Wall" (1906).

Victorian plant-hunting, scientific discoveries, evolutionary theory, and the uncomfortable questions it unleashed, imperialism, and the preoccupation with consciousness and states of dreaming provided late Victorian writers with a rich background for exploring the unfamiliar or unknown, whether in primitive or scientifically advanced settings. Both "The Door in the Wall" and "The Country of the Blind" are fantastic encounters with alternative realms of life and, to this end, like the scientific romances (see Stableford 1985: 4; Aldiss 1986: 25; Wolfe 1986: 113), draw on a variety of available forms and currents in prose writing: gothic, romance, utopia, travel literature and exploration narratives, menippean satire, fairytale and fantasy, philosophical enquiry, and scientific exposition. "The Door in the Wall" deals with a favorite Wellsian theme: the intrusion of mysterious forces into everyday life, which underlies many of his stories (for example, "The Sea Raiders," "The Flowering of the Strange Orchid," "The Beautiful Suit"). "The Country of the Blind" reverses this pattern and presents the protagonist venturing into an alien territory, as in "The Valley of Spiders," "The Empire of the Ants," "The Plattner Story," or "The Magic Shop." In extrapolating from the known to the unknown, Wells introduced his readers to new subject matter in the manner of scientific writing, without limiting the fantastic dimension to (pseudo-)science, while stimulating reflection in the manner of utopian literature, without implying the need for improvement of the status quo quintessential in utopianism. The worlds which Wells allows his readers to visit are not necessarily more or less humane, nor are they evolutionary dystopias or static utopian islands of bliss; they are essentially *different* – a term emphatically used in "The Door in the Wall" to describe the protagonist's sojourn in a wonderful garden.

Difference is the crux on which Wells's early aesthetic hinges. His stories create an awareness of irrational forces potentially coexisting with rational arrangements of life and, in this way, suggest the relative value of these arrangements. The "little possibilities" lying at the heart of his stories are all the more powerful for remaining *possibilities* and for leaving the reader in an unresolved state of hesitation. Wells's speculative stories are fantastic in a pragmatic sense, incessantly posing riddles without offering solutions. They have been labelled "pure fantasies" by critics usually praising the storyteller's original genius over the committed writer's didactic interests and his dedication to pamphleteering (Bergonzi 1961: 88). Still, "pure fantasy" in these stories is more than an intellectual game or *jeu d'esprit*. It is characteristically balanced by serious reasoning, by that "urgency for coherence and consistency" which science had taught him (Wells 1934: 1, 210):

> I found that, taking almost anything as a starting-point and letting my thoughts play about it, there would presently come out of the darkness, in a manner quite inexplicable, some absurd or vivid little incident more or less relevant to the initial nucleus. Little men in canoes upon sunlit oceans would come floating out of nothingness, incubating the eggs of prehistoric monsters unawares; violent conflicts would break out amidst the flower-beds of suburban gardens; I would discover I was peering into remote and mysterious worlds ruled by an order logical indeed but other than our common sanity. (Wells 1911: 8)

By projecting a different world order, Wells's speculative stories acquire a philosophical depth that places them at the crossroads between gothic mystery and the marvels of fantasy, on the one hand, and science-fictional explanation, on the other hand. Their logic is alternative rather than corrective and as such consistent with Wells's notion of plasticity, developed in his scientific writings and essentially connected with the "opposite idea," a term coined in "Zoological Regression" (1891; Philmus 1975) to counter rigid laws, especially those aligned with optimistic evolution. In the stories, little or apparently insignificant objects (a door, a suit, a harmless bacillus, an orchid), incidents or missions (a fall in the mountains, fighting an invasion of ants) are apt to trigger the most fanciful flights of the imagination and cause insoluble tensions between the mundane world and hinted realms beyond. "The Door in the Wall" and "The Country of the Blind" are representative of Wells's plastic outlook in that they do not so much subvert or supplant rational beliefs and assumptions as they *test* them, creating a richly suggestive symbolism while employing the prevalent discourses of empirical science, didactic exposition, and moral justification. The result is a profound skepticism, with regard to both the unknown *and* the known.

In both stories, the disappearance or death of a character, a vestigial echo of gothic sensationalism, furnishes material evidence of the impact which the supernatural has upon the real, while sealing the impenetrability of its meaning. In "The Door in the Wall," Lionel Wallace is all his life lured by a mysterious green door in a white wall. When he is eventually found dead in a railway excavation to which a little doorway in the hoarding led, the reader is left with a puzzle as to the nature of Wallace's experience: Was he merely deluded by the door in the hoarding? Or did the mysterious green door beckon death from his early childhood? And if so, how are we to explain the enchanted garden into which Wallace once came when entering the door as a child? Was it a daydream, a lie, a sign of the boy's vivid imagination, or a token of a hidden dimension accessible only to a "visionary" like Wallace? The questions remain unanswered and, what is more disturbing, the reader feels there *is* no answer to them, just as there is no answer why the little man who breaks out of his room one night, wearing his best suit, is found dead in the morning ("The Beautiful Suit").

The failure to understand what death means for the individual is inexorable in either story.

A similar sense of openness pervades Wells's explorative stories, with an individual or a group of people penetrating into strange, remote, or exotic regions and commonly faced with a different stage in evolutionary history. Both "The Valley of Spiders" and "The Empire of the Ants" appeal to archetypal fears of aggressive insects attacking the human body. Still, the ants do not so much serve the creation of horror as they call into question the superiority of civilization over primitive forms of life. Revealing Wells's obvious debt to Darwin and, especially, to T.H. Huxley, whose lectures he had heard at the Normal School of Science in South Kensington, evolution in these stories proves far more disconcerting than suggested in *The Descent of Man* (1871). Conceived of as a multi- or a-linear process that does not necessarily privilege *homo sapiens*, evolution is likely to imply the degeneration of the *genus humanum*, with lower creatures rivaling man's place in the universe. Wells's ants are gigantic – up to five centimetres – and have developed eyes and a brain, which enable them to operate intelligently rather than instinctively, i.e., with foresight and hindsight. Their poisonous weapons, possibly manufactured rather than being phenotypical extensions of their mutated bodies, prove superior to man-made technologies, and their strategic operations surpass human intelligence.

Systematically preyed upon by inferior species – spiders, ants, and octopuses – man is not necessarily the apex of evolution, nor is he the lord of the future. In Wells's speculative stories, evolution is prone to reverse, as in *The Time Machine*, with the biological logic working backwards from differentiation towards loss of specificity and eventual lifelessness. In a different environment, the fittest are those best adapted to the changed conditions. Thus the tentacles of a vampire orchid attack an unsuspecting plant-lover; the "sea raiders" endanger the contented life of an English village; and the more formidable Martians from *The War of the Worlds* prey on planet earth. The borderline between the real and the impossible is blurred by the actual casualties of such fantastically mutated or otherworldly species. These as well as the many instances of (quasi-)scientific explanation, such as the information about *Haploteuthis ferox* opening "The Sea Raiders," or the closing calculation of the year when the predatory ants will have conquered Europe, are not only superb instances of Wells's irony but a deft gambit by which the triumphs of modern civilization are made to appear slight, its optimism complacent. The invader becomes the invaded. The same pattern inheres in "The Country of the Blind" and, as a comparison with the 1939 version of the story shows, accounts for its plasticity.

Drawing on evolutionary, utopian, and imperialist paradigms, "The Country of the Blind" does not subscribe to any of these. Nunez is a mountaineer who has a fatal fall in the Andes, but survives and finds himself in the legendary valley of the blind. Motivated by adventure and the proverb "The One-Eyed Man is King in the Land of the Blind," his naive ambition to teach the blind the practical value of sight is doomed to failure, because blindness is neither an evolutionary defect nor a hereditary disease: it *is* evolution, envisaged as regressive. After fifteen generations, lack of sight is no longer perceived as an ailment by those affected, but represents the norm on the basis of which a wholly different world picture, philosophy, religion, and reason have been established. For the blind, their enclosed valley constitutes the world, sheltered by a cosmic roof and divided into cold and warm times, instead of night and day, which accordingly determine their shifts of work and rest.

The multiple subversive twists in the story are unsettling. What according to the legends appears to be a pastoral utopia – "The valley [. . .] had in it all that the heart of man could desire – sweet water, pasture, end even climate, slopes of rich brown soil" (Wells 1911: 345) – is denigrated by the inhabitants' blindness. Yet, the fact that evolution has wiped out sight with the only seeing man succumbing to the higher sensory faculties of the blind fundamentally challenges ameliorative concepts of evolution, hotly debated by leading scientists in Wells's time. The very idea of utopia is called into question, for not only is Nunez's civilized perspective pre-evolutionary, but his experience of life among the blind is distinctly dystopian. Tracing the rationale of a tribe living in blindness, Wells hints at the relativity of the attitudes and beliefs by which the seeing structure their world. To the blind, sight causes "constant irritation and distraction" (Wells 1911: 362) and is deemed a sign of insanity and depravity. Nunez's sense of superiority, which is both naive and arrogant, turns back on him: the outsider who attempts to impose the shape of his culture on to the new world is humiliated and persecuted. His language and his poetry prove inadequate in the light of a linguistic system without reference to the visual world. Significantly, he does not name the land in the manner of a colonizer but is himself renamed by the blind. Miscegenation is forbidden, too, and to marry the girl he loves, Nunez agrees to have his eyes removed, but eventually changes his mind and escapes into the mountains that separate the country of the blind from the civilization of Bogota.

Wells develops the imaginary encounter between one seeing man and a blind tribe into an irreconcilable confrontation between radically different societies and different stages of evolution. While the pervasive irony of the story brings to the fore its political undertone (Boulton 1995), using the ethical, biological, and social modes of justification characteristic of traditional conversion narratives against the imperialist cultivator ("Four days passed, and the fifth found the King of the Blind still incognito, as a clumsy and useless stranger among his subjects" (Wells 1911: 355)), the unmerciful subjugation of the intruder carries uneasy connotations. After doubting the validity of his own world, Nunez eventually prefers sight to marriage and social integration, but the evolutionary disparities persist, and the supremacy of reason appears doubtful in the light of *other* convictions:

And blind philosophers came and talked to him so impressively for his doubts about the lid of rock that covered their cosmic casserole that he almost doubted whether indeed he was not the victim of hallucination in not seeing it overhead. So Nunez became a citizen of the Country of the Blind, and these people ceased to be a generalized people and became individualities and familiar to him, while the world beyond the mountains became more and more remote and unreal. (Wells 1911: 360)

Such shifts of perspective or "standpoint" are a hallmark of Wells's aesthetic and, recalling the dialectic method of his scientific writings ("The Duration of Life," 1895; Phlimus 1975), guarantee the disturbing effect of both "The Country of the Blind" and "The Door in the Wall." In each story, hesitation is the result of mysterious phenomena and enshrined in the narrative.

Wells's typical narrator is either fantastically omniscient or a skeptical persona struggling against his own disbelief. Either way, he allows for the widest possible conception of reality, both in spatial and temporal terms, following characters into remote, otherworldly, or forgotten lands, communicating occult incidents, and even rising from the grave to be granted a new lease of life together with the whole of mankind on a different planet ("A Vision of Judgment"). Whether he is directly involved or a self-conscious mediator anxious to establish his credibility, his position typically straddles the boundaries between the strange and the everyday, while his rhetoric commonly serves the creation of plausibility. Though at times unfavorably compared with more daring modernist experiments in form (Orel 1986; Beachcroft 1968: 156), Wells's "unembellished" language and "absence of technical distinction" has been more positively seen as serving the free play of his imagination and his superb gift of playing with the reader's curiosity (Ward 1924: 131; Bates 1941: 109–10, Bergonzi 1961:70–1; Shaw 1983: 205). Wells proves a "Realist of the Fantastic," to use Joseph Conrad's phrase (Aubry 1927:1, 259–60), in the sense that he employs elements of literary realism and a semi-documentary style for fantastic purposes. Apart from specifying time and place, naming characters, and offering detailed descriptions of scenes, settings, or situations, Wells's stories are marked by strategies of persuasion. Characteristically, they provide for situations of telling and listening in which the narrator piques his readers' interest by anticipating their suspicion and self-consciously exhibiting his bewilderment. Wells's narrators are obsessed with their own reliability and insist on the authenticity of their stories, frequently calling upon reports and legends.

"The Door in the Wall" is a frame story. Redmond, the outer narrator, reports a conversation with his friend, the eminent politician Lionel Wallace, literally transcribing the latter's confessional account of a mysterious incident in his life. As a child Wallace had a vision of a green door in a white wall, through which he walked into a paradisal garden rich in mythological associations of joy and harmony. The door appeared several more times in his life, usually at crucial moments: when he won a scholarship to Oxford, when appointed to the Cabinet, and when his father was dying. Each time he ardently desired the door, but each time he rejected it in favor of more pressing concerns. Now, approaching middle age, he desperately longs for the door to lead him once more into this wonderful garden.

The disruptive power of the story rests upon Redmond, whose task is to convince the reader that his is a "true story" and that the solitary vision of a promising politician carries far greater weight than Wallace's immediate environment was apt to realize. For this purpose, he repeatedly asserts his trustworthiness, confessing to the reader his initial disbelief and, thereby, skillfully dispelling the latter's potential reservations. Uncertainty is built into the text at multiple levels: Redmond holds an exclusive right to Wallace's secret, which he passes on to the reader and, like the latter, is a listener who cannot verify or falsify the strange events told to him. Whenever Wallace had revealed his story, he met with doubt and hostility: he was punished by his father, called a liar by his aunt, and ridiculed by his classmates. Even Wallace himself, to whom "the Door in the Wall was a real door, leading through a real wall to immortal realities" (Wells 1911: 331), had his moments of doubt. This carefully constructed conflict between the real and the fantastic sets the pattern of Wallace's subsequent visions: whenever the door appears, duty calls, or vice versa. The garden, with its tame panthers and joyous playmates, becomes a haunting alternative, promising a life redolent with joy and "a keen sense of home-coming" (1911: 333), while painfully alerting Wallace to the shortcomings of his life: his stern father, his absent mother, fear, and conflict. This dual perspective is strengthened when an old woman shows the boy a book. It mirrors his real life until the moment he steps into the garden: "They were realities – yes, they must have been; people moved and things came and went in them" (335). Vicariously assuming the life of the living, the device of the book blends traditions of gothic, romance, and the fairy tale, while imparting a sterner utopian note to Wallace's recognition of the unrealized potentialities of his life. Subtly pointing ahead to the allegorical strain in Wells's later work, the door harbors a more complex vision than merely inverting the status quo or furnishing a key to Wallace's repressed emotional life. Neither psychology nor poetic irony has the final word. Wallace dies when he passes through a door in a hoarding and falls into a shaft. His dead body encapsulates an unfathomable mystery whose potency the narrator confirms in a semi-didactic gesture, once more pre-empting the reader's enquiry: "By our daylight standard he walked out of security into darkness, danger, and death. But did he see like that?" (344).

The narrator of "The Country of the Blind" leads us into an equally strange realm, this time conceived in topographical terms as a "mysterious mountain valley" which lies "in the wildest wastes on Ecuador's Andes" (Wells 1911: 345). The storyteller embarks on a *tour de force*, attempting to bridge the time span from the first population of this valley to its unique existence in the consciousness of a single visitor who is reported dead when the story begins and nearing his death when it ends. The story of this visitor, "a mountaineer from the country near Quito" (347), is established as part of a long tradition of legends and loose narratives which are joined together in an effort to overcome the gap between myth and speculation. For, to tell his story, the narrator has to adopt a fantastic standpoint and, to dissemble the vast impossibilities with which he is going to present his readers, he again inserts moments of uncertainty in his otherwise extraordinary panoramic account of the country of the blind, its history and inhabitants: "But the rest of his story of mischances is lost to me, save that I know of his evil death after several years" (346).

After this tortuous beginning, the narrator focuses on Nunez, the mountaineer. According to reports he had a fatal accident when guiding a group of English mountain climbers:

> The story of the accident has been written a dozen times. Pointer's narrative is the best. [. . .] Unnerved by this disaster, they abandoned their attempt in the afternoon, and Pointer was called away to the war before he could make another attack. To this day Parascotepetl lifts an unconquered crest, and Pointer's shelter crumbles unvisited amidst the snows. And the man who fell survived. (Wells 1911: 347–8)

This strikingly casual observation marks the shift from official documentation to fantasy. The narrator slips into the consciousness of the mountaineer and accompanies him as he vanishes from sight and lands in the valley of the blind, "cut off from the exploring feet of men" (Wells 1911: 345).

"The Country of the Blind" is an intriguing thought experiment, both thematically and technically. To make the reader see a different world through the eyes of one man who is left to die in the end is an extraordinary act of narrative dexterity. When climbing up the mountains at the end of the story, bruised from the stone and completely alone, Nunez has lost none of his reality for the reader, so that he can even glorify his freedom in an ecstatic poetic vision: "his imagination soared over them [the rocks, the sunlit ice and snow] to the things beyond he was now to resign forever" (1911: 364). Nunez's escape celebrates the power of imaginative literature over the exigencies of a world which, it suggests, is potentially richer, more variegated, and less fixed than it appears through the lenses of reason, duty, and science, persistently challenged in Wells's short stories. The end is open, but whether the lonely traveler survives or dies seems of little importance once it has been made clear that the vision he carries with him is *one* version of the world in a potential plethora of versions, all incompatible with one another and unlikely to be understood in Bogota, i.e., in real life.

Such unresolved tension, uncertainty, and shifts of standpoint affording fantastic glimpses into genuinely different worlds or modes of existence, are the gift of Wells's short fiction. They are the legacy of a great storyteller to the modern short story with its sense of openness, ambiguity, and interiority. Generically hybrid, Wells's speculative stories coincide with a formative phase in the development of the fantastic: far from declaring the unreality or impossibility of the events presented, they resort to strategies of realism, didactic discourse, and scientific exposition. The illusion of reality becomes indistinguishable from reality. In this, Wells's inventive stories open up a vast potential for tracing the magic within the real and the real within the magic. Precisely by interlocking alternative realms and progressively dismantling the frames setting off fantastic excursions, dreams or nightmares from the real world, Wells emphasizes the relative value of what constitutes our familiar world and our humanity. Calling into doubt social hierarchies, moral standards, and evolutionary processes by tracing opposite ways of looking at phenomena and events, his stories advocate the ultimately humanizing value of transgressive worlds – without reducing them to social allegories or vehicles of any particular ideology. Widening his readers' horizons of experience and expectation, Wells's short stories withhold answers in favor of disturbing insights into the value and validity of "little possibilities."

REFERENCES AND FURTHER READING

Aldiss, B. (1986). *Trillion Year Spree: The History of Science Fiction*. New York: Athenaeum.

Allen, W. (1981). *The Short Story in English*. Oxford: Clarendon.

Appleman, Philip (ed.) (1979). *Darwin: A Norton Critical Edition*, 2nd edn. New York and London: Norton.

Aubry, J.G. (ed.) (1927). *Joseph Conrad: Life and Letters*. Garden City: Doubleday Page.

Bates, H.E. (1941; 1972). *The Modern Short Story: A Critical Survey*. London: Michael Joseph.

Beachcroft, T.O. (1968). *The Modest Art: A Survey of the Short Story in English*. London: Oxford University Press.

Bergonzi, B. (1961). *The Early H.G. Wells: A Study of the Scientific Romances*. Manchester: Manchester University Press.

Boulton, A. (1995). "The Myth of the New Found Land in H.G. Wells's 'The Country of the Blind'," *The Wellsian* 18: 5–18.

Clute, J. and Grant, J. (eds) (1997). *The Encyclopedia of Fantasy*. New York: St Martin's Press.

Dickson, L. (1969). *H.G. Wells: His Turbulent Life and Times*. London: Macmillan.

Eilers, M.L. (2000). "On the Origins of Modern Fantasy," *Extrapolation* 41/4: 317–37.

Orel, H. (1986). "Joseph Conrad and H.G. Wells: Two Different Concepts of the Short-story Genre," *Literary Half-Yearly* 27: 2–25.

Philmus, R.M. (ed.) (1975). *H.G. Wells: Early Writings in Science and Science Fiction*. Berkeley, Calif.: University of California Press.

Schlobin, R.C. (ed.) (1982). *The Aesthetics of Fantasy Literature and Art*. Notre Dame, Indiana: University of Notre Dame Press; Brighton: Harvester Press.

Searles, A.L. (1991). "Concerning 'The Country of the Blind'," *The Wellsian* 14: 29–33.

Shaw, V. (1983). *The Short Story: A Critical Introduction*. London and New York: Longman.

Smith, D.C. (1986). *H.G. Wells: Desperately Mortal: A Biography*. New Haven and London: Yale University Press.

Stableford, B. (1985). *Scientific Romance in Britain: 1890–1950*. London: Fourth Estate.

Ward, A.C. (1924). *Aspects of the Modern Short Story: English and American*. London: London University Press.

Wells, H.G. (1911). *The Country of the Blind and Other Stories*. London: Aegypan Press.

Wells, H.G. (1934). *Experiment in Autobiography*. New York: Macmillan.

Wolfe, G.K. (ed.) (1986). *Critical Terms for Science Fiction and Fantasy: A Glossary and Guide to Scholarship*. Westport, Conn.: Greenwood Press.

15

D.H. Lawrence's Short Stories: "The Horse Dealer's Daughter" and "The Rocking Horse Winner"

Kathryn Miles

In his seminal essay on D.H. Lawrence, nature writer Scott Sanders asks readers a question that has plagued scholars for decades: "why do we continue to read Lawrence until the corners wear off his books, until the edges wear off his imagery?" (Sanders 1974: 167). The answer, Sanders concludes, rests in Lawrence's progressive notion of humankind's relationship with the natural world – a notion Sanders insists we are very much in need of in our postmodern era. According to Sanders, Lawrence's belief in the interconnectedness between humankind and the environment guarantees his continued currency in the face of theoretical backlash and a rapidly changing world of literary studies.

Sanders was not the first to make this claim. Lawrence's contemporary, George Orwell, characterized the British writer in a similar fashion, writing that Lawrence "was in essence, a lyric poet, and an undisciplined enthusiast for 'Nature,' i.e. the surface of the earth, was one of his principal qualities, though it has been much less noticed than his preoccupation with sex. And on top of this he had the power of understanding, or seeming to understand, people totally different from himself" (Orwell 2001: 228).

In many regards, these attributes made Lawrence uniquely suited for the task of writing short fiction. However, they also placed Lawrence on the margins of literary modernism, a movement often characterized as urban, cosmopolitan, and dedicated to the *avant garde*. In fact, much of Lawrence's literary and private life existed on one periphery or another. Born in 1885 and the son of working-class parents (his father was a miner) in the British midlands, Lawrence was raised in a family that prized piety, conservatism, and propriety. Their class meant that Lawrence was excluded by high society; his adoption of his mother's inhibitive speech meant that he was often ostracized both by classmates and fellow workers. Nonetheless, from a young age Lawrence was determined to make a name for himself as a modernist writer.

Success came early to the young author. At the age of 22 he won the "*Nottinghamshire Guardian* Christmas Story Competition" for his short story, "The Prelude." The paper restricted entrants to one story depicting an amusing Christmas anecdote or account of a historic building. Lawrence, ambitious from the start, determined to enter multiple drafts and thus called upon two of his friends to enter his stories under pseudonyms, lest he be disqualified for breaking the rule concerning submission restrictions. In the end, one of these two friends received the formal recognition after "The Prelude" was selected as the winner; however, Lawrence won something far more important: affirmation of his talent as a writer.

He also received a monetary prize – the first of many payments Lawrence received for his short fiction. Lawrence quickly discovered that *fin-de-siècle* writers had made popular the genre, which was once considered far inferior to the novel. During Lawrence's lifetime, the short story continued to gain both in marketability and profitability, and he repeatedly returned to the genre as a lucrative means of support in between novels. Throughout his life, Lawrence's short stories appeared in diverse publications such as *The Dial, The English Review,* and *Nation & Athenaeum.*

But according to Brian Finney, editor of Lawrence's *Selected Short Stories,* the genre represented far more than a paycheck for Lawrence. According to Finney, some of Lawrence's best writing appears in his short stories, and Finney contends that Lawrence possessed a special skill for the form, particularly insofar as it relies upon image clusters, narrative ambiguity, and a commitment to the inner-workings of the human mind. (Lawrence 1982: 11). Lawrence invested much in the development of each of these aspects.

In this regard, a great deal of Lawrence's short fiction reads as a testimonial to the evolution of twentieth-century fiction. As Finney adds, studying the development of Lawrence's short stories "is like retracing the history of the genre from its pre-Chekhovian social realism and watching it reach forward to the verbal play and self-conscious artifice of post-modernist writers such as Borges and Beckett" (Lawrence 1982: 11).

The perfection of this style took Lawrence decades to achieve. In his early stories, such as "The White Stocking" (1907) and "Love Among the Haystacks" (1911), Lawrence maintained the conventions of late nineteenth-century writers such as Thomas Hardy and Henry James, who relied heavily upon plot and social critique for their power. Nevertheless, even in these early stories we see glimmers of what would become Lawrence's signature style and theme: his interest in landscape, cognition, and human sexuality. With regards to the last of these elements, "Love Among the Haystacks" is a particularly noteworthy example, as it was rejected for publication by the *English Review,* which deemed it "too steaming" for early twentieth-century audiences. This would be the first of many such receptions his work received.

As Lawrence's narrative techniques developed, he gave himself over "to urgent thematic impulses which require new modes of narrative expression" (Lawrence 1982: 11). These impulses inspired Lawrence to subordinate traditional devices such as plot and conflict, preferring instead to focus on character interiority, metaphor, and the subtleties of interpersonal dynamics. With this evolution in style came an almost compulsive need to update earlier drafts, and he repeatedly returned to earlier stories, revising them often in an attempt to excise elements of the sentimental, stock characters, and other late Victorian conventions employed by the younger writer. In time, he came to reject what he called "the gross vision of all the nineteenth-century literature," which suffers from "emotional-democratic visions or motive" (Lawrence 1936: 205). Such constructs failed to render the nuances of human experience, claimed Lawrence, and thus he sought a new form of literature that would speak more honestly to emotion and interaction.

We see elements of this innovation in stories such as "The Horse Dealer's Daughter." Originally drafted in 1916, the story took five years to complete. Its final version combines elements of naturalism, human passion, and working-class characters to create what would had become Lawrence's fully mature – and trademark – literary style. On its surface, "The Horse Dealer's Daughter" is a deceptively simple story about one family's attempt to cope with financial ruin. As such, it chronicles the Pervins – four adult children who find themselves penniless and evicted after their father's loss of the family fortune, his misguided second marriage, and eventual death. Much of the action focuses on Mabel Pervin, the only remaining daughter who must bear the brunt both of the family's pecuniary crisis and the irresponsibility of her three brothers.

To this end, "The Horse Dealer's Daughter" offers a cautionary tale about overspending and the wisdom of marrying well. Nevertheless, the story's raw emotional power belies this seemingly straight-forward tale, and the story's account of Mabel's developing passion offers a pointed commentary on the redemptive aspects – and dangers – of desire. It also compels the reader to consider not only the plight of Mabel Pervin but also the ways in all human passion has the ability to both save and compromise one's sense of self.

In fact, the story's thematic core lies in Mabel's quest for self-definition and her attempt to actualize her emotional core. Lawrence begins the "The Horse Dealer's Daughter" with a singularly provocative query posed to its protagonist:

> "Well, Mabel, and what are you going to do with yourself," asked Joe, with foolish flippancy. He felt quite safe himself. Without listening for an answer, he turned aside, worked a grain of tobacco to the tip of his tongue, and spat it out. He did not care about anything, since he felt safe himself. (Lawrence 1982: 259)

This opening establishes the principal concern of the story: the emotion, physical, and financial well-being of Mabel, whose place in society and sense of self has been deeply wounded by the family's downfall. It also establishes a noticeable contrast between Mabel, who feels this compromise acutely, and her brother, Joe, who lacks both the introspection and tenuous social position endured by his sister. Indeed, Lawrence's repeated use of the word "safe" emphasizes both Joe's inability to question his own place and Mabel's awareness of her own insecurity.

Mabel's other two brothers – Fred Henry and Malcolm – offer little consolation or insight. The fifth sibling, Lucy, has already departed, most likely either in a new marriage or to assume a position in a neighboring town. All, however, are profoundly aware of the effects of their unfortunate inheritance. The Pervins' recently-deceased father, Joseph, is described as "a man of no education, who had become a fairly large horse dealer" (Lawrence 1982: 264) This success brought his family great comfort, including impressive grounds, a constant influx of horses and grooms, and a home full of servants. Their fortunes rapidly declined, however, and were only further compromised by an unfortunate second marriage. That we are never told the new wife's name nor anything about her station suggests the children's overt disregard for their stepmother's place. That Mabel continued to keep house during this marriage only furthers such a reading.

Admittedly, we also receive precious little description of Mabel, at least with regards to her physicality. Early in the story we are told simply that she is "a rather short, sullen-looking young woman of twenty-seven. She did not share the same life as her brothers. She would have been good-looking, save for the impassive fixity of her face, 'bull-dog' as her brothers called it" (Lawrence 1982: 259). This resolute countenance might be seen as determinedness, were it not for the fact that the narrator qualifies this description by also repeatedly referring to her as "mindless." So overcome by the shame brought on by sudden poverty, Mabel finds that she must detach both from society and her own sense of worth if she is to survive. Her brothers also meet their fate with an unexamined stalwartness, resigned to a life like that of the "subject animal" (Lawrence 1982: 260): not so unlike the horses so often bred, trained, and sold by the family at the height of their success.

Here we also see the development of Lawrence's metaphor and his persistent interest in animal imagery. As the four siblings reflect upon their fate, a group of horses are led across the grounds, "tied head to tail, four of them, and they heaved along to where a lane branched off from the highroad" (Lawrence 1982: 259). This image serves as an organizing motif for much of the story as the Pervin children similarly tread forward, yoked to one another in their own misery. But unlike her brothers, who seem content throughout the story to follow this pre-destined course, Mabel – like so many of Lawrence's spirited female protagonists – breaks the emotional bonds of her predicament and learns to yearn for something more. As we are told by the narrator, Mabel acquires a new sense of resolve: "she would not cast about her. She would follow her own way just the same. She would always hold the keys of her own situation" (Lawrence 1982: 264).

Initially, this key is death, which Mabel considers the only possible solution to her otherwise miserable life. As she retires to the town cemetery, where she regularly contents herself by tending to her mother's grave, Mabel begins to contemplate a reunion with her deceased mother. She determines to carry out this plan by drowning herself in a country lake not far from the cemetery. Thus, as the sun sets on a "grey, deadened, and wintry" day, Mabel makes the short walk to the lowland pond, passes through its gate, and steps to the edge of the lake: "there she stood on the bank for a moment. She never raised her head. Then she waded slowly into the water" (Lawrence 1982: 267).

Mabel would have no doubt succeeded in this suicide attempt, were it not for Jack Fergusson, a tired-eyed young physician and unlikely savior to our heroine. Up to this point in the story, everything about Fergusson has been unextraordinary: he is described as of "medium height," pale complexion, and Scottish descent. Like Mabel and her brothers, this everyman figure is equally tied to circumstance, a "slave to the countryside" who must serve the resident physician by tending to recovering surgery patients and dispensing cheap medications (Lawrence 1982: 265).

Mabel's suicide attempt is not the first time she – or the reader – has met Fergusson. To the contrary, this moment represents the third time the two have crossed paths in the story. The first occurred at the Pervins' kitchen table, where Fergusson appeared briefly to commiserate with Mabel's brothers. There, he initially offers her no greeting and pauses only briefly to ask her what she will do following their upcoming eviction. The two characters meet again a short time later while Mabel cleans her mother's tombstone. This encounter, which builds upon the first, indicates an increasing interest between Fergusson and Mabel:

> Their eyes met. And each looked again at once, each feeling, in some way, found out by the other. He lifted his cap and passed on down the road. There remained distinct in his consciousness, like a vision, the memory of her face, lifted from the tombstone in the churchyard, and looking at him with slow, large, portentous eyes. (Lawrence 1982: 265)

The above passage reveals both the development of feeling between Mabel and Fergusson as well as Lawrence's narrative technique. Although using a traditional third-person narrative, Lawrence succeeds in plumbing the depth of sentiment in both characters, teasing out the interplay of past memory, cognition, and the effects of desire. He also lays the groundwork for his critique of that desire by weaving elements of physical attraction with implied guilt and tremendous emotional gravity. That this occurs along with a juxtaposition of Mabel and the gravestone and the "hollow of the failing day" (Lawrence 1982: 266) also serves as clever foreshadowing for the event to come, and neither the reader nor Fergusson should be surprised to see Mabel enter the icy water in an attempt to end her life.

Mabel's desperate gesture emboldens and animates Fergusson, who finds himself capable of unimagined fortitude in the face of crisis. Not able to swim and never before considered brave, Fergusson nonetheless enters the slimy water and tries desperately to find the now-submerged Mabel:

> He went under, horribly suffocating in the foul earthy water, struggling madly for a few moments. At last, after what seemed an eternity, he got his footing, rose again into the air and looked around. He gasped, and knew he was in the world. Then he looked at the water. She had risen near him. He grasped her clothing, and drawing her nearer, turned to take his way to land again. (Lawrence 1982: 267)

Here Lawrence relies upon a resurrection motif that harkens back to classical and Christian antecedents. Fergusson and Mabel – two characters who had been languishing in their private misery – become reborn as passionate novices. Fergusson, emboldened by his new role as rescuer, carries the still-unconscious Mabel to her home, where he lays her before the hearth in a deeply-symbolic gesture. Next, he removes her "earthy-smelling clothing" and wraps "her naked in the blankets" (Lawrence 1982: 268).

Now removed of all material and earthly constraints, Mabel awakes to find herself immersed for the first time in all-consuming passion. From the moment she is conscious, Mabel seeks proof of his romantic attachment. She seeks in Fergusson proof of his heroism, but he recoils "afraid now, because he felt dazed, and felt dimly that her power was stronger than his" (Lawrence 1982: 269). Eventually, however, Mabel's insistence that their unlikely communion before the hearth is based on love sparks a possibility of such in the mind of Fergusson: "he watched the strange water rise in her eyes, like some slow fountain coming up. And his heart seemed to burn and melt away in his breast" (Lawrence 1982: 270–1). Overcome by the newness and intensity of this possibility, Fergusson finds himself paralyzed, unable to stand or respond.

As the sun sets and darkness falls upon the house, the two characters are slowly lulled back to reality. Fergusson dons a pair of clothes left by one of Mabel's brothers; she tidies her hair and changes into her best dress, then offers him a cup of tea. The quotidian elements of life exert a sobering effect on the two characters, who find their pronouncements of love somewhat awkward in the reality of the Pervin kitchen. Mabel shies away from Fergusson, embarrassed by her earlier passion, but he insists it is real and vows to marry her as soon as possible. She doubts his sincerity, claiming that she is too "awful" to warrant such affection. No, he swears, his desire remains strong. The story ends with his repeated affirmation of this vow, offered in a "terrible intonation which frightened her almost more than her horror lest he should *not* want her" (Lawrence 1982: 273).

Mabel's fear of all-consuming passion represents a second possible drowning and loss of self – an emblematic feature of much of Lawrence's fiction. But in spite of the familiar themes, the completion of this story did not come easy for Lawrence. Much of the delay in the final version of the story stemmed from Lawrence's quest for a new narrative form that would allow the kind of flexibility needed to accommodate his study of human cognition, emotion, and the process by which "two individuals indulge in mutual destruction" (Lawrence 1982: 18). However, this middle story tempers what would become a more encompassing examination of the destructive interplay of lovers seen in later stories.

Indeed, "The Horse Dealer's Daughter" mitigates what could so easily become the undoing of two disparate people and allows the possibility of a happy ending and domestic bliss. Mabel's immediate financial strife is solved, as is her solitary disconnectedness from the rest of society, and both characters uncover hidden possibilities within their emotional psyches. Originally titled, "The Miracle," the story allows

for the possibility of continued redemption and hope through its ambiguously determined ending, which Finney characterizes as almost impossible optimism. "The Horse
Dealer's Daugher," writes Finney, "prefigures this hope for the future while simultaneously stressing the painful nature of the regenerative process" (Lawrence 1982:
19).

The trauma associated with regeneration ought not be overlooked. Like many of
Lawrence's middle characters, Mabel and Fergusson experience both disenfranchise-
ment and fear throughout the story. These deleterious effects are no doubt indicative
of the pervasive feelings of chaos and unrest shrouding much of the Western world
in the early decades of the twentieth-century, a time in which World War I, advances
in mechanical reproduction, and an advancing economic depression – both in America
and Europe – exerted dramatic effects on notions of self and world.

Many of these same themes – and compromising conditions – underlie "The
Rocking-Horse Winner" as well. Written at the request of Lady C. Asquith, this story
was originally published in 1926 as part of Asquith's collection, *The Ghost Book, 16
New Stories of the Uncanny*. "The Rocking-Horse Winner" reveals an interest in genres
such as ghost and murder tales developed by Lawrence late in his life. Having perhaps
once again reached the limits of narrative and theme – this time through the constant
interrogation of passion and inner-consciousness – Lawrence sought new modes of
expression that would again open up possibilities for experimentation. He found them
not only by adopting these sensational genres, but also by subverting and ultimately
satirizing the genres as well.

"The Rocking-Horse Winner" is one of the finest examples of Lawrence's ability
to simultaneously embrace and subvert the conventions of these genres. There is much
of the uncanny in this story. The most notable examples, of course, include a house
and its furnishings that whisper furiously to its occupants, urging them to find more
material goods and more financial resources. Equally as supernatural, the story's main
character, a boy named Paul, finds that he possesses an preternatural ability to foretell
future victories at racetracks. This gift both allows him to provide financial support
to his family and ultimately results in his premature demise, as he is overcome with
the ferocity of his foresight and dies by the story's end.

These plot elements, however, represent the extent to which Lawrence upholds the
limits of the ghost story. Instead of following additional – and more traditional – conventions of the genre, Lawrence instead offers a far more chilling tale of a specter of
a family consumed by greed and materialism. This had been a pet project of Lawrence's
for some time. Throughout his life, Lawrence had maintained a profound contempt
for what he referred to as 'the god-damn bourgeoisie" (Watkins 1987: 296) as well
as capitalism's unrelenting push towards materialism. He explores the extremes of
this greed in "The Rocking-Horse Winner," showing how uncanny – and unfortunate
– its results can be.

The story focuses on one mother's quest for social stature and material wealth. Said
to be loosely based on Lady Sylvia Brooke, the mother – known only to us as "Hester"
– hardens her heart to all but her own sense of entitlement. Having watched her

marriage turn loveless, she finds that she is equally as incapable of feeling for her children:

> when her children were present, she always felt the centre of her heart go hard. This troubled her, and in her manner she was all the more gentle and anxious for her children, as if she loved them very much. Only she herself knew that at the centre of her heart was a hard little place that could not fee love, no, not for anybody. (Lawrence 1982: 444)

For Lawrence, who writes often of shared maternal and filial affection, this affliction must have been more frightening than any traditional tale of horror. The same could be said for Hester's insistence that her fortune – and the fortune of the entire family – is tied up in her perceived lack of luck. This unwillingness to assume responsibility of one's actions or one's fortune distinguishes Hester from so many of Lawrence's highly introspective, independent characters, and her negative portrayal throughout the story implies that we are to feel sympathy for the hard-hearted mother.

In fact, the only figure who does find Hester at all sympathetic is her son, Paul, who so desperately seeks her love that he is willing to overlook even her most egregious faults. Paul consistently seeks approval and affection from his mother and just as consistently finds himself rebuked. In one such instance, he insists that God has told him he possesses the very luck she lacks. She responds dismissively, which further incites him to seek her approval: "the boy saw that she did not believe him; or rather, that she paid no attention to his assertion. This angered him somewhere, and made him want to compel her attention" (Lawrence 1982: 446).

Paul discovers the means to do so through the Christmas gift of a wooden rocking horse – one of many extravagances indulged in by Paul's financially irresponsible mother. The horse joins in the material chorus of the house, continuously whispering along with all other possessions that "there must be more money." Unlike the other assets, however, Paul's rocking horse maintains a unique connection to the supernatural: it transports Paul into the future or, perhaps more exactly, transmits the future to Paul. By riding the rocking horse, "charging madly into space, with a frenzy that made the little girls peer at him uneasily," Paul finds he is able to predict the winners of high-stakes horse races (Lawrence 1982: 446). He enlists the assistance of Bassett, an injured veteran of World War I turned family gardener who places bets on behalf of the young boy. Before long, both Bassett and Paul have won thousands of pounds at the track.

Paul tells no one but his Uncle John of his winnings. John, an inveterate gambler who gives himself over to the family's addictive tendencies, is delighted to have a companion and fellow fan of the horses. He is even more thrilled when he discovers that his young nephew can, in fact, predict the race winners with astounding accuracy. He forms a loose partnership with Paul, agreeing to place the latter's winnings in trust in exchange for future tips. This trust is of the utmost importance for Paul: signed over to his mother, it represents the best chance he has to win her notice and affection. And, according to Daniel Watkins, it represents one of the most chilling aspects of the short story insofar as it emphasizes "not a sign of the occultish nature of Paul's religion, but quite the reverse a sign of the truly demonic quality of a Christianity that willingly and even insistently sacrifices human life in the pursuit of personal excellence and advancement" (Watkins 1987: 300). That Paul eventual fails in his quest (not to mention loses his life in the process) demonstrates how monstrous the living can be.

Nevertheless, we ought not be surprised by Paul's failed attempt to secure any more than a passing concern from Hester, whose heart is too hardened to be wooed by a few thousand pounds bequeathed anonymously. She spends this and every other gift at once, causing the chorus of "there must be more money" to become a cacophony:

> The voices in the house, behind the sprays of mimosa and almond-blossom, and from under the pile of iridescent cushions, simply trilled and screamed in a sort of ecstasy: "There *must* be more money! Oh-h-h! There *must* be more money! Oh, now, now-w, now-w-w – there must be more money! More than ever! More than ever!" (Lawrence 1982: 453)

The orgasmic nature of these exclamations have led some critics to suggest that sexuality lies at the heart both of Hester's anguish and Paul's desperate need for her affection. Indeed, these utterances along with sexualized nature of Paul's behavior on the rocking horse have led many to compare Lawrence's story with the theories of Sigmund Freud. This comparison is not without warrant. Indeed, much of Lawrence's own psychological theory bears a distinct resemblance to Freud. In his two essays "Fantasia of the Unconscious" and "Psychoanalysis and the Unconscious," Lawrence applies Freudian theory to topics such as dreams, sexual development, and the relationship between children and parents.

In his essay "Parent Love," Lawrence warns that not encouraging sensuality in children can lead to dire consequences. Too often, he warns, it results in skewed filial affection in which "one parent, usually the mother, is the object of blind devotion, whilst the other parent, usually the father, is an object of resistance" (Lawrence 1960: 118). This theory finds embodied existence in "The Rocking Horse Winner," where Paul's feelings towards his mother can only be described as intense devotion. The notable absence of Paul's father throughout the story only intensifies this correlation. What little we know of the unnamed character comes to us second hand: he graduated from Eton, he works at an office in town, he enjoys whiskey and soda. Still, his relationship with his children is so distant that he remains voiceless and passive throughout the death of his son. That this death occurs because Paul becomes blinded by his own foresight is an irony the aging Lawrence must surely have enjoyed.

Although by no means his most explicit tale, "The Rocking-Horse Winner" nevertheless points towards Lawrence's developing obsession with human sexuality. As this obsession grew, so too did his difficulties in placing some of his more risqué work. While early stories were simply rejected for being "steamy," later works were deemed obscene and banned – both in the United States and Britain, as were similar publications by contemporaries such as Oscar Wilde and Radclyffe Hall. This action against him both surprised and confused Lawrence, who maintained that he wrote about the most natural of all topics: human desire. Taking issue with the banning of his work, Lawrence wrote, "I am mystified at this horror over a mere word, a plain simple word that stands for a plain simple thing. . . . the words themselves are clean, so are the things to which they apply. But the mind drags in a filthy association, calls up some repulsive emotion" (Lawrence 1936: 280).

REFERENCES AND FURTHER READING

Coroneos, C. and Tate, T. (2001). "Lawrence's Tales," in *A Cambridge Companion to D.H. Lawrence*, pp. 103–18. New York: Cambridge University Press.

Hollington, M. (2004). "Lawrentian Gothic and 'The Uncanny,'" *Anglophonia: French Journal of English Studies* 15: 171–84.

Lawrence, D.H. (1936). *Phoenix: The Posthumous Papers of D.H. Lawrence*, ed. E.D. McDonald. New York: Viking Press.

Lawrence, D.H. (1960). *Fantasia of the Unconsciousness and Psychoanalysis and the Unconscious.* New York: Viking.

Lawrence, D.H. (1979). *The Letters of D.H. Lawrence*, ed., J.T. Boulton. New York: Cambridge University Press.

Lawrence, D.H. (1982). *Selected Short Stories*, ed. B. Finney. New York: Penguin.

Meyers, J. (1989). "D.H. Lawrence and Tradition: 'The Horse Dealer's Daughter'," *Studies in Short Fiction* 26/3: 346–51.

Orwell, G. (2001). "'The Prussian Officer' and Other Stories," *The Critical Response to D.H. Lawrence*, pp. 227–9. Westport, Conn.: Greenwood Press.

Sanders, S. (1974). *D.H. Lawrence: The World of the Five Major Novels.* New York: Viking.

Walterscheid, K.A. (2000). "The Double Quest in 'The Horse-Dealer's Daughter'," *D.H. Lawrence Review* 29/3: 58–9.

Watkins, D.P. (1987). "Labor and Religion in D.H. Lawrence's 'The Rocking-Horse Winner,'" *Studies in Short Fiction* 24/3: 295–301.

Worthen, J. (1991). *D.H. Lawrence.* New York: Routledge.

16

Virginia Woolf: "Kew Gardens" and "The Legacy"

Stef Craps

Virginia Woolf's reputation as a towering literary figure rests largely on her novelistic output, yet she was also an accomplished writer of short fiction. While short-story writing played an important role for her throughout her career, she published relatively few works of short fiction in her lifetime. *Monday or Tuesday*, which came out from the Woolfs' own Hogarth Press in 1921 (as its first full-length publication), was the only collection of short stories she ever published. In 1940 she began to contemplate putting together another book of short fiction, which became the posthumous *A Haunted House and Other Short Stories* (1944), edited and published by her husband Leonard. It included six of the eight stories from *Monday or Tuesday*, seven stories that had appeared in periodicals, and five previously unpublished pieces.

Criticism of Woolf's short fiction has been scarce, especially compared with the vast amount of critical attention bestowed on her novels. Few articles have been devoted to it, and critical studies and biographies tend to ignore or quickly pass over what they see as a sideshow to the author's core business of writing novels. This situation has changed somewhat since the publication of Susan Dick's *The Complete Shorter Fiction of Virginia Woolf* (1985; second edition 1989), which identified and included no fewer than forty-six complete works and a dozen incomplete ones. This authoritative edition managed to bring new attention to Woolf's achievement in short fiction, which forms the topic of three subsequently published book-length studies (Baldwin 1989; Benzel and Hoberman 2004; Skrbic 2004). Her stories are now no longer regarded as mere finger exercises, but as fully fledged literary works worthy of critical attention in their own right. However, despite the recent upsurge in critical interest, it remains true to say that Woolf's reputation as a short-story writer is "still emerging" (Baldwin 1989: xiii).

Confining ourselves to the stories collected in *Monday or Tuesday* and *A Haunted House*, we can divide Woolf's short fiction into three chronological periods (Baldwin 1989: 4–6): a radically experimental period, in which her concern with knowledge and perception led her to push the short-story form to its limits (1917–21); a period in which her main interest was in portraying the inner lives of characters associated with Mrs Dalloway's party (1923–9); and a remarkably conventional period, in which she employed traditional plot devices (1939–41). The variety and range of Woolf's short fiction is exemplified by the two stories that we will take a closer look at in the remainder of this chapter: the highly experimental "Kew Gardens" and the more conventional "The Legacy," written respectively near the beginning and near the end of her career.

"Kew Gardens"

Many critics have asserted that Woolf's short stories were testing grounds for themes and methods that she would take up and develop more fully in her novels. This is particularly true for the early, experimental phase of her career as a short-story writer, during which she produced two of her most famous stories: "The Mark on the Wall," which was published along with Leonard Woolf's "Three Jews" in *Two Stories* (1917), the first publication of the newly founded Hogarth Press; and "Kew Gardens," which was published as a small book by the Hogarth Press, with woodcut illustrations by Woolf's sister, the painter Vanessa Bell (1919). These two stories, along with "An Unwritten Novel" (1920), all of which were included in the volume *Monday or Tuesday*, led directly to *Jacob's Room* (1922), the first of her truly experimental novels. While Woolf initially saw "The Mark on the Wall" as no more than a playful distraction from the serious work of writing her long, conventional second novel *Night and Day* (1919), her diary shows that by January 1920 she had come to envisage "mark on the wall, K[ew]. G[ardens]. & unwritten novel" as "taking hands & dancing in unity" to form a radically new kind of fiction (Dick 1996). In fact, "Kew Gardens" is often singled out as a kind of ur-text of Woolf's literary corpus. In his memoirs, Leonard Woolf refers to it as "a microcosm of all [Woolf's] then unwritten novels, from *Jacob's Room* to *Between the Acts*" (Staveley 2004: 42–3). The critic John Oakland concurs that the story "contains in embryo many of the issues of form, theme, content, character, plot and action which occupied [Woolf] in all her work" (Oakland 1987: 264).

While "The Mark on the Wall" and "An Unwritten Novel" both revolve around the fanciful flight of the narrator's mind, the organizing principle of "Kew Gardens" is setting rather than character. A third-person narrator describes the goings-on on a July day in and around a flower bed in Kew Gardens, a public garden situated on the south bank of the River Thames which became a place of respite for the author after the Woolfs' move to Richmond in 1915. The narrator's attention alternates between the world of the flower bed, in which a snail is struggling to get past a leaf, and the thoughts and conversations of four couples passing by it. The characters are rather sketchy, and not a single thread of the story is narrated to completion. In addition to being utterly banal, the "progress" of the snail, the only consistent character, is not even recounted in full. The determinism of character-based plot development, that mainstay of realist narrative, has been superseded by the arbitrariness of spatial and temporal contiguity: what is narrated is narrated for no other reason than that it is what happens to occur in a given space within a given period of time. "Kew Gardens" challenges the traditional assumption that a short story must be unified and provide a sense of closure, thereby underlining the author's claim – in a 1919 review of a volume of stories by Chekhov – that "We are by this time alive to the fact that inconclusive stories are legitimate" (Benzel and Hoberman 2004: 4).

That, despite its fixed and tightly circumscribed setting, the story retains a distinctly dynamic feel is due in no small part to Woolf's experimentation with narrative perspective, one of the story's most original and subversive formal features. The flexibility of Woolf's narrative style is noticeable from the first paragraph, which begins with but soon moves beyond a conventional perspective on the garden scene it describes. The opening sentence starts with a description from a middle distance: the narrator is able to see the shape of the flower bed as a whole ("oval-shaped" (Woolf 1989: 90)), but also to discern individual flowers ("perhaps a hundred stalks" (90)). As the sentence continues, however, we move closer and closer, and by the end we can make out even the minutest component parts of the flowers: "from the red, blue or yellow gloom of the throat emerged a straight bar, rough with gold dust and slightly clubbed at the end" (90). The point of view gradually moves inside the flower bed as the paragraph goes on to describe the sunlight falling on the earth between the flowers. A breeze is said to stir the petals "overhead" (90), indicating that we are now down on the ground with the snail which is introduced here and whose slow progression across the base of the flower bed will become the focus of the narrator's interest. That we have literally come to adopt a snail's eye view by the end of the first paragraph explains why the area between the flower stalks through which the light makes its way is described as "the vast green spaces beneath the dome of the heart-shaped and tongue-shaped leaves" (90): what appears small to us is huge to a snail. This snail's eye view also manifests itself elsewhere in the story: depicted with corresponding size and perspective, the puddles, grass, pebbles, and leaves which the snail finds on its path become "[b]rown cliffs with deep green lakes in the hollows, flat blade-like trees that waved from root to tip, round boulders of grey stone, vast crumpled surfaces of a thin crackling texture" (92).

The perspectival shift that occurs in the first paragraph is reversed in the final paragraph, in which the narrative focus expands to include the entire city. The visual field widens as we are lifted up into the air – the drone of an airplane flying over Kew Gardens is mentioned at this point. From this distant aerial perspective, the human beings down in the garden appear as mere blurs upon the horizon, "dissolving like drops of water in the yellow and green atmosphere" (95). Even Kew Gardens itself, when viewed from a sufficient distance, is only one of "a vast nest of Chinese boxes"

(95) that make up the modern metropolis. Besides unsettling our accustomed perception of a landscape, "Kew Gardens" also contains the seeds of the kind of stream-of-consciousness narration for which Woolf's later prose would become famous. The story smoothly shifts between descriptions of the garden from the perspective of the snail and scenes in which the narrator adopts the points of view and enters the minds of the people who are passing by. As Susan Dick points out, "Such carefully patterned shifts of perspective, which occur throughout *Jacob's Room*, became a hallmark of Woolf's fiction" (Dick 1996).

The opening and closing paragraphs of "Kew Gardens" display not only the story's experimentation with narrative perspective, but also its affinity with visual art. In fact, the story's multiperspectivalism can itself be seen as a literary appropriation of a technique used in post-impressionist painting, to which Woolf had been introduced by her friend Roger Fry. "Kew Gardens" is often regarded by critics as a piece of verbal impressionism, an attempt "to capture in prose the way in which the light falls upon the flowers, pebbles, snails, drops of water" (Gordon 1984: 65). Like a modern painter, Woolf seeks to convey the immediate experience of reality rather than offering a representation of it, and does so by recording impressions of color and light. The first paragraph provides an elaborate description of the flowers – unidentified, as in a painting – which abounds with sensory details about the play of light and the diffusion of color, e.g., "when [the petals] moved, the red, blue and yellow lights passed one over the other, staining an inch of the brown earth beneath with a spot of the most intricate colour" (Woolf 1989: 90). No less visually charged is the last paragraph, which depicts the dissolution of "substance and colour" as all life in the garden seems to evanesce: "Yellow and black, pink and snow white, shapes of all these colours, men, women and children, . . . wavered and sought shade beneath the trees, dissolving like drops of water in the yellow and green atmosphere, staining it faintly with red and blue" (95). Another notable formal feature, which makes Woolf's prose even more sensuous and lyrical, is the abundant use of figurative language. Personifications, metaphors, and similes are scattered about the story, many of these blurring the boundaries between the human and the non-human world. The snail is personified, but so are the flowers, which are given "heart-shaped or tongue-shaped leaves," "throat[s]," and "flesh" (90); the men and women straggling past the flower bed are compared to butterflies, horses, and flowers; and the words they speak are likened to bees.

There is no denying, then, that "Kew Gardens" is a highly formalist story. However, one should be wary of overemphasizing form at the expense of content – a pitfall which, alas, few critics have managed to avoid. Writing in the *Times Literary Supplement* on the first appearance of "Kew Gardens," Harold Child praised this "new proof of the complete unimportance in art of the *hyle*, the subject matter" (Bishop 1982: 269). Child's review, which led to an outpouring of public interest in the story, set the tone for much of its critical reception, which, as Alice Staveley has recently observed, "reads in large part like a primer for traditional narratology, its emphasis on form in lieu of content, on universal generalizations about style and method obscuring specific interrogations for how history, gender, and class drive the story's manifold innovations of narrative form" (Staveley 2004: 43). Published in 1919, "Kew Gardens" can be productively read as a response to the shattering experience of World War I, which had discredited the social order inherited from the Victorian era (Johnson 2001). Far from being a neutral setting, the garden at Kew is a potent symbol of national imperial history – its mission, after all, was not only to attract visitors, but also to collect and display botanical specimens gathered from Britain's many colonies. Woolf's decision to set her story in this iconic site – which, moreover, being a garden, inevitably conjures Edenic connotations – allowed her effectively to portray and critique a world which had lost its innocence.

By privileging the perspective of an animal, dissolving the boundaries between human and non-human, and generally decentring the human presence, "Kew Gardens" gives literary expression to the dehumanizing effects of the war and the politics that propelled it. The world depicted in the story is marked by fragmentation and alienation (Séllei 1997). Having lost its bearings and its moorings, humanity seems condemned to wander senselessly through a disjointed world, following an "irregular and aimless movement" (Woolf 1989: 95). Though the passers-by are paired together, they do not actually connect with one another. Divided by disparate pasts, lost in separate thoughts, and talking past each other, they appear to be irrevocably isolated and incapable of meaningful communication. In fact, the story's social commentary manifests itself most explicitly in the fragmentarily recorded dialogs between the couples, which have tended to be overlooked by the critics (Staveley 2004: 43). World War I casts its shadow over the two central conversations, the one between a seemingly crazy old man and his younger male companion (presumably his son or keeper), and the one between two elderly women, possibly domestic servants. Delusional and rambling, the old man, who is haunted by "the spirits of the dead" from "this war," with whom he imagines communicating (Woolf 1989: 92), shows symptoms of what appears to be war trauma. This character is a precursor of Septimus Smith, the shell-shocked war veteran in *Mrs. Dalloway* who descends into madness and ends up committing suicide. The war is also present, albeit more obliquely, in the conversation between the two women, who are shown chattering about relatives and recipe ingredients. Their insistent repetition of the word "sugar" can be explained by the fact that sugar was a rationed and therefore precious commodity during the war (Staveley 2004: 56).

The story appears to suggest that the inherited social order has betrayed both men and women: while the conversation featuring the old man invokes the carnage into which the nation's young men had been sent by their government, the other three conversations foreground the crippling limitations imposed on women's lives by social conventions. Confined to the domestic sphere, the two women engaging in empty chatter find themselves in a position of economic dependence, as do the female partners in the story's two romantic male–female pairs, who are forced to adopt the subservient roles allotted to women in a patriarchal culture. By subtly linking militarism and patriarchal oppression, "Kew Gardens" anticipates the argument of Woolf's feminist and pacifist essay *Three Guineas* (1938), written some twenty years later, when Europe was facing the prospect of another devastating war.

"The Legacy"

Feminist concerns also inform "The Legacy," which, like other late stories, was commissioned by an American magazine. This transatlantic interest is probably attributable to the success of *The Years* (1937), which had become a best-seller in the United States. Woolf wrote "The Legacy" in 1940 in response to a request from the editor of *Harper's Bazaar*. However, much to her anger, he rejected the story, and she did not receive payment for it. "The Legacy" did not appear in print until after Woolf's death, when it was included in *A Haunted House*. The inspiration for the story is thought to have come from Woolf's visit to Philip Morrell shortly after the death of Lady Ottoline Morrell. During this visit, Woolf's host showed her his wife's diaries and pressed her to accept some of Ottoline's jewelry as a remembrance. "The Legacy" is a story in which a wife dies before her husband, leaving little gifts for all her friends and her diaries for him. From these, he learns that she had fallen in love with another man – who turns out to be the brother of her secretary – and committed suicide a week or two after his death. The method of suicide used recalls the death of Woolf's aunt Mary, who was run over by a car, as well as Milly Hamilton's remark, noted down by Woolf in her diary, that she wished she had the courage to step in front of a moving bus (Baldwin 1989: 70).

The fact that the intended audience of "The Legacy" were the editor and the readers of a middle-brow magazine may account for the relative conventionality of the story's form. Unlike with the self-published "Kew Gardens," Woolf appears to have felt a need to make at least some concessions to popular taste while writing "The Legacy." The story strays from the new path for fiction which Woolf had mapped out in her essay "Modern Novels" (1919) in that, like traditional realist fiction, it depends on plot and obeys the laws of probability and coherence. However, it does devote a great deal of attention to the elucidation of character in the manner called for by Woolf in both this essay and her essay "Mr. Bennett and Mrs. Brown" (1924). In these polemical pieces, Woolf argues that the methods used by Edwardian novelists like Arnold Bennett, John Galsworthy, and H.G. Wells tell us much about the material world of their characters, but fail to capture their soul. In "The Legacy," by contrast, Woolf employs a third-person narrator who gives the reader direct insight into the inner life of the protagonist, Gilbert Clandon, by focalizing the entire narrative through him.

What is more, the story thematizes the necessity of attempting to enter into the minds of other people by "punishing" Gilbert for his self-absorption and his incuriosity about his own wife. A successful politician, Gilbert is portrayed as being self-satisfied, self-centered, and insensitive. He condescends to his wife's secretary and friend Sissy Miller, who comes to visit him after Angela's death to pay her respects. While Angela, "with her genius for sympathy," had discovered numerous qualities in Sissy, to Gilbert "she was scarcely distinguishable from any other woman of her kind" (Woolf 1989: 282). It turns out that he also has trouble reading his own wife as an individual. He pictures her as the archetypal angel in the house: reading through Angela's early diary entries, he fondly remembers her as a charming, innocent, and ignorant little creature, content to bask in his reflected glory. Later entries, which he initially reads with less interest as "his own name occurred less frequently" (285), reveal that Angela had not been fulfilled in that role, and that she had found in another man the love and respect her husband had failed to give her. Gilbert's indignant reaction to these revelations, which betrays nothing but hurt pride, emphasizes his complacency and self-absorption. His thoughts are interspersed with extracts from Angela's diary, which disclose to him (and to the reader) the tragic truth of Angela's life and death. On learning that she would not leave her husband for him, Sissy's brother killed himself, closely followed, in true Antony-and-Cleopatra style, by Angela herself. Her death was not an accident, then, as Gilbert had been assuming (yet another misinterpretation on his part), but a deliberate suicide, a desperate attempt to escape from him and to rejoin her lover. This devastating insight is the "legacy" Angela has left her husband.

Gilbert's crime, if we may call it that, originates in a failure of imagination and a want of sympathy. In this respect, he closely resembles the Edwardian novelists lambasted by Woolf in the aforementioned essays. In "Mr. Bennett and Mrs. Brown," she argues that Bennett, Galsworthy, and Wells were "never interested in character in itself," but in "something outside" (Baldwin 1989: 86). Woolf makes this point by imagining them attempting in vain to capture in words the singularity of a woman sitting opposite them in a railway carriage, a woman she calls Mrs Brown. The reason for their failure, Woolf claims, is that "not one of the Edwardians has so much as looked at her" (Baldwin 1989: 89). Her predecessors' obsession with external details diverts their attention away from Mrs Brown herself, leading them to create "an image of Mrs. Brown, which has no likeness to that surprising apparition whatsoever" (Baldwin 1989: 95). Woolf even suggests that the Edwardian conventions and tools for portraying character cause "ruin" and "death" (Baldwin 1989: 90). If "Mrs. Brown must be rescued, expressed, and set in her high relations to the world before the train stopped and she disappeared for ever" (Baldwin 1989: 92), it falls on a new generation of modernist writers to carry out this life-saving, liberating, and restoring mission. One of these writers is, of course, the author of "The Legacy," who, sharing the "genius for sympathy" Gilbert attributes to Angela, offers her readers a sensitive and psychologically convincing portrait of a man whose world has collapsed about him without his quite realizing it yet.

Woolf's critique of the Edwardian novelists, which she translates into fictional practice in "The Legacy," is explicitly gendered and classed. The character Woolf presents in "Mr. Bennett and Mrs. Brown" as being victimized by the literary establishment is a powerless, impoverished woman, and the guilty party consists of male authority figures. The same power relations prevail in "The Legacy," which paints a bleak and damning picture of the gender and class politics of the time. The class prejudices of the powers that be, represented by Gilbert, show not only in the latter's interactions with Sissy, but also in his imperviousness to the suffering of the lower classes, which Angela wanted to help alleviate, and in his contempt for the socialist ideas and ideals to which – as he learns from her diaries – Angela had been exposed through her contacts with Sissy's activist brother. Even more central to the story than class snobbery, however, is the prevalent attitude towards women and the damage it causes. The fate chosen by Angela demonstrates that the restrictions imposed by patriarchal society can turn women's lives into a prison from which only death seems to provide release. Angela's sense of entrapment recalls the predicament of Clarissa Dalloway, another seemingly contented politician's wife, while her decision to commit suicide links her with Septimus Smith, Clarissa's doppelgänger, who also chooses death over a life of unrelieved misery. "The Legacy" thus bears witness to the havoc which an ingrained lack of empathy and understanding can wreak on people's, and especially women's, lives. As we saw with "Kew Gardens," far from being a retreat into empty formalism, Woolf's recourse to narrative innovation – here, the deployment of techniques for facilitating empathic identification with fictional characters – is rooted in, and prompted by, a particular historical reality which her work critically examines and interrogates.

References and Further Reading

Baldwin, D.R. (1989). *Virginia Woolf: A Study of the Short Fiction*. Boston: Twayne.

Benzel, K.N. (2000). "Woolf's Early Experimentation with Consciousness: 'Kew Gardens,' Typescript to Publication, 1917–1919," in A. Ardis and B. Kime Scott (eds), *Virginia Woolf: Turning the Centuries*, pp. 192–99. New York: Pace University Press.

Benzel, K.N. and Hoberman, R. (eds) (2004). *Trespassing Boundaries: Virginia Woolf's Short Fiction*. New York: Palgrave Macmillan.

Bishop, E.L. (1982). "Pursuing 'It' through 'Kew Gardens'," *Studies in Short Fiction* 19/3: 269–75.

Dick, S. (1996). "Virginia Woolf," in J.H. Rogers (ed.), *British Short-Fiction Writers, 1915–1945. Dictionary of Literary Biography*, vol. 162, pp. 357–71. Detroit, MI: Gale Group.

Fleishman, A. (1980). "Forms of the Woolfian Short Story," in R. Freedman (ed.), *Virginia Woolf: Revaluation and Continuity*, pp. 44–70. Berkeley: University of California Press.

Gordon, L. (1984). *Virginia Woolf: A Writer's Life*. Oxford: Oxford University Press.

Johnson, K. (2001). Critical essay on "Kew Gardens," in *Short Stories for Students, vol. 12: Presenting Analysis, Context and Criticism on*

Commonly Studied Short Stories. Farmington Hills, MI: Thomson Gale.

Oakland, J. (1987). "Virginia Woolf's 'Kew Gardens'," *English Studies* 3: 264–73.

Séllei, N. (1997). "The Snail and *The Times*: Three Stories 'Dancing in Unity'," *Hungarian Journal of English and American Studies* 3/2: 189–98.

Skrbic, N. (2004). *Wild Outbursts of Freedom: Reading Virginia Woolf's Short Fiction*. Westport, Conn.: Greenwood Press.

Staveley, A. (2004). "Conversations at Kew: Woolf's Feminist Narratology," in K.N. Benzel and R. Hoberman (eds), *Trespassing Boundaries: Virginia Woolf's Short Fiction*, pp. 39–62. New York: Palgrave Macmillan.

Woolf, V. (1989). *The Complete Shorter Fiction of Virginia Woolf*, ed. S. Dick. San Diego: Harcourt.

17

Katherine Mansfield: "The Garden Party" and "Marriage à la Mode"

Jennifer E. Dunn

Both "The Garden Party" and "Marriage à la Mode" were included in Mansfield's third collection of short stories, *The Garden Party* (1922). This collection was also the last of Mansfield's books published in her lifetime. Like other modernist short fiction, such as Joyce's *Dubliners* (1914) and Woolf's *Monday or Tuesday* (1919), Mansfield's stories center on the transitory, ephemeral nature of experience as conveyed through epiphany, symbols, and impressions, although they have a quality that is all Mansfield's own. Like Woolf, Mansfield may be labeled a practitioner of the plotless short story. Her texts shift the reader's focus from traditional, action-oriented plot to feelings and seemingly minor events, generating meaning through the myriad of symbols and their suggested associations. Yet, in Mansfield's stories, that which is small and fleeting is always deliberately and skillfully intertwined with larger themes: with issues of class and gender, with the nature of art and the consciousness of the artist, and with the difference between innocence and experience. While certain themes, tones, and tropes persist across her work, and may be traced to her influences in Chekhov, Wilde, and post-impressionist painting, "Mansfield, like other writers, cannot be confined to any single formula" (Nathan 1993: 96). A notable characteristic of her writing is the way it resists monological readings and generalizations, even as it neatly epitomizes the modernist aesthetic. Mansfield's resistance to unifying interpretations and labels is apparent when considering her work as a whole – her narrators are men and women of many ages and backgrounds, her subject matter is various, and her tone ranges from satire and irony to pathos and sentimentality – but is all the more striking when considering a single given text. As Head argues, the modernist short story works against critical approaches that seek to assimilate its ambiguities and gaps to a single, unifying interpretation. If the modernist short story often turns on moments of awakening, or what Joyce called epiphanies, then for Mansfield these moments do not necessarily offer a fixed and clear conclusion, but are "a point where different impulses converge and conflict" (Head 1992: 110).

"The Garden Party"

The title story of *The Garden Party and Other Stories* is one of Mansfield's most famous and frequently anthologized works (along with "Prelude" and "Bliss"). The story begins *in media res* as Mrs Sheridan and her daughters Meg, Jose, and Laura prepare for a summer garden party: "And after all the weather was ideal. They could not have had a more perfect day for a garden-party if they had ordered it" (Mansfield 2001: 245). Mrs. Sheridan has exempted herself from the preparations, and Laura, the youngest daughter and "artistic one" in the family (246), is sent to direct the workmen erecting a marquee in the garden. There, she revels in the beauty of the morning and the workmen's friendliness, dismissing "these absurd class distinctions" and imagining herself to be "just like a work-girl" (247–8). Her sense of euphoria is heightened by the deliveries of pink canna lilies and dozens of "beautifully light and feathery" cream puffs (252). She is momentarily diverted from these small joys by the news that a carter from the cottages across the road has been killed in an accident. Her desire to cancel the party out of respect for the dead is ridiculed by Mrs Sheridan and Jose, and Laura is swiftly distracted from the accident when her mother loans her a beautiful hat with a black velvet ribbon and golden daisies. The party proceeds as planned, and Laura enjoys herself as the guests compliment her newly grown-up and fashionable appearance. As evening approaches and the party ends, Laura is sent to the carter's cottage with the party's leftovers. There, she comes face to face with the "sleeping" corpse of the young man, and is profoundly moved by the "wonderful, beautiful" vision he presents, though at the same time she sobs and asks the man's family to "forgive" her extravagant hat. When she meets her brother Laurie on the road, he seems to understand her inexpressible emotions: "'Isn't life,' she stammered, 'isn't life' – ," to which Laurie responds, "*Isn't* it, darling?" (261).

"The Garden Party" is a plotless short story: there is little action, and the conflicts raised are not resolved by a neat and conclusive ending. The story's meaning seems to rest on Laura's conversation with her brother, although it is not clear what she means by her question about life, or what Laurie's answer signifies. Critical readings have focused on the nature of Laura's unexplained epiphany, often interpreting Laura's trip to the cottage as an awakening of social conscience that separates her from her frivolous and privileged family, or as an initiation, via the encounter with death, into adulthood. Laura's visit to the cottage has also been interpreted as the flowering of her "artistic" sensibilities into a broader vision of the nature of life itself:

> Gifted in vision, she is qualified, both because of and in spite of her youth, to discover what her mother and sister have always known, yet never known. The true subject of "The Garden Party," then, is not only the ultimate reality we perceive but, equally, the way an artistic one perceives it. (Kleine 1963: 371)

These readings draw on Mansfield's own comments that the story explores "the diversity of life and how we try to fit in everything, Death included" (Murry 1928: 196). But because the text upholds any and all of these interpretations, Head's argument for the *disunifying* function of the modernist epiphany becomes relevant here: "There is usually no simple 'solution' to the ambiguities of the characterization, but rather a denial of a solution" (1992: 110). As Nownes points out, the story, beginning "in midpassage" and ending with a question, "defies traditional notions of an ordered, unified text" (1993–4: 50). Approaching the story's ending as a "denial of a solution" shifts the focus from an attempt to stabilize the meaning of Laura's question and Laurie's answer to a more productive exploration of Laura's "ambiguity of characterization." More recently, Zivley (1995) and Atkinson (2006) have acknowledged that there are other, less positive, meanings suggested by Mansfield's ending, and they argue that Laura's so-called epiphany marks her assimilation into, rather than a break from, a problematic social order epitomized by her mother. Reading the story in this way, we see how Mansfield's ironic narrative voice, free indirect discourse, and ever-shifting symbolic meanings emphasize the frightening double-sidedness of life and of artistic vision, rather than their "wonderful, beautiful" unity or comforting totality.

From the very beginning of the story, Mansfield establishes a series of dichotomies that differentiate Laura from her family, only to undermine them. Laura is attentive to the natural beauty of the garden and laments that the marquee will obscure the "silent splendour" of the karaka trees (Mansfield 2001: 247), in contrast to the Sheridans' "attempt to 'methodize' nature and bring it under control" in the same way the weather itself is "ordered," "reduced to a matter of commercial transaction" (Magalaner 1971: 113). The Sheridan world is one built on affluence, materialism, and artifice, symbolized in Mrs Sheridan's self-indulgent order of too many canna lilies and Jose's contrived performance of the song, "This Life is Weary": the sad tune is followed by her "brilliant, dreadfully unsympathetic smile" (Mansfield 2001: 251). Laura's spontaneous delight in the natural and her instinctive sympathy for the carter seem out of place in this household, although it is important to note that Laura also poses and imitates. She tries to look "severe and even a little bit short-sighted" like her mother when she approaches the workmen (246), and repeats her mother *verbatim* when speaking to a friend on the telephone. When Mrs Sheridan places her hat on Laura's head, she passes on "the Sheridan heritage of snobbery, restricted social views, narrowness of vision – the garden party syndrome" (Magalaner 1971: 116–17). Laura is so astonished by her "charming" reflection that she forgets all about the carter's death (Mansfield 2001: 256). Thus, almost immediately we see Laura oscillating between the natural and the contrived, and the profound and the superficial, even in her well-meaning but pretended affinity with the workmen in the garden.

This pattern continues when Laura enters the carter's cottage, and destabilizes any suggestion that the visit allows Laura to fully transcend "the garden party syndrome." Mansfield's use of free indirect discourse is important here. As Laura descends upon the cottages, the omniscient narrative voice shifts to her perspective, but uses language more suggestive of Mrs Sheridan's views than Laura's sympathy. As the bright colors of the party fade with the sunlight, the cottages are portrayed as an underworld of "shadow" and "deep shade" (Mansfield 2001: 258–9), an underworld earlier described (again, perhaps from Laura's perspective) as "disgusting and sordid" and "far too near" the Sheridan house (254). When Laura meets two women in the cottage, they are described as monstrous and conniving. The widow with her swollen face is "terrible," while her companion is "sly" with an "oily" voice (260). These descriptions are at odds with Laura's interpretation of the corpse as "beautiful" and "peaceful," unless we consider her reaction as both a coping strategy and an extension of her earlier tendency to aestheticize her surroundings. The corpse presents for Laura "a blank screen" upon which she may project her *own* narrative or pleasing picture (Nownes 1993–4: 55). While her positive vision of life and death, and ensuing inability to articulate this vision, may be read in accordance with Mansfield's own comments about the diversity of life, "Death included," it can also be read as an upholding of the self-same class distinctions Laura earlier regards as "absurd."

As Magalaner points out, the reader – but also Laura – has been "prepared" for the story's final epiphany, which is foreshadowed in Jose's song, "This Life is Weary" (1971: 117). The lines "A Dream – a *Wa*-kening" refer both to Laura's "awakening" and to the carter's wake. Magalaner, like Nownes, reads Laura's initiation into adulthood as a refusal of her earlier generalizations and clichés, but there is equal evidence in the text that Laura's epiphany does not mark her departure from the social order represented by her family, but her initiation *into* and as *dictated by* that order, and specifically by her mother. There are clues earlier in the story that Laura's experience is fated or controlled by someone outside herself, especially when her mother's hat is forced upon her head. Significantly, Laura goes to the cottage unwillingly, under her mother's direction and wearing the hat. (Magalaner observes that "the reader quickly senses that the hands guiding the strings are the hands of the mother" (1971: 113).) As Nownes points out, the hat is doubly symbolic, its black color suggesting funereal garb, and its daisies symbolizing gaiety and festivity. Nownes argues that Laura's sobbed apology for the hat does not mark her knowledge of its inappropriateness, but her awareness of the inevitable "fact of class distinctions" (Nownes 1993–4: 56). Even as the facts of death and hardship sink into her consciousness, Laura chooses to excuse her genuine emotional reaction by recourse to etiquette. This is another pose, more akin to Mrs Sheridan's social codes than Laura's moral ones. As Atkinson has argued, Mrs Sheridan finds in the carter's death an object lesson for her daughter, a way

> to move her daughter from a mildly rebellious adolescence to a young-womanhood that does not question the status quo. In short, Laura's own transformation is entirely conventional; the subversiveness of the story lies in its uncovering of Laura's middle-class tendency to aestheticise the unfamiliar and thereby neutralise it. (2006: 54)

In this way, not only are the uncomfortable facts of death and poverty assimilated into Laura's "beautiful" vision of the world, but, as Atkinson argues, she can banish her earlier "inconvenient sympathies for those who are less fortunate than herself" (59).

Finally, it is significant that Laurie, rather than Jose or Mrs Sheridan herself, goes to collect Laura from the underworld of the cottages. Laurie's presence at the end of the narrative, like Laura's revelation at the wake, can be read in a number of ways. We know that Laurie had been Laura's partner in childhood explorations of the poor neighborhood, and this, along with their similar names, establishes them as counterparts. Laurie's self-assured attitude marks him as one of the already initiated; like Jose, he has already grown into his adult role. When he meets Laura at the end of the story, it is the final marker of *her* initiation into *her* adulthood, even as she (perhaps) realizes how problematic that adulthood is. As Zivley points out, as a male, Laurie is comfortably integrated into middle-class manhood. Laura's speechlessness, and Laurie's ability to close her sentence and the entire story with his own knowing pronouncement and slightly patron-izing use of "darling," mark the fact that men and women enter adulthood under very different terms. Zivley points out that when Laura "has experiences that transcend those of her family and society, she has no words or phrases with which to express those experiences – even to herself" (1995: 74). The conflict of the story, Zivley contends, is Laura's final isolation from her male counterpart and childhood companion, Laurie. Her brother's initiation into the adult world is an ascent into authority based on his male gender while, for Laura, initiation is merely an "extension from the powerless of childhood toward the powerlessness of womanhood and wifehood" (73). At the same time, neither Laura nor Laurie can explain their shared understanding, and Atkinson argues that "[w]e can see the non-exchange on life as Mansfield's sly representation of a class discourse that chooses not to inquire too closely into the inequalities and injustices of its power base" (Atkinson 2006: 60). Thus, in Mansfield's closing scene of awestruck aware-ness and emotional connection, we find an undercurrent of darkness and *dis*con-nection that can be read as an implicit acknowledgment of ineradicable power structures, an upholding of gender and class differences belied by the text's more explicit suggestions that Laura's narrative is one of transcendence and self-determination.

"Marriage à la Mode"

Although it is included in the same collection as "The Garden Party," "Marriage à la Mode" initially seems a very different and much simpler story. Mansfield again uses omniscient third-person narration interspersed with free indirect discourse, so that the narrator seems to be William, husband of Isabel and father to two young boys. William lives and works in London during the week, and as the story opens he is preparing for a regular weekend visit to his family in the country. The opening dilemma – the question of gifts to bring to his children – is swiftly replaced with the larger problem of the "new" Isabel. As his train travels away from the city, William feels a "familiar dull gnawing in his breast" (Mansfield 2001: 310) and remembers the early days of his marriage in a cramped but cheerful house in the city. Mimicking his wife, he condemns his sentimentality, and we learn that Isabel has since been "rescued" from the tedium of domestic life by a new circle of friends. These include Moira Morrison, who calls Isabel "Titania," Bobby Kane, Bill Hunt, and Dennis Green, all aspiring artists or writers. William dislikes these bohemian usurpers, and has a "horrible vision" of one of them stealing the fruit he has bought for his sons and "lapping up a slice [. . .] behind the nursery door" (310). Fears about the group's parasitical nature are not unfounded: Moira and the men take advantage of Isabel's impressionable nature, eating her food, littering her rooms, and spiriting her away from William. He spends a lonely weekend in the house while the rest of the group goes swimming, and even overhears them mocking him. He is granted one moment alone with Isabel just before he returns to London, when she dispatches him with a hurried kiss. Although these events seem to be the normal order of things, the weekend galvanizes William into writing a love letter to his wife. In the final scene of the story, we see Isabel reading this letter out to her friends, who laugh hysterically at William's sentimentality. Momentarily, Isabel is horrified by their laughter and her own heartlessness. She retreats to the bedroom, where she decides to reply to William, but is finally drawn away again, "laughing in the new way" (321) as she rejoins the circle.

At first glance, "Marriage à la Mode" is a satirical send-up of what Magalaner calls "the flamboyant, articulate, utterly silly pseudo-bohemian" (1971: 86). Bobby, Bill, and Dennis are ridiculous characters who take themselves and their worthless "art" far too seriously. William's nightmarish vision of one of them crouching in the nursery is fitting, since these young men are "playing at children and failing to carry off the pretense" (Magalaner 1971: 88). Moira, too, behaves like a little girl, whining and jumping as she wears "a bonnet like a huge strawberry" (Mansfield 2001: 314). The dichotomy in "The Garden Party" between the natural and the artificial is re-established here, as William's memories of his own childhood and Isabel's former freshness stand in stark contrast to the contrived play-acting of her new companions. The new Isabel, or "Titania," is bewitched by this group's fashionable posing, as seen in her rejection of all things traditional and "dreadfully sentimental" (309): she even discards the children's toys in favor of more exotic items from Russia and Serbia. As Weaver points out, life with the new Isabel is entirely à la mode: "The couple has no last name, implying how far they have escaped from family and traditions, how free they are from the conventional" (1990: 30). Of course, since we see Isabel from William's wounded perspective, it is her airs and antics, rather than William's "dreadful sentimentality," that seem ridiculous.

As in "The Garden Party," however, this story resists a unitary interpretation. On the surface, the text condemns Isabel's heartlessness; even she can see, if only for a moment, that her new ways are "shallow, tinkling, vain" (Mansfield 2001: 320). But her ultimate suppression of this awareness, and the allusions throughout the story to daydreams and fantasy, suggest that this is a modern "Midsummer Night's Dream" in which both husband and wife are spellbound by delusion. When William recalls their "poky" house in London, we are afforded a glimpse of Isabel's deep unhappiness:

> He hadn't the remotest notion in those days that she really hated that inconvenient little house, that she thought the fat Nanny was ruining the babies, that she was desperately lonely, pining for new people and new music and pictures and so on. (Mansfield 2001: 313)

Tropes of stagnation recur when the old Isabel temporarily returns. Reading William's letter, Isabel has a "stifled feeling" (319), and the "grave bedroom" that seems to admonish her conjures up the image of a tomb. Even as the text presents Isabel's epiphany as a possible escape from life "à la mode," the alternative on offer – a return to her former self – is even less attractive. Thus, even as the story generates sympathy for her husband, we see that "William is no Oberon" (Magalaner 1971: 90). If Isabel distracts herself from an unhappy marriage with silly escapades, William is equally in denial. Too much a "stranger" in his own family (Mansfield 2001: 312), he cannot regain Isabel's respect and love. His retreat into daydreams about the past is tinged with a nostalgia and desperation that recalls the bohemians' pointless and childish antics. He cannot even read his work papers, which seem to be divorce documents; the lines dissolve into ellipses as his mind wanders to the past.

This "marriage à la mode" is more tragic than it first seems, as it becomes apparent that the couple neither love nor really know one another. William is in love with a fantasy of the old Isabel, while she in turn pretends to be enamored of her bohemian friends. One of the group's paintings cruelly satirizes the situation with its depiction of a man with "wobbly legs" offering a flower to a woman with "one very short arm and one very long, thin one" (Mansfield 2001: 315). The picture mocks the artist's lack of talent, but also suggests Isabel's two-sided personality (two different arms, or sides) and William's inability to stand up for himself. Even William's letter and Isabel's epiphany cannot alter this new state of things. Under the story's satirical, witty surface, we see profound suffering in their desperate but ultimately futile attempts to wake from a dream life that is really a nightmare.

The conclusions of "The Garden Party" and "Marriage à la Mode" illustrate Head's assertions about the modernist short story's disunifying epiphanies. Thus, both aesthetically and thematically, the two stories conform to Hanson's definition of the short story as "a form of the margins" that lends itself to "the partial, the incomplete, that which cannot be [. . .] entirely satisfactorily explained" (Hanson 1989: 2). Laura's new consciousness after viewing the carter's corpse, and Isabel's fleeting awareness of her own frivolity and heartlessness, also position both women on the margins: they are momentarily cast outside their social circles, cut off from brother or husband, and alienated even from themselves, since their previous sense of identity has been entirely undermined. This fits O'Connor's oft-repeated maxim that the short story is suited to outsiders (1963). But in both "The Garden Party" and "Marriage à la Mode," nothing is finally accomplished by the characters' moments of transcendence and alienation. Distance from the old reality does not necessarily yield a lasting perspective or more profound understanding. Rather, there is in Mansfield a sense of futility that accompanies epiphany, even as these moments contain the potential for recognizing the truth, profundity, chaos, or darkness of life. Too often, Mansfield's characters turn away from these uncomfortable visions, or the visions are reducible to something bleaker and more mundane: the upholding of "absurd class distinctions" in Laura's case, or another pose or delusion in Isabel's. Life's sparkling surface sometimes illuminates its darker, deeper underside, even if only to banish it again to the margins: love is reduced once more to sentimentality, trust is made into an object of ridicule, or an ugly death is conveniently reframed as a beautiful picture. In the same way, Mansfield's exposed techniques, self-conscious ironic voice, and deliberately foregrounded images are the surface of her texts, and these bright and brilliant flourishes of her art reveal, even as they undermine and dispel, glimpses of other meanings and darker possibilities.

REFERENCES AND FURTHER READING

Atkinson, W. (2006). "Mrs. Sheridan's Masterstroke: Liminality in Katherine Mansfield's 'The Garden Party,'" *English Studies* 87/1: 53–61.

Dunbar, P. (1997). *Radical Mansfield: Double Discourse in Katherine Mansfield's Short Stories.* Basingstoke: Macmillan.

Fullbrook, K. (1986). *Katherine Mansfield.* Brighton: Harvester.

Hanson, C. (1989). *Re-reading the Short Story.* Basingstoke: Macmillan.

Head, D. (1992). *The Modernist Short Story: A Study in Theory and Practice.* Cambridge: Cambridge University Press.

Kaplan, S.J. (1991). *Katherine Mansfield and the Origins of Modernist Fiction.* Ithaca, NY: Cornell University Press.

Kleine, D. (1963). "'The Garden Party': A Portrait of the Artist," *Criticism: A Quarterly for Literature and the Arts* 5/4: 360–71.

Magalaner, M. (1971). *The Fiction of Katherine Mansfield.* Carbondale, Ill.: Southern Illinois University Press.

Mansfield, K. (2001). *The Collected Stories.* London: Penguin.

Murry, J.M. (ed.) (1928). *The Letters of Katherine Mansfield,* vol. II. London: Constable.

Nathan, R.B. (1993). "'With Deliberate Care': The Mansfield Short Story," in R.B. Nathan (ed.), *Critical Essays on Katherine Mansfield,* pp. 93–100. New York: Hall.

Nownes, N.L. (1993–4). "'The Garden Party': Responding to Katherine Mansfield's Invitation," *World Literature Written in English* 33/2–34/1: 49–57.

O'Connor, F. (1963). *The Lonely Voice: A Study of the Short Story.* London: Macmillan.

Pilditch, J. (ed.) (1996). *The Critical Response to Katherine Mansfield*. Westport, Conn.: Greenwood.

Robinson, R. (ed.) (1994). *Katherine Mansfield: In from the Margin*. Baton Rouge: Louisiana State Press.

Smith, A. (2000). *Katherine Mansfield: A Literary Life*. Basingstoke: Palgrave.

Weaver, G. (1990). *Katherine Mansfield: A Study of the Short Fiction*. Boston: Twayne.

Zivley, S.L. (1995). "Laura, Laurie, and Language in Mansfield's 'Garden Party,'" *Journal of the Short Story in English* 25: 71–7.

18
Frank O'Connor:
"Guests of the Nation" and
"My Oedipus Complex"

Greg Winston

When it appeared in the January 1931 issue of *Atlantic Monthly*, "Guests of the Nation" was Frank O'Connor's first published work of short fiction. Later that year, it became the title story of a collection published by Harold Macmillan at the recommendation of AE (George Russell). A debut work, it is also a representative one, announcing numerous features that characterize O'Connor's contribution to the short story. Its marginal characters, transformative action, multivalent symbols, and remarkable irony would all remain staples of O'Connor's writing over the ensuing four decades. For such formal techniques and for its effective rendering of the psychological trauma of war, "Guests of the Nation" has been widely anthologized and translated into a number of languages, including French, German, Slovak, and Flemish. Drawing upon his own experience as a Republican soldier in the Irish Civil War, O'Connor constructs a local tale with universal significance.

The story relates how, during the Irish war of independence, two British prisoners, Belcher and Hawkins, befriend their captors and community. Their prison is a rural cottage, where they help with chores, discuss politics, play cards, and debate theology. Over the course of several weeks, they forge a friendship with their two Irish guards, Bonaparte and Noble, as well as the woman of the house. The connection becomes such that, when the command comes from above to shoot the prisoners in retaliation for recent casualties, the captors find it difficult to carry out the orders. Two hard-line commanding officers arrive and the unpleasant task is done, but at no small cost to both the victims and their executioners. The climactic scene and its aftermath show the deeply personal impact felt on all sides.

One of O'Connor's own defining criteria for the short story is that instead of focusing, as does the novel, on a singular hero, it concentrates on "a submerged population group," those separated from the larger society through either material or spiritual shortcomings (O'Connor 1965: 18). Regardless of national and cultural identities, the key characters in "Guests of the Nation" exist at the margins; whether British or Irish, they are caught up in the fractured, isolating world of war. Guards and prisoners alike occupy a remote, interpersonal terrain that, through the climactic, almost fratricidal act, further separates them in death, leaving all equally and utterly alone.

The story is told by Bonaparte and through its first-person narrative ultimately comes to rest on the personal dislocation that he, Noble, and the old woman suffer as a result of the execution of Belcher and Hawkins. Instead of communing in grief, they move further apart from each other, as evidenced in the spatial imagery of the final passage. For Noble, the killing and burial site becomes magnified to the point that it is the only visible thing in the entire world, while for Bonaparte:

> it was as if the patch of bog where the Englishmen were was a million miles away, and even Noble and the old woman, mumbling behind me, and the birds and the bloody stars were all far away, and I was somehow very small and very lost and lonely like a child astray in the snow. And anything that happened me afterwards, I never felt the same about again. (O'Connor 1956: 16)

To Bonaparte's nihilistic perspective, the prayers of the woman and Noble come through only as "mumbling": human community and natural beauty are distant to the point of being unreachable. As Michael Steinman observes, the concluding sentence of the story paraphrases Nikolai Gogol's "The Overcoat" and O'Connor's short stories as "a transfiguring experience for its characters and the reader" (1994: 3). Indeed, that story is singled out in *The Lonely Voice* as the genesis for modern short fiction when O'Connor echoes a claim by Turgenev: "We all came out from under Gogol's "Overcoat" (1965: 14).

Along with underscoring Bonaparte's cold and isolated spiritual reaction to the murders, the final image of snow functions on an additional level that might properly be described as mythic. The image harkens back to a somewhat obscure allusion made earlier by the woman of the house when, at the end of the first section, Hawkins tries to make her curse the drought that has overtaken the countryside. But instead, "she gave him a great come-down by blaming it entirely on Jupiter Pluvius" (O'Connor 1956: 5). Hawkins and Bonaparte do not know what to make of the reference, but Noble tells them that among the pagans Jupiter Pluvius "had something to do with the rain" (O'Connor 1956: 5). J.R. Crider discusses how the pre-Christian deity Jupiter Pluvius represents not only rain and sky but also symbolizes, as Roman counterpart to Zeus, the sacred host–guest bond that the Irish soldiers will violate (1986: 409). The notion of the disrupted water-cycle becomes a background motif paralleling the war's disruption of human relations. Instead of water bringing an end to drought and a regenerative peace to the countryside, the only hint of relief comes in its frozen form, snow, which is confined through Bonaparte's thoughts, to a figurative and imaginary realm.

On several occasions O'Connor deploys significant imagery to foreshadow the Englishmen's tragic deaths. First, in a metaphorical account of their ability to assimilate into Irish culture, the narrator remarks, "it was my belief that you could have planted that pair down anywhere from this to Claregalway and they'd have taken root like a native weed" (O'Connor 1956: 3). Like Ireland's twelfth-century Anglo-Norman invaders, Belcher and Hawkins seem fast on their way to becoming more Irish than the Irish themselves. Within days, however, the two will be quite literally rooted in the bog behind the farmhouse. A few pages later, the taciturn Belcher is described "walking, in and out, like a ghost, without a word" (O'Connor 1956: 5), another subtle hint that the English prisoners are not long for this world. Similarly, the ashes (O'Connor 1956: 3) associated with Belcher in the opening image of the story imply his longed-for domestic comfort as well as "his later death and the larger mortality and transitoriness of all human life" (Evans 1998: 266). Like many images in the story, the possibilities cut both ways, contributing in microcosm to the broader irony of the entire story.

Symbolic naming in the story effectively conveys character traits, also in ironic fashion. For example, the surnames Hawkins and Belcher seem respectively to suggest soaring abstraction and boisterous humanity, yet the two Englishmen exhibit a grounded intellect and courteous respectability. These qualities surprise their guards as much as they surprise readers, and ultimately establish the friendship that makes their execution such a difficult task. On the Irish side, Bonaparte and Noble demonstrate neither the military command nor moral courage their names imply. The name symbolism applies to lesser characters, too. For instance, the coldly calculating Jeremiah Donovan is an echo of the nineteenth-century leader Jeremiah O'Donovan, popularly known as O'Donovan Rossa. As Earl Briden argues, this connection lends a "final irony" to the story by showing "that history may well fashion its legends of patriotic heroism from the stuff of such cold-blooded dullards as Donovan" (1976: 81). Even O'Donovan's quiet henchman Feeney evokes the glorified violence of the 1860s Fenian movement, to which both men are obvious throwbacks. And it is worth noting that Jeremiah O'Donovan also shares the author's own paternal surname – O'Connor was born Michael O'Donovan – a fact that suggests a possible hint of self-doubt surrounding the military period of his own life.

Indeed, several autobiographical threads weave through "Guests of the Nation." An incident from O'Connor's own stint as a Republican soldier in Ireland's Civil War of 1921–2 brought him close to the same dilemma that Bonaparte and Noble face in the story. "When he was ordered to shoot unarmed Free State soldiers who were walking out with girl friends, he brought the matter to higher authority and got the order rescinded" (Ellmann 1981: x). O'Connor himself noted two sources for "Guests of the Nation," one literary, the other experiential. Initially, he downplayed the tale as an attempt to imitate one of the war stories in Isaac Babel's *The Red Cavalry* (Steinman 1994: 3); later, he told in a 1963 BBC interview of how it originated from a conversation he heard in a civil-war internment camp:

> I overheard a group of country boys talking about two English soldiers whom they had held as hostages and who soon got to know the countryside better than their guards. It

was obvious from the conversation that the two English boys had won the affection and understanding of our own fellows, though it wasn't the understanding of soldiers who find they have much in common, but the understanding of two conflicting ways of life which must either fight or be friends. (qtd in Steinman 1994: 3)

Similarly, the dialog for Belcher and Hawkins developed from a boyhood recollection of hearing British soldiers while he played around the Cork army barracks (Matthews 1983: 392, n.9).

From its very title and unlikely bonding between enemies, "Guests of the Nation" announces the irony that defines much of O'Connor's short fiction. Irony is an essential stylistic ingredient to his writing. As noted, irony labels characters. It also divides sentences, marks twists in plot, and measures out the distance between narrator and other characters in numerous stories that followed "Guests of the Nation" (Evans and Magaw 1998: 150–5). Irony also seems to shape how he saw that story and wished for others to see it. When O'Connor revised "Guests of the Nation" in 1954 for inclusion in *More Stories by Frank O'Connor*, among dozens of other stylistic changes he added a fourth occurrence of each of two key words, "unforeseen" and "duty" (Liberman 1987: 440). Repeating these terms expands their thematic role and heightens their ironic function through the story. The betraying capacity of "duty" and its "unforeseen" consequences is constantly suggested by fleeting mention of both words, then finally and inevitably realized in the tragic conclusion. The words seem to echo like unheeded warnings across the story, their meaning only fully recognized when it's too late. In one view, this "penchant for paradox" on O'Connor's part generally comes as "a direct result of his attempt to look at the world accurately and to see it whole, with all its mess and complexities, all its mixed, hidden, or unsuspected motives, all its examples of virtue, vice, and everything in-between" (Evans and Magaw 1998: 155). In "Guests of the Nation," it allows the reader to enter into an intimate partnership with Bonaparte when all other connections have been severed or lost.

Unless one misses this ironic implication, it is difficult to read "Guests of the Nation" as anything but a condemnation of war. A number of critics have regarded the story along such lines, describing it as an "illustration of the cruelty of war, and its absurdity" (Ellmann 1981: x) and "undoubtedly one of the finest anti-war stories ever written" (McKeon 1998: 80). Another places it among "the most eloquent commentaries on the inhumanity of war" (Tomory 1980: 30). Perhaps the greatest part of that eloquence resides in the story's uncanny ability to convey the spiritual dislocation of war at the most basic and individual level.

While adept at writing the devastating, divisive effects of politics and war, Frank O'Connor was equally innovative and at home in telling a more light-hearted and humorous tale. For this, too, he was able to draw from his own experience. In his memoir *An Only Child*, he describes himself growing up as "a classic example of the Mother's Boy" (O'Connor 1961: 23). That early role was later underscored by his pseudonym, which combined his middle name with his mother's maiden name. The early and enduring bond between mother and son developed in large part because of the father's extended absences. Like so many thousands of Irishmen in the early twentieth century with little prospect of steady employment, Michael O'Donovan took the economic risk of soldiering. Whether he was attached to regional barracks or seeing overseas action during the Boer War, it was left for Minnie to raise their young son. When at last an army pension was secured and the three O'Donovans settled into home life together, it made for a trying and at times embittering domestic situation.

"My Oedipus Complex" renders this household stress in hilarious fictional terms. Although addressing a potentially traumatic psychology, the story manages to defuse the tension through witty tone and sympathetic characterization, achieving in the end an entertaining and tender commentary on family life. It is a down-to-earth domestic account that also brushes the realms of classical epic or historical allegory. On the formal level, the story showcases more of O'Connor's methods in the form in which he made his name as both theorist and practitioner. These techniques include a well-conceived storyline and calculated temporal strategy; yet the success of the story ultimately lies with its likeable characters and amusingly ironic narration.

The plot of "My Oedipus Complex" fuses ancient and modern elements in original, playful fashion. The experience of men returning from war, a common formula in Western literature since *The Odyssey*, combines with Freudian psychology, itself rooted in Greek myth, as the title reminds us. Such epic and tragic possibilities are comically offset by the mundane setting of middle-class Cork, where Larry, a young, only-child raised almost entirely by his mother, comes to know his father Mick for the first time upon Mick's demobilization. At first Larry experiences his father's presence as a rude intrusion into the intimate world he has constructed for himself and his mother. The initial equilibrium of paternal absence gives way to father–son conflict, as the two vie jealously with one another for the wife's and mother's attention. The conflict is only at last resolved by the unexpected alliance that forms when Mick and Larry find a common enemy in the new baby, Sonny, who manages to best both suitors and become the new object of the mother's affection.

The limited connection of father and son is established from the opening lines, narrated, like the entire story, in Larry's point of view: "Father was in the army all through the war – the first war, I mean – so, up to the age of five, I never saw much of him, and what I saw did not worry me" (O'Connor 1956: 249). When Larry does see his father, it's through half-sleep as "a big figure in khaki" or else he hears the slamming doors and clattering boots that mark his comings and goings. For these mysterious and intermittent visits, Larry likens his father to Santa Claus, a simple, child's metaphor that will take on greater significance by the end of the story.

Otherwise, the first part of the story serves to define the mother–son connection. The narrator ruminates on his personal paradise that follows a recurring pattern of lazy mornings, downtown shopping, and countryside rambles. This insular life with Mother is indirectly represented in the silly early-morning dialogs Larry stages between his two feet: "I put my feet out from under the clothes – I called them Mrs. Left and Mrs. Right – and invented dramatic situations for them in which they discussed the problems of the day" (O'Connor 1956: 250). Primarily familiar with his mother's world, Larry not surprisingly develops an imaginative discourse that is markedly domestic and female. For a little while, anyway, he lives in intimate isolation with Mother before the male world noisily intrudes; he characterizes the contrast in one simple, ironic declaration: "The war was the most peaceful period of my life" (O'Connor 1956: 249).

Peace is disturbed as the narrative shifts to present the conflict of the father's first days back in the house and, more specifically, the "big bed" Michael Steinman calls the structural center of the story (1996: par. 29). For it is there that the father–son quarrel announces itself most directly and physically, when Larry finds his morning routine disrupted by his father's presence: "There was no room at Mother's side so I had to get between her and Father . . . He was taking up more than his fair share of the bed, and I couldn't get comfortable, so I gave him several kicks that made him grunt and stretch" (O'Connor 1956: 253). So runs the first in a "series of skirmishes" (O'Connor 1956: 258) that render the home front an all-new theater of engagement.

From this point the main character rounds out the Freudian pattern predicted in the story's title. Larry's desire to be the sole object and recipient of his mother's affections is accompanied by his fervent rebellion against his father as man of the house – a rebellion which mostly takes the form of rational disregard or haughty contempt towards his father. Despite (or perhaps owing to) this tone of dismissive arrogance, one comes to sympathize all the more with Larry, while at the same time never entirely trusting in his version of events. He is an unreliable narrator but at the same time a rather likable intelligence, even in his most critical or manipulative moments. Most readers will probably not only forgive Larry his puerile offenses but even find them endearing.

At the same time, such moments engender empathy for the parents who must bear the brunt of this five-year-old personality. Take, for example, the following account of a father–son walk through town:

> Father had an extraordinary capacity for amiable inattention. I sized him up and wondered would I cry, but he seemed to be too remote to be annoyed even by that. Really, it was like going for a walk with a mountain! He either ignored the wrenching and pummeling entirely, or else glanced down with a grin of amusement from his peak. I had never met anyone so absorbed in himself as he seemed. (O'Connor 1956: 252)

The concluding remark could just as well apply to the narrator himself, who never seems to acknowledge that his own self-absorption might be the real problem.

It is such ironic distancing that contributes in large part to the effectiveness of the narration. Its well-conceived combination of childish impulses and mature vocabulary suggests that the story is being retold by Larry years later in adulthood. The result is an "alchemical mixture of language and voices: the urbane recollections of the adult narrator . . . seamlessly combined with the sensibility and perspective of a five-year-old" (Steinman 1996: par. 30). Although a precise narrative present is never established, it does not need to be, for the simple reason that, spurred on by the narrator's articulate words and winning personality, one rarely, if ever, pauses to consider the question of his age. Only the opening clarification that Mick returned from "the first war" seems to confirm that the narrator does in fact gaze back across several decades from sometime after World War II. In the inflated context of the story, it allows for the humorous exaggeration that the second war is the one fought between father and son.

Like Joyce's narrators in the childhood stories of *Dubliners*, Larry might be a sensitive five-year-old with the gift of the gab or else an adult with a sensitive and sieve-like memory of youth. Yet O'Connor goes further than Joyce in melding youthful innocence and adult hindsight to produce an ironically humorous result. While the young Larry might not have seen anything funny in the situation, time appears to have taught him the ability to laugh at his former self. This becomes particularly apparent, for instance, in Larry's unhappy realization that his father has returned to stay:

> Mother was pleased as anything. I saw nothing to be pleased about, because, out of uniform, Father was altogether less interesting, but she only beamed, and explained that our prayers had been answered, and off we went to Mass to thank God for having brought Father safely home.
>   The irony of it! (O'Connor 1956: 251)

The narrative gap between innocence and experience becomes the expanding conceptual center of the story when, by claiming to know irony, Larry unknowingly and repeatedly embodies it.

The skillful chronological structure of "My Oedipus Complex" exemplifies another purpose O'Connor relates in his well-known critical treatise on short fiction. In *The Lonely Voice* he distinguishes the short story from the novel on one level for its compressed, organic treatment of time. While for the novelist "the element of Time is his greatest asset; the chronological development of character or incident is essential form," different rules apply for the short-story writer, who replaces that "essential form" of time with its abbreviated version and "organic form, something that springs from a single detail, embraces past, present, and future" (O'Connor 1965: 22). The recurring temporal descriptions that mark the opening of "My Oedipus Complex" soon yield to more precise and regimented depictions of one-time events, as the story comes to focus on several key days in the life of the family. By focusing on a select series of mornings and evenings, O'Connor's narrative charts the progression and changes of the family dynamic. It measures out the pattern of stasis, conflict, and resolution, while at the same time re-creating the child's own gathering awareness of time itself.

Other ways of reading "My Oedipus Complex" include taking into consideration its historical realities and allegorical possibilities. The mythic, universal nature of the title suggests it might apply to any time or place, yet certain subtle details of late-colonial Ireland are indispensable to the story. Neither Cork nor Ireland are ever mentioned by name, but St Augustine's Church, where Larry and his mother pray for Mick's safe return, does confirm the writer's home city. Otherwise, O'Connor forgoes precise names for more generalized place description – "tall, red-brick houses terraced up the opposite hillside" (O'Connor 1956: 250) – that faintly suggests Cork. Personal names like the Geneys, Miss McCarthy, and Mick also imply but never overdo the Irish setting. This achieves the overall remarkable effect of reproducing the bounded geography of childhood. The named places that figure in Larry's plans are simply those local ones that evoke his romantic adventures with Mother: the Glen, the Fox and Hounds, and the Rathcooney Road, are as much as he wants – or the reader needs – to know.

From a historical perspective, however, it is difficult to ignore the fact that Larry's father, that "big figure in khaki" in his regimental uniform, resembles the Black and Tans, the British special-forces units deployed throughout the country during the war for independence. His invasive presence is associated with such details as "model tanks and Gurkha knives with handles of made of bullet cases, and German helmets and cap badges and button-sticks, and all sorts of military equipment" (O'Connor 1956: 249). These souvenirs of the soldier's life align Larry's father with the British imperial project around the globe. Meanwhile, like Larry, Irish republicanism could be said to suffer from its own Oedipus complex; indeed, the patriotic rhetoric of nationalism was often overtly described by a passionate male attachment to a Mother-Ireland figure: the goddess Eiru, the Poor Old Woman, and Cathleen ni Houlihan were among its primary manifestations. Having a father who is also a British soldier therefore represents a sort of double invasion for Larry on both the national and personal levels. To some extent, the child psychology of Larry suggests the portrait of a young nation. The complex negotiation that surrounds this father–son relationship points to preoc-cupations (to borrow Seamus Heaney's term) of a colonial as well as a psychological significance.

In this regard, Larry's Christmas present from Father in the final line of the story brings the narrative full-circle to a literal rendering of the Santa Claus simile from its opening paragraph. In addition, the gesture represents at least a temporary truce between warring factions. The model railway itself is a peace offering with symbolic political overtones beyond the story. For, along with such colonial improvements as the postal and telegraph networks, Britain also gave Ireland its first railways, starting in the mid-nineteenth century. O'Connor's toy train is a child's plaything and a father–son truce, but also the freighted symbol of a paternalistic Anglo-Irish history. As Michael Steinman observes, "My Oedipus Complex" "contributed to the paradox of O'Connor's reputation: those who know none of his other stories think of his fiction as limited to a world of precocious children, one where no dilemma is serious or irreparable" (Steinman 1996: par. 29). Yet, considered against the backdrop of the early twentieth century, even this funny story of childhood suggests as well the more serious growing pains associated with emergent nationhood.

In the end, though, any of history's longer shadows do little to dim the narrative brilliance and spirit of the story. Its predominant disposition is one of sweet forgiveness and celebration on all sides. Indeed, it is difficult for a reader not to join in Larry's uncontainable enthusiasm and metaphorical celebration of life when he says, "Next morning I woke at my usual hour, feeling like a bottle of champagne" (O'Connor 1956: 253). Even such a minor, passing comment holds something of the wit, energy, and artistry that mark the story as a whole. As Michael Matthews describes it, the narrative voice strikes "a tone of humorous congeniality, an innocent, self-effacing air that disarms the reader by its wise perspective and allows the author an escape hatch" (1983: 259). Yielding everything over to this wise-child narrator in his amusing family crisis, O'Connor does escape, but he never ventures far from his readers or, for that matter, his own experience.

In a 1963 interview, Michael Longley asked O'Connor the fundamental question of whether he preferred writing autobiography or short stories. "I prefer short stories," O'Connor replied. "You are more like God when you're writing stories and controlling the characters" (1990: 270). Yet, to a certain extent, "Guests of the Nation" and "My Oedipus Complex" demonstrate O'Connor's attempt to bring some of the extreme experiences from his own childhood and adolescence into comprehensible relief. In this regard, they parallel an effort that would eventually produce two volumes of memoir. They are also just two of many stories that clearly showcase Frank O'Connor as a creator of a rich, ironic brand of short fiction that depicts life in Ireland, or life anywhere, in its most devastating consequences and uplifting possibilities.

REFERENCES AND FURTHER READING

Briden, E.F. (1976). "'Guests of the Nation': A Final Irony," *Studies in Short Fiction* 13/1: 79–81.

Crider, J.R. (1986). "Jupiter Pluvius in "Guests of the Nation," *Studies in Short Fiction* 23/4: 407–11.

Ellmann, R. (ed.) (1981). *The Collected Stories of Frank O'Connor*. New York: Knopf.

Evans, R.C. (1998). "'Guests of the Nation': A Close Reading," in R.C. Evans and R. Harp (eds), *Frank O'Connor: New Perspectives. Locust Hill Literary Studies* 23: 263–96. West Cornwall, Conn.: Locust Hill.

Evans, R.C. and Magaw, K. (1998). "Irony and Paradox in Frank O'Connor's Style," *Frank O'Connor: New Perspectives*, in R.C. Evans and R. Harp (eds), *Locust Hill Literary Studies* 23: 149–58. West Cornwall, Conn.: Locust Hill.

Liberman, M. (1987). "Unforeseen Duty in Frank O'Connor's 'Guests of the Nation'," *Studies in Short Fiction* 24/4: 438–41.

Longley, M. (1990). "Interview with Frank O'Connor," *Twentieth Century Literature* 36/3 (autumn): 269–74 (reprint of 1963 Trinity College magazine interview).

McKeon, J. (1998). *Frank O'Connor: A Life*. Edinburgh: Mainstream.

Matthews, J. (1983). *Voices: A Life of Frank O'Connor*. New York: Atheneum.

O'Connor, F. (1956). *Stories by Frank O'Connor*. New York: Vintage.

O'Connor, F. (1961). *An Only Child*. London: Macmillan.

O'Connor, F. (1965). *The Lonely Voice: A Study of the Short Story*. Cleveland: World Publishing.

O'Connor, F. (1968). *My Father's Son*. London: Macmillan.

Steinman, M. (1990). *Frank O'Connor at Work*. Syracuse, NY: Syracuse University Press.

Steinman, M. (1994). *A Frank O'Connor Reader*. Syracuse, NY: Syracuse University Press.

Steinman, M. (1996). "Frank O'Connor," *British Short-Fiction Writers, 1915–1945, Dictionary of Literary Biography*, vol. 162, ed. J.H. Rogers. Gale Group. Ebscohost, August 15, 2006: <http://galenet.galegroup.com>.

Tomory, W. (1980). *Frank O'Connor*. Boston: Twayne.

19

The Short Stories of
Liam O'Flaherty

Shawn O'Hare

Liam O'Flaherty (Liam Ó Flaithearta) was born on Friday, August 28, 1896, in Gort na gCapall ("the field of the horses"), near the village of Kilmurvey, in the shadow of Dun Aengus, on Inishmore, the largest of the Aran Islands, County Galway, Ireland. He was the eighth of nine children born to Michael and Margaret Ganly O'Flaherty. Michael O'Flaherty was an Irish nationalist (a Fenian and a Land Leaguer) who is said to have been the first member of Sinn Fein on the island and led the island's resistance to land speculators. Tom O'Flaherty, one of Liam's older brothers, recounts some of the family's history in his story collections *Aranmen All* (1934) and *Cliffmen of the West* (1935), noting that the O'Flaherty household was the meeting place on the island for music, dancing, and stories, with his mother regarded as the best singer and his father the best dancer on the island. Faced with great poverty and hunger, as most of the islanders were, and an often-absent husband, Liam O'Flaherty's mother used storytelling and humor as a way to distract her children.

Growing up on Inishmore had a significant impact on Liam O'Flaherty's world view, as well as on his stories and novels, and the harsh natural world is often depicted in O'Flaherty's works. Inishmore is located in Galway Bay at the edge of the Atlantic Ocean off the west coast of Ireland, and is roughly sixteen square miles. It is a barren place dominated by rocks and stones with few trees, and the crops that are grown there (mostly potatoes) require diligent and difficult work from the farmers, who often have to gather seaweed from the ocean to fertilize the land. Powerful sea storms, along with blanketing fog, add to the isolation of Inishmore (which is a two-hour motorized boatride from Galway). Made famous in Robert J. Flaherty's 1934 "documentary" *Man of Aran*, Inishmore is an island of fishermen (sharks are the focus in Flaherty's film) and farmers who are often merely trying to survive. That relationship between the natural world – land, sea, wild and domestic animals – shapes O'Flaherty into one of Ireland's great realist/naturalist writers, and is most notably evident in his early short stories.

In 1908, however, at twelve years old, O'Flaherty left Inishmore to attend Rockwell College in Cashel, County Tipperary. In 1914, O'Flaherty moved on to Blackrock College, County Dublin, where he put together a corps of Republican Volunteers. From September 1914 until November 1914, O'Flaherty attended Holy Cross College, a Dublin seminary. In that same year, until 1915, O'Flaherty enrolled in University College, Dublin. However, in 1915, O'Flaherty enlisted in the Irish Guards of the British army, under the name Bill Ganly (his mother's last name). As a private in the infantry, he served in France and Belgium during World War I, until he was wounded by a shell explosion at Langemarck in September. Discharged from the military service because of his injuries, which were labeled *melancholia acuta*, in 1918 O'Flaherty was awarded a BA from University College, Dublin, for his service in the war. O'Flaherty spent the next years, 1918–21, traveling the world – Brazil, Turkey, Canada, and the United States – working manual labor jobs. In 1921, while back in Ireland, O'Flaherty became involved in the Irish Civil War, supporting the Republican struggle against the Irish Free State government. In January 1922, O'Flaherty and a group of unemployed mean seized the Rotunda in Dublin, raising a red flag. O'Flaherty was well read in Communist and protest literature, and was involved with the International Workers of the World while in Canada and was a member of the James Connolly Club while in Boston. Eventually the Irish government threatened to end the protest with violence, and the men acceded. O'Flaherty remained committed to Marxist and Communist ideology, though his attention soon turned to a writing career. The 1920s proved to be a very productive decade for the Aranman and many of his key works were published, including: novels, *The Neighbour's Wife* (1923), *The Black Soul* (1924), *The Informer* (1925), *Mr. Gilhooley* (1926), *The Assassin* (1928), *The House of Gold* (1929), and *The Return of the Brute* (1929); three short-story collections, *Spring Sowing* (1924), *The Tent* (1926), and *The Mountain Tavern and Other Stories* (1929); and a biography, *The Life of Tim Healy* (1927).

During the 1930s, O'Flaherty published three memoirs – *Two Years* (1930), *I Went to Russia* (1931), and *Shame the Devil* (1934) – that catalogued some of his youthful experiences as well as his political actions and ideas. He continued to publish novels at a breakneck pace, including *The Puritan* (1931), *Skerrett* (1932), *The Martyr* (1932), *Hollywood Cemetery* (1935), and *Famine* (1937), as well as *The Short Stories of Liam O'Flaherty* (1937). In 1932, he was a Founding Member of the Irish Academy of Letters, and in 1935 a film version of *The Informer*, by the American director John Ford, received the Academy award for Best Picture. After 1937, however, O'Flaherty's publishing pace dramatically slowed down, and the novels *Land* (1946) and *Insurrection* (1951) and the story collections *Two Lovely Beasts and Other Stories* (1950), *Dúil* ("Desire" in Irish, 1952), and *The Stories of Liam O'Flaherty* (1956) represent the extent of his publishing until his death in 1984. In his later years, O'Flaherty spent much of his time traveling and lived comfortably and quietly outside the spotlight.

As a novelist, O'Flaherty was most widely praised for *The Informer, Skerrett,* and *Famine*. His artistic vision is classically realist, and his prose style is smooth, clear, to-the-point, but, at times, highly metaphorical. In *The Informer*, O'Flaherty tells the story of Gypo Nolan, who, in the aftermath of the Irish Civil War, reveals the location of a comrade wanted by the Irish government. Nolan is paid twenty pounds for his information and the novel follows him as he spends the money in Dublin's pubs and brothels. Eventually he is tracked down by the revolutionary organization and he is ultimately executed by them for betraying the cause. *Skerrett* takes place in the west of Ireland and is based on a real-life battle between a schoolmaster and a parish priest. In this novel O'Flaherty presents a peasant past that is fading away. The conflict of the earlier period, represented by the schoolmaster, and changing Ireland, represented by the parish priest, results in Skerrett the teacher going mad. *Famine* is a historical novel about Ireland's Great Hunger during the 1840s (and it is also dedicated to film-maker John Ford). The novel is a Marxist critique of those in power (the British landlords) who denied the Irish peasantry the opportunity to survive when a severe blight attacked the potato fields in Ireland. With horrific detail, O'Flaherty describes the slow and painful death that a famine causes, physically, emotionally, and psychologically.

As a short-story writer, O'Flaherty was prolific, authoring almost 200 stories, and is best known for writing concise pieces that are often set in the west of Ireland. Although he is of the same generation as Seán O'Faoláin (b. 1900) and Frank O'Connor (b. 1903), O'Flaherty's short fiction is anchored more in the rich Irish oral tradition than the Corkmen's work, and as a stylist his prose is more direct and the stories more metaphorical. Since he wrote so many stories – and for many different purposes, publications, and audiences – his style and subject matter can vary greatly. However, O'Flaherty's best stories keep the focus on storytelling and for the most part on life on the Aran Islands, and the ways of the fishermen, peasants, and the natural world. Many of O'Flaherty's early short pieces focus on animals and the rural life of Inishmore, including "The Cow's Death," "The Wave," "The Rockfish," and "The Hawk." In these pieces, the natural world – which includes the land, the weather, and the animals – are often at the mercy of Chance, an extension of Nature. O'Flaherty's connection to literary realism is just as evident in this work as it is in his later novels. "The Sniper," the first story that brought him attention, is greatly shaped by O'Flaherty's war experiences; he also often wrote about the plight of the peasants, and in stories such as "The Arrest," "The Pedlar's Revenge," and "The Fanatic," loneliness haunts and controls the characters.

In his early stories, O'Flaherty often uses the natural world as an extended metaphor of the human condition. This is evident in stories such as "The Cow's Death," which opens with:

The calf was still-born. It came from the womb tail first. When its red, unwieldy body dropped on greenward it was dead. It lay with its head doubled about its neck in a clammy mess. The men stood about it and shook their heads in silence. The wife of the peasant who owned the cow sighed and said, "It is God's will." (O'Flaherty 1924: 19)

Eventually the cow discovers the corpse of the dead calf, which had been tossed over the cliff and has landed on the rock below. The cow, in an act of mourning that every parent can imagine, throws herself over the cliff to join the calf. Also from that first collection of stories, *Spring Sowing*, is a three-page story called "The Wave." This vignette has no living characters; it is merely an intense description of a wave crashing on to a cliff. O'Flaherty creates and describes the arc of action, much as he would often do for stories about humans. In this case, however, the climatic action is merely the wave hitting the shore. The last paragraph in the story is, in fact, rather anti-climatic:

> The cliff had disappeared. The land sloped down to the edge of the cove. Huge rocks stood awkwardly on the very brink of the flat rock, with the rim of the sea playing between them. Smoke was rising from the fallen cliff. And the wave had disappeared. Already another one was gathering in the cove. (O'Flaherty 1924: 26)

As with many of O'Flaherty's early stories, both "The Cow's Death" and "The Wave" bridge the ideas of Naturalist writers from the late nineteenth century, such as Emile Zola from France and Frank Norris from the United States, because of their emphasis on "environmental determinism." That is, the actions of O'Flaherty's characters – even a cow or a wave – are dictated by their environment. Although the stories about animals and nature may seem "simple," especially considering they were written during the experimental and complicated era of high modernism, O'Flaherty's early work remains effective because the emphasis is always on a condition that is universal: loneliness.

Frank O'Connor labeled such lonely and isolated characters the "submerged population," and argued that stories that focused on social outcasts formed the backbone of the twentieth-century short story. O'Flaherty is firmly in that tradition, and his best stories, including "The Arrest, "The Fanatic," and "The Pedlar's Revenge," are representative of not only O'Flaherty's corpus, but also themes widely examined in modern and Irish short fiction.

In "The Arrest," as in many of O'Flaherty's early works, the mood of the story is determined by the setting. The opening paragraph describes a grey twilight sky, without light from the stars or the moon, and surrounding mountains that are "terrifying" (O'Flaherty 1999c, vol. 3: 374). In the valley, Mary Timmons, nervous and jittery, awaits the arrival of her husband. Mary is from a village and, since she is accustomed to the business of village life and the sound of rumbling trains, her silent and isolated home in the valley is still foreign to her. She fears that her husband will come home drunk, and she notes that when people in her home village drink, they laugh and act the fool, but in the valley intoxication merely makes the locals "mad" (O'Flaherty 1999c, vol. 3: 374). Indeed, her worst fear does come true when her husband Jim returns home drunk with his cousin, Joe Sutton. The two men were drinking in a pub when Joe got into an argument with a police officer. The fight became very violent and Joe struck the Civic Guard in the head, killing him. The two men run to the house, only to have the police arrive. In the end, Joe is captured by the police, and Mary, who has fainted in the ensuing chaos, awakens to the voice of her husband explaining how the fight began in the pub and that he was going to raise his cousin's bail money. The story comes full circle in the final lines, as once again Mary feels trapped by the mountains. Mary's isolation is highlighted with the last line of the story that notes that "Dawn was breaking outside and a multitude of distant birds twittered" (O'Flaherty 1999c, vol. 3: 377). The meaning is clear: while the birds may be free, Mary is not.

"The Pedlar's Revenge" is the story of two neighbors, Old Paddy Moynihan – a mountain of a man who weighs 360 pounds – and The Pedlar, a diminutive man who makes his living repairing goods. The two men have been lifelong foes. Moynihan has used his size and strength to tease and taunt his smaller neighbor ever since they were boys. The Pedlar, on the other hand, has manipulated Moynihan because the larger man is mentally slow and very naive. When the townspeople and police find Moynihan dead in a ravine one day, The Pedlar is immediately the primary suspect because of their long-standing feud. As the police begin to put together the case, and as The Pedlar eventually confesses, Moynihan dies because The Pedlar tells him to fry some potatoes with candles if he is hungry. The Pedlar claims that he was scared for his life when Moynihan came to his house looking for food, so he gave his antagonist that advice, well aware, and proud, that it could lead to Moynihan's death. Indeed, The Pedlar rejoices in his revenge, and crows "I have a lovely satisfaction now for all my terrible shame and pain and sorrow. I can die in peace" (O'Flaherty 1999c, vol. 3: 231).

"The Pedlar's Revenge," like many twentieth-century Irish short stories, emphasizes loneliness and isolation. Paddy Moynihan and The Pedlar have known each other their entire lives, yet, in the end, the death of Moynihan is the result of the hatred built up over those years. Man's inhumanity to man, which O'Flaherty saw first-hand during his time on the battlefields of World War I, and the precarious nature of life, which he saw throughout his childhood on Inishmore, informed O'Flaherty's world view and his creative work. The story, however, that is most focused on loneliness is "The Fanatic."

Set in a dirt-floored dreary pub that doubles as a general store, "The Fanatic" is told in the first person. The speaker enters the pub to find only an old bartender there. They pass the time with the pleasantries of conversation, but the mood turns, fitting for the atmosphere, quite dark. The narrator comes to the opinion that the man in the pub is deranged, and such a conclusion is underscored with vitriolic rants against the British, the French, and, worst of all, the Americans. The bartender apologizes to the visitor for his comments, complaining that he is "half dead with loneliness" and that "loneliness is a terrible disease" (Trevor 1989: 305). In particular, the old man laments that American movies have ruined society. "Women are responsible for all the foreign filth that comes into this holy country," he tells the narrator. "Women are inclined to sin by nature and a hard discipline is needed to keep them on the right road" (307). The old man's sister, so he claims, was influenced by Hollywood, and he blames the films for encouraging her to leave Ireland for America. "Alone! Rotting with the loneliness! My heart broken! Oh! Indeed, the devil can have his fun now and plenty of it" (309). The last paragraph of the story illustrates a man who has lost connection with reality and is consumed by his loneliness. His voice, the things he says, and the style in which O'Flaherty writes the story is truly "fanatical."

Liam O'Flaherty's reputation as one of Ireland's masters of the short story center on the precision with which he draws his characters. For the most part, they are not remarkable. In fact, they are universal – the pain they have experienced, the disappointment they have encountered, and the loneliness that consumes human existence – serve as the foundation of O'Flaherty's artistic vision. From his earliest stories to his later writings, the realities of Liam O'Flaherty's world are present in his work, and for that reason he is one of Ireland's most important writers.

REFERENCES AND FURTHER READING

Doyle, P.A. (1971). *Liam O'Flaherty*. New York: Twayne Publishers.

Doyle, P.A. (1972). *Liam O'Flaherty: An Annotated Bibliography*. Troy, NY: Whitston.

Friberg, H. (1996). *An Old Order and a New: The Split World of Liam O'Flaherty's Novels*. Uppsala: Ubsaliensis S. Academiae.

Jefferson, G. (1993). *Liam O'Flaherty: A Descriptive Bibliography of His Works*. Dublin: Wolfhound Press.

Kelly, A.A. (1976). *Liam O'Flaherty the Storyteller*. London: Macmillan.

O'Brien, J.H. (1973). *Liam O'Flaherty*. Lewisburg: Bucknell University Press.

O'Flaherty, L. (1924). *Spring Sowing*. London: Jonathan Cape.

O'Flaherty, L. (1926). *The Tent*. London: Jonathan Cape.

O'Flaherty, L. (1929). *The Mountain Tavern and Other Stories*. London: Jonathan Cape.

O'Flaherty, L. (1932). *The Wild Swan and Other Stories*. London: Furnival.

O'Flaherty, L. (1937). *The Short Stories of Liam O'Flaherty*. London: Jonathan Cape.

O'Flaherty, L. (1950). *Two Lovely Beasts and Other Stories*. London: Victor Gollancz.

O'Flaherty, L. (1956). *The Stories of Liam O'Flaherty*. New York: Devin-Adair.

O'Flaherty, L. (1976). *The Pedlar's Revenge and Other Stories*. Dublin: Wolfhound Press.

O'Flaherty, L. (1999a). *The Collected Stories*, ed. A.A. Kelly, vol. 1. New York: St Martin's Press.

O'Flaherty, L. (1999b). *The Collected Stories*, ed. A.A. Kelly, vol. 2. New York: St Martin's Press.

O'Flaherty, L. (1999c). *The Collected Stories*, ed. A.A. Kelly, vol. 3. New York: St Martin's Press.

Sheeran, P.F. (1976). *The Novels of Liam O'Flaherty: A Study in Romantic Realism*. Atlantic Highlands, NJ: Humanities Press.

Trevor, W. (ed.) (1989). *The Oxford Book of Irish Short Stories*. New York: Oxford University Press.

Zneimner, J. (1970). *The Literary Vision of Liam O'Flaherty*. Syracuse, NY: Syracuse University Press.

20

W. Somerset Maugham's Ashenden Stories

David Malcolm

Somerset Maugham (1874–1965) wrote over 100 short stories in a long, multifaceted, successful and, ultimately, controversial career (Archer 1993: xi). Clare Hanson writes of him: "Perhaps no story teller besides O. Henry has been so reviled as Somerset Maugham. Yet he remains obstinately there, incapable of being dismissed by anyone interested in the forms and distinctions of the short story" (1985: 49). His detractors have included Edmund Wilson (Loss 1996: 237) and D.H. Lawrence (Curtis and Whitehead 1987: 176–7), although Angus Wilson (Archer 1993: 109–11), Evelyn Waugh (Loss 1996: 238), William Trevor (Hanson 1985: 29), and Graham Greene (Curtis and Whitehead 1987: 290–1) have warmly praised his work. Its technical conservatism is remarked on by critics (Loss 1996: 233–4), but his work has remained widely anthologized, and is, by any measure of commerce or canon, successful. Stanley Archer reckons that "Rain" made Maugham some one million US dollars, and was turned into a stage play and filmed three times (Archer 1993: 3).

Within Maugham's large output, the stories published in *Ashenden: or the British Agent* (1928) are of particular interest. They are seen as important in the development of the genre of espionage fiction, influencing writers such as Eric Ambler, Greene, John le Carré, and Len Deighton (Archer 1993: 118; Ochiogrosso 1989: 216). The protagonist breaks with the glamorous central figure of earlier spy stories, and a glance at (comparable) stories by William Le Queux will show how Maugham breaks with the melodramatic conventions of earlier examples of the genre (Occhiogrosso 1989: 217; see Le Queux 1911: 49–50 for a particularly good example of such melodrama). Savaged in a contemporary review by D.H. Lawrence, who felt they showed a mean and debased view of humanity (Curtis and Whitehead 1987: 176–7), the Ashenden stories were filmed by Alfred Hitchcock (*The Secret Agent* (1936)), and have been taken very seriously by critics such as Frederic Raphael, who sees *Ashenden* as being part of the "debunking literature" of the post-Great War period (1989: 53), and Richard Cordell, who remarks on the stories' objectivity vis-à-vis the participants in World War I (1961: 157–8).

The Ashenden stories present some textual enigmas and complications for the reader. Fourteen Ashenden stories were destroyed by Maugham (Curtis nd: 95). One story, "The Flip of a Coin" – a particularly cynical and inconclusive tale – was omitted from *The Complete Short Stories* published in 1951, and in the subsequent *Collected Short Stories* of 1975. In addition, the sixteen stories of the original edition were conflated into six in these editions (although with very few textual changes).

The Ashenden stories are only one aspect of Maugham's work in the short story. They have, however, consistently found defenders, and certainly played an important role in shaping the genre of espionage fiction in the twentieth century. Perhaps more than any other part of Maugham's output, they can be read with pleasure in the twenty-first century, which has a taste for their astringent, unillusioned world view, their shabby settings and dingy characters, their tensions between melodrama and control, their inconclusiveness, and their central figure's imaginative sympathy with those unlike himself.

In what follows, three of the Ashenden stories are analyzed in detail: "The Hairless Mexican," "Guilia Lazzari," and "Miss King." Together, they illustrate some of the power and complexity of Maugham's spy short stories.

"The Hairless Mexican"

"The Hairless Mexican" is different from some of the other Ashenden stories. The title announces an exotic subject, not the mundane "Miss King," "The Traitor," or "Mr Harrington's Washing." Other stories with glamorous-sounding titles – "Guilia Lazzari" and "His Excellency" – turn out to have more tawdry subjects than the titles suggest. But "The Hairless Mexican" does, indeed, have at its center the outré, but baroquely fascinating figure of Manuel Carmona, *soi-disant* revolutionary, cosmopolitan womanizer, and assassin. Some of the story's settings, too, are less shabby and dull than those of other stories. To be sure, Lyon, where R. and Ashenden meet Carmona, has "dull, busy and prosaic streets" (Maugham 2002: 40), and the sitting-room in the Lyon hotel is "cheerless" and full of "a cold, hard light" (42). In addition, the Hotel de Belfast, where Ashenden stays in Naples, is "a large second-rate hotel near the harbour frequented by commercial travelers and the thriftier kind of tripper" (67). But Ashenden and Carmona travel to Naples in a "salon-lit" that is a cut above normal compartments (54). Naples itself is seen by Ashenden in mostly positive terms, as "a sunny, dusty, lovely city," full of life and charm (68–70). Even after Carmona has murdered his victim and Ashenden's mood has darkened, the backstreets and low-class tavern that they visit have a sinister glamor which other settings in the Ashenden stories do not.

> Ashenden found himself in a long sordid room at one end of which a wizened young man sat at a piano; there were tables standing out from the wall on each side and against them benches. A number of persons, men and women were sitting about. They were

drinking beer and wine. The women were old, painted and hideous, and their harsh gaiety was at once noisy and lifeless. When Ashenden came in they all stared and when they sat down at one of the tables Ashenden looked away in order not to meet the leering eyes, just ready to break into a smile, that sought his insinuatingly. (Maugham 2002: 78)

The Mexico of Carmona's reminiscences and story is colorful and flamboyant.

It did not matter whether what he said was true or not, for those sonorous phrases of his were fruity with the rich-distilled perfumes of romance. He described a spacious life that seemed to belong to another age and his eloquent gestures brought before the mind's eyes tawny distances and vast green plantation, great herds of cattle and in the moonlit night the song of the blind singers that melted into the air and the twanging of guitars. (Maugham 2002: 60)

Despite the occasional glamor and "rich-distilled perfumes of romance" that emanate from the text, the organization of the story material occludes the sensational and underscores the relatively dull (see Archer 1993: 42). In the paperback edition of the third volume of Maugham's *Collected Short Stories* (2002), the first six pages of "The Hairless Mexican" recount R's and Ashenden's meeting in Lyon, their general conversation, their luncheon, and their discussion of Ashenden's next assignment. Carmona then appears, and the next six pages describe him and present his conversation about himself, his view of the world, and his plans with R. and Ashenden. The spy master and his agent briefly discuss Carmona, and then Ashenden waits (as he so often does; in this case in Lyon station). Ashenden and the Mexican assassin travel together to Naples. This section covers approximately fourteen pages, and contains an account of desultory conversation, card playing, and Carmona's story of a woman he loved and had to murder. Ashenden then waits in Naples, killing time pleasantly over two pages. The Mexican reappears to give information about his prospective victim's movements. This covers two pages and is followed by another two pages in which Ashenden again waits. When Carmona returns to the hotel, he and Ashenden search his victim's room for two pages, and then follows a long section (approximately seven pages) in which the two British agents walk the backstreets of Naples, dine in a dubious tavern (where Carmona dances with the sorry prostitutes), and, at the railway station, finally realize that the Mexican has killed the wrong man.

One should notice that the realization of the story material elides Carmona's pursuit and murder of his victim. The nearest the reader comes to the murder is when an alarmed Ashenden sees a spot of blood on the Mexican's cuff (Maugham 2002: 80). The text focuses on discussions preceding the mission, on Carmona's stories from his past, on Ashenden's waiting, on the shabby business of searching the dead man's room, and on killing time before leaving Naples. The story's ending – for all its shock value – is strikingly inconclusive. What happens next? What are the consequences of Carmona's error? The reader never learns. Espionage in this story too is a matter of arranging and waiting. Exciting action occurs off-stage. In the end, nothing much has been achieved, and the reader's knowledge – like Ashenden's too – is incomplete.

"The Hairless Mexican" adds to the richness of the Ashenden stories, particularly in terms of psychological complexity. Shading is added to R's character. The reader sees Ashenden put him socially in his place and deal with the spy master's social uncertainties (2002: 41–2). His lack of aesthetic sense (he thinks the "cheerless" hotel sitting room "very nice") (42); the clear indication that the war is treating him rather well (he now smokes Havana cigars not cheroots) (42); his cold withholding of information from Ashenden (44, 46); the sympathy that Ashenden feels for him with his "tired, lined and yellow face" (45) – all these help to make him a relatively complicated figure. Ashenden, too, is presented complexly – a worldly sophisticate (on macaroni and on holding bottles) (40–1), he suffers from extreme nervousness when catching trains (52–3). He maintains his usual sangfroid and disdain, but also worries about Carmona's victim (68). The murder he has been party to shocks him, so that the sight of a bloodstain on Carmona's cuff disturbs his equanimity (80). The sophisticated spy, too, we learn, wears glasses to decode secret messages (82).

However, the character of the eponymous Carmona dominates the text. He is a figure literally and metaphorically from another world. Ashenden thinks of him thus: "to the amateur of the baroque in human nature he was a rarity to be considered with delight. He was a purple patch on two legs" (50). It is as if he has stepped from the pages of a Le Queux novel, rather than the drab world of most of the Ashenden stories. His unabashed hypocrisy and luxury (the abstemious revolutionary buys silk pyjamas (50)), his lavish personal dressing (47), his drinking habits (51), his bon mots and stories drawn from a world of glamorous romance (60), his huge pistol and knife (57–8), his skilled and predatory dancing (80) – all these lead Ashenden (and the reader) to see him as "that chattering, hideous, and fantastic creature" (68), adding more than a touch of color to the gray shades of Ashenden's espionage work. He is at once Maugham's acknowledgment of his predecessors in the espionage genre, and an anticipation of the *galère* of grotesque villains and henchmen that one finds in later espionage texts (no Bond novel being complete without a couple at least).

"Giulia Lazzari"

"Giulia Lazzari" is one of the most complex of the Ashenden stories. It is full of tensions and contrasts. This is immediately apparent in the contrast between the story's title, containing more than a hint of exotic glamor, and the sordid and shabby story material. R and Ashenden use the hapless and, essentially, helpless Giulia Lazzari, a third-rate dancer cum prostitute of Italian origin who performs under the name of "La Malagueña," to entrap Chandra Lal, a dangerous (from the point of view of the British) Indian nationalist. Cynically, R, with Ashenden's connivance, forces Lazzari to barter her freedom for Lal's, and to play on her lover's feelings, enticing the love-stricken Indian across the French–Swiss border in order that British intelligence can capture and execute him. When apprehended by the French authorities, Lal commits suicide, and Ashenden sends Lazzari off to Spain as her reward.

The story is shaped around a contrast between its largely cheap and tawdry actions and settings, on the one hand, and motifs of romance and melodrama, on the other. Place settings, as in so many of the Ashenden stories, are at times unglamorous and mean. Geneva, which is Ashenden's base, is "agreeable" (2002: 84), and the meeting with R in Paris takes place in "a nicely furnished sitting room" (88); the hotel in Thonon in which Giulia Lazzari is held is "prettily situated" with a "charming view" (106); but, as the action develops, this last becomes transformed into something sordid. In the course of his blackmailing Lazzari, Ashenden sits at her dressing table, while she sobs in despair on the bed. He looks "idly at the odds and ends that littered" the table.

> The toilet things were cheap and tawdry and none too clean. There were little shabby pots of rouge and cold-cream and little bottles of black for the eyebrows and eyelashes. The hairpins were horrid and greasy. The room was untidy and the air was heavy with the smell of cheap scent. Ashenden thought of the hundreds of rooms she must have occupied in third-rate hotels in the course of her life wandering from provincial town to provincial town in one country after another. (Maugham 2002: 115)

Ashenden's sense of the unpleasantness of the hotel is even more marked after Lal's suicide. "When he entered the hotel he was seized on a sudden with distaste for its cold banality. It smelt of cabbage and boiled mutton" (124).

The central actions of the story are similarly mean and banal. Ashenden accompanies Lazzari to Thonon and waits while she entices Lal to cross to the French side of Lac Léman. He bullies her, deceives her, threatens her, and forces her to lie to and, in the end, utterly betray her lover. Her lover dies on the floor of a waiting room at a border crossing. Previous to all this, R has entrapped Lazzari, stolen her correspondence, had one of his agents seduce her, and threatened to send the terrified dancer to prison if she does not cooperate with him to sell her lover. Indeed, sex in this story is usually shabby and transactional. R describes Lazzari simply as a "prostitute" (94); the "good-looking boy" he sends to obtain information about Lazzari presumably uses sex to do so (97); Lazzari speaks wearily of the men whom she has met professionally ("they are not much, the men who haunt those places" (104–5)); in Thonon, Lazzari sells herself to a boatman to carry a message to Lal (112); Ashenden reflects on the prostitution that Lazzari must have engaged in during her life (116).

Even the great world that Ashenden takes R into in Paris is marred by R's gawky, gaping admiration (100). Ashenden himself sees the scene in the fashionable restaurant as full of "vulgar glamour" and "shoddy brilliance." Further, as in many of the Ashenden stories, much of the action is dull and consists of waiting. Ashenden confesses himself almost bored at the beginning of the text (85). In Thonon he must simply wait for Lal to fall into the trap laid for him. Earlier, as he is reading the report on the Indian nationalist, Ashenden is struck by the way in which the subject's exciting and dangerous life is rendered in dry official language (92). The strand of shabby, mean actions is completed at the story's end, when the griefstricken Lazzari asks for her dead lover's twelve pound wrist-watch (125).

However, these motifs of drabness and dullness are contrasted with those of passion and melodrama (see Cordell 1961: 156). Lal's life, through the official prose of the report, is one of "mystery and adventure, of hairbreadth escapes and dangers danger-ously encountered" (Maugham 2002: 92). Lal's and Lazzari's relationship is one of intensity and frequently melodramatic actions and utterances. When Ashenden tells Lazzari that he has a letter to her from her lover, her reaction is intense. "She gave a gasp and her voice broke. 'Oh, show it to me, I beseech you to let me see it'" (104). The content of the letter is similarly passionate. Lal has been led to believe that his lover will meet him in neutral Switzerland.

> He [Lal] was mad with joy at the prospect. He told her in passionate phrases how long the time had seemed to him since they were parted, and how he had yearned for her, and now he was to see her again so soon he did not know how he was going to bear his impatience. She finished it [the letter] and let it drop to the floor. (104)

Lazzari is frequently capable of behavior reminiscent of stage melodrama: she throws herself on the floor and embraces Ashenden's knees (110); she staggers and puts her hand on her heart (111); when about to be taken away by the police, she starts "vio-lently and flung her arms wide" and embraces Ashenden (117–18). Ashenden himself finds "something theatrical" in her conduct (111). When Ashenden reads one of Lal's letters, he is convinced that the writer is deeply in love with Lazzari. "Even the forced and elaborate language in which it was written could not dim the hot fire that burned the pages" (112). The cool British agent feels a "sudden thrill of horror" when he sees Lal's body (122), and describes his suicide as one of "these melodramatic devices" (124), although his own revelation of the situation to Lazzari comes straight from a sensational play.

> Her [Lazzari's] face changed suddenly as she caught sight of his and she sprang up so vehemently that the chair fell over.
> "What is it? Why are you so white?" she cried.
> She turned round and stared at him and her features were gradually twisted to a look of horror.
> "*Il est pris*," she gasped.
> "*Il est mort*," said Ashenden. (Maugham 2002: 124)

There are other tensions throughout the text. R's contempt for Lal's romantic feelings belies his own liaison with a woman, shown in the bowl of roses in his room (89, 93–4). He, himself a powerful man, is intimidated and enchanted by the "smart people" among whom Ashenden brings him (99–100). Above all, there is a tension between the voice of the narrator and Ashenden's voice and behavior, and the passion and melodrama of Lazzari's and Lal's. The narrator and Ashenden are, as always in these stories, very close. The point of view in the text is always Ashenden's, to the extent that, at times, it is not clear whether the narrator or Ashenden is making a comment. A good example of this is the passage in which Ashenden observes R in the Paris restaurant ("Luxury is dangerous to people" (100)). The narrator does distinguish himself from Ashenden, for example by the use of "I" in the long opening paragraph during the anecdote about Louis XIV (84), but for most of the text they are indistinguishable, and the third-person reference to Ashenden is merely a convention. Both are deeply controlled and reflective observers of action. The narrator's third-person stance vis-à-vis Ashenden indicates a distance from his subject. The generalized and confident reflections that pepper the text could be from either narrator or protagonist. Ashenden's coolness and detachment are emphasized. He sees himself as having "a cool head and an emotion well under control" (111). He sees the "comic" even in the melodrama of Lazzari's behavior (119). Such cool detachment and self-control – very evident in the story's opening paragraph, in which sophisticated lexis and syntax (within urbane limits) and breadth of cultural reference embody the nature of narrator and protagonist – clash with the intense passion of Lal's and Lazzari's affair. Lal, after all, is prepared to sacrifice himself for his love, coming to France, knowing, as he surely does, that it means his death.

There is a further tension, too, in Ashenden's cool commission of his duty to blackmail Lazzari and entrap Lal, and the imaginative sympathy he feels for both. The passage in which he reflects on Lazzari's previous life demonstrates this sympathy (115–16), and, from his first encounter with Lal, the British agent has considerable admiration for his enemy. He sees him as "a rather remarkable chap," brave enough "to take on almost single-handed the whole British power in India," a freedom fighter, someone who is even "justified in his actions" (100–1). Ashenden will still try to destroy his enemy (101), although at one point he hopes Lal will not fall into R's trap (117). Such complexity is representative of the tensions of "Guilia Lazzari" and typical of much later developments of the espionage genre by John le Carré and Len Deighton.

"Miss King"

The clash between dullness and melodrama, noted in "Giulia Lazzari," is present, too, in "Miss King," one of the best known of the Ashenden stories (Occhiogrosso 1989: 218). Ashenden reflects that "in the work" upon which he is engaged "the dullness of routine was apt now and again to slip quite shamelessly into the melodrama of the sixties" (Maugham 2002: 31). Later, as he sits by Miss King's bed, imagining what she may be wishing to say to him, he scolds himself for fancying "these idiotic things . . . it's cheap and tawdry fiction" (2002: 38). There is much else, too, in "Miss King" that echoes the other Ashenden stories: the narrational point of view that closely follows Ashenden's; the unglamorous actors (the old French lady with whom Ashenden exchanges messages and instructions, and Ashenden himself, described mundanely by the narrator as "an English writer approaching middle age" (19)); the mundane actions (the story proper starts with Ashenden in the bath (20), he passes information and receives instructions while buying half a pound of butter (19), much of the story involves Ashenden sitting at dinner and later playing cards); the tendency toward drab settings (although the settings in the Genevan hotel are far from shabby, the scene of Miss King's death is – "It all looked poor and mean in that trim hotel room" (37)); the moments in which Ashenden is able to exercise imaginative sympathy with another character (35–6). However, like much espionage fiction, "Miss King" is primarily organized round motifs of knowledge and ignorance.

Early in the text the narrator recounts how Ashenden receives and sends messages via the old French market trader, messages that are secret from the Swiss authorities (19–20). Ashenden is privy to much information about the glamorous Baroness von Higgins, her family background, and her income (21–2). Similarly, he is able to review the guests at dinner in his hotel, knowing a great deal about them that is not obvious to others, recognizing those that work for him and those that work for the Germans. He recognizes the German agent, Count von Holzminden. With regard to this figure, Ashenden's knowledge is more complete than that of most others, for he knew Holzminden before the war in England. Now they must pretend they do not recognize each other (23–4). However, motifs of knowledge are balanced by those of ignorance.

As he plays bridge with the glamorous Baroness and the Egyptians Prince Ali and Mustapha Pasha, Ashenden has a sense that the card game "was but a pretext and Ashenden had no notion what other game was being played under the rose" (28). He speculates as to whether the bridge party is an attempt to persuade him to disclose information, or to trick him into doing so (28). He wonders, too, if he is being recruited by the Central Powers.

> At one point he had a suspicion that he was being sounded upon the possibility of selling himself. It was done so discreetly that he could not be quite sure, but he had a feeling that a suggestion floated in the air that a clever writer could do his country a good turn and make a vast amount of money for himself if he cared to enter into an arrangement that would bring to a troubled world the peace that every humane man must so sincerely desire. (29)

Ashenden, in return, tries to suggest a willingness to listen further to such proposals. The whole card game is a matter of hidden currents, hints and innuendo.

At Miss King's bedside, Ashenden desperately tries to think what the old, dying, violently anti-British lady could have to say to him. He stares into her eyes and speculates wildly. Is it a desire to speak English in her last moments? Is it some patriotic impulse? Has it to do with the war? Has she some information, gleaned from her dissident Egyptian employers, to impart? Ashenden and the reader never learn. Miss King says only "England" and dies. Is she asking her country for forgiveness? Is she cursing it? Is there, indeed, some information to be passed? The story ends in an utterly inconclusive and enigmatic fashion (see Edward Shanks's 1928 review in Curtis and Whitehead 1987: 175). The world of espionage is a shadowy one. "Miss King" captures the epistemological uncertainties that are the stock in trade of spy fiction.

REFERENCES AND FURTHER READING

Archer, S. (1993). *W. Somerset Maugham: A Study of the Short Fiction*. New York: Twayne.

Cordell, R. (1961). *Somerset Maugham: A Biographical and Critical Study*. London and Melbourne: Heinemann.

Curtis, A. (n.d.). *Somerset Maugham*. London: Weidenfeld & Nicholson.

Curtis, A. and Whitehead, J. (eds) (1987). *W. Somerset Maugham: The Critical Heritage*. London and New York: Routledge & Kegan Paul.

Hanson, C. (1985). *Short Stories and Short Fictions, 1880–1980*. London and Basingstoke: Macmillan.

Le Queux, W. (1911). *Revelations of the Secret Service: Being the Autobiography of Hugh Morrice, Chief Travelling Agent of the Confidential Department of His Britannic Majesty's Government*. London: F.V. White.

Loss, A.K. (1996). "W. Somerset Maugham (1874–1965)," in J.H. Rogers (ed.), *British Short-Fiction Writers, 1914–1945, Dictionary of Literary Biography*, vol. 162, pp. 227–39. Detroit, Washington, DC, London: Bruccoli Clark Layman/Gale Research, 1996.

Malcolm, D. (2007). "Ashenden," in A. Maunder (ed.), *The Facts on File Companion to the British Short Story*. New York: Facts on File.

Maugham, W.S. (2002). *Collected Short Stories*, vol. 3. London: Vintage.

Occhiogrosso, J. (1989). "W. Somerset Maugham (1874–1965)," in B. Benstock and T.F. Staley (eds), *British Mystery Writers, 1920–1939, Dictionary of Literary Biography*, vol. 77, pp. 214–20. Detroit, Washington, DC, London: Bruccoli Clark Layman/Gale Research, 1989.

Raphael, F. (1989). *Somerset Maugham*. London: Cardinal.

21

Elizabeth Bowen: "The Demon Lover" and "Mysterious Kôr"

Sarah Dillon

Elizabeth Bowen (1899–1973) was a prolific writer of short stories, publishing six collections during her lifetime: *Encounters* (1923), *Ann Lee's* (1926), *Joining Charles* (1929), *The Cat Jumps* (1934), *Look at All Those Roses* (1941), and *The Demon Lover* (1945). In 1980, seven years after Bowen's death, seventy-nine of her stories – published over a period of thirty-three years between 1923 and 1956 – were brought together in *The Collected Stories of Elizabeth Bowen*. Reviewing that collection in February 1980, Eudora Welty commented in passing on the period of neglect that followed Bowen's death. It is only in recent years, however, that that neglect has been rectified and critical interest in Bowen's fiction has been revived – a revival prompted, not least, by Andrew Bennett and Nicholas Royle's *Elizabeth Bowen and the Dissolution of the Novel: Still Lives* (1995), an astonishing, inventive and provocative rereading of her novels. Subsequently, Hermione Lee's 1981 study *Elizabeth Bowen* has been reissued, further critical studies have emerged by contemporary literary critics such as Maud Ellmann and Neil Corcoran, and Bowen's novels have begun to make their long-awaited and deserved appearance on university courses in the UK. While lack of interest in her novels now seems to have been, or is at least in the process of being, remedied, critical attention to her short fiction lags behind. Most of the aforementioned studies include brief discussions of some of the short stories, but they do so mainly in relation to the novels, contradicting Bowen's own belief that "when a man engages himself in this special field his stories stand to be judged first of all on their merit *as* stories, only later in their relation to the rest of his work" (qtd in Lassner 1991: 127).

To judge Bowen's stories *as* stories, the reader must "pause to examine *how* the stories were told" (Bowen in Lassner 1991: 138). Poised between poetry and prose, concentrated and intense, short stories are very easy to read and very hard to read well. Good readings of Bowen's short fiction must attempt to be "as sensitive, [as] imaginative as to words themselves" (Bowen 1962: 212) as Bowen believes the writer must be, for "they are charged with destinies of their own, haunted by diverse associations"

(212). This demand for close reading is particularly challenging when confronted with "the strangeness and disturbing power of Bowen's writing" (Bennett and Royle 1995: 158, n.1). In *Elizabeth Bowen and the Dissolution of the Novel*, Bennett and Royle seek "to engage not only with a rereading of Bowen's work but also with the indissociable question of how to write about that work" (1995: 104). We need now to pose the same questions to the short fiction as Bennett and Royle posed to long fiction: not quite in their words, then, how might we present the short stories of Elizabeth Bowen in critically appropriate ways? What sorts of critical concepts and vocabulary do the stories themselves prompt? "What kinds of critical and theoretical thinking does Bowen's work seem to call for?" (Bennett and Royle 1995: 104). That these questions remain to be answered in relation to Bowen's short fiction points to the work still to be done in this area. Such work has begun in excellent readings of individual stories such as those by W.J. McCormack, Paul Muldoon, and Simon Buccleugh, but – if we understand theory, as J. Hillis Miller does, as "the displacement in literary studies from a focus on the meaning of texts to a focus on the way meaning is conveyed" (1991: 313) – the time is long overdue for a sustained theoretical study of Bowen's short fiction.

The following two readings attempt to make some start on that work. They take as their subjects two of Bowen's most popular and highly regarded stories, both of which are from her wartime writing: "The Demon Lover," first published in the *Listener* in November 1941; and "Mysterious Kôr," first published in *The Penguin New Writing*, Number 20, in 1944. Both appeared in the collection *The Demon Lover and Other Stories* (1945) which was published in the United States under a different title, *Ivy Gripped the Steps and Other Stories* (1946). In almost every period since it appeared in its modern form in the late nineteenth century, writers of the short story have argued that it is the most appropriate literary form for their moment in history: at the end of the nineteenth century, Henry James believed that "the short story could mirror contemporary life and epitomize modern conditions" (Shaw 1983: 17); in a contemporary piece on the short story, Jackie Kay concludes that "it is the perfect form for our times" (Kay 2006). Taking her own place in that tradition, in "The Short Story in England" (1945) Bowen observes that "it would still appear to me that the short story is the ideal *prose* medium for war-time creative writing" (qtd in Lassner 1991: 142). While the novelist suffers from "the discontinuities of life in war-time" (142), as well as from a lack of the perspective essential to good novel writing, "the short storyist is in a better position . . . he can render the great significance of a small event. He can register the emotional colour of a moment. He gains rather than loses by being close up to what is immediately happening" (142). In the preface to *The Demon Lover*, Bowen comments of her wartime stories that "twenty, forty, sixty years hence they may be found interesting as documents, even if they are found negligible as art" (1999: 99). Sixty years later, these stories do survive and are indeed rightly valued as a "diary" (Bowen 1999: 99) of "war-time London – blitzed, cosmopolitan, electric with expectation" (Bowen, cited in Lassner 1991: 142), but, by paying close attention to them here, I hope also to show that Bowen did herself a disservice in that prophecy, and that these stories are anything but negligible as art.

"The Demon Lover"

"The Demon Lover" is Bowen's most anthologized story. This is no doubt because it is regarded as one of her best, but it is also because it fits easily into "collections of tales of horror and suspense" (Morris 1990: 117) in the predominantly masculine tradition of such stories that comes down to us from Edgar Allan Poe. Taking its title and story idea from the traditional ballad of James Harris (also known as the ballad of the Demon Lover), Bowen's story tells the tale of Mrs Drover, a married woman who returns to her evacuated London home during the Blitz in order to gather more possessions. In the deserted and secure house, Mrs Drover's attention is drawn to a letter on the hall table which has no explanation for its presence there. On reading the letter, Mrs Drover is reminded of the "sinister troth" (Bowen 1980: 664) she plighted her former lover shortly before he went missing during World War I. The letter, the story implies, is from that lover, returned – whether dead or alive is uncertain – in order to claim her at the pre-arranged hour. Catching a cab in an attempt to escape him, the story ends as Mrs Drover confronts "eye to eye" (666) the driver of the cab and, screaming, is "made off with . . . into the hinterland of deserted streets" (666).

While appealing to the general reader simply as a well-written, spine-tingling ghost story, "The Demon Lover" has in fact provoked strong and conflicting critical interpretations. Douglas Hughes has argued that "The Demon Lover" is a tale of psychological collapse, "a masterful dramatization of acute psychological delusion, of the culmination of paranoia in a time of war" (1973: 411). Daniel Fraustino is keen to correct Hughes's "textual misrepresentation" and present "this short, enigmatic story in its original intent: a well-wrought mystery of high suspense" (1980: 483). Like Hughes, however, he does not entertain the fact that this is a ghost story, insisting that the lover – importantly only "presumed killed" (Bowen 1980: 664) – has returned in the flesh to kill Mrs Drover. Robert L. Calder provides an alternative, and compelling, interpretation of the story as a political allegory of Western civilization's "sinister troth" (Bowen 1980: 664) with war.

In provoking such conflicting interpretations, "The Demon Lover" demonstrates that "fulfillment in inconclusiveness . . . [which] is a specialty of the short story method" (Bayley 1988: 23). Indeed, Bowen valued the art of the short story precisely for its exemption "from the novel's conclusiveness – too often forced and false" (Bowen 1937: 15). The short story is not "weighed down (as the novel is bound to be) by facts, explanation, or analysis" (Bowen 1999: 128). Rather, "the plot, whether or not it be ingenious or remarkable, for however short a way it is to be pursued, ought to raise some issue, so that it may continue in the mind" (Bowen, cited in Lassner 1991: 125). In "The Demon Lover," the issue that continues is precisely that of the plot – the uncertainty the reader is left with at the end of the story as to what has actually happened, and what is going to happen next. For Mrs Drover is not murdered at the end of the tale, but driven "into the hinterland of deserted streets" (Bowen 1980: 666). Bowen's language here recalls her discussion in "Sources of Influence" of "the phantasmagoric hinterland" (qtd in Lassner 1991: 146) of fabricated memory from which the writer draws his or her inspiration. At the end of the story, Mrs Drover is not just trapped by the demon taxi driver, but also by the reader who makes off with her into the hinterland of his or her own fictional memories. Mrs Drover's name recalls what is arguably the first modern British short story, Sir Walter Scott's "The Two Drovers" (1827), and also originally means "troubling," "tribulation," or "disturbance," recalling Bowen's definition of the short story as "a crisis in itself" (1999: 128). As such, Mrs Drover is a figure of the short story and "the implications" it must have "when the story is done" (Bowen, cited in Lassner 1991: 127).

While a general feature of the short story form, the troubling nature of the "The Demon Lover" can be located specifically in the structure of the promise about which the story turns, and in the disturbance of identity caused by the demand for that promise now to be kept. Already perplexed by the desuetude of her former home, Mrs Drover's identity is spectralized when she reads the letter awaiting her. For Mrs Drover is no longer Kathleen, the addressee of the letter, the maker of the "unnatural promise" (Bowen 1983: 663) her former lover now calls upon her to keep. The specific nature of this promise remains undisclosed in the text, but the story works since *any* promise is unnatural: all those ultimate signifiers of fidelity – such as the oath and the promise – are, in essence, vows to refuse or resist the psycho-phenomenological truth that we change; that the "I" who promised then, at that time, is no longer the "I" that is called upon at a different moment to fulfill that promise. This is the "uncertain 'I'" (Bowen 1999: 98) to which Bowen refers in her preface to *The Demon Lover*. The rank of ghosts which rally to fill the vacuum of that uncertain "I" does not merely include the demon of a lover lost at war ("demon" may well now connote an evil spirit, but it also means the souls of ghosts or deceased persons, especially, in fact, deified heroes); it also includes the demon of Mrs Drover's former self – in "The Demon Lover," Mrs Drover is haunted by both. The semantic chain "lover," "drover," "driver" (as noted by W.J. McCormack) signals an inhabitation of her self by the Other: the former lover, driver of the taxi, and her own former self, "Kathleen," who shares her initial with that of the letter writer, "K." The (re)collection of her promise resurrects Kathleen in Mrs Drover, reminding her, very literally, of the self she used to be. This prompts a flashback in the narrative that in its turn draws the reader's attention to the multiplicity of narrative perspectives that constitutes "The Demon Lover."

"The Demon Lover" consists of three narrative perspectives: omniscient narration, free indirect discourse, and first-person narration. Omniscient narration characterizes the opening and – found in phrases such as "no human eye watched Mrs Drover's return" (Bowen 1980: 661) – is crucial to the build up of tension in the story, since it conveys knowledge to the reader that Mrs Drover herself does not have. In omniscient narration, direct speech or thought is appropriately introduced by "she thought" (662), or contained within quotations marks: "'The hour arranged . . . My God,' she said" (663). As the flashback precipitated by the letter merges back into the present, however, the omniscient narration is infected by free indirect discourse – "Who, in London, knew she meant to call at the house today? . . . The caretaker, *had* he come back, had had no cause to expect her" (664). As the story continues, the free indirect narration mutates into full-blown first-person narrative, in the section beginning "I will ring up the taxi now," and ending "So, wherever he may be waiting, I shall not know him" (665). Eventually, the three narrative perspectives become one in the sinister maxim, "You have no time to run from a face you do not expect" (665). The subject of this sentence is neither "I" nor "she" but "you." This draws you, the reader, into the text, causing you to identify with Mrs Drover and share in her situation, thus heightening your experience of horror at the end of the story. After this maxim, the story returns to, and closes with, the omniscient narration of the opening.

This movement between narrative perspectives in "The Demon Lover" is a crucial device in the story's creation of mounting tension and suspense since the reader is drawn from a distance into Mrs Drover's mind, with which she or he becomes one just in time to share in the fateful ending. At the same time, the narrational polyphony emphasizes the multiplicity of identity which the recollection of the promise forces Mrs Drover to confront. (Stephen Buccleugh makes a similar argument in his excellent reading of Bowen's early story "The Return.") Finally, the multiple narrational perspective is the cause of the inconclusive meaning of the story: the reader does not know if the lover is dead or alive because neither Mrs Drover nor the narrator does; the reader does not know if he is really sinister, or if Mrs Drover merely perceives him to be so; whether Mrs Drover is more shaken by the resurrection of her former self or by the return of her lost love remains unclear, and the so-called omniscient narrator does not provide elucidation for, in fact, she or he knows very little more than Mrs Drover does. The uncertainty and inconclusiveness of "The Demon Lover" stems, then, from a narrational heteroglossia that denies epistemological and ontological certainty and that is inextricably linked with the "uncertain 'I'" that Kathleen's unnatural promise was made to deny.

"Mysterious Kôr"

Although both were written during World War II, "The Demon Lover" and "Mysterious Kôr" represent two very different types of Bowen story. While "The Demon Lover" takes it place in the mystery, ghost, or suspense story tradition, "Mysterious Kôr" is very much part of the alternative tradition of the short story as a glimpse or snapshot. In the preface to *The Demon Lover*, Bowen indeed describes the stories as such: "taken singly, they are disjected snapshots – snapshots taken from close up, too close up, in the middle of the *mêlée* of a battle" (1999: 99). Although she may gently disparage them here, her use of the term "snapshot" highlights the intimate relationship between the short story and the visual arts – photography, film, and painting – and their important documentary role during the war. Bowen concludes the preface with an explicit analogy between her own writing and the work of painters and photographers:

> Painters have painted, and photographers who were artists have photographed, the tottering lace-like architecture of ruins, dark mass-movements of people, and the untimely brilliance of flaming skies. I cannot paint or photograph like this – I have isolated, I have made for the particular, spot-lighting faces or cutting out gestures that are not even the faces or gestures of great sufferers. This is how I am, how I feel, whether in war or peacetime; and only as I am and feel can I write. (Bowen 1999: 99)

Bowen uses similar visual language elsewhere when discussing her short fiction. In 1926, in the preface to *Ann Lee's and Other Stories*, she explains that her early stories were short, rather than long, because she "could not expand [her] vision outside the range of an incident or an hour" (qtd in Lassner 1991: 129): "I could spotlight," she writes, "but not illumine steadily" (129). Later, in the preface to *Encounters* written in 1949, she explains that she "snapshot" her characters "at a succession of moments when weakness, mistrust, falseness were most exposed" (Bowen 1999: 121). In a lecture delivered in 1950, she is less critical of this limited focus of the short story, celebrating its "poetic stress on the moment. The impression for its own sake – spotlit, isolated – only slight need for rationalization and explanation" (qtd in Lassner 1991: 122).

If all Bowen's short stories, as she notes, "have departed from a visual impression to which some poetic sign attached" (Bowen, cited in Lassner 1991: 122), this visual impression is perhaps nowhere so strongly manifested than in the moon-drenched blitzed London of "Mysterious Kôr," a story which "arose out of an intensified, all but spellbound beholding, on [Bowen's] part, of the scene in question" (Bowen 1999: 129). "Mysterious Kôr" opens with a brilliant snapshot of blitzed London at night, into which enter two figures, Pepita and Arthur, "a girl and a soldier who, by their way of walking, seemed to have no destination but each other, and to be not quite certain even of that" (Bowen, 1980: 729). The reader witnesses Pepita and Arthur's conversation in the moonlit London street, reluctant to return to the small flat in which Pepita's sexually naive flatmate Callie awaits them with cocoa. They inevitably have to return there, frustratingly, to separate beds. A document of war, this story is also, however, a story about stories, about fiction's power to imagine other times and places and the performative power of language to bring those places into being.

The opening of "Mysterious Kôr" signals this powerful self-referentiality, the language of spotlighting equating the moonlight which illuminates the scene with Bowen's description of the power of the short story: "full moonlight drenched the city and searched it; there was not a niche left to stand in" (Bowen 1980: 728). This self-referentiality has already been triggered by the title "Mysterious Kôr," the enormous derelict city of H. Rider Haggard's *She* (1887), a place and a novel by which Bowen was bewitched in her childhood. Just as Mysterious Kôr is the fictional city where Pepita takes refuge from the war even as she stands and sleeps in wartime London, the story "Mysterious Kôr" represents an alternative fictional space that coexists with and in another space and time, both the time of Bowen's writing and the time of any reading. The uncanny palimpsestuousness of this coexistence is brought home to the reader in the curiousness of one single phrase uttered by Pepita: " 'we'd be alone here' " (Bowen 1980: 730). With a simple shift from the expected "there" to "here," the phrase builds Kôr around Pepita and Arthur and/or, at the same time, transports them to it. The seemingly innocuous deictic marker "here" creates Kôr for them in the same way in which the story "Mysterious Kôr" creates their world for us. Imagining Kôr, Arthur and Pepita are literally in two places at once, as is the reader of fiction. "Mysterious Kôr" thus highlights the magical power of fiction to transcend physical limitations of time and space.

The need to escape to an alternative space and the related longing to find somewhere to be alone are the two desires that drive Pepita's imagination, and her dreams; they also drive Bowen's short fiction. They are present in very early stories such as "Breakfast," "Daffodils," and "The Return," where they seem to be associated with a need to break free from society and the oppressive codes of social intercourse; they are in the wartime stories, those "worlds-within-world of . . . saving hallucination" (Bowen 1999: 97); and they are challenged in the most disturbing way in one of Bowen's last stories, "Gone Away" (1946). A unique work of Bowenian science fiction, this story should be read not only in the context of the fears and anxieties of post-war Europe but also as a disturbing interrogation of art itself – as a vision of the potentially dystopian nightmare of the fabricated that cannot but alter the way one reads Bowen's fiction, and understands her relation to it. One of her most interesting and troubling short stories, it is also one of the many that deserve more critical and popular attention.

REFERENCES AND FURTHER READING

Bayern, L. (1981). "Scaling the Garden Wall: *The Collected Stories of Elizabeth Bowen*," *Alternative Review of Literature and Politics* 1 (September): 23–4.

Bayley, J. (1988). *The Short Story: Henry James to Elizabeth Bowen*. Brighton: Harvester.

Bennett, A. and Royle, N. (1995). *Elizabeth Bowen and the Dissolution of the Novel: Still Lives*. Houndsmills: Macmillan.

Bowen, E. (1937). *The Faber Book of Modern Stories*. London: Faber and Faber.

Bowen, E. (1962). *After-thought: Pieces about Writing*. London: Longmans.

Bowen, E. (1980). *The Collected Stories of Elizabeth Bowen*. Harmondsworth: Penguin.

Bowen, E. (1999). *The Mulberry Tree: Writings of Elizabeth Bowen*, ed. Hermione Lee. London: Vintage.

Buccleugh, S.H. (1990). "The Dialogic of Narrative: The Use of Free Indirect Discourse in Elizabeth Bowen's 'The Return'," *South Central Review* 7/2: 31–9.

Calder, R.L. (1994). " 'A More Sinister Troth': Elizabeth Bowen's 'The Demon Lover' as Allegory," *Studies in Short Fiction* 31: 91–7.

Corcoran, N. (2004). *Elizabeth Bowen: The Enforced Return*. Oxford: Clarendon Press.

Ellmann, Maud (2003). *Elizabeth Bowen: The Shadow Across the Page*. Edinburgh: Edinburgh University Press.

Fraustino, D.V. (1980). "Elizabeth Bowen's 'The Demon Lover': Psychosis or Seduction?". *Studies in Short Fiction* 17: 483–87.

Hughes, D. (1973). "Cracks in the Psyche: Elizabeth Bowen's 'The Demon Lover'," *Studies in Short Fiction* 10: 411–13.

Kay, J. (2006). "A Writer's Piece," *Story* [online]. Available from: <http://www.theshortstory.org.uk/thinkpiece/index.php4?pieceid=4>

Lassner, P. (1991). *Elizabeth Bowen: A Study of the Short Fiction*. New York: Twayne.

Lee, H. (1999). *Elizabeth Bowen*. London: Vintage.

McCormack, W.J. (1994). "Elizabeth Bowen's Infantilism," in *From Burke to Beckett: Ascendancy, Tradition and Betrayal in Irish Literary History*, pp. 401–10. Cork: Cork University Press.

Miller, J.H. (1991). "Presidential Address 1986: The Triumph of Theory, the Resistance to Reading, and the Question of the Material Base," *Theory Now and Then*, pp. 309–28, Durham: Duke University Press.

Mitchell, E. (1966). "Themes in Elizabeth Bowen's Short Stories," *Critique: Studies in Contemporary Fiction* 8/3: 41–54.

Morris, J.A. (1990). "Elizabeth Bowen's Stories of Suspense," in Clive Bloom (ed.), *Twentieth-Century Suspense: The Thriller Comes of Age*, pp. 114–29. Houndsmills: Macmillan.

Muldoon, P. (2000). "Bowen," in *To Ireland I*, pp. 18–25. Oxford: Oxford University Press.

Parsons, D. (1997). "Souls Astray: Elizabeth Bowen's Landscapes of War," *Women: A Cultural Review* 8/1: 24–32.

Shaw, V. (1983). *The Short Story: A Critical Introduction*. Harlow: Longman.

Wallace, D. (2004). "Uncanny Stories: The Ghost Story as Female Gothic," *Gothic Studies* 6/1: 57–68.

Welty, E. (1981). "Seventy-nine Stories to Read Again," *The New York Times* February 8 [online]. Available from: <www.nytimes.com>

Part II
1945–the Present

Introduction

22

The British and Irish Short Story: 1945–Present

Cheryl Alexander Malcolm and David Malcolm

1

The main outlines of post-war British and Irish history are well known and uncontroversial. Those aspects of British history since 1945 that can be seen to be relevant to the development of the short story are: a withdrawal from empire, and a consequent loss of status and independence; economic crisis; immigration; the development of a less deferential society in which many traditional norms have been breached; and the resurgence of regional nationalisms within the United Kingdom. Features of Irish history that find echoes in short fiction are: the conflict in Northern Ireland from the late 1960s (which is also a British issue); poverty, stifling conservatism, in the Irish Republic, and immigration from it, for over half the post-war period; and the economic and social transformation of the Irish Republic since the 1970s.

Britain emerged from World War II bankrupt, damaged, and with world commitments it was unable to meet. After World War II, it divested itself, or was compelled to divest itself, of its vast empire. Some commentators describe the process as one accomplished with relative good grace; others see it as a hasty, undignified, cynical, and often bloody withdrawal. Certainly, it was attended with great loss of life in India and Pakistan in 1947, and with considerable brutality on the British part in Kenya in the 1950s. Decolonization meant loss of status in the world. The Suez Crisis of 1956 was a watershed, both in terms of the United Kingdom's interference in the affairs of other people's countries, and in terms of its international standing. In the autumn of 1956, British, French, and Israeli troops, working in collaboration with each other, invaded the area round the Suez Canal in Egypt with a view to preventing its nationalization by the Egyptian government. Both the United States and the United Nations applied pressure on Britain to withdraw, which it duly did. In retrospect, 1956 can be seen as one of the years (like 1941) in which Britain's independence and status as a world power was seen to be materially limited. The process of decolonization continued remorselessly in the second half of the twentieth century; on June 30, 1997, the last British governor of Hong Kong handed authority over Britain's last major colony to the representative of the People's Republic of China. Within a century of Kipling's writing "The White Man's Burden," the British Empire had been wound up. The fact that the UK plays an important role in NATO and UN military activities, was able to mount a military force to retake the Falkland Islands/Malvinas from the Argentineans in 1982, and is an extremely close military ally of the USA, does not mean quite the same as the extensive "dominion over palm and pine" of the late nineteenth century. Alastair Davies and Alan Sinfield have even detected a "post-imperial melancholy" in British culture and society (2000: 2). Certainly, the United Kingdom in the early twenty-first century is (simultaneously) a client state of the USA, ready to do its interventionist bidding in Iraq and Afghanistan, and (since 1973) firmly embedded in the institutions of the European Union. Immediately post-war Prime Ministers Clement Attlee and Winston Churchill would have difficulty recognizing their country's role in the international arena.

Britain's relatively poor economic performance for much of the post-war period is similarly well documented. However, the economic life of Britain since 1945 is complex. Commentators at various times have talked alarmingly about Britain's economic decline. Yet the country is much wealthier than it was in 1945, and the grandchildren of people scarred by appalling poverty in the 1930s and 1940s now live in much better conditions. The 1950s and 1960s were years of very considerable material improvement in the lives of most British men and women. But economic success is relative. Certainly the UK has grown wealthier, but it has done so more slowly than most of its European partners. The economic face of Britain has changed over the past half-century. For example, the British motor manufacturing and shipbuilding industries have collapsed; there are many fewer steel mills and mines than even in the 1970s. Service industries are now much more important than ever before. In addition, the sense of economic crisis that has spread through British society at various times, in the late 1940s, and in the early and late 1970s, has formed the consciousness and memories of large numbers of people, and, indeed, driven them to political action, both on the right and the left. At various times, in the 1970s and the 1980s, for example, levels of unemployment have been very high, and a great deal of attention has been given to severe disadvantage and poverty in some sections of the population. But it must be emphasized that, at the beginning of the twenty-first century, the United Kingdom remains a very wealthy, major industrial country, by anybody's standards.

In the post-war period there were two periods of radical government social and economic policy: in the 1940s, under the Labour administration of Clement Attlee, and, in the 1980s, under the Conservative administration of Margaret Thatcher. The latter government's policies can be seen as an attempt to reverse what had been done by the former. The Attlee government, with a huge mandate from the British electorate, set out to take major industries – coal, rail transport, civil aviation, gas, iron and steel production, and others – into public control. It also set up a "welfare state" to provide certain social services for the population. The most notable, and one of the longest lasting, of these is the National Health Service, which aimed to provide health care, free at point of use, for all. The cost of relatively low economic performance was the gradual erosion of many of the socially egalitarian measures of this government in the 1960s and the 1970s. In addition, the Thatcher governments (with much smaller mandates than in the 1940s) set out to return state enterprises to private hands and to limit government expenditure on the Health Service and other social institutions, such as state education.

The relatively poor performance of the economy and the policies of the Thatcher government produced considerable social tension in the 1970s and the 1980s. Strikes by coal miners, for example, bitterly divided the country, especially in the mid-1980s. A wave of militant trade unionism in the 1970s was shattered by Conservative determination and legislation in the 1980s. The consensus of British politics from 1945 to 1970 (social democratic reformism, state intervention) shifted radically to a much more free-market, laissez-faire one by the 1990s.

A major legacy of the British Empire that has shaped post-World War II Britain is immigration from former colonial possessions. Post-war immigration into the United Kingdom was not just from former colonies, however. Almost a quarter of a million Polish troops (about half of a large Polish army that had fought very bravely alongside the rest of the Allies in the 1939–45 conflict) remained in Britain rather than return to a Poland dominated by the Soviet Union. Indeed, immigration was nothing new to Britain. Large numbers of Irish immigrants had been arriving in mainland Britain for over a century by 1945, and continued to do so throughout the 1950s and 1960s. The late 1880s and the 1890s had seen very substantial waves of Jewish immigration to Britain from Central Europe. But when the ship the *Empire Windrush* docked at Tilbury in London on 22 June, 1948, and almost 500 Jamaican men came ashore, a new chapter of British domestic history had opened.

These immigrants arrived in Britain with the full cooperation of the British government. They and those who followed, largely from the Caribbean and the Indian subcontinent, were encouraged to come, and sometimes directly recruited, to drive buses, to work in hospitals and in factories, to make up for a post-war shortage of labor. From the 1960s onwards successive UK governments have limited immigration to the country, but the changes were irreversible. Now almost 7 percent of the UK population is foreign born or of foreign descent (less than in France and Germany). People who trace their roots to the Caribbean or the Indian subcontinent, and elsewhere, have transformed many English cities.

However, this has not been a painless transformation. Black and Asian immigrants and their children have been discriminated against, and certainly have felt so, by individuals and institutions. Racist attitudes in employers, landlords, and the police, for example, produced, and produce still, much bitterness. Anti-immigrant and fascist political parties operate on the fringes of British political life. Terrible acts of violence are committed against members of racial and ethnic minorities by white extremists.

Full-scale race riots, battles between whites and blacks and with the police, have broken out at various times in UK cities, for example in Notting Hill in London in 1958, and Toxteth in Liverpool and Brixton in South London in 1981. Northern English towns, like Blackburn and Bradford, with their substantial populations that trace their roots to the Indian subcontinent, have been the scenes of bitter inter-ethnic conflict. Since 1976, the Race Relations Act and the Commission for Racial Equality have combated discrimination in many fields, although without complete success. Racial tensions still exist in professions, businesses, and on the street, although in a metropolis like London, black, Asian, and white populations do seem to mix amicably and successfully a lot of the time. Waves of immigration continue. The early twenty-first century has seen a large influx of people from Central Europe (particularly Poland) into the UK.

Commentators point to an erosion of traditional deference and hierarchy in post-war Britain. Davies and Sinfield put it thus: "For most social historians, the lives of both men and women in Britain have been transformed for the better since 1945, with the improvement of health, education and living conditions, the undermining of traditional social and cultural hierarchies and gender differences, and the extension of personal freedoms" (2000: 54). Robert Hewison notes that: "Contemporary Britain is not the militarized and masculine society of the forties. Deference and paternalism have declined, meritocracy has eroded class and Britain is an irreversibly multi-racial nation" (1995: 311–12). Davies and Sinfield, however, do point out that the poor and disadvantaged, many women, gays and lesbians, and black and Asian Britons might well dispute some of the above (2000: 54–5). One of the clear signs of the collapse of traditional hierarchies has been the devolution of political power to Scotland and Wales, accompanied by spurts of aggressive nationalism in both these parts of the United Kingdom. The Scots were, in many ways, important agents of British imperialism in the nineteenth century, but once the British Empire ceased to be a going concern, they clearly decided it was time to reconsider the Act of Union. In a referendum in 1998, Scots voted for a substantial degree of autonomy within the United Kingdom, and in 1999 the first Scottish Parliament since 1707 met in Edinburgh.

Since 1945 the history of the Irish Free State and, from 1949, of the Irish Republic has been quite different from that of the United Kingdom. Ireland in the late 1940s and 1950s was an introverted, stagnant, and extremely poor country, marked by lack of industrial investment, by rural conservatism, and by mass emigration (by 1961 the population had fallen to 2.8 million people). Social services were at a much lower level than in Britain and Northern Ireland, and tuberculosis was widespread until the early 1950s. Since the late 1950s, the situation has altered beyond recognition. The economic policy associated with the Whittaker Report attracted foreign investment, but Ireland's joining the European Common Market in 1973 changed its economic and cultural life very substantially. The European Union has lavished resources on Ireland, permitting the restructuring of agriculture, education, and road construction. Per capita GDP has responded. Ireland is now a very wealthy country that draws in immigrants from other parts of Europe. Like mainland Britain, it is also much more liberal. Homosexuality was decriminalized in 1993; divorce was made possible in 1995. The only blight on this success story has been the conflict in Northern Ireland, in which for thirty years Catholics and Protestants and British soldiers killed each other, and terrorist groups killed people with guns and bombs on both sides of the Irish Sea. Although the casualties from the conflict were relatively few, the late twentieth-century Troubles scarred lives and communities in irreparable ways.

One does not have to be a historical determinist to see how these events have found echoes in British and Irish short fiction. For example, the scrutiny of Englishness (discussed in James Lang's essay, chapter 24) is surely born out of the shocks of decolonization and economic crisis. According to Mitchell R. Lewis (chapter 30), Michael Moorcock's espousal of "dark fantasy" is born out of a discontent with the genre's inability in the 1950s to do justice to the post-war geopolitical realities that confronted Britain. The social tensions of the 1970s and 1980s and Scottish chauvinist self-assertion underlie James Kelman's short stories. Traditional British class antagonisms are Alan Sillitoe's material. Contemporary women's writing and the richness of gay and lesbian short fiction are unimaginable without the shifting norms and hierarchies of post-war Britain and Ireland. Ian McEwan's short stories, with their concern with incest, fetishism, and sexual mutilation, echo changes in social and personal mores. John McGahern and William Trevor write of the paralyzing conservatism of rural Ireland in the 1950s; Neil Jordan, Anne Enright, and Mary Dorcey tell of the complexities of the new Ireland of city and money. Bernard MacLaverty writes movingly of the tragedies and divisions of late twentieth-century Ulster. Hanif Kureishi and Ben Okri offer fictional voices that are extraterritorial, and look at the lives of immigrants in Britain. In a Britain and Ireland that are embedded in continental Europe it is striking, but appropriate, how much short fiction is set abroad.

However, besides economic and political events, cultural institutions have played a large role in the development of short fiction in the UK and Ireland. The situations in the two countries are quite different. Elizabeth Bowen's and H.E. Bates's prophesies of good times for the British short story in a post-war world were wrong (qtd in Beachcroft 1968: 212). Although a glance at Dennis Vannatta's bibliography of short fiction published between 1945 and 1980 shows the persistence of the short story, and although voices such as Clare Hanson's have occasionally announced its resurgence (Hanson 1985: 159), there is a scholarly and critical consensus that short fiction has not flourished in Britain since 1945. In 1965, Hilary Corke described it as "dying" (qtd in Beachcroft 1968: 213). Writing in 1985, Joseph M. Flora pointed to a belief that "the current state of the art [of short fiction] is moribund" (xv). In *Mislexia* (a journal by and for women writers) in 2003, Debbie Taylor called the short story an "Endangered Species" (9–13) and, in an article announcing a new short-story competition in the journal *Prospect* in 2005, Alexander Linklater declared "At some time during the last twenty years, the short story came to be viewed in Britain as culturally redundant and economically unviable" (24).

The reasons for this situation are twofold: a lack of publishing outlets for new short fiction, and British publishers' ingrained hostility to short stories. In 1968, T.O. Beachcroft declared: "Since the end of the Second World War, the outlets for short stories have altered. In the main, they have steadily diminished. Popular magazines as well as literary magazines have been disappearing" (216). In 1994, Dean Baldwin concurred (xiii), as did Linklater in 2005 (24). We have discussed this issue elsewhere (Malcolm and Malcolm 2006: xvi). The anti-short-story bias of British publishers is also well documented. Birgit Moosmüller provides many examples (1993: 108–15). Graham Swift writes about the situation thus:

> My publishing experience was that finding a publisher for my volume of short stories was by no means easy, and it was certainly the case when I began to appear in print, in the late 70s, early 80s, that a collection of stories that was also the author's first published work was exceptional. My own collection . . . was not published till I had already published two novels (though the stories were mostly written before my second novel), and I think this pattern was typical. (qtd in Moosmüller 1993: 113)

It is very clear that British publishers do not like publishing short stories and consider them (with justice) to be unprofitable (Taylor 2003; Linklater 2005). They appear only to do so if well-established authors threaten to take their work elsewhere unless their short stories are published.

The situation in the Irish Republic since 1945 has been very different. Journals, such as *The Bell* (1940–54), the *Dublin Magazine* (1923–58), and *Irish Writing* (1946–57) encouraged short story writing (Kilroy 1984: 11–12). Maurice Harmon sees the decision of the *Irish Press* in 1968 to devote a page every week to Irish writing (including short stories) as helping to create a climate receptive to short fiction (1979: 63–4). In 1979 Declan Kiberd declared that "For the past eighty years in Ireland, the short story has been the most popular of all literary forms with readers. It has also been the form most widely exploited by writers" (14), and the high status of the Irish short story has not changed in the last twenty-five years. Paradoxically, British publishers seem prepared to publish Irish short-story writers like John McGahern and William Trevor, although they are reluctant to publish English ones. The only way in which Irish short-story writers can be said to have a more difficult time than their British counterparts is that for most of the post-war period their work has been subject to state censorship under legislation substantially dating from the early years of the Irish Free State. Samuel Beckett, McGahern, Benedict Kiely, and Edna O'Brien, and many other Irish and non-Irish writers, have all had their work banned by the Irish Censorship of Publications Board.

Short fiction, thus, exists within multiple constraints and influences in both the UK and Ireland. One of these is the literary system, a manifold of influences and hierarchies, of traditions and innovations, that is operative at any one moment. It is striking that the short story in both Britain and Ireland tends to remain within the conventions of social-psychological fiction, in which a story will be concerned to delineate a character's psychological state or development within a social milieu that is rendered according to the norms of literary realism. This is scarcely surprising as the social-psychological novel has dominated British fiction for the past 200 years, and Irish fiction for the last 100. Like the novel, the short story has added exotic subject matters to its repertoire. Stories are set in Africa or continental Europe, or among new immigrant groups in the UK. Social-psychological fiction has reached down into non-canonical forms of writing for refreshment – pornography (McEwan), folktale (Carter), and working-class anecdote (Kelman), for example. But genre innovation and experimental writing are relatively rare. Even science fiction (J.G. Ballard's work, for example) seems at times to aspire to the status of social-psychological fiction. The work of Samuel Beckett, Gabriel Josipovici, and (sometimes) Adam Mars-Jones, and Carter's and Salman Rushdie's interest in folktale and legend, are among the few exceptions to this conservatism.

However, British short fiction in the post-war period is rich in complex and interesting texts. In what follows, we offer brief analyses of four short stories by contemporary British writers: Hugh Fleetwood, James Lasdun, Michel Faber, and Patricia Duncker. The Irish short story needs no critical defense, but these four stories, dating from 1980 to 2003, illustrate the strengths of the British short story in the last twenty-five years, despite readers' indifference and publishers' hostility.

2

The reception of Hugh Fleetwood's work illustrates the arbitrary nature of canon formation. He is the author of sixteen novels and four collections of short stories, all critically well received; yet his work is little known. The story "A Wonderful Woman" comes from his collection *Fictional Lives* (1980). All four stories in it involve writers and the dilemmas and complexities of literary life and work. "A Wonderful Woman" starts with Tina Courtland's hearing of the death of the one writer and man she has ever wholly admired, the successful novelist Joseph Braddon. Tina has given up writing and withdrawn from the world because of a sense of revulsion for it and a conviction that one cannot write and live honestly in it. Braddon, however, has seemed to her the only person who has been able to do this. Invited to write Braddon's biography, she travels to London, convinced that there is some flaw in Braddon's character, which she must find in order to justify her rejection of the world. In London, she meets Braddon's wife (the "wonderful woman" of the title) who turns out to be a terrifying figure, and Tina's clue to Braddon's corruption. Maragaret Braddon gives Tina her husband's diaries, which reveal that he has committed terrible acts in order to know the world better and write about it more accurately. Tina's dilemma is whether to write about what she knows or to conceal it.

The story is a traditional piece of social-psychological fiction, narrated in the third person, but entirely from Tina's point of view, with extensive passages of free indirect speech. Settings are mixed. Tina has fled from the world to Tuscany. Braddon has traveled in the Middle East and Asia. Both Tina and Braddon, it should be noted, are Americans. The story centers on Tina's dilemma as a person and a writer. Should she withdraw from the world? Should she lie about Braddon's wickedness? Tina herself is a complex figure: she wants to discover Braddon's flaw, for that will justify her retreat from society and make her safe there; her spirits rise when she meets the monstrously damaged Margaret Braddon; she refuses to read more than a few extracts from Braddon's diaries in order to preserve herself; finally, she knows that she will return to the world, having betrayed Margaret.

"A Wonderful Woman" is a powerful story, traditionally but sophisticatedly narrated. There is a literary focus, although the text is not self-referential in any substantial way (except in Fleetwood's usual complex and parallel syntax). It is partly non-British in settings and characters (again as much of Fleetwood's work). Its particular strengths lie in the intricacy of Tina's moral and literary dilemmas and her own psychological complexity, and in the picture of Margaret Braddon, a woman utterly destroyed by her husband's ambitions and another woman's cowardice.

Corruption is the focus, too, of James Lasdun's "Property," from his first collection of stories, *The Silver Age* (1985). Michael Hulse writes of this story that it belongs "with the best short fiction I have seen in the 1980s" (1986: 61). The story is narrated in the first person, by an unnamed narrator, who recounts the events over three days during a visit to his grandmother's. Although the language used is not that of a child, the point of view is entirely limited to that of the young boy; the adult he has become does not analyze his memories. Indeed, the striking narrational feature of this text is a refusal to interpret and draw conclusions from what is observed, as, indeed, elements of the story material are elided (who is Geoffrey Isaacs, for example, whom the grandmother seems to remember with such perplexity?). The story material centers on the grandmother's unease when she receives objects and money from a former servant to make up for thefts committed and lies told by the servant many years previously. These intrusions from the past release floods of memory. In the end the grandmother dies; the servant's attempts at compensation having, the text implies, utterly unsettled the old woman. The setting is contemporary, in an opulent Mayfair flat, which the narrator makes sinister, an unnatural, over-heated, too sweet-smelling place of death.

"Property" is one of those short stories that bears a resemblance to a lyric poem, organized, as it is, round recurrent motifs, full of metaphorical suggestion rather than direct statement. Hulse calls it "an ornate and oppressive investigation of greed" (1986: 61). The story's recurrent motifs are threefold: jewels, money and property, and decay and corruption. The narrator notes the rubies clustered on a ring on his grandmother's arthritic hand (Lasdun 1986: 7); he is allowed to spill out the lavish and colorful contents of his grandmother's jewelry box on the carpet (8–9); the condensation from a bunch of flowers gathers at his grandmother's dead throat "like a colossal jewel" (18); the bunch of flowers are red roses that recall the rubies at the story's start (14). Motifs of money and property run throughout the text: the narrator has begun to correlate money with happiness (10); the ex-servant returns money and objects to Mrs Cranbourne; the narrator steals money from his grandmother's purse (16); he plays with some of his winnings from a horse race in odd ways (for example, he fills his mouth with them) (17); at the story's end his grandmother lies dead, holding the notes of his winnings, and he pulls them from her grasp (18). Motifs of decay and corruption, and, ultimately, of death, are connected with the previous two groups. The rubies on the grandmother's hand are like cherries "on ancient trees in derelict orchards" (7). Grandmother and grandson love a story in which an old man cheats death (9). The grandmother's appearance (sparse hair, slack skin) is a *memento mori* (10, 11). Even the bubbles that the boy, and later the porter, blow are sinister and corrupt; they are certainly transient (15, 17). At one point, the boy records that he and his grandmother feel over-filled, satiated beyond endurance, in a way that is noxious (15). The grandmother's memories flow like dissolution. At the story's end, the grandmother lies dead, rubies on her finger, red roses behind her, pound notes clutched in her fingers, in an almost medieval image of the inevitability of death, even in material plenty. "Property" is a remarkable, ambiguous, and sinister story, hinting at intriguing complexities and viciousness.

Most of the stories in Michel Faber's collection *Some Rain Must Fall* (1998) are, like those of Fleetwood and Lasdun discussed above, social-psychological pieces. "Fish," however, is one of two stories (the other is "Toy Story") that break with the conventions of literary realism, and offer a vision of a different kind of world. The story is a dystopic vision of the future, with elements of science fiction and folktale. It operates within the conventions of the fantastic, rather than those of literary realism. "Fish" is an account of a day in the life of Janet and Kif-Kif, her daughter. The first five paragraphs of the text confuse the reader by suggesting, first, a mimetic world model, and, then, undermining it. A mother and daughter lie in bed; only slowly does it become apparent that fish have moved from the ocean into the air, and have rendered the human world a wasteland and one full of danger for surviving humans. Faber allusively sketches in what might be material for a science-fiction novel. A group of religious fanatics welcome the fish, and attack the homes of those unbelievers who have also survived. Janet and Kif-Kif visit a soup kitchen; killer whales attack a church; the two protagonists escape predatory moray eels. At the end of the story, Janet discovers to her horror that Kif-Kif has become accustomed to her world; her bad dreams are of other matters.

"Fish" is an impressive story, in the economy, complexity, and power of its vision of a world turned upside down, of a disturbing dystopia. This world is almost soundless, as there are no cars and fish make no noises; it is a wasteland, as the fish eat all the vegetation and have made traditional human life impossible; it is very dangerous, as religious fanatics and carnivorous aquatic creatures haunt the streets and air. The attack of the killer whales, which might easily have been against Janet and Kif-Kif, is one of the climaxes of the text, and is terrifying. The story is ambiguous and suggestive: how will the conflict between unbelievers and fanatics develop?; how can humans survive in such a world?; why do the whales attack a church? One of the most striking elements of the text, however, is its psychological focus. It starts with a reference to child psychologists, and the central moment of the text comes when Kif-Kif shows to Janet that she finds the world they live in bearable and even interesting. The killer whales are "amazing," she declares. This drives Janet to a rage; she wishes for death as an escape from the fish-dominated world. The revelation at the end that Kif-Kif does not have nightmares about fish, but "other stuff," is a psychological one. The young girl has adapted to a new, dangerous, and desolate world. Even when the short story moves outside the genre constraints of social-psychological fiction, psychological interests remain potent.

Patricia Duncker's short story, "Sophia Walters Shaw," comes from her collection *Seven Tales of Sex and Death*. In a note at the beginning of the book, the author gives the "narrative clichés of late night TV" as the inspiration of her stories. "Sophia Walters Shaw" certainly draws on these, and is a mixture of the pornographic, the dystopic, the crime story, and contemporary reworking of mythological motifs. The narrator is Sophia, a young, insubordinate woman who works in the sex trade. As she tells her story, it becomes clear to the reader that her world is a dystopic future world, in which women's roles are restricted to those of wife or prostitute, and in which pornography and prostitution (within certain limits) are legally tolerated activities. The vision of the future is complicated: alongside restrictions on women's activities, there are severe sanctions against racial discrimination and smoking is illegal. After the club she works in, called "The Underworld," has been raided by the police, Sophia is given a new role by Walters, her boss. He, she, and the sinister, but sympathetic Shaw, become a team of high-class assassins, murdering the rich and powerful for even more powerful clients.

Pornographic motifs are prominent in this story. There are graphic descriptions of sex acts; Sophia herself dresses at times in a full leather dominatrix outfit; the two murders depicted combine sado-masochistic sex with brutal violence. The story, however, is also full of mythological allusions, particularly to the story of Hades and Prosperpina. The trio of assassins have as one of their tasks the murder of Hades and the returning of Prosperpina to her mother. Sophia's working name is Cyane, the nymph that tries to prevent Hades's rape of Proserpina.

The story as a whole is a rich and complex piece that is hugely suggestive, and very difficult to interpret simply. The trio of assassins, for all the sexism and violence of the world they live in, and the inequality of Sophia's relations with her male boss, is seen very affectionately by Sophia. The dystopic society is not without redeeming possibilities. Is the reader to understand that Sophia and her companions are the damned in some urban wasteland, whose final job it is to return the kidnapped Persephone to nature? Perhaps they are to restore her to a powerful female figure, thus suggesting the possibility of reversing the restrictions on women in their world? It is the ambiguity of the story and its heady mixture of the dystopic, the pornographic, and the mythological that make it particularly interesting.

British short fiction in the post-war period is a rich field. Canonical and non-canonical authors offer considerable scope for research. Although social-psychological fiction is dominant, that in itself is not necessarily negative, and, indeed, there is considerable genre variety within the short story, a borrowing of motifs from the culturally high and the non-literary low (as in Duncker's work). The following essays aim to explore that richness and variety, as well as the much more widely recognized excellences of the Irish short story since 1945.

References and Further Reading

Baldwin, D. (ed.) (1994). *British Short Fiction Writers, 1945–1980. Dictionary of Literary Biography*, vol. 139. Detroit, Washington, DC: London: Bruccoli Clark Layman/Gale Research.

Beachcroft, T.O. (1968). *The Modest Art: A Survey of the Short Story in English*. London: New York and Toronto: Oxford University Press.

Davies, A. and Sinfield, A. (eds) (2000). *British Culture of the Postwar: An Introduction to Literature and Society, 1945–1999*. London and New York: Routledge.

Flora, J.M. (ed.) (1985). *The English Short Story, 1880–1945: A Critical History*. Boston: Twayne.

Hanson, C. (1985). *Short Stories and Short Fictions, 1880–1980*. London and Basingstoke: Macmillan.

Harmon, M. (1979). "First Impressions: 1968–78," in P. Rafroidi and T. Brown (eds) (1979), *The Irish Short Story*, pp. 63–77. Gerrards Cross, Bucks: Colin Smythe; Atlantic Highlands, NJ: Humanities Press.

Hewison, R. (1995). *Culture and Consensus: England, Art and Politics since 1940*. London: Methuen.

Hulse, M. (1986). "Stories and Histories: Recent Fiction," *Encounter* 67/3 (Sept.–Oct.): 57–61.

Kiberd, D. (1979). "Story-telling: The Gaelic Tradition," in P. Rafroidi and T. Brown (eds) (1979), *The Irish Short Story*, pp. 13–25. Gerrards Cross, Bucks: Colin Smythe; Atlantic Highlands, NJ: Humanities Press.

Kilroy, J.F. (ed.) (1984). *The Irish Short Story: A Critical History*. Boston: Twayne.

Lasdun, J. (1986). *The Silver Age*. Harmondsworth: Penguin.

Linklater, A. (2005). "Reclaiming the Story," *Prospect* (Sept.): 24.

Malcolm, C.A. and Malcolm, D. (eds) (2006). *British and Irish Short-Fiction Writers, 1945–2000. Dictionary of Literary Biography*, vol. 319. Detroit, New York, San Francisco, San Diego, New Haven, Waterville, London and Munich: Thomson/Gale.

Moosmüller, Birgit (1993). *Die experimentelle englische Kurzgeschichte der Gegenwart*. Munich: Wilhelm Fink Verlag.

Taylor, D. (2003). "Endangered Species," *Mislexia* 16 (Jan.–March 2003): 9–13.

Vannatta, D. (ed.) (1985). *The English Short Story, 1945–1980: A Critical History*. Boston: Twayne.

Topics and Genres

23

New Identities: The Irish Short Story since 1945

Greg Winston

Introduction

The title story of Benedict Kiely's collection *A Ball of Malt and Madame Butterfly* (1973) offers a brazen, comic look at urban Ireland near mid-century. Its rich array of characters – boisterous fireman, hard-drinking dockers, opportunistic "girls of the town" (Kiely 1980: 426), a pockmarked publican made in the Chicago speakeasies, and one lonely bureaucrat – provides a mix of personalities and social classes. The combination presents a challenge to conservative mores and is realized through a bawdy and unflinching narrative voice. First published in 1973, but set about three decades earlier, Kiely's story gives colorful testament to a Dublin red-light district that lingered on in numerous clandestine enclaves well after the notorious Monto neighborhood was shut down by authorities in the 1920s.

Alongside these social and historical truisms, the story constructs an allegory for the state of Irish writing at mid-century. This begins early in the tale, when Pike Hunter, a lonely civil servant with poetic aspirations, stumbles upon his literary paragon in Stephens Green: "Then on the park pathway before him, walking towards the main gate and the top of Grafton Street, he saw the poet" (Kiely 1980: 423). Although a name is never given, it is none other than Yeats, whose identity is confirmed by poetic allusions peppered through the rest of the story. Lines from "The White Birds" and "His Phoenix" evoke the aging Yeats and Maud Gonne McBride (the narrator sardonically dubs her "Gone Mad McBride" (Kiely 1980: 440)), whom the poet, still spied by Pike Hunter, encounters a few blocks later. Hunter observes their interaction in a quiet, sunlit street before moving on to the mystical promise of a pub called the Dark Cow. Their famous unrequited love soon translates into that of Hunter for the prostitute Butterfly, whom he first meets perched on a stool in the bar. In contrast to her name, Madame Butterfly displays little patience for literature or any of life's other romantic diversions. "Poor Pike," she'd say, "he'd puke you with poethry. Poethry's all very well but" (Kiely 1980: 433). Still, Butterfly hasn't the heart to dismiss the awkward bachelor who, if nothing else, is always good for a bottle of champagne.

There ensues a one-sided affair of the Yeats–Gonne variety, as Butterfly pursues her vocation while Pike pursues her. When he brings her on an outing to Howth in hope of securing a more intimate connection, another giant literary shadow looms over them.

> Pike told her about some fellow called Joyce – there was a Joyce in the Civic Guards, a Galwayman who played county football, but no relation – who had gone walking on the island one fine day and laid eyes on a young one, wading in a pool, with her skirts well pulled up, and let a roar out of him. By all accounts this Joyce was no addition to the family for, as Pike told the story, Butterfly worked out that the young one was well under age. (Kiely 1980: 439)

This dismantling allusion to the bird-girl epiphany from Joyce's *A Portrait of the Artist as a Young Man* provides a final hint of the doomed incompatibility of this mismatched pair. So doing, it invokes Ireland's other literary superstar of the first half of the twentieth century, thus rounding out the broad literary allegory to the story.

The passing of W.B. Yeats in 1939 and James Joyce in 1941 left enormous psychic space for Irish literary culture to fill. In Butterfly's rejection of Pike Hunter and, by extension, the Joycean and Yeatsian impulses he brings to their mismatched coupling, "A Ball of Malt and Madame Butterfly" enacts the need for Irish writing to leave off with the past and chart a fresh narrative direction appropriate to an emerging nation replete with new identities. Since 1945 the Irish short story has never ceased doing just that, and has taken a place alongside the preferred revival modes of poetry and drama. Three generations of practitioners have brought the short story to the forefront not just of Irish writing, but of world literature in general.

The past six decades of Irish short fiction are conveniently regarded in three twenty-year intervals, each in its turn a response and a record of socio-cultural change. At the same time, the growing awareness of not just a new national literature but a con-tinuous cultural discourse of storytelling within that literature becomes increasingly apparent. The period from 1945 to 1965 was marked on the one hand by the response of major short-story writers to their literary antecedents – namely, the Celtic revival and early twentieth-century genesis of modern Irish short fiction – and, on the other, to the insular, reactionary politics, social conservatism and censorship of de Valera's Ireland. During the mid-1960s to the 1980s, the short story is taken up by a wave of writers looking to explain their relocation from rural roots to urban lights. This microeconomic transition is matched on the national level by Ireland's political and economic emergence on to the world stage. Meanwhile, such modernizing tendencies are checked by renewed sectarian tensions and political violence, fueled by high unemployment and economic stagnation. Since 1985, a third wave of writers has the short story in the context of the Celtic Tiger economy, and of Good Friday peace accords. The ascendance of Irish film, music and digital media, as well as the internationalization of publishing, has supplied new forms and fodder for the short story, while attracting a global audience that would have hardly seemed imaginable only decades before. In some cases, a writer can be classified within a single generation. In others, a career might span two or sometimes even all three eras. Edna O'Brien, for example, began writing in the 1950s and continues to publish into the twenty-first century.

*Bell*wethers: 1945–1965

From its origins in George Moore's *The Untilled Field* (1903), and James Joyce's *Dubliners* (1914), the modern Irish short story had emerged by mid-century as a respected artistic medium and reliable barometer of national life. Moore's rural and Joyce's urban portraits represented significant benchmarks for writers, from both a literary and a commercial perspective. A number of Ireland's writers in the ensuing decades made their reputations through short fiction which, owing much to those first practitioners, had considerable marketability with editors in Britain and America. For some, like Elizabeth Bowen and Samuel Beckett, the short story was a stop on the way to other forms. Before proceeding towards his focus on drama and the novel, Beckett's first publication was his Dublin-based story collection, *More Pricks than Kicks* (1934). Bowen, better known for her Anglo-Irish novels, produced the short-story collections *Look at All Those Roses* (1941) and *The Demon Lover* (1945). For a host of others, however, short fiction remained the text of choice.

   Daniel Corkery and Liam O'Flaherty both published a prolific number of stories in magazines and book collections during the inter-war years. Most of these, including O'Flaherty's collections *Spring Sowing* (1924), *Civil War* (1925), and *The Tent* (1926), and Corkery's *The Stormy Hills* (1929) and *Earth Out of Earth* (1939), trained on the rural settings and folkloric subjects rooted in the writers' respective origins in Connacht and Munster. It was two of Corkery's students, Frank O'Connor and Seán O'Faoláin, who would lead the way in making the short story a significant literary form in Ireland after 1945. By that year, each had already published several books and each would maintain a steady output of stories for decades to come. Several other short-story practitioners, including Mary Lavin, Bryan MacMahon, and Michael McLaverty, would emerge during the 1940s and 1950s. Demonstrating a now continuous national tradition in the short story, this new crop of writers benefited from the artistic example and editorial influence of their predecessors.

   From 1945 to the mid-1960s, several established names in the short story led the way with a steady output of work in Irish, British, and especially American magazines, as well as book collections. By far the most dominant and pioneering voices in Irish short fiction were O'Connor and O'Faoláin, who were both at the height of their career during the World War II years. O'Connor, whose reputation was well established by 1945, cast an influential shadow over Irish short-story writers for at least the next three decades. O'Connor's early writing career had been inspired by the revolutionary political and military events of which he had firsthand experience as a republican soldier in the Irish Civil War of 1922–3. The title story of his collection *Guests of the Nation* (1931), which some critics still designate O'Connor's strongest work, came directly out of his own time spent in a wartime internment camp. In the post-war years, he remained highly productive, publishing his collections *The Common Chord* (1947), *Traveller's Samples* (1951a), and *Domestic Relations* (1957).

With his work appearing regularly in American magazines, such as *Harper's Bazaar*, *The Atlantic Monthly*, and *Today's Woman*, O'Connor was easily the country's greatest literary export since Joyce, and far less controversial. In stories from the period like "First Confession," "The Genius," and "My Oedipus Complex," a middle-aged O'Connor was perfecting the precocious child narrator who seemed to offer a positive counterpoint to his literary antecedents in the boyhood stories of *Dubliners*. O'Connor also made a noteworthy critical contribution with his study of the short story, titled *The Lonely Voice*. In that book, he defines several essential criteria for the short story, including the fact that an effective story arises not, like the novel, from focus on a singular hero, but instead from its focus on "a submerged population group," those who are separated from the larger society through either material or spiritual shortcomings (O'Connor 1965: 18). O'Connor's apt description of the underpinnings of short stories, by writers as diverse as Turgenev and Sherwood Anderson, would become a prescriptive manifesto for many future writers in Ireland and around the world.

During the 1940s and 1950s, President Eamon de Valera advocated returning Ireland to an austere, pastoral state in which the Catholic Church held moral sway. The Church's "special position" in the Constitution also gave it control of the Censorship Board, a fact of governance that would have a profound effect on the next two generations of Irish writers. Away from literary and artistic circles, the de Valera regime meant continual deprivation for many, especially in the countryside. De Valera's belief that no man required more than £1,000 per annum to survive led to salary cuts for civil servants and government employees that produced microeconomic ripple effects in households across the island. Few of the promises and improvements many had come to expect with the transfer from English to Irish leadership were realized during the period. Modernization, in the form of rural electrification and industrial development, were slow in coming to the Republic, leaving many to survive on dwindling small-acreage farms that were poor competition against the expanding agribusiness interests and protective subsidies of the United Kingdom. Economic limitations were accompanied by social bitterness and political disillusionment.

Perhaps the dominant literary expression of this came with Patrick Kavanagh's renowned long poem, *The Great Hunger*, with its multilayered consideration of economic, intellectual, and sexual deprivation. Short-fiction writers also adopted an inward gaze and backward look that continued to ponder the national growing pains of decolonization and civil war, and to question the status quo determined by Church and government in what historian R.F. Foster terms the "de Valera dispensation" (Foster 1989: 536). Within this context the two framing stories of Seán O'Faoláin's collection, *The Man Who Invented Sin* (1948), give a candid representation of the over-zealous social control by the Church during this period. The opening and title story of the collection concerns a group of two nuns and two monks studying Irish in a Gaeltacht summer college. Told in the first-person perspective of a young boy who shares their rural boarding house, the narrative lends a sympathetic portrayal to the secular enjoyments of dancing, drink, and late-night boat cruises, which are put to an end by the moralistic tyranny of a local curate who could as well be the reincarnation of any of George Moore's puritanical priests. Two decades on, chance encounters with one of the monks and the curate lend subtle confirmation to the grown-up narrator's original sense of the events.

At the other end of the collection, "Teresa" follows an Irish novice on her journey to a Carmelite convent in Normandy. When she ultimately decides against a spiritual calling, one has the hopeful impression she has escaped from the lonely, joyless destiny of the four clerics in the first story. The concluding paragraphs tell of her return to the convent two years later to show her new husband, a Protestant named George, the repressed life she might have lived. This ultimate escape from church-sanctioned social and sexual stagnation recalls the young narrator's comment in the title story regarding the more vivacious of the nuns: "Sister Magdalen was so dainty and gay and spirited that it seemed a shame to lock her away from the world in a convent" (O'Faoláin 1949: 4). While Magdalen does not escape that trap, one is relieved that Teresa does. Sounding a final open note to the collection, she points the way to intellectual and sexual freedom for many later O'Faoláin characters, such as the adulteress wife and her French diplomat lover in "The Faithless Wife," from the collection *Foreign Affairs* (1976). To be sure, the price of liberation is often a psychological peril, but few if any of O'Faoláin's characters would go back on the bargain if it meant reverting to the moral provincialism against which they rebel. As he challenged the clerical hold on society, it was no surprise that O'Faoláin had to look overseas for publication opportunities as he entered the mature phase of his career. Even as late as 1971, when O'Faoláin won a *Playboy* short-story competition, few readers in Ireland ever saw the issue because importation of the magazine was forbidden.

O'Faoláin also contributed to the development of the short story through his editorial role. Along with Peadar O'Donnell, O'Faoláin was a founder of *The Bell* literary magazine, which he edited for six years in the 1940s. *The Bell* charted a way for the Irish short story throughout the 1940s and 1950s. Its pages featured a roster of new and familiar voices, including Val Mulkerns, Brendan Behan, Elizabeth Bowen, and Michael McClaverty. O'Faoláin's editorial statement in the debut issue complained of the current social malaise and announced the mission for *The Bell* to be a force for artistic liberation: "a parochial Ireland, bounded by its own shores, has no part in our vision of the ideal nation that will yet come out of this present dull period." Mulkerns, who later served as an associate editor, proudly called the magazine a "thorn in the side of the establishment" (qtd in Lee 2006: 258). Notwithstanding such bold proclamations, the Church-controlled Censorship Board remained an obstacle to reaching a wide readership. *The Bell*, according to O'Faoláin's daughter Julia, "was often sold from under the counter with a furtiveness usually associated with pornographic magazines" (qtd in Thompson 1996: 269).

One writer who benefited directly from O'Faoláin's editorship was Bryan MacMahon, who published a number of his first stories in *The Bell* during the 1940s. In "The Exile's Return," from *The Red Petticoat* (1955), McMahon presents the themes of forgetting and betrayal that speak of a darker side to socio-economic separation. When a laborer returns from England to his rural Irish village, he encounters his old friend and new child with the realization that his friend is a little bit too familiar with the daily and nightly routines of his household. The result is a dark updating of the reverse-emigration theme famously explored in George Moore's "Homesickness."

Ulster writer Michael McLaverty published two major collections during the period, *The White Mare and Other Stories* (1943) and *The Game Cock and Other Stories* (1947). McClaverty's northern narratives trace what his friend Seamus Heaney calls "the worn grain of unspectacular experience" (1997). "Six Weeks on and Two Ashore," which first appeared in the magazine *Irish Writing* in 1948, tells of a lighthouse keeper and his wife whose temperament and routine have brought them at middle age to dwell on separate emotional shores. In a cruel parable of aging and marital isolation, they live within plain sight but beyond hearing, understanding, or communicative sympathy.

Finally, among the most prolific short-fiction writers of the post-war decades was Mary Lavin. Her career was well launched by 1945, with two story collections, *Tales from Bective Ridge* (1941) and *The Long Ago and Other Stories* (1944), already in print. She went on to publish six more collections over the next two decades, including *The Becker Wives and Other Stories* (1946), *At Sallygap and Other Stories* (1947), *A Single Lady* (1951), *The Patriot Son and Other Stories* (1956), *The Great Wave and Other Stories* (1961), and the first volume of her *Selected Stories* (1964). Lavin's steady output through the 1950s and 1960s maintained her status as one of the most important new voices in the Irish short story. "At Sallygap" is one of a number of Lavin stories concerned with the changing social and material conditions of an urbanizing mid-twentieth-century Ireland, especially in the realm of marriage and domestic relations. In addition, the story's geographic anchoring suggests a modern updating of the ancient Celtic *dindsenchas* (place-lore) tradition.

Modern Voices: 1965–1985

The power of broadcast technology and the televised image linked the island to the rest of the world more vividly and immediately than ever before. In his memoir, *44*

Dublin Made Me, Peter Sheridan recalls the advent of television to his family's north-side Dublin home as a historical watershed:

> Half an hour into 1960 we all sat staring at the television. It felt very different from 1959. The sound was perfect. A man was describing "traditional revelry" in Trafalgar Square. There was definitely something on the screen. Outlines that looked like human beings. I went right up close, but all I could see were dots and lines. Paddy touched something at the back of the set, and there it was – a perfect picture. Well, nearly perfect. Lots of snow, but a definite picture. We all clapped. It was a woman on a horse. She looked majestic. She looked regal. A big silver sword in her hand. (Sheridan 1999: 19)

Within the year, Irish households would not have to point their antennae towards England to receive snowy pictures. Radio Telefis Eireann (RTE) initiated radio broadcasts in 1960, followed a year later by the first Irish television programming. The image would prove both competition and inspiration for the printed word in Irish culture. If television was implicated by many as an agent of decline in the national reading culture, it was also true that it brought new opportunities for both employment and exposure. A number of authors found work writing for television and print journalism, which provided financial support as well as a practical training. Ireland entered the global stage in other ways as well. Its seat on the first UN Security Council reflected the young Republic's new role in international affairs. As people in the former colonial zones of Africa, Latin America, and Asia won independence, many emerging countries regarded the experience of Ireland as a sort of trailblazing for the rights of small nations everywhere.

These aspects of the period are well captured in John McGahern's "Sierra Leone," in which a fleeting love affair parallels the brinksmanship of the Cuban missile crisis. As the world holds its breath watching the Cold War showdown play out on television, two young Dublin sophisticates determine their own future direction. The fate of their liaison is inextricably tied to a diplomatic link between Ireland and the newly independent African nation of the title. International relations are not so much an allegorical thread as a literal indicator of a modernizing national consciousness and international awareness, proof positive that a new highly educated, cosmopolitan generation has completed the upwardly mobile circuit from rural farmhouse to Merrion Square.

A number of McGahern characters and narrators follow a similar trajectory from country to city, pre-modern to modern, starting with "Wheels," the lead-off story of his debut collection *Nightlines* (1971). In their urban sophistication, the narrators and central characters often share a growing tendency towards secular and international culture. Some stories move abroad, to London construction sites, Spanish villas, and Scandinavian cities. But no matter how far they wander, they always return. Notwithstanding the new occupations and identities they have found among city lights, and despite bitter memories and shattered relations, they continue returning to the

countryside on a ritual wheel of longing and responsibility. The cyclical migration
echoes that of an entire generation making the transition from agricultural to urban
life.

   One of McGahern's most autobiographical stories, "Oldfashioned," is also a vivid
portrayal of sectarian relations in 1950s village life. The story centers on Johnny,
son of a *garda* sergeant in a lonely Leitrim barracks, who finds a close connection
with a kindly Anglo-Irish couple. When the husband, a retired British army colonel,
offers to recommend the teenager for a place at Sandhurst, Johnny's father, who
fought in an IRA flying column in the War of Independence, breaks the connection.
The story is as much about Johnny's coming of age as it is Ireland's. Electricity and
the internal combustion engine have become a commonplace of a countryside now
repopulated by return emigrants. "The tide that had gone out to America and every
part of Britain now reaches only as far as a bursting Dublin, and every Friday night
crammed buses take the aliens home. For a few free days in country light they feel
important until the same buses take them back on Sunday night to shared flats and
bed-sits" (McGahern 2002: 269). Those who have relocated to urban opportunities
never totally cut the ties that bind, since such severance would mean losing that
over which they might feign a kind of generational superiority. In the final lines,
the grown-up Johnny returns some years later as a film-maker. The description of
his professional activities could just as easily be applied to McGahern's own writing
career in the 1960s and 1970s, with its mix of critical acclaim and censorial
disapprobation:

> he made a series of documentary films about the darker aspects of Irish life. As they
> were controversial, they won him a sort of fame: some thought they were serious, well
> made, and compulsive viewing, bringing things to light that were in bad need of light;
> but others maintained that they were humourless, morbid, and restricted to a narrow
> view that was more revealing of private obsessions. (McGahern 1992: 268)

The metaphor of illumination alludes to McGahern's 1965 novel, *The Dark*, which
dealt unflinchingly with the issue of child sexual abuse. Banning of the book and the
ensuing controversy ultimately cost McGahern his teaching job in one of the national
schools. McGahern's three short-story collections – *Getting Through* (1978) and *High
Ground* (1985) are the others – plus two new tales were published as *The Collected
Stories* (1992). The understated tone, realistic detail, and verbal economy of his work
have led some critics to consider him the greatest short-story writer from Ireland since
Joyce.

   Edna O'Brien, who settled in London to escape similar battles with the Censorship
Board, published her story collection *The Love Object* (1968). Established by that time
as a novelist for *The Country Girls Trilogy*, O'Brien maintained a bold female perspective throughout the eight-story collection. Her narrators and protagonists present a
rich cross-section of Irish women. Whether rich or poor, urban or rural, white collar
or blue, single or partnered, all are motivated by the same underlying desire for

intimacy and acceptance. Several find their love object in unreliable men; several others in actual objects and material prosperity. Most fall well short of their aim and, like the tragic heroine of "Paradise," even risk drowning – literally and metaphorically – in brutal social surroundings. Nearly all of them err in looking beyond themselves rather than finding strength and answers within. At the end of "Irish Revel," the dejected feelings of the protagonist Mary are conveyed through a limited omniscient narration that echoes the epiphany of Gabriel Conroy at the end of James Joyce's "The Dead":

> Frost was general all over Ireland; frost like a weird blossom on the branches, on the riverbank from which Long John Salmon leaped in his great, hairy nakedness, on the ploughs left out all winter; frost on the stony fields, and on all the slime and ugliness of the world. (O'Brien 1969: 114)

The lines sound an anti-climactic echo of Joyce's famous conclusion, underscoring the bleak environment of unrealized dreams not just for one adolescent female but an entire nation of women. With her meaningful parody of the most renowned moment in the modern short story, O'Brien asserts her own subject position within the tradition. Overall, the collection brings a totalized female perspective that, perhaps with the exception of Mary Lavin, is unprecedented in Irish short fiction. O'Brien followed *The Love Object* with the later collections, *A Scandalous Woman* (1974) and *Mrs. Reinhardt and Other Stories* (1978), before turning to a string of successful novels.

The modernizing social and political changes documented by McGahern and O'Brien were not uncontested. As many of their stories describe, the emergence of an enlightened secular culture was derided or dismissed by many whose own interests lay with maintaining the status quo of rural and revolutionary ideals. This bucolic dream eroded for many as the 1970s were marked by renewed sectarian tensions and paramilitary violence in the North, along with economic recession and high unemployment throughout the island. Ireland's entry into the European Economic Community subjected Irish agriculture to the new conditions of an international marketplace, with less benefit of protective tariffs and subsidies. The utopian vision of the family farm is laid bare in the dry second-person narration of Patrick Boyle's "Pastorale," which offers a cynical look at the rural rivalries and petty concerns that can remain an obsession to the bitter end.

> God knows no one would want to belittle a neighboring farmer and his family. The more so when there's been a chair for you at their kitchen fire every night for a score or more years. But not to put a tooth in it and to make due allowance for bitter tongues, the Bennetts are known throughout the length and breadth of the parish as notorious bloody landgrabbers. (Boyle 1980: 338)

So begins a narrative in which the neighbor's own jealousy cannot help but seep through, ultimately mirroring the very quality he denounces in the Bennetts. We are a long way from the celebratory speeches of De Valera, idolizing Irish farm folk. A retired bank manager, Boyle seems well aware of the material motivations in Irish life, which he recorded in three collections during the period, *At Night All Cats Are Gray* (1966), *All Looks Yellow to the Jaundiced Eye* (1969), and *A View from Cavalry* (1976).

William Trevor has described himself as a "a short story writer . . . who happens to write novels" (qtd in Podolsky 1994: 257). Trevor's immense short-fiction output – seven collections in two decades – often gazes at the fading embers of rural village society as well as Protestant Ascendancy culture. Such collections as *The Ballroom of Romance* (1972), *Angels at the Ritz* (1975), *Lovers of their Time* (1978), and *Beyond the Pale* (1981) made Trevor a name synonymous with Irish short stories during the seventies and eighties. Like Joyce and O'Brien, he has spent much of his career writing about Ireland from the perspective of exile – in Trevor's case, to England. His collections are populated by a wide array of strange, often isolated individuals, including coarse bachelors and lonely women, many of them grown-up children clutching at existence in the burned-out shell of the old class order. They seek insight and direction in a world that no longer dictates clear roles or obvious intentions. Many Trevor characters are trapped in a penitential existence of family obligations and delayed gratification. In the title story from *The Ballroom of Romance*, a daughter watches her prospects for happiness pass by as she cares for her invalid father. Ultimately, she opts to settle for anything but loneliness. "Death in Jerusalem," from *Lovers of their Time*, features two brothers, one a worldly priest, the other a cloistered shopkeeper, whose differing moral positions and filial connections deepen their spiritual divide during a tour of the Holy Land. Trevor's seven collections were published together as *Collected Stories* (1983; expanded edition 1992).

Several other notable contributors to the short story during the period began as print journalists before making the crossover to short fiction. Benedict Kiely was a columnist and editorialist for the *Irish Independent* newspaper, a role alluded to by the narrator of "A Ball of Malt and Madame Butterfly" when he counts himself one of the "merry newspaper men." Kiely shows the literary influence of William Carleton, about whom he authored a critical study in 1947, in the colorful characterization and generally apolitical flavor of his collections *A Ball of Malt and Madame Butterfly* (1973) and *A Cow in the House* (1978). Known from the 1940s for her numerous roles in Dublin newspapers and broadcasting, as well as an editorial stint at *The Bell*, Val Mulkerns produced the story collections *Antiquities* (1982) and *An Idle Woman* (1980). In contrast to Kiely, Mulkerns infuses a number of her stories with her own interest and activism surrounding social and political causes in modern Ireland (Lee 2006: 262). *Irish Times* columnist and popular novelist Maeve Binchy published the story collections *Central Line* (1977), *Victoria Line* (1980), *Dublin 4* (1983), and *The Lilac Bus* (1984). The majority of these stories are guided by imagery and motifs of movement. As one critic notes, "Binchy's works offer a compelling insight into Ireland at the close of the twentieth century. Her characters dwell in a world made homogeneous by media saturation and easy transportation" (Meche 2006: 37). In this regard, they predict key concerns facing the next generation of practitioners of the Irish short story.

The New Plurality: 1985–2005

From the mid-1980s, a widening international audience for Irish popular culture ushered in a period of unprecedented cultural awareness and international reception. Coinciding with the success of Bord Faílte and the expanding tourism, popular music (U2, Van Morrison, The Chieftains), movies (*The Crying Game, The Commitments, Michael Collins*), and entertainment (*Riverdance*), Irish identity underwent a process of revision and revitalization for the new global marketplace. As many cultural critics attest, the notions of Ireland and Irishness have become branded and saleable commodities in the past two decades. From the brink of economic collapse in the late 1980s, when some economists predicted a wave of emigration to rival that of the nineteenth century, financial investment and development led to an unprecedented rise in standard of living in Ireland. Within a decade, the opportunities and lifestyles for many, urban and rural alike, jumped from pre- to post-industrial conditions. Rooted in high-tech information, chemical, and pharmaceutical industries, the so-called Celtic Tiger roared to life in the late 1990s, and amid such gathering economic momentum the nation hardly had time to look back.

This new economic revolution effectively rendered obsolete the old political one. Economic opportunity and abundance led many to break from a narrow, protectionist definition of Irishness to a fluid notion of many Irelands. This sense of the plural is tied more to the nation's benefits from European Union and international investment than to any paramilitary or political victories in the longstanding ideological battle. The Good Friday Peace Accords of 1998 owed as much to the new prosperity on both sides of the border as to the politicians and diplomats who negotiated the treaty. Still, in place of the old divide, some new ones have arisen. Dublin, from the end of the 1980s to the start of the new millennium, was transformed into a city nearly as diverse and equally expensive as London or New York. With immigrants from Asia, Africa, Central and Eastern Europe joining thousands of repatriated Irish, entirely new questions of national identity are being considered from the Dublin streets to the *boreens* of Connemara.

These changes have their record and reflection in literature. On a quite pragmatic level, the global commodification of Ireland identity has opened up new intellectual and economic opportunities. Writers and critics who once would have competed for a scant number of academic posts at home found, by the late 1980s and early 1990s, American colleges and universities outbidding one another for the services of scholars, writers, and poets. John McGahern, Benedict Kiely, Seamus Deane, Paul Muldoon, Seamus Heaney, and Eavan Boland represent only a partial list of those who made the transatlantic hop to take advantage of the explosion of interest in Irish studies and literature. Amid the new mobility in literary and academic circles, and the rapid adjustment to image-driven consumer culture, the Irish short story has demonstrated its versatility and staying power. It has continued to thrive in the past two decades, remaining a vital genre capable of representing Ireland in its increasingly diverse and pluralistic identities. A host of emerging short-fiction writers joined those established names like O'Brien, Trevor, and McGahern who continued to produce memorable works of short fiction. These newcomers have given voice to a generation now living a life that, for its material abundance and demographic difference, would have seemed unimaginable to most people in Ireland only a few years ago.

If print journalism and television were a launch pad for short fiction writers in previous decades, the film industry has had a kind of opposite and reinforcing effect. The recent explosion in Irish cinema has increased its critical mass by drawing a number of potential short-storytellers into screenwriting. Perhaps the prime example is Neil Jordan, who began as a short-fiction writer with *Night in Tunisia and Other Stories* (1976).

The title story of the collection treats themes of sexual awakening, generational difference, religious beliefs, and gender identities. The two latter issues play out in the virgin–whore dichotomy that men impose on women across the story, especially in the contrast between Rita – the object of the narrator's desire who bears the stigma of village "hewer" – and the fishermen's statue of "a Virgin with thin fingers towards the sea, her feet layered with barnacles" (Jordan 1991: 1106). Neither of these opposed roles seems capable of providing women a means of escape from a world constructed primarily from voyeuristic male fantasy. By the end of the story, religion and sexual taboo become confusedly intertwined in the boy's perspective: "He looked at his sister's breasts across a bowl of apples, half-grown fruit. The apples came from monks who kept an orchard . . . He imagined a monk's hand reaching for the unplucked fruit, white against the swinging brown habit. For monks never sunbathed" (Jordan 1991: 1106).

Formalistically, such complex thematic arrangements resemble the forms of jazz and popular music to which the narrative constantly alludes, starting with the title, which is drawn from the name of a bebop composition by Dizzy Gillespie. The rapid scene shifts and musical motifs could be regarded as harbingers of some of the movies Jordan would write and direct over the ensuing decades, including *The Crying Game* (1992), *The Butcher Boy* (1997), and *Breakfast on Pluto* (2005). The latter two are adaptations of novels by Patrick McCabe, so to say prose fiction lost something to cinema on this score would be a misconception. In many instances film, the Internet, and even newer digital media have served to amplify interest and sales for Irish novels and short fiction.

In his critical study *The Lonely Voice,* Frank O'Connor famously described the short story as thriving most in "submerged population groups" (1965: 18). O'Connor's phrase takes on a revised meaning in prosperous, postcolonial Ireland. During the past two decades, a range of submerged or marginalized Irish voices have begun to be heard, particularly as these relate to issues of gender, sexual orientation, social class, and the new immigrant experience. In this sense, the plural identities of recent Irish short fiction can be said to resemble more and more the British and American short story. Nevertheless, national history remains a deep well for post-modern and experimental fiction, since new identities allow writers to excavate history anew and from fresh perspectives.

Ronan Sheehan's "Paradise" (1991) exemplifies a postmodern writing and fictional revisionist history that delves back into the psychosocial origins of Ireland's colonial experience. The story recounts the tragic story of Anne Greene, a servant in the upper-class British house of Jeffrey Reade. Following a brief love affair with Reade, Greene delivers a stillborn child. Discovery of the remains in a privy leads to a murder charge and a death sentence for the innocent and bewildered Greene. Reade, who narrates the story, learns about the case from a helpless distance when business responsibilities take him overseas. A botched hanging brings Anne Greene to the brink of death and into the hands of Sir William Petty. A doctor who takes charge of her recovery, Petty is a fictional version of the man who served as physician general to the English army in Ireland and wrote *Political Anatomy of Ireland* (1691). The bodily trope plays out as Anne Greene is ultimately reduced to a subject of medical experimentation at the hands of Petty: "The breath stopped in Margaret's throat when she saw her friend: her thighs bound, her bosom glistening and discoloured from the potion spread across it, livid weals about her neck from the rope, the first signs of bruises where the blows had struck her, her hair tied with Townsend's string" (Sheehan 1991: 1118). Anne Greene's treatment at the hands of society's legal and medical experts is certainly among the boldest and most heartrending metaphors of Britain's exploitation of Ireland. There develops through her tragic tale an allegory that shows how national ambitions can be rooted in individual appetites. Although she recovers from the physical injuries, Anne is left with incurable amnesia that suggests the permanent trauma of colonization.

Anne Enright represents another significant contributor to the Irish short story in the early 1990s. Enright's work has been described as "postmodern and deconstructionist while utilizing a cinematic style suggestive of both the celluloid quality and pace of contemporary life" (Moloney 2002: 89). Enright's sole collection of short stories, *The Portable Virgin*, has garnered comparison with Joyce's *Ulysses* for its artful, parodying blend of iconoclasm and naïveté. Its multilayered title points simultaneously to the sacred and the secular: holy-water figurines of the Virgin Mary on the dashboards of cars, and the notion of a self-contained, independent sexuality. *The Portable Virgin* took the Rooney Prize for Irish Literature in 1991.

The previous year, that honor was bestowed on Mary Dorcey's *A Noise from the Woodshed* (1989), a story collection that records lesbian experience in late 1980s Ireland. The book's success and critical acclaim demonstrated a new receptiveness to homosexuality that suggests something of the secular and social changes afoot. The stories, reflecting Dorcey's own experiences as an activist for women's rights, railed against those elements of religious and social conservatism that attempt to relegate women to the heterosexual and domestic spheres. The title story tells of a lesbian couple who establish their own domestic routine in a house in the country. Not long into their residence there, they hear noises from the woodshed behind the house: the sounds of other female couples making love. More days lead to discoveries of more lesbian lovers, in a kind of parable of the secrecy necessary to lesbian partnership in Ireland. As Moira Casey observes, "The experimental form of this short story indicates Dorcey's need to distance herself from conventional modes of narrative in order to write about the sexually unconventional lives of Irish lesbians" (2006: 65).

Other stories in the collection, more traditional in terms of narrative form, construct additional perspectives on lesbianism, including that of a man whose wife is preparing to leave him for her lesbian lover in "The Husband." His thoughts run the gamut: from sexual attraction towards both women, to a sense of disbelief that she can be satisfied by someone other than himself, to a feeling of hatred and disgust at imagining the sounds of their lovemaking. Overall, like the single story, the entire collection also charts a range of reactions to lesbianism, in a literary gesture that asks readers to engage in an open conversation about a sexual orientation and lifestyle once ignored or relegated to whispers.

Working-class experience has found a representation in writers like Roddy Doyle, whose own northside Dublin background is the basis for his novels known as the *Barrytown Trilogy.* Similarly, his short-fiction vignettes address topics of suburbia and family life, frequently from the perspective of characters not traditionally assigned a major place in literary fiction. "The Photograph" uncovers the buried life of a man facing the loss of a friend to cancer as he simultaneously becomes aware of the physical vulnerability of his own body. The title image – a literal image of the friend in his youthful prime – offers a meaningful (if only temporary) stand against time and change and death. The memorializing message is familiar from popular ballads or Shakespearean sonnets but rendered in a perspective and voice that are refreshing for their almost overlooked origin in the housing estates of north Dublin.

One can expect that in the coming years the Dublin of stories will alter as non-fiction Dublin and Ireland become ever more culturally diverse. An unprecedented experience of modern immigration to Ireland, mainly from Central and Eastern Europe, is now under way and having a direct impact on the social, economic, and cultural life of the island. Ireland now has four Polish newspapers. There is a new and sometimes hostile competition in higher education and the labor force. Irish society, just a few generations removed from life under British rule, is being forced to consider questions of economic and cultural subordination from the other side of the coin. The new cultural contact will likely reinvent the Irish short story, in the process challenging literary critics to reconsider geographic and ethnic distinctions once taken for granted in defining and assessing a so-called national literature. This has already begun to some extent with a work like Hugo Hamilton's *Dublin Where the Palm Trees Grow* (1997), a collection grounded as it is in the writer's dual Irish-German parentage. As more immigrants arrive from all over the globe to make their life in Ireland, one will expect to see more short fiction that seeks to document the first generation immigrant experience as well as the hyphenated identities that follow. As it has for literature in English around the world, short fiction will provide a space in which to work out the tension between assimilation and the drive for Irishness, on the one hand, and the primary linguistic and cultural ties on the other. There will be an Irish short story for the century ahead, but at least in content, if not in form, it will be moving ever further from the short fiction devised by Moore and Joyce a century ago.

Conclusion

In the editor's introduction to *The Oxford Book of Irish Short Stories*, William Trevor articulates his own opinion as to why the story, and not the novel, has flourished in Ireland like nowhere else:

> Stories, far more than novels, cast spells, and spells have been nurtured in Ireland for as long as imperial greed has been attempting to hammer its people into a subject class. The Irish short story has come to appeal to audiences far beyond its home one, but the confidence born of instinct and familiarity has encouraged the art of the spell to continue. (Trevor 1989: xv)

The short story, originally an effective literary mode in Ireland owing to the country's impoverished, colonized status, remains a dominant literary form in the present for virtually opposite reasons: Ireland's new prosperity, high-tech culture, and global marketability seem to be ensuring a place for Irish short fiction at home and abroad. Over the past six decades, the short story has constantly offered a way of seeing and representing the changes of Irish society as it made the transition from the Free State to the Republic and from economic stagnation to unprecedented wealth. Not in spite of, but rather owing to the recent ascendancy of broadcast radio, television, and digital media, the short story continues to hold a looking-glass to the changing faces of Irish life.

REFERENCES AND FURTHER READING

Boyle, P. (1980). "Pastorale," in Ben Forkner (ed.), *Modern Irish Stories*. New York: Viking Penguin.

Casey, M. (2006). "Mary Dorcey," *British and Irish Short-Fiction Writers, 1945–2000, Dictionary of Literary Biography*, vol. 319, pp. 63–7, ed. Cheryl Alexander Malcolm and David Malcolm. Detroit, New York, San Francisco, San Diego,

New Haven, Waterville, London and Munich: Thomson/Gale.

Doyle, R. (2006). "The Photograph," *The New Yorker* (October 16, 2006).

Foster, R.F. (1989). *Modern Ireland 1600–1972*. London: Penguin.

Jordan, N. (1991). "Night in Tunisia," in S. Deane (ed.), *The Field Day Anthology of Irish*

Literature, vol. III, pp. 1101–6. Derry: Field Day.

Kiely, B. (1980). *The State of Ireland: A Novella and Seventeen Stories*. Boston: Godine.

Lee, M. (2006). "Val Mulkerns," in *British and Irish Short-Fiction Writers, 1945–2000, Dictionary of Literary Biography*, vol. 319, pp. 257–62, ed. Cheryl Alexander Malcolm and David Malcolm. Detroit, New York, San Francisco, San Diego, New Haven, Waterville, London and Munich: Thomson/Gale.

McGahern, J. (1992). *The Collected Stories*. London: Faber and Faber.

Moloney, C. (2002). "Anne Enright," *Twenty-First-Century British and Irish Novelists, Dictionary of Literary Biography*, vol. 267, pp. 88–93, ed. Michael R. Molino. Detroit, New York, San Francisco, San Diego, New Haven, Waterville, London and Munich: Thomson/Gale.

Meche, J. (2006). "Maeve Binchy," *British and Irish Short-Fiction Writers, 1945–2000, Dictionary of Literary Biography*, vol. 319, pp. 34–8, ed. Cheryl Alexander Malcolm and David Malcolm. Detroit, New York, San Francisco, San Diego, New Haven, Waterville, London and Munich: Thomson/Gale.

O'Brien, E. (1969). *The Love Object*. New York: Alfred A. Knopf.

O'Connor, F. (1951a). *Traveller's Samples*. New York: Alfred A. Knopf.

O'Connor, F. (1951b). *The Short Story*. New York: Devin-Adair.

O'Connor, F. (1965). *The Lonely Voice: A Study of the Short Story*. Cleveland: World Publishing.

O'Faoláin, S. (1949). *The Man Who Invented Sin*. New York: Devin-Adair.

Podolsky, M. (1994). *British Short Fiction Writers, 1945–1980, Dictionary of Literary Biography*, vol. 139, pp. 255–66. Detroit, Washington, DC, London: Bruccoli Clark Layman/Gale Research.

Sheehan, R. (1991). "Paradise," *The Field Day Anthology of Irish Literature*, vol. 3, pp. 1107–21, ed. Seamus Deane. Derry: Field Day.

Sheridan, P. (1999). *44 Dublin Made Me*. New York: Viking Penguin.

Thompson, R. (1996). "Seán O'Faoláin," *British and Irish Short-Fiction Writers 1915–1945, Dictionary of Literary* Biography, vol. 162, pp. 265–81, ed. John Rogers. Detroit, Washington, DC, London: Bruccoli Clark Layman/Gale Research.

Trevor, W. (1989). "Introduction," *The Oxford Book of Irish Short Stories*, ed. William Trevor. Oxford: Oxford University Press.

24
Redefining Englishness: British Short Fiction from 1945 to the Present

James M. Lang

"Wanda! Have you any idea what it's like to be English?" (A Fish Called Wanda (1988; Dir. Charles Crichton))

There are times – temporal moments, say, such as great national events – when a nation does appear unified and homegenous as a national culture. These times only mask its actual heterogeneity. The English are a mingling of Celts, Romans, Germanic Angles and Saxons, Nordic Jutes, Vikings and Norman French, and that only takes you to 1500. So no one is purely English, not even the Queen. (Antony Easthope, Englishness and National Culture (1999))

Introduction

The short fiction of prolific English writer V.S. Pritchett spills over with characters in search of identities, a characteristically modern quest, but one that Pritchett also frequently links with the search for a specifically English identity following World War II. In his short story "The Fall," set at a business convention in "a large, wet, Midland city" (Pritchett 1982: 132), we encounter Charles Peacock, the ordinary brother of a famous film actor. Like his brother, Peacock has a talent for acting out different parts. The story opens with a description of him standing in front of a mirror and determining which part he will play for the evening. As he makes his way down to the ballroom of the hotel for the evening dinner, he greets everyone he meets in their native idiom, running through the accents and expressions of Scotland, York, Ireland, southern England, and finishing with "music-hall Negro" (Pritchett 1982: 132). Finally, the narrator explains, "having spoken to several human beings, the fragments called Peacock closed up" (Pritchett 1982: 132). He momentarily settles on an identity for the evening, in other words, and heads into the convention dinner; but not before his accents have toured the various regions of the United Kingdom.

Later in the evening, during a conversation with a dinner guest about his brother, over fine wine and pheasant, Peacock suddenly becomes aware that his brother's well-known biography – and hence his own humble origins – may be influencing his interlocutor's perceptions of him. In an interview, his brother had once referred to the family's trade as owners of a "bankrupt fried fish shop." Peacock's suspicions seem clearly paranoid, as the story offers no indication that the guest has any such ideas in mind. But in Peacock's origins and his embarrassed response to those origins are encapsulated nicely the complex trajectory of "Englishness" in the latter half of the twentieth century, and into the present day: a confused and shifting identity which has evolved beyond the qualities that defined it in earlier times – such as, in the case of the broader English identity, empire at home and abroad, clearly defined class boundaries, racial characteristics, and social propriety. Like Charles Peacock, though, England cannot seem unable to settle upon those qualities that will allow it to close up into a new identity.

The question of what makes individuals – or places, or things, or trends, or ideas – specifically *English* has formed an important theme in much of the literature of Great Britain following World War II. The writers who have addressed this question hail from all parts of the United Kingdom – including Scotland's Muriel Spark and Ireland's William Trevor – though in this essay the focus will rest exclusively on the question of *Englishness* – as opposed to *Britishness*, a more complex identity that would encompass all four countries of Great Britain, including Scotland, Wales, and Northern Ireland. Writers from all of these countries have certainly taken up the question of the national identities in their homelands, but they have also addressed themselves to the qualities of Englishness – indicating, perhaps, a special interest in the definition of the English identity around the United Kingdom.

Before attempting to define the ways in which Englishness has evolved in the latter half of the twentieth century, and into the twenty-first century, it is worth considering briefly the usefulness and plausibility of identifying "Englishness" – or "Frenchness," or "Italianness," or any other national character – in the first place. As the epigraph from Antony Easthope indicates, the English share no distinct racial heritage, and the ballooning and collapsing of the British Empire has resulted in a dizzying array of nationalities claiming a stake in the English identity.

Drawing upon the work of Ernest Gellner, Easthope makes a distinction between the structure of a society and its culture – structure containing its major legal and political institutions, especially those that establish clearly defined roles for its citizens (giving them their rights, their employment, their worth in the social hierarchy), and culture consisting of meanings, traditions, and rituals associated with those roles. In older, traditional societies, culture helped support structure; in modern societies, in which structure has become far more diffuse (everyone votes and can theoretically own property; career paths are theoretically open to all, etc.), culture has assumed a much more important role. Now, instead of having our identities defined for us by the structures of our society, we use elements of culture to construct our identities: "Deprived of structure," Easthope writes, "the subject is driven into culture; denied identity fulfilled in a significant role, he or she demands an individuality which will make up for what has been relinquished" (Easthope 1999: 52). In other words, because rigid social structures have dissolved, making it less likely for an individual to be pinned to an identity by his/her class, or his/her employment, people have had to find other ways to define themselves and their identities within a society. And one of the main planks in the formation of that individuality becomes the association with the nation – or, in this case, with Englishness.

Hence, as social structures become less and less rigid, as many would argue has happened in England in the post-war period, cultural associations such as Englishness become increasingly crucial to identity formation – and hence in the post-war period we see English writers caught in this same transition from structure to culture like the rest of us, staking increasingly aggressive claims on what it means to be English.

The historical factors that have contributed to the dissolution and uneasy reformation of the English identity are the same ones which have driven so many changes in British society and culture in the past fifty years: the collapse of the British Empire, accompanied by the open immigration policies that enabled millions of people from former colonies (especially India, Pakistan, and Bangladesh) to make their home in England; the rise of the welfare state, and the slow (though never complete) erosion of the class structures which governed English society for most of its history; explosive growth in development and urbanization, both modernizing English cities and gobbling up green and open spaces; and a liberalization of social policies that granted new rights to women, minorities, and English citizens in general (such the reforms of the divorce laws in 1969). All of these factors, and others, have contributed to four important areas in which the English identity has been reconsidered and reformulated in the post-war period: race and ethnicity; class; urbanization; and a certain nostalgia for an England of old, one in which identity markers still held its citizens firmly in their grasp.

Race and Ethnicity

In 1982, Booker Prize-winning novelist Graham Swift published *Learning to Swim*, a collection of short stories that range in subject matter from encounters with the supernatural to the everyday dramas of family life. The collection concludes with a story entitled "The Watch," which provides an excellent summary of the first and most crucial way in with Englishness has come to be redefined in the post-war period. Associations of English identity with white skin, and with ethnic heritages that produce the white skins born on English soil, date back at least as far as Shakespeare's depiction of the terrible consequences that occur when black Othello is "tupping" the "white ewe" – though the white skin in this ewe's case belongs to a Venetian, the sentiment is fully English.

The title piece of Swift's story is a magical watch that prevents ageing (but not death by accident) of the bearer of it, and it has passed through three generations of Polish watchmakers to the 160-year-old grandfather of the narrator of the story. Grandfather and grandson now work together in a decrepit watch repair shop in London. In the course of the narrative, the grandfather decides to forsake his ageless state and wanders into a lightning storm on the Sussex Downs, where he is struck by lightning and killed – at which point the watch passes into the hands of the narrator, now granted the mixed boon of agelessness. In the final moments of the story, the narrator follows the anguished cries from the apartment on the floor below him to the side of an East Asian woman about to give birth, alone and without any medical intervention. The narrator helps to deliver the child, who seems not destined to survive beyond his first minutes in the world; in an impulsive moment, the narrator gives the watch to the infant. The baby lives; the narrator walks into the street and suffers a heart attack.

Aside from the more general themes of the ways in which time and ageing grant and withhold meaning from our lives, the story's climactic moment – the transfer of the watch from the narrator to the infant – represents an ethnic transfer as well, from an old European male to the child of an Indian immigrant, taking place on English soil. The narrator remarks upon this himself as the scene begins: "I was an Englishman and I bent over this woman – whose mother had perhaps worn a veil in some village by the Ganges – as she suffered the most intimate female distress" (Swift 1992: 184). The narrator's status as an Englishman is worth noting, since the story repeatedly draws attention to his Polish heritage, and to the immigrant status of his grandfather. To be English in this story is purely a function of time – enough years spent living on English soil makes him an Englishman. The same, the story seems to imply, will eventually be true for the Indian mother and her small child – marked more distinctly from the narrator by the color of their skin, they too will assimilate themselves into the English identity, and the narrator's transfer-ence of his watch to the child functions in the story almost as a baptism into Englishness.

The post-war period's most important shock to the English identity mirrors the passing of the watch in Swift's story, in which the image of an English person as a white Anglo-Saxon, born and raised on English soil, has given way to a society of multiple ethnic backgrounds and of citizen-immigrants from all points of the globe (postcolonial and otherwise). Although geneticists may never have agreed, at one time it may have been possible to identify a particular set of bloodlines or ethnic traits as particularly English. As the British Empire imploded and immigrants from the former colonies sought their fortune in England, and as the rise of the welfare state made England an attractive option for immigrants from all around the world, the notion of Englishness as tied to a specific ethnic identity began to lose any hold it had in reality.

Two decades prior to Swift's allegory of the passing of Englishness to a new generation of immigrants, Muriel Spark, Scottish novelist and short-story writer whose first
collection of stories, *The Go-Away Bird and Other Stories*, had appeared in 1958, had
begun registering the discomfort of the English at this staining of the whiteness of
the English identity in "The Black Madonna." The story is set in what the narrator
calls the "new town of Whitney Clay," a modern place that had "swallowed up the
old village" (Spark 1985: 35). In that imagery, Spark prepares us for the more important symbolic transformation that occurs in the story – just as the traditional old
village gives way to the modern city, the traditional vision of the English identity
must give way in the face of new racial and ethnic presences.

The title of the story derives from a statue recently given to the local church, carved
out of bog oak which is responsible for its dark color. The protagonists of the story,
Raymond and Lou Parker, are Catholics living in a block of flats off the town center,
childless but hoping to conceive. They are members of the parish which houses the
black Madonna, and during the course of the story it becomes part of local legend
that the statue can answer prayers. Unsuccessful in conceiving a child, they decide to
pray to the statue for one. At the same time, the Parkers befriend two Jamaican men
who had worked with Raymond, and – with a self-congratulatory liberalism which
pleases them greatly – they begin introducing them to their friends and to English
society. Still, their liberal attitudes are thin enough. When one of the Jamaicans
accompanies them on a trip to visit Lou's sister Elizabeth in a shabby quarter of
Bethnal Green, and afterwards speaks knowledgeably about the "slum mentality" he
sees in her sister, Lou turns on him reproachfully, and then thinks: "What a cheek
him talking like a snob. At least Elizabeth's white" (Spark 1985: 42). The emphasis
on the word "him," and the fact that Elizabeth remains tied to her by both blood and
skin color, emphasize that Lou still sees Englishness in those traditionally white
markers of national identity.

The Jamaicans move away, and Lou becomes pregnant, thanks – in her mind – to
the intervention of the black Madonna. She continues to pray to it for the baby's
health and safe arrival. When it does finally come, though, it comes with a surprise:
the baby has dark skin and dark, curly hair. Of course everyone, Raymond included,
first suspects one of the Jamaicans to be the father. But when blood tests indicate the
baby to be born of Lou and Raymond, an alternate explanation emerges: " 'The doctor
says,' " Raymond reports to his wife, "that these black mixtures sometimes occur in
seaport towns. It might have been generations back" (Spark 1985: 49). To their horror
and dismay, they discover indeed a black ancestor on Lou's side, whose blood has
skipped generations and manifested itself – perhaps with the help of the black
Madonna – in their baby. Raymond and Lou are mortified, embarrassed at constantly
having to explain the baby's skin color, and eventually give the child away for
adoption.

But of course Lou cannot give away the black parts of herself, and neither as well
– in the symbolic layer of the story that reflects on the idea of Englishness – can the
English identity escape or ignore the presence of the immigrant in their midst, the

injection of color in the pale English skin. Spark's story not only depicts the entry of other bloods into the English body politic, but also calls into question the myth that the body was ever pure. The whitest English woman may have black blood running through her veins – does that make her, Spark forces the reader to ask, any less English?

Spark spent time living in South Africa, where her frequent interactions with white colonialists and black natives clearly made a strong impression. Many of her stories are set in Africa, and the ways in which blacks and whites make judgments about one another, and about their identities, form frequent themes in her work. "The Go-Away Bird," considered in more detail below, in part addresses the question of how the English maintain their English identity in the colonies, where they are surrounded by black, non-English faces. But incidental notices of the discomfort in England's racial make-up appear as well. In another of Spark's most well-known stories, "The Portobello Road," a ghost story narrated by a dead woman, the narrator responds uneasily to the news that a friend has married an African: "I must say I was myself a bit put-off by this news about the brown woman. I was brought up in a university town to which came Indian, African and Asiatic students in a variety of tints and hues. I was brought up to avoid them for reasons connected with local reputation and God's ordinances" (Spark 1985: 6). Spark's stories frequently depict the efforts of white English to avoid the presence of dark hues and tints in their midst, and frequently detail the futility and follies of doing so.

Such incidental references to the often-unnerving presence of darker skins on English soil, and hence in the English identity, occur throughout the canon of post-war England, even in writers whose focus seems clearly elsewhere. The short fiction of V.S. Pritchett, as I will address below, more consistently focuses on questions of class. But of course questions of class often coincide with questions of race and ethnicity, and this is the case in his story "Tea with Mrs. Bittell," the title character of which is an elderly and wealthy woman who has befriended Sidney, a working-class young man who visits her flat after church services on Sundays. During a period in which his visits have stopped, she ventures out to the streets to find a London completely changed from the London of her memories: "she saw that the city had become a swarming bazaar: swarms of foreigners of all colors – Arabs, Indians, Chinese, Japanese, and all people jabbering languages she had never heard – came in phalanges down the pavements, their eyes avid for loot . . . She noticed these things now because for three weeks Sidney had not been to church and when she was out walking she was looking at all the faces thinking she might see him. He had disappeared in the flood" (Pritchett 1982: 497). Mrs Bittell searches for Sidney by seeking the white faces amidst this sea of foreign complexions – symbolically, she seeks a time when Englishness meant white faces.

That time has come to an end by this point in English history, though some, as Pritchett depicts, no doubt continue to yearn for such a simple means of identifying their fellow English citizens. At least in terms of race and ethnicity, the features that define one as English have become far less about internal qualities or racial characteristics and far more about simple external ones: much like in the United States, to be English – no matter the color of your skin or the country of your ethnic origin – means simply to be an English citizen, born or currently living on English soil.

Class

Although race probably provided at one time the most simple and clean means of identifying outsiders to the English identity, class has never been far behind. The class system in England has taken on an almost mythical quality in the literature and culture of the post-war period, in part because of its surprising persistence to the present day. Although the rigid social structures that would at one time have reinforced class distinctions have largely disappeared, economic disparities and inertia have kept a more subtle version of it in place even into the twenty-first century. And while class markers may not be quite as clear as skin color, they can be ubiquitous: in accent and pronunciation of the language; in clothing; in one's address; or even the choice of one's favorite football team.

Class appears as a factor in many of the stories of V.S. Pritchett, including "Tea with Mrs. Bittell." The title character seeks not only a time when Englishness meant whiteness, but a time when her relationship with Sidney, the young man she befriends, would fit into the neatly defined categories of class. At the opening of the story, she describes to herself her teatime with the young man as "doing a kindness to someone outside her own class" (Pritchett 1982: 483). The differences in their class, and the persistence of class markers into the late twentieth century, are seen clearly enough when Sidney shows up for their first teatime and receives this greeting from the doorman: "Deliveries round the corner, second door" (Pritchett 1982: 483). The doorman assumes, based on Sidney's dress and manner of speaking, that he must be a delivery boy; he allows him in to see Mrs Bittell only with evident distaste. The story concludes when Sidney's boyfriend, who has accompanied him to one of their teatimes, and who studied the artwork in the apartment with rapacious admiration, breaks into Mrs Bittell's apartment and assaults her during an attempted robbery. The break-in both affirms and shatters class expectations: that the lower-class young men turn out to be thieves would come as no surprise to Mrs Bittell; but the men were cultured enough to come after her famous artworks, as opposed to just seeking money or jewels.

Pritchett frequently features just such characters, caught between class boundaries, or caught in a time period in which class has lost its ability to help them define their own identities. "Handsome Is As Handsome Does," for example, focuses on a man whose identity has become unmoored by his movement away from the simple and more clearly defined English landscape and class of his youth. Tom Coram is an industrial chemist from the Midlands, on holiday at the Mediterranean seaside, accompanied by his upper-class wife – "My family never earned a penny in their lives," his wife exclaims, "They would have been horrified at the idea" (Pritchett 1982: 63) – and in frequent contact with an elderly Frenchman and a young Jewish man. Their more clearly defined national identities inspire Tom's uneasiness at his own anchorless national identity: "He did not belong to the working class anymore. He did not belong to [his wife's] class. He did not belong to the class of the comfortable professional people he now met. He did not belong anywhere. He was lost, rough, unfinished, ugly, unshaped by the wise and harmonious hand of a good environment" (Pritchett 1982: 68–9). He longs instead for "the red streets of his childhood . . . the tap of his father's hammer, the workers getting off the trams with their packages and little bags in their hands, the oil on their dungarees . . . the Midland rain . . . That was his life" (Pritchett 1982: 81). That *was* Tom's life, but his inability to return to that simpler time in his life seems representative of a larger theme throughout Pritchett's stories – the longing backward glances at the pre-war years, when English identity was marked by boundaries of class.

Pritchett's stories do not make aggressive claims to redefine the English identity with the lower classes in mind; he works more to chronicle the class system's frequent failures, after World War II, to help define both individual and national identity. The short fiction of Alan Sillitoe, by contrast, does make an aggressive effort to locate the real English identity in the working classes, as opposed to the middle and upper classes whose lives and foibles have occupied the writers of some of England's most famous fictions, such as those of Jane Austen. Sillitoe's heroes are the criminals, factory workers, and slum-dwellers of England's industrial cities (much of his fiction is set in his home city of Nottingham). His most famous short story, "The Loneliness of the Long Distance Runner," focuses on a boy who has landed in a borstal – a reform school for criminals of school age – and who has been training to compete in a running competition against the boys from other borstals. Narrated in the voice of this borstal boy, the story depicts very clearly the young man's contempt for the upper-class supporters of the borstal who are urging him to compete:

> They're training me up fine for the big sports day when all the peg-faced snotty-nosed dukes and ladies – who can't add two and two together and would mess themselves like loonies if they didn't have slavies to beck-and-call – come and make speeches to us about sports being just the thing to get us leading an honest life and keep our itching finger-ends off them shop locks and safe handles and hairgrips to open gas-meters. (Sillitoe 2005: 2)

The borstal boy here turns upside down assumptions of the superiority of the upper classes; instead of the lower classes being dependent upon the industry and largesse of their betters, here we see that the upper classes are nothing without the slave labor of the lower classes. The moral superiority and integrity of the borstal boy comes through clearly at the close of the story, when the narrator nears the finish line with a commanding lead, but then slows down and deliberately loses the race, refusing to bow to the demands of the "snotty-nosed dukes and ladies" who seemingly have his best interest at heart.

Other stories from Sillitoe's first collection, *The Loneliness of the Long-Distance Runner and Other Stories*, first published in 1956, fill out his depiction of real life among the poor and working classes, and set hard his contempt, and that of his characters, for the wealthy and privileged. In another well-known story, "On Saturday Afternoon," a man describes his childhood recollection of seeing a man try to kill himself. The story opens with an extended discussion of the "blackness" that infects his family life, and especially that of his father, who toils at the "bloody great bike factory bashing away at the yard end" (Sillitoe 2005: 86), and still frequently has little money for fags or sweetener for his tea. One Saturday the boy overhears a man telling someone that he is about to hang himself, so he follows him into his apartment and observes with detachment as the man makes the effort, but botches it by not tying the rope to a stable enough support. At the end of the story a policeman discovers the man on the floor, releases him from his noose, and lets him know with irritation that he is arresting him for attempted suicide. The man is dumbfounded, and protests: "I only wanted to hang myself . . . It's my life, ain't it?" "You might think so," the policeman responds, "but it ain't" (Sillitoe 2005: 90). Not only the possessions and labor of the working classes are controlled by the moneyed and powerful members of society, but even their very bodies are not their own. In this story, though, as in "Loneliness," the poor man wins in the end; he jumps out of the sixth-story window of the hospital where they put him, succeeding in killing himself in spite of them. Both stories seem to highlight the fact that the poor and working classes can only win by opting out – losing the race or committing suicide.

The focus in Sillitoe's writing on the working classes, and on their struggle to survive and find meaning in English society, recurs throughout his five collections of short stories, which began appearing in the 1950s and have continued into the twenty-first century. His oeuvre works hard to establish the contrast between the upper and lower classes, and to demonstrate the harsh and gritty realities of lives spent in factories, in council housing, and in pubs. Many of his narrators and protagonists long for, and relish, time spent in more natural landscape settings, but they rarely have the time or energy to escape to such places. The narrator of "The Bike," a story from Sillitoe's second collection, *The Ragman's Daughter*, purchases a bicycle from a co-worker in part to allow him to escape the cramped confines of his life at the factory and at home: "I rode a dozen miles out into the country, where fresh air smelt like cowshit and the land was coloured different, was wide open and windier than in streets. Marvelous. It was like a new life starting up" (Sillitoe 2005: 202). The narrator eventually discovers that he has purchased a stolen bicycle, so his escapes from the city are short-lived, and he returns to the life he will lead until death.

That Sillitoe's fictions are so thoroughly populated with such characters, and such situations, helps establish his point that to be English has little to do with the lush landscapes, grand country houses, and elaborate social rituals that many associate with English culture. The vast majority of the English in the latter half of the twentieth century, Sillitoe seems to assert, are being forced to live cramped lives in cramped quarters, at home and in factories, with little chance to experience an England they might have read about in books (and many of his poor narrators are self-educated, bookish types). In the same way that the English identity must expand to include other races and ethnicities, now too it must expand to include these denizens of the dark and loud places of the cities, for whom the rich landscapes and cultural trappings of which England boasts are mythical remnants of the past.

Urbanization

In "The Disgrace of Jim Scarfedale," another story from Sillitoe's first collection, the narrator opens by describing his dream of leaving the city of his youth and traveling around the country. Then, in a moment of reflection, he acknowledges that he probably will not find any place all that different from the place he is leaving:

> Yes, I know every city's the same when you come to weight it up: the same hostels full of thieves out to snatch your last bob if you give them half a chance; the same factories full of work, if you're lucky; the same mildewed backyards and houses full of silverfish and black-cocks when you suddenly switch on the light at night. (Sillitoe 2005: 101)

This description captures succinctly Sillitoe's vision of the modern English city, and most of his characters rarely, if ever, escape that city setting. Cities are crowded, dirty, bleak, and impersonal places – and more and more of English soil is being gobbled up by just such cities. Sillitoe thus sounds a third theme by which the idea of Englishness is redefined in the post-war period – the movement from the perception of England as a land of greenery and rich countryside, the "other Eden" of Shakespeare, to an increasingly urbanized and bleak landscape of modern cities, accompanied by the massive and impersonal bureaucracies necessary to maintain such urbanization.

Novelist Ian McEwan, who began his literary career with two collections of short stories, joins Sillitoe in painting the modern urban landscape of England in bleak and dreary colors. McEwan's short stories, published in *First Love, Last Rites* (1972) and *In Between the Sheets* (1978), are disturbing tales of perversion, murder, and depravity. In a well-worn tradition of twentieth-century literature, they frequently depict individuals who are alienated from society; in McEwan's work, that alienation typically is either caused by, or leads to, violence – a young man raping his eleven-year-old sister, a man sexually assaulting and murdering a young girl, men locked in ovens and scalded with boiling water, animals tortured, and so on. And all of this takes place, in his work, against a background of harsh and discordant cityscapes.

In "Homemade," the first story of the first collection, the teenage narrator recounts the day he raped his sister, in a disturbingly neutral narrative voice. In the preliminary descriptions of his life, he explains that he used to enjoy watching cross-country races, seeing the runners emerge on "that vast dismal field, surrounded on all sides by factories, pylons, dull houses and garages" (McEwan 1994a: 20). The very words "cross-country" evoke a much more pastoral vision of the sport, with runners traipsing through the countryside; but in modern England, the runners are confined in the same dull landscapes as everyone else. An implied connection runs through McEwan's work between these settings and the behavior of his characters – the modern and featureless cityscape seems to provoke such acts of violence, as if individuals must take correspondingly extreme measures to create meaning in their lives. "Butterflies," a second story in the collection, also features a sexual assault by a neutral narrator on a young girl, though this story adds her subsequent murder to the plot. The setting for these events mirrors that of "Homemade," this time along a canal described by the narrator thus:

> The canal is the only stretch of water near here. There is something special about walking by the water, even brown stinking water running along the backs of factories. Most of the factories overlooking the canal are windowless and deserted. You can walk a mile and a half along the towpath and usually you meet no one. The path goes by an old scrapyard. (McEwan 1994a: 89)

Stinking canals, factories, scrapyards – these are the features that have come to replace green fields, flowers, and babbling brooks for many post-war English writers. McEwan asserts more actively than many a link between these growing urban spaces and the lives and characteristics of the modern English person, but he is by no means alone in redrawing the English landscape – and the English identity as well – in these harsh new tones.

Julian Maclaren-Ross's short fiction, first published in the early 1940s and continuing to appear through the latter half of the 1950s, tends to focus on one of two realms of human experience: army life, or the bohemian world of writers and artists constantly in search of money and drink. As Paul Willets observes of the settings of his short fiction, "the world of Maclaren-Ross's writing tends to be the dingy, down-at-heel world of smoke-veiled bars, rented lodgings, blacked-out streets, and wartime army garrisons" (Maclaren-Ross 2004: 7). A story which captures well the transition from the old England landscape to that of the post-war period describes the journey of the narrator and his girlfriend from London to Oxford. The two of them are "determined to get away from London for a bit" (Maclaren-Ross 2004: 83), in search of more picturesque settings. They settle on Oxford which, for the narrator, "was associated in my mind with grey stones and sported oaks and cloistral calm" (Maclaren-Ross 2004: 183). The narrator splurges on first-class train tickets, but the carriages are all full so they stand for the entire trip. Once there, the narrator's expectations of the beautiful scenery he hopes to find are immediately dashed: "My mental picture of the place may have been muddled, but I did expect to see from the window a perspective of dreaming spires. I saw instead a gasworks. This was immediately blotted out by an advertisement for timber and a line of trucks filled with coal" (Maclaren-Ross 2004: 183).

Hence not merely have the natural landscapes given way to the pressures of urbanization, but also the historical monuments and scenes upon which England's heritage and tourism industry largely rests. They have become blighted with the needs of life in the modern city (the gasworks and coal trucks), and the increasingly consumer-oriented culture of the late twentieth century (the advertisement). For the remainder of the story, the two main characters wander about in a futile search for a night's lodging, only to have to give up and catch the last train back to London. Symbolically, the England they sought in Oxford – the England of monuments and greenery – has disappeared.

English Nostalgia

Although those dreamy English settings, in much of the short fiction of the post-war period, have given way to the pressures of urbanization and overcrowding, their association with Englishness apparently dies hard – hard enough that nostalgia for an older, more pristine England seems to have entered the English identity as a distinctive trait in its own right. Characters who have difficulty escaping the England of their pasts, or who actively seek to recreate the England of their childhoods, form a regular part of the short fiction of the period, none so firmly as the title character in William Trevor's series of three short fictions collected under the title "Matilda's England."

Trevor, an Irish writer and one of the acclaimed masters of the short form in the twentieth century, has been producing work in the genre from the publication of his first collection, *The Day We Got Drunk on Cake*, which appeared in 1967. The stories that form "Matilda's England" appeared in his fourth collection, *Lovers of their Time and Other Stories* (1978). As one critic has noted, a frequent theme in Trevor's work is the "disturbance of those who try in vain to recreate an idealized happiness of the past" (Trevor 1992: 256). This description pinpoints the two major characters in the stories, Matilda and Mrs Ashburton. The first story, "The Tennis Court," is narrated by Matilda but focuses on Mrs Ashburton, an elderly woman who lives near Matilda's family at Challacombe Manor, a once-glorious estate now fallen into, as the story describes it, "rack and ruin" (Trevor 1992: 539). The bank foreclosed on the estate after World War I, but allowed the widowed Mrs Ashburton to remain in the main house for her life. In "The Tennis Court," Matilda recounts how Mrs Ashburton slowly entices her and her two siblings to come for tea, to play on her tennis courts, and eventually to help her clean and restore the tennis courts for a tennis party, a nostalgic replay of the grand parties that once were held at the estate. Although the party is a complete success, it reinforces for Mrs Ashburton the fact that her past is irrevocably gone, and the sight of her crying and alone in the kitchen after the party has a profound impact on Matilda.

In the second story, "The Summer-House," Matilda copes – though not very well – with the death of her father in the war, and her mother's acceptance of a man who courts her in the aftermath, and eventually marries her. The final story, "The Drawing-Room," makes evident that Matilda has joined Mrs Ashburton in her desire to recapture the days of her past, and the glory of the former manor house and the traditional English countryside estate. A nouveau riche family purchases the property, as Matilda enters her early twenties, and seeks to restore it to its former glory. Matilda's narration unwittingly begins to display signs of her deep ties to the past – discussing her mother's new stove, she says that her mother hated the old stove, "lighting it every morning with sticks and paper, the struggles she'd had with it during the war, trying to burn wood instead of coal. But I'd been sorry to see it go. I tried to stop myself being like that about things, but I couldn't help it" (Trevor 1992: 571). Matilda becomes "like that" – longing for the past, and retreating from the present – about so many things that eventually she marries the son of the family who has purchased Challacombe Manor, despite the fact that she does not love him, and gradually redecorates the house as it was in Mrs Ashburton's life. Slowly she descends into madness, as her narration faithfully but unknowingly describes the reactions of others to her obsessions. In the end, she drives her husband away, and he leaves her with the house and garden, where she sits as Mrs Ashburton once did, lost in the memories of the past. "Nothing," she concludes, "is like it was" (Trevor 1992: 594). Nothing in her life, of course, but on a broader scale nothing in England is like it was, and Matilda's despair at this reflects a broader cultural nostalgia for an England long gone by – the England of manor houses, and tennis parties, and old wood stoves.

Muriel Spark's "The Go-Away Bird" sounds a similar theme, though in this case the longing for a lost England is constructed by expatriates in a young girl who has never been there. Daphne du Toit, born of a Dutch father and English mother, has grown up in South Africa, but longs to see England. She listens with great interest to the descriptions of the land by those who have been there, and hears only what reflects her idealized descriptions of England. An artist at the school where she eventually is hired to teach ("The Go-Away Bird" is a three-part story that follows her through the course of her life) complains to her about the abysmal lack of support for the arts in England, describing how artists are forced to paint for patrons. Daphne hears selectively: "Daphne's mind played like the sun over the words 'Queen Anne's house,' 'Kensington,' 'Chelsea,' 'Studio,' 'Regent's Canal,' 'Henley.' She had ears for nothing else" (Spark 1985: 238). Fueled by her warped picture of pre-war England, Daphne finally moves there, only to find, of course, a different England. "I couldn't find that bootmaker in St. Paul's Churchyard," she writes in one letter back to South Africa, to the guardian who helped form her distorted views of England, "because it is all bombed" (Spark 1985: 247). Daphne eventually returns to South Africa, where she is murdered by an old farmhand. The last words of her life, before she sets out on the walk where she will be killed are, "God help me. Life is unbearable" (Spark 1985: 258). The unbearable nature of life, the story suggests, stems in part from the fact that her long stay in England destroyed the fantasies she had of a lost England, and left her with nothing but the cold and hard realities of life in a modern, post-war English city.

A final glimpse at this theme comes from Toby Litt, whose work in both short and long fictions has earned him a reputation as one of England's most daring and interesting literary talents. His first collection of stories, *Adventures in Capitalism*, appeared in 1996; a second collection, *Exhibitionism*, followed in 2002. Litt's penchant for innovation and experimentation pushes his stories all over the map both thematically and stylistically, and one story in his first collection, "Mr. Kipling," covers the familiar ground of nostalgia for England past. The narrator of the story has taken the story's title character, the brand name of "a rather soggy line of cakes and biscuits" (Litt 1996: 207), as both a real person and as a representative of what he sees as authentic England. Despite the corporation's explanation to the narrator that no such Mr Kipling exists, the narrator writes him frequent letters, and has constructed a full history and portrait of the man: Mr Kipling is a High Anglican, takes three sugars in his robust teas, smokes a long cigar, picks apples in the orchard for his Bramley Apple Pies. The narrator, in the meantime, spends his time trying to get money from the National Trust to repair his thatched roof, buys Mr Kipling's pastries in the village shop, and raises a glass of sherry to him on Christmas Eve. The arrival of a new sales clerk at the shop, Miss Ogbuku, he fears, "may diminish the pleasures of shopping [there]" (Litt 1996: 28). The surname, of course, indicates her status as an immigrant or minority in what the narrator describes as a small English village, and hence does not fit into the pastoral England of pre-war years that the narrator has constructed for himself, in the tradition of Matilda and Daphne du Toit. As in the case of Matilda, the story depicts the narrator's quest for the past as a form of madness – a madness whose frequent depiction in the post-war short story indicates that it represents an extreme version of a nostalgia shared by many English into the late twentieth century.

Conclusion

Of course, all of this longing for pastoral visions of Old England raises the question of whether such a land ever existed at all. It may once have, the short stories of the post-war period seem to imply – but it never existed for more than a small and exclusive segment of English society, and it certainly exists no more, except perhaps in the places and events of the booming heritage industry in England.

The England of the late twentieth and early twenty-first century has undergone massive social and cultural transformations, has experienced long-term effects from World War II and the fallow years following it, and the stories of the post-war period reflect the uneasiness many English have felt at these monumental shifts in horizon and perspective. The definition of Englishness has grown both increasingly fuzzy and increasingly subject to analysis and contestation. As the firm markers of English identity have dissolved, the literary interest in the question of what makes a person, or place, or era typically English has seemed to increase exponentially, and become a theme in its own right in the short fiction of the period. It would not stretch the point too far, indeed, to suggest that one final characteristic of Englishness that appears throughout the short fiction of the period is an interest in Englishness. As Aristotle famously defined the good life for humans as participating in conversation about the nature of the good life, it seems that to be English in the late twentieth and early twenty-first century means, at least in part, to be ever in search of the English identity.

REFERENCES AND FURTHER READING

Christopher, D. (1999). *British Culture: An Intro-duction*. London and New York: Routledge.

Easthope, A. (1999). *Englishness and National Culture*. London and New York: Routledge.

Litt, T. (1996). *Adventures in Capitalism*. London: Penguin.

McEwan, I. (1994a). *First Love, Last Rites*. New York: Vintage International.

McEwan, I. (1994b). *In Between the Sheets*. New York: Vintage International.

Maclaren-Ross, J. (2004). *Selected Stories*, ed. Paul Willetts. New York: DewiLewis.

Oakland, J. (2001). *Contemporary Britain: A Survey with Texts*. London and New York: Routledge.

Pritchett, V.S. (1982). *Collected Stories*. New York: Random House.

Sillitoe, A. (2005). *New and Collected Stories*. New York: Carroll and Graf.

Spark, M. (1985). *The Stories of Muriel Spark*. New York: Dutton.

Swift, G. (1992). *Learning to Swim and Other Stories*. New York: Vintage International.

Trevor, W. (1992). *The Collected Stories*. New York: Viking.

25
Scottish Short Stories (post 1945)

Gavin Miller

Although the 1920s and 1930s had seen a growth in Scottish nationalism, Scotland emerged from the World War II with a renewed faith in its Union with England. For many Scots, the massive governmental intervention required by wartime society held the promise of a post-war British state that could actively protect its citizens from economic insecurity: "Full employment, the Welfare State, and social reconstruction made it sensible for Scots to think of themselves as British" ("National Identity" 2001: 444). However, the Scottish short story in this period is marked from the beginning by skepticism towards the growing influence of the British state over community life – a skepticism that intensifies as narratives of British identity continue to wane in the decades after the war.

The Glaswegian author George Friel (1910–75) began his writing career during the 1930s by publishing a number of short stories that specialized in phenomena such as prostitution, the drudgery of female labor, the failure of the general strike, and the effects of unemployment. One might expect, then, that Friel would welcome the post-war construction of a more meritocratic society. Yet the short story "A Friend of Humanity," first published in 1952, examines skeptically this narrative of improvement. It tells of a young lower-middle-class man, Mr Glanders, who, after leaving the army, decides to train as a teacher. During his college entrance interview, he lectures his director of studies on the fallacy apparent, he believes, in Locke's argument from *Some Thoughts Concerning Education* (1693) that "'it doesn't matter what a man says or thinks if he says or thinks only what he is directed by another'" (Friel 1992: 152). During his teacher training, Glanders continues in this authoritarian vein, distinguishing himself by "his disputatious dogmatism and his constant appeal to the general good of mankind as his arbiter" (Friel 1992: 153). After qualifying as a non-graduate teacher, he enters a state school, where he begins to promulgate a narrative of improvement:

He was supposed to be doing the Tudors, but he didn't see what they had to do with the modern world, so he hurried past them to the Civil War and then by a mighty leap crossed the Channel to the French Revolution, solemnly explaining the necessity for the reign of terror. Proud of his eloquence, he returned to Britain to speak of the Reform Bills and the rise of the toiling masses in whose hands lay the future of mankind. (Friel 1992: 154)

His bored students have their revenge for "his attempt to direct them what to think" (Friel 1992: 157) – they mock his threadbare clothing, and build mocking constructions upon his name. The story ends as Glanders reverts to his army training, and singles out one boy, Hooper, for punishment, repeatedly beating him and denouncing him as "'an ill-bred, insolent little rat'": "The reign of terror had started," concludes the narrator (Friel 1992: 157).

The allusion to the Reign of Terror of 1793–4 invites a parallel between post-war Britain and post-Revolutionary France. The comparison with revolutionary ideology develops further in Glanders's ultimate ethical principle, "the general good of mankind," which clearly invokes Rousseau's argument in *The Social Contract* (1762) that recalcitrant citizens may be "forced to be free":

in order that the social pact shall not be an empty formula, it is tacitly implied in that commitment – which alone can give force to all others – that whoever refuses to obey the general will shall be constrained to do so by the whole body, which means nothing other than that he shall be forced to be free. (Rousseau 1968: 64)

To Rousseau, the state was an artificial, but far from fictional, person whose general will was always univocal: he who dissents from this will is "a rebel and a traitor to the nation" (Rousseau 1968: 2.5. 79). Likewise, Glanders's "general good of mankind" implicitly substantializes mankind into a single entity with a common will and purpose. The boys before him, who cannot perceive their historical role, do not deserve his "genial rule of reason" (Friel 1992: 157), and must be coerced into harmony with the general will.

Part of the irony of Glanders's aspirations is that he fails to perceive objectively his own sociological function. During his entrance interview, he is subject to a quite particular scrutiny: "the accent was passable," decides the director, "although the speaker would never entirely lose his more subtle variances from standard English" (Friel 1992: 152). Glanders is unwittingly entering an educational system designed to produce large numbers of citizens fit for modern industrial society. Such modern workers do not dirty their hands in manual labor; rather, as Ernest Gellner explains,

they must constantly communicate with a large number of other men, with whom they frequently have no previous association, and with whom communication must consequently be explicit, rather than relying on context. They must also be able to communicate by means of written, impersonal, context-free, to-whom-it-may-concern type messages. Hence these communications must be in the same shared and standardized linguistic medium and script. (Gellner 1983: 35)

Glanders thinks that he can educate a revolutionary vanguard; but his objective function is to discipline his pupils into the use of a standardized dialect, accent, and orthography.

A similar suspicion of post-war ideals is outlined in the early work of Muriel Spark (1918–2006), whose short story "You Should Have Seen the Mess," first collected in *The Go-Away Bird with Other Stories* (1958), provides a narrator who is typical of the rising lower middle class. With a certificate in typing, and her (only) talent for English, the teenage Lorna assesses any potential employer or acquaintance by how well they conform to standards of politeness, good speech, and – above all – the cleanliness that betokens distance from manual labor. Although her eventual employer "has not got a university education behind him," he is at least "well spoken" (Spark 1958b: 152), and the building where they work is modern and clean. Newness, too, is part of her post-war value system, for modern production requires a population of modern consumers. Lorna would "never keep a cracked cup" (Spark 1958b: 151), just as she would refuse to live in the "very cracked and old" fourteenth-century cottage owned by a friend's mother (Spark 1958b: 155). This clearing away of the old also erodes what Gellner would call "intimate, closed, context-bound communities" (Gellner 1983: 33). Lorna laments the condition of a modern block of flats which, although they are very clean, lack a "Welfare Centre [. . .], where people could go for social intercourse, advice and guidance" (Spark 1958b: 156). Community and tradition are being scoured away, so that a professionalized service is required to provide the "social intercourse, advice and guidance" that would once have been found in friends and family. Those who refuse to participate in this new value system will, in Spark's fiction, find themselves pathologized, and perhaps even disciplined into "health." Marjorie Pettigrew in "Come Along, Marjorie" (Spark 1958a), for instance, succumbs to the disciplinary power of the modern state. She is a resident in Watling Abbey, a religious institution that houses both clerical and lay members. During the narrator's stay at the abbey, she observes Miss Pettigrew's peculiar behavior: the latter refuses conversation, then starts to skip meals and to stay isolated in her room. This behavior eventually leads to Miss Pettigrew's involuntary incarceration in an insane asylum. Although isolation, fasting, and silence were acknowledged elements of the Catholic *vita contemplativa*, post-war Britain – at least according to Spark – can support only the *vita activa* and the *vita voluptuousa*.

Spark is well known for her conversion to Catholicism in 1954. Another Catholic convert, George Mackay Brown (1921–6), is also suspicious of the post-war British state. But where Friel uses urban Glasgow as his setting, and Spark ranges across the whole of Britain (and indeed the world), Brown almost always sets his short fiction in the Orkney archipelago in the north of Scotland. In "The Tarn and the Rosary," collected in *Hawkfall* (1974), the central character, Colm, listens as a local man bemoans "Progress," which he identifies as a modern religion:

> This island is enchanted with the idea of Progress. [. . .] Times are much easier for us than for our grandfathers. So, they argue, we have better fuller richer lives. This worship of Progress, it will drain the life out of every island and lonely place. (Brown 1974: 187)

For Brown, as for Spark, so-called progress assimilates everything heterogeneous to a single order of industrial production and consumption, of alienated labor and manufactured needs. To what he describes as the "false Gods" of "progress and money and mammon" (Murray 1996: 42), Brown opposes the cyclical temporality of the Catholic faith, which he represents as a source of spontaneous resistance to the (allegedly) Protestant narrative of secular historical progress. This is why Brown valorizes pre-Reformation Orkney in stories such as "Master Halcrow, Priest" (Brown 1967), first anthologized in *A Calendar of Love* (1967) – the protagonist marks time by the cycles of the seasons, rather than by the progressive time of the Reforming Church.

Suspicion of the post-war British narrative of improvement is not limited to Friel, Spark, and Brown. Since Britishness threatened also the homogenization of national identity in the United Kingdom, many self-consciously Scottish writers had some sense of opposition to the modern state. This widespread skepticism lends an extra significance to the formal properties of the short story. Iain Crichton Smith (1928–98) casts the short story as a form opposed to overarching "novelistic" narratives of communal identity. His short story sequence, *The Village* (1976), represents island life; but, unlike Brown, Smith depicts the island as complicit with the production of modern "individuals" suited to pre-allocated roles in economy and society. The minister in "Easter Sunday," for instance, imagines how the island's children "would turn out more or less exactly like their mothers," and suffers from "terrible dreams of a figure in a huge office with a stamping machine which duplicated people" (Smith 1976a: 9). A combination of rigid mores with the impossibility of privacy means that, if anything, islands are the harbingers of a modern society of surveillance, discipline, and economic (though not existential) individualism. "Easter Sunday" also explains some of the significance of the short-story form for Crichton Smith. In classic works of Scottish literature such as Lewis Grassic Gibbon's *Sunset Song* (1932), the church is a place of congregation for a village community, a location of *Gemeinschaft* rather than the merely social and political association of *Gesellschaft*. But in Crichton Smith's story, the island's female parishioners sit in various states of bored inattention, as they dwell on the separate short narratives that cannot be admitted into the sermon – stories of spousal abuse, the tedium of island life, and unplanned pregnancy. One young girl, for instance, worries during the sermon about her pregnancy by a local man, and the consequences of telling her mother:

> She'll throw me out. If it was the city it would be different but in a village everybody
> knows. Perhaps some of them know already. They'll sit in church but that's as far as
> it'll go. When it comes to helping there'll be a different story. (Smith 1976a: 9)

In presenting the short story as a stubborn footnote to overarching communal
narratives, Crichton Smith also mocks modernist short fiction, implying that the
coercive unity of island life cannot be challenged by the literary aesthetics of Joyce
or Chekhov. The narrator of "Moments" is a devotee of epiphanies in life and literature: "There exist in life [. . .] moments of vision," he tells the readers, that "shine
with an enormous significance, as if they meant to tell us something that we do not
quite understand or cannot put into words" (Smith 1976b: 101). His narrative duly
supplies two instances. The first is his own, which occurs when a local man, who
writes grandiloquent letters to bureaucrats for the villagers, dies at home while com-
posing such a missive ("'I would esteem it a great favour if you would make an
enquiry into this at your earliest . . .'" (Smith 1976b: 104)). The narrator discovers
the body:

> There the letter broke off and a scrawl trailed right down the page. As I said, I was
> struck and illuminated by something extraordinarily significant in the letter though I
> could not at the time see what the significance was. Nor do I now see it. For one can
> sense significance without understanding it. (Smith 1976b: 104)

The satirical bathos is clear:

> The other thing I remember, out of that storm of pathos and illumination, was that I
> noticed a chamber pot underneath the bed as if he had been using it not long before.
> (Smith 1976b: 105)

The other epiphany provided by the narrator equals his own in obscure pseudo-pro-
fundity. Another friend, a high-level physicist visiting from the USA, has his own
"moment" while observing the pallbearers at his mother's funeral: "'one of the men
in front had his arm round the other man'," explains the scientist,

> It was one of those moments such that if one is lucky one gets in a lifetime [. . .]
> The two things came together in my mind you see, the electron lacking both position
> and velocity and the arm of the man round the other man as they staggered under
> the weight of the coffin. The significance was stupendous and shattering. (Smith
> 1976b: 108)

The narrator's rather tepid conclusion is that such experiences "illuminate but at
the same time they don't necessarily lead to what you would call understanding.
And in any case one man's 'moment' is different from another man's" (Smith
1976b: 108). The Joycean epiphany for Crichton Smith is a futile verbal gesture

towards some private, merely psychological, and verbally inexpressible state of mind.

Although Alan Spence (1947–) frequently hints at moments of revelation or vision (and particularly associates them with music), he also uses the short story in implicit opposition to grander, novelistic narratives of social cohesion. The stories in *Its Colours They Are Fine* (1977) form a loosely overlapping sequence that traces Glasgow from the post-war period to the 1970s. One of the early stories, "Sheaves," refuses the redemption offered in George Mackay Brown's depiction of a spontaneous quasi-Catholic religion based around natural cycles. The story begins in urban Glasgow with an Eliotean "wasteground" (Spence 1977d: 21) where the working-class boys play amidst the weeds, conscious of the threat of modern policemen who "swore at you and moved you on for loitering and booked you for playing football in the street" (Spence 1977d: 25). The most academically able of the children, Aleck, attends a local Sunday school where the leader, Mr Neil, gives a sermon for the Harvest festival in which he explains to his audience that "deep inside" they are God's "golden sheaves" (Spence 1977d: 23). But Mr Neil is too honest to preach the gospel according to Brown: "it's only in the country that people can really be aware of the changing seasons and what they mean"; in Glasgow, "the food you eat is just bought by your mothers from the shops," and so it is difficult "to appreciate what harvest really means" (Spence 1977d: 32). This is precisely why Mr Neil's preaching (which parallels a strand of primitivist literary modernism) must fail: there is no spontaneous natural religion for these children, to whom the agricultural metaphors of the Bible are a distant irrelevance, if not a downright bourgeois imposition (as the story makes clear, only the middle classes have gardens and toolsheds, or know a sickle from somewhere other than the Soviet flag).

As the sequence progresses, the stories trace the increasing division and separation of the working-class community in which it began. Aleck and his friend Shuggie fall out with Les, their English-accented friend who moves with a traveling fairground. Aleck is then separated from Shuggie by his parent's educational aspirations. Shuggie drifts into the tribalism of gang violence, and then leaves Glasgow to enter the army. Much of the action of *Its Colours They are Fine*, therefore, comes to center on occasions of contact with a different community in a divided and increasingly individualized Glasgow: the narratives coalesce around such brief inter-community encounters as meeting somebody in the lift, visiting the traveling fairground, going to Sunday school, hitch-hiking (to be picked up by an apartheid-era white South African), and working with the mentally ill.

"Greensleeves" provides an architectural metaphor for the way Spence employs the short story. The central character has been moved into a new tower block from a comfortable tenement building that was demolished to make way for redevelopment. Unlike the cleared slums, the new estates have no shops, no cinemas, no places of entertainment, and even fewer areas for children. The nameless protagonist watches the 1932 Hollywood motion picture *Grand Hotel* on television, an experience interrupted by advertisements that show her an illusion of the home and family life that no longer exist. The tower block, reflects the central character, is like "the hotel and all the people in it, never really knowing each other, all their lives so separate but intertwined" (Spence 1977b: 177). This, of course, is also true of *Its Colours They are Fine*: the bound volume is like a building, a tower block, housing increasingly separate stories that are brought together not in a religious congregation or a national project but through the narrator's skills of observation and selection. In the penultimate story, "Auld Lang Syne," the first-person narrator (who is a writer by trade) looks out of his window at the other buildings, using the first-person plural to bring himself and reader together in this act of observation:

> Every window is a separate world, a little capsule of light. Here and there where the curtains haven't been drawn we can see right in; we can see a man singing; a glass raised in his hand; we can see a small family group round the TV; we can see a party, already well under way, a room and kitchen packed. (Spence 1977a: 234)

Whatever the merits of Spence's response to the separation and division that his narratives both represent and attempt to overcome, it is notable that his stories stylistically enact the very division they criticize. Spence's narratorial voice is always distinct from the dialect voice of his speakers. For instance,

> "C'mon wull look at the mirrors," said Shuggie. "Ye better no take any merr shooglin aboot jist the noo."
>   In the Hall of Mirrors they joined the hysterical laughing procession, convulsed and doubled up, howling with disbelief and glee at their own warped reflections. (Spence 1977c: 62)

The Scots-language poet Tom Leonard (1944–) compares this narratorial relationship with the relationship between psychiatric patient and doctor as described by the radical Scottish psychiatrist, R.D. Laing (1927–89):

> What Laing had to say about the status and nature of "schizophrenic" language as perceived by doctors and the relatives of a patient, had a bearing for me on the perception of non-standard English and dialect language in literature. The dialect speaker tends to appear in a narrative like Laing's patient in a hospital: there is complicity between author and reader that the speaker is "other", that the user of such language cannot be the person who has written or who is reading the work. (Mullan 1997: 90)

Elsewhere in Scottish writing, psychiatric "othering" seems to provide a model for "othering" on the basis of national identity. In the short story, "The Full Moon," by Brian McCabe (1951–), the narrator, who works as a therapist in a psychiatric ward, encounters some visiting clinical psychologists from the USA who assume that he is a patient, "a creature of a different species" (McCabe 2003: 53). They remark on the decorative full moon that he is creating as part of a Hallowe'en party:

> "Did you hear that?" she whispered excitedly. "He says that's the *dark* side . . . ain't that adorable?"
>
> I noticed that my status had changed, somewhere along the line, from the second to the third person singular. (McCabe 2003: 51)

As the relationship turn from I-thou to I-it (or, at least, from "I-you" to "I-he"), so the narrator finds himself unable to confidently access the language of power that would mark him as an educated equal:

> All I had to say was, "Actually, I'm not a patient at all; I'm a member of staff." I might add, just for good measure, that I was in reality a Philosophy Graduate, working here in the Therapy Unit as a preventative expedient against unemployment. In my confusion I was able to utter three words. All three were monosyllabic, and I said them without much conviction.
>
> "I . . . work . . . here," I said. (McCabe 2003: 52)

The narrator's experience is not merely a comment on psychiatric "othering": the recurrence of adjectives such as "gorgeous," "cute," and "adorable" in his visitors' comments also invokes the stereotypical discourse of US tourists in Scotland (McCabe 2003: 50–1). The young therapist is mistaken for a madman, but his inarticulate response to depersonalization is presented as typical for those who are recognized as Scots.

The best known statement on such "othering" of the dialect speaker is provided in the work of James Kelman (1946–). In Kelman's short story collection *Not Not While the Giro* (1983), this essentially anthropological mode of observation is satirized in "Roofsliding," where the narrator speculates on the meaning and significance of this custom in a voice that echoes those of anthropological classics such as E.E. Evans Pritchard's *Witchcraft, Oracles and Magic amongst the Azande* (1937) and Bronisław Malinowski's *Argonauts of the Western Pacific* (1922). A scholarly footnote explains that "[t]his account has been taken more or less verbatim from a pamphlet entitled *Within Our City Slums*; it belongs to the chapter headed 'Curious practices of the Glaswegian'" (Kelman 1983b: 179). This particular "curious practice," in which a number of men slide down tenement roofs, "can take place more than once per week and will always do so during a weekday mid morning," although "[a]s to the season of the year, this is unimportant; dry days, however, being much sought after" (Kelman 1983b: 179). It may even, the observer implies, be consequent upon some as yet unobserved rite of passage, for "no youth shall be admitted who has yet to attain his 14th birthday" (Kelman 1983b: 180). By so emphatically "othering" Glasgow in this way, Kelman mocks the implied reader of this text: for the fictional addressee of "Roofsliding," knowledge of working-class Glaswegians can only ever be scholarly – these tribes dwell in their own townships and reserves, separated by a de facto domestic and non-racial apartheid.

Kelman's essay, "The Importance of Glasgow in My Work," makes this point explicitly: "in the society that is English Literature, some 80 to 85 percent of the population simply did not exist as ordinary human beings"; "we all stumbled along in a series of behaviouristic activity; automatons, cardboard cut-outs, folk who could be scrutinized, whose existence could be verified in a sociological or anthropological context" (Kelman 1992: 82). Kelman, therefore, refuses to depict writer and reader as inevitably separated from working-class culture in the way implied, he believes, by the standard narrative techniques of canonical "English Literature":

> everybody from a Glaswegian or working-class background, everybody in fact from any regional part of Britain – none of them knew how to talk! What larks! Every time they opened their mouth out came a stream of gobbledygook. Beautiful! Their language a cross between semaphore and morse code; apostrophes here and apostrophes there; a strange hotchpotch of bad phonetics and horrendous spelling – unlike the nice stalwart upperclass English hero (occasionally Scottish but with no linguistic variation) whose words on the page were always absolutely splendidly proper and pure and pristinely accurate, whether in dialogue or without. And what grammar! Colons and semi-colons! Straight out of their mouths! An incredible mastery of language. Most interesting of all, for myself as a writer, the narrative belonged to them and them alone. They owned it. (Kelman 1992: 82)

Kelman's style is therefore partly a response to this stylistic hierarchy. To take an example almost at random: in this sentence from "Nice to be nice," the narrator, Stan, shares the same dialect and accent as Tony, whose speech is pointedly given without quotation marks: "Wiv knoaked it aff Stan, shouts Tony, grabbing it oot ma haun" (Kelman 1983a: 33).

Kelman's technique is not wholly original in the post-war Scottish short story. For example, the first-person narrator of Robert McLellan's *Linmill Stories*, which were variously broadcast and published in the early 1960s, shares the same voice as his community, and his orthography is notably free of the apostrophes which might otherwise mark it as a halting approximation to standard spelling. For instance:

> the fire settlet in the grate, and a muckle reid eizle [ember] fell oot on the fender, and my grannie opened her een.
>
>   She lowpit [leaped] for the eizle wi the muckle [big] tangs, and syne [then] turnt to me.
>
>   "I thocht ye were gaun to play ootbye, Rab?"
>
>   "Oh Grannie, I fand a nest of wee kittlins in the stable hey-laft." (McLellan 1990b: 12)

Or, in another instance (noted by J.K. Annand in his introduction to the Canongate edition of *Linmill Stories*), the Standard English speaker takes on the role of the "other":

> Fred Jubb was warking at the harness, but as sune as he tried to lowse the belly-band the stallion liftit its heid and tried to rise.
>   "Will one of you sit on its head?" askit Fred. He was an Englishman. (McLellan 1990a: 154)

However, it is fair to say that Kelman, along with Leonard, gave this technique its most explicit and compelling political interpretation.

Kelman's stories tend to focus on protagonists who, by virtue of their formal or informal education, are to some extent critical of their own community and its less palatable ideologies – be they sexist, racist, or politically quietist. Irvine Welsh (1958–), on the other hand, is far more willing to employ the voices and experiences of those who were traditionally dismissed as the lumpen proletariat by Marxist theory. As Willy Maley notes,

> Where Kelman can be seen to keep in place a distinction between the good working-class individual – conscientious, progressive, and resistant – and the bad guys who hover on the periphery – the addicts, hedonists, and time-servers – Welsh champions not only the socially excluded but the politically inarticulate and even the morally reprehensible. Which is not to say that he is amoral, merely that his subjects are not the deliberately dissenting individuals that a certain radical criticism finds it all too easy to countenance. (Maley 2000: 195)

So, for instance, in "Granny's Old Junk," first collected in *The Acid House* (1994), the narrator Graham, a heroin addict, sets out to rob his grandmother of the savings that she foolishly keeps in a tin under her bed in an old folks' home with its "rank, fetid smell of pish and stale bodies" (Welsh 1994a: 94). But the tables are turned on young Graham: Granny's tin contains heroin ("junk") for sale on the streets – his grandmother is both an addict and a dealer. The story concludes with the two entering into business together.

Welsh's fiction seems more intimately related than Kelman's to the short story as a form. His first, and most critically and commercially successful novel, *Trainspotting* (1993), has been described as "a loosely connected sequence of short stories stitched together, not just by common characters, but by a common language, a patchwork quilt of colloquialisms, criss-crossed by catch phrase, cliché, and cursing" (Maley 2000: 191–2). Welsh's affinity with the form continues in *The Acid House*, "a collection of short stories and a novella, which had, in large part, been written coterminously with much of the *Trainspotting* materials" (Kelly 2005: 79). To some extent, this reliance upon the short story reflects Welsh's strengths as a writer – his talent is very much for "spiky vignettes and swift explosive scenes" (Maley

2000: 191–2). It also owes something to the material culture of the Scottish literary scene: "the 'bittiness' of Welsh's writing, its episodic quality, is due in part to its origins in the pamphlet culture of small presses" (Maley 2000: 192). But such factors combine to produce a form that is exploited for its political meaning: "The civic and social specificity of Welsh's shorter fiction undermines the claims to inclusiveness of larger narratives of nation and empire, and sets up counternarratives of regional dissent" (Maley 2000: 192). Odd as it may seem, Welsh in certain respects inherits the short story aesthetic set out by Iain Crichton Smith. For Welsh, as for Crichton Smith, the short story communicates the various minor narratives that are repressed and excluded by the imaginary unity of a community, be this (for Crichton Smith) an island village, or (for Welsh) an island nation. Welsh's short story "Lisa's Mum Meets the Queen Mum" is told in the voice of an English mother whose young daughter, Lisa, has been picked to present a bouquet to the Queen Mother (the now-deceased mother of Queen Elizabeth II). The mother reflects on an appearance of continued Britishness, for she can remember when her own mother "met the Queen Mum at the Festival of Britain" (Welsh 1994b: 106). But the imaginary national unity left over from this 1951 celebration of Britishness cannot withstand the naïve perceptions enjoyed by young Lisa, who flees the Queen Mum in horror, citing the Royal personage's "bad breath," and claiming that she "smells of wee" (Welsh 1994b: 107). The daughter's realist mode ("truth at all times, madam, I tell her" (Welsh 1994b: 106)) contradicts the fantastic invented tradition and imagined community of Britishness. Even Lisa's Mum has her own oppositional narrative, albeit one that is submerged in cliché:

> They [the Royals] work ever so hard, you've got to give them that. Not like some I could mention, Derek, Lisa's dad, being a case in point. Not that I'm going into that little story just now, thank you very much. (Welsh 1994b: 107)

But it is such "little stories" that Welsh insists on going into: the stories of unemployment, alcoholism, and the decaying elderly, that are left out of the increasingly threadbare historical narrative of post-war Britain.

This use of the short story to present the "little stories" overlooked by mass narratives is also important to the work of A.L. Kennedy (1965–), and is particularly evident in her first published short story collection, *Night Geometry and the Garscadden Trains* (1990). The short story after which the collection is named features a narrator who promises to tell how "a Garscadden train [. . .] almost killed my husband" (Kennedy 1990a: 25). But the "incident involving my husband and a Garscadden train" (Kennedy 1990a: 33) does not allude to a near-disaster on the railways, but to an altogether different sequence of accidental causation. Frustrated by Garscadden trains passing through her station while none arrive for her, the narrator returns home, only to find her husband in bed with his lover, whereupon she is almost driven to stab him to death. The narrator's trick upon her readers has a serious point: only by pretending that her story is a (near-) disaster story, does her little narrative come to be worth reporting. Although "I am central to whatever I do and those whom I love and care for are more vital to my existence than statesmen, or snooker players, or Oscar nominees" (Kennedy 1990a: 25), their stories have no place in mass-consciousness. For instance,

> the television news and the headlines were the same as they always are when my mother died [. . .] Nations didn't hold their breath and the only lines in the paper for her were the ones I had inserted. (Kennedy 1990a: 25).

The "silent majority" only shove aside narratives of celebrity when they are caught up in "The Disaster," such as the Hillsborough football stadium disaster of 1989 – "a wall of pale faces, crushed against grillwork, one Saturday afternoon in spring" (Kennedy 1990a: 34).

The short story "Star Dust" presents a similar perspective. The narrator, an elderly woman called Mrs Mackintosh, imagines that if she were a director, then she "would film an ordinary person, their story, because they have good stories, too" (Kennedy 1990b: 88). At least if ordinary people were in films, they would not, she reflects, need to seek transient celebrity through television quiz shows or radio phone-ins. Mrs Mackintosh imagines her own film, based on the story of her life: as a teenager, she made a loveless marriage to escape an abusive father, and then fell in love with another man. When she told her husband that she was leaving, he coerced her back by threatening to refuse access to their daughter. She chose never to contact her lover again, and her life settled down to being something "sometimes uncertain and sometimes comfortable" (Kennedy 1990b: 91) – a long wait, in essence, for her daughter to grow up, and for her husband to die. Reflecting upon this narrative, Mrs Mackintosh concludes that the temporal flow of the motion picture is unsuited to her materials, for "there seem to be only tiny patches in my life that are at all important. There are images, or moments. It's material more suited to a series of photographs" (Kennedy 1990b: 91). She recalls how her lover once helped her across a collapsed wall on a day's outing in the countryside:

> That would only be a tiny moment in the picture, but it would show our hands and faces and be slow and watch the way that people choose things they'll remember. (Kennedy 1990b: 90)

Time has to be fragmented and elongated precisely because Mrs Mackintosh has not been able to take control of her own life. She could not choose to leave her husband without also leaving her daughter. And now, injured after a fall, she dreams of being helped to the local bowling club, but no one is willing to transport her there, despite their promises of assistance. Mrs Mackintosh's timeless epiphanies, her narrative implies, substitute for a life narrative in which her own agency barely features.

The uncovering of such "small" narratives in the short fiction of Kennedy and Welsh usefully illustrates the ambivalence of the short story in Scottish writing post-1945. On the one hand, the modern tower blocks erected over the demolished tenements of Glasgow are a central image. They stand as a synecdoche for a changing economy and society, and represent metaphorically both the increasing individualism of post-war Scotland, and the aesthetic properties of the short story (and, in particular, of the short story sequence). On the other hand, the short story is exploited as a way to represent narratives that contradict imaginary social unity, and which resist the homogenizing power of the modern socio-economic system. The Scottish short story post-1945 presents itself as both a symptom of a wider social malaise, and as a sign of rude hybrid vigor in the body politic.

REFERENCES AND FURTHER READING

Brown, G.M. (1967). "Master Halcrow, Priest," in *A Calendar of Love*, pp. 124–35. London: Hogarth.

Brown, G.M. (1974). "The Tarn and the Rosary," in *Hawkfall*, pp. 168–200. London: Hogarth.

Craig, C. (1999). *The Modern Scottish Novel: Narrative and the National Imagination*. Edinburgh: Edinburgh University Press.

Friel, G. (1992). "A Friend of Humanity," in G. Jarvie (ed.), *A Friend of Humanity and Other Stories*, pp. 151–7. Edinburgh: Polygon.

Gellner, E. (1983). *Nations and Nationalism*. Oxford: Blackwell.

Kelly, A. (2005). *Irvine Welsh*. Manchester: Manchester University Press.

Kelman, J. (1983a). "Nice to be nice," in *Not Not While the Giro and Other Stories*, pp. 30–7. Edinburgh: Polygon.

Kelman, J. (1983b). "Roofsliding," in *Not Not While the Giro*, pp. 179–81. Edinburgh: Polygon.

Kelman, J. (1992). "The Importance of Glasgow in My Work," in *Some Recent Attacks: Essays Cultural & Political*, pp. 78–84. Stirling, United Kingdom: AK Press.

Kennedy, A.L. (1990a). "Night Geometry and the Garscadden Trains," in *Night Geometry and the Garscadden Trains*, pp. 24–34. Edinburgh: Polygon.

Kennedy, A.L. (1990b). "Star Dust," in *Night Geometry and the Garscadden Trains*, pp. 82–91. Edinburgh: Polygon.

Klaus, H.G. (2004). *James Kelman*. Tavistock, United Kingdom: Northcote.

McCabe, B. (2003). "The Full Moon," in *Selected Stories*, pp. 49–55. Glendaruel, United Kingdom: Argyll.

McLellan, R. (1990a). "The Black Stallion," in *Linmill Stories*, pp. 151–8. Edinburgh: Canongate.

McLellan, R. (1990b). "The Kittlins," in *Linmill Stories*, pp. 9–16. Edinburgh: Canongate.

Maley, W. (2000). "Subversion and Squirrility in Irvine Welsh's Shorter Fiction," in D. Cavanagh and T. Kirk (eds), *Subversion and Scurrility: Popular Discourse in Europe from 1500 to the Present*, pp. 190–204. Aldershot, UK: Ashgate.

Mullan, B. (ed.) (1997). *R.D. Laing: Creative Destroyer*. London: Cassell.

Murray, I. (1996). "A Sequence of Images: George Mackay Brown," in I. Murray (ed.), *Scottish Writers Talking: George MacKay Brown, Jessie Kesson, Norman MacCaig, William McIlvanney, David Toulmin*, pp. 1–54. East Linton, UK: Tuckwell.

"National Identity" (2001). in M. Lynch (ed.), *The Oxford Companion to Scottish History*, pp. 437–44. Oxford: Oxford University Press.

Rousseau, J.-J. (1968). *The Social Contract*. London: Penguin.

Smith, I.C. (1976a). "Easter Sunday," in *The Village*, pp. 7–9. Inverness, UK: Club Leabhar.

Smith, I.C. (1976b). "Moments," in *The Village*, pp. 101–9. Inverness, UK: Club Leabhar.

Spark, M. (1958a). "Come Along, Marjorie," in *The Go-Away Bird with Other Stories* (pp. 159–73). London: Macmillan.

Spark, M. (1958b). "You Should Have Seen the Mess," in *The Go-Away Bird with Other Stories*, pp. 150–8. London: Macmillan.

Spence, A. (1977a). "Auld Lang Syne," in *Its Colours They are Fine*, pp. 198–217. London: Collins.

Spence, A. (1977b). "Greensleeves," in *Its Colours They are Fine*, pp. 157–66. London: Collins.

Spence, A. (1977c). "Gypsy," In *Its Colours They are Fine*, pp. 46–62. London: Collins.

Spence, A. (1977d). "Sheaves," in *Its Colours They are Fine*, pp. 22–35. London: Collins.

Welsh, I. (1994a). "Granny's Old Junk," in *The Acid House*, pp. 93–8. London: Jonathan Cape.

Welsh, I. (1994b). "Lisa's Mum Meets the Queen Mum," in *The Acid House*, pp. 106–7. London: Macmillan.

26

Hybrid Voices and Visions: The Short Stories of E.A. Markham, Ben Okri, Salman Rushdie, Hanif Kureishi, Patricia Duncker, and Jackie Kay

Michael Parker

The exile knows that in a secular and contingent world, homes are always provisional. Borders and barriers, which enclose us within the safety of familiar territory, can also become prisons, and are often defended beyond reason or necessity. Exiles cross borders, break barriers of thought and experience. (Edward Said, 2000: 185)

1

One of the many interesting cultural phenomena over the last twenty-five years has been a sudden surge in texts re-examining Britain's colonial past and its continuing legacy. While reflective of an increasing interest in history generally, it is also indicative of a growing need in British society to address issues of cultural difference and hybridity. Whereas in the late 1950s and 1960s, when the process of decolonization was gathering momentum, writing from and about the Caribbean and Africa – especially South Africa – attracted most attention in Britain, in the early 1980s, focus decisively shifted on to Britain's historical relationship with the Indian subcontinent. Novels such as Anita Desai's *Clear Light of Day* (1980) and *In Custody* (1984), Salman Rushdie's *Midnight's Children* (1981) and *Shame* (1983), films like *Gandhi* (1982), *A Passage to India* (1984), and television series such as *The Jewel in the Crown* (ITV 1984), quickened and sustained this appetite for versions of the Indian-British colonial encounter. However, this flurry of interest in the Raj among film-directors and television producers was not to everyone's taste. In his 1982 essay, "The New Empire within Britain," Salman Rushdie writes scathingly about the current "nostalgia for the Great Pink Age" (Rushdie 1992: 130), seeing it as a bi-product of the jingoistic national mood fostered by the then Prime Minister,

Margaret Thatcher. In later pieces such as "Attenborough's *Gandhi*" (1983) and "Outside the Whale" (1984), Rushdie raises specific, legitimate objections to historical inaccuracies and distorted representations of Indians in recent films and television dramas, yet refrains from discussing at any length the deeply unflattering portrait these present of "the nation that . . . ruled a quarter of the world" (Thatcher, qtd in Rushdie 1992: 131).

The writers of short stories discussed in this essay were undoubtedly beneficiaries of this significant, though problematic cultural turn, but also of other developments in the mid-1980s which witnessed a growing receptivity worldwide to the diversity of literatures in English following the Nobel Prize triumphs of Wole Soyinka (1986), Nadine Gordimer (1991), Derek Walcott (1992), V.S. Naipaul (2001), and J.M. Coetzee (2003). In the UK, meanwhile, throughout the 1980s, 1990s, and early 2000s, the foremost literary prize for fiction, the Booker, was repeatedly awarded to authors originating from Britain's former colonies for texts which, like the short stories examined here, explore complex negotiations within and between cultures and races. (Winners have included South Africa's J.M. Coetzee (1983, 1999), New Zealand's Keri Hulme (1985), Nigeria's Ben Okri (1991), Australia's Peter Carey (1988, 2001), Canada's Margaret Atwood (2000) and India's Salman Rushdie (1982), Arundhati Roy (1997) and Kiran Desai (2006)). Recently, *British* fiction-writers of mixed race origin have achieved considerable commercial success and critical acclaim. Jackie Kay's *Trumpet* (1999), Zadie Smith's *White Teeth* (2000), Monica Ali's *Brick Lane* (2003), and Andrea Levy's *Small Island* (2004) all movingly represent and reflect the cultural reconfigurations British society has undergone since World War II, making visible and audible individuals, communities, and histories that had long been marginalized and silenced. Preoccupied with issues of identity, the impact of colonial and post-independence history, and the migrant consciousness, their narratives have helped extend the borders of the literary terrain not only *in* universities, but also *for* the wider reading public.

The essay that follows considers the varied responses of writers to this quickening concern with empire and history at the close of the century, and the extent to which literary fiction from writers of African, Asian, and Caribbean origin both responds to and contributes to radical changes in British political and cultural discourse. What on one level many of these texts 'write back' against are the ideology and values promulgated by Margaret Thatcher's government following her election victory in May 1979, which some argue have been both maintained and extended by her Labour successors, Tony Blair and Gordon Brown (Wilson 2006). In a lecture on Britishness published in November 1997, Gordon Brown applauded Thatcher's recognition of "the need for Britain to reinvent itself and rediscover a new and vital self-confidence" and her understanding "that we could gain strength from the glories of our past which could point the way to a glorious future" (Brown 1997).

Mrs Thatcher's conviction that a failing economy and declining self-belief could be reinvigorated by market forces, individualist enterprise, and patriotic pride carried considerable sway over her party and the British electorate in the 1980s. While economic recession, spiralling unemployment, cuts to public expenditure, and increases in prices, were clearly potent contributory factors in the rioting which broke out in April and July 1981 and September–October 1985 in several major cities, as Sked and Cook point out, there was also invariably a racial subtext to the violence (Sked and Cook 1990: 351). Hostility within Britain's black communities towards the police had intensified in the period immediately before Mrs Thatcher assumed power. On St George's Day 1979, Southall in South London had witnessed an alarming confrontation between Asians and the police, after the National Front were given permission to host a meeting there. When the local Asian community and the leftist Anti-Nazi League jointly organized a demonstration to oppose what they viewed as a fascist "invasion" (Kureishi 2006), they were met with excessive violence from the police. Mounted officers and police vans were deployed to force back the protestors; and at some point a member of the Special Patrol Group struck and killed Blair Peach, a thirty-three-year-old teacher. Two years later, far more extensive riots broke out in Brixton (South London) and in Toxteth (Liverpool), which in turn triggered "copycat" incidents in Manchester and Birmingham, and other northern and midlands cities (Sked and Cook 1990: 352). What initially sparked the violence in Brixton was "Operation Swamp," a major police stop and search exercise designed to crack down on street crime, in which half of the 943 people questioned were of Afro-Caribbean descent. The name of this particular operation is said to derive from comments Mrs Thatcher made in January 1978, about a widespread fear

> that this country might be rather *swamped* by people with a different culture . . . The British character has done so much for democracy, for law, and done so much throughout the world, that if there is any fear that it might be swamped, people are going to react and be rather hostile to those coming in. ("Untold: Black History")

These events and this somewhat selective perception of Britain's history lay behind the Conservative government's decision in 1981 and 1982 to introduce legislation restricting the numbers of immigrants granted full British citizenship and therefore rights to residence in the UK. Appalled by these measures which were designed to reduce immigration from the subcontinent, the *Times of India* declared that Margaret Thatcher had "done more harm to race relations in Britain than any other post-war leader" ("Untold: Black History").

What also served to maintain attention on Britain's imperial past during Mrs Thatcher's first administration were negotiations over Rhodesia's transition to black majority rule and the Falklands War of April–June 1982. Mrs Thatcher's outrage at the invasion of this self-governing British dependency by Argentinian forces was shared by the British public, 76 percent of whom supported her plan for a military assault to regain the islands (Sked and Cook 1990: 414). Both at the time, and for a long period afterwards, the campaign was regarded by some as a "noble and principled crusade" (Sked and Cook 1990: 418). Mrs Thatcher's resolution in resisting a fascist enemy not surprisingly led to frequent comparisons with Winston Churchill, and did much to ensure the Conservatives' massive victory in the June 1983 election.

The strong working relationships she developed both with President Reagan of the United States and the Soviet leader Mikhail Gorbachev in the course of her first two terms in office secured Margaret Thatcher an important role in the global grand narrative. At home, however, unease and then opposition mounted to her consistent support for the United States' foreign policy, her assault on local government, and her industrial policies which saw distressed regions in the north being "left to rot and rust" (Schama 2002: 547–8). The unbending attitude she displayed during the Northern Ireland Hunger Strikes (1980–1), the Falklands War (1982), the Miners' Strike (1984–5), like her superciliousness towards her European allies, certainly played well amongst the "well-off middle and professional classes in the south of England" (Schama 2002: 547), but provoked intense antagonism elsewhere. Writers and artists were amongst her most hostile critics, indiscriminate in their loathing of every aspect of her domestic and foreign policies, including her philistine attitude towards the arts.

2

Rather than attempt a comprehensive survey of short fiction from the Thatcher and post-Thatcher era, this essay examines particular stories from single collections by E.A. Markham (*Something Unusual*, 1984), Ben Okri (*Incidents at the Shrine*, 1986), Salman Rushdie (*East, West*, 1994), Hanif Kureishi (*Love in a Blue Time*, 1997), Patricia Duncker (*Seven Tales of Sex and Death*, 2003), and Jackie Kay (*Wish I Was Here*, 2006). Of these writers, four have spent extended periods of their lives in Britain (Markham, Okri, Rushdie, Duncker), while two, Kureishi and Kay, were born in Britain. What their work contributes to literature in English is a widening of its parameters and possibilities; what it demonstrates is a growing self-belief and subtlety in exploring the problematic consequences of difference.

Born in 1939, on Montserrat, one of the Leeward Islands, E.A. Markham came to Britain in the year of the Suez crisis. His career as a writer has been accompanied by stints as a lecturer, director, editor, and media coordinator, which have seen him move extensively and frequently. Markham's reflections on the hybrid nature of the Caribbean poet is applicable to other writers represented here, who are similarly keen to add their "inflections" to language's "larger meaning" (Markham "Author's Statement"). Rather than seeing multiple cultural traditions as disabling, because of the uncertainty of identity they can generate, he argues that they can open up rich veins of creative possibilities:

Few West Indians are so self-contained as to regard the island/territory of their birth as fulfilling the sum total of their aspirations . . . Simply to go to school or to work

elsewhere constitutes leaving some of your emotional credit in that place . . . the geography of most Caribbean poets' lives suggest dual or multiple citizenship . . . We are
multi-national; cosmopolitan – some of us multi-lingual in ways that encompass and
extend beyond the standard-English nation-language debate and have residences on
earth that defy . . . the laws of immigration. (Markham 1989: 18)

The short stories in his 1984 collection, *Something Unusual*, demonstrate the plural-
ity of voices, tones and styles at Markham's command. "Digging," for example, is a
surreal, experimental piece. A parable about erased identities and histories, it dis-
orientates the reader from its outset with abrupt shifts in focus, language, and
location:

The name of the island has been lost, forgotten; in the basement, Sarah (I am satisfied
with the name, I worked it out my way) is still being tortured: her screams are muffled
but I can hear them . . . I hear them, as it were, fleetingly, or in moments of inattention.
I am speculating about what I have become . . . I'm surprised how transparent I've
become. (Markham 2002: 320)

Despite opposition from a nameless female companion who urges him to ignore
the voice he hears, the story's nameless protagonist is determined to investigate
what lies beneath the dark (ancestral, historical, artistic, psychological?) recesses of
his current abode. Any attempts to construct "something firm and resolute" out
of this uncertain narrative are repeatedly undermined, not least by the speaker's
confession a few paragraphs in that neither he nor she is in fact who they purport
to be, but rather descendants from a long line of diggers and opponents of their
mission: "I am in another time but my purpose is identical with the purpose of
the person I'm claiming to be" (321). He later informs us of many others similarly
engaged in quests for buried voices ("always retreating as you approached them"),
and how a whole industry and discipline had built up around the "shape, size and
depth of holes" (324). While allusions to "a school of philosophers" (322), "oppor-
tunists" (323), "lovers of Beauty and Truth" (325), suggest that Markham's story
might just be an elaborate allegory about the state of literature or of academic
English studies or of postcolonial studies, ultimately, like the hole, it defies
definition.

In language, form and characterization, "Mammie's Form at the Post Office" is
a far cry from "Digging," yet shares its preoccupation with ancestry and origins.
This depicts the difficulties the eponymous Mammie encounters in trying to send
money back to her Caribbean island to ensure the family gravestones are properly weeded and tended to. Focalizing the narrative through Mammie, Markham
presents the frustrations immigrants experience dealing with (sometimes well-
intentioned) bureaucracy in Britain. Even before she comes face to face with
the presumably young white man behind the counter, she is offended by the
"bullet-proof glass" that separates employees from customers. He queries her request
about sending "a hundred dollars *home*," and establishes that in reality she wants

to transfer money *"ABROAD"* (336; my emphasis). Indignant "that first they treated you like a foreigner, and then they denied you your home," her mood worsens when he hands her a form about making payments to the Indian subcontinent, and asserts that to the Royal Mail the "West Indies was the same as Bangladesh" (337). The options set out on the form further remind her and the reader of the cultural gulf between her native and adopted homes: ("Murial didn't live in a 'Road or Street'"). What finally makes her resolve to carry out the transaction in a different post office is a clash over language. She objects strongly to the proposed wording ("THIS IS TO WEED THE HEADSTONES"), and corrects the boy when he claims that

> ". . . it don't matter now . . ."
>   "It *does* matter. I'm not illiterate. You can't weed the headstones, you repair them."
> (Markham 2002: 339)

Though referring to the relationship between the English and the Irish, Seamus Deane's observation about "the incoherence that comes from sharing a common language . . . based on different suppositions" (Deane 1986: 22) could almost have been written with this exchange in mind. The close of Markham's story finds Mammie and her antagonist exhausted with each other. Feeling that she has wasted his time, he is "very rude" to her. Heading 'home' to put on the dinner, she wonders whether she should have specified "West Indian dollars," regretting that "her family would have to wait another day, choking on grass" (340).

Like Markham's, Ben Okri's work is in a number of literary genres, and displays a range of cultural influences, not least because of his hybrid family origins and the multiple relocations he has experienced since his earliest years. Okri was born in Minna, in central Nigeria in 1959, to parents from different ethnic groups; his father, Silver, was an Urhobo, brought up near Warri on the Niger delta, while his mother, Grace, was a delta or mid-western Igbo. While still in his infancy, Okri traveled with his mother to London, where his father was studying for a law degree. After settling into primary school there, he was dismayed to learn ten months later that his family were heading back to Nigeria (Fraser 2002: 14). Within months of their return, Nigeria was plunged into political instability, following military coups in January and July 1966, and a devastating civil war lasting from July 1967 until January 1970, in which over a million civilians died as a result of fighting and famine. Igbos in the eastern states had attempted to secede from the Nigerian federation and set up their own independent republic, Biafra. Fearing the havoc and "misery" (Michael Stewart, qtd in Phillips 2000) that similar secessionist movements might create in other newly independent African countries, Britain's Labour government backed and armed the federal regime led by Lieutenant-General Yakubu Gowon, and so were in part to blame for the terrible death-toll suffered by the defeated Igbos.

The publication of *Incidents at the Shrine* (1986), Okri's award-winning first short story collection, coincided with a period in which Africa was again the object of intense international focus, following another equally appalling humanitarian crisis, the Ethiopian famine of 1984–5. The opening and most powerful of its stories, "Laughter Beneath the Bridge," transports readers immediately into the civil war years. Its narrator is clearly *not* a ten-year-old (Fraser 2002: 49), but rather an adult recalling a profoundly disturbed time in his early life. By using a child-focalizer, Okri intensifies the defamiliarizing experience of war, and thus replicates a technique frequently deployed in news coverage and documentary film-making. The boy's fear and feelings of bewilderment and abandonment are swiftly established, conveyed in terse, simple statements. The first sentence juxtaposes prolonged discomfort ("pressed to the prickly grass") with terrified anticipation ("waiting for the bombs to fall"); from the second and third, we discover that the speaker was at school when conflict began, and how the adults charged with his and the other children's welfare deserted them: "Teachers disappeared; the English headmaster was rumoured to have flown home, and the entire kitchen staff fled" (Okri 1986: 1). In the second paragraph, the boarding school, a place once redolent of order, enlightenment, spiritual author- ity and companionship, becomes a site of violence and chaos. Vultures circling ominously overhead, like the planes the boys dread, are harbingers of this changed state, but the threat they embody seems minor in comparison to that posed by mad- dened, predatory humans. The school campus falls prey initially to "religious mani- acs . . . screaming about the end of the world," and then to a lynch-mob that has traveled from the city in search of "those of the rebel tribe" (1). Like the plague of rats in one of the collection's later stories ("A Hidden History"), the lizards which invade the school chapel, and then occupy the dormitory, function as both literal and symbolic "presences," reminding us of how easily human beings regress into animality.

Unlike the utterly isolated, increasingly savage schoolboys in William Golding's *Lord of the Flies* (1954), Okri's hunter-gatherers retain their victim status. Another key difference between Golding's and Okri's fables is the latter's emphasis on the burgeoning sexuality of his principal character and the sexual dimension within the inter-tribal violence. In the midst of his privations, the adult narrator informs us, his thoughts constantly turned to Monica, a girl from his home town, with "long legs and a pert behind" who moved "like a wild and beautiful cat" (2). She proves central to the story's preoccupation with war, male power and their casualties, and is the most dynamic of the three female characters. Significantly for the politics of the narrative, his account of Monica's risk-taking, transgressive history takes pre- cedence over his mother's arrival at the school to rescue him. The ten-year-old's erotic recollection of Monica bathing in the moonlight stands in marked contrast to his depiction of his mother, who initially appears in the story as a static, lifeless "figure," a mere "someone" resembling "a scarecrow in the middle of the field" (3). However, ominously from the outset, Monica's physicality sees her translated into an object of the male gaze, masculine desire: "She nearly drowned once trying to outswim the other boys across our town's river, *which was said to like young girls. I watched them* dragging her through the muddied water" (2–3). This opening portrait is proleptic in function, alerting us to Monica's frustration with the constraints the culture imposes on her gender, by, for example, excluding her as a female from the *egungun* rites, despite her greater proficiency as a performer than the boys (2).

For a short while Monica slips from view, as focus shifts to what the narrator initially terms the "beautiful" (3), unregulated time he enjoyed at school. Six lines later, in a moment of self-correction, his adult self concedes that "maybe it *seemed* beautiful" because of the novelty of his experiences. This admission follows an account of a mob beating a man to death, which again illustrates the doubleness and moral ambivalence of the narrative perspective. Recalled in the matter-of-fact, unemotional manner that a child witness might adopt – "So much blood came from him" – the incident serves as a preamble to the macabre violence the rest of the story records.

Misery accompanies menace on the boy's and his mother's journey home: "We saw whole families trudging along the empty wastes, children straggling behind, weeping without possibility of consolation" (5). This near-biblical vision of distress and displacement is followed by worse sights when the pair arrive at one particular army checkpoint. Wakened by the commotion the soldiers create, the boy spots instantly a pit containing the bodies of three men, "one . . . shot through the teeth". Acclimatized to brutality, the boy seems unable to grasp of the gravity of the situation in which they now find themselves, even after he has been smacked twice across the head by one soldier. During his mother's interrogation, he shows greater interest in what two soldiers are doing to a light-complexioned woman they have led away, a further indication of his scopophilic tendencies: "I was fascinated . . . I thought of Monica as the soldiers . . . struggled with and finally subdued the woman." By juxtaposing this off-stage rape scene with the verbal threats endured by his mother, the narrator intimates, however, the fate she faces if she cannot mask her ethnic identity: "They shouted to mother to recite the paternoster in the language of the place she claimed to come from: and mother hesitated as the woman's legs were forced apart" (7). Convinced by her linguistic fluency and abusive tirade against "the rotten pricks" and "the suppurating vaginas" which brought them into the world, the soldiers' attention switches from mother to son; they arraign him to establish his tribal origins. Hysterical from fear, disorientated by the raped woman's wailing, his mother's blows, and the marijuana he has inadvertently inhaled, he is for a long time incapable of uttering a single word in his father's dialect. Only by dredging from memory "the oldest word I knew" (8), the Urhobo word for excrement, is his life spared. Once they are freed and allowed to continue on their way, his mother repeatedly censures him for his slow-wittedness at the time of crisis: "They shoot people who can't speak their language" (9). His reaction is to speculate on what Monica might say "when", not if, "they came for her" (9), the first indication that she too is an Igbo.

On finally reaching home, he discovers that the terrible mark civil war has already made on Monica's life; she is traumatized by her brother's murder at the hands of local townspeople (11). It quickly becomes apparent that grief and anger have exacerbated her transgressive propensities. Despite his recent brush with the army, the boy follows her lead when she breaks the curfew the military have imposed. Heading straight for a bridge on the town's outskirts, they arrive at a manned roadblock, where a paunchy soldier takes a keen interest in her. Whereas the child-focalizer notes that the soldier looked at Monica "in a *funny way*," his older self speculates that the man must have been experiencing "the biggest temptation of his adult life" (16). His reaching out to touch her prompts Monica to recoil and then move away. Together, she and the boy descend towards the riverbank, despite the vile toxic smell that the water exudes.

Bridge and river clearly function in the narrative as symbolic locations, liminal spaces, boundaries where the living meet the dead, past present, puberty adolescence, sex war. Below the bridge, beside the stream, it becomes evident how much Monica has changed in the meantime. After confiding to the narrator that her brother's body was dumped here, she voices her need for revenge, to "Shoot a few people." Immediately afterwards, she tries reverting to an old pursuit, climbing a tree, only to find that she "Couldn't do it" (17). When the boy encircles her waist she responds passively, but then, "in a new voice", directs his desire away from her and towards the river which he suddenly realizes is clogged with bodies. Instead of her breasts, neck, legs, armpit, he is conscious of "the enormous eyes and bloated cheeks" of the corpses, "*bumped* along on the top of the water" (my emphasis). This image induces silence in Monica, then deranged laughter, then drooling at the mouth, leaving her young companion even more bewildered and appalled: "After a while I couldn't see her clearly *and* I called her *and* she laughed *and* then I thought it was all the swollen corpses that were laughing" (18). The simple grammatical structures and repeated conjunctions, along with the macabre misrecognition, convey effectively the focalizer's disorientation. Although the scene ends with first-person plurals and his and Monica's succumbing to a shared illness, the gulf between the pair is now unbridgeable.

Despite, or rather because of the pervasive smell of death in the town, clusters of children pour on to the streets to perform the *egungun* dance, a rite of "mourning, celebration and continuance" (Fraser: 50). Only partially recovered from fever, the narrator attaches himself to a group following the largest *Egungun*. Close to the bridge, a violent mêlée breaks out between competing troupes, prompting intervention by the military. In the midst of this bedlam, the main *Egungun* continues to whirl around the market-stalls, "provocatively shaking its buttocks, uttering its possessed language, defying the soldiers." Enraged by this act of insubordination, one soldier confronts the *Egungun*. Tearing off the mask, he exposes Monica, who, in expropriating a male role, has violated a taboo, and the Law of the Father. After slapping her hard, the soldier screams at her to "Speak your language!" Publicly shamed, she loses all control over her body and tongue: "she urinated down her thighs . . . She wailed. Then she jabbered. In her language" (21). This revelation of her identity as an Igbo results in "a terrible silence," and then her seizure by the military who throw her into the back of a jeep and drive off. In spite of the boy's father's efforts to discover her whereabouts, like the earlier rape victim at the checkpoint, she is never seen again; the reader, like the narrator, is left to imagine her fate.

Whereas Okri's story is an act of atonement to a young girl long dead, Salman Rushdie's "The Courter" pays tribute to a living ninety-one-year-old woman "who did as much as my mother to raise my sisters and me" (Rushdie 1994: 177). A miniature in comparison to *Midnight's Children* (1981), the final story in *East, West* is equally a skilled piece of storytelling, as moving, as affectionate as it is humorous, and partly autobiographical in origin (Goonetilleke 1998: 130). Set in the early 1960s, in Waverley House, a block of flats in Kensington, London, its main characters are two exiles, a diminutive *ayah* from Bombay and a porter from an unidentified country from behind the Iron Curtain. The text illustrates the disorientation of those forced by circumstances to inhabit a state and culture to which they can never really belong. Despite this emphasis on the difficulty of bridging huge cultural divisions, it opens positively, with the porter's efforts to reach out towards this foreign lady using a word from her own language. Observing Mary negotiating the steps in front of the building, Mecir thinks at first of someone scaling the Alps, but then hits on a more appropriate analogy, recalling a word "from his schoolboy atlas long ago, when India felt as far away as Paradise" (175). His mention of "ghats" triggers an avalanche of linguistic and cultural scree from the ayah. What he finds most attractive in her is her energy and purposefulness. Yet he also recognizes that, like him, she is compelled to operate in an alien language and context. (Much later we learn of the stroke which "had broken his tongue long ago" (205).) Thus in dubbing her "Certainly-Mary," he is not just commenting on her excessive use of the adverb, but commending her positive response to exile.

The story's opening section presents Certainly-Mary as a comic, almost Dickensian figure. The as yet unidentified third-person narrator draws attention to her problem in pronouncing the letter "p," noting how she generally changes it into an "f" or "c" sound. We are told how when heading out of the flats with her wheelie, she would inform the porter that she was "Going shocking"; on her return, she invariably responded to his offers of help with a "Yes, fleas" (176). In the course of the narrative, Mary translates Mecir and for a while helps him find contentment; misnaming the porter as "courter," she turns him into a suitor. His friendship and tuition in chess introduce her in turn to a new country, "beautiful and dangerous and . . . full of fuzzles" (Rushdie 1994: 195).

At the start of section two, however, the narrative voice strikes a different, humbler note, confiding to us how the tale came to be written out of a deep affection for an aged nurse. He admits also how patronizing and impertinent he had been as a sixteen-year-old to Mecir, whom he thought of nicknaming Mr Mxyztplk, "after a mischievous little comic-book character" (179). Incurious about, ignorant of the individual and the particularity of his culture, the expensively educated public schoolboy confesses that "he never even tried to learn" how to pronounce the porter's name, blathering instead about "Communist consonants . . . z's, and c's and w's walled up together without vowels to give them breathing space" (179). "To simplify life," he and his sisters refer to the porter as "Mixed-Up," their act of renaming unconsciously replicating those carried out by the British in India and elsewhere.

The delicacy of the chaste relationship that develops between Mixed-Up and Certainly-Mary is contrasted with the off-stage promiscuity of two wealthy Indian residents in the flats (the Maharaja of B and the sporting Prince P), and the thwarted sexual adventures of the adolescent focalizer. (In a further gesture of self-mortification, the narrator itemizes his brief encounters with Chandni, a "sort-of-cousin," and a Polish girl called Rozalia, whose name suspiciously echoes Romeo's first love.) The tender choreography of Certainly-Mary's and Mixed-Up's games of chess, like the constant references to the anodyne popular hits of the day ("Speedy Gonzales," "Jumbalaya," "Big Girls Don't Cry," "I Want to Hold your Hand," "Good Luck Charm"), initially create the illusion of a more innocent period.

What adds a darker counterpoint to the soundtrack of the boy's life, however, is the tyrannical figure of Abba, the narrator's father. A man who never consults his wife on any crucial family decisions, he consumes a bottle of Johnnie Walker every night, and is compared by his children at one point to the Minotaur. Another ominous figure is that of "a vulpine Englishman with a thin moustache and mad eyes" (189), who appears briefly on a television newscast. Rushdie is manipulating the chronology here, since this unidentified figure is the leading Conservative politician, Enoch Powell, who lost his Shadow Cabinet post in 1968 after prophesying rivers of blood if immigration remained unchecked in Britain. The story's most sinister presences are the thugs who direct their aggression on to Mecir, after failing to get their hands on the improvident Prince P and the sleazy Maharaja. (In an interesting reversal of racial stereotyping, these native English are depicted with "long hair and thick lips" (198).) Like the counter-clerk in Markham's story, Rushdie's tough-guys exhibit a limited grasp of English grammar. When Mecir informs them that the Prince is away, they leave him with what they euphemistically term their calling card, a fist to the mouth and a black eye. Even more menacing are the Pinteresque heavies who appear at the tale's climax. Though outwardly "well-turned-out young men with Beatle haircuts" (203), they too have business to transact with the Maharaja. They mistake the narrator's mother for the Maharani and assume Certainly-Mary is a member of his retinue. Polite, eloquent, courtly initially, their register changes dramatically when they referring to the Maharaja's sexual violence towards their ward:

> Fucking wogs . . . You fucking come over, you don't fucking know how to fucking behave. Why don't you fucking fuck off to fucking Wogistan? (Rushdie 1994: 204)

Just as one of them draws a blade in order to exact revenge, Mecir heroically rescues the innocent, bewildered women. Temporarily, the Beatle with the knife is amused at the sight of the yelling, flailing porter: "Who's this then? Oh oh fucking seven?" (205). The old man's breathless, broken explanation ("Sirs sirs sirs these not B- women . . . God's truth mother's grave swear") prompts an apology from the Beatles to the women. As they depart, however, one lunges at the porter and stabs him.

Although the knife attack on the porter is not fatal, it transforms the lives of many of Waverley House's residents. Not surprisingly, the Maharaja decides it is time to move on, "so we had no further visits from the Beatles or the Rolling Stones" (206), the narrator wryly notes. His mood switches, recalling the assault's impact on his ayah, since she rapidly starts to age. Fears about her frailty and "heart trouble" result in the narrator's entire family behaving impeccably over the Christmas period. Although at the time the boy enjoyed this outbreak of harmony and goodwill amongst his family, in retrospect he realizes "we were only play-acting" (207). In a telling flashback, he recalls "consoling" an American pupil at his boarding school following news of the assassination of JFK. By lying to the American that *his* father has just died, he exposes the depth of his animosity towards his father, and the intensity of his desire for individuation. Gaining British citizenship the very next year (1964) makes him at last *feel* free.

Ironically, his greater attachment to his adopted home coincides with Mary's decision to abandon Britain. After six months of fruitless medical tests, she diagnoses what she believes to be the source of her malaise: "it was England that was breaking her heart . . . by not being India. London was killing her, by not being Bombay" (209). The narrator, however, speculates that Mecir's decline since the stabbing may also be part of the story. In an analogy he keeps returning to, and which underlines his own westward leanings, he compares Mary's state to that of the horses in John Huston's film, *The Misfits*:

> was it that her heart, roped by two different loves, was being pulled both East and West, whinnying and rearing, like those movie horses being yanked this way by Clark Gable and that way by Montgomery Clift. (Rushdie 1994: 209)

The story concludes with an acknowledgment that while for some, like Certainly-Mary, a hyphenated existence (Anglo-Indian, Indo-Anglian), is intolerable, for others, like the writer-narrator, being "yanked" in contrary directions, by multiple cultural influences can be verifying. Neatly, in final paragraph of "The Courter," Rushdie plays one last variation on the motif of strangers meeting, though this time misunderstanding. Returning to Waverley a year or so after his departure, the narrator seeks out Mr Mecir:

> "Where's Mixed-up?", I cried . . .
> "I'm the porter, sir," the man said, "I don't know anything about any mix-up."
> (Rushdie 1994: 211)

3

Published in the year the Labour Party returned to power, Hanif Kureishi's first short story collection, *Love in a Blue Time* (1997), looks back on reconfigurations in British culture brought about during eighteen years of Conservative rule. That this has been a profoundly disorientating period is apparent from the opening, title story, its narration and characterization. Of the story's central character's background and origins, the reader learns almost nothing; it is as if Roy is entirely self-invented. He is defined not by family, home place, race or class, but primarily by his role within the media industry, his uneasy relationship with Clara, his pregnant, somewhat possessive partner, and his musical tastes. The narrative quickly establishes that he is on the verge of securing a major contract and about to become a father, These twin pressures generate a feeling of crisis, and he finds himself questioning the whole direction in which he is heading, not least as a result of the re-surfacing in his life of a university friend, a wastrel called Jimmy. Crucially, at both its beginning and conclusion, the text emphasizes how the latter is connected in Roy's mind with the Rolling Stones, with a pre-Thatcherite, alternative, responsibility-lite lifestyle. At Jimmy's flat he comes face to face with a "yellowing" Keith Richards poster, which reminds him of "how he'd longed for the uncontrolled life ... avoiding the ponderous difficulties of keeping everything together" (Kureishi 1997: 6). In one of the story's final scenes he conspicuously withdraws from a social gathering with Clara's complacent, bourgeois friends, since he harbors still a "delinquent" world view, one which he ascribes to the Stones: "the idea that vigour and spirit existed in excess, authenticity and the romantic unleashed self" (1997: 38).

Clara and Jimmy, and to a lesser extent, the film producer Munday, embody alternative temptations to Roy, a future of domestic constraint, reckless hedonistic self-destruction, or career advancement. Most of the attitudes and values he acquired at university – what the narrator terms "a charged conscience" (10) and which Roy sardonically characterizes later as "pieties" (15) – have long since fallen away: "Since then Roy hadn't settled in any of the worlds he inhabited, but only stepped through them like hotel rooms" (10). Roy's vacillation and sense of his own ephemerality is repeatedly attributed to the latter half of the Thatcher era, a period of "manic entrepreneurialism, prancing individualism, self-indulgence and cynicism" (15) from which he has never fully recovered. Although he had found the "Nietzschean pitilessness" of the time exhilarating (15), he now dimly senses the damage it has inflicted on culture and concepts of value:

> He had lived through an age when men and women with energy and ruthlessness, but without much ability or persistence excelled ... their ignorance had confused Roy, making him wonder whether the things he had striven to learn ... were irrelevant. Everything was to be the same: commercials, Beethoven's late quartets, pop records, shopfronts, Freud, multi-coloured hair. (Kureishi 1997: 16)

Kureishi's narrative strategy involves distancing the reader from his listless, morally unprincipled characterizations, an effect achieved primarily through his choice of focalizer and the worthless object of his admiration, the parasitical and ultimately treacherous Jimmy. In many ways, however, Roy and his double exemplify an urbanized, postmodern culture that has neither core nor coherence. As much as Jimmy's parents, they are refugees in a city "full of people" living "elsewhere in their minds" (8), but without any real sense of home.

This is a motif that runs through the other stories in *Love in a Blue Time*, most of which similarly deploy doubling devices in order to heighten the texts' dialogic qualities. The very title of the second story ("We're Not Jews") emphasizes how issues of racial difference continue to preoccupy Kureishi's fiction, despite Ranasinha's claims to the contrary (Ranasinha 2000: 19). Set during an earlier period of Conservative rule, in the late 1950s/early 1960s when Kureishi was himself growing up, the narrative traces the initiation of a child of mixed race into the prejudice rife in his native land. In so doing it presents the distress and repression daily life involved then and involves now for many in Britain's Muslim communities. The intense scrutiny and hostility his characters meet with is comparable, Kureishi's story implies, to that suffered by Britain's Jewish (and for that matter Irish) minorities in the latter part of the nineteenth and first half of the twentieth centuries. Activities as routine as going shopping and taking a bus journey home expose a young boy and his mother to threats, humiliation, and abuse from their neighbors. What makes matters worse is the tacit collusion at various levels within white society, represented initially by the bus conductor, who "had a laugh" with the perpetrators, and "let them ride for nothing" (41). The bullying Azhar has endured at school worsens after he followed his mother's advice on how to counter the insults directed at him; she "instructed him to reply" that Little Billy was "as common as muck." This jibe has clearly jarred on Big Billy, the bully's father, who shouts across the bus that "we ain't as common as a slut who marries a darkie" (43).

Kureishi's choice of focalizer is again absolutely crucial in shaping the story's reception and garnering the reader's empathy for characters who, as in "D'Accord, Baby," learn how "pitiless the world was" (Kureishi 1997: 54).

In quick succession over recent days, Azhar has learnt to his dismay that in South Africa, to which his best friend's family has recently emigrated, "people with white skins were cruel to the black and brown people," and that in Europe "there had been 'gassing' not long ago" (45). Although his parents sometimes discuss the possibility of emigrating themselves, the concept of Pakistan as "home" is problematized in the text. Azhar's white mother recoils from the idea of going to a sweltering alien place, full of "people who didn't speak English" (46), where women were expected to follow several paces behind their menfolk. It emerges that the "home" his father speaks of is somewhere he has never visited. A packer in a shoe-polish factory, Azhar's father has spent much of his life in Britain aspiring to become a writer, though without success: "Father didn't have a sure grasp of the English language *which was his, but not entirely*" (47; my emphasis). After the incident on the bus, the boy's mother takes him on a symbolic journey into a waste area, where "they could no longer feel anything firm beneath their feet" (49). Bewilderment, uncertainty, and isolation mark the story's ending, as they did its beginning. Ironically now, however, the disorientation the boy feels originates in those apparently closest to him; he is not even sure of the language swirling above his head:

> They were talking loudly in Urdu *or* Punjabi, but gesticulating . . . *in a way English people never did* . . .
>   Azhar was accustomed to being with his family while *grasping only fragments* of what they said. He endeavoured to *decipher the gist* of it, laughing as he always did, when the men laughed, moving his lips *without knowing what the words meant, whirling*, all the while, *in incomprehension*. (Kureishi 1997: 51; my emphasis added)

4

To conclude, I would like to consider the work of two outstanding women writers, part of a powerful new female presence in contemporary British writing. Born in 1951 in Kingston, Jamaica, and brought up there, Patricia Duncker is the daughter of an Englishwoman, a teacher, and a Jamaican businessman. Gender, sexuality, and politics, rather than race, are the predominant concerns in *Seven Tales of Sex and Death* (2003), her second short-story collection which, like its predecessor, *Monsieur Shoushana's Lemon Trees* (1997), is a work of remarkable psychological depth and complexity. In *Seven Tales*, as in Okri's "Laughter Beneath the Bridge," the calm exposition of appalling incidents accentuates their impact on the reader. Although the initial inspiration for these extremely violent narratives was primarily American B movies, Duncker takes their predilection for "rape, terrorism, sexual abuse, perverted desires . . . aliens, serial killers, stalkers" and uses it to expose the sadistic nature of male power, with which several of her female characters are complicit. Another recurring theme is men's incapacity to meet the intense sexual, spiritual, and psychological needs of women. In story after story female narrators depict themselves *performing* gender, mimicking and so subverting the roles patriarchy has assigned to them. For the teller of the opening tale, "Stalker," marriage is just an act, a display, a case of dressing up (Duncker 2003: 19). Repeatedly deploying the noun phrase "my husband" (4–6) as the subject of sentences, she signals her distaste at his patronizing attitude towards her, the way he smiles benignly at remarks which he deems "whimsical" and "infantile." An archaeology professor, he is adept at reading "the layers of time embedded in the earth" (4), but has no grasp of her, her history or present. The speaker in the second story, the aptly named Sophia, makes her living "marketing sex and death as a gourmet speciality" (75), donning costumes and roles at will to please her various male customers.

As well registering a more than nodding acquaintance with popular film genres and a penchant for theatrical metaphors, Duncker's stories frequently play with intertextual references in order "to deepen and complicate the surface narrative," and encourage readers "to reconsider both the normative bases of our moral perspectives and our assumptions of psychological verisimilitude and realism" (Matthews n.d.). Threaded through the grisly sequence of murders and mutilation that makes up "Stalker" are allusions to classical myth. Although it is not until the midway point that Duncker discloses that the narrator's name is Sem (short for Semele), she hints at a classical frame of reference at the outset. (In Greek myth, Semele was a priestess coveted by Zeus. News that Semele was bearing his child reached Zeus's jealous wife, Hera, whose machinations resulted in her rival being burned to ashes when the God revealed himself to her in his full glory. Her son, Dionysus, escaped her fate, and appears in Duncker's story at its close as the tall, young motorcyclist with a gold chalice emblazoned on his jacket.) It is established early on that Sem's husband is on a mission to unearth a lost Temple of Zeus. His lack of appetite for venery is set against the rapacious hunger of Sem's unseen admirer whose actions increasingly come to resemble that of the amoral, priapic deity represented in Ovid. The second victim of this serial rapist/"shape-shifter" (Duncker 2003: 41) bears "the fatal name" of *Helena* Swann – and heads a company called Leader Products (Leda). By naming the third victim, *Diana* Harrison, Duncker directs us back to a classical figure forever associated with voyeurism and forward to one of the highest profile, contemporary victims of stalking, the late Princess of Wales.

"Small Arms," like Kureishi's "Love in a Blue Time," pivots upon the gap between the narrator's 1960s political idealism and current, collusive state. In order to exemplify this falling-off, the narrative contrasts a fleeting acquaintance from her student days, a Vietnam war veteran, and a recent late lover, the embodiment of vacuous Thatcher-era materialism. The story begins quietly enough, meditating dryly on the instant forgettability of most men as sexual partners. Their deletion from memory, the narrator asserts, is because they lack the key skill possessed by the fictional Mr Rochester, an ability to listen to a woman "when she talks back" (Duncker 2003: 91). In a satirical sideswipe at her male counterparts' tendency to reduce their women characters to body parts, Duncker's narrator struggles to recall anything about one former partner, except his surname, the "blonde hairs on the back of his hand" (Duncker 2003: 92) and the fact that he drove a Citroen Diane.

The setting for her memorable encounter with Kelly is a grim West German bar near a US army base. A typical, late sixties, student radical – she tells us shortly how she had assiduously protested against the Vietnam War (2003: 96) – she sits alongside the only long-haired man in the bar. Although he speaks in "Bogart English" and surrounded by Peter Fonda and Jack Nicholson lookalikes, Kelly is more akin to the damaged characters in *The Deer Hunter* (1978), *Platoon* (1986), and *Born on the Fourth of July* (1989). Four terrible years spent in Vietnam have filled him with an intense hatred of politicians, generals, his family (especially his naïve, patriotic father), draft dodgers, and the "peace brigade who had betrayed him" (97). What particularly appalled him returning to his hometown was the anomaly between how others viewed him, "as a hero," and how he saw himself: he "felt like a ghost" (98).

Deploying skills acquired during the very time he was at war, she reads Kelly initially as a Shakespearean figure, Barnardine in *Measure for Measure*, a man in limbo, beyond redemption. Such are his powers of description and narration that she finds herself visualizing "the burning jungles, the vanishing bombers and the plastic bags full of dead white men" (99). In return she proffers her history, a tale of "small student jobs, vast ambitions" and "idealistic politics," "a narrative, small and pure, as fragile as fresh eggs" (100). This exchange between exiles enables both to "break barriers of thought and experience" (Said 2000: 185), as Kelly's final snatch of polemic demonstrates:

> Hey babe, you said they lied to you when they sold you all that crap about how being a woman was about marriage and motherhood. You didn't believe it. You didn't buy it. You refused to live your life just to suit someone else's fucking agenda . . . Well, they sold me a fucking load of lies too. (Duncker 2003: 101)

What consolidates the bond between them is first a symbolic grasping of hands (101), next a shared sleeping bag, shampoo and soap (2003: 102, 104), and a mad motorbike ride (104–6). Yet what she values as much as all these is their cliché-free dénouement. He disappears from her life with few words, having "kissed my cheek *gently*" (106; my emphasis).

At the start of the story's second half the narrator intimates how far she has traveled from this earlier "time of innocence," this "time of confidences" (Simon). Sentence after sentence demonstrates how she has metamorphosed into a passive, silent adherent of consumer capitalism: "I keep my head down and mouth shut," "I turned slick and cynical to suit the times," "What we all want is more money. And I'm no exception," "a girl has got to put something aside for her sell-by date" (108). The most obvious sign of collusion with and enslavement to capitalist ideology is her decision to yoke herself to a stock character, an "idiot called Charles" (109). (Her repeated mocking of his taste and behavior during her account of their holiday together in France suggests a subsequent change of stance.) As with the first boyfriend mentioned in the story, she does not give Charles "one hundred per cent attention," though she does recall him asserting that his former salary of £53,000 a year was totally inadequate: "No one can live on that kind of money" (110); "No, indeed not," she wryly quips.

Duncker manages effectively the story's unexpected climax, which occurs at a small restaurant, L'Auberge de la Croisade, where the ill-matched lovers' meal is disturbed by two French children, shooting at each other "with a variety of plastic gadgets" (116). Alongside the cacophony created by these junior "terrorists," and Charles's talk about outmaneuvering competitors, she hears "another voice," Kelly's, "louder and clearer than it had ever been" (117), urging her to reassume control of her life. As the speaker's attention oscillates between present to past, the changing quality of evening light and the choice of *tarte aux apricots* or tiramisu, the reader is intermittently made conscious of another presence. The narrative suddenly switches to the present tense, as a solitary cyclist on the opposite bank stops, and then unpacks what she at first takes to be his fishing equipment. Just as she recalls Kelly speaking about psychos exacting revenge on society, something clicks and the "fisherman" opposite starts machine-gunning the Auberge's staff and guests. What is almost as disturbing as the massacre itself is the narrator's chillingly distant account. For her the killing is primarily a spectacle, a cinematic experience:

> The blonde child has his brains *spattered in a satisfying mess* all over his plastic ray guns, which leap *like popcorn* off the table . . . Charles has three neat holes evenly spaced across his *splendid chest* . . . his raw silk shirt was ruined. The tie he had purchased in Paris was neatly pierced . . . *Good-oh*. I hated that tie. (Duncker 2003: 123; my emphases)

What conclusions should we draw from this ending? Is it a reminder of the arbitrary nature of terrorist violence, so much more horrific because so unexpected? Is it like the later story, "The Strike," a warning about the fragility of "normal" life and "order"? What does these word-choices, this resolution, disclose about the narrator and her state of mind? What or who is responsible for her brutalization, her amoral response? *Is* she in any way responsible for summoning this "spectral, authoritative . . . angel" (Duncker 2003: 124), or is he the product of some unspecified injustice? And are we *really* meant to view the "insouciance and humour" on display here as "well worth imitating" (Author's Note: viii)?

The last and youngest writer, whose work I would like to consider, is Jackie Kay, who was born in Edinburgh in 1961, to a Scottish mother and Nigerian father. Like her award-winning, début poetry collection, *The Adoption Papers* (1991), which narrates the story of a black child's adoption from the perspectives of a birth mother, her adoptive mother and the girl herself, Kay's second short story collection, *Wish I Was Here* (2006), reveals the author's versatility in conveying a diverse range of voices. In marked contrast to much of her writing in the 1990s, issues of race and identity are largely absent from this her latest book, which is peopled largely by individuals trying to cope with dissolved or dissolving personal relationships. These new fictions create a generically hybrid space somewhere between tragedy and comedy, one which is entirely appropriate for lives slipping into liminal, uncertain states.

The opening tale, "You Go When You Can No Longer Stay," provides a mostly alarmed, yet partly bemused account of a lesbian partnership breaking up. For Ruth, the aptly named narrator, a key indicator that things are falling apart is the intrusion of a male presence in their relationship. Hilary, her lover, insists on repeatedly quoting axioms drawn from Martin Amis's fiction, and, equally disturbingly, shopping in Harvey Nichols rather than M&S, drinking red wine rather than white, and losing interest in television crime series and the Sunday papers. At its close, feeling increasingly left behind, Ruth "writes" a reconciliation which readers are likely to dismiss as wishful thinking: "She smiled at me and I smiled back and both are faces looked the same" (Kay 2006: 15). Other characters in the collection lapse similarly into the delusion that the objects of their love are doubles or mirror images of themselves, and so find it difficult to conceive of parting. This is particularly true of the naïve, forty-four-year-old narrator of the title story. Paula is unable to anticipate the reception that awaits her once her long-time friend, Claudette, and her new partner, the affluent, thirty-year-old, Jan, discover that she has arranged to stay at adjacent premises to their holiday hotel. Convinced that since Jan has "not a lot going on upstairs" (33) Claudette will quickly tire of her conversation, Paula brightly confides to us that when that inevitably happens, "I'll be here to chip in" (27). Yet even before the smartly dressed lovers are first glimpsed together, "totally engrossed in each other" (38), "intermeshed" (39) together at the hotel bar, Paula's account betrays plenty of evidence as to why her hopes of a future with Claudette are likely to be dashed. Although she implies that she is intellectually superior to Jan – after all she has taken Charlotte Brontë's *Villette* as her choice of holiday reading! – she recognizes she cannot match her financially, or in years or looks. Revealingly, she allows herself to be conned by a manicurist into buying anti-ageing handcream which she can ill afford, and then succumbs to a two-drinks-for-one offer. A second pair of G and Ts leaves her ominously giggling one moment, admonishing herself the next: "You are not going to ruin Claudette's holiday. You are not going to get tearful and depressed" (39).

Separation is already a fact of life for the protagonists in two other early stories, linked by their subjects' desire to shut out the world. In "Blinds" a woman is observed adjusting to solo existence. Ill-at-ease in a new flat, she feels life away from her long-term partner is "play-acting" (66) merely. The strength of the "How to Get Away with Suicide" lies in its effective characterization, its black humor ("Will ye no come back again? No, frankly" (44)), and its evocation of place, which reminds us how rooted Kay is in Scottish culture. Her Glasgow comes across almost as vividly as Joyce's Dublin, as we follow the despondent Malkie on his odyssey up Buchanan Street, West George, West Nile, along Hope before ending up drenched in Sauchiehall Street. What makes Malkie such a sympathetic character is his far from "pernickety" concern at the emotional impact his suicide might have on his ex-wife, children and friends, hence his determination "to make it look like an accident" (46). Gradually, Kay discloses the factors behind his despair, how, hard on the heels of redundancy, his wife began an affair with the well-heeled Jamie; how, as a result of smashing a computer Jamie had given his bairns, Malcolm has been denied access to them.

One of the most intriguing, perfectly realized tales in *Wish I Was Here* is "My Daughter the Fox," a fable worthy of Angela Carter. This originated in a dream Kay had during pregnancy (Granelli n.d.), and must clearly therefore be intimately connected to her own experiences as a child. It opens uncannily in moonlight, with foxes howling outside, and a mother clinging closely to her (fox-) child. References to her fur, raised ears, wet nose, and paw alert us immediately to difference, and so prepare us for the story's focus on prejudice, ostracization, and, in this ecologically conscious new century, the proximity and interdependency of human and animal. Throughout the narrative Kay deftly maintains the reader's collusion in the fantasy by setting her creations in realistic, recognizable locations, and by imbuing parent and child with the very feelings one might expect. The narrator recalls in detail, for example, the exact sequence preceding Anya's conception, which took place in Room 2 of a small guest house beside Coniston Water. Her "sly and devious" (Kay 2006: 85), red-haired partner and the dead fox the couple had passed on their way to their bed-and-breakfast both appear to have played a part in the mysterious, inexplicable process by which she became pregnant. Childbirth itself is depicted as a dehumanizing process; the intensity of the contraction pains she likens to a descent into the earth, where she is compelled to "scrape and claw" (84); she feels as if her body is exploding or being ripped apart.

The midwife's horror at this Kafkaesque delivery is contrasted with the thrill the narrator experiences recognizing three traces of her own likeness in the newborn child: her "pointed chin," "high cheeks," "black eyes" (86). Hers proves the first of many rejections Anya's mother suffers, anticipating that of the ambulance men, her mother's, her neighbors', and the child's father's, who denies paternity and denounces his former lover as "barking" (90).

The closing stages of the story are particularly moving and expertly handled. Shunned by all but her best friend, the isolated narrator develops an intense bond with her offspring. Music performs a crucial role at this juncture, as it does throughout the lives of Joss, Millie, and Colman Moody in Kay's novel *Trumpet* (1999). In this story, however, there is an emphasis on hybrid influences; Ella Fitzgerald and Louis Armstrong's music plays alongside Mozart, Chopin, and Joni Mitchell's *Blue*, and mingles with the mother's own singing. Inevitably, however, in this collection about sundering, the moment when she has "to give her child up" (95) arrives. One snowy morning, the narrator observes pawprints leading up to the house. She sees immediately what this text signifies, that Anya's brother and sister creatures are asserting the claims of origin. Like so many other unwilling figures in *Wish I Was Here*, she ultimately has to resign herself to loss, to letting go the very being which gave life meaning.

5

The sheer diversity of the work discussed above illustrates how limiting categorizations such as "migrant," "black British," "postcolonial" writing can be. Rather than fix them within such a frame of reference, this essay has attempted to represent their work as reflective of major changes in political and cultural discourse over the past fifty years, yet as something more than that. Although there are points of affinity in terms of perspective and subject matter – their tales are concerned with "people on the edge of things. People on the border . . . People who feel they don't belong. People who aren't written about very much" (Kay, qtd in Granelli n.d.) – Markham, Okri, Rushdie, Kureishi, Duncker and Kay display uniquely individual traits in their short stories. Additionally, they remind us of the thriving, hybrid, "incorrigibly plural" (MacNeice 1966: 30) state of British fiction.

REFERENCES AND FURTHER READING

Books and Journals

Deane, S. (1986). Introduction. *Selected Plays of Brian Friel*. London: Faber.

Duncker, P. (2003). *Seven Tales of Sex and Death*. London: Picador.

English, J.F. (ed.) (2006). *Contemporary British Fiction*. Oxford: Blackwell.

Fraser, R. (2002). *Ben Okri*. Plymouth: Northcote House.

Goonetilleke, D.D.R.A. (1998). *Salman Rushdie*. Basingstoke: Macmillan.

Harrison, M.J. (2003). Review of *Seven Tales of Sex and Death. Times Literary Supplement* (March 28): 3–5.

Kay, J. (1991). *The Adoption Papers*. Newcastle-upon-Tyne: Bloodaxe.

Kay, J. (1999). *Trumpet*. London: Picador.

Kay, J. (2006). *Wish I Was Here*. London: Picador.

Kureishi, H. (1997). *Love in a Blue Time*. London: Faber and Faber.

MacNeice, L. (1966). *Collected Poems*. London: Faber.

Markham, E.A. (2002). *Taking the Drawing Room Through Customs: Selected Stories*. London: Peepal Tree Press.

Markham, E.A. (ed.) (1989). *Hinterland: Caribbean Poetry from the West Indies and Britain*. Newcastle-upon-Tyne: Bloodaxe.

Morris, M. (1990). *Contemporary Caribbean Short Stories*. London: Faber.

Okri, B. (1986). *Incidents at the Shrine*. London: Vintage.

Procter, J. (2003). *Dwelling Places: Postwar Black British Writing*. Manchester: Manchester University Press.

Ranasinha, R. (2000). *Hanif Kureishi*. Plymouth: Northcote House.

Rushdie, S. (1992). "The New Empire within Britain," in *Imaginary Homelands: Essays and Criticism 1981–1991*. London: Granta.

Rushdie, S. (1994). *East, West*. London: Cape.

Said, E. (2000). Reflections on Exile and Other Essays. Cambridge, Mass.: Harvard University Press.

Schama, S. (2002). *A History of Britain: The Fate of Empire*. London: BBC.

Sked, A. and Cook, C. (1990). *Post War Britain: A Political History*. London: Penguin.

Thomas, S. (ed.) (2005). *Hanif Kureishi: A Reader's Guide to Essential Criticism* Basingstoke: Macmillan.

Wilson, Richard. (2006). "Thatcherism Three," review of Simon Jenkins's *Thatcher and Sons. Times Literary Supplement* (December 15): 3–4.

Material from Internet Websites

Brown, G. (1997). "Britishness," *Spectator*/Allied Dunbar Lecture (November 4).

Duncker, P. (n.d.). "Author Statement." British Council Contemporary Writers:

<http://www.contemporarywriters.com/authors/?p=auth33>.

Duncker, P. (2000). "A Shadow at my Shoulder," interview with Nicholas Wroe, the

Guardian (August 12): <http://books.guardian. co.uk/departments/generalfiction/story/0,6000, 353237,00.html>.

Granelli, S. (n.d.). "On Matters of the Heart," interview with Jackie Kay: <http://www.liber-tas.co.uk/interviews.asp?ID=20>.

Kureishi, H. (2006). "Fear and Paranoia," the *Guardian* (April 22): <http://books.guardian. co.uk/review/story/0,,1757858,00.html>.

Markham, E.A. (n.d.). "Author Statement," British Council Contemporary Writers: <http://www. contemporarywriters.com/authors/>.

Matthews, S. (n.d.). "Critical Perspective: Patricia Duncker": <http://www.contemporarywriters. com/authors/?p=auth33>.

Phillips, B. (2000). "Biafra Thirty Years On": <http://news.bbc.co.uk/1/hi/world/africa/ 596712.stm>.

Simon, P. (1968). "Old Friends/Bookends," *Book-ends*. Columbia Records, ASINB00005ML9E.

"Untold: Black History" Channel 4 (2000). <http://www.channel4.com/history/microsites/ U/untold/programs/riot/timeline.html>.

27
The Anglo-Jewish Short Story
since the Holocaust

Cheryl Alexander Malcolm

The Final Solution aimed to put an end to Jews, not become their muse. Yet no other single event, not even the establishment of Israel, has had as great an impact on Jewish storywriters. Despite the difficulties of conveying its enormity with brevity, the Holocaust is the subject of an ever-growing number of short stories each year and underpins a multitude of concerns ranging from anti-Semitism to religious belief. If the literary output at the end of the twentieth, and beginning of the twenty-first, century is any indication, the Holocaust and the Jewish writer are by now inseparable. This essay will consider how the exter-mination of six million Jews inspires representations and responses in the short fiction of Ruth Fainlight, Jonathan Wilson, Gabriel Josipovici, Alan Isler, Dan Jacobson, Clive Sinclair, Wolf Mankowitz, James Lasdun, Elena Lappin, Michelene Wandor, and Neil Gaiman. It will suggest that whereas the perpetra-tors of the Final Solution used language to *de*form Jews, these writers are *re*form-ing images of survivors, witnesses, wanderers, tricksters, and exiles in the face of the Holocaust.

1   Survivors: Ruth Fainlight's "Another Survivor" and Jonathan Wilson's "From Shanghai"

After the Holocaust, every living Jew is a survivor. Whether you were spared the gas chambers by a liberating army, the British Channel, or the grandparent who immigrated to New York at the beginning of the last century, you realize what could have been. This is especially true for contemporary Jewish writers in Britain, many of whom come from recently immigrant backgrounds or are immigrants themselves, were evacuated from urban areas to the countryside for their safety during the war, and generally do not feel that Jewishness is tolerated, let alone welcomed, in Britain as it is in America. So it is not surprising that survival is the subject of so much Jewish literature. "Another Survivor" and "From Shanghai" contain several distinctive features of short stories about survivors. First, they are not trying to duplicate actual survivor testimonies. As these short stories illustrate, omniscient and third-person narrations set short stories apart from first-person survivor accounts and reflect the fact that neither writer is a Holocaust survivor but is an observer at a safe distance from the event. Fainlight was born in New York City in 1931 and lived there until moving to Britain when she was fifteen. Wilson was born in London five years after the end of the war. Other ways that short stories differ from conventional testimonies is that they are rarely chronologically linear, focus more on events years after as opposed to during the Holocaust, and concern the difficulty of representation more than survival itself. Second, these short stories concern psychological more than physical survival. They depict survivors as highly complex and frequently misunderstood characters who either cannot find a means of communicating their experience or someone able to comprehend it. A legacy of the Holocaust is thus an alienating of survivors from others, even other Jews. Third, "Another Survivor" and "From Shanghai" are set in Britain years after the Holocaust. Yet distance in time and terrain from the event does not diminish the trauma for their protagonists. Indeed, the contrast between peacetime British settings and characters' memories highlights the horror of the latter.

Fainlight's "Another Survivor," from her 1994 collection *Dr. Clock's Last Case: And Other Stories*, is about the ambiguity of survival. This is evident from its title, which underscores the ultimate failure of the Final Solution. Yet the word "another" hints at a lack of enthusiasm, if not weariness, towards survival. The first words of the story, "He's fifty now," would suggest that this is the malaise of middle age were they not followed by this piece of information: "but the day his mother and father took him to the railway station with the one permitted suitcase, clutching a satchel crammed with entomological collecting equipment he refused to leave behind – that chilly, too harshly bright day of a windy reluctant spring – was in 1938, and he was twelve years old" (Fainlight 1994: 75). The length of the last part of the sentence in contrast to its first few words symbolizes how the Holocaust is not diminished with time. Further on, Rudi explains "after more than thirty years, he was overcome with the most intense yearning for his mother" which "made him aware of how much grief had been repressed when they parted" (77). The shift in focus from the man to the boy and from contemporary England to wartime Germany in this first sentence foreshadows the eventual blurring of all demarcations of time and place when this survivor suffers a mental breakdown at the end of the story.

Fainlight suggests that Rudi's inability to speak of his Jewish background and *kindertransport* experience contributes to his collapse and gives him only a facsimile of a life. In contrast to his parents' attractive and comfortable home, Rudi's "bleak and characterless" house mirrors the emptiness of his *passing* identity when he marries a gentile (78). It is significant that the only one of his children who looks Jewish is called "Faith." Comparable to the wife of the same name in Nathaniel Hawthorne's "Young Goodman Brown," this daughter represents Rudi's conscience and invites parallels between the repression of his Jewishness in England and Young Goodman Brown's pact with the devil in the New England woods. Taking either path tarnishes all joy thereafter. The "anguish [which] came when he remembered visiting museums with his mother" casts a shadow over the same outings with his daughter Faith (79). After an apparition of his mother in a camp uniform appears when Faith puts on a dress from an antique shop "very like one his mother used to wear," Rudi realizes that he cannot erase the Holocaust from his past (81). He leaves the house with "such self-contempt and self-loathing that he cannot bear it, and starts to walk" (83). The story ends with Rudi deciding that he will "keep walking until a car knocks him down or someone fells him with a blow, until he reaches the end of his endurance and drops in his tracks" (83). The Jew on this death march is the *passing* Jew. The "self-contempt and self-loathing" which Rudi feels is for himself, not his Jewishness. Going out of the house can be read as "coming out." Ending on that note, this story of survivor trauma doubles as a cautionary tale for British Jews who believe that self-effacement of their Jewishness will bring happiness.

Wilson's "From Shanghai," from his 1995 collection of short stories called *Schoom*, is similarly set in England and concerns a middle-aged Jewish male who is a Holocaust survivor. But, as its title indicates, this story does not present a mono-lithic image of survival. Hugo arrives from Shanghai, not continental Europe, in the late 1950s, not immediately after the war, and he has considerable wealth. The latter is in the form of 20,000 volumes of Hans Christian Anderson stories in German. Hugo's refusal to sell the collection is unfathomable to the twelve-year-old narrator, who considers fairy tales childish, and a source of antagonism to Lotte, Hugo's voluptuous wife half his age. To the British Jews who "had only recently been freed from the restrictions of wartime rationing" and for whom "filling the larder" is a priority, Hugo seems out of step with the times (Wilson 1995: 78). Like Rudi, who fills his home with things that remind him of his pre-war German childhood, Hugo attaches meaning to objects, which those around him do not. Since both men are unable or unwilling to articulate the reason for their collections, they fuel the alienation from family and friends, which exacerbates their loneliness.

Both short stories end with specters of the Holocaust. The ghost of Rudi's mother haunts his house in an Auschwitz uniform. A letter notifies Hugo that his only son died sixteen years before. These incidents signal a loss of belief in preserving memories untainted by the Holocaust or in finding a loved one alive. With nothing else to believe in, since neither Rudi nor Hugo exhibits any belief in God, these survivors face lives without spiritual substance. And, like ghosts, their presence is disturbing. Fainlight and Wilson thus portray Holocaust survival as a country between death and life from which no one can emigrate.

2 Witnesses: Gabriel Josipovici's "He" and Alan Isler's "The Affair"

In terms of their writing and backgrounds, Josipovici and Isler could not be more different. Josipovici is an experimentalist. Isler is a humorist. Born in Nice in 1940, Josipovici lived in Egypt from 1945 until 1956 when he immigrated to Britain. Isler was born in London in 1934 and lived for over twenty years in New York before returning to Britain in the 1990s. Both survived the Holocaust through chance: Josipovici because he was hidden and Isler because Germany was defeated before it could invade Britain. While neither "He" nor "The Affair" directly draws from their writers' pasts, each does concern the ethics of witnessing. The dead are an absent presence in both short stories and the catalyst, which raises issues of remembrance and representation.

Josipovici's "He," from his 1987 collection of short stories, called *In the Fertile Land*, resembles a meditation. Devoid of plot or dialog, it consists of a first-person narrative in which a man reflects on the sudden death of a friend. As its title suggests, "He" is as much about the narrator as the deceased, and as much about the mysteries of survival as it is about the circumstances of the death. Just as the title is imprecise and ambiguous, there are no certain and clear answers to the questions which the death raises. In this regard, "He" resembles a mystery story but one without a solution. A suicide note is found "but it answered none of the questions" that haunt the dead man's friends (Josipovici 1987: 66). Why he killed himself remains a mystery and source of guilt to those who survive him. While this death is central to the short story, it drives the narrator into a meditation on remembrance as opposed to actual recollections about the friend.

The narrative is replete with questions, which begin with the particular and become increasingly general and philosophical. All, however, concern the role and responsibility of the witness and are summed up by these two: "But what end can there be for a memory or a lament? And what part of space can the survivors be said to occupy?" (72). As the questions in "He" become broader and less specific to one man's death, they seem more and more to spring from a post-Holocaust train of thought. The elegy for a suicide becomes a metaphor for poetry after Auschwitz. Josipovici suggests that words are by nature inadequate but recognizes this is half the battle to using them well. He writes:

> To speak it, to write it, is always to get it wrong. But to understand our distance from understanding is itself a form of understanding. To grasp our inability to pay our true respects to the dead is perhaps a form of respect. Our art, it is true, clouds or dazzles,

deafens with its too much noise or too much silence, distorts reality with its beginnings and endings. Yet, if we will let it, it can also make manifest that which it cannot express. (Josipovici 1987: 74)

The short story ends with the narrator looking up from the page of his friend's eulogy and realizing "that it was only another failure" but "that it was also the nearest he would ever come to success in this particular enterprise" (1987: 75). The final image of the writer/narrator sitting alone in a hotel room contributes to an impression that life is transitory, and words, however inadequate they may be, are all that the witness has.

Isler's "The Affair," from his 1998 collection *The Bacon Fancier: Four Tales*, could not be a more different short story. It is episodic, raucously comic, and contains decidedly Jewish characters. Yet it also concerns the responsibility of the writer as a witness, even when he or she does not experience events first-hand. Instead of a dead friend, the infamous Dreyfus case is the focus of a writer's attention in "The Affair." To the backdrop of a volatile affair between a Jewish singer and his Hungarian Christian girlfriend, the short story concerns the singer's refusal to take the lead role in *Dreyfus: The Musical*. Bruno Sorge turns down the part because he thinks that the play is "deeply offensive" for making "a fatuous mockery" out of the Dreyfus Affair (Isler 1998: 188). "[Y]ou *can't* write a musical about Dreyfus," he tells the playwright, "it's obscene" (198). In defense of his play, Duncan Greenglass tells Bruno that *West Side Story* and *Evita* treat serious subjects. What sets *Dreyfus: The Musical* apart from other musicals, however, is that it is about a Jew *and* is funny. Excerpts from the play suggest that Sorge misses the point of the play. It does not poke fun at Dreyfus but at anti-Semites by borrowing tunes from European opera, British and American musicals, and filling them with Yiddishisms and circumcision jokes. If its familiar melodies seduce the audience into listening to Dreyfus's story, its lyrics make clear this is no conventional romance. Even its "Love Duet" challenges anti-Semitism by changing the words of the 1916 British tune "If You Were the Only Girl in the World" to "If you were the only Jew in the world." When Dreyfus sings: "And you were the only *goy*," the Yiddish is empowering and dispels any notion that this song affirms the negative stereotype of an effeminate male Jew. Similarly, in "The Improbable Dream," a song based on "The Impossible Dream" from *The Man of La Mancha*, Dreyfus imagines circumcising a French general as the latter sings, "If a foreskin's not for him, it's most certainly not for me. / My, what a singularly brave young man, a brave young Jew must be!" (198). This combination of romantic melodies and coarse lyrics is obviously jarring but, rather than making the play a flop as Bruno predicts, it is a success. Isler is obviously evoking the hit musical about Hitler in Mel Brooks's *The Producers* and issues relating to the treatment of the Holocaust. There is, Isler suggests, a fine line between the writer bearing witness to and commodifying Jewish history. The success of *Dreyfus: The Musical* suggests that there is more than one way to bear witness and perhaps, in the end, as they say in show business: there's no such thing as bad publicity. Hallowing the past can be a form of erasure as much as ignoring it. Since the Holocaust, every Jewish writer is a eulogist.

3   Tricksters: Wolf Mankowitz's "The Finest Pipe-Maker in Russia," James Lasdun's "Ate/Menos *or* The Miracle," and Elena Lappin's "Noa and Noah"

If stereotypes are the cornerstones of group hatred, tricksters are the foundation of anti-Semitism. With Jewish tricksters from *Oliver Twist* to *The Protocols of the Elders of Zion* (never out of print or popularity), why would any Jewish writer want to create one? This question is especially relevant given that the trickster underpinned justification for the Final Solution. The three short stories in this section offer some answers.

Mankowitz's "The Finest Pipe-Maker in Russia" is one of a group of *shtetl* stories under the title "A Village Like Yours" in the 1957 collection *The Mendelman Fire*. While its publication predates the stories by Lasdun and Lappin by thirty-five and forty years and its setting by even more years, "The Finest Pipe-Maker in Russia" contains features which all three stories have in common. First, the trickster is a good character. Second, belief is integral to his or her trickery but it also has another significance which can justify the deception. Mankowitz introduces both features in the first words of his short story:

> My great-grandfather was certainly the finest pipe-maker in Russia [. . .] Once, however, my great-grandfather made a bad pipe – and even then he made it bad for a good reason. [. . .] It happens that this pipe was bad because of what took place on a Sabbath morning. Not that my great-grandfather made the pipe on a Sabbath. I would not like anyone to think that of him. (Mankowitz 1957: 69)

After establishing that the pipe-maker was a good craftsman *and* observant Jew, Mankowitz explains why he compromised one identity to maintain the other. The story has echoes of a fairy tale in which a tailor has to finish a whole suit in one night. In this case, a Russian lord orders a pipe with an eagle on it to be made on the Sabbath when, of course, work or any kind is prohibited. An exchange between the two men about duty foreshadows what happens next. The pipe is made on the Sabbath but the eagle's feathers are actually Hebrew letters and the wings form the Prayer for the Dead. By giving all his attention to the letters not the shape of the pipe, the pipe-maker compromises his craft but not his faith. The pipe is no good for smoking only for praying. Consequently, the pipe-maker observes the Sabbath and tricks the Russian prince into observing it as well. In this and other stories in *The Mendelman Fire*, Mankowitz *re*claims the Jewish trickster from the hands of anti-Semites and *re*turns this figure to God's. It is a bittersweet return, however, as anti-Semitism did eventually wipe out the *shtetl*. Like many of Isaac Bashevis Singer's stories, "The Finest

Pipe-Maker in Russia" is set in earlier times yet cannot help but evoke the Holocaust to come.

Whereas Mankowitz's writing moves in and out of Jewishness (and Irishness after he moved to Ireland for the later part of his life), Lasdun's writing seems to circumvent it entirely. Despite this, Lasdun's "Ate/Menos *or* The Miracle," from his 1992 collection *Three Evenings and Other Stories*, raises similar issues of identity, belief, and the empowering potential of words. And while there is nothing which says that Lasdun's trickster *is* Jewish, there is nothing which says that he *is not*. In fact, the trickster/narrator seems as blank as "the big blank freedom of the day" that he describes (Lasdun 1992: 3). No name. No address. No school. The short story is built on "nots." Its first sentence — "Sunday morning" — is not a complete sentence (3). The narrator is "not a believer, let alone a Christian, and had seldom been near a church since leaving school" (4). Yet, he takes Holy Communion, which is, in his own words, "committing a sacrilege" (4). When a woman in the street mistakes him for a theater director called Matthew Delacorta, he does not correct her then, after she invites him to her home, or while she seduces him. The word "no" ends the short story after the woman's husband exposes the fraud and she cries "drawing out the word into an anguished wail that pierced the air" as the narrator "ran from the house, repeating itself over and over, 'No, no, no . . . o . . . o . . . o . . .'" (28). Unlike the pipemaker's trickery, there is no higher purpose to this one since the narrator has no belief in anything. And that is his problem. Like Josipovici, Lasdun does not *make* his narrator Jewish but he does raise issues which may be called Jewish such as whether secularity is a form of belief or its negation and if the latter, as the motif of negativity suggests in "Ate/Menos *or* The Miracle," then is this self-erasure desirable or ultimately destructive? What comes through most in Lasdun's short story is how Christian-based British culture is and how alienating this can be for those who are not Christian. Jews are obviously not the only group who might feel the effects. But secular Jews are in the unique position of being from the only group that was subjected to religious expulsion in Britain, destruction under the Final Solution, and whose ability to assimilate is equated with trickery, conspiracy, and, as the infamous *Protocols of the Elders of Zion* suggests, plan to rule the world.

Lappin's "Noa and Noah," from her 1999 debut collection of short stories called *Foreign Brides*, is unique in that it depicts an Orthodox Jewish female trickster. This reclaiming of the trickster from male hands is an interesting twist on both the negative stereotype and the empowerment which *re*creation gives. Noa, like the narrator in "Ate/Menos *or* The Miracle," sees no higher purpose in her trickery. It is something which she seems almost accidentally to fall into. There is a snowball effect in Lappin's short story as in Lasdun's which begins when a character goes somewhere that he or she does not belong. For Lasdun's narrator it is a church. For Lappin's Orthodox wife, it is an Irish butcher's shop. There is a similar element of *passing* which both transgressors are aware of and which loads this act with an element of danger and mischief. The ease of *passing* is striking, so is the sense of spiritual trespass. Inherent in both short stories by Lappin and Lasdun is an acceptance by their protagonists that they do not have the same access to all of London as other Londoners. Physical space and objects, even for Lasdun's non-believer narrator, are weighted with spiritual significance which makes belief systems as tangible as bricks and mortar. Spiritually ghettoized by a lack of belief or different belief, these tricksters feel a strong sense of power when they break rules. Like poachers who trespass then shoot game which they later eat, these tricksters go where they should not and consume what they should not. Lasdun's narrator eats a communion wafer, drinks the cocktails meant for Matthew Delacorta, and sexually consummates his reunion with an actress. The Orthodox wife in Lappin's short story consumes and consummates as well, by cooking her husband non-kosher chicken and sleeping with the butcher. "Noa and Noah" ends more happily than "Ate/Menos *or* The Miracle" when it turns out that the deceived husband never wanted to observe *kashrut*. Declaring themselves vegetarians, Noa and Noah begin their marriage anew with an honesty that had previously been lacking. Lappin's female trickster betters life by her transgression and, in common with many of the women in *Foreign Brides*, is a Jewish seductress with smarts. A *New York Times* reviewer describes these women as having "the reckless spirit of tourists traveling without visas" who "would rather rely on improvisation and luck to get where they are going than follow a set of binding conventions. The men they desire are there to be outfoxed, not obeyed" (Amidon). In Noa and many of the other women in *Foreign Brides*, Lappin creates a feminist model of empowerment, a virtuoso of ingenuity, which recasts negative stereotypes of the trickster Jewish male and destructive Jewish seductress in the light of contemporary Jewish lives, emigration, Israel, and Central European experience.

4   Wanderers: Dan Jacobson's "The Zulu and the Zeide" and Clive Sinclair's "The Evolution of the Jews"

Wandering minstrels are romantic. So are gypsies and troubadours. Wandering Jews are another matter. Although in actuality, Jews left *en masse* at different times in history, the literary image is generally that of a solitary wanderer, driven out by necessity, not a desire for freedom, one who is essentially sad and lonely. After the Holocaust laid bare the precariousness of Jewish assimilation in Europe, the image of the wandering Jew has acquired new meaning. It might, after all, represent a preferred state of being, one without illusions which need not be wholly negative. Jacobson's much anthologized short story, "The Zulu and the Zeide" from *A Long Way From Home: And Other Stories* (1958), recreates the wandering Jew as a positive figure in a society with little about it to admire. This happens when a grandfather or "zeide" goes out walking, hand in hand, with Paulus, the young Zulu who looks after him. The deep friendship which the two develop is in marked contrast to the coldness and friction between the elder Grossman and his son. Despite the fact that they share no language, the *zeide* and the Zulu conduct long conversations as they walk. Their intimacy is not lost on the old man's son who eventually sends Paulus away, an act which results in the elder Grossman's death when a bicycle strikes him as he searches for his former companion.

Despite the *zeide*'s death, Harry is the tragic figure who cries in despair at the end of the narrative when he learns that Paulus had been saving his wages "to bring his family to this town also" (Jacobson 1958: 121). The word "also" likens the Zulu's hopes of migration from Zululand to the Grossman family's immigration from Europe. To this black servant, it is obvious that Jews and blacks are not naturally wanderers but people forced to be on the move. Given that it is the nineteen fifties, the proximity of the Holocaust makes the Grossman immigration particularly fortunate. Yet, survival comes at a cost. Family ties are broken not only with those who are left behind but also for future generations. As Paulus is the better "son" than Harry, this Zulu is the better Jew. Paulus's bearded face, unlike Harry's clean-shaven one, even suggests this as he resembles the old man. Perhaps what is most significant is that it takes a black man to remind this assimilated son what it means to be a Jew. Harry's tragedy is not merely that he strives to erase his Jewishness but that he replaces it with a model so similar to that which scorned and ghettoized his own family in Europe. "The Zulu and the Zeide" responds to the times and was in some regards ahead of them. It dares to racialize Jews even after the Holocaust made this anathema. It also introduces notions of performance which predate whiteness studies and pivotal works such as Karen Brodkin's *How the Jews Became White Folks and What That Says about Race in America* by four decades.

Sinclair's "The Evolution of the Jews" is a masterful short story from the 1979 (later edition 1983) collection *Hearts of Gold* which recasts the wandering Jew as a giraffe. In this first person tale of survival, the giraffe/narrator takes no personal blame for wandering but places this firmly on the shoulders of the anti-Semites, or lions, who threaten his existence. It begins thusly: "'Remember you are a Jew,' my father said when I was old enough to stand on my own four feet. As if the anti-Semites would let me forget! [. . .] Now they have my scent. And I am in danger" (Sinclair 1983: 65). Despite the short story's brevity, the short story evokes and tramples upon numerous negative stereotypes of Jews. According to its narrator, wandering is no more natural for Jews than anyone else. It does not stem from an inclination towards cosmopolitanism any more than an inability to become attached to any one habitat. It is the necessity of a group under threat for generations. To illustrate these points, Sinclair interweaves key words from the history of Ashkenazim with those from natural history as the narrator speaks of anti-Semites "killing Jews in the miombo" and "pogroms in the nyika" (64). This displacement of actual events from their real settings is a reminder of the displacement of Jews forced to flee as the giraffe/narrator must.

Unusual juxtapositions can be funny. In "The Evolution of the Jews," they are unsettling. By relocating anti-Semitic violence from Europe to Africa, Sinclair *resensitizes* the reader to the meaning of words such as *pogrom* and what is effectively an acceptance that Jews are subject to violence in Europe. The African words also remind the reader that this is a story about hunting and being hunted which is part of nature's order unlike the persecution of Jews which has no parallel in nature but is part of human history.

Sinclair's affably horned giraffe/narrator serves much the same purpose as the mice in Art Spiegelman's graphic novel *Maus* and Mickey Mouse in Horst Rosenthal's 1942 pamphlet *Mickey au Camp de Gurs*. It subverts the imagery of anti-Semitism, in this case the medieval image of the Jew as a horned devil. While the image of the wandering Jew is not altogether negative, it is also challenged by the giraffe/narrator's litany of persecution. He is not pursued merely to feed the lions but because giraffes are blamed for every calamity in Africa from droughts to floods. With the word "libel," the giraffe/narrator evokes the blood libels and expulsion of Jews from England. The tone of "The Evolution of the Jews" is nearer that of a stand-up comedian than of the narrator in Jacobson's "The Zulu and the Zeide." Yet, both short stories challenge the image of the Jew as a "natural" wanderer by evoking and challenging perceptions of Jews that were central to the Final Solution.

5 Exiles: Michelene Wandor's "Song of the Jewish Princess" and Neil Gaiman's "In the End"

Exile is inseparable from Jewish literature. They go hand in hand. In the Anglo-Jewish short story, exile often takes place beyond Britain's borders and in times outside the experience of its writers. Two interesting examples are Michelene Wandor's "The Song of the Jewish Princess" from *False Relations*, published in 2004, and Neil Gaiman's "In the End" from *Fragile Things: Short Fictions and Wonders*, published in 2006. Where Wandor finds her inspiration in history, Gaiman finds it in the Bible.

Wandor is a writer of short stories, poetry, plays for stage and radio, and a musician. Her short stories reflect this range by mixing genre and being highly adaptable for performance. The fluidity of Wandor's creativity mirrors the movement and resilience of her exiled characters. "Song of the Jewish Princess" is set during and just after the expulsion of Jews from Spain in 1492. While a languidly romantic tone might seem at odds with such violence, this is what makes the short story so powerful. Its narrator, a fiddler called Isabella, is the antithesis of the "Jewish American Princess" alluded to in the title. She is neither spoiled nor frigid. "Princess" also evokes images from fairytales, but happiness is short-lived after an Italian duke marries Isabella. In contrast to Cinderella or the derogatory image of a "JAP," Isabella explains: "*I am the original Jewish princess* [. . .] *The authentic article* [. . . .] *Play me. I shall sound true to you*" (Wandor 2004: 11). Italicized passages such as this are interspersed throughout the short story. They ostensibly concern fiddle playing but, as they become shorter and events around them become more violent, it is obvious that they express Isabella's feelings as a woman and a Jew. On the eve of the expulsion from Spain, for example, she compares herself to a string on a fiddle that is "ready to snap" and no longer sounds "true" to itself (15). Its sensuality distinguishes this short story from a fairytale as does the violent ending for its heroine. On the eve of her beheading, punishment for having an affair with the son of an Italian duke who married her, she plays her fiddle and remembers, for the first time, the color of her mother's eyes. Since the Inquisition, she could only recall her mother's charred body. Ending the short story on this note suggests that there is power in remembrance. Isabella goes to her death with this at least to hold. Similarly, she recalls a lover's smells of "cloves and chamomile, mixed with the acrid savour of satisfaction" long after he is gone (13).

Remembrance is the stuff of literature. For Jewish writing since the Holocaust, it has even greater significance. While Wandor chooses an earlier period in European history, its parallels are striking. Similarly, by giving voice to this victim of the Spanish expulsion, Wandor personalizes the event and surmounts the challenge which writers of the Holocaust face – how to give a face to the numbers. Passages such as *"Every text contains within it the music of a thousand others"* suggests that telling the story of one Jew is to tell the story of many others. Isabella is hunted as her mother was and more than six million Jews would be centuries later. Repeated scenes of hiding in this short story evoke similar patterns in those set during the Holocaust. Other parallels also arise through images of exile which are self imposed (Isabella and her mother's denial of their Jewish identities) and imposed by others (the expulsions). In common with other Anglo-Jewish writers, Wandor depicts the Jewish family as one whose heirlooms are stories of exile.

Exile is recurring in "The Jewish Princess" but is reversed in "In the End." This single page short story rewrites the expulsion of Adam and Eve from the Garden of Eden and, by inference, removes this legacy for all subsequent generations. In Gaiman's version, Adam and Eve are called "Earth and Breath" and are given the entire world *except* the garden which "the Serpent with the flaming sword" guards for "the Lord" (Gaiman 2006: 233). Earth and Breath bring the fruit to the garden and are let in. Although reversing all events, Gaiman maintains a tone that evokes the original thusly: "Then Earth and Breath knew their clothedness, and removed their garments, one by one, until they were naked; and when the Lord walked through the garden he saw the man and the woman, who no longer knew good from evil, but were satisfied, and He saw it was good" (233). Besides reversing their expulsion, Gaiman undoes creation. The short story ends with the Serpent going "proudly on four strong legs" out of the garden where "there was nothing but silence [. . .] save for the occasional sound of the man taking away its name from another animal" (233).

Although "In the End" is a reversal of everything in the original Garden of Eden story, its similar sequence of events suggests order not disorder. Its assured and reassuring tone reinforces the impression that inclusion rather than exclusion might have been given us all a better start. Alternatively, its convincing reproduction of the Bible chapter prompts a reconsideration of attitudes towards suffering, particularly to do with exile. Might history have been kinder with another first chapter or author? As a writer of fantasy fiction, Gaiman is known for creating unusual worlds. These often critique real life. In its recreation of the beginning of the Bible and, by inference, of the prototype for life to follow, "In the End" offers a new and more positive model. While loss can be negative, the gentle tone of the last sentences suggests that when Adam takes away each animal's name it is comparable to freeing them from a chain of pain and exile in the world.

REFERENCES AND FURTHER READING

Brauner, D. (2001). *Post-War Jewish Fiction: Ambivalence, Self-Explanation, Transatlantic Connections.* Basingstoke and New York: Palgrave.

Cheyette, B. (1998). *Contemporary Jewish Writing in Britain and Ireland: An Anthology.* Lincoln: University of Nebraska Press.

Fainlight, R. (1994). "Another Survivor," *Dr. Clock's Last Case: And Other Stories*, pp. 75–83. London: Virago Press.

Gaiman, N. (2006) "In the End," *Fragile Things: Short Fictions and Wonders*, p. 233. New York: HarperCollins/William Morrow.

Isler, A. (1998). "The Affair," *The Bacon Fancier: Four Tales*, pp. 159–215. London: Vintage (original work from 1997).

Jacobson, D. (1958). "The Zulu and the Zeide," *A Long Way from London: And Other Stories*, pp. 102–21. London: Weidenfeld and Nicolson.

Josipovici, G. (1987). "He," *In the Fertile Land*, pp. 63–75. Manchester: Carcanet.

Lappin, E. (1999). "Noa and Noah," *Foreign Brides*, pp. 1–17. London: Picador.

Lasdun, J. (1992). "Ate/Menos *or* The Miracle," *Three Evenings and Other Stories*, pp. 3–28. London: Secker and Warburg.

Mankowitz, W. (1957). "The Finest Pipe-Maker in Russia," *The Mendelman Fire*, pp. 69–77. London: Andre Deutsch.

Roberts, S. (1984). *Dan Jacobson.* Boston: Twayne.

Sicher, E. (1985). *Beyond Marginality: Anglo-Jewish Literature after the Holocaust.* Albany: State University of New York.

Sinclair, C. (1983). "The Evolution of the Jews," *Hearts of Gold*, pp. 64–9. Harmondsworth: King Penguin (original work from 1979).

Wilson, J. (1995). "From Shanghai," *Schoom*, pp. 75–92. London: Penguin.

Wandor, M. (2004). "Song of the Jewish Princess," *False Relations*, pp. 11–22. Nottingham, UK: Five Leaves Press.

28

Feminist Voices: Women's Short Fiction after 1945

Michael Meyer

A normative definition of feminist writing would ignore the great diversity of feminist theorists and writers of fiction concerning the position of women as social beings, discursive subjects, or others beyond representation (Eagleton 1996). Neither patriarchal society and discourses nor feminist responses are monolithic. The pragmatic approach taken here looks at how texts negotiate women's positions in a critical way in various aesthetic forms rather than prescribing in an essentialist manner that a story is only feminist if it presents "woman" in a particular aesthetic form. According to a basic and inclusive, rather than exclusive, definition, feminist texts expose patriarchal discourses and practices that discriminate against and marginalize women, and privilege female characters, perspectives, actions, and discourses. In the light of the feminist canon and the given era, this selection of writers is limited to female authors of post-war publications, bracketing the fact that some male writers take up feminist issues. The following survey roughly groups writers according to the criteria of whether they produce mimetic or non-mimetic fiction, and the time of publication of their texts. The analyses cannot be exhaustive and only cover a few characteristic examples by each writer.

The writers considered fall into three groups, as follows. (1) Irish realism: The Irish authors Mary Beckett, Evelyn Conlon, Edna O'Brien, and Julia O'Faolain tend to write realist stories with occasional forays into satire, farce, and gothic tales. The feminist view of Irish women's private lives and perspectives provides a counterpart to the rich tradition of short stories by male Irish authors. Frequently, the stories are located in rural settings and bemoan women's isolation, exploitation, and repression at the hands of hypocritical men and in the name of stifling religion. (2) From mimetic to non-mimetic fiction: Doris Lessing writes in the tradition of mimetic realism; Fay Weldon in that of mimetic and non-mimetic fiction. Lessing explores the impact of exile, ethnicity, and class on the female psyche in racist southern Africa and in Great Britain in realist and symbolic stories. Fay Weldon exposes female complicity in and rivalry under patriarchy, but also reveals ways to change in realist, satirical, and gothic stories. (3) Moderate postmodernism: Janice Galloway, Angela Carter, and A.S. Byatt can be called moderate postmodernists. Janice Galloway frequently offers disturbing female perspectives on Scottish lower-class life in fragmentary fiction. Angela Carter and Antonia S. Byatt rewrite patriarchal texts, experimenting with content and form in order to defamiliarize gendered norms. They often interlace references to real-world concepts with elements of fantasy, and employ inter-textual and meta-fictional strategies (Moosmüller 1993: 303, 318, 367).

Irish Realism

Mary Beckett (b. January 28, 1926, in Belfast, Northern Ireland)

Mary Beckett's stories, beginning with "The Excursion" (1980), which won a BBC contest in 1949, set the topic and the tone for much of Irish women's post-war realist fiction, because it portrays a woman's intense suffering from dependence, exploitation, and isolation, with her escapist dreams and her acts of resistance. The protagonist, Eleanor, who has been talked into a "sensible" marriage for financial reasons, finds herself stuck with a man who is as miserly with his words as with his affection and his money. She is reduced to being his servant and farmhand, albeit without pay. Thus, she cannot even go on an excursion to Dublin without asking him, like a child, for money and permission, which she avoids in order not to be humiliated by his denial. Instead, he joins the excursion, and her dreams of improving their relationship are now linked to his new experience instead of hers. When he comes home totally drunk, not having seen anything but a pub in Dublin, she gives vent to her pent-up frustration and gives him a murderous shove that almost lands him in the fire — simultaneously, an image of her duty to create a cozy home and of her burning rage. However, her single and limited act of rebellion will not dissolve their emotional and social paralysis.

A sense of missed opportunities, uselessness, emptiness, and waste also haunts Beckett's other female characters, who are often fettered to listless and unloving husbands. Many of these unhappy women are complicit in their repression, but a few muster the strength and courage to change their lives. In the story "Ruth," an illegitimate daughter leaves her community at her coming of age. The women gossip about her joyless character but also come to see that they enacted the misogynist social censure because they treated the illegitimate girl worse than a dog. In order to save her illegitimate and half-black baby from the orphanage, the eponymous protagonist of the story "Theresa" (1980) keeps her child, marries, and braves both her husband's and the community's racist ridicule.

In several stories, conflicts between Protestants and Catholics threaten women's lives. In "A Belfast Woman" (1980), the Catholic Mrs Harrison looks back on a life of persecution and repeated evictions. As extremist Protestants want to drive her out of her home again, the elderly Mrs Harrison takes her private stance of resistance: she refuses to leave but also refuses to endorse retaliation by the IRA. Beckett's short-story sequence *A Literary Woman* (1990) changes the setting from lower-middle class in Northern Ireland to middle-class Dublin. Her topics, however, remain the same. Beckett's realistic fiction delves again into women's frustration and alienation, but rarely explores attractive options for women beyond marriage, a fact that limits her criticism of patriarchal society.

Edna O'Brien (b. 1930 in Tuamgraney, Ireland)

Edna O'Brien explores her main topic of female desire in depth, which has given rise to praise, but also to criticism for transgressing norms of decency (Hosmer 2006: 274). O'Brien's women face a social and a psychological conundrum. The author asserts the sexual needs of women within and outside marriage, in the face of the repressive and hypocritical society that is patriarchal and Catholic Ireland. O'Brien maintains that, in contrast to the frequently cited oedipal complex, silence prevails about the daughter's desire for her mother, which can never be fulfilled (Hosmer 2006: 274). Her frequent choice of girls as narrators, witnesses, and protagonists in search of love is of psychological and aesthetic interest because of the drastic difference between the girls' romantic dreams and social reality, rendered with great sensitivity through the double perspectives of the experiencing and the narrating self.

The title story of the collection *A Scandalous Woman* (1974) is told by the ally and confidante of the beautiful Eily. Eily is caught in the act with her lover, who turns away from her when she is pregnant. They are forced to marry in order to make her "an honest woman." Her best friend, the witness and narrator, does not dare to stand by her under harsh social pressure. She registers with a shock that Eily, who gives birth to three children, goes mad under the strain of abuse, and seems to have been brainwashed because she reveals no memory of her painful past. O'Brien's female witness grippingly registers the girls' anxiety under an oppressive atmosphere, and the daring if futile attempt to escape it. The narrator's conclusion mounts a devastating criticism of Ireland: "I thought that ours indeed was a land of shame, a land of murder, and a land of strange, throttled, sacrificial women" (O'Brien 1984: 265).

The story "A Rose in the Heart of New York" (1978) belies the romantic associations of its title because it begins with a stark and naturalistic description of a woman giving birth to a daughter in impoverished circumstances. Mother and daughter develop a symbiotic relationship: "Her cup was full. Her mother was the cup [. . .] a gigantic sponge, a habitation in which she longed to sink and disappear forever and ever" (389). The daughter despairs when she is sent to a convent school, where a "nun became her new idol" (389), who is then replaced by her husband in a hasty marriage that fails, because she is unable to cope with the separation from her mother. She is haunted by strange dreams, such as "a bowl with her mother's menstrual cloth soaking in it and her sacrilegious idea that if lit it could resemble the heart of Christ" (393). The story focuses on the daughter's illegitimate desire for communion with her mother. The daughter, who feels abandoned, is haunted by a wish to kill her mother. After her mother's natural death, the daughter finds an envelope with money but no letter. The mother's death and her silence reassert that the daughter's desire can never be fulfilled. The representation of female desire, in an almost naturalist style with disturbing symbolic images, could have served Julia Kristeva as a case study for disruptive feminist writing and goes far beyond O'Brien's predominantly realist prose.

Julia O'Faolain (b. June 6, 1932, in London)

Julia O'Faolain was educated at a convent school in Ireland and has lived for long periods in Italy, France, and the United States. For Lorna Rooks-Hughes, both Edna O'Brien's and Julia O'Faolain's feminist criticism is limited: "although both authors are critical of the power of the Church and patriarchy, their fiction reinstalls the family as an inevitable and defining cultural structure within which women are effectively controlled" (1996: 86). O'Faolain shows sympathy for deviant women, but they are dislocated if they do not accept the identities of wife and mother (Rooks-Hughes 1996: 89). Her foregrounding of, and explicit descriptions of, sexual encounters have met with several critics' censure, whereas others have appreciated the shifting perspectives in her stories (Clandfield 2006: 290, 293). It is true that many, if not most, of her female characters are driven by passion, albeit in the double meaning of sexual desire and suffering. O'Faolain's ambiguous depiction of sexuality invites reflection rather than voyeurism, because her realism is often inflected by irony and a tendency towards the grotesque, farce, and satire.

O'Faolain's monologues by women strongly convey feelings of alienation, isolation, and despair in predominantly realist narratives, which prefer the ordering retrospect to recording the present disturbance in an aesthetic of disruption. The title story of O'Faolain's second collection of short stories, *Man in the Cellar* (1974), unravels her female character's typical double bond: "I was riveted by a resentful passion to one man. I resented his violence, also his having filled my mind with trivia, interrupted my independent life and drawn me into the game of playing house" (28). Since she can no longer bear the abuse and violence from her sadistic Italian husband, the protagonist chains him to a bed in the cellar. The story is written in the form of her letters to Carlo's mother asking her to release him, and to her husband, explaining her position. Her experience is fraught with irony. Having shackled her husband, she does not feel free at all because she has to take more care of him than before. In symbolic terms, the cellar represents her womb, and the chains the umbilical chord and the marriage that bind her to her husband as the potential mother she refuses to become. The story "Oh My Monsters!" (1982) can be read as a companion piece to "Man in the Cellar," because it also presents a woman's reflections on a relationship of love and hate. The story, however, has a different ending. The thirty-five-year-old Anne-Marie, who lives a fast life of pleasure, decides to return to her "monster," the schizoid Sam, rather than to her "normal" sister and the "Furies" of convention. In addition, her monstrous body threatens to overwhelm her: "Mentally I'm wound around, head between my own legs, eyes and brains swaddled in a monotonous cuntscape" (64). She escapes into dreams: "When I'm woken up I panic" (64). The escape from "normality" does not liberate her from the patriarchal world, but promises indulgence at the price of being punished by her insane lover.

The title story of *Daughters of Passion* (1982) is told from the perspective of Madge, who is on hunger strike in prison. Her reflections waver between associative thoughts of her present suffering from hunger and thirst and a – psychologically less convincing because more coherent – retrospect. Hers is a story about three female Catholic Irish friends, who get "involved" with the IRA. The orphan Madge, who loses her faith and her lover, tries to keep out of politics but assassinates a British Detective Inspector, who threatens to frame her political friend Dizzy and her friend Rosheen's husband, the victimized but abusive Sean. In prison, she is pushed by an IRA agent to claim political status, but drifts, instead, into a vision of her ex-lover, a dream that reveals her personal rather than political motivation. However, the story does not speak out against female political agency, but rather for a more complex consideration of women, politics, and violence.

Evelyn Conlon (b. November 5, 1952, in Rockcorry, Ireland)

Evelyn Conlon is more optimistic than Edna O'Brien and Julia O'Faolain about women's skills to manage their lives, to circumvent conventions if need be, and to develop new perspectives. She counters the silencing of ordinary women's experience in male fiction and history, and "explores everyday life in contemporary Ireland" (Nordin 2006: 56), its minor gratifications, and its discontent. She treats women's plight with both compassion and a sense of humor.

Her story "Telling" has a writers' workshop for women as its setting. A great male Irish writer tells the participants the true story of how a husband abuses and kills his wife who wants to leave him, taking their children with her. The writer offers them the subject matter as raw material because he does not need it, leaving the women smoldering with rage in "a kind of communal choking smothering their voices" (21). The story exemplifies the condescending dismissal by patriarchal institutions and individuals of women's suffering as a topic for serious male fiction, although it is deemed still useful to fledgling women writers for the subject of an exercise. The story "Taking Scarlet as a Real Colour, or And Also, Susan" (2000) explains why women's experience is relegated to the margins by male discourses. The first-person narrator realizes that public events that make the news and become history have nothing to do with her private existence, but rather leave her with "the aching embarrassment of being no one from nowhere" (47). She turns to books for solace but becomes so enraged about their image of women that her emotions gush out of her in a long monologue to her friend Susan: "What they didn't say about us is bad enough until you find out what they did say; yet, bad as that is, there is nothing worse than what they didn't say" (48). She points out that they omit, for example, female desire and agency; the process of giving birth to babies or aborting them. Conlon writes books about ordinary women, being aware that they cannot be pinned down because "the state of us, it varies so much there is no possibility of describing it" (53).

Conlon's story "Park-going Days" (2000) presents such lower-class women, for whom a simple day of sunshine and gossiping in the park is "a great day," as they remark time and again, just because nothing happens to them and their many children. They take the usual disappointments of being married to their husbands as part of their lot. However, such marginalized ordinary women form the substance of society: "Kathleen sighed. Bridie put her varicose veins on the wheel of the pram. These – the fat, the veins, the sighs – were the shapes of the backbone of the country" (198). Conlon's humor and her reassessment of the importance of ordinary lives could be mistaken as an effort to make light of women's experience and to endorse passivity and resignation, but she also gives examples of women who resist the limitations imposed upon them.

From Mimetic to Non-Mimetic Fiction

Doris Lessing (b. October 22, 1919, Kermanshah, Persia)

Lessing covers a wide range of female characters from various backgrounds in her stories, characters whose experience reveals more similarities than differences. Even if Lessing overtly condemns imperialism in southern Africa, where she mostly grew up, she sometimes reproduces colonial values, such as the dichotomy between African nature and patriarchal white culture (Hanson 1986: 113). Hanson argues that, according to the artist's own distinction, Lessing's style in the African stories is often masculine, highly selective, and abstract, dealing with "the *typical* rather than the particular event or perception" (1986: 110), as opposed to the indirect female style, "which is concrete, sensuous, and predominantly metaphorical" (1986: 108). Rick Oehling states that her characters "are exiled from the land, from each other, from themselves" (2001: 244); men appropriate the land, and women are alienated by it (Hanson 1986: 111). White women's isolation is multiplied because the problems of gender are compounded by differences of race, class, generation, culture, and the lack of social contact due to the scattering of farms over the vast territory.

In the story "Winter in July" (2003), after years of restless wandering, the competent and versatile Julia meets two half-brothers in South Africa, with whom she lives as if they were siblings. She marries the non-possessive and tolerant Tom, while being more attracted to the quick-witted younger brother, Kenneth. The strong, ageing woman experiences an identity crisis when her husband is absent for three years in the war and Kenneth marries. She realizes that, while her marriage had given her peace and freedom from material concerns, she is "still floating rootlessly, without support; she belonged nowhere" (2003: 230). After having dismissed the option of becoming a mother, the forty-year-old woman asks herself who she is, feeling that she still is a stranger and "a critical ghost" in Africa. Her exile on the arid continent becomes an allegory of women who have the potential to succeed in life, but are alienated by the hard, competitive world dominated by indifferent men. Julia's sensible marriage, her confusing, submerged "no-man's-land of feeling" (237), her inklings of evil and her flirtation with nihilism and death prefigure the story "To Room Nineteen" (Lessing 2002a): Julia's life could have resembled Susan Rawlings's fate if Julia had had children. Susan, the protagonist of "To Room Nineteen," is privileged because she has married a well-off husband, has nice children and a big house. Soon, the relationship between the insensitive husband and his wife disintegrates. She has given up her job in order to become a perfect mother and housewife, but she feels trapped in family life and tries to be "reasonable," repressing her frustration and her rage about his affairs. Visions of evil haunt her, possibly because of feelings of guilt, repressed jealousy, and aggression, disturbing her sense of sanity and reality. She retreats first into a room of her own in the house, then into an anonymous hotel room in order to feel free, and finally she commits suicide. The story takes the form of an intrusive and omniscient third-person narration, which wavers between detached observation and empathy, then often drifts into the technique of dual voice as if sharing the character's experience. The reason, order, and meaning provided by society no longer make sense to the woman protagonist and erase her as a person. Her suicide is an act of despair but one that establishes her as an agent, ultimately liberating her from patriarchal society.

Lessing's collected stories (2002a, b) castigate male chauvinism ("One off the Shortlist"), hypocrisy, and violence ("Mrs. Fortescue"). They also offer models of female independence and self-reliance ("Our Friend Judith"), liberation from heterosexual relationships by female bonding in a realist story ("The Other Woman"), or a fabulist one, in which a woman literally hands her transformed heart to another woman, rather than "losing" it again to one of the men she is attracted to ("How I Finally Lost My Heart").

Fay Weldon (b. September 22, 1931, in Alvechurch, England)

Fay Weldon is as concerned with moral issues in relationships as Lessing, but is less pessimistic concerning women's ability to cope. Weldon, who does not belittle women's suffering, has a satiric vein that ridicules men's and women's shortcomings alike. She depicts the absurd twists and turns of her characters' lives, but often ends her stories on a conciliatory or even optimistic note. Weldon deals with all sorts of social and sexual forms of private relationships and their psychological impact in mimetic and non-mimetic stories.

Instead of enjoying her leisure time, the "Weekend" (1981) adds to a plain housewife's chores. Her burden is compounded by providing for her husband's recently divorced friend and his new attractive girlfriend, who serves as a humiliating countermodel and a warning that a lover might replace her as well, if she cannot fulfill her husband's expectations. His voice dominates her submissive and tortured mind. A nervous breakdown is the result of the enormous pressure she experiences. The story

"In the Great War" (Weldon 1985) suggests an alternative solution to female competition for men. In the beginning, a daughter called Enid takes her plain mother's abandonment as a warning and strives to be a winner by displacing a professor's wife. In turn, Enid is abandoned and gives birth to a daughter. However, she is reconciled to and supported by her stepdaughters; she studies and enters a professional career. In recent stories Weldon (1995, 1998) deplores the return to ruthless competition in a post-feminist and individualist era that spurns her feminist ideal of women's solidarity.

In order to depict women's repressed psychological injuries and coping strategies, Weldon resorts to gothic stories, which deal with the subconscious and the return of the repressed, and to monologic narratives that externalize inner conflicts. Ghosts appear as manifestations of women's fears, sufferings, and desires in cyclical plots. The title story of Weldon's first collection, *Watching Me, Watching You* (1981), is about the third wife of a man who has replaced his previous spouses with younger ones. Two ghosts haunt the story, one in the shape of a feminist omniscient and intrusive narrator, the other as the shadow of a hanging woman, the spirit of a previous tenant, who was betrayed by her husband and committed suicide. The young wife manages to break the spell by separating herself from her husband and establishing a bond of solidarity with her two divorced predecessors. Weldon places female insight, agency, and solidarity against victimization by replacement or escaping by suicide. Weldon's monologic narrations form something like female talking cures in the professional setting of psychotherapy or in the confessions imposed upon others in chance encounters. In the narrative "A Gentle Tonic Effect" (1991), an amoral and competitive employee suffers from nightmares, which express her guilt for the neglect of her son and her promotion of a harmful pharmaceutical product, which causes birth defects. The story "Down the Clinical Disco" (Weldon 1991) criticizes the patriarchal imposition of what can be called "heterosexist" norms. A woman, who has been treated for sexual deviance in a mental institute, tells a stranger that the enforcement of offensive heterosexual practices erased her capacity to engage in loving relationships.

Moderate Postmodernism

Janice Galloway (b. 1956 in Saltcoats, Scotland)

Janice Galloway is more experimental and less traditional a writer than Lessing and Weldon. She often records the disturbing inner processes of her female protagonists in fragments that transcend the boundaries of realism, verging on the grotesque and the surreal (McGlynn 2001: 7–10). Galloway's collection *Blood* (1991) provides a frame of two stories about shy girls' embarrassing bodily experience of their first menstruation and molestation. Galloway also presents robust responses to male abuse. A little girl proves not to be afraid of "Fearless" (Galloway 1991), a small but aggressive derelict, who stares and shouts obscenities at her mother. She stares back and kicks him. While she is told off by her anxious mother, the experience proves to be seminal for her defiant attitude towards aggressive men.

Galloway both draws on and debunks traditional tales. In the sketch "It Was" (1991), an elderly woman has lost her bearings and finds a little face in the dirt, which suddenly turns into her old uncle George. He takes her for a cup of tea but does not know that he is dead. Probably, the kind uncle is a figment of her imagination fed by her loneliness. In "Fair Ellen and the Wanderer Returned" (1991), the wanderer's romantic expectations are disappointed since the woman, who indeed had been waiting for years, finally married, and even if she were widowed, would prefer to be free now.

The collection *Blood* contains several dramatic scenes, which are numbered but disconnected from each other and apparently chosen at random. These dramatic pieces have a defamiliarizing effect on three levels: (1) they frustrate the reader's expectation of a coherent narrative and create an awareness of the art of representation; (2) the scenes with stage directions and explicit authorial comments on characters and the spectators' responses reveal theatrical conventions and prevent the readers' identification with the characters; (3) the scenes depict the performative and theatrical quality of life. We become witnesses of fragments of offensive male gossip in "Scenes from the Life No. 29: Dianne," the stretching of time in an old woman's solitary existence in "No. 26," or twenty-four hours in the life of a single everyman as a strange pantomime in "Scenes from the Life No. 27: Living In."

Galloway's second collection, *Where You Find It* (1996) also "re-creates her characters' fragmented impressions and moments of realisation, suggesting the elusiveness of love, human warmth, and happiness" (Sánchez Calle 2006: 83). This is a darker collection than her first. The new volume often explores deviant desire and destructive relationships. In the ironically titled story "Valentine," a woman submits to being the sexual object of a callous control freak, a substitute for love, which is formally "celebrated" on Valentine's Day without any corresponding emotion on his side. At the hairdresser's, a female customer is "Waiting for Marylin," a sexy hair stylist whom she desires, but she angrily realizes that Marylin is engaged. In the stories "Bisex" and "Not Flu," a woman struggles with her boyfriend's homosexual contacts and their dire consequences. The monologue "Someone Had To" displays a sadistic father's rising anger about his six-year-old stepdaughter's passive resistance: "STAND UP KIMBERLY curling in a corner NOT EVEN TRYING TO STAND UP just watching while I shook her, I lifted her up put the cigarette onto the skin of the wrist it was MEANT TO BE A LESSON all she needed to was say she was sorry to STOP not knowing when to STOP" (1996: 138). Of course, he himself does not know when to stop and reacts with a shocking incremental repetition of violence.

Angela Carter (b. 1940 in Eastbourne, England;
d. February 16, 1992. in London)

Angela Carter also offers sex and violence as key topics, but prefers fantasy and historical fiction to realism and a depiction of contemporary life. Carter won fame by her retelling of tales with gothic elements. Critics are divided over the question whether she repeats traditional tales and reaffirms gendered norms or rather revises them in a defamiliarizing and feminist way (Benson 2001: 33–7). However, by retelling tales and foregrounding their gendered and sexual dimension, Carter exposes their ideology (Benson 2001: 43–4). She reiterates female desire with a difference in an ambivalent way, which invites both identification with the voyeuristic spectacle of sado-masochism and reflection on its gendered bias and function.

Carter plays upon variations of the story of Beauty and the Beast, in plots full of sex and violence and with surprising turns of plot. In "The Loves of Lady Purple" (1974), the Beauty is the Beast. A puppet master performs a play about an oriental whore, who allegedly turned into a puppet because she was only driven by desire. The puppet master's kiss inadvertently revives the lifesize puppet. She sucks his breath and blood, burns his theater, and leaves for the nearest brothel. The fact that she is a mute puppet, who is animated by her master's "articulating fingers" and his voice, reveals her status as a figment of his imagination and as his other. His reduction of her to an expression of his own desire and fear turns against him when she becomes alive as a man-eating vampire. She frees herself from the strings that attached her to him without escaping her prefigured role. Thus, the story both enacts and takes issue with the patriarchal and orientalist script of the other, because the ending reveals the lure and the danger of reverse colonization by the oriental in the shape of a prostitute that offers risky pleasures for Western male consumption.

In "The Bloody Chamber" (1979), Carter rewrites the tale of Bluebeard with sensationalist scenes of sado-masochism, but reveals "that 'complicated economic, social, and psychological forces contribute to the objectification, fetishization, and violation of women'" (Robin Ann Sheets, qtd in Benson 2001: 39). A young poor piano-player from Paris makes an excellent marriage by marrying the richest man of France, a Marquis. He, however, sadistically "deflowers" her and orders her not to visit his secret chamber while he is away. She discovers the victims of his sadistic murders in the secret, locked torture chamber. The young woman's mother saves her from execution for her transgression. The story enacts and revises gendered scripts. The semi-orphaned teenager at first seems to follow the script of romance, but it turns out that she has consciously sold herself to the Marquis in order to escape poverty. However, she resents his treatment of her as if she were a prostitute. She musters courage and defies him after having had a glimpse of both her own strange desire and his perversion. She survives with female instead of male help, and forms something like a patchwork family with her mother and a blind piano-tuner, who cannot subject her to the possessive male gaze. Carter's self-reflexive voyeurism is an effective strategy for confronting male and female readers with the desires and terror of the misogynist text.

Carter combines the legends of the werewolf with the tale of Little Red-Riding Hood in "The Company of the Wolves" (1979). She transforms Little Red-Riding Hood into a curious and fearless adolescent girl, who sleeps with the werewolf instead of being devoured by the predator. It is remarkable that she has sex with the animal

male in the bed where he has just killed her grandmother, an act that recklessly discards any traditional female role model.

Carter's historical meta-fiction similarly rewrites representations of deviant and
marginalized historical characters. Jeanne Duval is the "Black Venus" (1985), whom
Baudelaire "saves" from a brothel, only to take her as his mistress and as inspiration
for his poetry. Carter shows the erotic and melancholic relationship of two alienated
souls. Upon the poet's death, the elderly black woman goes to the West Indies and
runs a brothel, which infects bourgeois men with the decadent poet's venereal disease.
The process of contagion can be taken as an ironic form of a subversive, bodily revenge
of the repressed on a hypocritical, racist, and sexist society. Even if Carter stresses that
the black woman has a mind and soul of her own that is beyond the male gaze and
grasp, she can only survive by performing a role within the patriarchal economy of
desire.

A.S. Byatt (b. August 24, 1936, in Sheffield, England)

A.S. Byatt shares Carter's interest in the body and in inter-textuality, but also attaches
importance to inter-mediality. Byatt began her career as an academic and became a
full-time writer of fiction in 1983. Her poetic language abounds with aptly chosen
words, memorable phrases, precisely rendered sense perceptions, and pertinent metaphors. Sabine Coelsch-Foisner succinctly characterizes the complexity of her fiction:
"The solid, visible, tangible world constantly points to realms that are the province
of fantasy – hesitation, uncertainty, and ambivalence – and the province of experiment
as far as narrative strategies are concerned" (2006: 43). Byat's self-reflexive fiction
focuses on the gendered construction of reality, the rewriting of tales, and the functions of visual art.

"Sugar," the title story of her first collection of stories (1988), provides an insight
into Byatt's feminist analysis of verbal representation as fabrication. A female writer
tries to find her identity and origin by reconstructing the history of her family. Her
memory is as full of scattered impressions and gaps as the reports she receives. The
truth is inaccessible because experience itself is already a "storied event, already lived
over and over, in imagination and hope, in the invented future." Byatt's story takes
its cue from a poem by Goethe, which deploys and undermines the gendered binary
system, because it suggests the combination of serious male control and humorous
female fabulation, defying the search for original meaning and identity. Quoting
Goethe, Byatt foregrounds inter-textuality and renounces any claim to the alleged
originality of male authorship, as her first-person narrator does. In Kristevan terms,
patriarchal discourse thwarts the representation of women's desire and identity. It is
highly symbolic that the narrator's father was a judge, who was interested in evidence
and truth, and who denies his wife's claim to truth. Ironically, his daughter has to
take recourse to her mother's unreliable tales and myths, which are characterized by
a digressive, cyclical structure, and by fabrication; these subvert the masculine power
game of linear "truth and consequences." The unreliable female narrator combines

her father's and her mother's fragments and episodes in a complex feminist "confection," marked by uncertainty, process, and possibility, rather than by coherence and truth.

Byatt rewrites tales as Carter does, negotiating generic and gendered conventions. "The Story of the Eldest Princess" (Byatt 1994a) is a meta-fictional tale about a princess, who knows about, and feels trapped in, stories of failure, but who, nevertheless, leaves the path of her given quest in order to pursue one of her own. She passes tests and arrives at the house of an old wise woman, who praises her thus: "You had the sense to see you were caught in a story, and the sense to see that you could change it to another one. And the special wisdom to recognize that you are under a curse" (66). The oldest princess becomes the wise woman's companion, while her younger sister fulfills the quest and rules the country. Women are successful in various ways: the old, wise and single woman establishes a private space of her own; the oldest princess rewrites gendered scripts and retreats from the heterosexual order; and the youngest princess masters the conventions and rises to a powerful position in the public sphere. The story about the princess is a good example of Byatt's rejection of those traditional tales which imprison female characters in "stories of stopped energies" and "strangling, willed oblivion" (Byatt 1994a: 121).

"The Chinese Lobster" (Byatt 1994b) deals with the gendered production of and response to visual art. A young, anorexic, and depressed art student, who hides her body in "hideous" clothes, spreads faeces on reproductions of Matisse's paintings of women. Her own body is part of her counter-art, a protest against the masculine cult of the voluptuous but mute female body. In opposition to Matisse's depiction of women, she deflects the male gaze from her outward appearance and directs it to what in Kristeva's term could be called the abject. The artist accuses the Distinguished Visiting Professor, who advocates the aestheticist separation of life and art and rejects her work, of sexual harassment. The Dean of Women's Studies, who suffers from her ageing body and depression, understands his aestheticist stance but also feels for the feminist student, whose art is "meant to disgust and desecrate." The academic dandy's aggressive reaction can be explained by the fact that he can cope neither with the criticism of the sexist aesthetics he shares, nor with the (Kristevan) abject as a reminder of the repressed m/other and his own corporeality.

The feminist appropriation of realism is more overtly political than the experimentalist subversion of it. Realist stories invite readers to identify themselves with specific types of patriarchal practice and with forms of women's resistance in their society. However, experimental feminist fiction also takes issue with linear and logo-centric patriarchal discourses as inadequate ways of constructing female experience. In both realist and experimental fiction, the (dialogic) female monologue, in the shape of a letter, asymmetric oral communication, or the recording of mental processes, provides a pertinent form for women's central experience of being "alone together" in alienating relationships. The experimental use of fantasy externalizes women's fears and desires, which realist fiction often relegates to women's muted inner lives. Intertextual and self-reflexive fiction defamiliarizes and inverts gendered and generic conventions that are usually taken for granted. In spite of the devastating criticism of repressive male-dominated relationships, the stories under discussion only provide a few examples of women moving beyond the heterosexual matrix. Some stories offer models of self-reliant single women and female solidarity, but most of the feminist British writers of short fiction would not go as far as Jeanette Winterson's story "The Poetics of Sex" (in *The World and Other Places* (1999)), which endorses lesbianism and satirizes heterosexual prejudice in the shape of rather narrow-minded questions in an interview about lesbian experience.

REFERENCES AND FURTHER READING

Beckett, M. (1980). *A Belfast Woman and Other Stories*. Dublin: Poolbeg Press.

Beckett, M. (1990). *A Literary Woman*. London: Bloomsbury.

Benson, S. (2001). "Angela Carter and the Literary *Märchen*: A Review Essay," in D.M. Roemer and C. Bacchilega (eds), *Angela Carter and the Fairy Tale*, pp. 30–58. Detroit: Wayne State University Press.

Byatt, A.S. (1988). *Sugar and Other Stories*. London: Penguin.

Byatt, A.S. (1994a). *The Djinn in the Nightingale's Eye*. London: Chatto & Windus.

Byatt, A.S. (1994b). *The Matisse Stories*. London: Vintage.

Byatt, A.S. (2004). *Little Black Book of Stories*. London: Vintage.

Carter, Angela (1997). *Burning Your Boats. The Collected Short Stories*. London: Penguin.

Coelsch-Foisner, S. (2006). "A.S. Byatt," in C.A. Malcolm and D. Malcolm (eds), *British and Irish Short-Fiction Writers, 1945–2000, Dictionary of Literary Biography*, vol. 319, pp. 39–47. Detroit, New York, San Francisco, San Diego, New Haven, Waterville, London and Munich: Thomson/Gale.

Conlon, Evelyn (2000). *Telling: New and Selected Stories*. Belfast: Blackstaff Press.

Clandfield, P. (2006). "Julia O'Faolain," in C.A. Malcolm and D. Malcolm (eds), *British and Irish Short-Fiction Writers, 1945–2000, Dictionary of Literary Biography*, vol. 319, pp. 289–97. Detroit, New York, San Francisco, San Diego, New Haven, Waterville, London and Munich: Thomson/Gale.

Eagleton, M.(ed.) (1986). *Feminist Literary Theory: A Reader*. Malden, Mass.: Blackwell.

Galloway, J. (1991). *Blood*. London: Secker & Warburg.

Galloway, J. (1996). *Where You Find It*. New York: Simon & Schuster.

Hanson, C. (1986). "The Woman Writer as Exile: Gender and Possession in the African Stories of Doris Lessing," in C. Sprague and V. Tiger (eds), *Critical Essays on Doris Lessing*, pp. 107–14. Boston: Hall.

Hosmer, R.E., Jr (2006). "Edna O'Brien," in C.A. Malcolm and D. Malcolm (eds), *British and Irish Short-Fiction Writers, 1945–2000, Dictionary of Literary Biography*, vol. 319, pp. 270–9. Detroit, New York, San Francisco, San Diego, New Haven, Waterville, London and Munich: Thomson/Gale.

Kristeva, J. (1980). *Pouvoirs de l'horreur. Essai sur l'abjection*. Paris: Seuil.

Lessing, D. (2002a). *To Room Nineteen. Collected Stories*, vol. 1. London: Flamingo (original work from 1978).

Lessing, D. (2002b). *The Temptation of Jack Orkney. Collected Stories*, vol. 2. London: Flamingo (original work from 1978).

Lessing, D. (2003). *This Was the Old Chief's Country. Collected African Stories*, vol. 1. London: Flamingo (original work from 1951).

McGlynn, M. (2001). "Janice Galloway," *Review of Contemporary Fiction* 31: 7–40.

Matthews-Kane, B. (2006). "Mary Beckett," in C.A. Malcolm and D. Malcolm (eds), *British and Irish Short-Fiction Writers, 1945–2000, Dictionary of Literary Biography*, vol. 319, pp. 12–16. Detroit, New York, San Francisco, San Diego, New Haven, Waterville, London and Munich: Thomson/Gale.

Moosmüller, B. (1993). *Die experimentelle englische Kurzgeschichte der Gegenwart*. München: Fink.

Nordin, I.G. (2006). "Evelyn Conlon," in C.A. Malcolm and D. Malcolm (eds), *British and Irish Short-Fiction Writers, 1945–2000, Dictionary of Literary Biography*, vol. 319, pp. 56–62. Detroit, New York, San Francisco, San Diego, New Haven, Waterville, London and Munich: Thomson/Gale.

O'Brien, E. (1984). *A Fanatic Heart. Selected Stories*. London: Weidenfeld and Nicolson.

Oehling, R. (2001). "Doris Lessing," in E. Fallon, R.C. Feddersen, J. Kurtzleben, M.A. Lee, S. Rochette-Crawley, and M. Rohrberger (eds), *A Reader's Companion to the Short Story in English*, pp. 241–51. Westport, Conn.: Greenwood.

O'Faolain, J. (1974). *Man in the Cellar*. London: Faber and Faber.

O'Faolain, J. (1982). *Daughters of Passion*. Harmondsworth: Penguin.

Rooks-Hughes, L. (1996). "The Family and the Female Body in the Novels of Edna O'Brien and Julia O'Faolain," *The Canadian Journal of Irish Studies* 22: 83–97.

Sánchez Calle, P. (2006). "Janice Galloway," in C.A. Malcolm and D. Malcolm (eds), *British and Irish Short-Fiction Writers, 1945–2000, Dictionary of Literary Biography*, vol. 319, pp. 80–4. Detroit, New York, San Francisco, San Diego, New Haven, Waterville, London and Munich: Thomson/Gale.

Weldon, F. (1981). *Watching Me, Watching You*. London: Hodder and Stoughton,.

Weldon, F. (1985). *Polaris and Other Stories*. London: Hodder and Stoughton.

Weldon, F. (1991). *Moon over Minneapolis, or, Why She Couldn't Stay*. London: Collins.

Weldon, F. (1995). *Wicked Women: A Collection of Short Stories*. London: Flamingo.

Weldon, F. (1998). *A Hard Time to be a Father. A Collection of Short Stories*. London: Flamingo.

Winterson, J. (1999). *The World and Other Places*. London: Vintage.

29

British Gay and Lesbian Short Stories

Brett Josef Grubisic

1

As a literary subgenus, the "gay and lesbian short story" raises immediate questions relating to definition, identification, and utility. For instance, most generally – and viewed in relation to the complete absence of the "heterosexual male and female short story" as a recognized category of literature – it initiates what could be an acutely political discussion about the need for identification at all. As novelist David Leavitt points out in his introduction to *The New Penguin Book of Gay Short Stories*, such a label is *imposed*, and is reflective of ongoing debate about a culturally divisive topic. The significance of labeling, then, extends well beyond the need for a convenient, strictly literary taxonomy: "Many people ask me if I consider myself a "gay writer." My answer is that the question is irrelevant; as long as the culture I live in considers me a gay writer – and it considers every writer who tackles gay matter a gay writer – I'm stuck with the label" (Leavitt and Mitchell 2003: xxviii).

That broad consideration aside, situating the subgenus historically and defining its core characteristics proves equally challenging. As a historically contingent genre, an argument could be made, for example, that the "gay and lesbian short story" has existed only since the partial decriminalization of homosexuality and concomitant gay liberation in England circa 1967 since that "moment" also inaugurated the political desire to claim specific literary territory for depictions of homosexual lives. Determining its salient characteristics raises additional questions: is a "lesbian short story" necessarily written by a lesbian author? Must it contain central characters that are lesbian (or else risk becoming a "heterosexual short story")? How does a story with one homosexual character get categorized? Need a "gay short story" dramatize one "gay theme" or another (and, if so, what are those)? And what of quantifying an elusive attribute like "gay sensibility"? Consider the case of the London-based poet, editor, novelist, and short-story writer William Plomer (1903–73), who made no overt reference to homosexuality in his numerous publications (though, arguably, he alluded to it: "Local Colour" (1934) is included in Leavitt's gay short-story anthology). Even so, he instructed a colleague to make certain that his biographer treat his sexual orientation seriously because it was important to his work. How can or should one discern the significance or role of his apparently influential gay sensibility, given its textual absence?

These questions are seemingly inherent to the broader scholarship pertaining to "gay and lesbian literature." If nothing else, surveying prefatory comments of anthologists and historians of gay and lesbian literature further illustrates the complexities of defining necessarily restrictive category boundaries, such as those raised by the "gay and lesbian short story." While in *A History of Gay Literature* Gregory Woods confidently asserts that "[i]t is easy to tell where gay literature begins – in openly gay authors' writing explicitly about the experience of being gay" (Woods 1998: xx) (which would mean that *Monopolies of Loss*, gay author Adam Mars-Jones's 1993 short-story collection about the lives of gay men in 1980s London would be eligible for consideration while anything written by Oscar Wilde, for instance, would not), such ease is an exception. Comparatively, Gabriele Griffin, in *Heavenly Love?: Lesbian Images in Twentieth Century Women's Writing*, expresses notable trepidation and introduces frequent qualifiers when she seeks to solve similar puzzles that Woods explains with seeming assurance. She states that the "drawing of the boundaries between what is and what is not lesbian writing is a problematic exercise, highlighting the provisional nature of such categorization" (Griffin 1993: 3). Griffin continues, highlighting the difficulties that continuously arise with acts of definition:

> The answer to the question, "What is 'lesbian writing'?" depends, in part, on where the locus of the establishment of meaning in relation to the text is sited. One may consider this meaning, in this instance the "lesbian identity" of a text, to be determined primarily by the author, by the text itself, or by the reader. This ignores, for the moment, the possibility of a multiplicity of interrelating factors determining meaning. As I shall indicate, each of these ways of determining writing as "lesbian" has implications which question the category such classification is seeking to construct. (Griffin 1993: 3)

Griffin's reference to a multiplicity of interrelating factors atop an already complicated author-text-reader lens for determining meaning is remarkable insofar as it suggests that potentially endless permutations or strata of "lesbian writing." Interestingly, Griffin's study does not ultimately arrive at any definitive or categorical explanation of the lesbian/non-lesbian boundary; instead, she remains content to draw attention to the endeavor's inherent challenges. Following the introduction in *Heavenly Love?*, she subsequently chooses to examine lesbian images in fiction written by women who were for the most part known as lesbian.

In a similar (though far less scholarly) vein, in *The New Penguin Book of Gay Short Stories*, David Leavitt defines – after the customary preliminary handwringing – a gay story "[f]or the purposes of this anthology" as "one that illuminates the experiences of love between men, investigates the kinds of relationships gay men have with each other, their friends, and their families, or explores the nature of homosexual identity. The sex or sexuality of the [story's] author is, according to the definition, irrelevant" (Leavitt and Mitchell 2003: xxiii). Even if that somewhat broad and ambiguous definition is accepted (a story that "explores the nature of homosexual identity," for instance, could be conceptualized from numerous vantage points), an earlier comment by Leavitt also warrants attention because it points out how his later working definition for the anthology required suppression of knowledge about the arbitrariness of that very definition:

> What makes a "gay story" gay? This is a more complicated question than it may first sound. Traditionally, anthologies of so-called gay fiction have collected stories by gay male writers writing about the lives of gay men. And yet, numerous gay male writers, from antiquity to the present day, have written fiction that at least explicitly has nothing to do with gay experience – even though it may exhibit a "gay sensibility" or "gay style" (two more problematic terms). Likewise, numerous heterosexual written have written fictions that deal eloquently with male homosexuality. What about them? (Leavitt and Mitchell 2003: xxii–xxiii)

Like Griffin, Leavitt here acknowledges the complex, politically provocative nature of definition. Yet, as his anthology-tailored definition makes plain, he sidesteps the seemingly messy philosophical quagmire inherent to the simple question, "What makes a 'gay story' gay?" because a contingent, site-specific and provisional definition suffices. (Leavitt's anthology and others, such as *The Faber Book of Gay Short Fiction* edited by Edmund White, may prompt further concern from purists, though not about sexuality: in selecting, for instance, an excerpt from D.H. Lawrence's 1911 novel *The White Peacock* or Ronald Firbank's 1926 novel, *Concerning the Eccentricities of Cardinal Pirelli*, and identifying them as "short fiction," the editors are in essence inventing discrete short stories where none previously existed.)

Since the philosophical conundrums listed above render plain the essential complications of the "gay and lesbian short story" as a label and a historical phenomenon, and refute the comforting notion of an objective categorical definition, provisional guidelines necessarily serve to mark the way to a workable model that takes into account literary changes (that are closely tied to the transforming historical visibility of homosexuality, which in turn relates to the relaxing of hostile social attitudes and the status redefinition in legal and psychiatric fields). In keeping with Leavitt, then, author sexuality, while suggestive, does not provide an adequate basis for category eligibility. After all, an author who is lesbian might choose to stock her work exclusively with heterosexual characters. Or author sexuality may need to be historically situated (and here the example of a figure like Oscar Wilde, who was by no means an "openly gay author writing explicitly about the experience of being gay," is illustrative; despite being openly gay in neither life nor print, Wilde plays an iconic role in any gay literary history). Moreover, given that homosexuality has long been deemed criminal, a sin, and a sickness, there is no surprise in learning that Woods's politicized gay-writers-writing-gay become rare to the point of being fully camouflaged in the decades preceding the sexual revolution. Though the intentional visibility and self-conscious (literary) territory claiming that were part of the gay liberation politics that began in the late 1960s well serve the reader or scholar in search of unequivocally gay literature that is specifically defined as being that written by "openly gay author writing explicitly about the experience of being gay," its relative absence in pre-liberation discourse also encourages scholarship to scrutinize texts that stand beyond the patently "lesbian" (lesbian characters in a lesbian community enmeshed in lesbian plots and themes) or the self-defined "gay" (gay author writing gay character, setting, and theme). While that requires reliance on such eye-of-the-beholder terms as "homosocial" and "homoerotic" (as well as the "gay style" and "gay sensibility" that Leavitt found ambiguous and problematic), it also emphasizes the cultural imposition that made such invisibility necessary in the first place.

2

Late Victorian and Edwardian England witnessed an unprecedented growth in awareness and visibility of the discourse about sexuality. Pioneering European psychiatrists and sexologists such as Sigmund Freud, Karl Heinrich Ulrichs, Havelock Ellis, Magnus Hirschfeld, and Richard von Krafft-Ebing were not yet household names, but their works and ideas circulated extensively and their provocative case studies and hypotheses percolated throughout mass culture. This emergent discourse, which must be viewed in relationship to Wilde's profoundly public 1895 trials and their aftermath (for example, commenting on W. Somerset Maugham's careful avoidance of homosexual themes and characters, the novelist Glenway Wescott contended that, "Willie's generation lived in mortal terror of the Oscar Wilde trial" (Summers 1995: 469)), led to generalized consciousness of both the variety of sexualities and the repercussions for those who expressed or made visible their "perverse" and punishable non-normative sexuality.

An integral aspect of discursive dissemination, period literature expressed "fact," opinion, utopian visions, alarm, and conjecture in differing ways and to divergent degrees. Hence, while the era's activists and ideologues wrote increasingly of sexuality – for instance, Edward Carpenter spoke approvingly in radical tracts about the "intermediate sex" and "homogenic love" (1894) and later championed homoerotic pairing in *Iolāus: An Anthology of Friendship* (1902); John Addington Symonds remarked on homosexuality's official "unspeakableness" in his *Memoirs* (composed between 1889 and 1893, circulated privately, and unpublished until 1984) and called for law reforms based on sexological research in *A Problem in Modern Ethics* (1891); and Max Nordau loudly protested the various symptomatic perversions (Wilde amongst them) of *fin de siècle* Europe in his best-selling, era-defining treatise *Degeneration* (1895) – it cannot be said that short fiction of the era was explicit in the same manner. The lack of directness relates of course to the undeniable danger – for publishers and authors alike – that being homosexual or writing about it without condemnation could represent. Alan Sinfield argues in *The Wilde Century* that "[u]ntil the Wilde trials, effeminacy and homosexuality did not correlate in the way they have done subsequently" and "the trials helped to produce a major shift in perceptions of the scope of same-sex passions" (Sinfield 1994: 4). At that point, Sinfield continues, "the entire, vaguely disconcerting nexus of effeminacy, leisure, idleness, immorality, luxury, insouciance, decadence and aestheticism, which Wilde was perceived, variously, as instantiating, was transformed into a brilliantly precise image (Sinfield 1994: 3). In short, Wilde and his work embodied homosexuality, and that "brilliantly precise image" was both dangerous and a cautionary tale. Nor does this pervasive caution and hesitance to directly textually represent sexuality and explore minority sexualities remain restricted to Victorian or Edwardian England. While the successful banning of Radclyffe Hall's putatively obscene novel *The Well of Loneliness* in 1928 and, as late as 1960, the censorship trial of D.H. Lawrence's "pornographic" novel *Lady Chatterley's Lover* have numerous political implications, the anxiety their print depictions produced also speaks volumes about the disruptive power widely accorded to frank images of sexuality, normative or otherwise.

Heightened wariness about public examination of sexuality does not, however, mean virtual suppression of discourse. Instead, it produced discreet or clandestine discussion, one that might be called inferential. In his study *Homosexuality and Literature 1890–1930*, Jeffrey Meyers speaks of how the "clandestine predilections of homosexual novelists" created a tension between repression and expression that in turn produced a characteristic mode of discourse; the supposed "inarticulate feelings" in the novels, according to Meyers, "force the authors to find a language of reticence and evasion, obliqueness and indirection" (Meyers 1977: 1) to convey their themes. And, indeed, Meyers's view finds support with literary historians such as Claude J. Summers, Terry Castle, and Gabriele Griffin, who trace a lineage of stories, though the detective work tends to rely on inference: the scholarship refers to the necessarily coded expression and to pointed allusions, oblique references, subtexts, and even "apparitional" presences within texts. An example of this practice of detection (evident as well in scholarship about authors whose work was ostensibly focused on heterosexual relationships, such as Elizabeth Bowen, Charlotte Mew, and Ivy Compton-Burnett) can be witnessed in analyses of the fiction of Saki (H.H. Munro). In particular, "Gabriel-Ernest" (circa 1910) has been explicated as a covert and anxious contemplation about the disturbing physicality of male homosexuality. While that short story – about a foundling with "savage propensities" whose short-lived stay at a well-mannered, "primly ordered house" eventually causes chaotic discord – can easily be viewed as reflecting imperialist anxiety about the colonized non-white subject, the very ambiguity of the story does not preclude the alternate "homosexual panic" interpretation.

As progenitor figures of homosexual literature (and specifically of gay and lesbian short fiction), Oscar Wilde, E.M. Forster, and Radclyffe Hall are paramount. Even so, their bequeathal can be understood with ambivalence: while all three did incorporate discussion of homosexuality in their work to varying degrees, they were reticent in their depiction and arguably more apologetic than championing in attitude. Wilde, for instance, widely viewed as *the* grandfather figure of gay literature, published numerous works – from *The Importance of Being Earnest* and *Salomé* to *The Picture of Dorian Gray* – that have been studied as exemplifying coded and clandestine investigations about homosexuality through their artifice, epigrammatic humor, allusion, and veiled references. Though *Lord Arthur Savile's Crime and Other Stories* (1891) contains recognizable elements of Wildean wit and characterization, it is Wilde's lengthy short story – a game of indeterminacy and ambiguity in Peter Ackroyd's view – "The Portrait of Mr. W.H." (1889; extended and revised version published 1921), that has drawn critical attention for its investigation of homosexual themes. With its effete aesthete characters and highly mannered style, the story does not veer far from the dialog-laden essays of *Intentions* (1891) that celebrate aestheticism, such as "The Decay of Lying" and "The Truth of Masks." Claude J. Summers notes that while the lengthy story has be read as playful investigation of the identity of the young man to whom Shakespeare dedicated his *Sonnets* ("To the Onlie Begetter Of These Insuing Sonnets Mr. W.H. All Happiness"), it can also be interpreted as an idealization of homosexual relationships, a cautious defense of homosexuality, and an enunciation of the "continuity of homosexual feeling from the past to the present, even as that recognition culminates in an acknowledgement of the dangers of self-discovery and an awareness of gay oppression" (Summers 1995: 745). The narrator's conclusion – a repudiation of the hypothesis explaining the identity of the mysterious W.H. – offers the possibility that knowledge can have significant drawbacks if revealed in a discouraging cultural context.

Born nearly three decades after Wilde, E.M. Forster approached the topic of homosexuality in his fiction with anxious caution: the gay short stories were direct and explicitly gay, but were also written over a number of decades and designated as not publishable. Symptomatic of their author's anxiety presumably, an unknown number of them were also destroyed. Forster's diary for April 8, 1922, records that during an intermittent "smut scratch" the author had burnt his "indecent writings or as many as the fire will take" (Martland 1999: 163). While an early published story, "Story of a Panic" (1904), in which the intense friendship of two boys is broken up, can be discerned (like Saki's "Gabriel-Ernest") as cautiously examining the workings of heteronormative social regulatory forces, it is Forster's "indecent" writings that develop more fully diverse representations of homosexuality. Alongside *Maurice*, Forster's suppressed novel of a gay romance, these stories were published in *The Life to Come and Other Stories* (1972), following Forster's death in 1970. The stories, written between 1922 and 1958, include the title story (1922), "Dr. Woolacott" (1927), "Arthur Snatchfold" (1928), "The Classical Annex" (1931), "What Does It Matter?: A Morality" (circa 1930s), "The Obelisk" (1939), "The Torque" (circa 1958), and

"The Other Boat" (1958). In depicting (in the order they were written), the love between an Indian chief and an English missionary; the relationship between a sickly young man, an apparition, and their doctor; an aristocrat and a milkman; sexual adventure between a museum curator's son and a statue; a Pottibakian politician and a policeman; between a married schoolmaster and a sailor; an early Christian and a pagan; and a failed shipboard romance between a British officer and an Indian named Cocoanut, the stories are remarkable for their sophisticated and diverse incorporation of homosexual character and theme. The satiric fantasy of "What Does It Matter?: A Morality" and "The Classical Annex," and the humor of "The Obelisk," are well counterbalanced by the solemnity of "The Other Boat" and "Dr. Woolacott." That said, critics have questioned the literary value of the unpublished stories. For instance, Meyer dismissively assesses them in *Homosexuality and Literature* as banal "guilt-ridden and joyless episodes," trapped by their Edwardian conventionality: "It is both surprising and depressing to discover that these puerile, sentimental and thoroughly unimaginative fantasies, which lack Forster's characteristic subtlety and wit, actually excited the elderly novelist and occupied his creative mind for forty years" (Meyers 1977: 108).

Part of Forster's social network, Radclyffe Hall, whom Terry Castle identifies as "the most famous and intransigently 'sapphic' personality of the postwar years" (Castle 1996: 59), was not an isolated figure but rather an integral aspect of an overall flowering of lesbian discourse. In fact, historians of lesbian literary history cite burgeoning discussion and representation of lesbians, and what Jane Rule identifies as "lesbian sensibility," in the early decades of the twentieth century, taking note of diverse prose and verse from Ivy Compton-Burnett, Charlotte Mew, Sylvia Townsend Warner, Elizabeth Bowen, Virginia Woolf, H.D., Naomi Jacob, and Rosamund Lehmann. In *Surpassing the Love of Men*, Lillian Faderman contends that generally the discussion was antagonistic: "Twentieth-century fiction, reflecting society, played a large role in keeping women down through associating feminism with lesbianism and lesbianism with everything horrible" (Faderman 1981: 341). In support, she cites numerous early twentieth-century British novels, from Clemence Dane's *Regiment of Women* (1915) and Dorothy Sayer's *Unnatural Death* (1927), to Naomi Royde-Smith's *The Tortoiseshell Cat* (1925) and *The Island* (1930), Compton Mackenzie's *Extraordinary Women* (1928), and G. Sheila Donisthorpe's *Loveliest of Friends* (1931).

Far more sporadic than their novelistic counterparts, lesbian short stories nonetheless reflect ambivalence at best about lesbianism's origins, psychology, and rightful place in society. Hall's "Miss Ogilvy Finds Herself" (1926) exemplifies such a conflict of attitudes. Hall, whose 1928 novel *The Well of Loneliness* "remains *the* lesbian novel" (Rule 1975: 50), according to Jane Rule, directly experienced social reprisal when that novel was banned weeks after its publication. Its very appearance inspired outrage, best exemplified by a *Sunday Express* editorial: "I would rather give a healthy boy or a healthy girl a phial of prussic acid than this novel. Poison kills the body, but moral poison kills the soul" (qtd in Castle 1993: 5). If Hall's earlier novel *The Unlit Lamp* (1924) had examined the psychological and biological origins of "inversion," the strange Wellsian title story of *Miss Ogilvey Finds Herself and Other Stories* (1934), described by Hall as an "excursion into the realms of the fantastic," proposes a solution of a sort to the problem that the existence of inverts causes: thanks to a voyage through time, soon-to-be-dead Miss Ogilvy, an alienated former member of an all-woman ambulance brigade in World War I France, comes to understand that she and "her kind" are out of place in contemporary England (and are in fact at home only in the literal caverns of pre-history). As Griffin remarks, "Miss Ogilvy Finds Herself" constructs the "invert as a rather sorry anachronistic outsider, a lower-order rather than a higher-order being" (Griffin 1993: 20), for whom death is not an unwelcome option.

Beyond the prominent literary troika of Wilde, Forster, and Wells, authors such as Ronald Firbank, D.H Lawrence, and Elizabeth Bowen have likewise be analyzed as engaging (if in a circumlocutory manner) with the politics of sexualities within short fiction. Their approaches are as individual as their styles. For instance, Ronald Firbank's eccentric novels and short stories' "unserious treatment of the unusual" in E.M. Forster's view (Hollinghurst 2000: xvi) are often viewed in relation to aestheticism, Proust and, especially, Wilde, and stand out as well for their unconventionality – in particular their formal modernist experimentation and adulation of both style and artifice. Alan Hollinghurst notes that Firbank's "unignorably gay presence" (Hollinghurst 2000: xvii) is evident throughout his droll elliptic novels (such as *Concerning the Eccentricities of Cardinal Pirelli* of 1926), which are generally populated by perverse clerics, lesbian nuns, gay altar boys, and decadent aristocrats. Overall, the often female-centered fiction is remarkable for being fantastical, fashion-conscious and accessorized, oblique, camp, trivial, and pointedly theatrical. True to form, Firbank's "contes" (as he, a dedicated Francophile, called his short stories) are equally notable for their repudiation of realism and their luxuriant detail (i.e., "She glanced stealthily at the sleeping Bishop, and opened her dressing case noiselessly, her hands fluttered undecidedly between her powder-puff and a mysterious-looking box. Would she have time for both?"). The stories, only eight of which were published before his death in 1926 (the remaining manuscripts labeled "Not to be published"), include "A Study in Temperament" (1905), "A Study in Opal" (1907), and "The Wavering Disciple: A Fantasia" (1906). While Hollinghurst observes that Firbank utilized female characters as a sly means of expressing his own homosexuality in later fiction, the short stories serve as examples of juvenilia, and are not so much sly as inferential about homosexuality, implicit principally through Wildean aestheticism and mannered camp.

Forster's contemporary, D.H. Lawrence, influenced by the work of Edward Carpenter, exhibits great fascination with erotic relationships and sexuality in his fiction (as well as in essays such as "Pornography and Obscenity"). There is extensive scholarship about the sexuality of the self-proclaimed "priest of love" that introduces a complex and unfinished debate about the man's true nature (that, variously, labels Lawrence a homophobic heterosexual, an erratic bisexual, a repressed homosexual, and a visionary man whose sexuality aims to subvert the problematic heterosexual/

homosexual binary of Western culture). Accordingly, then, as Summers notes in *The Gay and Lesbian Literary Heritage*, "[p]erhaps no other major modernist author was so continually absorbed in the subject of homosexual desire" (Summers 1995: 438). While Summers diagnoses him as "highly conflicted," it is evident too that he returned to male and female homosexuality over and again in his fiction: when his 1915 novel *The Rainbow* was suppressed and all copies destroyed, a lesbian scene was cited as being obscene; *Women in Love* (1920) depicts the protagonist's unfulfilled quest for a transcendent bisexuality; Faderman's evaluation of *The Fox* (1922), however, suggests that the short novel was serially published in *Dial* because of its conformist moralizing that "[w]omen cannot find satisfaction with each other, to try to do so is sick, and some terrible disaster will befall those who test those truth" (Faderman 1981: 351).

Lawrence's well-documented preoccupation with spirituality, freedom, sexuality, and social roles is also ambiguously conveyed in the short stories, notably "The Prussian Officer" (1914), much anthologized, and the subject of decades of critical debate. Depicting the interactions between an aristocratic Captain and a peasant orderly who hates and eventually murders him, the story anatomizes the possible ecstasy and consequence of extreme experiences and explores the sexual politics of authority. Moreover, its evocation of the Captain's homoerotic attraction and concomitant sadism, and the young innocent orderly's "passion of relief" as he chokes the cruel officer, offers a weird and decidedly anxious parable about same-sex "courtship." "The Blind Man" (1924) envisions a triangular erotic skirmish between the titular character, a primal phallic figure whose magnetic virility (he is called both a "tower of strength" and "a strange colossus") draws the fevered attention of a friend of his wife, a cerebral but impotent man who cannot "approach women physically." The story's crisis, precipitated by physical contact between the two men, disarms the reserved intellect, who is reduced to being "like a mollusk whose shell is broken." Likewise, in another triangular struggle, "Jimmy and the Desperate Woman," a cosmopolitan, albeit disagreeable, author travels to a "demonish" coalmining region in search of a "wild-blooded woman." He meets a married poet whose virile and barbaric husband influences her to such a degree that the eventual marriage between the urban author and rural poet can be accomplished only because the miner is involved. The ultimate, if unexpressed, erotic attraction, then, exists between the two men; the woman acts as a socially sanctioned conduit for their eroticism.

In comparison to the intense passion and violence of Lawrence, Elizabeth Bowen's fiction is resolutely subdued. Likewise, her examination of sexual politics is subtle. Feminist literary historians have nonetheless asserted that the decorous novels and short stories of Bowen have a place in the canon of Western lesbian literature. Rule is characteristic when she claims that Bowen's "work manifests a pattern she seems to see in life, lesbian experience bracketing the heterosexual experience of love and marriage," subsequently noting that Bowen is "reticent about love between women, presenting it always as an emotional need rather than a physical attraction" (Rule 1975: 115). Rule concludes that Bowen "finds nothing unnatural in the love between women, [and] a great deal that is hostile in the world in which they try to survive" (Rule 1975: 124); and she also acknowledges that the affinity between women is not manifested physically. With the distinction between sorority, romantic affection, and erotic attraction effectively blurred, discerning specifically lesbian qualities in the fiction is challenging. For example, Summers cites "The Apple Tree" (circa 1934) and "The Demon Lover" (circa 1944) as examples of "coded" stories containing "homo-erotic pairings" (Summers 1995: 111). The former describes a woman haunted by memories of the death of a girlhood friend. With the help of another woman, the memory is exorcised and she can then disappear into her marriage as one half of a "sublime nonentity," her feminine individuality subsumed by her role as wife. The latter story describes a middle-aged women pursued by and attempting to escape the contract-minded ghost of her dead husband. Summers suggests that the story "might be read as a woman running away from heterosexuality" (Summers 1995: 111). While the story's ambiguity does render that interpretation possible, that same ambiguity does not preclude other readings relating to sexual politics, masculine violence, and marital obligation. Two World War II stories, "Mysterious Kôr" and "The Happy Autumn Fields," feature intimate female friendships that seemingly flourish in response to the absence of men; likewise, "The Jungle" (1929) depicts a charged physical bond between two teenaged girls.

Meyer places Angus Wilson's "gentle satire, elegant style and certain thinness of substance" (Meyers 1977: 107) as part of a tradition of English writers – including Forster, Plomer, and Christopher Isherwood – whose fictional treatment of homo-sexuality was polite but fundamentally anxious and apologetic. In contrast, his biog-rapher Margaret Drabble views the author as someone whose redefinition of the homosexual and exploration of homosexual society in fiction led to a redefinition in society at large. That redefinition involved, for instance, depicting supportive homo-sexual community, announcing the unexceptional nature of homosexuality, represent-ing a range of homosexuals beyond camp or aesthete stereotypes, and identifying homosexuality as part of the ordinary social fabric. This post-war broadening impulse can also be detected in fiction by a diverse assortment of novelists, including Iris Murdoch, Maureen Duffy, Jocelyn Brooke, Mary Renault, Anthony Burgess, and Pat Arrowsmith.

Wilson himself identified a key characteristic of his fiction as positing "the pos-sibility of homosexual happiness within a conventional framework" (Summers 1995: 753) and it is easy to view his first novel, *Hemlock and After* (1952), as evidence of his belief since it features a relatively well-adjusted gay protagonist (about whom, W.H. Auden claimed, reviewers were "horrified, not at the subject, but at [Wilson's] portrayal of queers as no more unhappy than anyone else" (qtd in Woods 1998: 295)). When the comic and gently satiric stories in *The Wrong Set* (1949) and *Such Darling Dodos* (1950) do feature gay or lesbian characters they are the not case studies of depravity or tragic examples of social outcasts that Faderman mentions in her survey of early twentieth-century fiction. Instead they are, like Tony in "Such Darling Dodos," remarkably ordinary, merely one element in a complex social world that include various genders, political allegiances, and moral sensibilities. In contrast, the short stories of Wilson's contemporary Denton Welch, are less hopeful, tending – if they touch on sexual identity at all – to emphasize the deleterious results of self-realization. Published in *Brave and Cruel and Other Stories* (1949), "When I Was Thirteen," for instance, describes moments from the innocent narrator's Christmas vacation skip trip, during which his homoerotic friendship with an acquaintance of his brother results in his being physically attacked by his brother. When the brother yells "Bastard, Devil, Harlot, Bugger" during his assault, the boy realizes that he has learned new words others may soon use to describe him. Noted for his self-obsession and gothic sensibility, Welch was also acutely sensitive to the prevailing political climate. Robert Phillips, who edited *The Stories of Denton Welch* (1985), notes:

> In a number of stories, Welch almost certainly adopted the Proustian Albertine strategy and changed the sex of the protagonist from male to female. These include "The Fire in the Wood," "The Hateful Word," "Anna Dillon," "Weekend," and "Alex Fairburn." Censorship was more strict and sexual freedom less prevalent than it is today. (Phillips 1985: xii)

John Lahr describes Noël Coward's witty and style-conscious work as promoting a frivolity that in turn serves to mask despair about the futility of life. Coward's numerous short stories, written over decades like Forster's, exhibit a progression from implicit to frank depiction and discussion of homosexuality. While earlier collections like *To Step Aside* (1939) and *Star Quality* (1951) are pervaded with a highly mannered stylishness that recalls both Wilde and Firbank, later stories are where Coward focuses on specifically gay characters and situations. Set in Singapore, the lengthy "Pretty Polly Barlow" (1964), for example, tells of the title character's brief stay with her uncle, who has the "amiable, self-centered assurance of a determined bachelor" (Coward 1985: 52). Sophisticated and knowing, her discretely homosexual uncle teaches her how to sidestep the rules of convention and offers life-affirming wisdom to his ward that reflects his own life experiences: "Enjoy yourself and try to remember that life is real, life is earnest and the grave is not the goal" (Coward 1985: 141). Diary-like, "Me and the Girls" (1964) features the reminiscences of a hospitalized former chorus dancer whose recovery from surgery is uncertain. His humor-flecked bedside recollections about his involvement with a touring troupe called the Bombshells is punctuated by wry observations about a woman wearing a "camp hat," an Italian woman who looks like a "wrestler in drag," and "a few poufs round the bar hissing at each other like snakes." Early in the story the voluble narrator also exhibits pensiveness about his sexuality:

> I never was one to go off into a great production about being queer and work myself into a state like some people I know . . . You're born either hetero, bi or homo and whichever way it goes you are stuck with it. Mind you people are getting a good deal

more hep about it than they used to be but the laws still exist that make it a crime and poor bastards still get hauled off to the clink just for doing what comes naturally as the song says. (Coward 1985: 155)

Such directness is wholly absent from the dozen stories published in Coward's two earlier collections. Similarly, while later publications of Graham Greene contain gay and lesbian characters, it is as members of a fictional universe marked by human foible and moral inconsistency. First published in 1962, the darkly humorous title story of Greene's 1967 collection, *May We Borrow Your Husband? and Other Comedies of the Sexual Life*, depicts a narrator watching the strategies of a gay couple who plan to seduce a newly married man on his honeymoon in Antibes. Greene's story deftly anatomizes the *human* capacity for self-deception. Likewise, brief and witty, "Chagrin in Three Parts" offers an account of a luncheon conversation between two French women; the elder one consoles her heartbroken companion by declaring that romance between women and men is hampered by insuperable masculine shortcomings. She explains: "I adored my husband, yet it was only after his death I discovered my capacity for love. With Pauline."

3

Faderman's survey of mid-century fiction publications notes that ludicrous depictions of lesbians stocked popular literature throughout those conservative decades; by her account, the rare exceptions were invariably veiled and "inexplicit" crypto-lesbian representations designed to save publisher and author from reprisal. In her like-minded survey of American lesbian fiction, Bonnie Zimmerman concludes:

> More lesbian novels were published in the United States during the 1950s and early 1960s than at any other time in history. Most, however, were pulp paperbacks that depicted lesbians as tragic maimed creatures trapped in a world of alcohol, violence, and meaningless sex. The plots either doomed them to a cycle of unhappy love affairs or redeemed them through heterosexual marriage. (Zimmerman 1990: 9)

These popular and pulp images were soon to be challenged by a burgeoning alternative publishing industry dedicated to disseminating the work of openly homosexual authors writing explicitly about the experience of being homosexual. Interestingly, while "Claiming Our Space," Griffin's chapter discussing activist lesbian texts in the 1960s and 1970s in *Heavenly Love?*, remarks on the historical invisibility of British Asian or black lesbian fiction, it fails to mention that many of her sample works are not British, but American. With gay liberation politics (and publishers) effectively headquartered in the United States (the novels of British writers Brigid Brophy (1969) and Maureen Duffy (1966) being the exception rather than the norm), the literary component of the queer sexual revolution was likewise dominated by American publishing houses that tended to focus on and support American authors. In short, while the unprecedented growth of gay and lesbian literature was nominally multinational and Western in its reach, there was nonetheless a distinctly American predominance in the output.

Zimmerman also notes that since 1969, the vast majority of lesbian literature has been published by small presses whose overall aim is to establish a "literary and symbolic 'place' for lesbian writers and readers" (1990: xii). Early anthologies, such as *The Lesbian Reader* (1975), favored non-fiction and originated from American publishers. A decade later, however, England accords with Zimmerman's American grass-roots model. Onlywomen Press, Pandora, Virago, Third House, Sheba Feminist Publishers, and The Women's Press, for example, have published scores of books, including anthologies of short stories such as 1984's *The Reach* (the first lesbian feminist fiction anthology published in Britain) and *Everyday Matters 2*, 1985's *The Needle on Full* (lesbian science fiction) and *Girls Next Door* (lesbian short stories), 1986's *Stepping Out* (short stories about friendship between women), 1988's *Incidents Involving Warmth* (lesbian feminist love stories), 1989's *The Pied Piper* (lesbian feminist fiction) and *Out the Other Side* (lesbian short stories), and 1990's *In and Out of Time* (lesbian feminist short stories), to name only a few. Like periodicals, these anthologies provide a popular forum to which new and established authors can contribute, or utilize as venues to further disseminate their stories. *What Did Miss Darrington See?: An Anthology of Feminist Supernatural Fiction* (1989), for example, features "Dreaming the Sky Down" by London's Barbara Burford, whose stories in *The Threshing Floor* (1986) are notable for their often solemn depictions of black working-class lesbian lives (such as "Miss Jessie," which first appeared in *Everyday Matters 2* (1984)).

Such pointedly activist enterprises – the mission statement of Onlywomen Press, for example, declares that it "publishes fiction, theory and poetry by lesbians to express and illuminate a developing Radical Feminism" – have also brought to market numerous collections of lesbian short stories, such as Anna Livia's *Saccharin Cyanide* (1989), J.E. Hardy's *Stranger Than Fish* (1989), Mary Dorcey's *A Noise from the Woodshed* (1990), Caroline Natzler's *Water Wings* (1990), and Cherry Pott's *Mosaic of Air* (1992). The sheer quantity of short stories – hundreds rather than the sporadic offerings of past decades – renders any summary fruitless. The variety, which according to book jacket copy runs from "[m]ore than dykes in space" science fiction, to fiction that examines "family confrontations and connections, futuristic fantasies, struggles with anti-lesbianism, [and] the exhilaration of love," makes plain the breadth of both lesbian experiences and the avenues of expression. Moreover, it is the view of Patricia Duncker, editor of *In and Out of Time*, that the "Utopian impulse in Lesbian writing" (Duncker 1990: 225) seeks not only to celebrate and render increasingly visible lesbian actuality, but to combat such social ills as patriarchal oppression, economic disparity, and racism. Likewise, while Emma Donoghue, editor of *The Mammoth Book of Lesbian Short Stories* (1999), does not adopt a storm-the-barricades posture for her anthology, there is no doubting the political dimension in her identification of lesbian pervasiveness and culture-building industriousness. Lesbian literature, in short, exhibits no shortage of ambition.

Though less overtly politicized than their lesbian counterparts, British anthologies of gay male fiction such as *Mae West is Dead* (1983), *Oranges and Lemons* (1987), and *The Freezer Counter* (1989) express a self-consciousness that their physical presence has a political dimension – if not to the world at large, then to the gay men who read them. The publisher's book jacket overview of *The Freezer Counter* describes the collection of nineteen stories as displaying a broad range of interests, from the mundane to the explicitly topical: "Age-old interests like coming out, forming relationships and the scene are touched on but urgent and more contemporary issues are also examined: AIDS and living in Margaret Thatcher's Britain." Moreover, their purview is not restricted to strictly local cultural formations. Adam Mars-Jones notes, in his acerbic introduction to *Mae West is Dead*, that "America, where social change is chronic as well as epidemic, has played a large part in the shaping of gay attitudes in Britain," and that publishers have paid attention to the relative affluence of gay men with resultant "spectacular success" (Mars-Jones 1983: 14). As indicated by popular anthologies of gay fiction written by an "international" (though in fact largely Anglo-American) assortment of authors – including *The Gay Nineties* (1991), *The Faber Book of Gay Short Fiction* (1991), *Another Part of the Forest* (1994), *The Mammoth Book of Gay Short Stories* (1997), and *The New Penguin Books of Gay Stories* (2003) – "gay" does not require a national affiliation or focus to be successfully marketed; nor does its purview necessarily restrict itself to geographical borders. Like the lesbian anthologies, these anthologies are nurturing forums, granting authors venues for individual short stories that may later be collected into a volume. Story collections like Tom Wakefield's *Drifters* (1984), Simon Burt's *Floral Street* (1986), and Joseph Mills's *Obsessions* (2000), for instance, contain stories that first appeared in earlier gay fiction anthologies. While novels by Neil Bartlett, Alan Hollinghurst, Pat Barker, Michael Carson, Patrick Gale, Timothy Ireland, Ronald Frame, Jamie O'Neill, and Stephen Fry have captured critical acclaim and public attention for their explicit renderings of gay characters, Adam Mars-Jones's 1992 solemn and accomplished volume of stories, *Monopolies of Loss* (featuring four stories from *The Darker Proof: Stories From A Crisis* (1988), his earlier co-collection with Edmund White), might best emblematize Woods's definition of gay literature as "openly gay author writing explicitly about the experience of being gay." The stories range in topic from a gay man improvising a funeral ritual for his eccentric aunt who has suddenly died in front of him on a Scottish beach (in the elegiac "Summer Lightning") to a social network's divided response to the suicide of an HIV-positive friend ("Bears in Mourning"). Observing gay men struggling with universal experiences – love and sex, death and grieving, family and friends, anger and joy – in a specifically gay milieu, the stories have merit both as historical portraits of moments of a particular community and as an evocation of human problems and resolutions.

With *The Line of Beauty*, Alan Hollinghurst's satiric tale of a gay man's engagement with circles of power in Thatcherite England, winning the 2004 Man Booker Prize, Sarah Water's Man Booker Prize-nominated lesbian period romps, *Tipping the Velvet* and *Fingersmith*, being made into popular television serials, and Jeanette Winterson's

Whitbread Prize-winning lesbian coming–of-age novel, *Oranges are Not the Only Fruit*, becoming a best-seller later made into an award-winning feature film, it is abundantly plain that the former criminal and sinful status of homosexuality has been radically transformed. In fact, the "unspeakableness" about the brute fact of homosexuality that John Addington Symonds privately agonized about in his *Memoirs* over a century ago may been both bizarre and incomprehensible to a young generation that witnessed, for example, the fifty-eight-year-old pop star Sir Elton John wed his forty-three-year-old boyfriend David Furnish – alongside 699 other gay and lesbian couples – in 2005. In keeping with that progression, British gay and lesbian short stories have transformed from secretive, anxious, indirect, and coded representations of the forms, concerns, and conditions of homosexuality to being direct, diverse, and unapologetic. If there has not been a revolutionary shift in the short story form, the change in content – the willingness or ability to portray homosexual lives – is nothing short of remarkable.

REFERENCES AND FURTHER READING

Bowen, E. (1981). *The Collected Stories of Elizabeth Bowen*. New York: Knopf.

Castle, T. (1993). *The Apparitional Lesbian: Female Homosexuality and Modern Culture*. New York: Columbia University Press.

Castle, T. (1996). *Noël Coward and Radclyffe Hall: Kindred Spirits*. New York: Columbia University Press.

Castle, T. (ed.) (2003). *The Literature of Lesbianism: A Historical Anthology from Ariosto to Stonewall*. New York: Columbia University Press.

Coward, N. (1985). *The Collected Short Stories. Volume Two*. London: Methuen.

Drabble, M. (1996). *Angus Wilson: A Biography*. New York: St Martin's Press.

Duncker, P. (ed.) (1990). *In and Out of Time*. London: Onlywomen Press.

Faderman, L. (1981). *Surpassing the Love of Men: Romantic Friendship and Love between Women from the Renaissance to the Present*. New York: William Morrow.

Firbank, R. (1990). *Complete Short Stories*, ed. S. Moore. Elmwood Park, Ill.: Dalkey Archive Press.

Fone, B.R.S. (ed.) (1998). *The Columbia Anthology of Gay Literature*. New York: Columbia University Press.

Foster, J.H. (1985). *Sex Variant Woman in Literature*. Tallahassee, Florida: Naiad Press.

Griffin, G. (1993). *Heavenly Love?: Lesbian Images in Twentieth-Century Women's Writing*. Manchester: Manchester University Press.

Hall, R. (1926). *Miss Ogilvy Finds Herself and Other Stories*. London: Heinemann.

Hollinghurst, A. (2000). "Introduction," in *Ronald Firbank: Three Novels*. London: Penguin.

Lahr, J. (1982). *Coward: The Playwright*. London: Methuen.

Lane, C. (1995). *The Ruling Passion: British Colonial Legacy and the Paradox of Homosexual Desire*. Durham, North Carolina: Duke University Press.

Lawrence, D.H. (1994). *Collected Stories*. New York: Everyman's Library.

Leavitt, D. and Mitchell, M. (eds) (2003). *The New Penguin Book of Gay Short Stories*. London: Viking.

Mars-Jones, A. (ed.) (1983). *Mae West is Dead*. London: Faber and Faber.

Martland, A. (1999). *E.M. Forster: Passion and Prose*. London: The Gay Men's Press.

Meyers, J. (1977). *Homosexuality and Literature 1890–1930*. Montreal: McGill-Queen's University Press.

Phillips, R. (ed.) (1985). *The Stories of Denton Welch*. New York: E.P. Dutton.

Rule, J. (1975). *Lesbian Images*. New York: Doubleday.

Sinfield, A. (1994). *The Wilde Century: Effeminacy, Oscar Wilde and the Queer Moment*. New York: Columbia University Press.

Summers, C.J. (ed.) (1995). *The Gay and Lesbian Literary Heritage*. New York: Henry Holt.

Welch, D. (1985). *The Stories of Denton Welch*, ed. R. Phillips. New York: E.P. Dutton.

White, E. (ed.) (1991). *The Faber Book of Gay Short Fiction*. London: Faber and Faber.

Wilde, O. (2003). "The Portrait of Mr. W.H.," Foreword by P. Ackroyd. London: Hesperus.

Wilson, A. (1987). *The Collected Stories of Angus Wilson*. London: Secker and Warburg.

Woods, G. (1998). *A History of Gay Literature: The Male Tradition*. New Haven: Yale University Press.

Zimmerman, B. (1990). *The Safe Sea of Women: Lesbian Fiction 1969–1989*. Boston: Beacon Press.

30

Science Fiction and Fantasy after 1945: Beyond Pulp Fiction

Mitchell R. Lewis

Post-war science fiction (sf) and fantasy were related genres linked to pulp magazines, paperback publishers, conventions, and devoted audiences of fans who occasionally produced their own amateur periodicals known as fanzines. Examples of mainstream sf and fantasy existed, but the two genres were primarily popular forms of writing. In the 1960s, however, "new wave" writers like J.G. Ballard and Michael Moorcock attempted to move science fiction and fantasy toward the mainstream, a trend most notable in the celebrated magazine *New Worlds*. Subsequently, it became more common for mainstream writers to dabble with the two genres, as seen in such short-story collections as Sylvia Townsend Warner's *Kingdoms of Elfin* (1977) and Martin Amis's *Einstein's Monsters* (1987). The result has been some blurring of the distinction between genre and mainstream fiction, but this is a result that is largely recognized only by a minority of readers, writers, and publishers. For the majority, sf and fantasy remain distinguished from the mainstream. In spite of this popular perception, innovative and accomplished short stories, informed by the conventions of fantasy and science fiction, have continued to reveal the literary potential of their genre materials. They often do so, moreover, in the pages of *Interzone*, an important contemporary British magazine that has continued the work of *New Worlds* while also breaking new ground, becoming a vehicle for the publication of all kinds of science fiction and fantasy.

Arthur C. Clarke and Genre SF

In post-war science fiction the most distinguished and popular British writer is Arthur C. Clarke. Influenced by golden age pulp magazines like *Amazing Stories*, *Astounding Science Fiction*, and *Wonder Stories*, Clarke is a genre writer, working within the traditions and conventions of science fiction, but to his stories he brings a philosophical and scientific sophistication rarely seen in the pulp fiction before his time. Clarke's brand of sf, in fact, is often grounded in the "hard sciences" of mathematics and physics. His career began with the publication of "Loophole" (1946) in *Astounding*, but his first celebrated short story is "The Nine Billion Names of God" (1953). This brief third-person story is about a Tibetan monastery that purchases an advanced computer from a Manhattan corporation to complete their long-standing project of compiling all the possible names of God. The monks believe that the computer will allow them to do the necessary work in 100 days rather than in the projected 15,000 years. They also believe that once all the names are tabulated, the world will come to an end, God's purpose for humanity finally being achieved. The head of the corporation, Dr Wagner, finds the project ludicrous, as do his two engineers who assist the monks with the installation and maintenance of the computer, but he thinks to himself that the "customer [is] always right" (Clarke 2002: 418). After three months elapse, the computer prints out the last name and, to the shock of the engineers, the monks were right. They look above at the night sky, witnessing the beginning of the end. In the famous concluding sentence the narrator simply notes, "Overhead, without any fuss, the stars were going out" (422).

The combination of mysticism and science leading toward some kind of transcendental knowledge or evolution is a well-known feature of Clarke's work, but what makes this story interesting is the ambiguity of its conclusion. Clarke could be portraying the transcendental quest for knowledge and the spiritual evolution of humanity, taking the big-picture view of human development that he learned from fellow British science fiction writer Olaf Stapeldon and famously depicted in his novel *Childhood's End* (1953), or he could be portraying a natural catastrophe brought about by the collaboration of science and religion, a plausible reading in the context of Cold War anxieties. The Western engineers are portrayed as cynical businessmen who have no faith. They view a television commercial as "manna from heaven" (419) and a plane as a "silver cross" (421). Their technology is up for sale to anyone who can afford it, and they do not seem to have any purpose beyond profit. The monks, on the other hand, claim that they are on a special divine mission, but their dispassionate, inhuman regard for the consequences of their endeavor is disturbing. Neither the monks nor the engineers are portrayed in a particularly appealing way, and the reader is left contemplating the destruction of the world by people who do not particularly seem to care for it. And yet one could argue that Clarke is portraying the union of science and religion, the latter supplying the mission and purpose to the former. Clarke typically portrays humans as evolving toward divine status in their search for knowledge and understanding. But the conclusion of the story argues for neither reading. The narrator simply gives us the famous last sentence, offering a disturbingly ambiguous ending, and leaving the reader to think about the relationship between science and religion, as well as the East and the West.

Another of Clarke's celebrated stories is "The Star" (1955). In this poignant first-person narrative a Jesuit astrophysicist joins a crew of astronauts whose mission is to investigate a distant phenomenon known as the Phoenix Nebula. A nebula is the gaseous remains of a dead star that explodes at the end of its life cycle. The star first expands, engulfing, and destroying most if not all the planets in its system, and then it explodes, going supernova, propeling dust and gas outward as a small core of matter condenses into a white dwarf, an ineffectual star in what becomes a stellar wasteland. A supernova is so bright that it can be seen across vast reaches of space. While investigating the Phoenix Nebula, the crew discovers what is essentially a time capsule of an ancient alien race that was completely exterminated by their dying star. The narrator struggles to reconcile the extinction of this race with his faith. To compound matters, the narrator finally realizes that the exploding star was seen millennia ago on Earth at the birth of Jesus Christ. It was the so-called Star of Bethlehem whose extraordinary brightness led the three wise men to the manger of the newborn Jesus. The realization that God had killed an alien species to provide a beacon for the wise men irrevocably undermines the faith of the Jesuit scientist. Clarke concludes his short story with yet another resonating, open-ended sentence: "What was the need to give these people to the fire, that the symbol of their passing might shine above Bethlehem?" (Clarke 1959: 119). The question is poised between requiring an answer and simply making a rhetorical point that no answer or justification is possible. What Clarke accomplishes here is a thoughtful and skillfully-crafted meditation on religious and scientific ways of reading the universe and dealing with death, tragedy, and human suffering. As with "The Nine Billion Names of God," in "The Star" Clarke demonstrates the literary and philosophical potential of the pulp science fiction that proved so inspirational to him as a young man.

New Wave SF and the Mainstream

The "New Wave" was a movement of independent sf writers who attempted to bring science fiction toward the mainstream. Although it began in the late 1950s, the new wave flourished in the counter-culture of the 1960s, particularly in the pages of the acclaimed sf magazine *New Worlds*. Under the editorship of Michael Moorcock the magazine became a major venue for new-wave sf from 1964 to 1970. A largely British movement, the new wave included many writers, but three have come to be identified as major figures: Brian Aldiss, J.G. Ballard, and Moorcock. Their best work is original, ultimately transcending the movement for which they are best known, but in general it is characterized by an emphasis on style, self-conscious narrative technique, and imagery, and by a focus on such themes as entropy, the near future, and time. Perhaps the most distinguishing characteristic of their work is its focus on the "soft science" of psychology. The result is a persistent concern with the nature of identity and perception, which usually takes the form of a tragic existentialism.

This concern with the nature of identity can be seen in Aldiss's "The Impossible Star" (1963). The story concerns four astronauts on a cartographic expedition in the Crab Nebula who, in order to repair their ship, are forced to land on what they believe to be a small planetoid. The focus of the story, however, is on the disorientation of the crew whose conventional sense of reality is tested by their terrifying environment. They must deal with a planetoid dubbed Erewhon whose horizon is 100 yards from the ship, and whose rotation period is two hours. To compound matters, a large star named Bertha, possessing twenty-five million times the mass of the sun, constantly redefines the crew's sense of gravity, pulling the crew in its direction as it quickly passes overhead, completing a day in one hour, while also dragging about the planetoid a vapor cloud of melted ice. Bertha, moreover, is so large that light cannot escape it, so it appears as a colossal black hole in the sky, around the edges of which the smaller stars of the heavens are distorted by its huge gravitational effect, appearing to melt. It is finally discovered that the planetoid is really an asteroid that is plummeting into Bertha, not revolving around it. Under the strain of these unsettling conditions one astronaut kills two crew members and eventually strands the other, successfully escaping the planetoid with a lightened ship.

The stranded astronaut, Edy Sharn, articulates the story's concerns with identity. As Erewhon rapidly approaches Bertha, the disillusioned Sharn writes in his notebook, "As this rock is stripped of all that made it seem like a world, so I become a human stripped of all my characteristics" (Aldiss 1971: 100). The last thing he writes before he throws the notebook aside is "I –," and he reflects on the "appositeness" of this final entry (100). The story thus stresses the alienation of the subject, the *I* that is cut off from its environment, unable to comprehend it, to label it. Losing all his conventional frameworks, Sharn must face the existential angst of his situation, that humanity is insignificant in the context of the universe. This theme reflects Aldiss's whimsical definition of sf as "hubris clobbered by nemesis" (Aldiss and Wingrove 2001: 4). Indeed, tracing the history of sf back to Mary Shelley's *Frankenstein* and gothic literature more generally, Aldiss has stressed the importance of sublimity to science fiction, and it is clear that the sublime plays a crucial role in "The Impossible Star." Aldiss's sense of the sublime, however, is not about beauty. It is not uplifting, ennobling, or spiritually transcendent. It is humbling, disorienting, and ultimately terrifying. The story, in fact, clearly distinguishes between these two senses. As the third-person narrator notes, "To begin with, the four men were elated at the sheer magnificence of the new environment. Later, the magnificence seemed not of beauty but of annihilation. It was too big, they were too insignificant. The four men retreated into silence" (Aldiss 1971: 80). Aldiss's sense of the sublime is later reinforced when the narrator characterizes Bertha as a "whirlpool" (84), a clear allusion to Edgar Allan Poe's "A Descent into the Maelström," another story about nature's terrifying sublimity. In effect, Aldiss melds the gothic and science fiction traditions to articulate an existential view of identity.

Ballard's portrayal of psychology draws on the gothic as well, but his work is largely shaped by surrealism. Critiquing the Enlightenment emphasis on consciousness and rationality, Ballard's stories emphasize the unconscious, his dream-like settings

working as externalized representations of the self. In "Manhole 69" (1957), for
instance, Ballard depicts an experiment designed to liberate three human subjects
from the necessity of sleep. Dr Neill, the project leader, sees this liberation as the
next step in the evolution of mankind, the conscious mind's warding off of the unconscious. After an operation, the human subjects are placed in a permanently lighted
observation room with no windows. To pass the time they read, play games, and listen
to music. The subjects do remain awake for an extended period of time, but the prolonged consciousness proves disastrous, as the three subjects withdraw into psychosis,
each believing that the room is encasing them into a "manhole" (Ballard 1978: 37).
The story concludes with Dr Neill reflecting on his mistaken assumptions as he
paternally looks after one of his subjects whose voice seems to come from "the bottom
of a well" (42).

The plot clearly illustrates the surrealist thesis that the unconscious is necessary
for psychological well-being, but what is interesting is how Ballard uses the setting
of the observation room to make this point. Neill explicitly concludes that for the
human subjects the room becomes an "external projection of their own egos" (42),
establishing a connection between a closed, lighted room and perpetual consciousness,
but several allusions flesh out this use of setting even further. The first involves
repeated references to the room as "windowless," which recall the rationalist philosophy of Gottfried Leibnitz, particularly his characterization of the mind as a "windowless monad." Leibnitz believed that this self-contained mind could become a "living
mirror of the universe" through systematic thinking alone, but, like Samuel Beckett,
Ballard satirizes Leibnitz's rationalism, portraying it as a kind of solipsism, a self-
created fantasy or projection. Far from reflecting the world, the mind merely reflects
itself. Not surprisingly, Ballard picks up on Leibnitz's mirror imagery, having Neill
say that each of the human subjects were like "the man in the spherical mirror, who
can only see a single gigantic eye staring back at him" (41). Neill's image is of a self-
contained mind contemplating its own reflection.

Two allusions to Anton Chekhov's "The Bet" (1889) further enhance Ballard's
use of setting. Chekhov's story is about a young idealist lawyer who accepts a
gentleman's bet that he cannot live in a house isolated from human contact for
fifteen years. The lawyer passes his time much like the human subjects in Ballard's
story, reading, studying, and listening to music, learning everything there is to
know, but in the end he goes insane and disappears, leaving a note that says he
despises life, freedom, and health. Ballard uses this story to add further significance
to the setting, the observation room being like the lawyer's house, and the lawyer's
academic pursuits being comparable to rationalist inquiry, as the lawyer cannot rely
on experience or observation. In effect, with "Manhole 69" Ballard reworks Chekhov's story into a surrealist parable about the nature of identity, making explicit
Chekhov's critique of rationalism and working in the surrealist emphasis on the
unconscious.

In "Islands" (1966), Moorcock looks at competing views of identity, with uncertain outcome. The story concerns a sociologist and a psychologist arguing with each

other over the nature of individuality. The sociologist, who is the unnamed narrator, believes that identity is a function of class and social environment, whereas the psychologist, Dr Schmelling, dismisses social influences as superficial, believing that every individual is fundamentally unique. To prove his thesis that "every man exists in his own space–time continuum" (Moorcock 1978: 168), Schmelling recounts his recent experience with a patient named Nicholas Davenport who is suffering from recurring hypnagogic illusions that transform his sense of who and where he is. Schmelling has verified Davenport's claim that he is "an island existing in [his] *own* space, [his] *own* time – in fact, in [his] own universe which has little contact with the universe around it" (173). Moreover, Schmelling develops a machine that can induce the hypnagogic state and, as he reveals to the sociologist at the end of the story, he has built many such machines, set them at strategic points around the world, and plans to flood the planet with their effect, creating a "New Era – the era of salvation" (179). The sociologist dismisses this nonsense but, not long after Schmelling leaves, the narrator begins to experience a hypnagogic illusion.

With this story Moorcock extends the new wave's concern with psychology to include a classic political topic, the relationship between the individual and society. Schmelling argues for a Romantic individualism, emphasizing freedom, individual rights, and "the infinite variety and complexity of human experience" (165). His argument approaches the visionary when, under the influence of the hypnagogic machine, he claims he "saw heaven" and "bands of angels living a peaceful and ordered personal existence – freed from the chains of so-called conformity" (177). The state in which the angels exist "precludes any interference with the lives of their fellows" (177), and Schmelling believes that such a social order "is what politicians have been shouting about for years and never achieving" (177). The hypnagogic machine, Schmelling contends, liberates mankind so that "there will be only independent men and women" (177). The narrator, however, is horrified by Schmelling's argument, which he believes to be anarchic and irresponsible. In his sociological view, "without organization we cannot have civilization – we could not have buildings, or railways or even newspapers" (177). The narrator also sees the rhetorical persuasion of Schmelling, his delight in performing and sophistry. Moorcock himself seems to be ambivalent about the opposed arguments. There seems to be some satire evident in Schmelling's name, which appears to combine the name of the romantic philosopher "Schelling" with the word "smell," yet at the same time Schmelling's argument is the most extensive and passionate in the story. This ambivalence can also be seen in Moorcock's original title for the story, "Not by Mind Alone," which seems to take the side of the sociologist, whereas the later title, "Islands," seems to validate Schmelling's position. On record, Moorcock has argued for the necessity of "an ideal liberal democracy" (Moorcock 1978: 8), a balance between individual and society, but in practice Moorcock's short stories explore all facets of this classic topic in political philosophy, showing how the new wave can situate their psychological concerns in larger social and cultural contexts, much like Sigmund Freud in *Civilization and Its Discontents* (1930).

Michael Moorcock and Dark Fantasy

In the 1960s, Michael Moorcock participated not only in the revitalization of sf, but also in the reinvigoration of epic fantasy, helping to establish one of the dominant modes of contemporary fantasy fiction, dark fantasy. As he explained in his essay "Epic Pooh" (1976), later collected in *Wizardry and Wild Romance* (2004a), Moorcock had been dissatisfied with the Christian allegories of C.S. Lewis's *The Chronicles of Narnia* (1950–6) and J.R.R. Tolkein's *The Lord of the Rings* (1954–5). Their conservative, 1950s portrayal of an ideal rural world – of a pastoral greenwood – encouraged escapism in the face of the harsh realities of the twentieth century, promoting infantilism, nostalgia for an imaginary past, simplistic morality, and sentimental consolations. In fact, in his infamous criticism of *The Lord of the Rings*, Moorcock claimed that the popular trilogy of novels is "*Winnie-the-Pooh* posing as an epic" (Moorcock 2004a: 127). Explaining the historical basis for the rise of such fantasy, Moorcock argued that it was the product of a "morally bankrupt middle class" (127) attempting to evade the decline of Britain, "dreaming of a sweeter past" by turning "to the fantasy of rural life and talking animals, the safety of the woods that are the pattern of the paper on the nursery room wall" (138). Behind the escapist fantasy of the 1950s, Moorcock argues, are the collapse of the British Empire and post-war economic and political problems.

Charting new territory for epic fantasy, Moorcock wrote a series of successful short stories featuring the character Elric of Melniboné. Beginning with "The Dreaming City" (1961) and concluding with "The Singing Citadel" (1967), the ten original Elric stories are situated in a pre-modern world characteristic of epic fantasy, but Elric is a more complicated character than the usual fantasy hero. An anti-hero, Elric is a cynical, brooding outsider who seeks the meaning of life, but who always remains frustrated, alienated, and disillusioned. In contrast to the typical fantasy hero, whose plot concludes with a comic resolution, Elric is a tragic character who never finds consolation. He is also a deposed king, the last of a dying race in an age that is coming to an apocalyptic end. He is further distinguished by his dependence on his sentient magic sword, Stormbringer. Physically weak because of his albino condition, Elric derives sustenance from his sword, without which he would slowly die. The sword, however, must kill to sustain itself. Capable of manipulating its bearer, the sword often compels Elric against his will to kill those closest to him. Elric and Stormbringer become vampires, parasites whose existence depends on killing. Elric's condition, moreover, is often figured as a loathed but irresistible addiction. The Elric stories, at the time, were decidedly unusual for a fantasy genre often shaped by Christian pieties and consolations. They raise ethical questions about the use of violence to whatever end, portraying the psychological, physical, and social consequences of warfare. They also blur the distinction between good and evil characters, even as they conclude with no simple answers or resolutions. And they also portray a world in decline whose moral ambiguities and apocalyptic scenes are surely better reflections of post-war England than the pastoral fantasies of Lewis and Tolkien.

A good representative Elric story is "While the Gods Laugh" (1961). This story reworks the typical conventions of epic fantasy toward dark fantasy, focusing on the conventional allegorical quest. Elric sets out to find the Dead Gods' Book, which he believes will provide all the answers about life he has been seeking. He hopes to learn whether there is a god and a divine plan beyond the seemingly meaningless struggle between order and chaos that shapes Elric's world. He is joined by Shaarilla, who hopes the Book will help her mend the birth defect that has deprived her of the wings her people normally possess. After a brief series of adventures Elric finds the book, but it crumbles to dust once he touches it. Deprived of consolation again, Elric concludes with bitterness, "I will live my life without ever knowing why I live it – whether it has purpose or not. Perhaps the Book could have told me. But would I have believed it, even then? I am the eternal skeptic – never *sure* that my actions are my own, never certain that an ultimate entity is not guiding me" (Moorcock 1995: 473). Shaarilla tries to console him, but Elric responds, "There is no salvation in this world – only malevolent doom" (474). The frustrated spiritual quest and the decidedly agnostic themes markedly distinguish "While the Gods Laugh" from the usual consolations of epic fantasy, offering the reader existential rather than Christian allegory.

Moorcock's Elric stories helped to establish dark fantasy as one of the dominant genres of post-1960s fiction. Understood broadly, the genre includes such diverse writers as Angela Carter, Tanith Lee, Sylvia Townsend Warner, and Neil Gaiman. Perhaps the most acclaimed contemporary dark fantasist is China Miéville, who has openly acknowledged Moorcock's influence, claiming that "Epic Pooh" was an "absolute revelation" and a "hinge-point" in his life (Miéville 2004: 14). Primarily known for such novels as *King Rat* (1998) and *Perdido Street Station* (2000), Miéville has also published some thought-provoking short stories. His "Looking for Jake" (1998) is an interesting case in point. The unnamed narrator, as the title suggests, is on a quest for a lost friend named Jake. He wanders through an apocalyptic contemporary London decimated by an unspecified cataclysm, causing people to disappear, and apparently linked to strange winged creatures circling the city. The narrator describes London as a collapsed, nearly abandoned city strewn with rubbish and suffering from some "vague entropy" (Miéville 2005: 12). He claims to have been close friends with Jake and even to have found him once, only to lose him again. Struck by the futility of his quest, the narrator eventually gives in to the dark forces around him, willingly entering the Gaumont State Building, "the generator of the dirty entropy that has taken London" (20). The story is cast in the form of a letter addressed to Jake, giving the story greater immediacy and realism, but the reality of the situation becomes doubtful as the story proceeds. In fact, Miéville suggests that the narrator is simply an alienated, dispossessed inhabitant of a London in decline, a lost man generating a fantasy world reflective of his alienation.

In "Looking for Jake," Miéville's reworking of classic epic fantasy elements links the story to dark fantasy. In place of rural romance is a modern London with its labyrinthine streets. A psychological quest replaces the usual literal quest. And, most interesting of all, a troubling blend of fantasy and realism exists. This blending, moreover, concerns not only the psychology of the narrator, who is likely psychotic, but also the nature of communication and interpretation, both of which are portrayed as possible acts of fantasy creating alienated worlds of fantasy. These reflections on interpretation, communication, psychosis, and alienation also serve as meta-fictional commentary on the fantasy genre itself, revisiting the subject of escapism in fantasy initiated by Moorcock in his criticism of Tolkein and Lewis. In fact, like Moorcock, Miéville also draws a historical parallel between fantasy and the collapse of the British Empire. This parallel is most explicitly drawn when the narrator has a hallucination in which he sees a British cavalry soldier "on duty as the cataclysm fell, sensing the change in the order of things and knowing that the queen he was sworn to protect was gone or irrelevant, that his pomp meant nothing in the decaying city, that he had been trained into absurdity and uselessness" (2005: 18). As this hallucination suggests, Miéville's story is clearly commenting on the relationship of fantasy to its historical situation, much like Freud's work does, and in its textured richness and philosophical sophistication it breaks new ground for dark fantasy in the new millennium.

Interzone

What *New Worlds* did for British sf and fantasy in the 1960s, *Interzone* has done from 1982 to the present. First published by a coalition of fans and writers, *Interzone* revived the flagging market for short stories that ensued after *New Worlds* ended its run as a magazine in 1970. The editors, especially David Pringle, took their inspiration from Moorcock's *New Worlds*, deriving the title of their magazine from a major influence on the new wave, William Burroughs's novel, *The Naked Lunch* (1959). The magazine naturally became an outlet for new-wave writers to publish their work, as seen in the regular contributions by Aldiss, Ballard, and Moorcock, but it also became and continues to be a high-profile venue for new generations of sf and fantasy writers, including such prominent figures as Josephine Saxton, Stephen Baxter, Nicola Griffith, Ian Watson, and Mary Gentle. Breaking new ground for science fiction and fantasy, their work is every bit as accomplished as their new-wave predecessors.

For instance, Josephine Saxton's "No Coward Soul" continues the new-wave concern with psychology, but unites it with a feminist sensibility. First published in a 1982 issue of *Interzone*, the story focuses on a frustrated artist named Nadine Quilling who seeks peace and contentment through an autosurgical operation on her brain. Plagued since childhood by uncontrollable rage and resentment, Nadine had found temporary outlets in painting, sculpture, and performance art, but she turns to autosurgery as the ultimate work of art, planning to operate on her own amygdala, an almond-shaped part of the brain associated with fear and aggression. With the aid of mirrors, specialized training, and appropriate medical equipment, Nadine completes the operation and, manipulating the biochemistry of her brain, proceeds to experience a series of hallucinations in which she finds herself on a strange desert planet named Amygdalanea. During these surreal hallucinations she becomes a heroic warrior on a quest for some kind of vague ideal involving the planting of crops in a wasteland, but getting in her way are a series of nightmarish male characters with whom she must do battle, including a Lizard Lord and a disreputable psychiatrist known as the Chief who was "white, clean, bespectacled, masculine, self-assured, unscrupulous, self-controlled, reasonable, rational, patronizing, helpful, fatherly, brotherly, friendly, efficient, trained, qualified, educated, powerful, potent, virile, monied, God-fearing, authoritative, secure, polite and democratic" (Saxton 1985: 174). Nadine defeats all the men she encounters, but her story ends unresolved. At first Nadine feels that the experiment is a success and that she will make the wasteland blossom, but when telephoned by a friend to be invited to a party, her rage prompts her to throw the phone against the wall. Believing herself to be Mary Amygdale, Nadine begins to lose confidence in the success of her experiment and wonders if "she would never be able to return to Earth" (182).

Saxton's story is disturbingly realistic in its unresolved conclusion and in its clinical descriptions of a brain operation, but it is an effective use of surrealism that prevails, one whose dream-like imagery calls for a symbolic reading. The archetypal imagery, in fact, suggests a psychological quest in which the male figures are all embodiments of a patriarchy that has taken root in Nadine's psyche, frustrating her dreams and ambitions. Through the figurative use of the conventions of fantasy and science fiction Saxton presents a feminist exploration of female identity, one influenced by Carl Jung's archetypal symbols of transformation. With these conventions Saxton also presents a meta-fictional reflection on the nature of science fiction and fantasy, which she portrays as a kind of autosurgery in which the artist explores her deep self, reaching some kind of universal mythic dimension through self-examination. Saxton's reference to Emily Brontë's poem "No Coward Soul is Mine" (1850) reinforces this psychological focus on fearlessly facing the "God within."

Published in *Interzone* in 1994, Mary Gentle's "Human Waste" also focuses on the nature of female identity, but it takes a sociological rather than a psychological approach. The story is narrated by an unnamed female scientist responsible for remarkable breakthroughs in nanotechnology. Gentle focuses the story on the narrator's relationship to her son Thomas whom she has genetically engineered to her own design specs, producing a boy who is now six years old but who has the intelligence of a two-year-old. In her mind, the boy is a pet as a well as an object for her bottled-up aggression against men. Her constant physical abuse of the child is aided by her nanotechnology implanted in his body that can repair nearly any injury done to him, including the broken neck Thomas suffers in the disturbing opening scene. Picking up on a venerable science fiction theme most famously embodied in Shelley's *Frankenstein*, the narrator thinks of herself as a creator who has supplanted nature, "that outmoded concept whom I flatter myself I somewhat resemble" (Pringle 1997: 478). Gentle suggests, however, that in spite of her attempts to manipulate her son and her environment to her satisfaction, the narrator remains dissatisfied. In fact, she confesses at the conclusion of the story that she has two fears, that she will "get bored with Little Thomas" or she will "start to love him" (482).

In this story Gentle articulates the classic science fiction theme that scientists should not interfere with nature, but more importantly she criticizes the postmodern celebration of the social construction of identity, depicting a woman who is alienated precisely because she lives in an advanced technological world out of touch with nature and humanity. Gentle presents a woman who tries to engender and organize a world that is a reflection of herself, a woman whose only mode of communication with others comes through the Internet, and whose aggression towards men, stemming from a world in which hostility towards women is rife, is continuously displaced on to her child. It is, finally, a portrait of alienation in which identity is seen as a function of social environment, of technology and science, of gender distinctions, and even of class. Gentle does not celebrate this person who "inhabit[s] a different planet" (482), a strategy typical of postmodern fiction. She celebrates neither the cyborg nor the mastery of nature, as is common in science fiction stories informed by the Enlightenment rhetoric of domination. Instead, Gentle creates sympathy for an angry and frustrated woman who can find no fulfillment in a world of postmodern illusions in which fundamental human needs and desires are sublimated by technology.

As Gentle's and Saxton's stories suggest, the science fiction and fantasy short story is alive and well in the pages of *Interzone*. Well-written and sophisticated, it has progressed beyond its modern origin in pulp fiction. Since the 1980s, moreover, significant women authors have emerged, supported not only by *Interzone*, but also by the Women's Press in London, whose line of sf books promoting women writers was founded in 1985. The influence of the legendary *New Worlds* is still felt on the contemporary scene, but so is the influence of Arthur C. Clarke, especially in the case of Stephen Baxter, a frequent contributor to *Interzone* whose stories share Clarke's interest in the hard sciences. Clarke and Baxter have even co-written novels and short stories, including "The Wire Continuum" (1998) and *The Light of Other Days* (2000). Science fiction and fantasy now thrive in many forms, due in part to the amorphous nature of the two genres, but, in spite of their literary accomplishments and of the pervasive postmodern concern with breaking down the distinction between high and low culture, they are still generally perceived to be distinguished from the mainstream. This ivory-tower perception of sf and fantasy has always been unwarranted, but it is especially so now in the twenty-first century. In fact, science fiction and fantasy may be the forms of writing best equipped to explain the advanced technological and scientific world in which we live.

REFERENCES AND FURTHER READING

Aldiss, B. (1971). *Best Science Fiction Stories of Brian W. Aldiss*, rev. edn. London: Faber and Faber.

Aldiss, B. and D. Wingrove. (2001). *Trillion Year Spree: The History of Science Fiction*, new edn. North Yorkshire: House of Stratus.

Amis, K. (1960). *New Maps of Hell: A Survey of Science Fiction*. New York: Harcourt, Brace.

Ballard, J.G. (1978). *The Best Short Stories of J.G. Ballard*. New York: Henry Holt.

Clarke, A.C. (1959). *The Other Side of the Sky*. New York: Signet.

Clarke, A.C. (2002). *The Collected Stories of Arthur C. Clarke*. New York: Orb.

Clute, J., Greenland, C. and Pringle, D. (eds) (1985). *Interzone: The First Anthology*. New York: St Martin's Press.

Clute, J., Pringle, D. and Ounsley, S. (eds) (1987). *Interzone: The Second Anthology*. New York: St Martin's Press.

Clute, J., Pringle, D. and Ounsley, S. (eds) (1988). *Interzone: The Third Anthology*. New York: Simon & Schuster.

Clute, J., Pringle, D. and Ounsley, S. (eds) (1990). *Interzone: The Fourth Anthology*. New York: Simon & Schuster.

Clute, J. and Nicholls, P. (eds) (1995). *The Encyclopedia of Science Fiction*. New York: St Martin's Press.

Greenland, C. (1983). *The Entropy Exhibition: Michael Moorcock and the UK "New Wave"*. London: Routledge & Kegan Paul.

James, E. (1994). *Science Fiction in the 20th Century*. Oxford: Oxford University Press.

Kaveney, R. (ed.) (1987). *Tales from the Forbidden Planet*. London: Titan Books.

Kincaid, P. (1995). *A Very British Genre: A Short History of British Fantasy and Science Fiction*. London: British Science Fiction Association.

Lefanu, S. (1988). *In the Chinks of the World Machine*. London: The Women's Press.

Luckhurst, R. (2005). *Science Fiction*. Cambridge: Polity.

Miéville, C. (2004). Introduction, *Wizardry and Wild Romance: A Study of Epic Fantasy*, pp. 11–14. Austin, Texas: MonkeyBrain Books.

Miéville, C. (2005). *Looking for Jake*. New York: Ballantine Books.

Moorcock, M. (1978). *Dying for Tomorrow*. New York: Daw Books.

Moorcock, M. (1993). *Earl Aubec and Other Stories*. London: Millennium.

Moorcock, M. (1995). *Elric: Song of the Black Sword*. Clarkston, Georgia: White Wolf.

Moorcock, M. (2004a). *Wizardry and Wild Romance: A Study of Epic Fantasy*. Austin, Texas: Monkey-Brain Books.

Moorcock, M. (ed.) (2004b). *New Worlds: An Anthology*. New York: Thunder's Mouth Press.

Pringle, D. (ed.) (1997). *The Best of Interzone*. New York: St Martin's Press.

Pringle, D., Montgomerie, L. and Clute, J. (eds) (1991). *Interzone V*. London: New English Library.

Saxton, J. (1985). *The Power of Time*. London: Chatto & Windus.

31
Experimental Short Fiction in Britain since 1945

Günther Jarfe

1

The history of the British short story from 1945 to the present can easily be divided into three distinct phases. The first covers the twenty years from 1945 to 1965. This is a period when lots of stories were produced and a number of established writers like Graham Greene, Angus Wilson, Doris Lessing, Alan Sillitoe, and others practiced short fiction. But they told their stories (as if nothing much had happened) in a fairly traditional way, i.e., realistically. The one obvious exception to this realist bias is Samuel Beckett to whom even in the 1930s the limitations of realism had become apparent. Beckett, however, was fairly unknown at the time and only much later turned out to be extremely influential for the innovative writers of the 1970s.

Then, in the mid-sixties, a new mode of telling stories established itself that for want of a better term is often called postmodernist. This phase lasted roughly twenty years. After 1985, postmodernist attitudes and practices slowly petered out. Writers did not totally forget the experimental spirit that had shaped the short story during the two decades before. But they felt that the anti-realist bias of postmodernism and its meta-fictional games had landed fiction in a stalemate. And so another mode of writing developed, often called neo-realism.

2

The following essay, then, confines itself to the years 1965–85. This is the period, the only period, when a whole generation of writers felt forced to deviate from the then current form of storytelling, and to adopt an experimental attitude toward form and content of fiction. It has to be admitted at the outset, though, that there are different kinds and degrees of experimentalism, and that British writers, on the whole, prefer the less radical variant. But even writers such as Ian McEwan or Graham Swift, who are not often counted among experimental writers, will be shown to participate in some postmodernist procedures.

Experimental writing presupposes a widely accepted and practiced aesthetic norm from which to deviate. In the mid-sixties this was still basically realism. Realism as employed at the time by prominent short-story writers involves certain important features: it usually serves as a vehicle for a coherent story about one or more figures whose experience, no matter how brief or casual it seems to be, is significant either for the figures concerned or the reader or both. This is only possible because the story, although invented, clearly refers to what we are accustomed to call reality, i.e., the people and world around us. Even though what we are told did not happen that way, we are convinced that it could have. This aspect of the story is called verisimilitude. The illusion of likeness to life created by the writer can only be upheld if the process of narration remains fairly unnoticed. We forget, so to speak, that there is a narrator. It is this kind of realistic writing that met with more or less furious resistance on the part of many experimental writers. They were opposed to it because they were convinced that in most cases life is not meaningful and, consequently, should not be represented in meaningful stories. At the same time, the realist mode of writing was said by some to have exhausted itself, to be unsuitable for dealing adequately with the explosive state of the world in general and of late capitalism in particular. How could realism cope with the all-pervasive presence and influence of the media? There was also the growing influence of Samuel Beckett and the Argentinian Jorge Luis Borges who had long since given up writing within realistic conventions. In addition, the radical theories of some French philosophers, above all Roland Barthes who declared "The Death of the Author," Jacques Derrida who initiated post-structuralism, and Jean-François Lyotard who attacked realism as arbitrary and propagated postmodernism as a continual rebirth of modernism, slowly but surely transformed the academic world. It was this explosive mixture of political, philosophical, and literary influences that exercised a profound impact on literary theory and, often indirectly, on practicing writers too. They got the message: fiction can no longer represent the experience of reality mimetically.

Such writers, then, were determined to defy realism on all counts. It is obvious which aspects of a fictional text writers eager to experiment can tackle most effectively: (1) they can refuse to tell a story or the story told can be inconsistent, pointless; (2) they can compose stories that no longer automatically and inescapably refer to "reality" (which is seen to be a social construction, anyway), but that become self-reflexive or auto-referential; (3) the act of narration is given special prominence or the arbitrary whims of the narrator are focused on. If this becomes the center of attention it is called meta-fiction. These three areas for experimentation, namely: (a) the degree of story-ness to which a text aspires or which it denies; (b) the question of who or what the text refers to; and (c) the foregrounding of the narrative process, are clearly interrelated. The more meta-fictional a story becomes, the less compelling is its reference to reality and the less interesting is its anecdotal aspect. Thus it cannot always easily be determined whether a story's experimental character is due to its obtrusive narratorial intrusions, or rather to its lack of story-ness. Anyway, within the three areas a great number of variants and variations can be found, the more important of which will now be listed.

The writer can deviate from the expected norm by something as simple, and yet effective, as the introduction of typographical innovations (such as doing without commas, inverted commas, etc.). Or he/she can employ an intrusive narrator, constantly breaking the spell of the narration. He/she can also offer different endings to a particular story, thus letting down an unsophisticated readership. The most complicated and confusing strategies are those that have been termed *metalepsis, mise-en-abyme* and *regressus ad infinitum.* McHale groups them together under the heading "Chinese-Box Worlds" (McHale 1987: 112–30). *Metalepsis* (sometimes referred to as *trompe-l'oeil* or "variable reality") is a mixing-up of different levels of reality, or a blurring of the distinction between fiction and reality (as when a fictional figure suddenly objects to what its author has decreed). The figure of *mise-en-abyme* is a story within a story (there must, however, be a close connection between the two). The *regressus ad infinitum* is a special case of *mise-en-abyme,* a kind of aggravation of the device: compare, for example, the "Story of someone reading a story of someone reading a story" (William Burroughs, qtd in McHale 1987: 114). All these devices ostentatiously parade the fact of the stories' being constructed and, thus, disturb or destroy the readers' illusion. The traditional reader's trust, his/her expectation of mimesis, are to be disappointed, not in order to alienate or even antagonize the reader so much as to win him/her over to a different view of things. I shall now discuss one or two stories each by those writers I consider relevant and representative within this period. The word "experimental" I shall use as a comprehensive term covering not just those experiments thought to be radical, but all devices frustrating readers' expectations for story-ness and mimesis.

3

Ian McEwan started his career with two collections of short stories. Most critics consider them traditional. Among them is Walter Evans. He calls McEwan's stories "determinedly traditional . . . reassuringly conventional beneath the surface. Despite his sometimes radical subject matter, McEwan for the most part refuses to concern himself with novelties of technique or with intellectual posturings" (Evans 1985: 140). Clare Hanson, on the other hand, unhesitatingly counts McEwan among the innovators and demonstrates in what way "Solid Geometry," "Disguises," and "Reflections of a Kept Ape" are about fiction-making and thus have a self-referential quality (Hanson 1985: 159–64). The truth, as so often, is even more complex, as I hope to show by a more extensive look at "Psychopolis." This is the final story in McEwan's second volume of short stories, *In Between the Sheets* (1978). It marks the climax of McEwan's postmodernist achievement because it shows important traditional notions such as personality, identity, and truth in dissolution, and was written with a keen awareness that "genteel escapism" (the narrator's term for traditional art) was no longer acceptable.

"Psychopolis" is about an Englishman, told by himself, who spends some time in Los Angeles. We never know why he is there or what his job is. But it soon becomes clear that he has no particular duties and feels bored most of the time. It is extremely difficult to summarize the story because it lacks a narrative thread. One could say perhaps that it is made up of four major episodes, which, however, are only loosely connected. The first one deals with the weekend when the narrator's new girlfriend Mary has herself chained to his bed. The second one describes how the narrator meets an old friend of his, Terence Latterly, who tells him about his latest abortive attempt at winning a woman's favor. The third episode reports how the narrator and his host George spend some time together going to bars and listening, among other things, to a stand-up comedian telling his sad story. The last episode is about the farewell party organized for the narrator by George.

What do these episodes have in common? One thing is the inability of the people described to form more than fleeting relationships. They are basically singles who enter only into momentary alliances. Indeed, Mary's statement "Everyone here . . . has got some kind of act going like that" (Bradbury 1988: 353), which is made with reference to the comedian and challenges the genuineness of what he says, claims the right for herself, her friends, and her fellow countrymen and countrywomen to consider identity as a provisional and makeshift arrangement you can redefine at any moment according to your whim. This also means that the clear-cut distinction between truth and fiction collapses. That is why the narrator, after listening to Terence, remarks: "I wondered if Terence's story was invented or dreamed." While the lack of a stable identity and the blurring of truth and fiction are high on the postmodern agenda, they are, nevertheless, predominantly thematic aspects of the text. But there are formal factors of considerable interest, too, in this story. I suggest taking a closer look at the kind of information we get and at the way it is presented. Here is the first paragraph of McEwan's story:

> Mary worked in and part-owned a feminist bookstore in Venice. I met her there lunch-time on my second day in Los Angeles. That same evening we were lovers, and not so long after that, friends. The following Friday I chained her by the foot to my bed for the whole weekend. It was, she explained to me, something she "had to go into to come out of." I remember her extracting (later, in a crowded bar) my solemn promise that I would not listen if she demanded to be set free. Anxious to please my new friend, I bought a fine chain and diminutive padlock. With brass screws I secured a steel ring to the wooden base of the bed and all was set. Within hours she was insisting on her freedom, and though a little confused I got out of bed, showered, dressed, put on my carpet slippers and brought her a large frying pan to urinate in. She tried on a firm, sensible voice. (Bradbury 1988: 341)

In this paragraph we get a lot of information, mainly of a factual sort. No causes are given; motivations, if at all, in small doses only. The human interest part of the story is largely left out. All we get is starkly related facts. Further, the events mentioned extend over several days. This hurried and breathless résumé is, according to David Lodge, a typical feature of postmodern texts. He calls it:

> the summary narration of events which would have occupied a considerable length of time in reality, and which would be sufficiently important to the people involved to be worth lingering over in a more conventional kind of fiction. . . . It seems to me a distinctively postmodern phenomenon in that it deviates from the norms of both classic realism and of modernism. (Lodge 1990: 26n)

This "foregrounding of diegesis" (Lodge 1990: 28) is, however, only one aspect of the narrative strategy. The lack of coherence is another. The single sentences are straightforward enough. But the way they follow one another, and the way pieces of information are joined together consecutively, does not result in the actions and events mentioned forming a psychologically plausible sequence. Read through, they do not offer the reader a coherent picture of anything. What is true of single paragraphs is true of each episode and of the story as a whole. Each of the episodes leaves the reader dissatisfied because so many of their ingredients seem irrelevant. As to the whole story, it seems to lead nowhere special. What we are told may have happened in a roughly chronological order. The point is, though, that the chronological order turns out to be meaningless. One might say that lack of coherence seems to be the principle underlying everything that is told. This narration, that fails to weave the different threads of the story properly together, finds a counterpart in the aimlessness and openness of the lives of those people whom the narrator meets in LA. These thematic and formal features are certainly in accordance with basic tenets of postmodernism.

The narrator's flute-playing is an important motif in the story. Whenever he is bored, he takes out his flute and plays a Bach sonata. I take it that, in this story, flute-playing is the central symbol for the modern artist's (and the modern writer's) temptation to fall back on the forms and achievements of his/her predecessors. This danger the protagonist suddenly recognizes, while he is at the party playing his flute and nobody is listening. He has a sudden revelation: "I was weary of this music and of myself for playing it. . . . Why did I go on doing what I couldn't do, music from another time and civilization, its certainty and perfection to me a pretense and a lie . . .?" (Bradbury 1988: 360). The protagonist/narrator looks at his friends lying on the floor, everyone preoccupied with him- or herself, and he realizes that whatever is happening to them and between them: "my music was inane in its rationality, paltry in its over-determination." He calls practicing old art forms "genteel escapism" and is sure: "I could play no more of it" (361). Since this insight occurs at the farewell party, and the story is not composed until after his return to Great Britain, it is to be supposed that before actually writing down the story the narrator had got rid of "genteel escapism" and "over-determination" and found the kind of "music" he had been looking for. In other words "Psychopolis" is proof of what the narrator has learned in the United States, namely, to do without "genteel escapism" – to represent the fragmented lives of people by a fragmented style.

4

Graham Swift is not normally mentioned in connection with postmodernist experimentalism. His novels belong basically to the realist tradition. Nevertheless his stories from the 1970s, which were not published in book form until 1982, show the influence of postmodern thinking in several respects. Thus, Ulrich Broich, in his essay "Muted Postmodernism," chooses Swift's story "Seraglio" as a pertinent example for his thesis that postmodernism in Britain is a rather half-hearted affair. The metafictional aspect of the story is bound up with the intricate pattern in the text of the married couple's relationship. Broich explains:

> their relationship is a kind of autopoietic system in which external events are only used to perpetuate a pattern in which one partner wounds and blames the other in order to be wounded and blamed by him in turn and so on in infinite regress. (Broich 1993: 37)

The crucial passage, for which I have selected this story, is the conclusion of the husband's description of their relationship:

> We were not like real people. We were like characters in a detective novel. The mystery to be solved in our novel was who killed the baby. But as soon as the murderer was discovered he would kill his discoverer. So the discovery was always avoided. Yet the story had to go on. (Swift: 1986: 120)

As Broich notes:

> Solving the enigma would mean getting down to reality, to truth. This in turn would mean death, death for the relationship between the husband and the wife in the story. Their relationship can go on only if it retains that autopoietic closure which I tried to describe and if it is not opened towards the truth. (Broich 1993: 37)

Another aspect of Swift's flirtation with postmodernism is his use of first-person narrators. Ten out of eleven stories of his are told in this way. First-person narrators are not in themselves exceptional. It is the type of speaker Swift employs, and the way he employs him, that makes the difference. Some of Swift's first-person narrators are very similar to those that Ansgar Nünning calls "mad monologists" (Nünning 1990: 36ff.). A mad monologist is isolated, obsessed by a certain idea, deviates from widely accepted norms of behavior, has a view of the world and other people that is restricted to his private needs and subjective opinion, and is therefore unreliable. All this applies, more or less, to several of Swift's stories. His narrators, too, often have a false opinion of themselves and other people, suffer breakdowns, and end up as failures. The point is that the narrators of "Hotel," "The Hypochondriac," and "Cliffedge" do not have a genuine self of their own, but live on borrowed identities. This is revealed when, after his breakdown, the narrator of "The Hypochondriac," sitting in an armchair and watching his substitute, remembers a decisive event from his childhood when his uncle dissected their dead cat and induced in him the wish to become a doctor. He decided on his future profession because he admired his Great-Uncle Laurie, a successful surgeon. But as his inability to treat his patient M. shows irrefutably, the doctor has never been able to live up to his chosen profession.

Similarly the narrator of "Hotel," who has just been treated for a mental disturbance, wants to be a kind of healer himself, and so decides to become the keeper of a hotel where people can come and stay for "therapeutic visits" (Swift 1986: 107). He has the obsessive idea that everybody has some hidden guilt and is in need of someone's understanding, and that he is the one who can provide care and consolation. People do come and enjoy themselves at the place but not, as it turns out later, because they are in need of the hotelkeeper's care. This whole illusion collapses when one day a couple comes to stay – a father and a daughter, it seems – who may really be guilty. Whether or not this is the case remains open. Soon the other guests show themselves to be outraged and begin to check out. At last the hotelkeeper realizes that his whole scheme of offering understanding and forgiveness was a delusion and beside the point. "I went down to my hotel office, shut the door and wept" (1986: 112).

Swift's first-person narrators do not really know themselves. They model their lives on what they admire in others. Swift's insistent use of first-person narration as a means to explore minds that have been thrown off balance has allowed him to articulate his skepticism with regard to what constitutes the self. In this he echoes an ongoing concern (the deconstruction of the autonomy of the self) of postmodernism throughout the 1970s.

5

During his lifetime B.S. Johnson was known only to a small circle of friends. Today it seems certain that "a promising, adventurous and, in retrospect, very important career was halted suddenly by his suicide" (Bradbury 2001: 395). Johnson felt, and said openly, in the introduction to the collection of his shorter pieces, *Aren't You Rather Young to be Writing Your Memoirs?*, that realism was no longer viable: "it is anachronistic, invalid, irrelevant and perverse" (Johnson 1973: 14). He also militantly denounced his contemporaries as "stultifyingly philistine" (29). Despite this certainty of assertion, Johnson found himself in a dilemma. He wanted to be a writer and he wanted to tell the truth. However, he was convinced that "Telling stories really is telling lies" (14). Therefore, he experimented with different kinds of non-stories or anti-stories. Gottfried Schröder describes his 1973 collection thus:

> The "pieces" are not homogeneous; many contain bits and pieces of narrative, but causality and closure are avoided. Narrative elements are rather anecdotal, sketchy, sometimes just extended (and obscene) jokes ("Instructions for the Use of Women"). Other devices to break up the flow of (traditional) narrative are: the montage of two independent narratives ("Mean Point of Impact"), which are centuries apart; the presentation of events or characters like forms filled out; catalogues of behavioural strategies; long lists, containing dozens of items each; descriptive parts are artificially broken up into separate categories. (Schröder 1993: 13)

Two of the texts will be dealt with here. In his brief text "A Few Selected Sentences" (which, meanwhile, has been accorded a special prominence through repeated reprinting in anthologies) Johnson carries the refusal to tell a story, and the ensuing loss of coherence, to extremes. To call this piece of fiction a story would be grossly misleading. It is made up of twenty-seven paragraphs, the briefest of which consists of one word ("Life"), the longest of fourteen lines (in Bradbury's *Modern British Short Stories*). It is a sequence of very heterogeneous fragments from vastly different sources, some of which can be read as anecdotes or sentences (with a play on the meaning of "sentences" as "judicial punishments"), others as reports on accidents or situations, or simply as isolated statements. Thus, one of the passages describes how the vice chancellor of some institution met his death when a wheelbarrow fell into a lift shaft he was inspecting. There is one statement which seems pertinent to the formal principle underlying "A Few Selected Sentences": "I love anecdotes. I fancy mankind may come in time to write all aphoristically . . . ; grow weary of preparation and connection and illustration, and all those arts by which a big book is made" (Bradbury 1988: 283). One cannot help reading this as a meta-fictional comment on Johnson's device of putting together miscellaneous fragments. Since this is a collage of seemingly random components, it is apparently meant to remind the reader that what we call reality is, in fact, a chaotic muddle of many different processes, all going on at the same time, independently of one another. And if this is what "Life" amounts to, it is without recognizable meaning. It seems that this is what the speaker considers it is his duty to record as a chronicler. For, at the beginning and at the end of "A Few Selected Sentences," we find the succinct statement: "Someone has to keep the records" (Bradbury 1988: 282, 285).

Johnson's brief text "Aren't You Rather Young to be Writing Your Memoirs?", which gave his 1973 collection its title, not only shows a number of the experimental features typical of many stories of the 1970s and early1980s; but it also reveals the existential motive behind these devices and explicitly demonstrates the consequences for the reader. "Aren't You Rather Young to be Writing Your Memoirs?" is told by a first-person narrator and deals with two fishing trips he takes to an old mill. He describes the location at some length and also supplies technical details about fishing.

He does not catch a fish, though, and soon suspicion grows that fishing may be just a red herring. This is confirmed when the narrator lets the reader know that "It was on my second visit that the thing in which I hope to interest you happened" (Johnson 1973: 37). He witnesses a minor incident: while he is standing on a bridge, fishing, a car rushes past him and stops where two young men have just climbed over a fence. The driver jumps from his car and addresses the young men – angrily, it seems. One of them is holding a shotgun. Suddenly there is a gunshot, but nobody is hurt, the man drives off, and the two young men also leave in the opposite direction. That is all. And the narrator comments:

> The elements of this situation were such that further speculation as to motives, indeed, as to what had happened, were pointless, on my part, in the circumstances. (Johnson 1973: 39)

Soon after this, on his way home, the narrator again comes upon the man who is now talking to a policeman on a bicycle. He imagines how what he had seen might continue:

> The conclusion I hoped for was that the informed and uniformed policeman rode off, down a mile or so to the mill, over the bridge, along towards the level crossing, and over it . . . And failed to find the two men with the shotgun. (1973: 40)

This ending, apart from being pointless, is purely hypothetical, because the narrator does not have a clue whether there is going to be a sequel to the incident. So he suggests that the reader come up with his own solution:

> But you can provide your own surmises or even your own ending, as you are inclined. For that matter, I have conveniently left enough obscure or even unknown for you to suggest your own beginning; and your own middle, as well, if you reject mine. (1973: 41)

And to those readers who may be disappointed or taken aback by this insignificant and anti-climactic episode, and by the narrator's refusal to make sense of it, he puts the indignant question: "Why do you want me to tidy up life, to explain? (41). The narrator concludes his comments with the defiant remark "I am a professional!" (41). This last remark makes it clear that to Johnson (and, I would add, to many other experimentalists) being a professional writer means the refusal "to tidy up life," in the sense of entertaining people by telling gripping stories, or of inventing stories with a beginning, a middle, and an end. Even those experimental writers who still do tell gripping stories punctuate them with narratorial intrusions, thus disturbing the reader's natural consumer mentality and inertia. So, in spite of much postmodern paraphernalia, many experimental writers still have the intention to produce stories that are not only self-referential but also, at the same time, critically focus on certain aspects of the world around us. This is particularly true of Gabriel Josipovici.

6

Josipovici is easily the most brilliant and the most radical of the experimentalists discussed here. (I am using this term for the sake of convenience, although Josipovici himself, by exposing the shallow use of the term by a number of critics, has made it abundantly clear why he does not want to be called an experimental writer. See his "True Confessions of an Experimentalist" in Josipovici 1983: 173–80.) His approximately 40 stories cover an impressive range of topics and show the author to have all the major narrative strategies of realism and postmodernism at his disposal. I want to present an early and a later example from his production to show his wide range.

The early story is called "Mobius the Stripper" and has meanwhile achieved the status of a classic example of a postmodernist story. It is made up of two stories which, ideally, should to be read at the same time. Both are printed on the same pages, the first one filling the upper part of the page, the second one the lower part. The first story is told in the third person and deals with a fat man called Mobius who earns his living by stripping in a club. The second story is told in the first person and presents a would-be writer who is suffering from writer's block and is, therefore, sitting in front of an empty page. The two stories have some important things in common. Both Mobius and the writer claim to be in search of the truth. Mobius explains that his true motive for stripping is metaphysical, that he wants to get "to the centre of me" (Josipovici 1974: 65). At first sight, this may sound absurd and paradoxical. But Dominique Pernot elucidates the paradox thus:

> his show does not necessarily comply with our prejudices since Mobius rejects the overtly libidinous aspect of his stage act by means of his highly idiosyncratic commentary. In fact Mobius "desexualizes" his exhibitory act . . . The essence of stripping which normally appeals to instinct and bodily drives, that is to the lower part(s) in man, is radically refined by his elevated speech, giving it a metaphysical, even religious dimension. (1999: 355)

The writer also believes that, as soon as he can start writing, he will get back "my lost self" (Josipovici 1974: 85). Apart from that, Mobius is not totally unknown to him. His girlfriend has been urging him for some time not to miss "Mobius the Stripper." But the true relationship between the two stories can be derived from the title, which contains a pun on the mobius strip. A mobius strip is a strip of paper made into a band by gluing the ends together after twisting one end 180 degrees. It results in "a mathematical model of a surface with only one side" (Korte 2003: 154).

The pun on the mobius strip implies that both stories have to be read consecutively, beginning either with the first or the second one. Should you begin with the first one, then the second one must be one of the voices Mobius keeps hearing. The first sentence of the second story, "I first heard of Mobius the stripper," is identical with one of the voices mentioned in the first story. Should you begin with the second story, then the first one must be that story the writer will eventually be able to put down on paper. The idea of presenting the two stories in the form of a mobius strip, and of having the reader recognize and read them as a continuous story, has obviously an element of playfulness about it. But "Mobius the Stripper" is more than a game. The postmodern author's dilemma, namely, to know that traditional means of telling a story are no longer valid, and yet "to be dangerously threatened by the size and the *assurance* of all the great men who had come before me" (Josipovici 1974: 68), and, on top of that, not to know beforehand how to go about writing a story – this existential dilemma is shown in a sophisticated manner. The suffering individual (Mobius), who used to be the writer's subject, has lost his autonomous self. Both Mobius and the writer are in search of identity and truth. Both want to free themselves from the fetters they have been put in by society and tradition. The painful truth, however, seems to be that the more Mobius strips, the less he finds. There is no self beneath all the societal layers he removes. In the end nothing remains for Mobius but to take his own life. And the ambitious writer, who, after some kind of revelation, seems finally able to fill the empty page in front of him, will have to write about Mobius's failure. The more one thinks about this story, the more challenging and disturbing it becomes. Is the writer Mobius's creation or is Mobius the writer's invention? Who is the subject, who the object? "Mobius the Stripper" leaves the reader completely baffled and yet fascinated.

A postmodern short story which glaringly reveals its fictitiousness, and yet brilliantly manages to tell a moving story at the same time, is Josipovici's "Goldberg." It was first published in 1989 and later became the first chapter in Josipovici's book *Goldberg: Variations* (2002). Taking as a kind of stimulus an anecdote about how Bach's famous *Goldberg Variations* came to be composed, Josipovici, in this story, has Mr Goldberg, a fictitious eighteenth-century Jewish writer, write a letter in which he explains how he took up his temporary position as reader to Mr Westfield. His duty is every day to write something new that during the night he can read out to Mr Westfield until he falls asleep. But on his very first day he realizes that it is impossible for him to fulfill this task: he is up against writer's block. In the evening, he decides to write a letter instead, describing to his wife his situation, his problems, and also imagining the conversation between Westfield and himself that will possibly take place later that night, as a consequence of his failure. This is the most dazzling part of the piece. While reading it, you know this is an imagined conversation, and, at its beginning, the narrator leaves no doubt about this:

> I knew of course what he would say. He would call me in and sit me again by his bed, as he had on the previous night.

— Well, my friend, he would say, why do you sit there in silence when you are acquainted with my wishes? (Josipovici 2002: 9)

But hardly has the conversation got under way when all the "woulds" disappear, and we seem to be overhearing the actual conversation:

— Are you a writer, my friend?
— I am, sir.
— Then why have you not written?
— One single day, sir, to prepare for a whole night's reading, appears to have been beyond my powers.
— You have enough then for half the night?
— No sir.
— For a quarter then?
— No sir.
— For an hour perhaps?
— Alas, sir, no.
— For half the time?
— No.
— How can you explain this state of affairs, my friend? (Josipovici 2002: 9)

While we read, we realize that not only is Mr Goldberg desperately defending himself, but also the modern writer is trying to explain why writing has become so difficult. Eventually Mr Goldberg explains how he resolved the impasse:

— I have inevitably found that when I am at a loss for a subject, when the elusive thread of which I was speaking remains resolutely hidden from sight, then there is one way in which I can perhaps call it into being.
— And that way, Mr Goldberg?
— That way is to cease to search for themes or for subjects and to start from the actual position in which I find myself. If that happens to be a labyrinth from which there seems to be no exit, that will become my theme. If it is the frustrating search for a subject which refuses to emerge, then that will be my theme. (Josipovici 2002: 10)

So Mr Goldberg sits down and writes a letter to his wife describing his problems. This letter contains the conversation I have been quoting from. In this imagined conversation, Goldberg refers to the letter that he is in the process of writing, and that is to be a substitute for the fiction he finds himself unable to produce. Not only different levels of time are mixed up here, but also different kinds of (fictitious) reality. All this is postmodern par excellence.

As I suggested before, this is not just a story about Mr Goldberg. In his last (but one) sentence (still part of the imagined conversation), Goldberg uses the first-person plural:

> But we, today, can only do what we can, not what we would, and this was a solution
> of sorts, not perhaps entirely without its own kind of elegance. (Josipovici 2002: 11)

This clearly refers to the contemporary writer's problems of how to come to terms
with the fact that vital constituents of what used to make up fiction (character, plot,
mimesis, etc.) have been called into question and can no longer be employed with
impunity.

7

David Lodge has primarily distinguished himself as a very successful contemporary
novelist and a prominent literary critic. But he has also published some shorter
pieces of fiction. Among these, "Hotel des Boobs" is a fascinating little masterpiece,
which, by deliberately confusing different levels of reality – McHale speaks about
"variable reality" (1987: 116) – puts postmodern meta-fictional devices brilliantly
to the test.

The text begins – or so it seems – quite realistically, as a story about Harry and
Brenda, a couple spending their holiday at a hotel in the south of France. There most
of the women who lie sunbathing around the pool are topless, thus giving Harry who
"had always had a thing about women's breasts" (Bradbury 1988: 327) the opportunity for "boob-watching" (329). After a few pages this narrative is interrupted by the
sentence "The author had reached this point in his story, which he was writing seated
at an umbrella-shaped table on the terrace overlooking the hotel pool" (330), which
makes it clear that this is really a story about the author and his wife, and that what
we have just been reading is a story in the making. Like his hero Harry, the author
is on holiday in the south of France and watches the women around the pool while
he is writing a story. As it happens, a sudden gust of wind scatters many pages of the
author's manuscript. This puts him in an awkward position. His story about Harry
and Brenda is peopled with guests from his own hotel, who, should they pick up a
page and read it, might find that the author has described them not always to their
advantage. So when the author's wife comes back from her shopping trip, he announces
that he wants her to find another hotel:

> "I can't stand the thought of staying on here, on tenterhooks all the time in case one of
> the guests comes back from a walk in the woods with a compromising piece of fiction
> in their paws. What an extraordinary thing to happen."
>   "You know," said the author's wife. "It's really a better story."
>   "Yes," said the author. "I think I shall write it. I'll call it 'Tit for Tat'."
>   "No, call it 'Hotel des Boobs'," said the author's wife. (Bradbury 1988: 333)

It is at this moment that we realize: this is the story we have just been reading. So,
miraculously, the fictitious author has turned into a real one, and we could call this
a triply embedded story. But this is not all. This brilliant example of a *mise-en-abyme*

could also be read as a hoax deconstructing postmodernism by treating it as a joke. For, whereas it is one of the premises of postmodernism that to assume fiction's mimetic function is mistaken, the Chinese-box device, as employed in this story, can only be made to work because there is such a close resemblance and parallelism between Harry and Brenda (fiction) and the author and his wife ("reality"). In writing this story, Lodge deliberately caters to a widespread cliché, namely. that authors always write about their own experiences, thus undermining the seriousness of his story.

Meanwhile, the postmodernist phase of the British short story has become a historical phenomenon. Looking back at it from today's vantage point, British writers' relative immunity from being too thoroughly infected by French deconstructionists may seem to be a boon rather than a disadvantage.

References and Further Reading

Bradbury, M. (ed.) (1988). *Modern British Short Stories*. Harmondsworth: Penguin.

Bradbury, M. (2001). *The Modern British Novel 1878–2001*, rev. edn. Harmondsworth: Penguin.

Broich, U. (1993). "Muted Postmodernism: The Contemporary British Short Story," *Zeitschrift für Anglistik und Amerikanistik* 41: 31–9.

Evans, W. (1985). "The English Short Story in the Seventies," in D. Vannatta (ed.), *The English Short Story 1945–1980: A Critical History*, pp. 120–72. Boston: Twayne.

Hanson, C. (1985). *Short Stories and Short Fictions, 1880–1980*. London: Macmillan.

Johnson, B.S. (1973). *Aren't You Rather Young to be Writing Your Memoirs?* London: Hutchinson.

Josipovici, G. (1974). *Mobius the Stripper: Stories and Short Plays*. London: Victor Gollancz.

Josipovici, G. (1983). *The Mirror of Criticism*. Brighton: Harvester Press.

Josipovici, G. (2002). *Goldberg: Variations*. Manchester: Carcanet.

Korte, B. (2003). *The Short Story in Britain*. Tübingen: Franke.

Lodge, D. (1990). *After Bakhtin: Essays on Fiction and Criticism*. London: Routledge.

McHale, B. (1987). *Postmodernist Fiction*. London: Routledge.

Nünning, A. (1990). "Kurzgeschichten von Ian McEwan in einem Englisch-Leistungskurs: Darstellung grotesker Welten aus der Perspektive des 'verrückten Monologisten'," *Literatur in Wissenschaft und Unterricht* 23: 36–50.

Pernot, D. (1999). "Biblical, Modern and Postmodern Winding and Unwinding in Gabriel Josipovici's Fiction," *Germanisch-Romanische Monatsschrift* 49: 351–60.

Schröder, G. (1993). "Recent British Short Stories," in H.-J. Diller et al. (eds), *Recent British Short Story Writing*, pp. 7–31. Heidelberg: C. Winter.

Swift, G. (1986). *Learning to Swim and Other Stories*. New York: Washington Square Press.

Reading Individual
Authors and Texts

32

The Short Stories of
Julian Maclaren-Ross

David Malcolm

Julian Maclaren-Ross (1912–64) is an enigmatic figure in the history of twentieth-century British fiction, and especially of the British twentieth-century short story. Successful and highly regarded at the start of his career in the mid-1940s, he never lived up to the expectations of his admirers, his potential destroyed by a bohemian way of life, indigence, and alcohol and amphetamine consumption. He is a non-canonical writer of short fiction, but one whose work has been revived and revalued in the early twenty-first century, largely as a result of the efforts of his biographer and editor, Paul Willetts. At his death Maclaren-Ross left three considerable volumes of short fiction – *The Stuff to Give the Troops* (1944), *Better Than a Kick in the Pants* (1945), and *The Nine Men of Soho* (1946) – and one substantial novel, *Of Love and Hunger* (1947). His novel *Bitten by the Tarantula* (1946) is slim, but acidly interesting. A later volume of miscellaneous prose, *The Funny Bone* (1956), contains several short stories, as well as literary parodies and memoirs. In addition, Maclaren-Ross wrote many reviews, humorous pieces (for *Punch*, among other journals), essays on film, screenplays, memoirs, and the beginnings of several unfinished novels. Despite his achievements, his story is one of promise unfulfilled.

Yet Maclaren-Ross's early work, especially his short-story prose, was largely positively received. Willetts lists the praise (and the criticism) that the early volumes met with. Walter Allen called *The Stuff to Give the Troops* "as good a series of sketches of army life as has yet appeared," and it was similarly endorsed by Anthony Powell, John Lehmann, and the anonymous reviewers in *John O'London's Weekly* and the *Times Literary Supplement*. Although the latter had reservations about some of the collection, the "best of the others" were seen as possessing "a nice descriptive zest and vigour." In *The New Statesman*, Philip Toynbee wrote that "These stories . . . give reason to hope that Maclaren-Ross may prove the considerable satirist of whom we are in such evident need" (Willetts 2003: 166–7; "Army life" 1944: 389). *Better Than a Kick in the Pants* received much more hostile comment from reviewers, Henry Reed condemning some stories as "no more than pub anecdotes" (Willetts 2003: 185–6). But of *The Nine Men of Soho*, Willetts notes that "it enjoyed brisk sales, aided by some excellent reviews" (2003: 194). Anthony Powell praised it (as he had *The Stuff to Give the Troops*), and Elizabeth Bowen wrote of the volume that it showed that Maclaren-Ross was a "writer due for the first rank." She went on to declare that "Better, and more dire, pictures of the Bohemian extremity – in pubs and the Soho purlieus, in dun-beleaguered bungalows along half-made roads, in and out of bookshops and under the duress of the Army – are not . . . to be found" (Willetts 2003: 194–5). More recent commentary has also seen much to praise in Maclaren-Ross's work. Bernard Bergonzi writes that his "memorable stories of army life" are marked by "sharp descriptive writing, accurate dialogue, nicely paced development, and a keen sense of the absurd" (1993: 42), and the contributor to *The Reader's Companion to Twentieth-Century Writers* calls him "a considerable and much underrated writer" ("Julian Maclaren-Ross" 1995: 468). D.J. Taylor argues that "his best work . . . retains an extraordinary sparkle: things borrowed from another time, but still capable of startling us with their intensity" (2002: xiv). Willetts notes that "his work *is* uneven, but the best of it matches, and from time to time surpasses, anything produced by his more celebrated contemporaries" (2004: ix). Elsewhere Willetts argues: "He was, in many ways, ahead of his time, not least in his literary output. As a writer of fiction, he pioneered a style that was often slangy and conversational, its unpretentious clarity, casual tone and mordant humour contributing to its enduring appeal. What's more, in short stories such as 'The Rubber Cheque,' he indulges in jokey formal games that prefigure the post-modern trickiness of many current writers" (2005: ix).

Maclaren-Ross's short fiction falls into three main groups: army stories, childhood stories (usually set in the South of France, where Maclaren-Ross did, indeed, spend much of his childhood and youth), and "Soho" stories (largely set in the bohemian milieu of the pubs and clubs in that seedy area of central London). Army stories make up the whole of *The Stuff to Give the Troops*, but Maclaren-Ross returned to his wartime experiences in stories in *The Nine Men of Soho* ("Lulu" and "The Swag, the Spy and the Soldier") and in *The Funny Bone* ("The Triple Life of Major Trask" and "Old Ginger"). Four childhood stories make up one section of *Better Than a Kick in the Pants*, under the general title of "The Mandrake Root," and childhood materials recur in *The Funny Bone* in "The Bird Man" and "The Gondolier of Death." Soho stories make up Part Four, "London is in Soho," of *Better Than a Kick in the Pants*, and predominate in the fictional section, "Part Two: Plots Ten-and-Six," of *The Funny Bone*. *Better Than a Kick in the Pants* also contains a miscellaneous group of stories that deal with pre-war life: the Indian stories ("The Hell of a Time" and "A Bit of a Smash in Madras") and those presenting an existence on the margins of social respectability (and at times outside them), such as "Happy as the Day is Long," "Petty Cash," "Five Finger Exercises," and "Civvy Street." Of this group, "Action Nineteen-Thirty-Eight" is a sobering account of a meeting with two lumpen pre-war British fascists, while "I'm Not Asking You to Buy" offers material about working as a vacuum-cleaner salesman later incorporated in *Of Love and Hunger*. *The Nine Men of Soho* contains one unusual story, a lightly fictionalized account of Maclaren-Ross's father's and mother's lives, entitled "My Father was Born in Havana," a highly innovative condensed family-saga novel, in which copious fabular material is covered breathlessly in thirteen pages.

Apart from his two Indian stories, in which he writes about people and places he did not directly know, Maclaren-Ross based his fiction closely on his own experiences of army life, childhood in the south of France, and the shabby pubs of Soho. It is, thus, not surprising that he usually adopts a first-person narration, even when those narrators – as he is at pains to stress in the first part of *Better Than a Kick in the Pants* ("The 'I' in these stories is not Me") – are, at times, nothing like Maclaren-Ross himself. Elsewhere, however, he courts identification with the narrators, for example, in *The Nine Men of Soho* ("The 'I' in these stories is always Me. All other characters are imaginary") and in some army stories in which the narrator is called "Rossy" ("Are You Happy in Your Work," "Lulu"). But several stories are told in lower-class voices that are not Maclaren-Ross's own, for example, "The Tape" and "A Bit of a Stink." The language used by Maclaren-Ross's narrators varies in formality and closeness to standard English. However, almost all narrators use a relatively informal lexis and syntax, and at times his narrators speak thoroughly non-standard varieties of the language. Examples of substantial informality and linguistic deviance can be found in the voices of narrators of "The Tape" and "I Had to Go Sick" in *The Stuff to Give the Troops*, although all the narrators in this collection speak at the informal and colloquial end of any linguistic spectrum. Their language is also permeated by the slang, argot, initials, and acronyms of the mid-twentieth-century British army. In *Better Than a Kick in the Pants*, the narrator in "Petty Cash" employs a highly informal, non-standard language, while the middle-class narrators of "A Hell of a Time" and "A Bit of a Smash in Madras" use very colloquial, if standard, English. The narrators in the childhood stories are usually marked by a much more neutral discourse, and those of the bohemian "Soho" stories, while often employing quite sophisticated lexis, favor short, frequently simple, sentences. Commentators have remarked on Maclaren-Ross's deployment of informal and colloquial English, and seen it as an important and innovative aspect of his writing ("Army Life," 1944: 389; *Reader's Companion* 1995: 468; Willetts 2005: 9). His commitment to a demotic English is also exemplified by the widespread use of dialog in his stories.

Place settings are similarly homogeneous in Maclaren-Ross's short stories. If one excludes the childhood stories, with their picturesque southern French locations, his short fiction is permeated by shabby milieux. This is as true of his army stories as it is of his Soho fictions. Note the descriptions of soldiers' beds in "Gas," the sordid lavatory in "They Can Have It," the billets in "Are You Happy in Your Work?," and the shabby restaurants and tea room, the miserable seaside town of "Seven Days of Heaven" (*The Stuff to Give the Troops*). Compare these with the dismal Oxford of "The Oxford Manner" (*Better Than a Kick in the Pants*), the desolate landscape and mean provincial realia of "Lulu," the sordid bohemian life of "The Swag, the Spy and the Soldier" which is matched only by the tawdriness of the military barracks depicted in the same story (*The Nine Men of Soho*). Further unsavory settings are to be found in "The Man from Madagascar" and "The Gem" in *The Funny Bone*. The reader's sense of the shabbiness of the environment in Maclaren-Ross's work is further enhanced by the human material that inhabits it. Soldiers pass the time squeezing another's blackheads ("Are You Happy in Your Work?"). The patients in "Y List" suffer from thoroughly unglamorous and inglorious ailments. The fascists in "Action Nineteen-Thirty-Eight" are stupid; the girls in the seedy dance hall bored and cold. The old soldier in "Old Ginger" is physically and verbally grotesque. The officers in the night club in "Seven Days of Heaven" are crass and coarse; waitresses are rude and civilians treat private soldiers with contempt.

There are four sets of recurrent motifs in the created worlds of Maclaren-Ross's short stories: the absurdity and arbitrariness of authority; chaos; cruelty coupled with emotional aridity; and fraud. Bergonzi writes that Maclaren-Ross "presents the military-medical bureaucracy as something out of Kafka rewritten by the Marx brothers" (1993: 43). Examples of absurdity certainly abound in *The Stuff to Give the Troops*. In "I Had to Go Sick," the hapless narrator is caught in a web of army bureaucracy, and left in an unresolved limbo; in "Jankers," the narrator falls foul of a lance-corporal and his life is made miserable by the complexities of regulations and the arbitrariness of petty authority; in "Ack Beer Charlie Don," obscure rules and codes and arbitrary decisions by officers make the narrator's life very difficult. Civilian life is scarcely better. In *Better Than a Kick in the Pants*, the children in "The High Priest of Buddha" become subject to the whimsical cruelties of bullies; the protagonist in "Civvy Street" is powerless vis-à-vis state bureaucracy; and the narrator in "The Spy Who Was a Character from Conrad" is mistaken for a German agent because he is wearing a corduroy coat, a motif that is repeated in *The Nine Men of Soho* when Sandy in "The Swag, the Spy and the Soldier" is accused of treason because of his notes for a novel. "The Rubber Cheque" recounts the futile attempts of the narrator to extract payment from a publisher and an officious bank. In *The Funny Bone*, Major Trask is driven mad by the contradictions of his role in army bureaucracy ("The Triple Life of Major Trask").

The regulations of army life do not produce order, but rather its reverse. "Gas," "A Bit of a Stink," "Ack Beer Charlie Don," "They Can Have It," and "Invasion according to Plan" all present the military world as one of utter chaos. The civilian world is less so, but it is equally cruel. The indifference towards others and the casual brutality of army life in "This Mortal Coil" and "Jankers" (*The Stuff to Give the Troops*) are echoed in the childhood savagery of "The High Priest of Buddha" (*Better Than a Kick in the Pants*), "The Far West" (*The Nine Men of Soho*), "The Bird Man," and "The Gondolier of Death" (*The Funny Bone*). Human relations have an emotional aridity and exploitativeness about them. One sees this clearly in the love affairs that go nowhere in "A Sentimental Story" (*The Stuff to Give the Troops*), "Welsh Rabbit of Soap," and "Lulu" (*The Nine Men of Soho*). One has a sense of futility, both in the army stories, and in accounts of civilian lives – conversations that go nowhere, relationships that never develop, afternoons that tail off into inconclusiveness ("Happy as the Day is Long" in *Better Than a Kick in the Pants*; "The Virgin" in *The Nine Men of Soho*).

Maclaren-Ross's stories are also full of tricksters, frauds, and deceivers. Petty crime, evasion of regulations, and trying to avoid the demands of military service abound in the army stories. "Dodging the Column," "The High Jump," "The Soldier Who Had a Complex and the Psychiatrist Who Miraculously Cured Him," and "Dead Men Do Tell Tales" all illustrate this motif. It is present, too, in civilian stories, such as "Petty Cash," "Call a Policeman," and "The Honest Truth" (*Better Than a Kick in the Pants*). Deception is central to "Welsh Rabbit of Soap," "The Great Writer," "The Token Sheep," "Edward: A Detective Story," and "The Swag, the Spy and the Soldier" (*The Nine Men of Soho*). *The Funny Bone* is full of criminals and liars – the thieves in "The Gold Fish," the crooked film producers of "The Shoestring Budget," and the literary conman of "The Man from Madagascar." In this collection, even Old Ginger's grotesque behavior, it is hinted, is assumed in order to get out of the army ("Old Ginger").

Two stories which embody Maclaren-Ross's disaffected vision of the world, and which illustrate his skill as a short-story writer, are "They Put Me in Charge of a Squad" from *The Stuff to Give the Troops* and "A Bit of a Smash in Madras" from *Better Than a Kick in the Pants*. If Maclaren-Ross is to find a place within the canon of British short fiction it is with stories like these that he will do so.

The title of "They Put Me in Charge of a Squad" already expresses something of the world and experiences of the text. The narrator has no choice; arbitrary authority ("They") orders him to do something. The narrator, although only a private soldier, is ordered to take a squad of derelict and disobedient soldiers into town to shift furniture from one building to another. The soldiers are reluctant to obey orders; the task seems futile; the narrator barely retains control over his refractory subordinates. The action is utterly banal, the conflicts trivial. The story has a highly restricted focus; there is little sense of before or after; the war is not even mentioned. The text has features of an oral anecdote: the "So" that begins the second paragraph (Maclaren-Ross 1944: 53); the inconsequential conclusion ("Somehow I don't think I'll ever make an officer" (59)). The very banality of the action and the lowness of the anecdotal shape of the text are crucial to the meaning of the story. This is a sordid world taken up with rather trifling matters.

The narrator is a typical one in Maclaren-Ross's army stories, a private soldier, but one clearly from a middle-class background who is on his way to becoming an officer. He is, thus, socially superior to both the derelict private soldiers he has to command and to the corporal who gives him orders, but, by virtue of his military rank, in an ambiguous position, not an officer, but not quite one of the other ranks either. (Such figures abound in Maclaren-Ross's fiction, military, civilian, and childhood.) The narrator's social rank is reflected in his language, which is grammatically correct throughout. However, like most of Maclaren-Ross's educated narrators, his lexis and syntax are relatively informal and accessible. His syntax shows some range of sentence type, but simple and compound sentences usually predominate. The following paragraph is typical.

At 9.20 hours I reported back to the Company Office. A squad of men shivered sullenly on the kerb outside. Their denim suits, buttonless, flapped open in the bitter wind. My heart sank when I saw them. Dexter must have got them together on purpose. All the worst janker wallahs were there, mixed with a few well-known malingerers and a man just back from detention barracks who had no top teeth. Behind them was the frozen grass plot facing the office and beyond that again, the sea. Against this background they looked terrible. But their faces, covered with pimples and blue with the cold, brightened when they saw me. (1944: 54)

Lexis is informal. Of the nine sentences in this paragraph, six are simple sentences. Three are complex, but one of those, the fourth sentence, is a very short one, and the others are really long simple sentences with short subordinate clauses tacked on to their ends (the sixth and final sentences). Most characters' language contrasts strikingly with the narrator's. Dialog, of which there is a great deal in most Maclaren-Ross stories, is frequently non-standard. "You're an OCTU wallah aincher?" says Corporal Dexter to the narrator. "In for a pip? Well then, how the hell you going to lead men if you don't never have charge of nothing?" (1944: 53). The corporal's triple negative is grammatically very irregular, as is his "aincher?" (ain't you/aren't you?), and his speech also illustrates the peppering of language in "They Put Me in Charge of a Squad" with the acronyms and slang of the mid-twentieth-century British army (OCTU: Officer Cadet Training Unit; "wallah": man, fellow).

The informality and slang nature of language in the text is appropriate to setting and character. Time setting is striking by its trivial indefiniteness. This is a wartime story, yet the great international conflict is entirely absent. Place setting is lightly alluded to, and is unpleasant and sordid whenever it is mentioned. "It was December," the narrator laconically comments, and he talks of "the frozen pavement" and his fingers' being "frozen stiff" (53). The squad, in the passage quoted above, stands "blue with the cold" against a desolate background (54). Characters themselves are physically and morally unglamorous. The first paragraph of the text tells the reader that "One of our corporals had scabies" while another is being "court-martialled for slackness" (53). It seems suitable that one of the soldiers in the squad wipes "an icicle of snot from his nose" at one point (57).

The story's recurrent motifs are very much of a piece with language and setting in their inglorious tawdriness. Hostility among characters is very marked, Corporal Dexter bears a grudge against the narrator (53); the soldiers in the squad try to injure the narrator (57); one abuses him (58). Disobedience is rife throughout the text. The squad is ill-disciplined and insubordinate. They try to avoid tasks; most of the company is trying to avoid a route march in any case (54). One of the squad pretends to have broken his leg (56). Most of them attempt to run off and hide (58). Disorder reigns and the squad cannot form ranks or march properly (55–6). The job of shifting furniture seems futile. The narrator is utterly incompetent as an officer. No wonder the former World War I soldier who observes the squad's antics mutters disparagingly (57). "They Put Me in Charge of a Squad" is a meticulous and integrated study of incompetence and futility, couched in a language that is both tawdry and vivid, like the conscripts' malingering and blue pimpled faces.

"A Bit of a Smash in Madras" (the story that won Cyril Connolly's attention) is similarly carefully integrated in language, character, and action. It tells the story of a few days in the life of Adams, an employee in a British firm in India in the late 1930s, who injures two Indians while driving home drunk. Adams himself recounts the subsequent police investigation, an attempt to blackmail him, his Indian lawyer's devious methods, his trial, and the imposition of fines on him. Like "They Put Me in Charge of a Squad," "A Bit of a Smash in Madras" has qualities of the oral anecdote: direct addresses to the reader (for example, "look what he did for Cornford" (Maclaren-Ross 1945: 34)), especially the text's concluding "Don't know of any good jobs going, do you?" (50).

Adams gives his account in a very informal language, with an uncomplicated lexis and syntax, and a discourse full of colloquialism and slang. "Absolute fact, I knew damn all about it," the story begins (32), and it continues in this vein. The narrator drinks "socking great cups of tea" (33); his lawyer is "a damn good scout" (35); there are "bags of natives" in the court (48); Adams "went on a binge for a bloody month" after his trial (50). Anglo-Indian slang (for example, "*chota hazri*" (early morning tea)) adds further colloquial color to the text. It is striking that the narrator's language contrasts markedly with the much more formal "BBC accent" (36) and "Oxford-English" (43) of the educated Indian characters, Krishnaswami, Menon, and Shankran (for example, 39, 43).

Very few details are given about time and place setting (perhaps because these are so familiar *mutatis mutandis* from dozens of Kipling stories and other tales of imperial adventure and encounters), but where there are some details, in the description of the site of the doctor's office, these are, typically for Maclaren-Ross, unsavory (47). The story's main focus (and in this it may be attempting to capture time and place) is on characters and their relationships. Adams is a typical Maclaren-Ross central character, incompetent, dissolute, careless, vulgar, and unfortunate. There is a shabby banality about his vision of things and people, and about his language. He is, however, not a racist, and is well aware that he needs Shankran to get him out of the mess he is in. He is also not without regret for what he has done and has sympathy for the injured "coolies" (46). Indeed, the lack of any sense of European superiority vis-à-vis Indians (as opposed to privilege) is striking both in Adams's own words and the story as a whole. (This makes it very different from the Kipling stories of colonial service, of which it seems at times to be a parody.) But the aimlessness of Adams's life (the story never shows him working) fits in with the pointlessness and absurdity of the action in so many other Maclaren-Ross texts. "A Bit of a Smash in Madras" echoes other stories, too, in the motif of fraud. Krishnaswami and his associate Turpin try to blackmail and defraud Adams; Menon is also interested in what he can get out of the case; while Shankran arranges false documentation for Adams and bribes witnesses. In the end, Adams evades punishment for his actions, and at the story's end has learned nothing, and will presumably go on with his aimless boozy life back in England.

Maclaren-Ross's output of short fiction is small, but his stories are skillfully integrated, linguistically innovative and vigorous, and present a consistent and disturbing vision of a shabby, aimless, and compromised world. His is a voice for the early twenty-first century as much as for the mid-twentieth, and one hopes that his most powerful short stories, particularly the texts about the British army, offering an account of an often forgotten historical experience, that of the unwilling and much put-upon conscript in World War II, will receive a wider readership and the critical attention they deserve.

REFERENCES AND FURTHER READING

"Army Life" (1944). *Times Literary Supplement* (August 12): 389.

Bergonzi, B. (1993). *Wartime and Aftermath: English Literature and Its Background 1939–60.* Oxford and New York: Oxford University Press.

Maclaren-Ross, J. (1944). *The Stuff to Give the Troops.* London: Jonathan Cape.

Maclaren-Ross, J. (1945). *Better Than a Kick in the Pants.* London: Lawson and Dunn.

Maclaren-Ross, J. (1946). *The Nine Men of Soho.* London: Allan Wingate.

Maclaren-Ross, J. (1956). *The Funny Bone.* London: Elek Books.

Maclaren-Ross, J. (2004). *Selected Stories,* ed. Paul Willetts. Stockport: Dewi Lewis.

Parker, P. (ed.) (1995). "Julian Maclaren Ross," *The Reader's Companion to Twentieth-Century Writers,* pp. 468–9. London: Fourth Estate; Oxford: Helicon.

Taylor, D.J. (2002). "Introduction," in J. Maclaren-Ross, *Of Love and Hunger,* pp. vii–xiv. London: Penguin.

Willetts, P. (2003). *Fear and Loathing in Fitzrovia: The Bizarre Life of Writer, Actor, Soho Dandy Julian Maclaren-Ross.* Stockport: Dewi Lewis.

Willetts, P. (2004). "Introduction," in J. Maclaren-Ross. *Collected Memoirs,* pp. ix–xxi. London: Black Spring Press.

Willetts, P. (2005). "Introduction," in J. Maclaren-Ross, *Bitten by the Tarantula and Other Writing,* pp. ix–xx. London: Black Spring Press.

33

Alan Sillitoe: "The Loneliness of the Long Distance Runner"

Michael Parker

"The Loneliness of the Long Distance Runner" (1959) is a deftly executed story that continues to challenge readers and prompt them to reassess their attitudes towards the interrelated issues of social inequity, emotional deprivation, and criminality. Voiced by Smith, a young male offender who at first appears to be providing his account from inside a borstal, the narrative depicts and reflects upon critical moments in his life, which on several occasions he compares to an extended race (Sillitoe 1994: 19, 43–4). That it is a contest he is determined to "win" on his own terms is made apparent from the outset, when he states that he has no intention of satisfying the governor's ambitions to secure the grandly titled "Blue Ribbon Prize Cup for Long Distance Cross-Country Running (All England)" for the borstal. Whereas in the 1962 film adaptation, an element of suspense surrounds the race, six pages into the original story there is a clear indication of its outcome. Smith's unspoken response to the governor's assertion "I know you'll get us that cup" is "Like boggery, I will" (13). At the story's climax and in sight of the finishing line, Smith stops running, thereby enabling another competitor, a public-school boy, to overtake him and take the prize. Far more important to Sillitoe than this one single calculated act of defiance are the factors that go into its making, not least amongst which is the death of his father. Disempowered, embittered, alienated even in his own home, the almost anonymous narrator represents a whole underclass in British society, generations of lives which have been (as Thomas Hobbes puts in *Leviathan*) "solitary . . . brutish and short."

In a pioneering, early study of Sillitoe's writing, the American critic Allen R. Penner argues that the insights into "the psychology of poverty" (Penner 1972: 14) it contains arise directly from the author's formative years, growing up during the Depression of the 1930s. The author's father, Christopher, a semi-skilled laborer, was frequently on the dole and so unable to provide adequately for his wife and five children, who thus experienced intense economic want. What Penner is less attentive to, however, are the political, economic, social, and cultural circumstances of the period immediately *prior* to the composition of Sillitoe's early fiction. When Sillitoe returned to Britain in 1958, after a five-year stint teaching, translating, and writing in Majorca (during this time, he wrote *Saturday Night and Sunday Morning* and many of the stories in *The Loneliness of the Long Distance Runner*), it was to a country in which the Conservative Party was in the ascendant and in government. Their popularity had plummeted in the wake of the Suez debacle, when they slipped to thirteen points behind Labour in the opinion polls, but rose once more when Harold Macmillan became Prime Minister in January 1957 (Sked and Cook 1990: 139). Post-Suez, the process of decolonization gathered momentum, as did debates over Britain's future defense policy. Partly in order to reduce growing costs, the government decided to phase out conscription to the armed forces, and so entrust the defense of the nation to a smaller, fully professional body of men. Financial considerations, as well as national pride, influenced the Conservatives' decision to opt for an independent nuclear deterrent, a move strongly opposed by the recently formed Campaign for Nuclear Disarmament (Sked and Cook 1990: 143).

Traces of this macro-narrative can be detected throughout the short story. The constant references to the army *might* be simply attributable to the fact that the central character must have been born immediately before or during World War II. At the outset Smith compares the warders at the borstal to "German generals" (Sillitoe 1994: 8), and later comments several times on the resemblance between the detective who arrests him and Hitler (31, 35, 38). The borstal boy's suspicion is that on his release he will be pressganged into national service (12), though at the story's close he reveals how a diagnosis of pleurisy enabled him to escape the "khaki" (54), an allusion to contemporary British counter-insurgency operations in Malaya and Kenya. With an insight worthy of George Orwell's Flory, and in an image resonant of colonial malpractice, Smith comments at one point on the negative psychological effects of wielding power: "Maybe as soon as you get the whip-hand over somebody you go dead" (14). A reference two pages later to the possibility of nuclear conflict seems directly linked to the intermittent tensions in the Cold War and to a specific crisis of November 1958 when the Soviet Union threatened to use force to incorporate Berlin in the German Democratic Republic (Sked and Cook 1990: 151).

Primarily, however, it is the class war that Smith sees himself as being engaged in, and which he speaks of being "born into" (17). Unlike the aspiring working-class characters in John Wain's *Hurry on Down* (1953), John Braine's *Room at the Top* (1957), or David Storey's *This Sporting Life* (1960), he remains consistent in his utter contempt for the middle classes, their values, and for the whole inequitable system "them bastards over us" operate; the very structure of this phrase replicates socio-economic actualities. From the very opening sentence, he represents British society in binarist terms; an unidentified "I" pitches himself against a determining "they" who "*made me* a long-distance cross-country runner" (Sillitoe 1994: 7; my emphasis). Although this first utterance is couched in a standard, formal register, he soon starts signaling his class difference by deploying colloquial words and expressions ("a fair lick," "cops," "Borstal slum-gullion," "a mug's game"). In his over-extended second sentence, he speculates on what "*they* thought" about his physique. The fact that his body is "long and skinny" equips him for his allotted role, but for the reader it also hints at his straitened economic origins. By then informing us that "running had always been made much of in our family, especially running away from the police" (7), he demonstrates a recurring tendency to explain himself to himself – and anchor his identity – in terms of class and kin.

What greatly enhances Sillitoe's story are the complexities and ambiguities in his principal character, and the way in which the readers' attitudes shift towards Smith and his partial narration. The dehumanizing portrait of borstal life he provides fosters a degree of empathy for him and his plight, at least initially. To him the borstal is a panopticon where the powers-that-be "spy on us all day" (10), constantly "watching out" (8) for signs of recalcitrance and transgression. In phrases evocative of Orwell's *Animal Farm*, its setting and inhabitants, he describes the "crumbly manor house" that dominates the borstal grounds, where warders sit "like spiders" or "jumped up jackdaws," in the service of a "pig-faced" establishment (8). Repeatedly he equates his status, and occasionally that of his fellow prisoners, to that of animals. "They're training me up" for the sports day, he tells us, as if he were a race horse (9, 12) or derived from "a long line of whippets," monstrously compelled "to run on two legs" (43). Resentment at being "cooped up" (9) – both inside the borstal and outside – has made him embrace the chance to run *and* to give vent to the "thoughts and secrets and bloody life" locked up inside him. The way he reads his situation demonstrates both genuine insight and naive generalization, as his mood oscillates between a cocky self-regard and self-condemnation, and from perky optimism to fatalistic resignation. One moment he declares "I'll win in the end," and that "what I'm scribbling down is worth a million" compared to what the governor "could ever scribble down" (13); the next he concedes that "it's dead blokes like him as have a whip-hand over blokes like me, and I'm almost dead sure it'll always be like that" (14). Amongst his many fatalistic pronouncements is a constant conviction that "every minute of my life a big boot is always likely to smash any nice picnic I might be barmy and dishonest enough to make for myself" (18). Were he ever to achieve a position of power, he chillingly informs us, he would stick up against a wall "all the cops, governors, posh whores, penpushers, army officers, Members of Parliament" and "let them have it" (15).

In characterizing "life" as "bloody" and the governor and his ilk as "dead," Smith unconsciously draws attention to a critical absence, that of his father, which continues to haunt him and dictate his behavior. Tellingly, reference to his father's death does not occur until the flashback at the start of part two, and is then mentioned almost in passing. Indeed, he gives greater prominence to the £500 compensation money his mother receives and the goods she buys with it, and recalls how suddenly having "all the money we needed" (21) transformed the family for a few months. Intruding on the euphoria created by becoming a free-spending family – with new clothes, a twenty-one inch television, a fur coat, and "bags of grub" – is a reminder of the terrible actuality that brought these things into the house, the cost his father bore: "Poor old dad, he didn't get a look in, and he was the one who'd done the suffering" (21). In contrast to the other items, the new bedroom carpet was virtually a necessity, since "the old one was covered with blood from dad's dying and wouldn't wash out" (20). That the cause of death was throat cancer adds impetus to Smith's passion to speak out on behalf of his silenced father and his ill-used class.

The disclosure of this loss sheds a different light on some of the borstal boy's comments and choice of metaphors in part one. There he had spoken of the pleasure of running at daybreak when "Everything's dead, but good, because it's dead before coming alive, not dead after being alive." He adds that though "frozen stiff at first," and unable to "feel my hands or feet or flesh at all, like I'm a ghost," he knows shortly that he will undergo a kind of rebirth, which will leave him as warm as "a potbellied stove," "as happy as a dog with a tin tail" (11). At each of the major turning points in the narrative, the bakery robbery and the big race, Smith's identification with and separation from his father come to the fore. Following the break-in, he imagines how he might explain away the bulky shape he has stuffed up his jumper if stopped by a policeman: "'What is it?' he'd ask, and I'd say 'A growth . . . Dad died of it last month, and I'll die of it next month by the feel of it'" (27–8). The macabre humor here seems like a defense measure, an attempt to repress the intensity of his emotions, rather than merely a sign of callousness. Two-thirds of the way through his climactic run, he returns once more to his father's final agony, comparing a pain in his chest to a knife "that has somehow got stuck there" (47). This prompts a flashback to his gruesome discovery of his father's solitary death, "when he filled his bedroom with hot blood and kicked the bucket that morning when nobody was in the house." The metaphors deployed at the close of this key episode reinforce the conviction that the son reads himself as the image of his father. Returning to the *nail-dead* house," he

> stood leaning my head against the *cold* mirror above the mantelpiece, trying not to open my eyes and see my *stone-cold* clock – because I knew I'd gone as *white* as a piece of chalk since coming in as if I'd been got by a Dracula-*vampire*. (Sillitoe 1994: 47–8; my emphases)

However much he tries refocusing on the race – both at the time and in his recollection of it – his telling constantly shifts in tense, the past becoming insistently present ("now . . . I see my bloody dad behind each grassblade," "now I'm making up for it by going over the rotten life mam led him ever since I can remember"(48, 49)).

Bearing an imprint of the multiple betrayals and sufferings his father endured, and the memory of his stubborn resistance at the end, Smith's animosity towards the governor becomes even more comprehensible. To the borstal boy, the governor is a false father, an interpellator and instrument of the state's repressive and ideological apparatuses, another purveyor of "false consciousness" or, as Smith has it, "magic lantern slides" (48). Having glimpsed a copy of the *Daily Telegraph* beneath his "lilywhite workless hands" during their first encounter, the youngster never has any doubt about the governor's allegiance to the ruling Conservative Party. Thereafter any pronouncement he makes is read negatively, as Smith brings to bear the skills in textual analysis acquired from his father and "the comrades" (28). As early as the fourth paragraph in the story, he quotes the governor's address on his arrival at the borstal, picking up on his iterated use of the word "we" and its import. The first-person plural signals the governor's representative status, not just as the head of the borstal staff, but of the millions of conforming citizens or "In-law blokes" (9) ranged against him and the other new boys, should they consider any further "false moves." The very idea of "playing ball" with the authorities is written off as laughable, especially when the governor's sporting analogies and soothing rhetoric are immediately followed by "the barking sergeant-major's voice" of one of his officers, "calling" Smith "to attention" and to a recognition of the quasi-military nature of the regime.

Despite the lack of reference to petty theft as a political strategy in *The Communist Manifesto*, Smith clearly regards himself and fellow delinquents as foot soldiers in a continuing class war. Alert to the way political and economic establishments manipulate language and discourse, he is determined to construct his own text as a site of alternative meanings. Thus, when the governor extols the virtues of being "honest," he decodes the word, arguing that in reality what it amounts to is inferiority, passivity, resignation:

> Be honest. It's like saying: Be dead, like me, and then you'll have no more pain of leaving your nice slummy house for Borstal or prison. Be honest and settle down in a cosy six pounds a week job . . . I know what honest means according to me. (Sillitoe 1994: 14–15)

For him, being honest entails loyalty to the patrilineal line and to class origins. Subsequently, in the light of the reflections generated by the big race, he extends the term to embrace within it an acceptance of the terrible solitariness of human beings, a knowledge that "it would be no different ever . . . all I knew you had to do was run, run, run, without knowing why you were running" (43). The only "realness" in life, he perceives, is death, and "when you tripped over a tree-trunk . . . or fell into a disused well . . . and *stayed dead in the darkness forever*" (44: my emphasis). This Beckett-like take on existence is not unconnected to his materialist political stance, or unaffected by the trauma of loss he has sought to contain. Given his experiences thus far and this frame of mind, it is hardly surprising that he should dismiss as fripperies the symbols placed in his path by the system, winning posts, bits of blue ribbon, and "clothes-line" (44, 52).

Smith's precocious gifts as a reader of signs are displayed in the extended flashback of the story's middle section, which demonstrates that he is not immune to the enticements disseminated by the dominant ideology. He gives a revealing account of the impact made by television advertising in the late 1950s, and how it fueled a "new consumer passion among the working class" (Daniels and Rycroft 1993: 471). Adverts on television made a much greater impression than those in the cinema, on posters, or in the newspaper, he observes retrospectively, since in the privacy of their homes people were more susceptible to the fantasies they wove:

> To begin with, the adverts on the telly had shown us how much more there was in the
> world than we'd ever dreamed of . . . and the telly made all these things seem twenty
> times better than we'd ever thought they were . . . We used to cock our noses up at
> things in shops that didn't move, but suddenly we saw their real value because they
> jumped and glittered around the screen. (21)

The dread expressed in Richard Hoggart's *The Uses of Literacy* (1957) that working-
class affluence might result in increasing "cultural sterility" (Hitchcock 1989: 24) is
not one that Smith would share. He and his partner-in-crime, Mike, find television
intensely alluring, not only because of the apparent accessibility of the commodities
on display, but also because of the films shown. In particular, they relish heist dramas,
where the thieves get away with the money "until the last moment" (Sillitoe 1994:
22); this anticipates his own situation, when for a long time he is able to evade arrest
for his part in the bakery robbery. So engrossed was he in these fictions, he explains,
that he often found it difficult to refrain from putting his hand "into the screen" in
order to prevent the coppers arresting the robbers. The implicit messages in these
films that crime does not pay, or that the police always get their man, is utterly lost
on him; he identifies totally with the supposed anti-hero, even if "he'd knocked off a
couple of bank-clerks" (22). His allusion to the television as a "box of tricks" (23)
might be taken as indicating an awareness of its ambiguity as a medium, and how
through the power of its illusions it can foster an illusion of power. Certainly, what
he finds deeply satisfying and empowering about owning a set is being able to
manipulate the volume control. He recalls nostalgically how at home, for a while at
least, he had been able to silence the voices of authority and at the same time gain
approval from his "*whole* family":

> It was best of all though when *we* did it to some Tory telling *us* all about how good his
> government was going to be if *we* kept on voting for them . . . you could see they didn't
> mean a word they said, especially with not a murmur coming out because *we*'d cut off
> the sound. (Sillitoe 1994: 22: my emphasis)

This is an illuminating example of Smith's wish-fulfillment, and of Sillitoe's use of a
character's "private pronouncements" to reflect what is "more like collective desire"
(Hitchcock 1989: 102).

At first reading, it is easy to come to the conclusion that for Smith the pinnacle
of his achievement to date is that instant when he deliberately throws the race and
warms to the recognition that the other borstal boys have grasped his meaning. It is
a turning point in his life, since at that moment he refuses inscription and becomes
instead a maker of texts. In the story there are recurring, sometimes self-deprecatory
references to the act of writing (Sillitoe 1994: 13, 15, 18, 23, 26, 46). At the close,
Smith tells us how after contracting pleurisy, brought on by the borstal running
regime, he has resumed his career in crime and so "had the peace to write all this"
(54). Ten lines later, in the final paragraph, he provides a brief critique of the shortcomings of contemporary writing, when he informs us that the books he has read

recently were "useless . . . because all of them ended on a winning post and didn't teach me a thing" (54). This acutely solitary young man concludes his narrative by affirming local loyalties, confiding to us that

> I'm going to give this story to a pal of mine and tell him if I do get captured again . . . he can try and get it put into a book or something . . . the bloke I give this story to will never give me away; he's lived in our street for as long as I can remember, and he's my pal. That I do know. (54)

The identity of this reliable "pal" he is clearly unwilling to disclose, though it could possibly be Mike, with whom he undertook the bakery robbery. The informal term "pal," of course, has a long association with northern working-class solidarity, though the preceding text has displayed little illustration of this. Indeed, as Peter Hitchcock suggests, Smith is "not typical of the working class, yet voices a structure of feeling that is specific to it" (Hitchcock 1989: 102). In this he resembles a considerable number of gifted working-class writers whose books, plays, films, and television work came to prominence at this juncture and during the 1960s.

On publication in 1959, Alan Sillitoe's "The Loneliness of the Long Distance Runner" met with instant acclaim. Reviewing the book in which the short story appeared, Malcolm Bradbury cited it as evidence that its author was "a major writer who ought to be read" (Bradbury 1960: 5). Sillitoe's skill as a creator of vividly realized working-class "leads" resulted in his work being swiftly taken up by directors from the British new wave. Following his own successful adaptation of *Saturday Night and Sunday Morning*, his award-winning novel, Sillitoe was asked by Tony Richardson to write the screenplay for *The Loneliness of the Long Distance Runner* (1962), which further enhanced his reputation and the impact of his fiction.

References and Further Reading

Bradbury, M. (1960). Review of *The Loneliness of the Long-Distance Runner*, *New York Times Book Review* (April 10): 5.

Daniels, S. and Rycroft, S. (1993). "Mapping the Modern City: Alan Sillitoe's Nottingham Novels," *Transactions of the Institute of British Geographers* 18/4: 460–80.

Hitchcock, P. (1989). *Working-Class Fiction in Theory and Practice: A Reading of Alan Sillitoe.* Ann Arbor: UMI Research Press.

Hoggart, R. (1969). *The Uses of Literacy.* Harmondsworth: Penguin (original work published 1957).

Penner, A.R. (1972). *Alan Sillitoe.* New York: Twayne.

Sillitoe, A. (1994). *The Loneliness of the Long-Distance Runner.* London: Flamingo (original work published 1959).

Sked, A. and Cook, C. (1990). *Post War Britain: A Political History.* Harmondsworth: Penguin 1990.

34

The Short Stories of
Elizabeth Taylor

Robert Ellis Hosmer, Jr

Elizabeth Coles Taylor (1912–75) lived a quiet, modest life, a life she herself described as one in which "nothing sensational, thank heavens, has ever happened" (Taylor 1953: 23). Born on July 3, 1912, in Reading, she was educated at the Abbey School, where Jane Austen had been a student long before her. With that, her formal education ceased. Then, as she noted, "I drifted into being a governess and went on writing novels in the evenings as I had done for years" (Taylor 1953: 23). In 1936 she married John Taylor and settled in the village of Penn, Buckinghamshire, where she spent most of the rest of her life. The village life of the Thames Valley would furnish her with much of her fictional subject matter.

While bringing up two children and running a household, Taylor continued to write. Her first publication, a short story, appeared in 1942, followed by her first novel, *At Mrs Lippincote's*, in 1945. Though Taylor's reputation rests largely on the twelve novels she wrote, she never abandoned the short story, publishing in a variety of magazines and journals (*The London Magazine, The Cornhill, Vogue*, and *The Saturday Evening Post*), most frequently in *The New Yorker*, where the longtime fiction editor William Maxwell took a special interest in her work. Indeed, Taylor herself seems to have had a decided partiality, to judge from a comment she made in a letter to her agent, Patience Ross: "I feel happier about my stories than about my novels" (Knight 1995: 2).

By the end of her career, Taylor had published four volumes of stories: *Hester Lilly and Twelve Short Stories* (1954); *The Blush and Other Stories* (1958); *A Dedicated Man and Other Stories* (1965); and *The Devastating Boys and Other Stories* (1972). Biographical evidence suggests that she continued to write both novels and stories during her last several years as she suffered from cancer: two of her uncollected stories, "The Blossoming" and "The Wrong Order," can be dated to 1972 and 1973 respectively; and another work, title unknown, was sent to her agent on March 8, 1974, some twenty months before her death (Knight 1995: 8).

A resurgence of interest in Taylor's work prompted Virago to republish all four collections during the 1980s and early 1990s, and then issue *Dangerous Calm: The Selected Stories of Elizabeth Taylor* in 1995 as well. If recalled at all today, Taylor is remembered as a novelist, with some critics comparing her favorably with Jane Austen: Arthur Mizener called her "the modern man's Jane Austen" (1953: 25), and William Pritchard followed suit in a review titled "Almost Austen." Nonetheless, her stories deserve attention, for she was an accomplished practitioner of the form; and they sometimes please as much as the novels, since in both, "she wove fancies from fragments of fact" (Liddell 1986: 66).

In some measure, it makes little difference which volume of stories is chosen to examine Taylor's achievement. To consider several dozen stories with an eye toward discerning "development" would be a waste of time. To borrow a line from an essay on Elizabeth Bishop by Howard Moss, an estimate equally applicable to Elizabeth Taylor, "she was herself from the beginning" (Moss 1986: 303). Each of the four collections illustrates her strengths without disguising her weaknesses. Perhaps *The Devastating Boys*, her most famous and readily accessible collection, affords best insight in Taylor's way with the short story.

The Devastating Boys received favorable reviews on publication in 1972. Already well known as the author of eleven novels, including the popular *Angel* (1957), and many short stories as well, Taylor met with more critical and popular acclaim with this fourth collection of eleven typical tales. These are stories of disruption, disappointment, and deception (especially self-deception); not of anguish, catastrophe, or death. And so they are very much Taylor's. Characters are English – either on home territory or transplanted to foreign parts, as in "Flesh," "Hotel du Commerce," and "Crepes Flambees," though it is a mistake to subscribe to the accepted notion that Taylor wrote exclusively about the English: a sketchy, stereotypical Arab, Habib, a hustler of sorts, is integral to "Crepes"; a detailed and carefully individualized West Indian living in London is the fully realized center of "Tall Boy"; and two "coloured" boys are instrumental in the collection's title story. Indeed, one clear distinction between Taylor's novels and stories lies here: the world of her stories tends towards a racial diversity not found in the longer fiction.

One of her most appreciative readers, the novelist Paul Bailey, notes in his introduction to *The Devastating Boys*, that, "the short-story form is one that attracts the swift glance rather than the long, cold stare, and Elizabeth Taylor is one of the great glancers" (1984: x). Certainly, the most successful stories here are glances. Many of the stories are ten-to-fifteen pages long, illustrating a typical economy; indeed, when the stories are substantially longer – as in the case of "Excursion to the Source" (thirty pages) and "Crepes Flambees" (twenty-two pages) – they are noticeably weaker efforts. The glance has turned into a long, though not cold, stare.

All of the stories feature a singular ability to paint a scene; in that service, Taylor's apt choice of detail, which serves her so well in constructing character through significant feature and telling gesture, enables her to set a carefully framed context with a few quick strokes. Finally, the stories share a characteristic Taylor tone: wry, humorous, compassionate, understanding, if not always accepting. Taylor consistently resists the cheap shot and rejects an easy laugh at her character's expense. Her third-person narrator imperceptibly guides and unfolds the narrative most often, in keeping with her stated intention, "When I move characters from place to place, I like to go with them. I am rather like a ghost, unobserved; and *they* are the real ones at that moment" (Taylor 1965: 10).

Five of the stories from *The Devastating Boys* show Taylor in fine form. First, the title story, deemed "an absolute stunner" by Bailey (1984: xi). The title of the story would lead a reader to think that it is about "the devastating boys," two six-year-old boys who leave London for two weeks' summer holiday at the home of an Oxford don, Harold, and his wife, Laura. Certainly Taylor's story spends some time describing the antics of the boys, Septimus Alexander Smith and Benny Reece, one "coloured," the other "half-caste." Taylor exploits their behavior to rich comic effect, whether they are playing cricket, fooling around on the telephone, taking three baths daily, or visiting a stuffy neighbor. Her acute ear captures and renders most plausibly the speech patterns of the boys, particularly their marvelous gift for mimicry: the boys' mimicking of the neighbor's remark, "you strike me entirely rigid," adds both plausibility and humor to the story.

Further, Taylor pokes gentle fun at the liberal, agnostic Harold, who tells Laura, "We could have two boys or two girls to stay. . . . No stipulation, but that they must be coloured" (Taylor 1984: 10). His political sympathies and patience are tested when he is unexpectedly forced to take the boys to church for Sunday service. Particularly discomfiting is the vicar's after-service greeting, "We are especially glad to see *you*" (30).

But despite the boys and the comedy, "The Devastating Boys" is a serious story, and it belongs to Laura, "a woman who never had a very high opinion of herself" (31), and who has spent most of her adult life as caregiver and traditional home-maker. Now that her two daughters are grown and married, she is adrift and terrified by the void. The story itself opens in the "empty space" between children and grandchildren, and, in middle age, Laura feels dread, panic, and menace. The story's opening paragraphs perfectly capture Laura's existential situation and state of mind with clarity, its images culminating in a "closed door . . . looking more closed, she thought, than any door she had ever seen" (9). In a quick stroke, Taylor's narrator summarizes Laura's plight: "Life had fallen away from her" (11). So deep is her dread and fear that when the boys arrived, "she stooped and clasped them to her in terror" (12).

By the end of the boys' stay, Laura realizes that their visit had been "a success for her and for Harold" (31). She has found a place for herself once again. Harold is noticeably pleased by Laura's dealings with the boys, and uncharacteristically generous as well ("There had been almost a note of praise in his voice" (32)). This portrait of a marriage, with its power dynamics and condescension on his side and its subservience to male domination on hers, disturbs a twenty-first-century reader, but this is the way it was, this was real life in the Thames Valley circa 1960, untouched by the feminist revolution. "The Devastating Boys" ranks as one of Taylor's several best stories.

"Praises," a brief seven-page story, concerns a moment in the life of Miss Smythe, a dignified, lonely older woman, on the day of her retirement from the gown department of a great store now "due for demolition." The story is really a double demolition, for Miss Smythe, a woman who, like Laura, has consistently defined herself through what she does in a patriarchal world, life is effectively over. Taylor's description of the store, its employees, some Miss Smythe's friends, others her critics only now able to express their feelings as she prepares to leave, and its director, whose farewell speech echoes with typical platitudes and clichés, creates a finely detailed context for Miss Smythe's exit. The final image of Miss Smythe, unseasonably smothered in a Persian lamb coat on an unfamiliar train home, staring out the window, is heart-wrenching: "She sat back idly, her hands clasped over the bag on her lap, and looked out of the window at the evening scene as if for the first time, not the last" (87). The delicacy of Taylor's telling of the story is an ironic counterpoint to the brutality of one woman's destruction.

"Tall Boy" is an unusual story for Elizabeth Taylor, with a male figure, a West Indian man, at its center. Taylor gave few interviews and was reticent to talk much about her craft, but in a short piece for *London Magazine*, "Some Notes on Writing Stories," she wrote about the genesis of this story:

> Sometimes, in my own experience, the being hit upon by the idea [for a story] is almost unregistered at the time. Once, from a bus, I saw a West Indian sprinting along in the rain, as if running simply for the pleasure of using his stride. Where to, I wondered. Sitting in the bus, I began to guess, to ponder, to stretch my imagination. The small picture of him stayed in my mind for a long time before I began to write the story. (Taylor 1970b: 9)

Jasper Jones, nicknamed "Tall Boy" by his co-workers at a van-loading operation, lives a lonely life in a bed-sitter on St Luke's Road, far from his mother and sisters. Taylor excels at creating the touching detail that illuminates character so beautifully; here the childlike Jasper (one must ignore political correctness for the moment) takes comfort in believing that the time in London coincides with the time at home in the West Indies: "He imagined home having the same time as England" (Taylor 1984: 70).

Jasper works hard, sends money home to his family, and has few, if any, pleasures other than an occasional glass of beer at a local pub. He is an outsider and Taylor lets us see the world from his point of view: to him, Londoners are afflicted with "a greyness of soul and taste, to match the climate" (69). His approaching twenty-sixth birthday fills him with dread and Taylor creates a narrative of great tenderness and gentle humor as she details the means by which Jasper tries to stave off the loneliness of a birthday spent away from home.

Like "The Devastating Boys" and "Praises," "Sisters" is one woman's story: here, she is a woman far less attractive than Laura or Miss Smythe, however. She is Mrs Mason, ex-mayoress, comfortable widow of a dentist who lives a genteel life of morning coffees, shopping, gardening, charitable committees, and afternoon bridge games in a picturesque village. Hers is a little world, hermetically sealed, and self-deception is the sealing fluid. Only her late husband knew a secret she considers shameful: her oldest sister, Marion, had been a successful novelist of scandalous bohemian lifestyle during the 1920s and 1930s. Nothing has disturbed Mrs Mason's little world for years now, but, "on a Thursday morning, soon after Mrs Mason returned from shopping – in fact she had not yet taken off her hat – a neat young man wearing a dark suit and spectacles, half-gold, half-mock tortoiseshell, and carrying a rolled umbrella, called at the house, and brought her to the edge of ruin" (126). That first sentence of "Sisters" attests to Taylor's characteristically engaging opening and to her skill at creating the illuminating detail, here one that sets a menacing tone for what follows.

The young man is writing a book about Marion and, by a bit of literary detective work, he has discovered Mrs Mason and come to interview her. Their conversation, really not much more than an elliptical monologue to begin with, becomes an exemplum of the unspoken, before Mrs Mason makes a stunning declaration, *sotto voce*, and the young man pounces, but to little avail. He leaves unsatisfied; she leaves for her afternoon card game, at which she will play badly, so unsettled is she at the prospect of the young man's revealing family secrets to the world. That others will talk about her is the feared "ruin" for this self-centered, self-deceived widow of considerable means.

Taylor's typical economy and clarity, enhanced by evocative, detailed delving into Mrs Mason's past, make this story a haunting, psychologically revealing tale that resonates beyond the confines of its ten pages, an infrequent achievement for Taylor's short stories.

Just the title of another story, "Flesh," creates unusual expectations for a story by Elizabeth Taylor, and expectations are significant here. The plot is, indeed, somewhat clichéd: Phyl, wife of a publican, is off on holiday without her husband, part of a group trip of English men and women to an unnamed Mediterranean resort. Phyl and Stanley, a recent widower, are drawn to each other by a certain shared fondness for drink. They plot a side trip, for a little tryst. It would spoil the story to say more, but it's really a French farce.

Taylor's humor and compassion make "Flesh" something more than a trite little tale of a holiday liaison, though. Neither Phyl nor Stanley would qualify for tourist board brochures: she is a large, middle-aged woman recuperating from a hysterectomy, spending her days by the pool "basting herself with oil" (105), and her evenings in marathon drinking. No oil painting himself, Stanley is well past a prime he may never have had; his interests are limited: drink, food, sex (in that order). Both Phyl and Stanley are easy marks for mockery, but that is clearly not Taylor's purpose. Rather, she seems to be interested in presenting a little slice of real life, told with some affection, and a considerable humor that sustains this twenty-page story.

These five stories illuminate Elizabeth Taylor's strengths as a writer of short stories: character construction, choice of subject matter, economy, tone, scene painting, and detail. Of these, detail – what she herself called "the illuminating detail" or "the enlivening detail" – is likely her greatest strength. At her best, Taylor creates details are exactly what she wanted them to be: "strokes of reality, highlights, dashes of colour; breath to the abstract, death to the vague " (Taylor 1970a: 15).

The remaining six stories, though some do show signs of her strengths, are weaker, less satisfactory efforts. "The Excursion to the Source" suffers from a singular improbability of climactic episode as well as excessive length (thirty pages). "In and Out the House" is a portrait of village life disrupted by a little girl who makes a daily rota of visits to her neighbors and carries tales from one to another; "Hotel du Commerce" takes Taylor off-territory, following a honeymoon couple to a two-star French hotel, and the narrative is assigned more significance than it can bear. "Miss A. and Miss M." tells of the disruption of a partnership between two women who have lived together for years, the cause entirely predictable, the narrator atypically first person and unconvincing. "The Fly Paper," a clever enough horror story of a young girl's seduction, seems derivative of Elizabeth Bowen. And "Crepes Flambees" is an unconvincing study of marriage, no more than a weak variation on "Hotel du Commerce"; it seems clear that Taylor most often needs the length of the novel when she deals with marriage, so many of her novels being perceptive and knowing studies of that institution (especially *At Mrs Lippincote's*, *The Wedding Group*, and *In a Summer Season*). Judged by her own criteria, none of her weaker stories succeeds: "For success there must be immediate impact, less going into anything, more suggestiveness and compression, more scene and less narrative, all beautiful and exciting restrictions to my mind" (Taylor 1970b: 9).

In his introduction to *The Devastating Boys*, Bailey noted that "Elizabeth Taylor wanted to be a painter" (1984: xiii), and a simple analogy between the verbal and painterly arts may be most useful in evaluating Taylor's achievement: her best stories are genre paintings, carefully defined personal spaces, small canvases with clearly etched characters illuminated with a worldly wise appreciation as they go about the business of everyday life. In that realm, Taylor's sharp eye for detail, gesture, shades of light – in sum, her extraordinary technical control – serves her well. In the best stories Taylor does what William Pritchard has said she does in her novels, "she gives us a sense of the real, of life going on (as it were) without the help of a presiding, shaping, manipulative spirit' (1984: 160).

But readers may require something more from stories. A certain lack of agenda, an absence of greater concerns in most of Taylor's stories, seems refreshing at first; but after reviewing her work in the short story, a reader might well want more. Her refusal or inability to deal with greater issues of the human condition is puzzling. Bailey's defense of Taylor, "Elizabeth Taylor couldn't be bothered to be important" (1984: x) seems inadequate. Set alongside the likes of Bowen's "The Demon Lover," Pritchett's

"The Camberwell Beauty," Lessing's "To Room Nineteen," or Spark's "Portobello Road," even "The Devastating Boys" pales. That failure to deal with larger issues, both personal and political, weakens Taylor's stories; only rarely do the central concerns of the story echo beyond the confines of the text. All her charm, technical polish, assurance, and humor cannot make the majority of her stories more than glimpses of a largely vanished way of life.

Certainly the verdict of an anonymous *TLS* reviewer, "Elizabeth Taylor must surely now be among the four or five most distinguished practitioners of the art of the short story in the English-speaking world" ("Escape" 1972: 649), is a judgment substantially wide of the mark. Too many of her stories seem like staples of women's magazine writing of the 1950s and 1960s, from the days before feminism subverted so many received notions of gender and role definition. Taylor's stories remain carefully crafted period pieces, valuable, perhaps as cultural documents or models of technique, enjoyable as narratives, but ultimately precious, lesser achievements in the tradition of short fiction in English.

References and Further Reading

Bailey, P. (1984). "Introduction," *The Devastating Boys and Other Stories by Elizabeth Taylor*, pp. ix–xiii. London: Penguin Books/Virago Press.

Knight, L. (1995). "Introduction," *Dangerous Calm: The Selected Stories of Elizabeth Taylor*, pp. 1–8. London: Virago Press.

Liddell, R. (1986). *Elizabeth and Ivy*. London: Peter Owen.

Mizener, A. (1953). "In the Austen Vein," *The New Republic* (November 2): 25.

Moss, H. (1986). "The Poet's Voice," *Minor Monuments: Selected Essays by Howard Moss*, pp. 293–303. New York: Ecco Press.

Pritchard, W. (1984). "Almost Austen," *The New Republic* (March 26): 36–9.

Taylor, E. (1953). "Elizabeth Taylor," *New York Herald Tribune* (October 11): 23–5.

Taylor, E. (1965). "Setting a Scene," *Cornhill Magazine* 1045 (autumn): 68–72.

Taylor, E. (1970a). "Choosing Details that Count," *Writer* 83/1 (January): 15–16.

Taylor, E. (1970b). "Some Notes on Writing Stories," *London Magazine* (March): 8–10.

Taylor, E. (1984). *The Devastating Boys and Other Stories*. London: Virago Press.

Times Literary Supplement (1972). "Escape into Irony: *The Devastating Boys* and Other Stories by Elizabeth Taylor," *Times Literary Supplement* (June 9): 649.

35

The Short Fiction of V.S. Pritchett

Andrzej Gąsiorek

In *Why Do I Write?* (1948) V.S. Pritchett contributed to an exchange of letters between himself, Graham Greene, and Elizabeth Bowen. He emphasized that a new society was emerging but insisted on the writer's freedom of expression and refused the lure of political *engagement*, emphasizing instead the writer's inwardness and his right to challenge entrenched assumptions. The writer, Pritchett suggested, is "the incurable instance that cuts across the general pattern; the man with shocking dreams, a timeless creature like the invalid, the lover", whose writing should be characterized by "party disloyalty" (Pritchett 1948: 16). The "world of art", he wrote, "is the world of what has been experienced, but not noticed" (34). This ability to "notice" was for Pritchett linked to the writer's position as an outsider. Hence his claims that the writer is "a man living on the other side of a frontier" (Pritchett 1968: 238) and, of himself, that although he is "often described as a traditional English writer, any originality in [his] writing is due to having something of a foreign mind" (Pritchett 1971: 215).

It is for his stories that Pritchett is best known. They are wide-ranging in subject matter but are principally concerned with the lives of ordinary people. Pritchett's ability to observe the nuances of behavior and to hint at what lies beyond its surface is reminiscent of Chekhov's understated style; no less understated is his depiction of far-reaching social changes. Pritchett was sceptical about the politicization of literature and had a modest view of the writer's social placement, noting of an earlier observer's work that the "revival of Henry James has taught us that writers who live passively within history may be more deeply aware of what is really going on than those who turn up in every spot where the news is breaking" (Pritchett 1965: 154). His view that the writer notices what others have unconsciously experienced points to an aspect of his work that goes beyond realism and draws on the fantastic. The latter lies at the heart of his comic talent. The fantastic – grotesque, delusional, monstrous, or hilarious – is the anarchic spirit that animates Pritchettian comedy. It is a comedy sustained by its observation of the discrepancy between what is enacted by characters but not noticed by them, in short, between their lack of self-awareness and the stories' exposure of that lack. Jeremy Treglown has observed that Pritchett "valued and exploited the traditions of realist prose fiction" (Treglown 2005: 23), but we should also note that he was aware of their limits. He remarked the unimaginativeness of a "quotidian art" that "goes on describing and describing" and praised "romance" for its power to awaken the imagination (Pritchett 1965: 56). Equally importantly, with respect to the English tradition of comedy about which he wrote so perceptively, Pritchett was attuned to those comic strains in which the private imagination vies with public reality, giving rise to "fantasticating" modes of writing dominated by self-inventing solipsists, madmen who "speak as if they were the only persons in the world" and who live entirely "by some private idea or fiction" (Pritchett 1970: 20).

Pritchett's stories typically give us snapshots of intermeshed lives caught in an instant of time. The short story, he notes, "is a flash that suddenly illumines, then passes" (Pritchett 1971: 214). The brief revelations thus vouchsafed to us disclose a world that is both familiar and strange, since Pritchett spotlights aspects of life that have often been ignored in literature. His focus is on lower-middle-class characters who are making their way in a rapidly changing social landscape. In stories such as "Sense of Humour," "Handsome Is As Handsome Does," "X-ray," "The Scapegoat" (all published in 1938), and "When My Girl Comes Home" (1961), to name only a few, class is the omnipresent theme. Pritchett was not a polemical writer; he does not proselytize on behalf of any class in particular but shows how the behavior, attitudes, and life possibilities of *all* social strata in England are conditioned by class. That said, he displayed a special interest in the lower middle class and in his accounts of it followed Gissing rather than Wells or Dickens. Of his own class preoccupations, he noted: "I was much less interested in the 'People' than in the condition of individual people. I was particularly concerned with their lives and speech. In their misleading sentences and in the expressive silences between would lie the design of their lives and their dignity" (Pritchett 1971: 213).

"Sense of Humour" was Pritchett's first successful story. It is told from the perspective of a first-person narrator who reveals his obtuseness as the tale unfolds while "assuming an air of reasonableness and virtue" (Pritchett 1971: 214). This technique is classic Pritchett. The narrator is a commercial traveler who embarks on a relationship with a bored hotel receptionist, Muriel. He supplants her boyfriend, a car mechanic called Colin, who is lower in the social scale than the traveling salesman. The narrator assumes an air of cosmopolitan superiority over the provincial mechanic, who lacks status and power. Unable to compete with the narrator's glib confidence, the mechanic starts to haunt the couple on their weekend jaunts by following them on his motorbike. When Colin is killed in a head-on collision, he takes on a strange role in the couple's relationship. His death brings them together sexually, but from Muriel's behavior it is not clear to whom she thinks she is making love and which of the two men she actually cares for. Has the narrator been the means by which she could escape a dead-end job in a boring town? Did she care for Colin at all or does she simply feel guilty at her role in his death? The narrator has no clue: "Did she love Colin all the time? Did she think I was Colin? And every time I thought of that poor devil covered over with a white sheet in the hospital mortuary, a kind of picture of her and me under the sheets with love came into my mind. I couldn't separate the two things. Just as though it had all come from Colin" (Pritchett 1990: 12).

If Colin is an inarticulate character, then the narrator is shown to be equally limited. His is a surface confidence that rests on his social status. Muriel's refusal to divulge what is in her mind leaves him bewildered, but seemingly content to pass over the truth of their relations in silence. This is unsurprising, however, for he is depicted as a man whose view of life is narrow. His language is one-dimensional and cliché-ridden, revealing a character whose thoughts run in pre-set grooves. Everything he does begins and ends in a business calculus through which he works out whether his actions will profit him. The narrator's penny-pinching business mentality is inseparable from his *amour propre*, his need to see himself as above the class from which he is trying to escape. His company car is the visible symbol of his success, and when Colin fails to get it ready for a visit to his parents, he is incensed: "I felt quite lost on the railway after having a car. It was crowded with trippers too. It was slow – stopping at all the stations. The people come in, they tread all over your feet, they make you squeeze up till you're crammed against the window, and the women stick out their elbows and fidget. And then the expense!" (8). This enforced journey with the hoi polloi is ironically reversed at the end of the story. When the couple return with Colin's body in a luxury hearse, they embark on a stately progress through the region in which they imagine themselves to be royalty.

Colin's death brings the story's strands together. The narrator wants to be rid of him so that he can pursue his affair with Muriel, even though he half grasps that in some indefinable way Colin is implicated in their relationship. But the narrator's character has already been clearly visible to the reader; it is the hitherto somewhat shadowy Muriel whose personality is now illuminated: "'Colin loved me. It is my duty to him,' she said. 'Besides,' she said, suddenly, in her full open voice – it had seemed to be closed and carved and broken and small – 'I've never been in a hearse before'" (14). It is not any sense of "duty" but a wish to extend her range of experience that motivates Muriel, who proceeds to have a thoroughly good time on the drive back. Muriel, it transpires, is as desperate to escape her background as the narrator, and their return trip symbolizes their shared desire for upward social mobility. But Colin's ghostly presence in the hearse cannot be exorcized. He is a reminder of those who get left behind in the drive for self-improvement and a disturber of the new couple's assumptions. The narrator acknowledges that the consummation of their relationship has "put [his] calculations out" (15), since Muriel might get pregnant, but he does not grasp that Muriel, too, is making calculations and that he may represent nothing more to her than a route to a better life. What is missing from this relationship between two social climbers is revealed through the narrator's obtuse view of Colin: "He couldn't save money so he lost her. I suppose all he thought of was love" (7).

Although the protagonists in "Sense of Humour" are ironized, they are taken seriously as representatives of an emerging social stratum. It was among the members of this group that Orwell identified "the germs of the future England," which he described as "a rather restless, cultureless life, centring round tinned food, *Picture Post*, the radio and the internal combustion engine" (Orwell 2002: 314). Orwell treats this emergent class with a suspiciousness that borders on disdain, but Pritchett gives it a voice. He also challenges assumptions about this class, which in his view originate in an earlier comic tradition. Pritchett says of his narrator: "His emergence as a type is commonly misunderstood by literary critics who, owing to the stamp that Dickens and Wells put upon him in their time, have thought of the lower-middle class or petty bourgeois as whimsical 'little men'. But in this century all classes have changed and renewed themselves; they . . . carry inside them something of the personal anarchy of unsettled modern life" (Pritchett 1971: 215–16).

Pritchett's sense of the "unsettled" nature of contemporary social life leads at times to amusing stories and at others to profoundly sad ones. In the beautifully economical tale "X-ray," a cross-section of the population is brought together in a hospital waiting room. Embarassed and awkward, their communal silence is punctured by the impersonal sounds of the hospital staff going about their business, and, in its depiction of their brisk efficiency, the story becomes a study of power in microcosm. The nurses are not just indifferent to their patients but relish the authority they have over them, while the doctors, like absent gods, do not deign to grace the waiting room with their presence. One character, Beale, a "chicken-breasted, trembling little man, stringy of skin, red-nosed and wearing a white choker," is singled out to be victimized, and by being turned into a scapegoat frees everybody else: "There is a movement of delight and pity. All gaze at Beale the hero, the idiot, the man who HAS COME ON THE WRONG DAY" (Pritchett 1990: 101). Beale's discomfiture allows the others to unbend socially, his abject suffering overwhelming any anxiety they are feeling. Beale is the sacrificial victim in a tale that quickly moves from observation to fantasy:

> Nurses scatter to the walls, and suddenly there appears with great strides a tall red-haired doctor, fat, whiskered and gleaming, cannibal, with his white coat flying behind him and out of it great legs leaping with the gusto of striped tigers. He dashes through the sun, a hand covered with golden hairs shoots out of his sleeve, back flies the swing door and he is gone, the spices of the Indies with him. Thermometers have risen. But when the air has settled again the nurse comes and intones, "Beale," looking at the empty corner. Where is Beale? What is he doing in that room? Is he praying or weeping or has he hanged himself? With what awful garments is he struggling? Will he be found crushed on the heel of the doctor's shoe? (Pritchett 1990: 102–3)

The theme of the victim resurfaces in "The Scapegoat," but whereas in "X-ray" the observers of Beale's humiliation are indifferent to his plight, here they rally round the scapegoated figure in an act of empathy. Two rival working-class communities vie with each other for social prestige and in preparation for the Jubilee try to out-do each other in the amounts of money they can raise. The narrator's community reveals its casual anti-Semitism when it refuses to let a Jewish tailor take charge of their money: "We had nothing against Lupinsky but when we saw him raking in the money on his God Saves and Kiss-me-quicks and his flags of all the nations, we thought he was collecting enough as it was. He might mix up the two collections" (Pritchett 1990: 107). They select instead a widower called Art Edwards who steals the money, loses it all in gambling, and hangs himself. But this leads the community to question itself, acknowledge its anti-Semitism, and recognize that it has over-burdened Edwards: "He was ourselves, our hero, our god. He had borne our sins. You couldn't see the hearse for flowers. . . . Art Edwards our king. It looked like a wedding. . . . Earl Street couldn't touch that. And Lupinsky collected the money" (119).

"Handsome is as Handsome Does," by contrast, discloses Pritchett's sense that "class-ache was and is profoundly true to the inner English life" (Pritchett 1991: 528). A warring couple live in mutual detestation but are bound by a shared sense of grievance and shame. The story's class dimension is explicit, for the husband cannot "forgive his wife for coming from a rich family" (50), while she cannot accept that he is a failure who is "always spending his energy on reacting from something which no longer existed" (56). Husband and wife tear at each other in a demented fashion but cannot part since they are "two ugly people cut off from all others, living in their desert island" (55). Thus what seems at the outset to be a story about mutual destruction turns out to be more complex, for it depicts a couple who are embroiled in a *folie à deux*. The husband's inner turmoil, which originates in his class origins, has turned him into a man marked by *ressentiment*, while the wife's self-hatred is inseparable from her abasement before him. When her husband refuses to save a drowning man, who is rescued by a young Jew who has spurned her advances, she pretends that it was the other way about, and through this act of defiance asserts their rejection of the world that has injured them.

"When My Girl Comes Home" is Pritchett's longest and, possibly, his best story. It traces the reactions of an extended family to the post-war homecoming of a woman (Hilda) who they mistakenly believe has been interned in a Japanese prisoner-of-war camp. The story turns on misunderstandings and misperceptions, but its real interest lies in why these come about in the first place: those who observe Hilda project their fantasies on to her until she too becomes a scapegoat figure. "When My Girl Comes Home" begins *in medias res* with the family celebrating Hilda's return, for which an officious in-law, Mr Fulmino, takes credit. Most of the family assume that Hilda has been mistreated by the Japanese in the same way that another member of their community – the sullen Bill Williams – has been. But Hilda turns up well-fed and rich, to amazement and mistrust. It gradually transpires that Fulmino has made an awful mistake. Having married a Japanese, Hilda has been an internee, not a prisoner, and her experiences bear no resemblance to those of Bill Williams. A grim account ensues of how the family react to what they see as a betrayal of their collective dream about Hilda.

Class and race are at the heart of these conflicts. Events are narrated by a young man who is an outsider in two respects: he has just started dating the Fulminos' daughter, so is not a family member, but he is also middle class and educated. His understated narration is quietly observant; he records events as they happen and has no omniscient overview. The story builds through a slow accumulation of sharply perceived details, and it wonderfully evokes the texture of urban life, social frustration, and family history. It is gradually disclosed that Hilda is perceived by those around her to be guilty of a double betrayal on racial and class grounds. Her first marriage was to an Indian, her second to a Japanese, but in addition to this both of them were educated men who belonged firmly to the middle class. Hilda has twice chosen to marry outside her endogamous group, and racial antipathy quickly combines with class resentment. Mr Singh, we discover, "spoke a glittering and palatial English – the beautiful English a snake might speak, it seemed to the family," and reactions to him range from Mrs Fulmino's refusal to be alone with him for fear of sexual assault to Mrs Draper's suspicion that he is nothing but "a common lascar off a ship" (455). When at the end of the story it turns out that Bill Williams has stolen Hilda's money, whereas the family had thought that she was planning to elope with him, her reaction is revealing: "'Go off with Bill Williams!' Hilda laughed. 'My husband was an officer'" (489).

Hilda is the scapegoat upon whom social and personal grievances can be projected. Her *difference* from everybody else is noted early on in the story, and this emphasis on difference is central to the ways in which she is (mis)judged and (mis)treated. Hilda resembles an oriental woman, is described as a foreign exotic, and seems to embody the possibility of an alternative existence. As the narrator admits, when he notes that the Hilda who has returned is quite unlike his expectations, "we had all dreamed of Hilda in our different ways" (445). Grasping that "Hilda" represents a kind of collective fantasy to the family, the narrator eventually recognizes that they have "been disturbed in a very long dream" (454). This dream is "an effect of the long war," seen by the narrator as a bleak incarceration during which, "like convicts, we had been driven to dwelling on fancies in our dreary minds" (454). Such reflections move the story from social notation to the inner space of the private and collective mind. By blurring the boundary between the social and psychological self, it suggests that one of the consequences of war has been the erosion of identity. As the narrator drily observes, when commenting on the incorrect newspaper account of Hilda's wartime experiences: "Even Hilda was awed when she read it, feeling herself drain away, perhaps, and being replaced by this fantasy; and for the rest of us, we had become used to living in a period when events reduced us to beings so trivial that we had no strong feeling of our own existence in relation to the world around us" (468). There is only one exception, a character whose humanity has not been destroyed by the war and who grasps that the suffering it has caused knows no national boundaries: "Jack Draper had fought in the war and where we thought of the war as something done to us and our side, Jack thought of it as something done to everybody" (456).

Hilda ultimately represents a dream of the possibility of escape from the drudgery and irreality of a post-war London existence in which people feel themselves to be adrift. The family is riven by rivalries, jealousies, and disagreements, but they are trapped in a social space that is at once fragmenting and constricting. Hilda is almost broken by the treatment to which she has been subjected, a form of torture that contrasts with the fantasized suffering she did not, in fact, undergo in Japan: "There was in all of us a sympathy we knew how to express but which was halted – as by a fascination – with the sight of her ruin. We could not help contrasting her triumphant arrival with her state at this moment. It was as if we had at last got her with us as we had, months before, expected her to be" (489). In a furious response to this voyeuristic exultation, Hilda condemns her tormentors for their inhumanity and, reversing the gaze that has been so relentlessly directed at her, exposes their vicious and small-minded mentality. This shift in perspective is central to the story's end. After Hilda has left, a book is published about the community by an American who had befriended her, and this book examines her persecutors with an anthropological eye: "Mr Gloster's book came out. Oh yes. It wasn't about Japan or India or anything like that. It was about us" (491).

It is impossible in a short space to do justice to Pritchett's gifts as a writer of stories. He did, after all, produce close to a hundred of them, and they range widely in theme and technique. But his greatest contribution to the genre surely lies in his even-handed representation of ordinary people in all their glorious multiplicity. His biographer, Jeremy Treglown, rightly notes that: "Few writers have been more fair-minded than V.S. Pritchett" (Treglown 2005: 13). His stories reveal him as a wonderful observer of human foibles; always in his work an awareness of how general social pressures determine behavior and attitudes is combined with a sensitivity to particular individual responses to the situations in which people find themselves. Above all, perhaps, he is a chronicler of social change who saw that England's classes were being transformed. Pritchett never viewed the aspiring working or lower middle classes as simply a subject for comedy; he took them seriously without treating them sentimentally. He was as attentive to the reality of class conflict as he was attuned to the delusions of self-mythologizing individuals desperate to make themselves appear more significant than they really were. Pritchett's special gift lay in his ability to combine close observation with wry humor. But his penchant for the sardonic never distracted him from the lesson he learned from Gissing: "To most English novelists, invigorated but narrowed by class consciousness, one class has always seemed comical to another; that is where Gissing is so un-English, a foreigner or an exile. He sees nothing comic in class. He writes as if it exists chiefly as a pathos or a frustration, a limitation of the human keyboard" (Pritchett 1965: 67).

REFERENCES AND FURTHER READING

Orwell, G. (2002). *Essays*, ed. J. Carey. New York: Alfred A. Knopf.

Pritchett, V.S. (1948). *Why Do I Write? An Exchange of Views Between Elizabeth Bowen,* *Graham Greene and V.S. Pritchett*. London: Percival Marshall.

Pritchett, V.S. (1965). *The Working Novelist*. London: Chatto and Windus.

Pritchett, V.S. (1968). *A Cab At The Door: An Autobiography: Early Years*. London: Readers Union/Chatto and Windus.

Pritchett, V.S. (1970). *George Meredith and English Comedy*. London: Chatto and Windus.

Pritchett, V.S. (1971). *Midnight Oil*. London: Chatto and Windus.

Pritchett, V.S. (1990). *The Complete Short Stories*. London: Chatto and Windus.

Pritchett, V.S. (1991). *The Complete Essays*. London: Chatto and Windus.

Treglown, J. (2005). *V.S. Pritchett: A Working Life*. London: Pimlico.

36
Edna O'Brien: "A Rose in the Heart of New York"

Sinéad Mooney

Edna O'Brien's short story, "A Rose in the Heart of New York" was originally published under the title "A Rose in the Heart" in the *New Yorker* in May 1978, the same year it appeared with variants in her *Mrs Reinhardt and Other Stories*. It was later collected in *A Fanatic Heart: Selected Stories*. Like many of her other fictions, it concerns the complex and ambivalent bond between mother and daughter, against an Irish context freighted with the proliferation of religious and political constructions of the maternal. Alongside "Irish Revel" (1968) and "A Scandalous Woman" (1974), it is perhaps the strongest single exemplar among her stories of her consciously post-Joycean creation of a recognizable fictional world, the stultifying rural Irish midlands of the mid-twentieth century, and, more specifically, her recovery of the previously unvoiced female experience of that world. O'Brien consciously constructs a feminocentric rewriting of the family romance: the home is an eerily-personified farmhouse where decay symbolizes sexual violence, the father is exposed as an alcoholic brute, and the mother's mute submission is observed and violently rejected by the daughter, who, nonetheless, fears replicating it. However, the element of the family romance which most engages O'Brien is the dark inter-generational conflicts that emerge from the mother–daughter dyad, which her fiction constructs as poised between ecstatic symbiosis – inevitably becoming suffocation – and insurmountable loss. "A Rose in the Heart of New York" charts, over the course of some forty years, the stifling intimacy of a mother–daughter relationship in which the daughter moves from intense childhood love for her martyred mother, to a largely unsuccessful adult desire to break loose from the filial bond.

"A Rose" tells the story of Delia and her daughter, from the birth of the latter until the mother's death, when the daughter is aged about forty. The plot of the story continues to elaborate themes familiar from O'Brien's earliest published work, *The Country Girls* trilogy, of which the first novel appeared in 1960, notably a heroine incapacitated by adoration of a smothering, victimized mother, which sets her daughter off on a career of abject suffering at the hands of her lovers, the first of Edna

O'Brien's lopsided, desperate women athirst for a resumption of the primary object of love, but unable to regain it. However, while Cáit Brennan's mother drowns during her daughter's adolescence, leaving Cáit, haunted by her absence, to go through the motions of 1960s sexual rebellion in Dublin and London before her own possible suicide by drowning, Delia remains a living presence throughout her daughter's first forty years. After a harrowing description of the birth of her daughter, as her drunk husband ransacks the bedroom for hidden alcohol, the focalization switches gradually, over the course of a few paragraphs, from mother to child. Domestic life is animalistic, as observed by the daughter, herself conceived as a result of marital rape: in the eerie farmhouse, the father takes a hatchet to the mother, and on another occasion shoots at her, but misses as he is "not a good aim like William Tell" (O'Brien 1984: 382), and is threatened with the asylum, where the insane are "brought in on all fours, like beasts of the earth" (381). The mother–daughter dyad, close and consoling, offers an all-encompassing totality of mutual love, eluding spousal brutalization, and the current of violence at the heart of the family romance. However, the maturing daughter, first at boarding school and later in the capital and abroad, attempts to struggle free of the maternal bond, recognizing Delia as a thwarted, deeply disappointed woman who requires "her pound of flesh from life" (396). The story veers from the maternal idealization of the child to the matrophobia of the adult daughter, who, terrified of repeating in her own life the mother's censored tragedy, nonetheless perseveres in attempting to effect some kind of reconciliation despite her own dread of the maternal inheritance, a struggle which ends only at the mother's death.

O'Brien has frequently been attacked by critics for her repeated portrayals of "throttled, sacrificial women", her relegation of men to grotesquely violent impediments to her protagonists, and for her depiction of the Irish female psyche as defined by suffering and lack. Such criticism, however, erroneously assumes that O'Brien's stories are confined to a documentary or social realist mode. "A Rose in the Heart of New York," while it does document the sufferings of women in patriarchal rural society, aims less for a seamless realism than a more unorthodox form of narrative, in which a fractured and problematic verisimilitude is cut with elements of fairy tale and gothic. As Bruno Bettelheim has argued, fairy tales "depict in imaginary and symbolic form the essential steps in growing up and achieving an independent existence" and "represent in imaginative form" the process of human development as tales of *Bildung*, reducing a complicated process of socialization to its essential paradigm (Bettelheim 1976: 73). The opening of "A Rose in the Heart of New York" deliberately echoes the fairy tale, with its childlike evocation of "Jack Frost," a winter landscape, an approach to a mysterious house, and its repeated emphasis on "story." As a whole, it also replicates, in the daughter's violent attachment to, and detachment from, the mother, the way in which, in fairy tales, maternal representations are bound to a binary pattern of idealization and defilement, the good (often dead or lost) mother and the wicked (step)mother.

The story's gothic elements, as well as signaling the obviously patriarchal abuses of power – the half-crazed father and his murderous impulses – also emerge in fears of maternal power, the nightmare of female confinement within a domestic space presented as haunted, with states of living death and live burial, family curses, and hidden stories. The happy homestead beloved of De Valera is rewritten as a place of gothic horror, "a kind of castle where strange things happened and would go on happening" (O'Brien 1984: 383). Its windswept rooms, "cold inside and for the most part identically furnished" and furniture painted an oppressive "oxblood red, with the sharp end of a nail dragged along the varnish to give a wavering effect" (375, 385) are redolent of female lack of identity and suffering. Wardrobes contain the hidden bottles that unleash male aggression and the "bottom drawer" retains, poignantly, only the memory of the wedding gifts, while the paraphernalia of childcare – the cot that rattles like a cage, the "dark, mottled teat" – is given a sinister aura. Often, realist and fantastic modes are combined: the midwife's stories of rural infanticide which open the narrative, as she makes her way towards the protagonist's laboring mother, are both an exposé of the reality of a state in which Catholic doctrine forbade women control of their own fertility – both mother and daughter attempt to prevent conception with tissues – and, in the stuffing of the dead baby into a drawer, supply a haunting image of the unlived life and the stifling of female experience. O'Brien's story moves between a harsh, post-Joycean verisimilitude, in which an intensity of maternal–filial love offers the only solace in a vicious environment, and a mythic dimension in which the archetypes of the lethal or devouring mother and the rebellious daughter confront one another.

The story also achieves important narrative effects via inter-textuality with others of O'Brien's works, in which characters, settings, motifs, and images are repeated: the beloved, then resented, mother-figure, martyred by the alcoholic father, is familiar from as far back as *The Country Girls*; the convent crush on the nun, the "new idol" who replaces the mother (389) and prefigures the distant husband, also features in "Sister Imelda" (1982); motifs such as the humble, twine-wrapped food parcels from home, and the slitting of the child's fingers on a discarded razor-blade reappear from "Cords" (1968), while the narrative movement from rural Ireland to exile in England recurs in much of her work. The effect of such dense inter-textuality suggests less that O'Brien writes "the same story over and over again" as Lynette Carpenter argues (Carpenter 1986: 263), but that the repetitions constitute a set of enforced returns to what O'Brien terms in her *Mother Ireland*, "that trenchant childhood route" from the family to exile (O'Brien 1976: 89), an expulsion from a less than ideal Eden, which is nonetheless perpetually mourned. It is perhaps also the presence of the prototypical O'Brien female protagonist – nameless and archetypal, a figure of wounded or compromised subjectivity – that provides the most significant link to her other work, the namelessness in particular suggesting "a porous feminine consciousness that subverts the notion of an individual identity and an individual story line," as though attacking the notion of the conventional *Bildungsroman* and its central idea of the coherent, perfectible self (Schrank and Farquharson 1996: 23).

As is so frequently the case with O'Brien's protagonists, insufficiency and lack form the ground of the daughter's being, and hamper her attempts to forge a selfhood independent of the all-encompassing figure of the mother who dominates her early life. From the agonized experience of the mother, giving birth at Christmas to a daughter after a succession of dead children, emerges gradually the growing daughter's narrative, structurally indicating both the closeness and the suffocating nature of the bond which forms the body of the story. As both narratives are third-person and the daughter is never named – while the mother's name, Delia, appears only once, the shortened form of "Cordelia," from the Latin *cor* (heart), suggesting again the central symbolism of the story's title, and of course, in a story about female silencing, King Lear's silent daughter – it is not always possible to discern immediately which "she" is speaking, so that maternal and filial narratives cannot be disentangled. This confusion enacts the conflicting desire of the daughter both to uncover the mother's unwritten history and to violently reject the possibility of reduplicating, calamitously, the mother's unlived life in her own, as a form of inherited matrilineal curse. Throughout, the daughter's wavering quest for self-fulfillment operates on this fundamental ambivalence; as an adult woman thinking of her mother from her city home, paradoxically, she is "recalling someone she wanted to banish", hating her mother's humble food parcels "despite the fact that they were most welcome" (O'Brien 1984: 391).

The story obviously demands to be considered in psychoanalytical terms. O'Brien, as in her other well-known story "The Love Object," is consciously playing with the Freudian family romance, and with psychoanalytic binaries in general, such as Freud's vision of human love as being out of phase, and adult sexuality as a bleakly deterministic replication of the child's earliest experience. Freud insists that the mother remains an important figure in the adult woman's life, often determining the nature and quality of sexual relationships, and that adult femininity, at its best, is the result of a long, conflicted, and discontinuous developmental course, marked by what Elizabeth Abel has termed "a series of costly repressions" (Abel 1983: 271) O'Brien, turning away from the masculine Oedipal plots which have dominated twentieth-century Irish literature, seeks to explore precisely these "repressions" and, in doing so, to investigate the ambiguities and divisions in the female psyche. More radically, also, "A Rose" attempts to narrativize what Freud and others have termed the almost entirely repressed and inaccessible pre-Oedipal imaginary This is the period before human desire emerges as rule-governed, subject to a basic "thou shalt not" that ensures that it will always be mediated by lack. Freud links nostalgia in relation to masculine fantasies of recovering the mother's body in his essay on "The Uncanny": "There is a joking saying that 'Love is homesickness.' Whenever a man dreams of a place or country and says to himself while he is still dreaming: 'This place is familiar to me, I've been here before,' we may interpret the place as being his mother's genitals or her body" (Freud 2001: 245). But where desire is joined to threat for the boy it is joined to nostalgia for the girl. As Jane Gallup puts it, "the boy's fear of losing what he has as the mother lost hers is matched by a feminine nostalgia" (Gallup 1985: 147). Male desire is linked to menace, the threat of castration; women's to a wistful reminiscence. While In O'Brien's work, the lyrical evocation of a beloved landscape – "fields full of herbiage and meadowsweet, fields adorned with spangles of gold"

(O'Brien 1984: 394) – is always a displaced longing for what at the conclusion of *Mother Ireland* she calls "the leap that would restore one to one's original place [. . .] the radical innocence of the moment before birth" (O'Brien 1976: 89).

The daughter's life in "A Rose" is warped by precisely this form of nostalgia for union with the mother's body: in childhood, daughter and mother are "together, always together [. . .] eating off the same plate, using the same spoon, watching one another's chews, feeling the food as it went down the other's neck" (380). Bodily boundaries collapse and identity becomes porous, or rather has not yet emerged into separateness and loss: "Her mother's knuckles were her knuckles, her mother's veins were her veins, her mother's lap was a second heaven" (380). The daughter "feasts" on the sight of the mother, attempts to assuage the horror of maternal loss by praying continually for her mother's safety when she is absent on an errand, and desperately fears her death at the hands of the father. The father's incursions into the narrative are brutal, always violent, intrusions into the originary bliss of the mother–child dyad, terrifying and inexplicable to the daughter. His sexual needs interrupt the mother and child's nights sleeping together "entwined like the twigs of trees or the ends of the sugar tongs" (382). Yet he remains a curiously impotent figure, accorded little narrative importance: "it was of her mother and for her mother she existed" (387).

Later, mother–daughter symbiosis becomes suffocation. The daughter's doomed pursuit of romantic love – her unsatisfactory courtship by a baker's apprentice, her short-lived marriage to her "censuring" husband, and her later relationship with a married man – is defined by its failure to live up to the all-consuming totality of maternal love. The "orgies" of kisses and ersatz cream cakes with the "notable hurley player" with whom she starts a perfunctorily-narrated "kind of courtship common to their sort" (390), cannot appease her larger "hunger." Following the daughter's emotional logic, the narrative immediately skips from these unsatisfying male kisses to an atavistic maternal memory of the mother's perpetually smudged lipstick that "appeared like some kind of birth mark," and their identical mole "on the back of the left hand [. . .] made to seem paler when the fist was clenched" (390–1). Female desire is sent back into the potent closed circuit of filial love, with the shared birthmark signaling both a fall from language into a wordless feminine terrain, a return to an infantile pre-symbolic space in which primal drives reassert their force, and a doomed replication of the mother's fate of mute suffering and internalized anger is written on the body. The shared mole operates as a version of the *croix de ma mère*, the token traditionally affixed to or engraved on the abandoned orphan which enables at the denouement the establishment of identity. Here it suggests, bleakly and ironically, the reverse – an icon of the daughter's lack of identity and sense of illegitimacy, as well as the almost biological, thanatological pull back towards the mother.

In a story which has as its central concern the mother's body, whose representation, as in so many contemporary Irish writers, can never be innocent of the maternal iconography of mariolatry and Irish nationalism, the maternal body is presented in a manner similar to the symbolically marked and tortured bodies of Christian martyrs, bearing the tools of their own martyrdom. In "A Rose," the mother's physicality is continually evoked in terms of injury – the wounds of childbirth, or the "rim of a bucket, or a sledgehammer" with which the father menaces her (393), or the artificial roses, "the point of each petal seared like the point of a thorn" (385) which unite, poignantly, the symbolism of the story's title and the "speared head" of Christ in a picture on the farmhouse landing. That the child characterizes her mother as "the tabernacle with God in it" (388) suggests also the fantasy of maternal omnipotence, the archetype of the Blessed Virgin which offers for emulation a corrosive ideal of self-effacing motherhood, by which Irish Catholicism both lauds mothers as incarnations of the mother of God and refuses to cede them social value. However, the mother is also, more ambivalently, "the lake with the legends in it [. . .] a gigantic sponge, a habitation in which she longed to sink and disappear for ever and ever," yet she is also "afraid to sink, caught in this hideous trap between fear of sinking and fear of swimming" (388). The daughter's interiority is submerged in the fluid domain of the mother, seen only in terms of her memories of and internal struggles with the mother; she finds no voice of her own, no independent life outside of this drowning, increasingly threatening closeness.

With its preponderance of fluids, particularly bodily fluids, scenes of birth, death, menstruation, and excretion, and the concluding confrontation with the corpse, all multiply linked to the central figure of the mother, "A Rose in the Heart of New York" requires to be read in terms of the Kristevan theories of abjection. Essentially, this is the process of sacrificial logic by which the pre-Oedipal infant, to constitute itself as a subject, rejects, or *ab*jects, "unclean" aspects of bodily function and, with it, the maternal (Kristeva 1982). This process, of course, can never be accomplished once and for all, but continues into adult life, as categories of waste, disgust, and pollution establish, and thereafter sustain, the boundaries of the self against non-self. As previous critics such as Lorna Rooks-Hughes and Patricia Coughlan have seen, O'Brien's struggling, incapacitated heroines, their sense of independent selfhood so wavering that they frequently appear to seek fusion or self-annihilation in the maternal other, strongly resemble what Kristeva calls "abjects," or those who have not successfully relinquished the longing for the mother's body in favor of a more acceptable "love object" (Rooks-Hughes 1996; Coughlan 2006). The protagonist of "A Rose," in particular, evokes Kristeva's stress on the incompletion of the abjection process, and the porosity of the resultant subject. From being in childhood ecstatically "part of the lovely substance of [the] mother," in a tender image emphasizing the sustaining mutuality of the mother–child dyad (O'Brien 1984: 380), the adult heroine, fleeing to England and sexual rebellion to "start afresh," is inexorably "staggered by the assaults of memory" (393). A surreal, dissociated collage of visceral maternal memories follow: she is tormented by memories of "a bowl with her mother's menstrual cloth soaking in it"; sharing the exact "hurt to the quick" of a splinter under the mother's nail; her mother's sputum, which she can "taste [. . .] like a dish"; her mother turning into "bursting red pipes [. . .] brown blooded water," into a streetwalker "taking down her knickers in public, starting to do awful things"; her mother's imagined deathbed (393–4). The irruption of the maternal, the abject, the repugnant, and all that is supposed to have been rejected by the formation of the self, signals the refusal of the abject to remain banished, and advertises its presence at the heart of the subject. Horrified at the revelation that she has been unable to extricate herself from the maternal which she repudiates yet mourns, the protagonist resolves "to kill [. . .] to take up arms and commit a murder" (393).

The murder, however, is primarily a symbolic one, though the story does end with the mother's death. The protagonist (still, significantly, referred to as "the girl") takes her now-septuagenarian mother on a strained holiday, away from the domestic space of the family romance and domestic violence, "away from that house, and its skeletons, and its old cunning tug at the heartstrings" (395). In a hotel by the sea, the daughter attempts to uncover a maternal narrative other than the familiar story of domestic self-sacrifice and endurance. Specifically she seeks to hear the tale of a possible "long-sustained clandestine passion" for a long-lost sweetheart, which would cathartically allow her mother some form of separate identity outside the family romance, even if only in terms of thwarted romantic desire, and thereby release her own life from its condition of "curtained shame" (398). However, the mother – as signaled by her earlier letters "written on blotting paper and almost indecipherable" – maintains a self-censoring silence, "refused to speak, balked, had no story to tell, said that even if she had a story she would not tell it" (394, 396). She will tell only of embroidery done as a girl in America, of stitching the gnomic statement that "there was a rose in the heart of New York" (398), and of maternal suffering and loss. No dialog between generations of women is possible; maternity remains ineffable.

The mother's desire to confine her daughter within the supposedly safe arena of the mother–child dyad, pitted against the daughter's desperate need to affirm her own tenuous difference from the mother, is strongly evident in her reaffirmation that love between the sexes was "all bull" and "that there was only one kind of love and that was a mother's love for her child" (399). Both endeavors are doomed; instead of the daughter's hope that "they could be true at last, they need not hide from one another's gaze" (398), suggesting a condition of achieved mutuality between mother and daughter, there passes between them, climactically, "a moment dense with hate" (399). The daughter resolves to deny her mother's fervent wish that they be buried in the same grave. Here, the narrative point of view, having been exclusively the daughter's since early in the story, opens out for the only subsequent time to encompass both women, and again produces a significant confusion as to which "she" is meant. Here it is the mother who is "curled up on the bed, knotted as a foetus," while the "grown girl," downstairs, remembers "a woman she most bottomlessly loved, then unloved" (400), in a recognition that maternal-filial identities are destined to remain definitively sundered, and, paradoxically, inextricably commingled.

"A Rose in the Heart of New York" ends with the daughter's confrontation with the mother's corpse, her death having foreclosed the possibility of reconciliation. The funeral convoy makes its way through "Joyce's Ireland [. . .] the great central plain open to the elements, the teeming rain, the drifting snow" (401), as the story moves more consciously and evocatively on to Joycean terrain, with the returning exile revisiting Mother Ireland for the mother's funeral. As the undertaker leads the daughter into the dark chapel to allow her to see "the remains," we are again in the realm of the abject and gothic. In her discussion of the corpse as a "sign of horror," Kristeva links abjection and Freud's perception that death rituals mask hostility towards the dead and that taboos concerning corpses represent the fear of the invasion of the dead into the space of the living (Kristeva 1982: 108–11). The daughter, as she approaches her mother's coffin, fears "something fateful has happened, the skin has turned black," but the "worst" would be if the mother is not in fact dead, but has "merely visited the other world" (O'Brien 1984: 403). In fact, the confrontation with the dead maternal body, is characterized by being "unfinished": "The mouth was trying to speak. [. . .] One eye was not fully closed" (403). Desperate for some communication, the daughter then searches the house "as if for some secret," to discover, gothically, her mother's pathetic letter to her youthful sweetheart, undelivered and unread, which she crumples instinctively "as if it had been her own" (403). As if, almost parodically, to underline the overdetermined and gothic nature of the enterprise, the daughter eventually finds another "cobwebby" hidden envelope, this time addressed to her, which turns out to contain money, but no note, despite the daughter's longing for "little tendernesses her mother might have written [. . .] some communiqué" (404).

In O'Brien's fiction, the boundaries between the realms of the dead, especially the dead mother, and the living are continually, fearfully, blurred, an extension of the porous boundary of the "abject" self, and the way in which mother–daughter economies dangerously feed off one another. O'Brien's vision of the family romance is essentially, a bleakly deterministic one: kinship determines identity, and there seems no possibility of fully dissociating maternal and filial identities. The final lines of "A Rose in the Heart of New York," however, if hardly optimistic in their evocation of "spilt feelings," filial bereavement, and silence, nonetheless suggestively elide these into a tender image of maternal care: "there was a vaster silence beyond, as if the house itself had died or had carefully been put down to sleep" (404).

References and Further Reading

Abel, E. (1983). "Narrative Structure(s) and Female Development: The case of *Mrs Dalloway*," in E. Abel, M. Hirsch and E. Langland (eds), *The Voyage In*, pp. 161–85. Hanover: University Press of New England.

Bettelheim, B. (1976). *The Uses of Enchantment*. New York: Alfred A Knopf.

Carpenter, L. (1986). "Tragedies of Remembrance, Comedies of Endurance: The Novel of Edna O'Brien," in A. Wertheim and H. Brock (eds), *Essays on the Contemporary Irish Novel*, pp. 263–81. Munich: Max Hueber.

Coughlan, P. (2006). "Killing the Bats: Abjection and the Question of Agency," in K. Laing, S. Mooney and M. O'Connor (eds), *Edna O'Brien: New Critical Perspectives*, pp. 171–95. Dublin: Carysfort Press.

Fogarty, A. (2002). "'The Horror of the Unlived Life': Mother–Daughter Relationships in Contemporary Irish Women's Fiction," in A. Giorgio (ed.), *Writing Mothers and Daughters*, pp. 85–118. Oxford: Bergahn.

Freud, S. (2001). *Standard Edition of the Complete Psychological Works of Sigmund Freud*, vol. 17

(1917–19), trans. James Strachey. London: Vintage (original work published 1919).

Gallup, J. (1985). *Reading Lacan*. Ithaca and London: Cornell University Press.

Kristeva, J. (1982). *Powers of Horror: An Essay on Abjection*, trans. Leon S Roudiez. New York: Columbia University Press.

O'Brien, E. (1968). *The Love Object*. London: Cape.

O'Brien, E. (1974). *A Scandalous Woman*. London: Weidenfeld & Nicolson.

O'Brien, E. (1976). *Mother Ireland*. London: Weidenfeld & Nicolson.

O'Brien, E. (1978). *Mrs Reinhardt and Other Stories*. London: Weidenfeld & Nicolson.

O'Brien, E. (1982). *Returning: A Collection of Tales*. London: Weidenfeld & Nicolson.

O'Brien, E. (1984). *A Fanatic Heart: Selected Stories*. London: Weidenfeld & Nicolson.

Rooks-Hughes, L. (1996). "The Family and the Female Body in the Novels of Edna O'Brien and Julia O'Faoláin," *Canadian Journal of Irish Studies* 22/2: 83–97.

Schrank, B. and Farquharson, D. (1996). "Object of Love, Subject to Despair: Edna O'Brien's *The Love Object* and the Emotional Logic of Late Romanticism," *Canadian Journal of Irish Studies* 22/2: 21–36.

37

Doris Lessing: *African Stories*

Don Adams

Doris Lessing's *African Stories* was first published in 1964, and published in an expanded form in two volumes in 1973. The 1964 collection included stories from her first book of short fiction, *This Was the Old Chief's Country* (1951), and from her collection of five novellas entitled simply *Five* (1953). In 1977, a revised one-volume American edition included two stories not collected in earlier editions: "The Story of a Non-Marrying Man" and "Spies I have Known." This edition of *African Stories* was reprinted in 1981, following the 1980 publication of *Stories*, in which were collected all of Lessing's non-African stories. The separate publication history of the stories set in Africa indicate that the stories stand together as a group, apart from Lessing's other short fiction, and that they are meant to be considered as a whole. A reading of the volume confirms that the stories contribute to form a general impression of the setting, and of the author's fictive response to it.

The African stories are generally autobiographical in nature. Although Lessing was born as Doris Tayler in Persia (now Iran) in 1919, where her father was posted as a bank clerk in the British colonial apparatus, the family moved to a farm in Southern Rhodesia (modern Zimbabwe) in 1925, and this is where Lessing grew up and began her career as a writer. The farm was not as prosperous as had been hoped, and the difficulties of living in the African countryside as part of a colonial minority contributed to a tense home-life, from which the young Doris as a child and adolescent sought release by venturing into the countryside, or "bush."

Lessing's parents decided rather precipitously to leave Persia and to emigrate to Africa after attending a 1924 British Empire Exhibition at Wembley, when they were in England on leave (Rosner 1999: 61). The exhibition was designed to attract emigrants to the empire's extensive overseas colonies, including the newest one of Southern Rhodesia, which had been granted self-governing colony status in 1923. All of Lessing's stories are set during the period of colonization (1923–65). Although the governing white minority in Southern Rhodesia never made up more than 5 percent of the country's population, 50 percent of the country's land area was set aside for white ownership, while just 2 percent was set aside for collective farming by blacks. The desired result was to force a large percentage of the black population to work as hired help on white-owned farms and projects.

Lessing's African stories can be divided into two groups: those stories that focus almost exclusively on the white minority colonialists, and those that focus on the relationship between the white minority and the black majority. Only one story ("Hunger") is set almost exclusively within the world of the black majority, and although the story was a "favorite" with Lessing's early readers, the author herself has dismissed it as being overly sentimental and moral (Klein 2000: 144). Certainly the story has a dissatisfying moralistic and doctrinaire Marxist conclusion in which the healthy future of the collective is posited as the release from present individual misfortune and unhappiness. But the fundamental problem with the story stems from the fact that the central figure is never allowed the existential freedom necessary for fictive characters to become real.

This is the most obvious and recurrent weakness in Lessing's fiction – her tendency to treat her characters as sociological and psychological case histories, rather than as existential beings. All too often Lessing's characters seem the unconscious fictive products of the dehumanizing social systems they were created to critique. Along this line, Harold Bloom has remarked that "the power [Lessing] seeks to gain over the text of life is always reductive: tendentious, resentful, historicizing" (Bloom 1986: 4). This is an acute and damning observation. Nevertheless, a sociological writer such as Lessing can tell us a great deal about ourselves and our problems – information that may be more useful, perhaps, in some pointed ways, than the information provided by a more profound creator. For Lessing's very fiction suffers from our time's maladies: a using and abusing world is reflected in stories in which characters are employed as symptomatic figures.

The most affecting of the African stories are those in which Lessing herself is present as a young witness and (more crucially) participant. Her biographer, Carole Klein, notes that Lessing "seems to experience life at a remove, perhaps to soothe a painful sense of homelessness" (Klein 2000: 2). But in these first-person autobiographical narratives, the remove is itself removed. It would almost seem that Lessing is an instinctive confessional writer who has been forced by unbearable emotional circumstances – as Klein implies – to project her pain and unhappiness upon fictive victims. But in the clearly autobiographical narratives, the pain stays close to home.

Perhaps the most emotionally honest and thematically comprehensive of the stories is "The Old Chief Mshlanga," which is the felt "heart" of the entire collection. The overtly confessional story begins tellingly in the third person, as Lessing describes the experience of the as yet voiceless first-person narrator as a young girl adventurously "ranging the bush over her father's farm," but dreaming all of the while about "a pale willowed river, a pale gleaming castle – a small girl singing: 'Out flew the web and floated wide, the mirror cracked from side to side . . .'." (47). The quotation from Tennyson's "Lady of Shalott" foreshadows a break in the child consciousness of Lessing's autobiographical character, as she approaches adulthood and begins to be "presented" with "questions" concerning herself and her surroundings, the answers to which "were not easy to accept" (49).

The first five paragraphs of this story, which depict the inevitable confusion arising from the child's inclination imaginatively to inhabit the interiorized European fairy-tale dream-world while "ranging the bush" in southern Africa, are presented to us in prose that is itself at times grammatically and syntactically confused, as in the passage below:

> Pushing her way through the green aisles of the mealie stalks, the leaves arching like cathedrals veined with sunlight far overhead, with the packed red earth underfoot, a fine lace of red starred witchweed would summon up a black bent figure croaking premonitions: the Northern witch, bred of cold Northern forests, would stand before her among the mealie fields (47).

Of course it is a small girl fearful of witches who is pushing her way through the green aisles of the mealie stalks, and not the "red starred witchweed," as the sentence's syntax mistakenly informs us.

One might argue, of course, that such syntactic confusion serves the purpose of emphasizing the girl's mental–physical disconnect, but such an argument is countered by the presence of numerous such examples of syntactic dissonance scattered throughout Lessing's prose, often in places in which the purposeful meaning of the confusion is much more difficult to construe, as in the first paragraph of this very story (unquoted), which is casually and frustratingly ungrammatical. Even ardent proponents of Lessing's fiction have felt compelled to comment on the sometimes slack prose: "There are few admirers of [Lessing's] work who would defend the careless homeliness of her style" (Sukenick 1973: 534). Whether such carelessness disqualifies Lessing's work from serious consideration is, of course, a matter for the individual reader to decide. The author and editor already have had their say.

The confusion regarding the physical and emotional homes of the autobiographical character in "The Old Chief Mshlanga" becomes more painful and acute as she enters self-conscious adolescence. She is able to suppress her confusion, however, by force of will, as she interacts vigorously with her expanding environment:

> Later, when the farm grew too small to hold her curiosity, she carried a gun in the crook of her arm and wandered miles a day, from viel to viel, from *kopje* to *kopje*, accompanied by two dogs: the dogs and the gun were an armour against fear. Because of them she never felt fear (48).

The repetition of the last sentence is indicative of Lessing's insistence in these stories of driving home an argument that is pointedly political, as the characters in their circumscribed social situations are employed metonymically to represent the bigger picture of racist power structures and colonial oppression.

As the story's tellingly unnamed central figure approaches the truth of the dreadful social, historical, ethical, and spiritual circumstance in which she finds herself, she metamorphoses from a third-person character in someone else's story into the first-person narrator of her own.

> One evening when I was about fourteen, I was walking down the side of a mealie field that had been newly ploughed, so that the great red clods showed fresh and tumbling to the viel beyond, like a choppy red sea; it was that hushed and listening hour, when the birds send long sad calls from tree to tree, and all the colours of earth and sky and leaf are deep and golden. I had my rifle in the curve of my arm, and the dogs were at my heels (49).

This brief paragraph contains in miniature the positive and alluring aspects of the colonialist experience of making fertile land productive amid an expansive, enlivening, and embracing pastoral landscape; and it calls to mind similar idyllic passages in Willa Cather's "pioneer" fiction set in the Great Plains of America.

But the final sentence of the Lessing paragraph points to a crucial difference between the colonial experience in South and East Africa and the pioneer experience in the Great Plains. In Cather's pioneer fiction, the potentially threatening native population presence is telling primarily in its absence, reflecting the historical conditions under which a much smaller native population had been effectively neutralized and marginalized in relation to the later waves of settler immigrants. In Lessing's Southern Rhodesia, however, in which millions of native Africans outnumbered thousands of colonial immigrants by a ratio of more than twenty to one, the native population is a palpable presence – so palpable, in fact, that the gun-toting young narrator of the passage has been accustomed to take their servile presence for granted, and is all the more surprised to come upon an old Chief whose polite dignity of engagement is more shocking even than his failure obsequiously to yield the right of way on the path to the young white "Chieftaness."

For all intents and purposes, the old Chief is the first native African that the young colonial narrator has come to recognize as a fellow human being, and the shock of coming into contact with the depth and richness of his reality as both a product and heir of this strange, outsized, and (for the European colonialist narrator) un-mythologized landscape quite suddenly forces her into its margins, and she becomes, for the first time in her budding adulthood, both afraid and lonely within her physical environment, in which she no longer feels herself naturally at home.

The profound theme underlying all of Lessing's most successful African stories is that of the enervating effects of uprootedness upon the human spirit, and of the brutalizing of human relations and destruction of individual psychic health that are its consequence. Although these stories sometimes seem to suffer from, more than they render artistically, their painful subject matter, they nevertheless serve a diagnostic social and psychological function as they expose the misery that results from both the willed and unwilled loss of one's individual and collective past.

Writing during the same mid-twentieth-century time period in which these stories are set (1930s–40s), philosopher Simone Weil noted in *The Need for Roots* that an individual receives "well-nigh the whole of his moral, intellectual, and spiritual life by way of the environment of which he forms a natural part" (Weil 1952: 43) – a natural domestic environment which the colonial emigrants in Lessing's African stories have abandoned, thereby becoming emblematic of a modern Western world in which we "have thrown [our past] away just like a child picking the petals off of a rose" (Weil 1952: 119). "For people who are really uprooted," Weil claimed, "there remain only two possible sorts of behavior":

> either to fall into a spiritual lethargy resembling death . . . or to hurl themselves into some sort of activity necessarily designed to uproot, often by the most violent methods, those who are not yet uprooted, or only partly so. (Weil 1952: 46)

So it is that, at the conclusion of "The Old Chief Mshlanga," a property dispute between the narrator's father and the old native Chief results in the forced resettlement of the Chief and his people "two hundred miles east" in a "proper Native Reserve," opening up their traditional homeland for further "white settlement."

It was of course the white *men* in Southern Rhodesia – those who ran the colonial government and farmed and mined the confiscated lands – who were most actively and aggressively uprooting the land's native inhabitants; while the colonists' wives and daughters, who were largely confined to their isolated farmhouses by both an exaggerated sense of propriety and a much-cultivated fear of the natives, proved particularly prone to a disabling spiritual lethargy. Several of the most memorable of Lessing's African stories are concerned with the plight of these housebound colonial farm wives.

Perhaps the most successful of these stories is "Getting Off the Altitude," which is told from the point of view of a first-person adolescent autobiographical narrator who is fearful of becoming a cloistered and embittered farm wife like the adult women of her acquaintance. The story is focused on a neighbor woman, Mrs Slatter, whose bullying and headstrong husband is prototypically patriarchal and stereotypically masculine in his aggressive and violent behavior – a violence inflicted no less on his wife and children than on the abused native laborers in his employ. Lessing is expert at detailing the implacable social and psychological mechanism whereby colonists living with the daily spectacle of institutionalized violence and injustice inflicted on a subject people become themselves victims of and participants in violence and abuse between family members and neighbors.

In stories such as "Getting Off the Altitude," "Old John's Place," and "Winter in July," the native subject people in the midst of which the white colonists lived their lives are either marginalized within or absent entirely from the narrative. But their disenfranchised and suppressed existence is felt throughout in the manner in which the colonists undermine their social relations among one another through bad faith, suspicion, cheating, and intolerance. Living in a situation in which they are confined within their superior social realm, apart and aloof from the natives, as both exemplars of "civilized" domesticity and guardians of the family hearth, the female colonists in particular find that their in-group social relations become easily over-heated and super-sensualized. Lessing dramatizes repeatedly the heavy irony whereby these isolated and aloof, symbol-laden colonial domestic goddesses "go to the bad" under the influence of an unaccustomed conviviality, furtively coupling with itiner-ant farm managers and traveling salesmen, or with the husbands of desperate house-wives like themselves.

Mrs Slatter is a sympathetic figure precisely because she feels the impossibility of her situation so keenly. Her brutal husband openly cheats on her with a neighboring farmer's wife, prompting her to bar him from her bedroom, into which she invites, in his spite and out of a desperate loneliness, their young farm manager, who is not much older than her sons. This unseemly situation is unsuited to her formal and gentle nature, however, and she soon locks the door on the young lover as well, prompting her vulgar husband's scorn and her gentlemanly lover's protests. Mrs Slatter seems equally appalled by the situation in which she finds herself and by her own behavior in response to it. And yet she can imagine no alternative, other than to pray to God that she will get old soon. The author obliges, and the story concludes with a vision of the encroaching twilight of a hateful life and marriage.

In his disaffected essay, Bloom claims that Lessing's fiction is entirely humorless (Bloom 1986: 6). But that is not exactly the case, for there is a certain amount of social humor, but it is always bitter and didactic. Perhaps the story in the collection that is most effective in conveying the bitter humor of the colonialists' plight in Africa is "A Home for the Highland Cattle," which is concerned with the darkly comic and satirized experience of an emigrant couple newly arrived from England. The husband has emigrated with the high-minded mission of helping the colonial government to put its land-management practices in order. But the wife has the seemingly more modest goal of finding "a nice house, or a flat, with maybe a bit of garden" (251). What ensues, for the wife, is a brutal crash-course in the impossibility of living in this racially divided and overtly unjust environment while maintaining even a small amount of individual human dignity. As the story concludes, she has begun to adopt the attitudes and habits of racial and social prejudice that she at first scorned in her neighbors.

Like most of the stories in this collection, "A Home for the Highland Cattle" is in essence an indictment of human history. Apart from Chief Mshlanga, who is himself more symbolic than real, there are no truly admirable characters in these stories, although there are many who earn and deserve our sympathy. Repeatedly one is driven to ask oneself, "But what should these people do? How should they act? How can they make it right?" To which there is no apt response. For they live in a world in which all avenues for right action and feeling and response have been closed off. Although Lessing is skillfully and acutely realistic in her renderings, these characters and their world seem smaller than life. And that is because they have no future – no potential for creative change or availability to happy accident.

It is an odd fact about realistic writing, that when everything that happens in a story is all too entirely likely to have happened, then the story and its characters come to seem fictively false. The author of such a work has left out the world of potentiality that always exists alongside our world of necessity. For we are saved by what we cannot imagine, as Marcel Proust famously dramatized for us. So it is that Proust's characters become increasingly real as they encounter situations and behave in manners that seem less and less likely. Lessing's characters, by contrast, suffer from the ideological rigidity of their author, which does not allow them the existential freedom of acting uncharacteristically in a world in which anything is possible.

The strength and weakness of Lessing's African stories stem alike from the righteous indignation of their author. When Lessing writes about characters and situations in which she does *not* display this passionate engagement (as in "The Trinket Box," "The Words He Said," "A Mild Attack of Locusts," "A Road to the Big City," "Flight," "Flavours of Exile," "Plants and Girls," "A Letter from Home," "The Sun Between Their Feet," "The Story of Two Dogs," "The Story of a Non-Marrying Man," and "Spies I Have Known,") the stories seem obvious and derivative, and suffer from sentimentality and a lack of vitality. For better and worse, Lessing's authentic subject matter in these African stories is the impossibility of feeling oneself naturally at home in an environment that one has taken by force, and the bitter inheritance this condition of violence prepares for one's heirs.

When Lessing is able to qualify the bitterness through sympathy for characters entangled in a hopeless situation, the stories engage our own sympathetic interest. But it is the situation and not the characters embroiled in it that Lessing is most concerned with portraying. And our ability to sympathize with a situation is limited to an intellectual response, while our potential for responding in a more visceral manner is not evoked by characters who are trapped in their circumstance and seem smaller than life.

D.H. Lawrence, with whom Lessing sometimes has been compared, remarked in his essay on "Morality and the Novel" that immorality in fiction results from a writer's inability or unwillingness to enable the free operation of "the trembling instability of the balance" between the human figure and its environment – that is, when a writer allows his or her individual "predilection" to impair the existential freedom of the fiction (Lawrence 1936: 528). In these stories, Lessing could not prevent herself from putting her finger on the scale of her characters' lives, and while we may agree with her opinions regarding their generally self-ignorant and self-defeating behavior amid deplorable circumstances, we resent that we ourselves are not allowed the freedom to respond in a more instinctive and holistic manner to their fictive experience.

That being said, however, we may note that there are poignant moments throughout these stories in which existential freedom does seem possible for author, characters, and readers alike. These moments are most often evoked by the lovingly rendered beauty of the natural world in which these characters are living out their constrained and embittered lives. The scene near the conclusion of "The Old Chief Mshlanga," in which the narrator's father and the Old Chief come to a final impasse in their dispute over a herd of goats owned by the Chief's tribe that the farmer has confiscated as reparation for its destruction of his crop, is entirely emblematic in this regard:

> It was now in the late sunset, the sky a welter of colours, the birds singing their last songs, and the cattle, lowing peacefully, moving past us towards their sheds for the night. It was the hour when Africa is most beautiful; and here was this pathetic ugly scene, doing no one any good.
>
> At last my father stated firmly: "I'm not going to argue about it. I am keeping the goats."
>
> The Old Chief flashed back in his language: "That means my people will go hungry when the dry season comes."
>
> "Go to the police, then," my father said and looked triumphant.
>
> There was of course no more to be said. (57)

The Chief does, though, have one final, entirely damning comment to make, when he states flatly that all of the land that the colonial farmer calls his own in reality belongs to the Old Chief's people.

It is perhaps little wonder that, when faced with the task of representing such desperate, demeaning, and disheartening situations in fiction, Lessing would be prone to be tendentious and humorless. There is, after all, little in this subject matter to be light-hearted about, and myriad causes for complaint. To which one might respond idealistically that the author's duty is not to render the failure of the historical world, so much as it is to envision a more successful world of the future. To her credit, Lessing herself makes such a response in her later fiction.

REFERENCES AND FURTHER READING

Bloom, H. (1986). Introduction, in H. Bloom (ed.), *Doris Lessing*. New York: Chelsea House.

Klein, C. (2000). *Doris Lessing*. New York: Carroll & Graf.

Knapp, M. (1984). *Doris Lessing*. New York: Ungar.

Lawrence, D.H. (1936). "Morality and the Novel," in E. McDonald (ed.), D.H. Lawrence *Phoenix: The Posthumous Papers, 1936*, pp. 527–32. London: Penguin.

Lessing, D. (1981). *African Stories*. New York: Touchstone.

Pickering, J. (1990). *Understanding Doris Lessing*. Columbia, South Carolina: University of South Carolina Press.

Rosner, V. (1999). "Home Fires: Doris Lessing, Colonial Architecture, and the Reproduction of Mothering," *Texas Studies in Women's Literature* 18: 59–89.

Sprague, C. and Tiger, V. (1986). *Critical Essays on Doris Lessing*. Boston: G.K. Hall.

Sukenick, L. (1973). "Feeling and Reason in Doris Lessing's fiction," *Contemporary Literature* 14: 515–35.

Weil, S. (1952). *The Need for Roots*. Boston: Beacon.

38

The Desire for Clarity: Seán O'Faoláin's "Lovers of the Lake"

Paul Delaney

In his critical study *The Short Story* (1948), Seán O'Faoláin suggested that writers are by necessity oppositional. "The moment an opinion becomes popular," he remarked, "a writer [must] at once abandon it. The moment an idea becomes general it is useless to the individual artist" (O'Faoláin 1948: 23). O'Faoláin's comments are revealing, particularly when they are read in the context of his work during the middle decades of the twentieth century. Only two years earlier, in April 1946, O'Faoláin had stepped down as editor of the literary journal *The Bell*, and it was in the pages of that journal (which O'Faoláin had helped to found in 1940) that this middle-class liberal secured a reputation for being one of the most prominent dissident voices in Ireland. Under O'Faoláin's editorship *The Bell* led the fight against censorship and cultural isolationist policies in Ireland. It also provided, in the words of Roy Foster, "the record of an alternative culture" to the principal ideologies of the day, laying waste to many of the shibboleths and tired prejudices which were endemic in post-independence Irish society (Foster 1988: 548). Favorite targets for O'Faoláin included myopic nationalist movements which were crudely Anglophobic as well as organizations and individuals who propagated a sentimental approach to questions concerning religion, nationality, the Irish language, or the past.

In his *Bell* editorials O'Faoláin relentlessly attacked those who championed the cause for a lost essence or spiritual purity of "Irishness," advancing instead the thesis that national identities are hybrid, synthetic, and self-fashioned. O'Faoláin also denounced those who traded in romantic idealizations of the peasant, seeing in this an ignorance of the harsh realities of rural life in Ireland and also a denial of the changing conditions of Irish society as it negotiated the pressures of modernization, urbanization, and globalization. Seamus Deane has noted that a persistent concern in O'Faoláin's work at this time was the desire "to resituate Ireland in a wider and less oppressively devotional context" (Deane 1986: 210). It was in this context that a broader sense of the international could be traced through the cultural life of the nation, as social and intellectual developments in Britain and on the Continent could be shown to have influenced supposedly "native" traditions and cultural practices.

Such thoughts found expression in many of O'Faoláin's editorials and critical writings, where he repeatedly situated himself as a discordant figure – someone who presented and, it has been claimed, "continues to present a challenge to our private icons and national ideas" (Dunne 1991: 3). If O'Faoláin was unequivocal in his adoption of this stance, however, it is striking to note that in much of his short fiction he appeared far less confident than this stance would seem to suggest. Indeed, it would be closer to the mark to claim that O'Faoláin's short stories explore many ideas and beliefs which are "popular" or widely shared, but that very few of those stories dismiss these ideas with any degree of certainty as "useless."

O'Faoláin's stories are typically characterized by contrasts and oppositions (the relationship between conventional beliefs and personal freedom is a key concern as is the relationship between traditional values and modern practices), but they rarely suggest that either of these points of contrast can be advanced or easily privileged. Rather, as John Hildebidle has noted, "a conflict of loyalties and intentions is at the heart of all of O'Faoláin's fiction," and much of the power and suggestiveness of his stories resides in the fact that that conflict defies any resolution (Hildebidle 1989: 131). Instead of engaging with themes, events or situations which are always original or oppositional, O'Faoláin's stories – or at the very least the vast majority of his stories – deal with issues and questions which are conflicted and deeply ambiguous. This is certainly the case in one of O'Faoláin's most celebrated stories "Lovers of the Lake," which was first published in 1957.

In "Lovers of the Lake" an adulterous couple, Jenny and Bobby, travel from the wealthy suburbs of Dublin to Station Island on Lough Derg, an ancient penitential site in the remote northwest of the country. Jenny undertakes this journey out of desperation, in an attempt to find the strength that will enable her to end her relationship with Bobby. Bobby sees the journey as "lunacy," but nonetheless follows Jenny on pilgrimage to confront her religious beliefs with skepticism and a declaration of love (O'Faoláin 1981: 22). O'Faoláin is clear from the outset that the characters' love for one another is genuine. However, he is also clear that Jenny is trapped in a hopeless situation since, as a practicing Catholic, she has no option other than to submit to the prior claims of her marriage – even if that marriage has become loveless.

This is the dilemma which provides the central thrust of the story, and it is a dilemma which is denied any easy outcome by O'Faoláin as he holds back from offering his characters any neat or simple answers. Instead of allowing or forcing Jenny to choose between the dictates of her conscience and the desires of her heart, the story enunciates states of uncertainty, ambiguity, and irresolution. O'Faoláin's point seems to be that such states are a basic condition of life, and that "the desire for clarity and faith remains part of the confusion of actual living, not separable but distinct from it" (Deane 1986: 213).

This sense of uncertainty is reiterated time and again in the course of the story as readily drawn associations are undercut or re-presented by O'Faoláin. From the outset, Jenny and Bobby are identified as confident, well-heeled citizens of upper-middle-class society. Both characters are articulate, intelligent, and well traveled, and they clearly enjoy the comforts of a very particular close-knit world (there is even a suggestion that Bobby knows Jenny's husband quite well). In this respect, they are quintessential O'Faoláin characters. However, although both characters are of a type, they are nonetheless also associated with a range of attributes which place them – in the early sections of the story at least – in conflict. Jenny is ostensibly imagined in terms of faith, conscience, and impulsiveness, for instance, whereas Bobby is depicted as the voice of cynicism, rationality, and science.

This potential for conflict is expressed in the opening exchanges of "Lovers of the Lake," when Bobby sets himself against the idea of Jenny's pilgrimage. The idea is so alien to Bobby that he initially misinterprets Jenny's request that he drive her to Lough Derg, mistaking the ancient site of pilgrimage and penance with "the other Lough Derg," a popular tourist spot in the southwest of the country (O'Faoláin 1981: 18). That Bobby should make this mistake is, of course, telling, and it is significant that once he is corrected his body language instantly changes – he rises from "the lazy deeps" of an armchair in search of cigarettes, nervously checks his watch, and abruptly ends the conversation by stating that it is time to leave for work (O'Faoláin 1981: 18). The tone of Bobby's voice also noticeably alters – his first words to Jenny are spoken "amiably" but they quickly become "cold" – and his choice of words becomes condescending and flippant (O'Faoláin 1981: 18). "Do you mean *that* place with *the* island where *they* go around on *their* bare feet on sharp stones, and starve for days, and sit up all night ologroaning and ologoaning?" (O'Faoláin 1981: 18; emphasis added). Bobby's stress on the definite article and the third-person plural draws a clear distinction, at least in his mind, between the inhabitants of his world and the sort of people who, he thinks, routinely undertake this type of journey.

Jenny, for her part, is committed to the idea of the pilgrimage, but the reasons why she wants to go on the pilgrimage so suddenly – "next week" – are not articulated in this brief but richly suggestive exchange. Indeed, Jenny declines to say anything about the pilgrimage in the opening sequence of the story. She chooses not to rise to Bobby's description of the demands that are put on pilgrims in "*that* place," and she repeatedly rebuffs his questions by changing the topic or performing some kind of role. When Bobby asks her "are you going religious on me?," for instance, the reader is told that "she walked over to him swiftly, turned him about, smiled her smile that was whiter than the whites of her eyes, and lowered her head to one side" (O'Faoláin 1981: 18). This fails to provoke any kind of response, so Jenny instead compliments Bobby for being able to act impulsively and "doing things on the spur of the moment" (18).

Jenny explains that she is forever praising Bobby to her friends because of this ability (theirs seems to be a very public affair at a time when such practices would not have been widely condoned in Irish society), and suggests that this is an ability that distinguishes him from the other men in his circle. Interestingly, it is this praise that wins Bobby over as he agrees to take Jenny to the island. Given all the subtle role-playing which is recorded in the opening exchange, it is of added interest that the scene should conclude with an image of Jenny briefly transformed into the dominant figure in the relationship: the closing sentence describes her behaving patronizingly towards her lover, patting his cheek and kissing him "sedately," before seeing him to the door with the playful double-edged comment "you are a good boy" (19).

This transformation is reconfigured within a few lines of the second section of the story, when the couple are depicted traveling – ironically, "like any husband and wife off on a motoring holiday" – across the face of Ireland (19). As they drive through the countryside, Bobby continues to press Jenny to discover the motivations behind her impending pilgrimage. "All of this penitential stuff is because of me, isn't it?" he asks, only to hear Jenny retort, "Don't be silly. It's just something I thought up all by myself out of my own clever little head" (19). Jenny reverts to perform another role – that of the child – in her subsequent exchange with Bobby, as he dismisses her decision to go on pilgrimage as juvenile nonsense, or "fal-lal," and she, in turn, begs him to "stop bullying me" by demanding answers from her (20). Searching for a reason to explain why she needs to make the trip so urgently, Jenny remarks:

> And I tell you I don't know. The impulse came over me suddenly last Sunday looking at those boys and girls playing tennis. For no reason. It just came. I said to myself, 'All right, go now!' I felt that if I didn't do it on the impulse I'd never do it at all. Are you asking me for a rational explanation? I haven't got one. (O'Faoláin 1981: 20)

Jenny's explanation is founded upon a basic dichotomy that is important to the overall structure of O'Faoláin's story. This dichotomy speaks to a classic piece of chauvinist logic and imagines human behavior to be divided along strict gender lines, with men and women associated with various characteristics and traits which are essentially organized and exclusively embodied. Chief amongst these associations is the division between rationality and impulsivity, where rationality is associated with men and impulsivity is seen as the preserve of women. Jenny and Bobby identify themselves and each other along these lines throughout the story. O'Faoláin's narrator also repeatedly identifies both of these characters in this way. Jenny sees herself as rash and spontaneous in the above exchange, for example, and this act of self-identification is in keeping with many of her thoughts and actions, in addition to the comments of the narrator and Bobby, which are expressed elsewhere in the story. This identification of Jenny is set against the image of Bobby, and also, crucially, the self-image that Bobby likes to project of himself (as rational, cynical, and scientific), which is repeated *ad nauseam* in "Lovers of the Lake."

However, this dichotomy is not as straightforward as it might otherwise appear. For one thing, as has been noted, the image of Bobby as rational and reserved – or, to put it another way, anti-impulsive and masculine – is undermined in the very first page of the story, when Jenny praises him for "doing things on the spur of the moment" and "never looking beyond the day" (O'Faoláin 1981: 18). It is significant, once again, that this praise is said to distinguish Bobby from the other men in Jenny and Bobby's world; it is also significant that this praise immediately precedes Bobby's change of mind, as he abruptly agrees to take Jenny to Lough Derg. The reader is never told how or why this change comes about, but there is a suggestion that Jenny's praise flatters some kind of self-image (of recklessness, spontaneity, and independence of thought) which Bobby secretly harbors.

What is more, in the opening exchange Bobby alludes to the fact that Jenny has previously brought questions of faith and conscience to bear on their relationship. "I've noticed this Holy Joe streak in you before," he patronizingly remarks. "You'll do it once too often" (18). Jenny returns to this point several times in the pages that follow. As the couple drive across the Irish midlands, for instance, Jenny attempts to explain – to Bobby as well as to herself – why she has continued to perform her religious duties in spite of her commitment to an adulterous relationship. "It was never routine," she says of her attendance at Confession and Mass. "It's the one thing I have to hang on to in an otherwise meaningless existence. No children. A husband I'm not in love with. And I can't marry you . . . ; All I have is you, and God" (22). The suggestion is that Jenny has agonized about this situation for a number of years – the hesitation which is induced by the inclusion of the comma after "you" signifies as much. Indeed, she subsequently confesses that she has often promised to end her relationship with Bobby, but that she has always been too weak to follow this through (33). The implication is that her decision to travel to Lough Derg is the result of ongoing thought and reflection, and that it has not been rashly undertaken.

Jenny explains that "the impulse" to go on the pilgrimage "came over me suddenly last Sunday looking at those boys and girls playing tennis. For no reason. It just came." This explanation refers back to the opening scene and sentence of the story, where Jenny is heard to remark "They might wear whites" of a group of tennis players she can see from her window (18). Jenny's initial comment receives no response from Bobby and remains unglossed by Jenny. Indeed, the second sentence of "Lovers of the Lake" appears to change the apparent direction of the story, as it gives neither the context for nor an explanation of Jenny's words. The second sentence is spoken by a different voice (O'Faoláin's conventional external narrator), and instead of following through with the reference to the tennis party, it provides the first in a series of animal metaphors to describe the attitude which has been adopted by Jenny – the reader is informed that "she" (as yet unnamed) turned her head in such a way "that always reminded him [as yet unidentified] of a jackdaw" (18). This image, in turn, is abandoned by the narrator (although it is presumably intended to introduce the idea that Jenny acts suddenly and is scatterbrained), as Jenny regains control of the narrative and asks Bobby to drive her to the island.

Given the importance that is attached to this opening comment, it is significant that neither the narrator nor the characters feel the need to annotate these words. "They might wear whites" might be taken to suggest an innate conservatism on

Jenny's part – the tennis players are not traditionally attired. It might be interpreted as a metaphorical reflection on the state of Jenny's soul – white obviously indicates the state of grace and spiritual purity. It might even be thought to anticipate the many uncertainties that inform the larger story – things are not black or white in this world, and the pervading color on Lough Derg is grey. Any of these readings – in addition to any of a number of other readings – are possible since the comment is ambiguously worded and left without any kind of immediate explanation. Jenny's words are not closed down or clarified in any way.

The equivocal nature of Jenny's words is in keeping with the design of "Lovers of the Lake," as it seeks out and traces various states of ambiguity and irresolution. O'Faoláin might add, however, that the ambivalent nature of the opening remark is also a consequence of the specific demands which are placed on writers of short stories more generally. "Telling by means of suggestion or implication is one of the most important of all the modern short story's shorthand conventions," he remarked in *The Short Story* (O'Faoláin 1948: 150–1). "It means that a short story writer does not directly tell us things so much as let us guess or know them by implying them" (151). Because a short story writer has "no time for explanation," characterization has to be kept to a minimum, and extended reflections and interpretations can only be sparingly provided (169). O'Faoláin clearly believed, as a consequence of this, that readers have a vital role to play in the explication of short stories. He was also of the opinion that readers play a part in the production of the meaning of stories. O'Faoláin considered the relationship between reader and text (in an almost proto-post-structuralist manner) engaged and dynamic, and argued that "the alertness of the reader," and also the imagination of the reader, is something "on which every short story writer counts" (205).

One of the many ways in which readers are invited to produce or make play with "Lovers of the Lake" is through the story's constant engagement with binaries and oppositions. O'Faoláin's story is framed by a set of binaries and antitheses which impacts upon and helps to shape the relationship between Jenny and Bobby. This set of binaries is extensive and includes medieval rituals vs. modern cultural practices, the claims of marriage vs. life alone, reason vs. impulsiveness, religion vs. science, masculinity vs. femininity, land vs. water, appearances vs. reality, social obligations vs. personal independence, aestheticism vs. hedonism, and spiritual penance vs. physical delight. Each of these terms is carefully organized and patterned into an antithetical opposition by O'Faoláin.

At first glance, the significance of each of these terms is obvious and allows the two central characters to be clearly placed. However, in the course of the story each of the terms escapes the restraints of this patterning and risks blurring into its opposite. If Bobby likes to think of himself – and is imagined by Jenny and the narrator – as rational and judicious, for instance, he also appears and is happy to be considered impulsive on occasion. Moreover, if Bobby is explicitly associated with skepticism and science (one of the few things the reader knows for certain about him is that he is a surgeon and a lapsed Catholic), he nonetheless also participates, perhaps fully (the reader can never be sure), in the pilgrimage as the story develops. Jenny, in turn, undertakes this pilgrimage in search of spiritual clarity and to gain the inner strength that will allow her to deny that which her body most desires. Jenny's scruples and reflections on the complexities of her situation appear genuine, even if a recent critic, Marie Arndt, has suggested otherwise. ("Jenny is really more concerned with social respectability than with the religious implications of her love affair, and does not have a problem with negotiating between the two" (Arndt 2001: 175).) One of the ironies of the story, though, is that whatever clarity Jenny gains is achieved through the experience rather than the negation of the body. "We must understand one another. And understand this place," Bobby observes at a critical juncture:

> I'm just beginning to . . . Can't you see how the old hermits who used to live here could swim off into a trance in which nothing existed but themselves and their visions? I told you a man can renounce what he calls the Devil, but not the flesh, not the world. They thought, like you, that they could throw away the flesh and the world, but they were using the flesh to achieve one of the rarest experiences in the world. (O'Faoláin 1981: 30)

Body and spirit transcend their simple designation at this point in the text and are shown to be mutually interrelated. Something similar can be said of each of the other antithetical terms that O'Faoláin calls on his readers to imagine in the story. As David Pierce has pointed out, each of these terms combines to the point where they provide "not so much opposites as accompaniments to a larger symphony" (Pierce 2000: 695). It is because each of these terms is stretched beyond the limits of this careful patterning that "Lovers of the Lake" avoids the risk of appearing reductive or overly schematic.

An added irony of the story is that in the closing movements Jenny and Bobby are said to return from Lough Derg "by the road they had come" (O'Faoláin 1981: 37). The reader can never be sure whether anything has changed as a result of their pilgrimage, nor can the reader be certain how to interpret Bobby's remarks that he might return to the island and do the pilgrimage "properly" next year (42). How one reads the final image — where the couple book into a hotel together but separate to sleep in adjoining rooms — remains a vexed question. Does this image signal an end or the beginnings of an end to their relationship? Does it bear witness to the impossibility of Jenny and Bobby's situation? Or does it simply suggest that the couple are continuing to perform part of their penitential duties for one more night? Interestingly, problems to do with the interpretation of this image led to the difficulties O'Faoláin initially encountered in securing a publisher for "Lovers of the Lake." Seemingly, the final image proved "something of a curiosity to non-Irish, non-Catholic readers" and this led to a delay in the publication of the story (Harmon 1994: 193). Fifty years on, "Lovers of the Lake" remains as equivocal, expansive, and open-ended as ever. It is one of a number of stories by O'Faoláin which are best characterized by their absence of any kind of resolution and which creatively engage with states of uncertainty and productive tension. In this respect, as the critic Michael Neary has so eloquently remarked, it is one of O'Faoláin's several "hymns to ambiguity" (Neary 1995: 11).

REFERENCES AND FURTHER READING

Arndt, M. (2001). *A Critical Study of Seán O'Faoláin's Life and Work.* Lewiston: Edwin Mellen Press.

Bonaccorso, R. (1987). *Seán O'Faoláin's Irish Vision.* New York: State University of New York Press.

Butler, P. (1993). *Seán O'Faoláin: A Study of the Short Fiction.* New York: Twayne.

Deane, S. (1986). *A Short History of Irish Literature.* London: Hutchinson.

Dunne, S. (ed.) (1991). *The Cork Review* (a special issue on Seán O'Faoláin).

Foster, R.F. (1988). *Modern Ireland 1600–1972.* London: Allen Lane.

Harmon, M. (1966). *Seán O'Faoláin: A Critical Introduction.* Notre Dame: University of Notre Dame Press.

Harmon, M. (ed.) (1976). *Irish University Review* 6/1 (a special issue on Seán O'Faoláin.)

Harmon, M. (1994). *Seán O'Faoláin: A Life.* London: Constable.

Hildebidle, J. (1989). *Five Irish Writers: The Errand of Keeping Alive.* Cambridge, Mass.: Harvard University Press.

Le Moigne, G. (1979). "Seán O'Faoláin's Short-stories and Tales," in P. Rafroidi and T. Brown (eds), *The Irish Short Story*, pp. 205–26. Gerrards Cross, Bucks: Colin Smythe.

Neary, M. (1995). "Whispered Presences in Seán O'Faoláin's Stories," *Studies in Short Fiction* 32: 11–19.

O'Donnell, D. (1954). "The Parnellism of Seán O'Faoláin," in *Maria Cross: Imaginative Patterns in a Group of Modern Catholic Writers*, pp. 95–115. London: Chatto & Windus.

O'Faoláin, S. (1948). *The Short Story.* London: Collins.

O'Faoláin, S (1981). "Lovers of the Lake," in *The Collected Stories of Seán O'Faoláin*, vol. 2, pp. 18–43. London: Constable.

Pierce, D. (ed.) (2000). *Irish Writing in the Twentieth Century.* Cork: Cork University Press.

Walshe, E. (ed.) (2000). "Seán O'Faoláin: Reassessments." *Irish Review* 26: 1–59.

39

The Short Stories of Muriel Spark

Robert Ellis Hosmer, Jr

Born February 1, 1918, in Edinburgh, Muriel Sarah Camberg had an extraordinarily prolific literary career, launched early. At the age of nine, she revised Browning's "The Pied Piper of Hamelin" to give it what she called "a happy ending." That confident creative spirit and bravado became one of the distinguishing features of a nine-decades long writing life. As a young (and brilliantly talented) pupil at James Gillespie's School for Girls, she continued to write poetry, winning the first of many prizes, this one to mark the centenary of Sir Walter Scott's death (1932); she became known as the school's dreamer and poet ("I was famous for my poetry," she told more than one interviewer).

Emigration to Africa and marriage at the age of nineteen to Sydney Oswald Spark did not dampen her literary enthusiasms: during her six years in Southern Rhodesia (now Zimbabwe) and South Africa she wrote and published more poems. On her return to England in 1944 she wrote an unusual kind of fiction: so-called "black propaganda" or disinformation for the war effort. After the war, she became General Secretary of the Poetry Society and editor of its publication, *Poetry Review*, while publishing poems there and elsewhere frequently.

In the tense time of post-war rationing, Muriel Spark, poor and hungry, entered the *Observer's* Christmas story contest. She describes the experience in her memoir *Curriculum Vitae* in 1992:

In that year 1951 came the first real turning point in my career. In November *The Observer* announced a short-story competition on the subject of Christmas. The first prize was two hundred and fifty pounds, quite a fortune in those days, with various secondary prizes. The rules were that the story should be not more than three thousand words, and the entry should be anonymous. The story was to be accompanied by an envelope signed by a pseudonym on the outside, the real name inside. I put aside my work on Masefield and wrote 'The Seraph and the Zambesi' on foolscap paper, straight off. Now I had to type it but I found I had no typing paper. I scrounged some from the owner of an art shop nearby in South Kensington, typed it out, put my pseudonym "Aquarius" on the Envelope and my name and address inside, and mailed it off to *The Observer* that afternoon. (Spark 1992: 198)

From 6,700 entries, "The Seraph and the Zambesi" took the prize. From then on, Spark continued to write both stories and poems, even as she became a novelist with the publication of her first novel, *The Comforters*, in 1957.

In the course of her writing life, Muriel Spark published twenty-two novels, four volumes of poetry, two biographies (Mary Shelley, John Masefield), several editions of letters (Shelley, Newman, the Brontës), plays, both for radio and stage, an autobiography, a screenplay (for her novel, *The Takeover*), stories for children, and dozens of uncollected essays on diverse subjects (the Book of Job, Proust, traveling the backroads of Tuscany). In addition, she had eight collections of short stories published: *The Go-Away Bird and Other Stories* (1958); *Voices at Play* (radio plays and short stories, 1961); *Collected Stories I* (1967); *Bang-Bang You're Dead and Other Stories* (1983); *The Stories of Muriel Spark* (1985); *Open to the Public: New and Collected Stories* (1997); *All the Stories of Muriel Spark* (2001); and *The Ghost Stories of Muriel Spark* (2003, all stories previously published).

Spark never abandoned the short story, publishing her first in 1951 ("The Seraph and the Zambesi") and her last in 2000 ("One Hundred and Eleven Years Without a Chauffeur"). If *All the Stories of Muriel Spark* be true to its title, then Spark left a legacy of forty-one stories upon her death, on April 13, 2006.

From first to last, the stories bear a certain indelible Spark stamp. To read her work is to endure immediately the shock of dislocation into a world at once so familiar and so alien. Each story is always grounded in what appears to be a common and conventional world of everyday circumstances, a world where the forces of good and evil do battle, and only the rare character is able to negotiate successful passage. Evil is an existential reality, and an abiding sense of menace poisons the atmosphere. In a BBC Radio 3 interview late in life, she put things emphatically: "I really do think that the devil exists. I think evil exists. I think we see it everywhere" (Tusa 2001).

Crucial and axiomatic to all Spark's fiction is an understanding that this world and the world beyond, the temporal and the spiritual, the quotidian and the transcendent, are inseparably integrated. No parallel reality theories ever captivated Spark. The natural and the supernatural are complementary, not contradictory. As one critic has noted, "Muriel Spark sees no line separating the supernatural from the natural. For her, they are neither contradictory, nor even merely analogous. Instead she insists, 'they are implicitly in each other'" (Glavin 2000: 223). The things of this world point to the other; the good things of this world possess a sacramental efficacy, the bad things, a cautionary, allegorical significance. Perhaps one of Spark's characters, Barbara Vaughan in *The Mandelbaum Gate*, puts it best: "Well, either religious faith penetrates everything in life or it doesn't. There are some experiences that seem to make nonsense of all separation of the sacred from the profane – they seem childish. Either the whole of life is unified under God or everything falls apart" (Spark 2001b: 308).

It follows, then, that the characteristic point of view for Spark's stories must be divinely omniscient. Even when a first-person narrator is used, a more frequent occurrence in the stories than in the fiction it might be noted, the point of view is ultimately Beyond.

Everything in Spark's short fiction takes place *sub specie aeternatatis*, with the narrator constructing, demolishing, dispatching, prolonging, and propeling with a detachment for which Spark is renowned; it is "the genius of her fiction" for John Updike (Updike 1960: 161). That detachment should not be taken as a lack of compassion or concern for her characters, a frequent and ridiculous criticism of her work; rather, it is a bracing tonic against sentimentality and an altogether just moral attitude towards those endowed with intellect and free will. Likewise, the typical tone of Spark's fiction – variously and accurately described as astringent or acerbic or withering – is appropriate. The angle of vision is always and quite deliberately off accustomed center. In her own words, she explains the choice: "Being at an angle I found a help. It means one has a different perspective, a new angle of absurdity" (Dalgano 2006). An acerbic, caustic, and detached tone not only works against sentimentality ("We were encouraged not to be sentimental, self-pity was something to be avoided," she told one interviewer (Wavell 2006)), but also underscores a rational, adult attitude toward human behavior.

Several other features distinguish Spark's short fiction, perhaps most prominent among them a sly, seductive, never-to-be-completely-trusted voice, but none of those so important as her often-stated sense of fiction as poetry. In a "Special Message" written for the first edition of her novel, *The Only Problem* (1984), Spark reminisces:

> Before I became a novelist I was a poet. . . . I know that the practice of poetry . . . contributed to my work in the novel form. . . . The American critic, the late Allen Tate, made a claim in a broadcast discussion, to the effect that a good novel should be a poem. He meant this in a very special sense; he was not thinking of ornate language or of the prose-poem; he meant the intrinsicconstruction, the conception, the vision. I would wish all my novels . . . to be judged under this deep and haunting light. (Spark 1984: np).

Elsewhere, she put it even more emphatically: "Allen Tate said a novel is a poem or it is nothing. . . . To me, poetry is the first thing and a novel is, to me, a poem" (Ross 1984: 455). That understanding applies to her short stories as well. The sense of prose fiction as poetry has little to do with the altogether obvious poetic qualities and strategies that grace the stories (rhythm, repetition, symbol, etc.); or with the ways in which they partake of the Border Ballads she acknowledged as formative (tales of violence, betrayal within a compressed lyrical structure); nor even with the wit and lyrical grace of her best stories. Rather, the stories are poems in their vision and scope: Spark's stories, with so much meaning compressed into an integrated, balanced, and tightly constructed entities, are indeed poems.

Two early stories cast long shadows over the remaining thirty-nine, and they shall be the focus of the discussion that follows. Spark wrote other, fine stories, of course, but these two, if not paradigmatic, establish the essential template for all her fiction, whether short or long.

The title of "The Seraph and the Zambesi," Spark's first published story, aptly suggests the coexistence of the supernatural and the natural. The place itself made an indelible impression on the young Muriel, and she conveys that in her memoir:

> The Zambesi River itself was another unforgettable marvel I went on a steamboat among rhinoceroses and crocodiles, with low trees lining the shore crowded with chattering monkeys and alive with happy and agile small boys making fun among the voracious-looking orchids. (Spark 1992: 129)

As is appropriate for such an exercise, categories of time are collapsed into an eternal present as Samuel Cramer, a character from Baudelaire's novella, *The Ballad of the Fanfarlo* (1847), appears as the proprietor of a petrol pump and rooming house in Africa circa 1946. The utter fictionality of the construct serves to underline the fictionality of all characters – except the Seraph, who finds himself locked in a heated contest with Cramer over the staging of the town's Christmas pageant. In a carefully contextualized and characterized story, Cramer loses control of the proceedings, of course. No mere mortal can be a match for divine intelligence. The sheer heat generated by the weather, by the angelic presence, and by the discourse, at once witty and deadly serious ("this is my show," shouts Cramer at one point, to which the Seraph responds, "it's been mine from the beginning" (Spark 2001a: 82)), erupts into a holocaust of sorts, consuming the stage set for Cramer's masque.

On an elemental level, it is a struggle between the forces of good and evil, told with what would become one of Spark's distinctive narrative voices from the start, "You may have heard of Samuel Cramer, half poet, half journalist, who had to do with a dancer called the Fanfarlo. But, as you will see, it doesn't matter if you have not" (Spark 2001a: 77). It expresses a marvelous devil-may-care attitude characteristic of all Spark's work, derived from her religious faith; as she told one interviewer who questioned her about her conversion to Roman Catholcism in 1954, "Nothing matters very much of things that previously seemed to matter a great deal, and yet *everything* matters a great deal. It's a paradox" (Ross 1984: 455).

The whole enterprise is not just viewed from beyond, with detachment and wit, as well as a terrifying economy (seven pages); it leads into the beyond. At the end of the story, the Narrator, with Cramer and others, follows the Seraph towards the river: "by the mute flashes of summer lightning we watched him ride the Zambesi away from us, among the rocks that look like crocodiles and the crocodiles that look like rocks" (84). That last line imbues the narrative with a poetic finish, of course, but it does far more in directing our attention to another, real world, beyond. In the battle for control of words, the Seraph has not only the first word but the last as well.

Spark's other African stories are fascinating. In Africa, Muriel Spark said that she "learned to cope with life" (1992: 119); in addition, as "The Seraph and the Zambesi" and a number of other stories testify, she found context for some of her best stories (though not for any novel, curiously). "Bang-Bang You're Dead" may be read, like "The Seraph and the Zambesi," as an African fable, indeed a fable of identity. Sybil Coleman, a young woman with an uncanny resemblance to a schoolmate, Desirée, marries and goes to Africa with her husband, Donald, an archaeologist. The couple are a classic mismatch: she reads Kierkegaard's *Journals*, he reads nothing, not even the literature in his field. Donald is soon mauled to death by a lioness. Meanwhile, Desirée and her husband have moved to Africa. The widow Sybil, colossally bored with life, accepts invitations to spend weekends with them. She becomes involved in a peculiar dynamic that results in Desirée's being shot by a man who has mistaken her for Sybil. Though several other stories use an African locale – "The Pawnbroker's Wife," "The Curtain Blown by the Breeze," "The Go-Away Bird" – none ranks with the first.

"The Seraph and the Zambesi," a dramatic and highly original re-scripting of a traditional Christmas pageant story, is so breathtaking, so audacious in the territory it stakes out, in the claims it asserts, and in its technical bravado, that it took the rest of Spark's career for her – and her readers – to work out its profound implications.

Spark's other real masterpiece in the short story is also an early one, "The Portobello Road," written in 1956. It opens like a conventional, comfortable narrative with four friends – George, Kathleen, Skinny, and the narrator – on a high summer holiday in the Scottish Borderland years beforehand. Frolicking in a haystack, the Narrator plunges her hand in and pricks her thumb on a needle, earning her the nickname "Needle." Several paragraphs into the story, years having passed, the narrator "mooching down the Portobello Road" (Spark 2001a: 2), spies Kathleen and George rummaging through the bins of knickknacks and bric-à-brac. She calls out "Hallo, George" several times, eliciting nothing more than a terrified, silent response from George, who tells Kathleen, "It's Needle" (3).

And then comes the Spark punch: the narrator announces, "I must explain that I departed life nearly five years ago. But I did not altogether depart this world" (3). The rest of this twenty-page story, up until the last several pages, flashes backwards in order to explain the cause of George's terror, if not exactly Needle's hovering presence throughout: that is simply a given, part of Spark's essential vision of the supernatural and the natural being "implicit in each other."

The account of Needle's murder by George is both grisly and gruesome, the sudden eruption of unexpected and terrible violence among the fields of Kent shocking, as George stuffs Needle's mouth with hay. The lead-in to the murder gives one of Spark's most famous lines, "he looked as if he would murder me and he did" (17).

Needle's point of view is explicitly Roman Catholic: an adult convert to the faith, she is not altogether likable (typical for Spark), being overtly racist and given to storing up venom, "which spurted out indiscriminately on Skinny or on anyone who crossed my path" (9). Needle is a voice from beyond, penetrating the here and now in the most familiar, matter-of-fact way. When the confirming bishop had brushed her cheek, as "a symbolic reminder of the sufferings a Christian is supposed to undertake" (12), she had thought, "how lucky, what a feathery symbol to stand for the hellish violence of its true meaning" (12). Along with Kathleen, she is the mediating, if disturbing and disruptive, Catholic point of view, which, as Kathleen asserts at one point, "takes some getting used to" (17). Indeed – but this point of view is Spark's perspective, set forth early on in the story, when Needle details her habits: "But most Saturdays I take my delight among the solemn crowds with their aimless purposes, their eternal life not far away" (4). The double-edged irony of that last phrase is not to be lost: eternity is already now and "not far away."

These two stories are Spark's finest. She went on to write dozens more, easily classified into sometimes overlapping categories: fables of identity; ghost stories; tales of murder and menace; stories concerned with literary matters (reputations, estates, archives). Several of these are first rate: "The Gentile Jewesses," a lovely memory/fable of identity; "The Dark Glasses," a haunting vignette of double vision; "The Go-Away Bird," a riveting African tale of murder and mayhem, virtually novella-length; "Come Along, Marjorie," a sly tale of a religious eccentric slipping into insanity; "Alice's Long Dachshunds," a shocking story of violence in a small village; and "A Hundred and Eleven Years without A Chauffeur," a further exploration of identity construction. Of the remaining, none is less than assured, polished entertainment but some are noticeably weaker efforts ("Quest for Lavishes Ghast," "A Member of the Family," "The Thing About Police Stations") nonetheless.

Just as the best stories cannot be confined to one period of Spark's career, so, too, the less than best. The intriguing question to ask is: why are "The Seraph and the Zambesi" and "The Portobello Road" so distinctive, so accomplished? The answer has likely nothing to do with the vicissitudes of inspiration or circumstances or routine. More likely, Spark found that the concerns she explored in these two stories needed greater consideration than the limits of the short story allowed. Indeed, examination of Spark's novels demonstrates that the concerns she articulated in these two early stories are explored, to greater depth and extent, in novels of greater aesthetic distinction and bravado (*The Driver's Seat, The Prime of Miss Jean Brodie, The Girls of Slender Means*) than the bulk of her stories.

The short story was not Muriel Spark's strongest suit. Her best stories are highly wrought, deeply textured contemplative exercises; they have about them the precision, vision, crackling intelligence, rhythm, wit, and economy of poetry. They are explorations, quite metaphysical, inquiries into what has to be called, for better or worse, the human condition. If these stories be read as dialogs, then the conversation continues well beyond the last word into the Beyond. As one critic has pointed out about her work in general, "There is a moral but no catechism" (Kimball 2006). Her best stories, like "The Seraph and the Zambesi" and "The Portobello Road," are ultimately about mystery and indeed they are mysteries themselves:

never fully comprehended, always with a sense of something greater to be derived.

Roger Kimball has suggested the "the presentiment [created by Spark's use of what seems "unvarnished reportage"] often terminates in an ellipsis" (Kimball 2006). I would extend the use of that subtle graphic marker and argue that "The Seraph and the Zambesi" and "The Portobello Road" – and a half-dozen others cited – should end not with a period, but with an ellipsis. They have about them some of the poetic mystery Spark ascribed to the Book of Job: "it will never come clear. It doesn't matter; it's a poem" (1984: 121). The beauty of the experience is in the process of contemplation as well as whatever vision might come.

A thrifty Scot always, Spark wasted nothing. She took to heart what John Masefield told her, "All experience is useful for an artist" (Spark 1991: 13), and took great pride in telling interviewers, "I don't want to throw anything away" (Fergusson 2006). She wrote short stories throughout her career, using materials not suitable for a novel and crafting entertainments of a slighter, lighter nature. Never merely "trivial" or "mechanical," as David Lodge would have us understand (Lodge 1985: 39), but always entertaining, some stories do seem like rehearsals for those longer texts that burnished her reputation to the end. Yet, perhaps the words of another writer, Shirley Hazzard, put it best: "She writes to entertain, in the highest sense of that word – to allow us the exercise of our intellect and imagination, to extend our self-curiosity and enrich our view" (1968: 1). What more could any reader ask?

References and Further Reading

Dalgarno, P. (2006). "The Funeral," *Sunday Herald* (April 17): <http://www.sundayherald.com/55201>.

Fergusson, J. (2006). "Dame Muriel Spark: Author of *The Prime of Miss Jean Brodie* and Other Acerbic Twentieth-century Parables," *The Independent Online Edition* (April 17): <http://news.independent.co.uk/people/obituaries/article358213.ece>.

Glavin, J. (1988). "Muriel Spark's Unknowing Fiction," *Women's Studies* 15: 221–41.

Glavin, J. (2000). "Muriel Spark: Beginning Again," in A.H.P. Werlock (ed.), *British Women Writing Fiction*, pp. 293–313. Tuscaloosa and London: The University of Alabama Press.

Hazzard, S. (1968) "A Mind Like a Blade," review of *Collected Stories* by Muriel Spark, *New York Times Book Review* (September 29): 1, 62.

Hosmer, R.E., Jr (1989). "Muriel Spark: Writing with Intent," *Commonweal* 116: 233–41.

Kimball, R. (2006). "Muriel Spark, 1918–2006," *The New Criterion* (April 16): <http://www.newcriterion.com/weblog/2006/04/muriel-spark-1918-2006.html>.

Lodge, D. (1985). "Marvels and Nasty Surprises," *The New York Times Book Review* (October 20): 1, 38–9.

Ross, J.W. (1984). "Muriel Spark," *Contemporary Authors: New Revision Series*, vol. 12, pp. 455–7. Detroit, New York, San Diego etc: Thomson/Gale.

Spark, M. (1984). *The Only Problem*, 3rd edn. Franklin Center, Pennsylvania: The Franklin Library.

Spark, M. (1991). *John Masefield*. London: Pimlico (original work from 1953).

Spark, M. (1992). *Curriculum Vitae*. New York: Houghton Mifflin

Spark, M. (2001a). *All the Stories of Muriel Spark*. New York: New Directions Press.

Spark, M. (2001b). *The Mandelbaum Gate*. New York: Welcome Rain Publishers (original work from 1965).

Taylor, A. (2006). "Scottish by Formation," *Sunday Herald* (April 17): <http://www.sundayherald.com/55201>.

Tusa, J. (2001). *The John Tusa Interviews*, Radio 3, interview with Muriel Spark. BBC Radio, (December).

Updike, J. (1960). "Creatures of the Air," review of *The Bachelors* by Muriel Spark, *The New Yorker* (September 30): 161–2, 165–6.

Wavell, S. (2006). "Blithe Spark Dies Still in Her Prime," *Times Online* (April 16): <http://www.timesonline.co.uk/article/0,,2087-2136608.html>.

40

Jean Rhys: "Let Them Call It Jazz"

Cheryl Alexander Malcolm

"Let Them Call It Jazz" is no bastard child. Yet it can seem so different from Rhys's other creations that it can be taken for one. This is a shame if it deters the reader. Selina's voice does distinguish her from other Rhys protagonists and narrators, but her message links her to them all. This short story, which so resembles the outsider among Rhys's stories because it is the only one told by a black West Indian, is, in fact, Rhys's quintessential story of an outsider. "Let Them Call It Jazz" does not merely belong in Rhys's repertoire; it is essential reading for anyone wishing to understand this writer. Other short stories can seem more accessible, such as the whimsical "Illusion" about a plain English woman in Paris with a hidden cache of exotic dresses, or the comic "On Not Shooting Sitting Birds" about a date gone terribly wrong between a white Caribbean girl and an upper-class Englishman. They are lighter in many ways. Their narrators view events with a measure of emotional distance or the still fierce optimism of youth. Selina, in "Let Them Call It Jazz," has no such distance or optimism. For admirers of *Wide Sargasso Sea*, the injustices in "Let Them Call it Jazz" can lack glamour both in themselves and their wrappings. Cultures clash in too close a proximity to our present times, in rooms with mold on the walls and with none of the flounces or flora of Antoinette's life on a Caribbean island in the 1800s. There is also no unfolding like a flower of a symbiotic relationship to another work of literature. If *Wide Sargasso Sea*, as David Cowart points out, "affects the way readers experience its host text," "Let Them Call It Jazz" should impact the way readers view the English, who are Selina's hosts (1993: 48). This essay would rather propose that reading "Let Them Call It Jazz" *for* its sound will impact all future readings of Rhys's fiction.

Most likely inspired by Rhys's own noisy run-ins with neighbors and consequent brief incarceration in Holloway Prison, "Let Them Call It Jazz" begins noisily and obstinately: "One bright Sunday morning in July I have trouble with my Notting Hill landlord because he ask for a month's rent in advance" (Rhys 1987: 158). Selina is in trouble, money troubles that have a way of finding nearly all of Rhys's protagonists. Yet "One bright Sunday morning in July" is a charming beginning uncharacteristic of Rhys. Look a little further, though, and the sentence seems infused with sarcasm – as if to say: England may be warm at the times but the English remain cold. The irony of bad news coming with good weather is implicit, as is Selina's outrage. She has been paying her rent weekly since winter. Her landlord's change of policy comes without warning, explanation, or apology, and is accompanied by verbal and physical abuse. This is classic Rhys territory. Acceptance turns to rejection as swift as the flip of a coin. Elsewhere in Rhys's writing, pregnancy sends lovers on their way. Sadness, too. Her women are decorative objects and subject to the whims of collectors. But there are no lovers in "Let Them Call It Jazz" and Selina is no coquette in a black dress. She *is* black. What can seem to set "Let Them Call It Jazz" apart from the rest of Rhys's writing is in fact what makes it so much a part of it. Rhys plays with blackness as a symbol throughout her fiction. It is central to the figure of a "petite femme," or fragile woman, whose black dress is a virtual uniform of doomed vulnerability. Selina, who is doomed by her skin and her distinctly black voice, is not anomalous but characteristic of the underdogs for whom Rhys rallies. "Let Them Call It Jazz" is the model child not the bastard. Although it postdates too much of Rhys's writing to be a prototype, it offers an excellent introduction to this writer.

The opening sentence of "Let Them Call It Jazz" takes its power from one word. "Ask," instead of "asks," designates Selina's West Indian background. In common with its African American usage, "ask" for "asks" also makes Selina a racial as well as ethnic "outsider" in England. As a result, it "others" Selina from all of Rhys's other protagonists who, whether they are European or West Indian, are white. For these reasons, "Let Them Call It Jazz" can seem an anomaly. Yet, through the West Indian voice of Selina, Rhys is doing what she always does, only more so. Rhys is speaking out for the silenced, and she is voicing intimate thoughts about her Anglo-Caribbean identity. This essay will examine how Rhys shatters silence through sound and song. First, it will consider the way sound battles silence. Second, it will investigate the relationship between song and memory. Third, it will consider the significance of music in selections from Rhys's personal essays and autobiography. Despite the lack of critical attention, music is a presence in Rhys's writing, which this essay will argue is worthy of further exploration and study.

In common with music, "Let Them Call It Jazz" is built on silences and sound. A pivotal combination of both occurs early in the short story after Selina is robbed of all her money and accepts a room in a rundown house from a stranger called Mr. Sims. Although she is grateful to have a place to live, its silence disturbs her. Selina thinks: "I listen but I can't hear one sound" (159). To combat her loneliness, she sings to herself. "When I sing," she explains, "all the misery goes from my heart" (160). From this point on, Selina is associated with sound and England with silences. The former prompts the latter such as when she tries to make friends with her neighbors. "At first" she explains, "I say good evening" but the woman "turn away her head, so afterwards, I don't speak" (161). Selina confronts silence with sound, however, when she laughs at the man who "stare as if I'm wild animal let loose" (161). By evoking the laughter of apes, Selina challenges the man's feelings of superiority by seemingly confirming her wildness and, by inference, his civilized difference. With her West Indian background, Rhys would have been well aware of the racist implications in comparing a black woman to a "wild animal." Whereas money is a source of power in all of Rhys's writing, whiteness empowers in "Let Them Call It Jazz." With laughter as with song, Selina refuses the passive role of the observed object.

Her West Indian voice enhances the imagery that places this story in the realms of postcolonial literature. The neglected garden evokes a fallen Eden. The abandoned house which Selina's old white neighbors lament "could have been saved, but nothing done of course" brings to mind the loss of empire (160). When they call it "shameful" and Selina says "many things shameful," agreement is tinged with dissent (160). Selina does not tell her neighbors what those "many things" are, but the reader is privy from the first sentence of the short story and its message is damning. Selina's fall into homelessness, the hands of a pimp, and prison, begins with her unlawful eviction by a landlord. Each step of Selina's descent is marked by sounds ranging from her singing to her smashing of a window in the house. But these are always in response to the silences of whites who ignore and abuse her. Breaking silences, like the breaking of the window, are acts of resistance. It can be argued that the distinctive rhythms of her West Indian voice make even her ordinary speech a form of protest song in England.

When Selina remembers a song that she hears from the prison punishment cells, sound takes on religious overtones. Evoking the biblical fall of Jericho to explain what the Holloway Song means, she reflects: " One day I hear that song on trumpets and these walls will fall and rest" (173). Those walls that do fall are spiritual although not in a strictly religious sense. The Holloway Song is a gendered spiritual, and appropriately so, given that Holloway Prison was where suffragettes were incarcerated at the start of the twentieth century. While the singer's words "tell the girls cheerio and never say die" empower women in a decidedly British English, Selina's response: "I don't want to stay lock up here" reminds us of her black West Indian origins (173). "Lock" instead of "locked" *re*locates "The Holloway Song" from the British mainland to former colonies with their own history of song and resistance going back to spirituals and slavery. As with "ask" for "asks" in the first sentence of the short story, Rhys is not merely impersonating black speech. She is iconizing non-standard English to convey how Selina iconizes sound by imbuing it with her own meaning.

It is important to remember that song in "Let Them Call It Jazz" is both an aural and oral site of remembrance. Selina first experiences the prison song as a listener. Only later does she become its performer. When a man at a party jazzes it up, she is not disturbed to be made a listener again but that he alters it. The spirit of it is removed. Like so many of the songs and sounds in Rhys's fiction, the original song evokes absence and longing, which extends beyond its prison walls or initial singer. To Selina, the Holloway Song comes out of England but becomes iconic of her lack of belonging there. The song also becomes a solace to Selina who identifies it with a brief period of connection and inclusion with other prisoners. Songs generally have the power to include and exclude those who do and do not belong to groups based on race, ethnicity, age, or good fortune and they function in all of these ways in "Let Them Call It Jazz." What Rhys does in this short story is relate how a song, like a person or nation, can include then later exclude.

Rhys's autobiographical writing frequently recalls the Dominican island of her birth in terms of the dichotomy between white and black attitudes toward sound. Generally, whites hush and blacks make noise. When the former impinges on her play as a child, such as when she is told to stop swinging because the ropes creak, it is no wonder that she would more fondly remember the effervescent sounds of blacks in the town. Thus, she immortalizes the market women's calls of "Salt fishcakes, all sweet an' charmin', all sweet an' charmin'" at the start of the highly autobiographical *Voyage in the Dark* about a young Anglo-Caribbean woman's loneliness and loss of innocence in Edwardian England (Rhys 1978: 1). Anna Morgan, its narrator/protagonist modeled after Rhys, recalls these sounds as another émigré might the lullabies of a mother. If family voices are remembered, they are sources of pain, rejection, and criticism. When Anna's English aunt despairs of her making a success as an actress in London, she puts it in terms that are also highly racist:

> I tried to teach you to talk like a lady and behave like a lady and not like a nigger and of course I couldn't do it. Impossible to get you away from the servants. That awful sing-song voice you had! Exactly like a nigger you talked and still do. Exactly like that dreadful girl Francine. When you were jabbering away together in the pantry I never could tell which of you was speaking. (1978: 56)

"Sing-song voice" suggests that black speech is more musical. "Jabbering" evokes the calls of apes or other beasts. Although all languages have a rhythm depending upon which syllables are stressed, Anna's aunt regards her own English as devoid of these features. Comparable to regarding whiteness as a norm not a race, the aunt hears "song" or rhythm only in voices that differ from her own. She thus equates musicality with something savage.

Another of Rhys's Anglo-Caribbean characters also runs into trouble when her speech contradicts her looks. In "On Not Shooting Sitting Birds," an Englishman is confused when his date dresses like a lady but is unruffled by the open door to a bedroom adjoining their dining room. When she describes an imaginary hunting party in an effort to impress him, he is aghast that her brothers shot sitting birds. Like Anna in *Voyage in the Dark* whose voice carries too keen a Caribbean rhythm for her to be a lady, the young woman in "On Not Shooting Sitting Birds" appears unladylike less for what she says than what it suggests to the listener. The real hunt is for the woman. If, as is the case here, she acts unafraid, then the roles of hunter and hunted are reversed. For this Englishman, like Anna's aunt, Rhys's Anglo-Caribbean women disrupt racial distinctions and social order. Given the declining fortunes of the former plantation families such as Rhys depicts in *Wide Sargasso Sea*, the demarcation lines separating white from black, owner and owned, are so blurred that accent and manners become the last vestiges of white "superiority." While British writing has a long tradition of voices indicating class position, Rhys connects this to racial identity, empire, and the colonial past.

The impact of Rhys's first sixteen years in Dominica cannot be overestimated when exploring sound in her fiction. Of the many types of sound she would have known, those to do with religious rite and celebration were outside her family experience but inside the island life that she remained so wistful about for years afterward. In *Smile Please: An Unfinished Autobiography*, she reveals that the happiest time of her life was at convent school and she even considered becoming a nun despite her parents' disapproval (Rhys 1981: 81). When she visited Dominica years after going to England at sixteen, Rhys visited the nuns and was warmly welcomed (Angier 1990: 353). The regimentation and gendered exclusivity of Rhys's convent education may seem at odds with a writer who appears to have spent her life bucking the system then craving its acceptance. But it is totally fitting, for the students were almost exclusively black. For Rhys, like Selina in Holloway Prison, acceptance does not come easily and when it does it can be in surprising places. Rhys's identification with blacks is deserving of more attention than this essay has space for. It is worth noting, however, that sound is integral to her concepts of race.

If black sounds were for all to hear, white sounds were for restricted audiences. The sounds in the streets, which come from the descendents of slaves, are thus more positive sites of remembrance for Rhys than musical evenings in her family home from which she was excluded. In *Smile Please: An Unfinished Autobiography*, she describes her fascination with the music that she was not supposed to hear:

> Before I was old enough to be allowed down during the musical evenings, I would sit on the staircase and look through the banisters into a dark passage. Beyond was the room where the music came from. "Night has a thousand eyes," someone sang, and suddenly I don't want to listen any more but go up to my bedroom and undress quickly. (Rhys 1981: 65)

Too young to understand that the "thousand eyes" do not refer to insects, Rhys flees to her room. Her undressing, though done in innocence, evokes the voyeurism alluded to in the song. There are worse things than insects. But no one is willing to tell her that.

In contrast, processions at Corpus Christi are fondly recalled and exude a positive and open sensuality that is absent from her descriptions of Anglo-Caribbeans and the English. The memory of sneaking a peak at the black women in the Corpus Christi procession on their way to Mass is altogether satisfying:

> They were dressed in their best, sweeping trains, heavy gold earrings and necklaces and colourful turbans. If the petticoat beneath didn't make the desired frou-frou voices, they'd sew paper in the hems.

Frou-frou, frou-frou,
Par son jupon la femme
(Frou-frou, frou-frou)
De l'homme trouble l'âme . . .
      (Rhys 1981: 51)

The sound of rustling is erotically charged in an age when a glimpse of a petticoat would have been taboo for the women in Rhys's family. It announces that women have hips and those hips can move in ways that beat out a rhythm. Thus even in a religious procession, blacks proclaimed their freedom from white social constraints. The lack of border between procession and dance, speech and song, mirrors other changing orders.

In "Let Them Call It Jazz," dances are despairing. Selina dances on her own after too much drink until the neighbors complain. And there is the parody of a dance when she is forced to walk in circles with the other inmates in the exercise yard at Holloway Prison. Despite fine weather and blue skies, Selina calls the yard "a terrible sad place" (Rhys 1987: 172). Her high heels, meant for dancing not marching, tire her feet and make going around in circles a cruel reminder of her getting nowhere in England. Such negative circularity is a frequent feature in Rhys's writing. After Anna has an abortion at the end of *Voyage in the Dark*, the doctor who thinks she is a prostitute says "Ready to start all over again in no time, I've no doubt" (Rhys 1978: 159). The harshness of these words reverberates in Anna's mind and the novel ends with her thinking: "starting all over again, all over again" (159). Sacha in *Good Morning, Midnight* regrets starting over again after a failed suicide attempt. Going around in circles has an altogether different meaning for Rhys in one memory from childhood. In *My Day*, a short collection of personal essays, Rhys recounts how she and some other white children did a circular dance called "Loobi Li" until their mothers stopped them. The dance, it seems was indecent. Rhys gives considerable attention to this memory and the origins of the dance. She suspects it was originally English, not West Indian, because, whether the latter had Spanish, American, or African influences, "it was always sad" (Rhys 1975: n.p.). Rhys did not have a simplistic view of blacks any more than of black music. When she reminisces about her childhood – "Every night someone gave a dance, you could hear the drums. We had few dances. They were more alive, more a part of the place than we were" – she envies black belonging, not a skewered idea that blacks were born happier (1981: 50).

Besides being narrated by a black West Indian, "Let Them Call It Jazz" stands apart from Rhys's other writing because Selina is so entirely alone. However abusive or merely insensitive they might be, lovers, friends, and family fill the pages of Rhys's fiction. Selina's story *makes* a confidante of the reader by inference, because she is such a solitary figure. In Rhys's other fiction with Caribbean characters and settings, their difficult relations with other characters discern outsiders, whereas Selina is designated as an outsider in England from the first tones of her voice. There is less emphasis on a single confrontation between two characters and more on its telling. The irony underpinning the power of Selina's narrative voice is that she rarely has anyone to talk to or who is willing to listen. Yet, she listens to others. She listens to her neighbors say what a shame it is that the neighborhood has become run down. She listens to the woman singing from the punishment cell in Holloway Prison. The same neighbors later call Selina shameful when she dances barefoot in the garden. Whereas their hostility overshadows all future relations, the Holloway Song remains the same. "So let them call it jazz," she thinks, "and let them play it wrong. That won't make no difference to the song I heard" (175). "No" does more here than draw attention to Selina's West Indian origins. That would be redundant and Rhys is not a writer who is verbose or repetitive. "No" resonates with resistance that the closing words explain. A single sentence paragraph ends the short story thusly: "I buy myself a dusty pink dress with the money" (175). The missing "will" after "I" ends the narrative in dialect, which by implication links her blackness to resilience. Selina says she "could cry" when she receives a letter saying the song has been sold and enclosing five pounds (175). But that is different from saying that she does cry. Buying a dress suggests that her eyes are on the future not the past. Its color signifies innocence although faded by the gray of age and experience. "Dusty" sets this pink dress apart from the "pink milanese silk underclothes" in "On Not Shooting Sitting Birds" that an Anglo-Caribbean woman buys to wear on a date, then she takes off with regret when he sends her home early (Rhys 1987: 328). The unnamed woman remains an innocent who thinks: "Some other night perhaps, another sort of man" (330). Selina holds out no such hope that she will meet another sort of English person from those she has met. "On Not Shooting Sitting Birds" ends with its protagonist still intent on finding love. "Let Them Call It Jazz" ends on a note of independence. While a series of encounters, rather than one oppositional relationship, sets "Let Them Call It Jazz" apart from other Rhys short stories, they actually highlight what is true of them all. As Judith Moore puts it in "Sanity and Strength in Jean Rhys's West Indian Heroines," "Rhys's world is in fact less one of personal relationships than of impersonal and unequal power structures in which blackness and femaleness are significant and inescapable disadvantages, to be recognized certainly, resisted when possible, but decisively changed only in some future none of her heroines has the security to imagine" (Moore 1987: 30).

Rhys is a writer of subtleties. Even when her characters charge in with fists flying, the narratives are controlled, their power often hinging on a single word. Although "Let Them Call It Jazz" appears flamboyant, it is Rhys at her most refined. Kenneth Ramchand points out in "West Indian Literary History: Literariness, Orality and Periodization" that Rhys signifies dialect rather than duplicates it. Selina's non-standard use of English tense is "the clue" for readers to "hear 'Ah' for 'I' and 'mih' for 'my' throughout" (Rhys 1988: 105). While imagery has garnered the bulk of critical attention, it is a pity to ignore the sound of Rhys's writing. As Ramchand argues: "Rhys's story doesn't die if we miss out on the dialect tone, but it becomes much less dramatic, and the narrating character does not leap into life when the ear does not come into play" (1988: 105). Tone is more than mood. It can suggest complex forms of speech. In "Let Them Call It Jazz," Rhys exhibits a West Indian sensibility, which has drawn comparisons to Derek Walcott's subtle use of dialect tone over total duplication of dialect (Ramchand 1988: 105). The many more sighted than aural readings of Rhys support the belief that "the language of West Indian literature conveys more to the West Indian reader, who is attuned to it below the level of phoneme, than to the non-West Indian reader" (Ramchand 1988: 106). But perhaps this essay will spark change.

References and Further Reading

Angier, C. (1990). *Jean Rhys: Life and Work.* Boston, Toronto, and London: Little Brown and Company.

Cobham, R. (1993). "Revisioning our Kumblas: Transforming Feminist and Nationalist Agendas in Three Caribbean Women's Texts," *Callaloo* 16/1 (winter): 44–64.

Cowart, D. (1993). *Literary Symbiosis: The Reconfigured Text in Twentieth-Century Writing.* Athens: University of Georgia Press.

Davidson, A.E. (1985). *Jean Rhys.* New York: Frederick Ungar.

Emery, M.L. (1990). *Jean Rhys at "World's End": Novels of Colonial and Social Exile.* Austin: University of Texas Press.

Gardiner, J.K. (1989). *Rhys, Stead, Lessing and the Politics of Empathy.* Bloomington and Indianapolis: Indiana University Press.

Howells, C.A. (1991). *Jean Rhys.* New York: St Martin's Press.

James, L. (1978). *Jean Rhys.* London: Longman.

le Gallez, P. (1990). *The Rhys Woman.* New York: St Martin's Press.

Malcolm, C.A. and Malcolm, D. (1996). *Jean Rhys: A Study of the Short Fiction.* New York: Twayne.

Moore, J. (1987). "Sanity and Strength in Jean Rhys's West Indian Heroines," *Rocky Mountain Review of Language and Literature* 41/1 & 2: 21–31.

Morrell, A.C. (1990). "The World of Jean Rhys's Short Stories," in P. Frickey (ed.), *Critical Perspectives on Jean Rhys*, pp. 95–102. Washington, DC: Three Continents Press.

Morris, L. (2001). "The Sound of Memory," *The German Quarterly* 74/4: 368–78.

Ramchand, K. (1988). "West Indian Literary History: Literariness, Orality and Periodization," *Callaloo* 11/34 (winter): 95–110.

Rhys, J. (1975). *My Day.* New York: Frank Hallman.

Rhys, J. (1978). *Voyage in the Dark.* Harmondsworth: Penguin (original work published 1934).

Rhys, J. (1981). *Smile Please: An Unfinished Autobiography.* Harmondsworth: Penguin.

Rhys, J. (1987). *The Collected Short Stories*, ed. D. Athill. New York and London: Norton.

Staley, T.F. (1974). *Jean Rhys: A Critical Study.* Austin: University of Texas Press.

Wilson, L. (1986). "'Women Must Have Spunks': Jean Rhys's West Indian Outcasts," *Modern Fiction Studies* 32 (autumn): 439–47.

Wolfe, P. (1980). *Jean Rhys.* Boston: Twayne.

Zimring, R. (2000). "The Make-up of Jean Rhys's Fiction," *Novel* (spring): 212–34.

41

George Mackay Brown: "Witch," "Master Halcrow, Priest," "A Time to Keep," and "The Tarn and the Rosary"

Gavin Miller

The Scottish author George Mackay Brown (1921–96) is most admired for his poetry, which distinctively combines universal themes and imagery with representations of mundane life in his native Orkney, the archipelago in which he lived for most of his life. Brown, however, was also an accomplished writer of fiction. As well as five novels, including the Booker Prize shortlisted *Beside the Ocean of Time* (1994), he also produced fifteen volumes of short stories. Brown's stories, like his poetry, are essentially modernist, even primitivist in spirit. They invite the reader to discern eternal mythic patterns underlying a contemporary wasteland, and to renew forgotten rituals that once filled human existence with meaning.

Bill, the protagonist of "A Time to Keep," a story first anthologized in the 1969 volume of the same name, exemplifies Brown's depiction of the modern psyche. This Scottish crofter-fisherman is an atheist who is openly hostile to organized religion. Yet he is also an implicit believer whose everyday life is filled with hints of private consecration. The story is set in the early part of the twentieth century on a Scottish island, so Bill's atheism is unusual within his community, and derives (so his bookshelf tells us) from the tradition of nineteenth-century rationalism. Bill is a self-made man, driven by what he sees as an unflinching commitment to rationality and intellectual integrity: the local minister is a "missionary" (Brown 1969a: 42), and even the midwife who attends the birth of his son is merely "some kind of priestess" (Brown 1969a: 57). Yet he is also depicted as *naturally* and *unconsciously* religious. As Berthold Schoene persuasively argues, Bill needs neither scripture nor revelation, for, although unrecognized as such, the divine is everywhere evident to his senses:

> although Bill is obviously determined not to believe, Brown presents his way of perceiving the world as marked by a primal understanding of the religious import of life and nature in the sense of a *naturalis gentium religio* [a natural religion of the people]. (Schoene 1995: 154)

Schoene points out, for example, the connection between Bill's perception of the harvest and the practices of Christian religion. The language is indeed laden with religious significance:

> My oats had heaved at the sun like a great slow green wave all summer. Now the sun had blessed it. The whole field lay brazen and burnished under a blue sweep of sky. And the wind blessed it continually, sending long murmurs of fulfilment, whispers, secrets, through the thickly congregated stalks. (Brown 1969a: 54)

The vocabulary of congregation and blessing, and the probable sun/Son pun, point to a hidden Christian religiosity in Bill's perceptions. The hints deepen when his wife Ingi dies, and he grudgingly accepts as his second wife her best friend, the conventionally religious Anna. The story ends on Christmas Eve with a further revelation of Bill's spontaneous religion. As they walk home, Bill, Anna, and his son pass through their byre, which contains "five kneeling animal," and so form their own Nativity scene – a point emphasized by Anna's remark that the church service was beautiful, "All about Mary and Joseph and the baby and the shepherds and the three kings. [. . .] Who would ever think such things could happen in a byre?" (Brown 1969a: 62).

Inside their house, the hearthfire – in a typical piece of Brown's poetic symbolism – conveys the revival of Bill's life after the death of Ingi:

> The fire wasn't out after all. There was a deep glow in the heart of the peats. Anna broke the red core with the poker; flames flowered everywhere in the fireplace, and the room was suddenly alive with the rosy shifting dapple. (Brown 1969a: 62)

This fire, throughout the narrative, is central to Bill's latent religiosity. He thinks of it as "the red heart of the house" (44), as a precondition of "food and companionship" (38), and feels that because of it, the house is "alive" (39). Ingi's maintenance of the fire means that she is an unofficial priestess of Bill's religion, and their home is a church. The house is filled with the incense-like "blue hot reek of baking" (46); when Ingi brings home pails of water, they ring "like bells" as she sets them down on the stone floor (40); and when she dies after the birth of her son, she is as "long and pale as a quenched candle" (58).

Bill's religion is latently Christian, but it is also recognizably a Catholic Christianity in its imagery of candles, bells, and incense, and its emphasis on "companionship" (literally, the sharing of bread, from the Latin *com-panis*). It may therefore come as little surprise that Brown was received into the Catholic Church in 1961. As Schoene notes, this act was a conscious rejection of the Scottish tradition of Presbyterianism:

> By converting to Catholicism, Brown denies the four-century-long tradition of the Reformed Church in Orkney any constructive influence on Orcadian life. He branded

it a serious mistake, detrimental to all spiritual genuineness and in urgent need of correction. (Schoene 1995: 206)

Brown's consequent idealization of pre-Reformation Orcadian life is apparent in "Master Halcrow, Priest," a story first anthologized in the collection *A Calendar of Love* (1967). Halcrow is a Catholic priest in sixteenth-century Orkney, who is abruptly expelled from his kirk at Stromness by the forces of the Scottish Reformation. Although the story is nominally set "in the year of Our Lord 1561" (Brown 1967a: 124), Halcrow is strikingly indifferent to quantified, progressive time. He marks time, instead, by the agricultural cycles of his community. He dates the writing of his story merely to "a harvest evening" (124), and throughout his narrative, positions events according to the seasons. When the bishop arrives, warning of the proscription of the Catholic Faith, it is to Halcrow, "the time of tall green corn, before the last burnish comes upon it and the heavy ears droop" (126). Similarly, the day of his expulsion from the Church is the day after the community "began the cutting of the oats" (129).

Brown's temporal imagery in this narrative introduces a motif found throughout his stories, as Halcrow describes how one labourer "was in the oatfield, making bright circles with his scythe" (133). Although "Master Halcrow, Priest" only marginally introduces this circular imagery, it forms an integral part of stories such as "The Whaler's Return" (collected in *A Time to Keep*), where the protagonist, Andrew Flaws (who, as his name suggests, has a few masculine vices), returns home to find his wife is spinning wool in order to make a blanket for their bed, a christening shawl for their child-to-be, and two shrouds for their eventual death. The natural cycle of sex, birth, and death is symbolized in the spinning wheel, and made explicit in Flaw's earlier anticipation of the "ritual of the corn, the cycle of birth, love, death, resurrection" in which "the seed was buried, the ripe corn fell, bread was broken." (Brown 1969b: 121).

Halcrow's fear of the Reformation therefore centers around the loss of the Host, the Catholic Church's expression of the "ritual of the corn" which symbolically binds men and women to the agricultural cycle: "What might such men do," he wonders, "to the Bread of Heaven, seeing that for them now it was no longer the Body of Our Lord but mortal bread over which five invalid words had been uttered?" (133). But although the Reformation successfully takes over the organization of the Scottish Church, it is less successful in suppressing the sacred rituals of agriculture. The story ends with Halcrow being passed the Host by Master Anderson, a Catholic priest who has decided to conform to the Reformed church, yet has secretly preserved these sacred materials. As with "A Time to Keep," the narrative is one of a *natural* religion that can be driven underground by institutional religion as much as by rationalism, yet which may be preserved and maintained in a covert religious life of the folk.

As Brown's connection of communion to cyclical temporality suggests, his religion is essentially opposed to any notion of progress. Part of his dislike of the Reformation is conveyed by one of Halcrow's taunts to the lascivious Master Anderson, who seems to have accepted the Reformation partly in order that he can marry:

> "I trust that Mistress Angela is well," I said. "She is an immense piece of territory, your Newfoundland, but doubtless in time you will be able to chart the geography of her to your satisfaction, and wring much fruitfulness out of her, Father." (Brown 1969b: 132)

This anachronistic ventriloquism, by which Brown alludes to John Donne's well-known and much anthologized "Elegy 19. To His Mistress Going to Bed" (first published 1669), reveals what happens when man breaks free of cyclical time, and worships progress. Donne's colonial metaphor for his lover – "O my America, my new found land, / My kingdom, safeliest when with one man manned, / My mine of precious stones, my empery" (Donne 2000: ll. 27–9) – is extended in Brown's sexual-imperial comparison. The Reformation will set Scotland on course, with an already Protestant England, towards a future in which "fruitfulness" will be wrung out of the British Empire.

The antagonism between what Brown calls the "false Gods" of "progress and money and mammon" (Murray 1996: 42) and, as he sees it, the inner truth of the Catholic faith, is set out in a short story, "The Tarn and the Rosary", collected in *Hawkfall* (1974). The central character, Colm, is a representation of Brown, growing up in Orkney, and re-evaluating his cultural inheritance. Jock Skaill, the island's local (pseudo-)atheist, and Colm's closest confidante, bemoans "Progress," which he identifies as a modern religion:

> This island is enchanted with the idea of Progress. [. . .] Times are much easier for us than for our grandfathers. So, they argue, we have better fuller richer lives. This worship of Progress, it will drain the life out of every island and lonely place. (Brown 1974: 187)

Predictably, Brown re-employs his favored opposition of cyclical Catholic time to progressive Protestant temporality. Colm in the local smithy feels the heat of the recently extinguished forge dwindling – in an echo of the fire symbolism in "A Time to Keep" – as the men gathered there begin to criticize Roman Catholicism. According to one local bourgeois, "Your Roman Catholic takes out his rosary beads. He counts them over and over. He mumbles the 'vain repetitions' that we are warned against in scripture" (Brown 1974: 191). Yet, despite whatever may be said in Matthew 6: 7, it is repetition that the adult Colm identifies as at the heart of agricultural life. In a letter to a friend which he writes while in temporary exile in Edinburgh, Colm takes the example of an island "peasant" who is "bound upon the same monotonous wheel year after year" (195), and yet who is, in truth, "at the very heart of our civilization" (196). The agricultural peasant is a central figure because:

the humble earth-worker [. . .] represents us all. He it was who left the caves and, lured on by a new vision, made a first clearing in the forest. There he began the ceremony of the bread. (Brown 1974: 196)

According to Colm, communion ceremonies – of all kinds – are what reconcile mortal and divine: "What saves us is ceremony. By means of ceremony we keep our foothold in the estate of man, and remain good citizens of the kingdom of the ear of corn. Ceremony makes everything bearable and beautiful for us" (198). Colm views the ritual of communion as a figurative communication of the truth of God's reality, a *Credo* that bypasses rational thought and the conscious mind, and which may be found even in those who are indifferent or hostile to organized religion. Every participant believes, at some level, that Christ "came up out of the grave the way a cornstalk soars into wind and sun from a ruined cell" (197). The act of breaking bread together is a metaphor for the way in which "the brutish life of man is continually possessed, broken, transfigured by the majesty of God" (197).

Such ceremony, Colm implies, is, or should be, at the heart of literary art. In his letter, he refers to "a few random pieces of verse and song – those ceremonies of words" that have touched him "to the heart's core" (198). Among them are Gerard Manley Hopkins's "The Wreck of *The Deutschland*," Chaucer's *The Canterbury Tales*, and Federico García Lorca's "Oda a Walt Whitman." "I want a black boy," writes Colm, citing Lorca, "to announce to the gold-minded whites / The arrival of the reign of the ear of corn" (149). Brown therefore follows Lorca's call for a renewal of poetic and communal ceremony by voices that we would now identify as "subaltern" because of their position in lower social classes or marginal social groups. In "The Seller of Silk Shirts" in *A Calendar of Love*, the role of the "black boy" is taken by Johnny, an Indian clothes salesman who visits the islands. As this Sikh visitor distributes his gifts, and encourages the ceremonies which the islanders might otherwise neglect, his ear arranges in poetic form the speech of the islanders. He sells to one woman a shirt, which she gives to her boyfriend for his birthday, along with a small cake. Johnny overhears the boyfriend discussing the gifts in a voice that "seems like singing":

> "So, then, what could I say?
> For my birthday
> Had she not baked a small cake
> And brought on her arm
> A shirt yellow as buttercups
>   this very afternoon?
> That way
> All our troubles are ended."
>   (Brown 1967b: 3)

In Brown's fiction, as Schoene concludes, the verbal ceremonies of poetry are to be found in the everyday speech of farmers, fisher-folk, and traveling salesmen:

His poetry is influenced by the medieval Church's literary ideal of *claritas*. *Claritas* describes a poetic style that, in the face of God's immanence in everything on earth, humbly renounces artistic virtuosity for a plain voice of religious celebration. (Schoene 1995: 265)

Brown's vision of spontaneous religion and poetic ceremony means that all his characters inherit and participate in religious forms derived from, or analogous to, those found in medieval Christendom. Like the sexual drive in Freudian psychoanalysis, religious communion is a constant which can never be wholly eliminated: the only issue is whether it is celebrated in religious or para-religious ceremony, or whether it is driven so far underground as to return in a perverted or sinister form. The story "Witch" from *A Calendar of Love* explores this latter possibility. It is the tale of a fictional Orcadian girl, Marian Isbister, who is accused in the early 1600s of witchcraft, put on trial, and finally burnt at the stake. The trial and burning of Marian is a scapegoating and a distraction organized by the Earl of Orkney to buttress his unpopular regime. Marian's accusers are a collection of the earl's cronies: a factor on his estate, his chaplain, and the local sheriff (equivalent in Scotland to a judge). Marian's supernatural intervention, the sheriff finally concludes, has led to the death of dogs, stormy weather, infertile cattle, sick and dying children, fires in haystacks, and her boyfriend's impotence. She is eventually burnt on a day decreed by the Earl to be "a public holiday" (Brown 1967c: 121), thereby providing a temporary carnival or Saturnalia designed to appease the population.

Marian's accusers, though, are not motivated solely by political cunning. Part of their pleasure in tormenting Marian is in the symbolic sexual gratification of the "tests" to which they subject her. As they prick her to find the insensitive areas supposedly indicative of commerce with the devil, Brown piles on the sexual imagery: "These parts were probed: the breasts, buttocks, shoulders, arms, thighs. Marian displayed signs of much suffering, as moaning, sweating, shivering, but uttering no words" (106). This "return of the repressed" is echoed in the perversion of Christian doctrine and ritual in Marian's trial and execution. The sheriff in the closing address to the jurors, for example, draws upon the imagery of agriculture and communion in order to justify murder by the state. Marian's actions are, he claims, "the first shoots of a boundless harvest of evil":

> it is well to choke the black shoots early. For if we neglect them, then in the fullness of time must we eat bitter dark bread indeed – blasphemy, adultery, fratricide, tempest, flood, war, anarchy, famine. (Brown 1967c: 119)

The torture and execution of Marian extend this debasement of Christian narrative: Marian is an actor in a perverted Passion Play or mystery play that has merged ritual with reality. The Christological hints are intensified by her "meekness" before her tormentors (120), her public humiliation through the streets of Kirkwall, her death on a hill, and her forgiveness of her executioner. Typographically, the ritualized aspects of the story are emphasized by the way the narrator, a town clerk, frequently records dialog in playscript form: the characters are speaking parts written for them long ago in the original drama of the Christian Passion.

When ceremony is debased, in Brown's fiction, then communion bread and religious ceremony are perverted into the "bread and circuses" by which political repression is maintained. But regardless of whether ceremony is used or abused, Brown's essential vision of temporality is maintained. To Brown, time is a wheel or recurring cycle in which apparent progress is really endless repetition. We are bound to this wheel, and our only choice, it seems, is to wholeheartedly live through the cycles and celebrate them in our rituals, or to deny them in the name of post-Reformation "progress," and so have them return in an alienated, debased, and fanatical form. In literary terms, such temporality leads to an essential "typological" view of history. As Schoene notes, "Brown believes in the existence of historical patterns and anthropological constants, firmly anchored in the Fable of a religious master plot that lies at the heart of our human existence" (Schoene 1995: 231). Brown sees all reality and culture as a network of correspondences that find their purest expression in the events of biblical narrative.

Yet, despite his avowed Catholicism, Brown's vision is anything but medieval. There is no real eschatology or soteriology, no doctrine of the end of things or of our salvation, in Brown's vision of endless repetitions. His "Catholicism" is a twentieth-century response to a narrative of progress that Christianity, in all its various sects, helped to compose. The search for a unifying myth of regeneration in a contemporary cultural wasteland marks Brown as essentially a late-modernist poet turned short-story writer and novelist. He is therefore exploring a primitivist poetic terrain already thoroughly mapped by T.S. Eliot, W.B. Yeats, Robert Graves, and many others. Fortunately, Brown does not resort to the state-political authoritarianism found in many of these primitivist writers – Graves, for example, denounced democracy and called for a government headed by a cultic élite of moon-worshipers in his poetic-political manifesto, *The White Goddess* (Graves 1952). Brown's gender politics, however, are manifestly limited by his identification of women with cyclical temporality. Brown can depict the cruelty of the European witch craze, but that seems the extent of feminist sensibility in his fiction. Brown's womenfolk are wholly fulfilled by church, children, and the kitchen. Anna in "A Time to Keep," for example, marries the misanthropic Bill, who calls her an "ugly bitch," so that she can have a child and a house to look after: "Somebody must look after this bairn and this house," says Anna to Bill, "I don't like *you* at all, but I love this bairn of Ingi's" (Brown 1969a: 60). Those few women who move outside these sacred domains generally have some slur on their femininity. The schoolmistress in "The Seller of Silk Shirts," for example, is a graduate of Edinburgh University, and so must be afflicted with "long black hairs on her lip, and a wart" (Brown 1967b: 75).

But despite these limitations in his range, Brown can also be seen as a more original figure – as a writer who anticipates contemporary Scottish fiction. His fascination with communion rituals such as the breaking of bread positions him amongst authors such as George Friel (1910–75) and Alasdair Gray (1934–) who find in communion an image for the interpersonal life that has been eroded by contemporary culture and society (Miller 2005). Furthermore, Brown's insistence on the aesthetic validity of common speech puts him in some interesting company. It may be hard to think of the Edinburgh working-class dialect of Irvine Welsh's *Trainspotting* (1993), or the Glaswegian demotic of James Kelman's fiction or Tom Leonard's poetry, as sharing much in common with the medieval *claritas* that Brown finds in Orcadian speech. Yet, although the ideology that underlies Brown's valorization of demotic language is very different, he shares with Welsh, Kelman, and Leonard their opposition to a cultural hierarchy in which metropolitan culture and speech occupy a privileged position. Brown's work is also what might be called "anti-essentialist." Although he works within a small Orcadian canvas, his fiction is remarkably welcoming of "foreign" influence and representation. From the Vikings to Indian immigrants, Brown accepts that there is no pure-blooded Orcadian ethnicity, or even a distinct and homogeneous culture, that might be offered in some literary vision of the island's identity.

REFERENCES AND FURTHER READING

Bold, A. (1978). *George Mackay Brown*. Edinburgh: Oliver & Boyd.

Brown, G.M. (1967a). "Master Halcrow, Priest," in *A Calendar of Love*, pp. 124–35. London: Hogarth.

Brown, G.M. (1967b). "The Seller of Silk Shirts," in *A Calendar of Love*, pp. 73–76. London: Hogarth.

Brown, G.M. (1967c). "Witch," in *A Calendar of Love*, pp. 104–23. London: Hogarth.

Brown, G.M. (1969a). "A Time to Keep," in *A Time to Keep and Other Stories*, pp. 38–62. London: Hogarth.

Brown, G.M. (1969b). "The Whaler's Return," in *A Time to Keep and Other Stories*, pp. 115–30. London: Hogarth.

Brown, G.M. (1974). "The Tarn and the Rosary," in *Hawkfall*, pp. 168–200. London: Hogarth.

Delmaire, D. (2001). "L'Oeuvre fictionnelle de George Mackay Brown. Un Fantastique qui laisse à désirer?," *Études Ecossaises* 7: 41–60.

Donne, J. (2000). "Elegy 19. To His Mistress Going to Bed," in M.H. Abrams and S. Greenblatt (eds), *The Norton Anthology of English Literature*, pp. 1256–7. New York: W.W. Norton.

Graves, R. (1952). *The White Goddess: A Grammar of Poetical Myth*. London: Faber and Faber.

Miller, G. (2005). *Alasdair Gray: The Fiction of Communion*. Amsterdam: Rodopi.

Murray, I. (1996). "A Sequence of Images: George Mackay Brown," in I. Murray (ed.), *Scottish Writers Talking: George MacKay Brown, Jessie Kesson, Norman MacCaig, William McIlvanney, David Toulmin*, pp. 1–54. East Linton, Scotland: Tuckwell.

Schmid, S. (2003). *"Keeping the Sources Pure": The Making of George Mackay Brown*. Oxford: Peter Lang.

Schoene, B. (1995). *The Making of Orcadia: Narrative Identity in the Prose Work of George Mackay Brown*. Frankfurt am Main: Peter Lang.

Valdés Miyares, J.R. (1987). "'The Story Teller': Una narración clave en el conjunto de la obra de George Mackay Brown," *Revista Canaria de Estudios Ingleses* 15: 139–46.

Zagnoli, M. (1988). "Story and Fable in the Purgatorial Ghost Stories of George MacKay Brown," *Studies in Scottish Literature* 23: 77–86.

42

William Trevor: Uncertain Grounds for Assured Art

John Kenny

Lest there linger any doubts about his cultural roots and place in national literary tradition, William Trevor has recently been claimed definitively for Mitchelstown, County Cork, as one side of a festival double-header with his Cork precursor, Elizabeth Bowen. Mitchelstown Literary Society's new Trevor-Bowen Summer School establishes a pairing that is critically natural and publicly popular. Both writers were natives of the same locale in the northeast of the county; both were born into Protestant families in a largely Catholic society; both are major figures in the development of modern Irish prose fiction in English; both are arguably at their very best in their short stories, not their novels. Aside from geographical and religious proximity, and a mutual excellence when practicing one particular form, it is clear that Trevor's broadly realist mode, his stately sentence rhythms, controlled emotiveness of theme, and restrained authorial voice owe much to Bowen's example. She will remain the appropriate local starting point for a comparative assessment of Trevor's work.

A particular divergence should always be emphasized nonetheless. While Bowen famously felt there was a productive tension between her Irish and English cultural inheritances, Trevor, who has lived by far the greater portion of his life in England, has always accentuated his further experience of a kind of psychological homelessness, what might be termed a micro sense of in-betweenness. Again and again, he has insisted, as he did to his *Paris Review* interviewer in 1989, that "being a Protestant in Ireland was a *help*, because it began the process of being an outsider – which I think all writers have to be . . . I didn't belong to the new, post-1923 Catholic society, and I also didn't belong to the Irish Ascendacy" (Paulson 1993: 123). Thus, in crucial aspects, Trevor is not Bowen-like, from his point of view at least. On top of feeling, as she did, that Protestantism can be vitally formational for a particular sense of cultural (dis)placement in Ireland, he has also always had an acute sense of himself as removed from the ascendancy Protestant establishment which was Bowen's background and which was central to the Irish literary revival that continued to considerably influence the agendas of literary taste for Trevor's generation. Within a Protestant tradition that was now outside the new post-independence mainstream, Trevor therefore came to regard himself as doubly an outsider. In a repeated image, he has always clearly put himself retrospectively in his place: "Had my family remained in Mitchelstown I would have been one of the small boys who were employed every summer to field the tennis-balls when they bounced out of court at nearby Bowen's Court" (Trevor 1993: 2).

William Trevor Cox was born in Mitchelstown in 1928, into a middle-class Protestant family that, because Cox *père* was a bank official and was frequently transferred in the traditional manner, experienced a respectably peripatetic life in various Irish towns, largely in Munster and Leinster, but also in Connaught. William equally had to move schools a number of times, then finished his secondary education in Dublin. He took a BA in history at Trinity College Dublin in 1950, then became for a while a teacher at home and subsequently in England. He settled permanently in England in 1953, and tried, with considerable success, to become an independent sculptor. Due both to reaching what seemed a relatively early impasse in what he could express through sculpture and to the financial imperatives of a developing family life (he had married in 1952; by 1960 he was a father), Trevor had begun by the mid-1950s to channel his sculpting skills into the art of narrative. He published his first and unremarkable novel, *A Standard of Behaviour*, in 1958; his second, *The Old Boys* (1964), was a clearer sign that a talented new fiction writer had appeared on the English scene. These and others of Trevor's early novels are in the vein of the black English social comedies of Evelyn Waugh, Kingsley Amis, Muriel Spark, and V.S. Pritchett, and while this is often considered to be one of the more outmoded tendencies in his work, then and since, he has retained such a particularized fascination with the mood of creeping despair, claustrophobia, and vague threat that comedies of social manners facilitate that this aspect of his writing can only be regarded as a conscious aesthetic choice.

With only occasional exceptions, Trevor's fictions, and especially his major short stories, are set either in Ireland *or* in England (or, frequently, on the continent); while in his English stories Irish people sometimes come and go, and in his Irish stories English people and Irish emigrants come and go, sometimes these are not together long enough or complexly enough to invite sustained reflection on their integral significance, as in the title story from *The Hill Bachelors* (2000) where Trevor's repeated use of "gum boots" to refer to the footwear that in Ireland would only ever be called "wellingtons" is perhaps a miniature suggestion of the inattentiveness that can sometimes mar the accuracy of his Irish stories. In *A Writer's Ireland*, his major non-fictional work on his native literary tradition which he wrote in the years subsequent to his award of an honorary CBE in 1977, Trevor describes the historical Anglo-Irish world with which, by tone and judgment in this instance at least, he has some sympathy if not necessarily background allegiance: "Enlivened by the edginess of mixed loyalties, it was a world always capable of finding answers to its innate problems, of smoothing without apparent effort what should have been a perpetually ruffled surface" (Trevor 1984: 55–6). This could perform as a virtual stylistic self-description. Trevor in his stories often sets up Inside Ireland/Outside Ireland and Old/New Ireland thematic axes that are so awkward or obvious that his elegance of style is very busy steadying them, as in the relatively recent stories "Of the Cloth" and "Men of Ireland." This does not necessarily detract from the integrity of his intentions, however. It is simply that Irish writers generally, of whatever living generation, are currently so in thrall to the imposing theme of rapid social change in the country that even a veteran of style such as Trevor can sometimes allow his sophisticated imagination to be imbalanced by an overweening determination to analyze or depict actualities.

Trevor has always been culturally nationalistic to a considerable degree and even as a young man was proudly conscious of his nuanced Irishness. After he launched his career in fiction in the 1950s, his distance from his home country soon encouraged him towards a creative re-examination of the geographical, political, and social context of his own background. By the 1970s and 1980s, surely inspired to some degree by the international attention newly directed at the Ireland of the political Troubles, he had begun to explore both historical and contemporaneous dimensions of home subject matter. The relevant "Irish" works – short stories such as "The Distant Past," "Beyond the Pale," and "The News from Ireland," and novels such as *Fools of Fortune* (1983) and *The Silence in the Garden* (1988) – would come to be regarded as among his best, and the many successful screen adaptations of his work have largely evolved from this area of thematic concentration. Whatever the exact cause and effect, one could speculate that his move into the short story and his move into Irish settings and themes occurred organically round about the same time. It was with his second collection of stories, *The Ballroom of Romance* (1972), that he began to emerge as a writer with a fundamentally Irish voice.

For a major and much anthologized writer, recipient of an honorary knighthood in 2002, comparatively little critical attention has so far been devoted to Trevor. More extensive examination of the way his background feeds into his aesthetics is due before readings of his individual stories can properly proceed in context. This critical lack is to some degree attendant on his own views of the potential for easy generalizations about his work. While his short fiction is clearly that of a dedicated craftsman, with a homogeneity of style and voice that some commentators see as the hallmark of a premeditatedly cohesive vision, some as a relentless and unadventurous sameness, he has always resisted the intellectualization of his fiction, in terms both of the way he himself approaches the writing of a story and in the way interviewers have sought to elicit from him grand overarching statements. He has admitted to "a great fear of analyzing why and how one writes. There is a considerable element of mystery. One does not *know* how the magic of a good story works" (Paulson 1993: 109). Political aspects of his Irish work, nevertheless, would provide particularly rich territory for full-scale critical examination. Even though he has often admitted to probably being politically naïve and has regularly insisted that art is under no compulsion whatsoever to be politically engaged, much of his Irish work, if only because of its socio-historic specificity, is either directly or, more usually in his hands, obliquely political.

Trevor's general sense of the way in which his Irish background seems to regularly, if sometimes discreetly (and, by his own account, mysteriously) insinuate itself within his sensibility is inseparable from his conception of the art of short fiction. He holds to established but nonetheless crucial distinctions concerning the widely perceived intimate connection between the inheritances of Irish ethnicity and the seemingly natural ways in which Irish writers continue to approach the short-story form. Certain joys of national influence, it would appear, are unavoidable for a writer, even when their relevance is not overtly paraded in the work itself. "Nationality seems irrelevant in the loose, uncharted world of art," Trevor commented in the introduction to a collection of his occasional non-fiction pieces; but it then "suddenly raises its voice; fiction insists on universality, then equally insists that a degree of parochialism can often best achieve this" (Trevor 1993: xi). This is potentially a divisive statement since it arguably proposes a false equivalence between Irish nationality and parochialism, which Trevor then turns into a too easily resolved dichotomy between the parochial and the universal. But Trevor is presumably offering his own version of the classic alignment of the parochial and the universal that Patrick Kavanagh argued for in his famously nuanced distinction between a benevolent Irish "parochialism" and malevolent "provincialism" (Kavanagh 2004: 237).

Trevor's choice of vocabulary and oppositions is often potentially unfortunate when he attempts to explain the interaction of Irish ethnicity and Irish literary tradition as he sees it. In explaining the well-documented failure of the novel as a genre to take root in nineteenth-century Ireland in the way it did in England, he has commented that Victorian England was "the perfect hierarchical environment for long afternoons of cricket, for keeping up the eighteenth-century gardens that were decaying in Ireland, for writing and reading the novels that were edifices in themselves." This is incontestable. But then, inadvertently or otherwise, he simply inscribes too much passing judgment within his alignment of a native preference for miniature prose forms with a certain lack in Irish aesthetic sensibility: "Ireland, compared, lay in fragments, a battleground for seven centuries, a provincial wilderness beyond the pale of Dublin and the life of the big country houses, sick at heart and with half of its population starving." The worthiness of the invocation of historical tribulation aside, this is, at best, a lazy propagation of a threadbare colonial stereotype: the British administrative center of Dublin and the Pale with its regional figurations in the Big Houses as the citadels of civilization, symbols and powerful actualizations of culture beyond which all was "provincial wilderness." To quickly counter this, one need not indulge in easy politicizing about the question of whether it was the British administration's responsibility to look to the cultivation of its own wildernesses; the real issue is that in propagating the stereotype Trevor is ironically dismissing those very residual "wilderness" zones of Gaelic folk and oral culture, outside the establishment definition of the literate, which contributed to the emergent health of the short story in Ireland. Trevor's terms of analogy thereafter approach the absurd. Victorian Ireland, he says, had "neither the mood nor the stomach for a new art form, just as it hadn't the leisure for the ceremony and subtlety of the game of cricket. Like the novel, that sport has since only intermittently flourished in Ireland" (Trevor 1984: 104). Assessing Ireland's preference for the short story and seemingly endemic resistance to the novel, in its English version at least, by measuring its fondness, or lack thereof, for cricket would be akin to inquiring into the great tradition of the English novel while wondering about the curious fact that English cricketers have never taken to the much older Irish small-ball field game of hurling.

All this is not to submit Trevor's non-fiction to overly close reading nor to accuse him of an adopted perpetuation of English cultural colonialism in his own Irish context. The carping encouraged by his expressed sense of his own background and of the interaction of Irish ethnicity with literary preference is testament to the complexity of that background and of that interaction. In any case, the world stature of Trevor's own career as a short-story artist is its own argument that an end must be put to any entertainment of the idea that the novel is to be thought of as the pinnacle of literary achievement in prose and that other prose genres are to be measured thereby. It is important that Trevor's work and culturally specific ideas be carefully scrutinized, but it is equally important to speculate that his devotion to and productivity in writing short stories has emerged somehow organically from his continued angular attempt to resolve, or at least to probe, the sense of problematic but simultaneously useful outsiderness that he feels his background was bound to bring with it and that cannot be so comprehensively resolved as to suit a novel. The story "Attracta" from *Lovers of Their Time* (1978) reveals just how determined, but contrived and awkward, Trevor can be when on uncertain thematic ground. To study Trevor's short stories and the intelligence behind them in depth would be to productively engage not only with twentieth-century Irish prose as a whole but with the entire history of prose genres in Ireland and with the question of the relative worth of direct and angular treatments of imposing socio-political actualities. That his stories sustain a quietly polished surface beneath which a potentially untidy cultural irresolution can yet be extracted and examined is not the least badge of his artistry.

Trevor also writes a second, less politically charged brand of Irish short story where his thematic concentration is on the personal, the familial, or the local rather than the national context. It is perhaps in keeping with the received critical idea of the short story as more sympathetic than the novel to the private rather than the public world that Trevor's better Irish stories are of this second brand. Even if the relevant stories are less amenable to thesis-driven analysis, certain Irish sociological realities are usually refracted through their more private setting and are sufficiently manifest for debate. The title story of *The Ballroom of Romance*, with its outlining of the state of national affairs through the absence of intimate affairs in the life of Bridie, the protagonist with a fear of spinsterhood, is still considered his foundational work in this regard, even though it is a conventional epiphany-driven story and would not perhaps have attained the status of Trevor's nonpareil were it not for Pat O'Connor's consummate television version of 1982.

A writer is at least as much an individual as a symptom of nationality, and the assured appearance of Trevor's stories probably owes most to his personal determinations as a craftsman, his apparently instinctive sense of what makes a good story, this innate talent that he calls mysterious. He also finds himself standing on some certain grounds for general cultural confidence however. In his introduction to his widely used anthology of Irish short stories he reports that in thinking about his selection he found himself returning repeatedly to "a consideration of the part that storytelling has played, and continues to play, in Irish life." An Irish "flair" for stories, he says, has long been recognized as a natural "national" trait: "Stories of one kind or another have a way of pressing themselves into Irish conversation, both as entertainment and as a form of communication" (Trevor 1989: ix). Such is his conviction of the centrality of the story to the Irish art of prose that he determinedly sees Bowen's and James Joyce's genius in their stories rather than in their more fêted novels. The appropriate way to similarly approach Trevor's stories as the acme of his own work in fiction is firstly to think of them, in Elizabeth Bowen's phrase, as "free stories" (Schirmer 1990: 85–6). While some formulas of style, theme, character, tone, and structure can be readily discovered from story to story and from collection to collection, the sheer extent of Trevor's output and his widespread popularity necessitate the broadest possible initial approach.

Within fifteen years after his first collection, *The Day We Got Drunk on Cake* (1967), Trevor published four further collections, and such was their readership that by 1983 *The Stories of William Trevor* was published to bring all five together. The count at that stage was already sixty stories. Two collections of new stories followed before *The Collected Stories*, containing eighty-five stories, was published in 1992. Four other collections, containing forty-eight stories in total, have since issued, and by the evidence of the most recent, *Cheating at Canasta* (2007), even the smallest of the short story's developmental possibilities will continue to hold Trevor in thrall. Many of the stories have been redistributed for the purposes of thematic collections. Aside from the two original collections whose titles have clear Irish import, *Beyond the Pale* (1981) and *The News from Ireland* (1986), he published a selection of eleven of his Irish stories as early as 1979 under the title *The Distant Past*. Evidence of the clear axes of focus in the stories as a whole was provided by the simultaneous publication in 1995 of the selections *Ireland* and *Outside Ireland*.

Sheer weight of numbers and rearrangements should not dissuade the pattern seeker. Writing short stories, Trevor has pointed out, is "a repetitious business anyway if you write, as I do, in order to experiment, and I consider myself, like all fiction writers, an experimentalist. I find that in a lot of my stories I'm investigating the same theme so see what happens a second or third, even a fourth or fifth, time." Analogies from the visual arts apply in Trevor's concentration, especially at the openings of stories, on a relatively old-fashioned kind of character portraiture, but they apply also in the case of a thematic repetitiveness that is clearly conscious: "I would liken that to a Renaissance painter who painted over and over again the Virgin and Child or the Nativity" (qtd in Paulson 1993: 116). Despite this description of himself as an investigative experimenter, Trevor's preference for the Joyce of *Dubliners* over the Joyce of the subsequent tomes of novelistic experimentalism effectively highlights the generally plain aesthetic of his own stories. Even though he has written through decades that witnessed extraordinary changes in the practice of fiction, Trevor has proven formidably resistant to fads of theme and technique. While his stories often mention other writers and books, these are incidentals that relate organically to setting and character. He is not an allusive or deliberately intertextual writer. His story "Two More Gallants" is clearly a nod to Joyce's "Two Gallants," but it is important to realize that this is very much an isolated occasional story, written for the Joyce centenary of 1982. While there are elements of allegory and symbolic intensity in his stories, especially the earlier ones, his characteristic style is more descriptive than imagistic or metaphoric. He does not always rely on plot, but simultaneously does not ever entirely eschew anecdote and storyline; he is interested in the problems of psychological and narrative authenticity but retains a confidence in the revelatory power of realistic investigations of character and society. His most patent radical side concerns his frequent refusal of both structural and thematic resolution whereby his early use of varieties of epiphany – inherited, not least, from Joyce – has given way to stories that are more minimalist in design, less explanatory of human decision and motivation, and he has gradually become adept at the kind of ambiguity that means, in a story such as "Gilbert's Mother" from *After Rain* (1996), that it is ultimately impossible to decide whether Gilbert is a murderer or, instead, his mother paranoically imagines him to be one.

Rather than having a handful of major enduring themes, Trevor has suggested he has hundreds of littler ones, and it is this microcosmic concentration, rather than the grander variations on Irish themes, that is his true métier. His has written poignant little masterpieces on the subject of children ("Access to the Children," "Mrs Silly," "Child's Play") and the elderly ("The General's Day," "Widows"). He is unbeatably accurate on the atmosphere of places of social assembly ("Downstairs at Fitzgerald's," "The Paradise Lounge," "Lunch in Winter," "After Rain," "Cheating at Canasta"). From the very outset he became renowned for the kind of dry-eyed ironic treatment of affairs of the heart that characterized his signature Ballroom story ("Office Romances," "Teresa's Wedding," "Lovers of Their Time," "The Wedding in the Garden," "The Piano Tuner's Wives," "A Bit on the Side"). The morally threatening material for which he became more noticeable after Atom Egoyan's 1999 film version of his novel *Felicia's Journey* (1994) also figures to great effect in stories such as "Cocktails at Doney's" and "A Bit of Business." His general preoccupation with ideas of good and evil has frequently taken the form of religiously themed stories ("Death in Jerusalem," "Of the Cloth," "The Virgin's Gift," "Lost Ground," "Justina's Priest," "Sacred Statues," "Faith"). Multiple other stories cover these and related areas.

Even when these stories involve tension or threat or collapse of some kind, Trevor's treatment is usually so quiet that, once read, his stories do not tend to stay with or worry the reader as do, for instance, the more sinuous stories of John McGahern. On the obverse, McGahern's stories might be said to achieve much of their provocative effect through the common presence of an authorial mood of philosophical tribulation, while Trevor's mastery is reflected in his disabling of any intrusive third-person statements. Trevor's honorary title of the Irish Chekhov stands because his stories are illustrations of his enduring Chekhovian view that the writer's function lies in asking the right questions in the right way, not in pronouncing or in providing answers. "There aren't," Trevor insists, any "firm answers at all. I have spent four years writing a story; I have also spent a single day . . . Sometimes I endlessly rewrite; sometimes not at all . . . I have no rules; it seems to me there aren't any" (qtd in MacKenna 1999: 229). Thus the Trevor stories keep coming, standing fast to their indispensable uncertainty.

REFERENCES AND FURTHER READING

Kavanagh, P. (2004). *A Poet's Country: Selected Prose*, ed. A. Quinn. Dublin: The Lilliput Press.

MacKenna, D. (1999). *William Trevor: The Writer and His Work*. Dublin: New Island.

Morrison, K. (1993). *William Trevor*. New York: Twayne.

Paulson, S.M. (1993). *William Trevor: A Study of the Short Fiction*. New York: Twayne.

Schirmer, G.A. (1990). *William Trevor: A Study of His Fiction*. London: Routledge.

Thomas, M.W. (1998). "William Trevor's Other Ireland: The Writer and His Irish in His England," *Irish Studies Review* 6/2: 149–56.

Trevor, W. (1984). *A Writer's Ireland: Landscape in Literature*. London: Thames & Hudson.

Trevor, W. (ed.) (1989). *The Oxford Book of Irish Short Stories*. Oxford: Oxford University Press.

Trevor, W. (1993). *Excursions in the Real World*, with illustrations by L. Willis. London: Hutchinson.

43

John McGahern: *Nightlines*

Stanley van der Ziel

Like many of John McGahern's works, *Nightlines* describes the clash between two cultural systems: that of a disappearing traditional, rural world whose routines and values go back to the time of the Famine in the mid-nineteenth century, and that of a simultaneously emerging modernity. Often this cultural clash is represented as that between a father and son. As Terence Brown (1979: 293ff) points out, *Nightlines* must be read as a literary experiment to find a style suitable to engage with the psychological turmoil and complexity of life in the modern world; as a deliberate and conscious adaptation of a previous provincial, predominantly rural literary tradition (that of O'Connor and O'Faoláin) into an art form capable of expressing the realities of Ireland's transition into modernity. This essay will examine some of the stories' strategies for making the disjunctions and uncertainties of modern life bearable, and the way in which art itself may bring salvation from the metaphysical crises faced by protagonists adrift in a world which often seems chaotic, confusing, and alien.

Tragedy and Comedy

The opening story of the collection, "Wheels," is not only set in a major railway station, one of the principal sites of modernity, but it is also written in a characteristically detached tone that is associated more with the existentialist novels of Camus than with the social-realist mode of the Irish post-revivalists: "Grey concrete and steel and glass in the slow raindrip of the morning station, three porters pushing an empty trolley up the platform to a stack of grey mail-bags, the loose wheels rattling, and nothing but wait and watch and listen, and I listened to the story they were telling" (McGahern 1970: 11). As Denis Sampson points out, the images of a bleak, urban, man-made world dominate the opening paragraph and seem to be the subject of the long descriptive sentence, "until, at the end, the withdrawn 'I' finally appears" (Sampson 1993: 92). The narrator has, syntactically, almost been lost in his own description of the station, reflecting the existential anxiety – so severe that he has in the past tried to commit suicide – of his own perceived insignificance in the larger scheme of things. The modern world is, in this opening scene and elsewhere in the collection, represented as a sort of existential hell, stripped of all meaning and purpose. The three porters pushing the empty trolley with the "loose," "rattling" wheels up the platform may therefore be an oblique echo of Beckett's *Watt*, where a solitary porter is seen wheeling empty cans up and down the platform, "perhaps [as] a punishment for disobedience, or some neglect of duty," like a modern version of Sisyphus, Camus's emblem of existential man's absurd, futile, repetitive existence (see: Ackerley and Gontarski 2006: 529). A similar eternally repeated Sisyphean task, a cosmic punishment with no hope of ever being stopped or interrupted, is also present in "Hearts of Oak and Bellies of Brass," where Tipperary – who as a boy had been taken to be educated by the Christian Brothers "but hadn't been able to pass the exams that would have qualified him a teacher," after which he was first put to work in the kitchens before leaving to work on the building sites in England, where his mocking companions have nicknamed him the Professor – continually asks the protagonist, who has attended secondary school for two years, questions about the merits of Shakespeare and Shaw: "puzzling over and over perhaps his failure to answer satisfactorily the questions they'd put him at the exams before they'd sent him to the kitchens" (McGahern 1970: 53–4). Tipperary inhabits another of the collection's many purgatories.

The first paragraph of "Wheels" reveals that the narrator has nothing to do but "wait and watch and listen," and suggests an amount of boredom in his resolve to listen to the porters' story to pass the time. McGahern shares with Beckett an acute sensitivity of the boredom encountered in the modern world and the great amounts of time spent waiting for something else to happen. (Compare this sentence from *The Pornographer* for its identical Beckettian preoccupation: "passing time, and killing time, and lessening time that'd lessen anyhow" (McGahern 1979: 30).) The repeated act of waiting, of passing the time on a railway platform, becomes an act of almost heroic endurance, a necessary ordeal amounting to that of a Prometheus in the age of mass-transit. (It may be interesting to remember that Beckett originally wanted Lucky in *Waiting for Godot* to be dressed as a railway porter (Mercier 1990: 53).) The men on the building site in "Hearts of Oak and Bellies of Brass" are also acutely aware of "the burden of the slow passing of the minutes, a coin for each endured minute," and the narrator of that story remembers with something like fondness the time when he first started his laboring job: "There was no boredom those first days" (McGahern 1970: 51). The story seems to suggest the only available way to make this existence bearable is to turn their monotony into a series of anaesthetizing chants and habits, repeated regularly throughout the short course of the story: "The shovels drove and threw: gravel, sand, gravel; gravel, sand, gravel; cement . . . 'Our fukker who art in heaven bought his boots for nine-and-eleven,' he sang out as he sledged. 'Come on: shovel or shite; shite or burst'" (McGahern 1970: 49, 52, 56, 59). Thus the boredom of repeated experience is transformed into a *ritual* act – far removed from the painful reality of actually felt experience and capable of assuming a formal beauty all its own. (Bergson (1911: 4–5), in a ploy to transcend the "tragedies" of modern life, had suggested a similar strategy of decontextualizing experience in order to achieve an "absence of feeling" by making it appear *mechanical*, when he proposed one definition of the comic is to watch a room full of dancers but with one's ears stopped to block the sound of the music.)

The outline of the porters' story in "Wheels" itself is heavily indebted to the climax of the action in Act 2 of *Waiting for Godot*:

> Took to fishing out beyond Islandbridge, bicycle and ham sandwiches and a flask of tea, till he tried to hang himself from a branch out over the river, but the branch went and broke and in he fell roaring for help. (McGahern 1970: 11)

The fate of the porters' unfortunate colleague in the story duplicates Vladimir and Estragon's tragic resignation at the impossibility of suicide. McGahern's reliance on black humor in this instance is also similar to *Godot*. The sequence in *Godot* ends with the play's cheapest laugh when Estragon's trousers fall down after the rope that had held them up is snapped in an attempt to see if it might be strong enough to hang themselves with. In McGahern's story it is the branch, not the rope, that breaks, but the author plays for a similar cheap laugh with the comic image of the man trying to commit suicide "roaring for help" at the thought of drowning, and his colleague's tasteless joke (which originates in a profound feeling of despair, like the audience's thunderous uproar at the spectacle of a trouserless Estragon in *Godot*): "No use drowning naturally if you'd meant to hang yourself in the first place" (McGahern 1970: 11). Humor is necessary here to make a moment of extreme crisis bearable; laughter functions as a safety valve when life's absurdity becomes unbearable. McGahern has himself made the same argument in a review of Jack Common's *Kiddar's Luck*: "Common's world can't afford tragedy. His defence is laughter. Even the horrible humiliation of the crippled mother's arrest in charge of a pram becomes just another little comic Calvary" (McGahern 1976: 159). And in *Memoir* he writes of the shattered illusion of continuity that occurs when a loved one dies: "The only way it can be articulated openly is as a joke, when the clash between the inevitable and the unimaginable can be resolved in laughter" (McGahern 2005: 116–17). McGahern's analysis of this function of humor is indebted to Freud's famous essay on humor which argues it enables a detachment from a world that had previously seemed dangerous and threatening (Freud 1990: 432–3), and to Bergson's influential book on *Laughter* (much admired by McGahern (see: van der Ziel 2004)), which describes "the *absence of feeling* which usually accompanies laughter . . . for laughter has no greater foe than emotion," so that "the comic demands something like a momentary anesthesia of the heart. Its appeal is to intelligence, pure and simple." Bergson's solution for coping with potentially tragic or unbearable situations is very similar to that proposed by McGahern in his review of Jack Common: if one were to "step aside, look upon life as a disinterested spectator: many a drama will turn into a comedy" (Bergson 1911: 4–5). Furthermore, it is interesting to note that McGahern's 1976 review shares a preference for the use of the theatrical terms *tragedy* and *comedy* with Bergson's essay; and that the narrator of "Wheels" – after overhearing the porters' conversation and deciding the story of the suicidal railwayman is "too close to the likeness of my own life for comfort" (McGahern 1970: 11) – also seems to be aware of the existence of this Bergsonian mechanism to turn "tragedy" into "a joke" when he recalls a comment his drinking companion had made the previous evening:

> "Looked at with the mind, life's a joke; and felt, it's a tragedy and we know cursed nothing," he'd said last night over the pints of Guinness. (McGahern 1970: 12)

In a later story, "Like All Other Men," Bergson's theory makes another appearance, as a young couple's "nervousness found release in laughter" (McGahern 1985: 62) – even as it eventually breaks down in the face of a question whose implications are so serious and unanswerable that "It could not be turned aside with sarcasm or even irony" (McGahern 1985: 64).

Note also that when "a comic incident on the train generalizes his [the narrator's] experience *into the social domain*" (Sampson 1993: 92; emphasis added), this is in accordance with Bergson's idea that "Our laughter is always the laughter of a group . . . laughter always implies a kind of secret freemasonry, or even complicity, with other laughers, real or imagined," that laughter being "a sort of *social gesture*" (Bergson 1911: 6, 20). The same is true for the estranged couple in "Peaches," who temporarily renew their intimacy through their shared laughter at an absurd thought (McGahern 1970: 118).

Throughout the *Nightlines* stories we can find more examples of the use of humour. Take Lavin's crude tasteless joke in the eponymous story of rural sexual frustration (Sampson (1993: 87) calls it an updating of Joyce's "An Encounter," but as a study of the dangers of sexual repression it also owes something to Kavanagh's *The Great Hunger*):

> "Know the only place the stiff get in: the cunt and the grave," Lavin joked and I noticed his mouth full of the black stumps of teeth as he laughed. (McGahern 1970: 96)

McGahern employs the familiar Renaissance trope of the identification of sex and death, "the cunt and the grave." But the analogy between these two abstracts does not here carry the passionate ecstasy of the seventeenth-century poets, but instead is full of an existential despair at the proximity of the cradle and the grave, embodied most memorably by the image of the obstetrician-turned-gravedigger putting on the macabre forceps in *Waiting for Godot* which would be echoed by McGahern in *The Pornographer* (McGahern 1979: 30). The association between sex and death is a recurring theme in the collection: it is also present, for example, in the comic sequence in "Hearts of Oak and Bellies of Brass" in which the ageing prostitutes offer their decaying bodies in the condemned row of houses (McGahern 1970: 57–9), as well as in the narrator's association between the stinking, rotting sweatband of his father's old felt hat and the thought of the "body that had started my journey to nowhere" in "Wheels" (McGahern 1970: 15), and (less explicitly) that between the smell of the decaying shark on the beach and the estranged couple's spontaneous lovemaking in the sea in "Peaches." It is furthermore reinforced by the overwhelming image of decay in that same sentence from "Lavin," as the randy old bachelor's mouth is full of "the black stumps of teeth." Sexuality is usually seen in these stories as something to be feared, and is imbued with connotations of violence, decay, and the disgust of the unnatural. The image in "Lavin" of Casey inserting a dried reed into a frog, as well as the two boys' fantasies of whipping gipsy girls into submission before taking them from behind "the way the bull does" (McGahern 1970: 98–9), reinforces the theme of a violent sexuality, far removed from the sacred live-giving force it would become in McGahern's later fiction, notably in his last novel, *That They May Face the Rising Sun.*

Lavin shares his despairing, vulgar laughter with Sinclair in the story "Why We're Here," as the latter mocks his own self-destructive interest in women in a casual obscenity that fails to mask his anxiety at his present situation: "*All candles were made to burn before the high altar of their cunts*" (McGahern 1970: 26). His mocking tone at his own interest in women — as well as the mock-ecclesiastical overtones of the "*high altar* of their cunts" — is motivated by his economic downfall at the hands of the Marriage Laws after wedding a Catholic girl. Sinclair's is a tragic story: reduced from his one-time stature as a small Protestant gentleman-farmer, he was last seen by "The crowd up for Croke Park . . . outside Amiens Street with an empty shopping bag. They said he looked shuck [sic]. Booked close to the jump" (McGahern 1970: 24); and the only way he can allow himself to speak of his life is in terms of a vulgar joke. Most of the humour in *Nightlines* consists of the self-effacing laughter of despair.

The Absurd

Many of the stories in *Nightlines* are concerned with the end of childhood and the loss of innocence: they "recall a past experience, the pivot of which is initiation or disillusionment" (Sampson 1993: 87). One of the most accomplished stories in the collection, "Korea," deals with a father and son, the last men to fish the rivers and lakes of the Leitrim–Roscommon border region for a living because of an encroaching modernity threatening their traditional way of life and their meager livelihood: they have been refused a renewal of their fishing license because the tourist board "said we impoverished the coarse fishing for tourists – the tourists who came every summer from Liverpool and Birmingham in increasing numbers to sit in aluminium deck chairs on the riverbank and fish with rods" (McGahern 1970: 89). The son has completed his school exams and is waiting during this last summer in the boat with his father for his results, and the future these will allow him. But as the son knows it would be too expensive for his father to hire anyone else in his place, "the guilt of leaving came: I was discarding his life to assume my own" (McGahern 1970: 89). The turning point of the story comes when the son overhears his father's intention for him to be sent to fight for the American army in the Korean War and perhaps be killed in order that the father may receive the compensation money: "In the darkness of the lavatory between the boxes of crawling worms before we set the night line for the eels I knew my youth had ended" (McGahern 1970: 90). In the last paragraph of the story, remembering his childhood happiness with his father while the boat slowly moves through the calm water for the last time, "Each move he made I watched as closely as if I too had to prepare myself to murder" (McGahern 1970: 91). The deliberate ambiguity of the grammatical object of the verb "to murder" in this last phrase (is the son getting ready for his own murder at the father's hand, or is he preparing himself for the murder of his father?) sums up the terrible truth that whatever his decision – to go to America and be enlisted or to follow his own course in life – it will amount to an effective death sentence for one of them. The son's cruel epiphany at the end of the story is of the vicious way of the world, far removed from the bliss of Sunday afternoons lived in childhood which he had then imagined to be the only reality. Adult experience is random and at times unjust, and does not conform to a set of *fair* rules like a children's game.

In "Christmas," the nameless Homeboy, looking back on past events like the narrator of "Korea," also realizes the fragility of happiness:

> There was no reason this life shouldn't have gone on for long but for a stupid wish on my part, which set off an even more stupid wish in Mrs. Grey, and what happened has struck me ever since as usual when people look to each other for their happiness or whatever it is called. (McGahern 1970: 39)

The narrator grows cynical of his own childhood wish for "happiness or whatever it is called." This cynicism is brought about during a farcical scene in his employer's kitchen on Christmas Eve, and the story ends with a resolve never to form any human attachments again for the disappointment they inevitably bring:

> I was glad, as I quietened, that I'd torn up in the train the letter that I was supposed to give unopened to Moran. I felt a new life for me had already started to grow out of the ashes, out of the stupidity of human wishes. (McGahern 1970: 46)

A sneering, world-weary, and street-smart character, suspicious of human contact and the possibility of happiness, rises like a Phoenix out of the ashes of his own destroyed childhood innocence. And the story's angry and frustrated final phrase must be understood as a deliberate comical, parodic (with its coarsened, countrified diction) misquotation of the title of Samuel Johnson's verse satire *The Vanity of Human Wishes*. The problems facing the youthful protagonists of many of the stories in McGahern's first collection are those of Johnson's poem: to cope with the folly of human aspiration, and the difficulty of not being deceived by a world made up of illusions; of finding a point of view from which to see the world as it really is, and yet at the same time finding a happiness that can last. It is here that McGahern's affinity with the European sensibility of the mid-twentieth century also becomes clear, as the narrators in the latter two stories are both faced with the challenge of "absurd" existence described by Camus: how to find happiness in "a universe suddenly divested of illusions and lights" and of the infallible governing laws of divinity (Camus 2000: 13 and *passim*).

In two other stories, the turning point comes after a revelation about sex or sexuality. In "Coming into His Kingdom," the boy discovers how he has come into the world through the sexual act, "like the bull and the cow" (McGahern 1970: 35):

> it was growing so clear and squalid that there was hardly anything to see. The whole world was changed, a covering torn away; he'd never be able to see anything the same again. (McGahern 1970: 35–6)

In this extract, the description of the radical change in the narrator's perception of the world as "a covering torn away" is perhaps an ironic echo of Yeats's *The Trembling of the Veil*, as McGahern's character experiences a negative version of the glimpse of advent or revelation referred to by Yeats. The boy feels he has been enlightened (quite literally, as the imagery suggests) in the ways of the world: "it was good to stand in the daylight of the others for once and not to be for ever a child in the dark" (McGahern 1970: 37). "Lavin," finally, chronicles the moment when the two young boys – the narrator and his friend Casey – reveal to each other their homosexual desires. From that moment on, they "avoided each other's eyes," and "in the evenings we avoided each other, as if we vaguely glimpsed some shameful truth we were afraid to come to know together" (McGahern 1970: 99–100). What all these child characters – recollected from maturity – have lost is the perception that the world around them makes sense, is whole. This would make *Nightlines* a bleak and pessimistic collection, were it not for the possibility of redemption from this state which is also offered.

The Role of Art

In a later essay, McGahern described the ideal work of art (in the guise of Ó Criomhthain's *An tOileánach*) as "a complete representation of existence" (McGahern 2004: 217); and, as Sampson points out, McGahern's work can be seen to follow John Butler Yeats's suggestion that "Art embodies not this or that feeling, but the whole totality – sensations, feeling, intuitions, everything – and when everything within us is expressed there is peace and what is called beauty" (qtd in Sampson 2005: 146). The narrator of "Wheels" is anxiously waiting for exactly this "rich whole that never came but that all the preparations promised" (McGahern 1970: 22). For McGahern, this "rich whole" of experience can be found only in Art, and thus this narrator is unwittingly anticipating the moment when he will become an artist, capable of feeling "the whole totality" (Sampson 2005: 146), of attaining a "persistent way of thinking and feeling" that will make sense of all of existence (McGahern 2004: 217). Two other stories in *Nightlines* explicitly suggest that Art or literature may offer this elusive vision of a "whole" world. The narrator of "Lavin" remembers how, when a boy, he had tried to get a friend to read *David Copperfield* "so that we could share its world" (McGahern 1970: 95); and in "Strandhill, The Sea" the narrator's comic books contain "whole worlds" (McGahern 1970: 67). For the latter, this "world of imagination" (McGahern 1970: 70) forms an escape: "hours of insensibility" to the boring, imperfect real world he sees around him in the seaside boarding house (McGahern 1970: 67). It is suggested in these stories that Art may offer a "whole" vision of existence to replace the imperfect shattered worlds of disillusion, confusion, and hurt that the collection's many disillusioned characters have discovered in their various moments of enlightenment.

"Why We're Here" is also concerned with the redemptive power of Art. Consider for a moment Sinclair's central question in that story about the nature of existence, recalled and mimicked by Boles:

> *No reason why we exist, Mr. Boles. Why we were born. What do we know? Nothing, Mr. Boles. Simply nothing. Scratching our arses, refining our ignorance. Try to see some make or shape on the nothing we know. . . .* (McGahern 1970: 25)

Sinclair's predicament describes the function of Art and the artist. (In fact, his desire to "*refin{e} our ignorance*" – rather than our *knowledge* – seems to be a version of Beckett's artistic imperative to "Try again. Fail again. Fail better" (Beckett 1983: 7).) His seemingly hopeless search for the meaning of life describes the artist's task to make sense of the random chaotic reality he sees around him by imposing upon it the ordered vision of Art. For the purpose of Art, according to McGahern, is the transformation of "life in the raw" into an ordered "vision" (McGahern 1977: 45) (see also Maloney's speech on the function of Art in *The Pornographer* (McGahern 1979: 27)). McGahern also wrote of this need for Art "to be true to a central idea or vision," which distinguishes it from life, which is governed by "accident," in his short Preface to *Creatures of the Earth* (McGahern 2006: viii). In other words, in Art, everything happens for a reason (according to the plot, scheme, or plan), unlike in life, which, as the protagonists of many of the *Nightlines* stories find out to their distress, is not subject to such laws but is instead completely random. Therefore, if life could be made to assume the *wholeness* of Art, its accordance to an ordered vision – if it could be made to be more like a novel, or a story – it could be made liveable again.

It becomes clear from many of these stories, told in the first person past tense, that many of these narrators seek to make sense of their imperfect past by reinventing it "in the shape of a story," as the narrator of "Wheels" puts it (McGahern 1970: 22). This act of becoming the narrator of one's own past in order to "*see some make or shape on the nothing we know*" is something McGahern owes to Proust's long novel about the search for a clear way of seeing through narrative and memory. (McGahern describes the act of writing as one long Proustian search for "the lost image that gave our lives expression, the image that would completely express it again in this bewilderment between our beginning and end" in an essay called "The Image" (McGahern 1968: 10), which appropriately was reprinted as a Preface to the French edition of *Nightlines* (McGahern 1971: 17–18).) This strategy is especially evident in the two stories which frame the collection, "Wheels" and "The Recruiting Officer," both of which consciously re-examine the past through the act of narrating it. Thus, these stories – and especially "The Recruiting Officer" – can be seen as thematic precursors to McGahern's next two novels: *The Leavetaking*, in which the Proustian theme of "memory becoming imagination" (McGahern 1974: 45) in order to come to terms with a traumatic and puzzling past is once again central; and *The Pornographer*, which takes the opposite approach of unraveling truth from fiction in order to once again uncover life's reality with all its inconsistencies, flaws, and imperfections.

References and Further Reading

Ackerley, C.J. and Gontarski, S.E. (eds) (2006). *The Faber Companion to Samuel Beckett*. London: Faber and Faber.

Beckett, S. (1983). *Worstward Ho*. London: Calder.

Bergson, H. (1911). *Laughter: An Essay on the Meaning of the Comic*, trans. C. Brereton and F. Rothwell. London: Macmillan (original work published 1900).

Brown, T. (1979). "John McGahern's *Nightlines*: Tone, Technique and Symbolism," in P. Rafroidi and T. Brown (eds), *The Irish Short Story*, pp. 289–301. Gerrards Cross: Colin Smythe.

Camus, A. (2000). *The Myth of Sisyphus*, trans. J. O'Brien. London: Penguin (original work published 1942).

Freud, S. (1990). "Humour," in J. Strachey (ed.), *Art and Literature. The Penguin Freud Library*, vol. 14, pp. 426–33. Harmondsworth: Penguin (original work published 1927).

Jordan, N. (1978). "Word and Image: John McGahern's and Cathal Black's 'Wheels'," *Film Directions: A Film Magazine for Ireland* 1/2: 10–11.

Kennedy, E. (1989). "Sons and Fathers in John McGahern's Short Stories," in J.D. Brophy and E. Grennan (eds), *New Irish Writing*, pp. 65–74. Boston: Iona College Press/Twayne.

McGahern, J. (1968). "The Image," *Honest Ulsterman* (December 8): 10; rev. edn *Canadian Journal of Irish Studies* 17/1 (July 1991): 12; see also McGahern 1971.

McGahern, J. (1970). *Nightlines*. London: Faber and Faber.

McGahern, J. (1971). *Lignes de Fond: précédé de l'Image*, trans. Pierre Leyris. Paris: Mercure de France.

McGahern, J. (1974). *The Leavetaking*. London: Faber and Faber.

McGahern, J. (1976). "Memories of Newcastle," rev. of *Kiddar's Luck* and *The Ampersand* by Jack Common, *Times Literary Supplement* (February 13): 159.

McGahern, J. (1977). "Brian Westby," *Threshold* 28 (spring): 37–50.

McGahern, J. (1979). *The Pornographer*. London: Faber and Faber.

McGahern, J. (1985). *High Ground*. London: Faber and Faber.

McGahern, J. (2004). "What is My Language?," in M. Massoud (ed.), *New Readings of Old Masters*, pp. 205–19. Cairo: Macmillan.

McGahern, J. (2005). *Memoir*. London: Faber and Faber.

McGahern, J. (2006). *Creatures of the Earth: New and Selected Stories*. London: Faber and Faber.

Maher, E. (2003). *John McGahern: From the Local to the Universal*. Dublin: Liffey.

Mercier, V. (1990). *Beckett/Beckett*. London: Souvenir.

Quinn, A. (1989). "Varieties of Disenchantment: Narrative Technique in John McGahern's Short

Stories," *Journal of the Short Story in English/ Les Cahiers de la Nouvelle* 13 (autumn): 77–89.

Sampson, D. (1993). *Outstaring Nature's Eye: The Fiction of John McGahern.* Washington, DC: Catholic University of America Press.

Sampson, D. (2000). "The 'Rich Whole': John McGahern's *Collected Stories* as Autobiography," *Journal of the Short Story in English/Les Cahiers de la Nouvelle* 34 (spring): 21–30.

Sampson, D. (2005). "'Open to the World': A Reading of John McGahern's *That They May Face the Rising Sun*," *Irish University Review* 35/1 (spring/summer): 136–46.

Tosser, Y. (1979). "Théorie de l'image, sensibilité absurde et aspects de la pratique textuelle dans *Nightlines*," *Cahier du Centre d'Études Irlandaises* 4: 7–31.

Whyte, J. (2002). *History, Myth, and Ritual in the Fiction of John McGahern: Strategies of Transcendence.* Lewiston, Queenston, Lampeter: Edwin Mellen.

Ziel, Stanley van der (2004). Unpublished tapescript of a conversation with John McGahern at the Gresham Hotel, Dublin (October 12).

Ziel, Stanley van der (2005). "John McGahern – an Annotated Bibliography," *Irish University Review* 35/1 (spring/summer): 175–202.

44

The Clinking of an Identity Disk: Bernard MacLaverty's "Walking the Dog"

Jerzy Jarniewicz

There is a museum in Berlin which does not attempt to guide its visitors from one room to another, nor to display an ordered sequence of historical exhibits, all carefully numbered, labeled, and conveniently distanced from the viewers. David Libeskind's Jewish Museum is more like a sculptural environment to be experienced directly, a designed space which the visitor is asked to enter and wander about along unmapped corridors, arriving at dead-ends and dark empty chambers, looking out through slanted windows like scars on the surface of its walls, grappling with the feelings of anxiety, fear, and confusion, which in an incomparably more powerful manner affected those who perished and to whom the museum is dedicated. There is no one proper way of visiting the museum; cool detached observation is replaced by the sense of being inside, of experiencing rather than perceiving the bits of reality which challenges all modes of representation. In Libeskind's museum "our perception of space and structure, and our own vantage point, is no longer a matter of course – it becomes a new experience" (Schneider 2005: 57).

Bernard MacLaverty's short story "Walking the Dog" from the 1994 collection of the same title, works in a similar way: it is a piece of narrative writing which does not purport to give an account of the (supposedly fictitious) incident, but invites the reader to enter and experience it by being exposed to the same uncertainties as its main protagonist. MacLaverty carefully introduces his readers as much into the narrative, as into the world represented in it. This illusion of being inside the fictional world of his short story is carefully built by gradually providing the readers with regular doses of details, and, consequently, by delineating the limits of our knowledge of the world-within-the-story.

The story itself is set in Belfast, in a city stricken by sectarian violence. The protagonist, who leaves his house to walk the dog on a wintry night, is kidnaped by a paramilitary squad. The kidnappers claim they represent the IRA. It turns out, however, that they are Protestants, whose alleged republicanism was only a trick aimed at forcing the victim, whom they take to be an Irish nationalist, to declare his political and religious allegiances. During a brutal interrogation the kidnaped man manages to avoid answering their questions directly and is eventually let free to pass into the city's darkness again. This dramatic event in the man's life during which he has to face an absurd life-or-death alternative lasts no more than ten minutes: a short, seemingly trivial incident in trivial circumstances that might have cost him his life.

The narrative starts significantly with an act of leaving, going outside into the uncharted territory where anything may happen. The main character, who remains for a longer while anonymous, later to identify himself, however dubiously, as John, leaves his flat and goes out with his dog into the dark wintry night. In an analogous move, readers of MacLaverty's story leave the reassuring safety of their homes and go out with the protagonist into the new dark territory of possible events, knowing about it all as much, or as little as he does. The protagonist's experience is thus not *reported*, but *mirrored* in our experience of reading the story: his cognitive recognitions and misapprehensions run parallel to our recognitions and misreadings of the details of the narrative. In order to achieve this cognitive parallelism, the narrator assumes a limited point of view, confining himself to what is experienced, felt or thought by one character within the story, whom Henry James called "focus" or "central consciousness." The narrative material presented to the reader is filtered through the character's mind, to the effect that the reader feels all the events unfold gradually and partially in front of his or her eyes.

"As he left the house" are the very first words of MacLaverty's narrative, establishing from the outset the theme of dislocation, shared by both the protagonist and the readers. The protagonist leaves a safe abode, leaves his private, personal territory, which is under his control: enclosed, familiar, and domestic. Reading the story is a repetition of the same act of leaving the familiar and the domestic. To leave is to be ready to face the unfamiliar and the unexpected, which may be fascinating, or terrifying, or both. Leaving home, as John does, presumes thus the existence of another reality, and MacLaverty indicates its tangible presence immediately after the initial phrase of the story. The domestic nature of walking the dog suggests the deeply rooted familiarity of the world, which the protagonist is going to leave and which will soon be shattered by an intrusion of outsiders. In the course of the narrative, John's engagement in the routine activity from the title of the story, whose ordinariness and repetitiveness may seem to guarantee the unproblematic perpetuation of the world in which he lives, turns out, ironically, to be an act of going beyond the safe borders of his familiar territory.

The way MacLaverty handles the narrative indicates that this familiar world (symbolized in walking the dog) does not constitute the whole reality – there are other worlds, which in our everyday duties we tend to forget. It is already in the first sentence of the story that we learn that "As he left the house he heard the music for the start of the Nine O'Clock news" (MacLaverty 1995: 3). This bit of information not only sets the time of the incident, but also recalls these numerous other, often more dramatic, worlds, which exist outside one's domestic domain, outside one's daily routines such as walking the dog. The music of the News which the protagonist hears brings information from and about a larger political, social, and cultural context, which most palpably exists and in which he lives, but of which he is not entirely conscious. Thus, in the first sentence the protagonist's reality is symbolically split, or doubled: there is the world of the dog on the leash and the world beyond about which the News at Nine reports, the inside world of controllable familiarity and the outside world of ignorable public events. The story will focus on the dramatic collision of the two, making it one of its most intriguing themes.

It is interesting that the Nine O'Clock news comes to the protagonist not as noise, but as music. What is most probably chaotic, random, and violent takes the shape of an ordered, harmonious structure — music. The news of the bigger world, when they come from the safely distanced "elsewhere" and enter the smaller world of one's home, comes as disempowered and adjusted to the reassuring order of the house. The terrifying chaos of world politics is tamed and filtered, before it is communicated to us via the media. But leaving the house means also leaving the sheltering function of the media and exposing oneself to the raw, unstructured, convex outside.

To intensify the unsettling unfamiliarity of the outside world MacLaverty decides to set his story at night — in darkness. The protagonist cannot see the world beyond the safety borders of his house. More than this, the narrative is full of ominous signs, indicating that something dangerous might happen. First comes, as if randomly mentioned, the cul-de-sac, the dead-end street, offering no escape and suggesting entrapment, functioning also as a veiled commentary on the protagonist's future plight. The sense of anonymous threat intensifies in the first paragraph of the story, even though nothing unusual happens yet, with the details of the path taken by the protagonist, which, as we learn "sloped steeply" (3). Furthermore, the narrator observes that the weather conditions of the evening "could be dangerous" (3), because of the frozen snow.

MacLaverty's story, just as much of his writing, is set in the context of the Northern Irish Troubles. However, instead of providing information about the political background of the story and introducing readers directly into the realities of the terror-stricken Belfast, MacLaverty implies the fragility of the apparent calm of the evening by creating an oppressive scene of the backstreets of a big city on an unfriendly wintry night. That the city in question is Belfast is disclosed to us, also indirectly, later on in the story with the reference to Lisburn.

All the elements of the initial scene: the anonymity of the setting, its ominous, claustrophobic character, treacherous wintry weather, and eventually darkness, contribute to the general atmosphere of the threatening unknown world, which the protagonist is soon to enter.

In one of his essays in *Mythologies* Roland Barthes contrasts two famous vessels from the nineteenth-century French literature, Jules Verne's "Nautilus," and Arthur Rimbaud's "Drunken Boat." "Nautilus," the underwater ship of Captain Nemo from

2000 Leagues under the Sea, stands for a human habitat, as a symbol of closure and absolutely finite space, where man can organize "the enjoyment of a round, smooth universe, of which, in addition, a whole nautical morality makes him at once the god, the master, and the owner" (Barthes 1973: 67). The vague world outside, beyond man's control, decentered and slanted, is exorcised, observed only from a safe distance through a large window-pane. Rimbaud's "Drunken Boat," on the other hand, stands for the "genuine poetics of exploration" (Barthes 1973: 67), the readiness to confront the new and unpredictable, in which one gives up one's desire to own and control, and is carried by the waves of events.

MacLaverty's protagonist leaves his cozy habitat, the finite world of his private Nautilus, and will be captured, literally captured, by the uncontrollable forces of the outside vagueness. He has to abandon his function of "the god, the master, and the owner," which he entertained inside and hoped to entertain, as the master of the dog, during his short excursion into the outside world. He may still cherish this power, his mastery over the dog even when he lets it free: the dog responds to his calls and comes back to him obediently.

The kidnaping will break this illusion of order and control, introducing chaos to his world. The man and the dog form a kind of a team, based a hierarchical order, with their respective roles recognized and acknowledged. The kidnaping not only shatters the man's sense of being "at home," but also breaks the link between him and the dog. The two are no longer a team; they may be beside each other, but the link of control and cooperation had been broken. While reflecting on the destruction of the old order in the early twentieth-century Europe, W.B. Yeats comments on the situation in a famous image: "Turning and turning in the widening gyre / The falcon cannot hear the falconer; / Things fall apart; the centre cannot hold" ("The Second Coming"). The relationship between man and dog in MacLaverty's story can be seen as an instance of the Yeatsian cooperative link between the falcon and the falconer, which is broken by a violent intrusion of "mere anarchy." In both cases, the relation is built on a clear hierarchical order, which gives man the privileged central position and guarantees the successful cooperation of the two.

The world in which MacLaverty's protagonist finds himself when kidnaped is the unmapped realm of disorder. What exactly happens, when the car stops and a stranger forces him to get into it, is as unclear as who these people in the car are, and what intentions they may have. John's uncertainty: finding himself in a world without center, with no points of reference, immersed in the darkness of the night, and furthermore being forced to keep his head down and eyes closed, is also the uncertainty of the readers of the story. The kidnaped man knows as little as we do about the incident. His desperate search for meaning will also be our search. We follow his perceptions and the course of his thoughts. Things, covered in darkness, vague and chaotic, reveal themselves gradually: John has to revalue his perceptions, constantly groping for meaning, when first he thinks the man from the car was pointing with one of his hands, only to realize later that he was "not pointing, but aiming a gun at him. Was this a joke? Maybe a starting pistol" (4). This is another wrong recognition – it is not a joke and the thing in the hand is not a starting pistol.

And yet these small recognitions do not make the incident meaningful. The protagonist tries to fit them as small pieces of a scattered jigsaw puzzle in his picture of the world, so that the mystery of kidnapping will be explained. The picture of the familiar inside – the world of everyday routines such as walking the dog or listening to evening news – has all of a sudden fallen to pieces; its finite concavity, with fixed rules to obey and well-defined roles to play, opened itself to the infinite, unmeasured, and consequently threatening possibilities: here anything can happen. The protagonist, and we as readers in our encounter with the text, have moved beyond the pale, have gone down the slippery path and ventured into the unknown, leaving the outskirts of the home city behind – not so much geographically (we may still be in Belfast), but psychologically (the territory is no longer under our control). We are in Libeskind's museum: confused and at a loss.

In the shattered world of darkness, which urgently demands deciphering, even trivia may become meaningful. Rage for meaning starts. The kidnaped protagonist begins to collect even the most trivial sensory data in order to create a comprehensive picture of the new reality into which he has been thrown. The new reality communicates with him through various senses, offering fragmentary, inconclusive, and discontinuous information. In just one paragraph of the story we learn that the protagonist, with his head down, forced to get into the car, *sees* the upholstery, *hears* the dog panting, and *feels* the gun against his neck. His intensified perceptual powers work hard to map out the new terrain, as hard as readers trying to pinpoint meaningful details and reconstruct the situation that slowly, partially, with utter resistance emerges from the dark. He perceives accidental fragments which do not add up to any convincing picture, just as readers go on reading about the incident and still find themselves in the dark, asking: Who? Why? What?

An attempt to answer these simple questions, vital for the proper functioning of any narrative, is an attempt to reconstruct the story from the random multitude of details and collected evidence, bringing to mind detective work. That is what John actually engages in, though not without doubt: "What was he playing the detective for?" (MacLaverty 1995: 6). The protagonist looks for items that together would make up a convincing story. In the light of the street lamps he notices "a Juicy Fruit chewing-gum paper" (6). The surprising specificity of the observation is puzzling, suggesting some importance: if the narrator speaks about a particular brand of chewing gum, he provides us with information that we have to process, answering questions such as: what difference would it make if it had been a different brand? The high degree of specificity with which the worthless found object is described is undoubtedly a red herring – the chewing gum found on the floor of the car has no meaning and will lead us nowhere. It can never be a part of a meaningful narrative, being a waste, a throwaway article, so blatantly deprived of meaning. Focusing on the chewing gum and its brand says nothing about the new threatening reality in which the protagonist finds himself, but it says much about his emotional state: he is desperately looking for clues and hints. Being in the darkness, without any interpretative guidelines, he is ready to ascribe importance even to the most contingent phenomena, including a piece of waste. However, the details which he observes slip away from him, do not yield to the mastery and control which he exercised just a few minutes earlier, while walking the dog; separated by commas, they refuse to form any coherent sentence, entering into paratactic relations with no hierarchy and no grammar. It is a mere accumulation of partial perceptions that does not lead to the understanding of the whole to which they belong. The chewing gum is followed by similar details of the gunman's apparel, such as Doc Martens and stone-washed denims, which again do not reveal much about his possible intentions nor about the sense of the whole incident (and that is what John tries to establish).

Other observations help the protagonist to identify the part of the city they might be driving through. The outside world of the city comes to him only as reflection in the fragments of the inside of the car: "The reflections from the chrome inside the car became red. Traffic lights. John heard the beeping of a 'cross now' signal. For the benefit of the blind" (9). If signals designed for the blind provide John with crucial information, he becomes metaphorically blind himself. Through MacLaverty's skillful handling of the narrative, we as readers partake in this condition: the blindness is ours, too.

We wander in the story, groping blindly for meanings in the fragmentary scene, clutching at every, true or imagined, signal of information. We walk through the narrative as along the corridors of Libeskind's museum, unable to take our bearing, sharing with John not only his angst, fear, or terror, but primarily his uncertainty as to the meaning of the incident in which he got himself involved and in which we, in turn, are trapped in our act of reading.

One of the key uncertainties that the story examines concerns the identity of the main protagonist, who is introduced as an anonymous pronominal "he" and remains nameless well into the story. And, even though when he tells his name to the gunman we learn that it is John Shields, we remember that he is under enormous pressure, terrorized by the kidnapers. He might have lied to his persecutors, choosing one of the most popular names, which contrary to, say, William or Seamus, would not say anything about his political, religious, or cultural alliances. MacLaverty makes it a crucial moment in his story, when the abducted man does not respond immediately to the gunman's question:

> "Who are you?"
> There was silence. He was incapable of answering.
> "What's your name?"
> He cleared his throat and made a noise. Then said, "John." (MacLaverty 1995: 5–6)

The initial question with its philosophical echoes is redefined to stand for a very concrete life-or-death issue, a matter of survival, but is nevertheless followed by silence. The unnamed man cannot, or does not want to, answer it. When the question is repeated in a modified version, what follows is, first, an inarticulate noise, an attempt at providing self-definition. It is only later that the answer is given, though again the captive decides to give his first name only.

But even the full name, John Shields, does not mean much to the terrorists: it does not identify its bearer enough. From their point of view, it proves to be an empty sign, a free- floating signifier. Further inquiry starts, in a series of aggressive questions that are supposed to disclose the captive's identity: other names, the school that he attended, his denomination, his parents'. These inquiries fail, either because John does not want to provide answers that would betray his position, or – more interestingly – because whatever he has to say about himself is destined to be vague, unfixed, and indeterminate. He may be in fact a feature-less person, and, indeed, he has been presented as such in the story so far: we know nothing about his age, physical appearance, family, or background: a true man without qualities. When asked to declare himself as either a Protestant or a Roman Catholic, he responds in weighty words: "I suppose I'm nothing." My name will tell you nothing, I am nobody, he seems to declare. We can however modify this statement – he is nobody within a set of identities established by his oppressors, or more generally, by the politicized situation in Northern Ireland. The two labels, as the words of that external, imposed identity discourse that he rejects, do not apply to him, leaving him out of the world which for the terrorists, who do not accept his declaration of religious indifference, is the only one.

MacLaverty leaves all these interpretative possibilities for us to decide. If until now we have been looking at the world through John's eyes, in this scene we become associates of the terrorists who do not know whom they have abducted – we do not know either. Is he a cunning man who has well-grounded suspicions that the terrorists might, in fact, be some other group than they claim to be, and who, consequently, tries to give answers that would not be used against him by any side of the conflict? Possibly, but he may also be true to himself: someone who wants to stay outside the conflict, refusing to be categorized in terms of either of the two warring camps. And, finally, he may be a man who has erased his identity, one of the many anonymous, non-involved citizens who walk their dogs in the evening every day.

There are hints that he may well be calculating carefully his answers, so as to avoid any traps that might have been set against him. Hence long silences before he answers; hence slow responses and evasions. The interrogation, having proved useless so far, turns to linguistic examination, when he is asked to recite the alphabet. Paradoxically, this is the most difficult identity test: it is believed that the way you pronounce one of the letters betrays your identity, marks you as a member of one or the other side of the Northern Irish conflict, more categorically than your name or schooling. The eighth letter of the alphabet functions here as the latter day shibboleth from the Book of Judges, 12: 5–6:

And the Gileadites took the passages of Jordan before the Ephraimites: and it was so, that when those Ephraimites which were escaped said, Let me go over; that the men of Gilead said unto him, Art thou an Ephraimite? If he said, Nay; Then said they unto him, Say now Shibboleth: and he said Sibboleth: for he could not frame to pronounce it right. Then they took him, and slew him at the passages of Jordan: and there fell at that time of the Ephraimites forty and two thousand.

This simple identity test in which the Ephraimites had to pronounce a difficult Hebrew word, meant a death sentence for those who were unable to cope with the articulation. The biblical story seems to suggest that identity rests not so much in the name, which can be misappropriated or changed, but in the language, as linguistic differences divide "us" from "them" better than anything else.

John is aware of this shibboleth, so he tries doing it both ways: he says "aitch" as Protestants would do, and "haitch" in the manner of Irish Catholics, as if nullifying the distinction, and more generally – the dualistic divisions in the sectarian society. The evasive nature of identity as one of the themes of the story is reflected also in the fluctuating labeling of the terrorists. Their declared identity ("we're from the IRA") soon proves false, when we learn that they are Protestants. They also, without being aware of it, face a linguistic test which they fail: they use the term "Roman Catholic," which is used almost exclusively by Protestants in Northern Ireland.

John's non-being, his anonymity saves him. His self seems to remain undecided and split. When at the end of the story he is asked to stand against the tree with his head down, he notices two shadows of himself crawling on the ground: "In the headlights his shadow was very black and sharp againts the tree. There was a double shadow, one from each headlight" (MacLaverty 1995: 11). He sees himself as dual, tentative. This duality may be in fact a sign of his indefiniteness. He is one of the city's anonymous crowd. After the ordeal he has just come through, he realizes that there is no sense in calling home, because "he wouldn't even have been missed yet" (12). In these ten minutes, which for him might have meant so much, but were insignificant for others, his absence from home could hardly have been noticed.

The story that focuses on the issue of identity and the salutary condition of anonymity, ends with a telling acoustic image (because it is darkness, sound remains the first, primary impression): "The street was so quiet he could hear the clinking of the dog's identity disk as it padded along beside him" (12). It is only now that we realize that the answers to the gunman's questions, and consequently, the life-or-death information might have been there all the time, ready for inspection, on the dog's neck. We cannot be sure the protagonist's name was really John Shields; the narrator starts calling him so only after he identified himself as such to the terrorists, and he did it under pressure. We cannot be sure he really was an E.O. in the Gas Board. His true name, the dog's owner's name, was inscribed on the disk, but remains to the readers, and to the kidnapers as well, a blank – an unknown, uncertain, always dangerous identity that clinks in the empty streets of Belfast.

References and Further Reading

Barthes, R. (1973). *Mythologies*, trans. A. Lavers. London: Granada (original work published 1957).

MacLaverty, B. (1995). " Walking the Dog," in *Walking the Dog*, pp. 3–12. London: Penguin.

Schneider, B. (2005). *Daniel Libeskind – Jewish Museum Berlin: Between the Lines*. Munich: Prestel.

Yeats, W.B. (1982). *Collected Poems*. London: Macmillan.

45

Angela Carter's *The Bloody Chamber:* A World Transformed by Imagination and Desire – Adventures in Anarcho-Surrealism

Madelena Gonzalez

The Othering of Angela Carter

The Bloody Chamber has come to be seen as emblematic of Angela Carter, the writer. For Rushdie it is "the likeliest of her works to endure" (2003: 43). This collection of short stories published in 1979 is the book for which she is best known and which brought her to the attention of the public gaze in a way that her first seven novels had not. Possibly, as Helen Simpson (Simpson 2006) suggests, her choice to retell fairy tales brought her an audience she would not otherwise have reached. It was this interest that encouraged obituaries to pay tribute to her as a benevolent witch or postmodern fairy godmother, perhaps as a way of dealing with the strangeness of her writing. As I hope to show, and as others have remarked, including Carter herself before her death, nothing could be further from the reality of her aesthetic ambitions as a writer and the tales collected within *The Bloody Chamber*.

In fact, at the time, and for many years afterwards, this slim volume was the source of much controversy and debate, alternately vilified for being complicit with male dominance and even pornography (Duncker), or praised for the new configurations of independent subjectivity it provided for womanhood (Jordan and Makinen). Published in the same year as *The Sadeian Woman*, Carter's polemical essay, it was perceived as its fictional counterpart. Indeed, some of the more virulent criticism of the stories reads as if it were talking back to the essay rather than the fiction. The stark opposition between such points of view illustrates the difficulty critics have had in pinning down the poetics of Carter and fitting her into a recognizable category. Classified as magic realist, postmodernist, or mannerist, to name but a few, she did indeed try her hand at many different genres, sometimes simultaneously. She can be all things to all critics, it would seem, either complicit with patriarchy or radically feminist, amazingly innovative (Atwood, Sage), or vulgarly predictable (Bayley). These varied and conflicting interpretations of her work and character, a certain talismanic othering which helps to explain her frequently evoked foreignness or un-Englishness (Broughton and Bristow; Peach), could be interpreted as the logical consequence of the othering she herself effects on her fictional material, making familiar forms and structures unrecognizable and luxuriating in an ornate and arcane prose style which obliges even an educated reader to reach for the dictionary.

At first sight, the stories which make up *The Bloody Chamber* seem eminently readable and easily decoded, for they appear to be reworkings of "Bluebeard," "Beauty and the Beast," and "Little Red Riding Hood." However, even on the level of form and structure, it is rapidly clear that they are not only refusing to follow fairy-tale conventions, but also subverting them. The borders between different tales become blurred, and endings are left open instead of providing comforting finality, or provide an ironic comment on the concept of the happy ending, thus upsetting reader expectations. This is compounded by the *recherché* language Carter uses, very different from the simple hand-crafted imagery of fairy tale, which she saw as one of the domestic arts, like cooking. It is this verbal richness that entices us into a fictional world where we become voyeurs or even accomplices of sexual excess and violence, as in the scene from "The Snow Child" where the Count imagines into being a daughter and then rapes her dead body, furnishing us with a troubling image of both sexual and textual relations. If readers are perfectly willing to suspend disbelief in keeping with the conventions of the fantastic, it is more difficult to accept the tension between the realist mode and the fantastic mode that Carter makes visible in her text. It is at this point that we cannot help but recognize that something else is in play here; there is a subtext to be decoded and it is ideological as well as aesthetic, for Carter refuses to separate the two.

When is a Story not a Story? When it's a Tale

For some, the stories in *The Bloody Chamber* are postmodern versions of traditional fairy tales (Bacchilega 1997: 140–6), with the exception of "The Erl-King" which hails form German Romantic legend and Goethe's well-known poem, while for others they are completely new stories more reminiscent of Poe and the gothic (Armitt 1997: 89). Most critics have noticed the tendency for one tale to "dissolve" into another, to foreshadow what follows, to comment on and embellish, or even rewrite the same story. They form a cycle in the Chaucerian or Boccaccian sense or can be seen as reminiscent of Ovid's *Metamorphoses* and its variations on a theme, in this case, gender and power, sex and death. They are constructed within a set of frames or Chinese boxes, or even chambers, which present the reader with an endlessly proliferating series of *mise en abyme*, not least of which is the title story of the collection, to be interpreted literally as a chamber of horrors or metaphorically as a womb, a heart, the unconscious or sexuality. In this way meanings and symbols are disseminated throughout the text in its entirety in order to build up an elaborate system of signification that is visible lying just beneath the surface structure.

In other words, although the short story is traditionally a hermetic, self-sufficient form, it would seem that Carter's project is more epic in scale and more picaresque in character, as it uses "shifting structures derived from orally transmitted tales" to deal with "the shifting structures of reality and sexuality" (Carter, qtd in Tucker 1998: 25). It is important to note the term "derived" here, for although much has been made of the orality of the Carterian tale, when it does in fact occur, as in "Puss-in-Boots," it is more of a deliberate performance intended to defamiliarize than an example of authentic oral narrative. As Carter herself pointed out in her introduction to *Angela Carter's Book of Fairy Tales*, "speaking is a public activity and reading a private one" (Carter 2005: xi). Certainly the stories in *The Bloody Chamber* do not lend themselves to the improvisation of the oral storyteller; they are far too elaborately crafted for that, each one a perfect gem of jeweled prose. However, like Rushdie, Carter does consciously imitate certain conventions of orality in a highly stylized way as part of her complex contract with a knowing postmodern reader who is expected to possess a sound knowledge of de Sade, French Symbolism, Dostoevsky, classical music, opera, film, and a highly literary vocabulary. This obviously works against the spontaneity of the oral or at least shows it up here for what it is, that is to say, a knowing imitation of the impromptu:

> See a black barque, like a state funeral; and Puss takes it into his bubbly-addled brain to board her. Tacking obliquely to her side, I rub my marmalade pate against her shin; how could any duenna, be she never so stern, take offence at such attentions to her chargeling from a little cat. (Carter 1981: 71)

The cat narrator of "Puss-in-Boots" mixes Cockney with Latin and French, bawdy and the demotic with erudition and sophistication in an alliterative and ebullient rococo mode which is obviously meant to remind the reader of the architecture of the building he scales in the first pages: "Nothing to it, once you know how, rococo's no problem" (69). Naturally he has more trouble with the smoothly classical surfaces of the Palladian a few pages later.

Carter's choice of the tale stemmed from both ideological and aesthetic concerns. It was a way of reconnecting with the margins and challenging grand narratives, because the tale interprets rather than presents, using "a system of imagery derived from subterranean areas behind everyday experience, and therefore the tale cannot betray its readers into a false knowledge" (qtd in Tucker 1998: 5). Unlike the short story, she perceived it as decidedly non-mimetic and opposed to traditional realism. Thanks to, rather than in spite of, its limited trajectory, she also saw it as opening up imaginative possibilities for the writer, a maximalist, rather than a minimalist form where "sign and sense can fuse to an extent impossible to achieve among the multiplying ambiguities of an extended narrative" (qtd in Duncker 1984: 8). It is precisely this fusion that creates "the heightened diction of the novelette" for which

Carter was aiming (qtd by Simpson 2006). However, at first reading, sign dominates sense, and gives the impression of an endless chain of signifiers constantly
deferring meaning. Thus the rose, which is one of the recurring motifs in several
different stories, is not rooted in a stable signified, but thrusts out new shoots of
meaning every time it appears, sometimes confirming, sometimes challenging its
own symbolism.

A seemingly inexhaustible reservoir of signs means that the unnatural dominates
the rational, a clash which is graphically played out in "The Lady of the House of
Love," a twentieth-century gothic version of "Sleeping Beauty," where the reasonable
young hero chases away the vampire curse of the heroine with a kiss. However, the
supposedly normal existence to which he returns is defamiliarized by the unseasonably
blooming rose picked from the lady's garden, a hint at the madness of a world where
thousands are about to meet "a special, exemplary fate in the trenches of France" (97).
Carter's tales have an almost tactile, some might say, edible, quality as they lure us
into their "wicked, glamorous, fatal world" (qtd by Simpson 2006), and make us
consumers of their lush, cholesterol-rich textuality, vampire readers greedily feeding
on the excess of fantastic imagery which flavors the volume at the expense of verisimilitude. However, they also raise important questions about the nature of reality
and how to represent it in words.

The Pleasure Principle versus the Reality Principle: Dancing the Kitsch Fantastic

In her introduction to *Angela Carter's Book of Fairy Tales*, Carter notes that fairy tales
are "dedicated to the pleasure principle," but that "there is always more going on than
meets the eye" (2005: xiv). In her later novels, readers may feel at times that there is
perhaps too much going on as she transforms the fictional form into the all-dancing,
all-singing road show of *Wise Children*. She is very much more at home with the high
diegetic than the low mimetic and this is how she makes her fictional worlds irresistible, but also encodes into them questions of narrative voice and point of view, focusing the reader's attention on the way the tale is told as much as on the events of the
tale. Like the traditional storyteller, she sees her role as that of entertainer whose creative lies are truer than the mimetic illusion. Her impulse towards the fantastic and
the unnatural and her blend of exoticism and eroticism promise readers untold
aesthetic and imaginative pleasures.

Emulating the "moral pornographer" she conjured up in *The Sadeian Woman* (Carter
1993a: 18–20), who, ideally, would create a world of absolute sexual license for all
the genders, she aims for a similar sort of artistic freedom in these tales, in order to
escape the stranglehold of respectable literature and try on different generic identities
at will, whether they be classical or sub-literary. This mirrors the way subjectivity is
conceived of as a process and identity a performance, for characters cross not only
gender, but ontological, barriers. Thus, after a painful journey of self-discovery, the

heroine of "The Tiger's Bride" exchanges her stifling humanity as an oppressed female for a liberating "beastliness," and the predatory male sexuality of the terrifying Marquis of "The Bloody Chamber" or the mysterious Erl-King is momentarily disturbed by the irruption into their portraits of the word "housewife" with its connotations of the homely and the domestic. This comparison unsettles received notions of gender, suggesting the supposedly pacific female resonance of the term, but applying it to a man – "He is an excellent housewife. His rustic home is spick and span" (87) – and also revealing the latent menace within woman – "I saw him watching me in the gilded mirrors with the assessing eye of a connoisseur inspecting horseflesh, or even of a housewife, in the market, inspecting cuts on the slab" (11). Whether we find this strangely empowering or obscurely offensive, it encourages us to look again at clichéd representations of gender roles.

These repetitions with a difference, mimicking the traditional strategies of fairy tales, which tend to tell the same story over and over again, enable Carter to keep her narrative at play, constantly reconfiguring meanings within new contexts. The order in which she places the stories provides intratextual commentary by juxtaposing different versions of similar tales. Thus the passive and petulant "Beauty" of "The Courtship of Mr. Lyon" is swiftly rewritten in the next story as a feisty "woman of honour," the ironically over-determined happy end of the former preparing us for the transformation. The ethereal "Snow Child" as archetypal victim is reinvented as fin-de-siècle vampire preying on naive young men in "The Lady of the House of Love," hardly surprising in view of the carnivorous rose with which the earlier tale concludes. Carter's poetics of allusion, echo, and accumulation create endless variations on her themes, turning her collection into an impressive examination of power, sexuality, and identity in a fugue-like mode. Instead of restricting herself to binaries, the straitjacket of "either/or," she imagines a world where we can be "both and" at the same time – man and woman, animal and human, lamb and tiger – and weaves this into the very texture of her stories thanks to a transvestite aesthetics which ceaselessly reinvents itself.

Signs are taken from many different registers and styles, the bygone and the folksy (the "Wolf" tales and "The Erl-King"), the oriental and the exotic ("The Bloody Chamber" and "The Courtship"), and mixed into what is at first sight a kitsch hybrid. Different references and genres are aped and combined discordantly, symbolism and sadomasochism ("The Bloody Chamber"), Lacan and lycanthropy ("Wolf-Alice"), the carnivalesque and the gothic ("The Company of Wolves"), with imitation providing an ironic comment on the absence of originality, as, for example, in the encounter with the wolf of legend that Carter invents for one of her female characters:

She saw how his jaw began to slaver and the room was full of the clamour of the forest's Liebestod but the wise child never flinched, even when he answered: All the better to eat you with. The girl burst out laughing; she knew she was nobody's meat. (Carter 1993a: 118)

As has been remarked, oxymoron and zeugma, the yoking together of different objects and effects within the same syntax, disruptive figures which question any single univocal reading, are typical of her style (Jordan, in Tucker 1998: 38). It is at this point that kitsch tips over into camp, thanks to sexual but also textual self-consciousness. Thus, the heroine's positively medieval deflowering in the title story of the volume is followed by "the shrilling of the telephone" (17) which awakens protagonist and reader to possibilities of escape unavailable to Bluebeard's wife. Of course it is also an ironic comment on our expectations of the fairy tale and its constraints.

The obsession with artifice and theatricalization, the idea of writing as spectacle, are clearly imaged by the numerous references to specularity and mirrors in which protagonists are made to study their reflections, both literal and metaphorical. In the same way the text comments on its own textuality by changing tense, narrative voice, and focalization, and obliges the reader to take another look. Rather than gratuitous stylistic acrobatics, Carter's pantomimic poetics is performative, a risky high-wire act, no doubt (Rushdie 2003: 46), but also an example of how self-conscious fiction can transform reality and reader.

Ideological Aesthetics: Writing For and Against

For Carter, language is never neutral, a "rational glass" (Carter 1981: 126) reflecting an unproblematic reality. Indeed in "Wolf-Alice," from which this formulation is taken, she shows us the transformative powers of reflection, thus questioning the idea of representation as stable and transparent and foregrounding her own meta-textual strategies. As she puts it in *The Sadeian Woman*, "the notion of the universality of human experience is a confidence trick" (12), and it is through freedom of expression that freedom of thought is to be gained. Despite her extra-fictional pronouncements, Carter's work is not openly political in any obvious way, but in the more subtle sense of literature against itself, or what Linda Hutcheon has termed "complicitous critique," a way of writing that exposes its own position within the cultural hegemony at the same time as it undermines it. In true postmodern fashion, Carter's fiction is skeptical of the meta-narratives and myths which have come to be regarded as truths. She claimed to be in the "demythologising business" (Carter, in Tucker 1998: 25), writing against traditional fairy tale, against Bettelheim, even against a certain type of militant feminism which denies woman any complicity in her seduction, the heroine of the title story being a case in point: "And, as at the opera, when I had first seen my flesh in his eyes, I was aghast to feel myself stirring" (15). The consciousness of her "shame" (41) with which the story concludes can be interpreted either unsympathetically as Eve's sempiternal and well-deserved guilt or, alternatively, as proof of her victimhood, an illustration of the way in which the female's subjectivity cannot exist outside the male gaze in a patriarchal society.

Once again, Carter leaves the final interpretation open to her reader. This typically postmodern indeterminacy that both "encourages and resists different readings" (Lee

1997: 13) helps to explain why so many contradictory accounts of these tales and their possible significance have flourished. She provides the reader with a series of interpretive challenges that are inherent to her multivocal mode. One of the most striking aspects of the stories is the way in which they prevent us from relaxing into familiar fairy tale and leaving critical judgment at the door. Thus the "Erl-King" starts with recognizable extradiegetic omniscience even if terms such as "anorexic" trees or "sick-room hush" (84) used to describe the archetypal fairy-tale wood have a defamiliarizing effect, rapidly emphasized by the sudden appearance of the pronoun "you" in the next paragraph, which ironically, even violently, foregrounds its traditional role of projecting the reader into the text. When a "me" intrudes two paragraphs further down, it becomes impossible to read the story in any conventional way, particularly as it provides incessant metatextual commentary on itself and the rest of the volume, an ironic and deconstructive baring of the device:

> The woods enclose and then enclose again, like a system of Chinese boxes opening one into another; the intimate perspectives of the wood changed endlessly around the interloper, the imaginary traveller walking towards an invented distance that perpetually receded before me. It is easy to lose yourself in these woods. (Carter 1981: 85)

Each successive story is a rewriting and a comment on the one which preceded it, as well as a comment on textuality itself.

Changes of tense, including frequent recourse to the rarely used narrative present, and shifting focalization create a denaturalizing effect, giving rise to the ontological flickering so characteristic of postmodernism and directing attention to the processes that govern narration and reading themselves. In the following passage taken from "The Bloody Chamber," Carter uses free indirect speech to blur the boundaries between the real and imagined, but it is also to comment on how the script of the Marquis converges with that of the girl, and to some extent, at least, is desired by her:

> A deal, an enterprise of hazard and chance involving several millions lay in the balance, he said. He drew away from me into that waxwork stillness of his; I was only a little girl, I did not understand. And, he said, unspoken to my wounded vanity, I have had too many honeymoons to find them in the least pressing commitments. I know quite well this child I've bought with a handful of coloured stones and the pelts of dead beasts won't run away. (Carter 1981: 18)

However, she also encodes here the girl's consciousness of her value on the marriage market – her youth and innocence in return for untold luxury – thus inserting a critique of woman as commodity and providing an ideological dimension. At the end of "The Werewolf," a grasping and unattractive Little Red Riding Hood inherits her grandmother's cottage after driving the old woman out and helping the neighbors to stone her to death. This appears to be a blackly humoristic parody of a traditional fairy-tale ending, but also of Freudian wisdom, and a cynical comment on power relations and self-interest: "Now the child lived in her grandmother's house; she prospered" (110).

Carter's much discussed and documented use of inter-textuality also serves her skepticism of meta-narratives for it allows her to denaturalize the mythic pretensions of source texts. The hybrid textuality she favors is certainly enriching and enthralling, but also disconcerting, for it emphasizes the postmodern theory that there is no fixed origin and no final authoritative text. However, in writing against, Carter is also writing for, telling a different story or stories to replace received wisdom and truths. This suggests that her recycling of fairy tales is doubly subversive. Not content with disrupting the ideological status quo, she offers us alternatives, moving beyond the limits of what it is usually possible to think and express, endlessly transforming her fictional world for readers who must take responsibility for their own interpretations.

Permanent Revelation and Permanent Revolution

The face of the werewolf Duke with which the last tale closes, echoes the human/beast dialectic of the whole volume. It is an invitation to the reader to confront the Other and bring to light its hidden potentialities. The refusal to choose, to privilege one mode of being over the other, the denial of the existence of a universally accessible truth or reality which is so clearly discernible in *The Bloody Chamber* can be construed as a continuation of Carter's "adventures in anarcho-surrealism" (Carter in Tucker 1998: 25) as she shows us "a world transformed by imagination and desire" (Carter 1993a: 70). Her admiration for the surrealist movement which based its artistic and political agenda on "permanent revelation" and "permanent revolution" (1993a: 69) can perhaps give a clue to what she was trying to achieve with these tales, but also make the link with the novel that followed it, *Nights at the Circus*, as part of her ongoing project for the reinvention of fictional form.

REFERENCES AND FURTHER READING

Armitt, L. (1997). "The Fragile Frames of *The Bloody Chamber*," in J. Bristow and T.L. Broughton (eds), *The Infernal Desires of Angela Carter: Fiction, Femininity, Feminism*, pp. 88–99. Harlow: Longman.

Atwood, M. (1994). "Running with the Tigers," in L. Sage (ed.), *Flesh and the Mirror: Essays on the Art of Angela Carter*, pp. 117–35. London: Virago.

Bacchilega, C. (1997). *Postmodern Fairy Tales: Gender and Narrative Strategies*. Philadelphia: University of Pennsylvania Press.

Bacchilega, C. and Roemer, D.M. (eds) (2001). *Angela Carter and the Fairy Tale*. Detroit: Wayne State University Press.

Bayley, J. (1992). "Fighting for the Crown," *The New York Review of Books* (April 23): 9–11.

Bristow, J. and Broughton, T.L (eds) (1997). *The Infernal Desires of Angela Carter: Fiction, Femininity, Feminism*. Harlow: Longman.

Carter, A. (1981). *The Bloody Chamber and Other Stories*. Harmondsworth: Penguin (original work published 1979).

Carter, A. (1993a). *The Sadeian Woman: An Exercise in Cultural History*. London: Virago (original work published 1979).

Carter, A. (1993b). *Expletives Deleted: Selected Writings*. London: Vintage.

Carter, A. (1998). "Notes from the Front Line," in L. Tucker (ed.), *Critical Essays on Angela Carter*, pp. 24–30). New York: G.K. Hall.

Carter, A. (2005) (ed.). *Angela Carter's Book of Fairy Tales*. London: Virago.

Duncker, P. (1984). "Re-imagining the Fairy Tale: Angela Carter's Bloody Chambers," *Literature and History* 10: 3–14.

Jordan, E. (1998). "The Dangers of Angela Carter," in L. Tucker (ed.), *Critical Essays on Angela Carter*, pp. 33–45. New York: G.K. Hall.

Lee, A. (1997). *Angela Carter*. New York: Twayne.

Makinen, M. (1992). "Angela Carter's *The Bloody Chamber* and the Decolonization of Feminine Sexuality," *Feminist Review* 42: 2–15.

Peach, L. (1998). *Angela Carter*. London: Macmillan.

Rushdie S. (2003) 1995. "Angela Carter," in *Step Across This Line*, pp. 40–7. London: Vintage.

Simpson, H. (2006). "Femme Fatale," the *Guardian* (June 24): <http://books.guardian.co.uk/departments/classics/story/0,,1804398,00.html>.

Tucker, L. (ed.) (1998). *Critical Essays on Angela Carter*. New York: G.K. Hall.

46

J.G. Ballard: Psychopathology, Apocalypse, and the Media Landscape

Mitchell R. Lewis

J.G. Ballard's short stories are unflinching portraits of the modern world. Commonly thought to be science fiction (sf), in reality they are not so easily classified. While drawing on sf conventions, Ballard's stories also show the influence of William Burroughs, surrealism, psychoanalysis, and high modernism. Their unique fusion of different artistic and intellectual traditions has placed Ballard's works at the margins of traditional sf, even as their genre elements have kept them at the fringes of mainstream fiction. Bridging high brow and popular culture, Ballard's stories are generally apocalyptic in nature, examining the intersection of psychology and technology, especially mass media. Taken as a whole, they can be viewed as reflections on the psychopathologies endemic to Western capitalist societies since the end of World War II.

Ballard's early work is associated with the British "new wave," a literary movement in the 1960s that attempted to revamp the sf genre. Including such writers as Michael Moorcock, Brian Aldiss, and Pamela Zoline, new wave sf focuses on style, imagery, experimental narrative technique, near future stories, apocalyptic visions, time, entropy and, above all, psychology. These new-wave concerns are reflected in Ballard's essay, "Which Way to Inner Space?" (1962), which spells out the program for much of Ballard's fiction. Calling for the reinvigoration of science fiction, Ballard dismisses rocket ships, ray guns, and space operas, arguing that the form and content of traditional magazine sf, established in the 1930s under the influence of H.G. Wells, have become dated to the modern reader. In place of Wells's "simple plots" and "journalistic narrative" (Ballard 1996: 197), Ballard chooses surrealist imagery and avant-garde narrative technique, and, for subject matter, in place of the hard sciences he chooses psychology. As Ballard explains, "The biggest developments of the immediate future will take place, not on the Moon or Mars, but on Earth, and it is *inner* space, not outer, that needs to be explored" (197). Indicating the extent to which his work diverges from traditional sf, Ballard notes that "the first true s-f story . . . is about a man with amnesia lying on a beach and looking at a rusty bicycle wheel, trying to work out the absolute essence of the relationship between them" (198). The issue of technology aside, the focus of Ballard's exemplary story is not on spaceships and aliens, but on psychology and epistemology. Characterizing much of Ballard's work is this concern with inner space and its corresponding nightmarish landscapes inspired by Salvador Dali.

Reflecting this concern, Ballard's early short stories often transform a common sf plot into a surreal narrative about the unconscious. In "The Illuminated Man" (1964), for instance, Ballard rewrites the disaster story, a staple subgenre of sf including H.G. Wells's "The Star" (1897) and John Wyndham's *The Day of the Triffids* (1951). The disaster story typically concerns a global catastrophe of apocalyptic proportions, such as the impact of a meteor, the spread of a deadly virus, or a cataclysmic deluge. It also depicts the political, scientific, and military responses to a catastrophe. Usually disaster stories are told with objective realism, but in "The Illuminated Man" Ballard tells a psychological story in which the earth and its inhabitants are slowly becoming "encased in a mass of crystalline tissue like an immense glacé fruit" (Ballard 2001: 610), an inexplicable process dubbed the "Hubble Effect," which has taken root in the Florida everglades. The narrator provides a brief scientific explanation of the phenomenon, but the clear intention of the story is to depict a surreal environment, an "enchanted world, where by day fantastic birds fly through the petrified forest and jewelled alligators glitter like heraldic salamanders on the banks of the crystalline rivers" (627). The protagonist of the story investigates the phenomenon with the intention of stopping it, but in the end he wants to become part of its "transfiguration of all living and inanimate forms" (627). Using the material world to depict the unconscious life of his protagonist, Ballard makes the crystallization process into an apocalyptic event symbolic of psychological transformation. Some science fiction fans and writers have found the story to be pessimistic and depressing, but they generally have failed to see the story's surreal imagery as psychological and symbolic rather than as realistic. Ballard does indeed invert the traditional plot of the disaster story by having the protagonist willingly submit to the Hubble Effect, rather than resist it, but the story is meant to be read neither as a realistic documentary, nor as a "what if" story. Instead, it is meant to be read as a symbolic story of psychological metamorphosis, as surreal in its depiction of the unconscious as the interior landscape depicted in Dali's "Persistence of Memory."

The same reworking of sf conventions toward a psychological focus can also be seen in "Thirteen to Centaurus" (1962). In this story Ballard rewrites the well-known "generation starship" plot, the most famous examples of which include Robert A. Heinlein's "Universe" (1941) and "Common Sense" (1941) – both later collected in *Orphans of the Sky* (1963) – and Brian Aldiss's *Non-Stop* (1958). The generation starship story centers on a slow-moving spaceship traveling on a long voyage between solar systems, during which time generations of crew members succeed each other because of the centuries of time it takes to travel between stars. In the stories of Heinlein and Aldiss, with the passage of time the crew members forget their original mission, begin to conceive of the ship as the universe, sink into various superstitions supported by crude political and religious institutions, splinter into various factions, and often fight among themselves. Typically the protagonist discovers the reality of the situation, finding out that he is aboard a ship. This moment of "conceptual breakthrough," as it is popularly known, replays the Enlightenment narrative of scientific discovery that informs so much sf, depicting the acquiring of knowledge, the conquering of darkness by light, the overcoming of superstition and politics, and the progression from infancy and savagery to maturity and reason. This Enlightenment narrative of conceptual breakthrough is a master plot of sf, and it often finds its most felicitous expression in the generation starship story.

In "Thirteen to Centaurus," however, Ballard undercuts this master narrative. In this story there is indeed a crew of astronauts making a multigenerational "non-stop journey to . . . Alpha Centauri" (Ballard 2001: 335), but it turns out that they are really a part of a psychological experiment to determine how human beings would handle such a trip. They are actually on earth, their ship in a large hanger overseen by scientists, politicians, and military officials. The crew has been brainwashed to believe they are on an actual generation starship. They are monitored by scientists, one of whom, Dr Francis, can enter the ship to pose as a crew member. When the project faces closure because of the controversy surrounding it, Dr Francis seals himself up in the ship with the crew, "deliberating accepting the illusion" of the ship itself (337). Calling into question the scientific objectivity that informs Enlightenment narratives, Dr Francis thinks, "Earth itself is in orbit around the Sun . . . and the whole solar system is traveling at forty miles a second toward the constellation Lyra. The degree of illusion that exists is a complex question" (337). What the doctor contemplates in this passage is the relativity of knowledge in which the idea of scientific objectivity is undermined and replaced with the idea of the psychological nature of space, time and, ultimately, perception. Indeed, the doctor discovers that several of the crew members have known about the experiment, but have chosen to accept the illusion of the ship, as the doctor has. In place of the optimism about rationality and science typical of generation starship plots and classic pulp science fiction, Ballard provides a psychological story about psychotic withdrawal and the necessity of subjectivity and relativity.

What Ballard also presents in "Thirteen to Centaurus" is a descent into psychopathology, a dominant theme in Ballard's work. This psychological retreat into madness can be seen in a number of Ballard's stories. In "The Overloaded Man" (1961), for instance, the protagonist, Faulkner, attempts to transcend the intolerable material world with the help of his recently acquired ability to strip objects of their significance and meaning. In a kind of bizarre mysticism Faulkner strives for a state of pure consciousness, leaving behind the world as well as his body, but his increasing alienation and mental instability prompts him to kill his wife as the last step to transcendence, his psychotic fantasies equating women with the material world, a common if disturbing idea in Western philosophy. Many of Ballard's characters, in a parody of rationalist inquiry, strive for such a state of pure consciousness as they retreat from the world, but the body, the unconscious, and the material world usually return with a vengeance. As the allusions to Descartes' *cogito* in "The Overloaded Man" suggest,

Ballard's grand theme is the demise of the Enlightenment, the end of the age of reason.

In this questioning of the rationality of human beings, Ballard is attempting to depict what in *The Introductory Lectures on Psycho-Analysis* (1917) Freud calls the "third and most wounding blow" to "human megalomania," the idea that "the ego . . . is not even master in its own house, but must content itself with scanty information of what is going on unconsciously in its mind" (Freud 1977: 352). Following the revolutions of Copernicus and Darwin, the two other "blows" of which Freud speaks, the psychoanalytic revolution decenters human consciousness, emphasizing the unconscious world of drives, instincts, and other irrational, impersonal processes. It is this Freudian unconscious world that is the concern of so many of Ballard's stories, in which the ego has only a bit part in a compulsory psychodrama beyond its conscious comprehension. Not surprisingly, along the way, Ballard's stories cover many familiar Freudian topics. In "The Gioconda of the Twilight Noon" (1964), for instance, Ballard deals with the Oedipus complex. Recovering from temporary blindness at his Mother's house, the protagonist, Richard Maitland, becomes obsessed with the world of phantasmagoric images that his imagination has unleashed in the wake of his blindness. Soon after his recovery, rather than give up his surreal fantasy world of beaches, caves, labyrinths, and enchantresses, Maitland permanently blinds himself, becoming "an eager, unrepentant Oedipus" (Ballard 2001: 657). In "I Smile" (1976) Ballard tells his version of E.T.A. Hoffman's "The Sand-Man," a story that preoccupied Freud in his essay "The Uncanny" (1925). In Ballard's story the unnamed protagonist falls in love with an uncanny Mannequin, who turns out to be a real woman who has died and been preserved by a taxidermist. The protagonist's obsessive love allows Ballard to explore wounded masculinity, compensatory fantasies and the illusory nature of love. Ballard's "Manhole 69" (1957) depicts an experiment to eliminate the need for sleep, stressing the necessity of the unconscious while also revealing the influence of the death drive, as discussed by Freud in *Beyond the Pleasure Principle* (1920). Such stories read like Freudian case histories, and they also reinforce Brian Aldiss's well-known assertion in *Trillion Year Spree* (2001) that sf has its roots in gothic literature. In fact, with its emphasis on psychopathology and its critique of the Enlightenment Ballard's work may be more gothic than sf.

Complementing Ballard's focus on psychopathology is his use of apocalyptic imagery. In Ballard's stories apocalyptic events are symbols of psychological transformation. In "Now Wakes the Sea" (1963), for instance, Richard Mason, an unhappily married man, repeatedly witnesses an apocalyptic flood at night, during which he also sees a strange enchanting woman, but no one else can corroborate his visions. In his wife's opinion "it's only in [Richard's] mind" (Ballard 2001: 473). In this story Ballard uses apocalyptic imagery to represent the changing psychology and relationship of his two principle characters. In "Venus Hunters" (1963), a man named Kandinski is convinced that he has seen a Venusian spaceship. Having a messiah complex, Kandinski sees an impending catastrophe for the earth if humanity does not abandon its space programs. He becomes a new age prophet predicting an imminent apocalypse.

A scientist by the name of Cameron does not believe Kandinski, but in a passage that reflects Ballard's own views of apocalyptic imagery, he claims to see the figurative, psychological truth of what Kandinski preaches, explaining, "The real significance of [Kandinski's] fantasies . . . is . . . as an expression of the immense psychic forces stirring below the surface of rational life, like the isotactic movements of the continental table which heralded the major geological transformation" (497). Operating out of a Jungian understanding of symbols of transformation, Cameron sees Kandinski's visions as saying something about the collective unconscious and how it responds with apocalyptic imagery to the anxieties of the time. Kandinski also raises the issue of the traumatic origins of fantasy, a recurring concern of Ballard's work. Finally, in what might be a dig at overly rational or realistic sf fans and authors who take apocalyptic stories literally, Ballard has Cameron say, "It is unfortunate for Kandinski, and for the writer of science fiction for that matter, that they have to perform their tasks of describing the symbols of transformation in a so-called rationalist society, where a scientific, or at least a pseudo-scientific explanation is required *a priori*" (498). In these meta-fictional passages Cameron seems to speak for Ballard, pointing out how readers should interpret Ballard's use of apocalyptic imagery.

In "The Voices of Time" (1960) Ballard presents more apocalyptic imagery influenced by Carl Jung. Psychologist Dr. Powers participates in a genetic experiment that may well bring about the evolution of humanity, but he ends up developing a keen sense of the entropy of the universe. As he contemplates a mandala, reflecting on the decaying universe, Powers mystically joins his consciousness with the universe, his body gradually dissolving. Once again Ballard stresses the psychological significance of the apocalyptic imagery that he employs, presenting a mythical merging of psychological and cosmological time in a vision of entropic decline signifying psychological transformation. But as the references to the historians Oswald Spengler and Arnold Toynbee suggest, Ballard's apocalyptic imagery is also related to the sense of living at the end of an historical era. This era can be understood as the age of "Enlightenment . . . running from the birth of modern science up to 1933 and the arrival of Hitler" (Vale 2005b: 53), but as Ballard's essay "First Impressions of London" (1993) suggests, this era might also be the heyday of the British Empire (Ballard 1996: 185). Ballard has even indicated that the era in decline may be that of the American empire. Whatever the case may be, Ballard's apocalyptic imagery usually has the twofold sense of an ending and a beginning. As Ballard has explained, "my fiction is littered with the debris of mythological end-points . . . Ends [however] are also the beginning of the next step forward" (Vale 2005b: 167). This positive view of apocalyptic imagery, moreover, is in keeping with Ballard's view of the disaster tale as a "celebration of the possibilities of life" (Ballard 1996: 209).

Linked to the themes of apocalypse and psychopathology, finally, is Ballard's attention to the media landscape. Typically Ballard's characters, attempting to escape the material world, find a temporary haven in the disembodied world of media imagery. In "Motel Architecture" (1978), for instance, the main character Pangborn lives all alone in "a fully equipped television studio, in which [he] was simultaneously the star, scriptwriter and director of an unending domestic serial of infinitely more interest than the programs provided by the public channels" (Ballard 2001: 992–3). Like Faulkner in "The Overloaded Man" or Powers in "The Voices of Time," Pangborn seeks the "absolute abstraction of himself . . . the construction of a world formed entirely from the materials of his consciousness" (993), but a visiting repair woman named Vera reminds him of his body and his sexuality, prompting him to kill her in a reenactment of Hitchcock's *Psycho.* A similar kind of psychological disintegration keyed to the media landscape is seen in "The Intensive Care Unit" (1977), a story about a family in the future in which all human relationships are mediated by television screens with all the artistry of Bergman, Fellini, and other film *auteurs.* The father decides to see his family in the flesh, but unused to the absence of media artifice, the family finds itself torn apart by their repressed hostilities and incestuous desires that suddenly surface now that they are denied the sublimation of information technology.

In some cases, Ballard's characters are manipulated by mass media as the world crumbles around them. Tapping into fantasies of fear, desire, and aggression, mass media in Ballard's stories can become a form of escapism, compensation, or evasion, a substitute for the renunciations of civilization, as Freud puts it in *Civilization and Its Discontents* (1930). In "A Guide to Virtual Death" (1992), for instance, Ballard's narrator presents one of the remains of a now extinct humanity, a schedule of a day's television programs, which reveals the extent to which mass media had colonized the unconscious, presenting a virtual reality of sex and violence that distracted humanity from the political realities that finally drove it to extinction. Similarly, in "Report from an Obscure Planet" (1992) the inhabitants of a planet abandon their world for a virtual one, a kind of "electronically generated amusement park" (Ballard 2001: 1186) that they have come to regard as more real than the original on which it was based. As the narrator explains, "Driven by the need for a more lifelike replica of the scenes of carnage that most entertained them, the people of this unhappy world had invented an advanced and apparently interiorised version of their television screens, a virtual replica of reality in which they could act out their most deviant fantasies" (1186). In this virtual world "they could assume any identity, create and fulfil any desire, and explore the most deviant dreams" (1186).

Ballard also extends his analysis of media to the political realm. In "The Secret History of World War 3" (1988), for instance, American citizens become consumed with the continuous televised coverage of the failing health of their President who has become little more than a media construct. Meanwhile, relegated to the margins of media coverage, brief news stories about an exchange of nuclear strikes between the USA and a rival superpower go all but unnoticed. This idea of politics as grounded in media imagery charged by the unconscious desires of its audience is a dominant preoccupation of Ballard's. It can also be seen in the controversial stories "Why I Want to Fuck Ronald Reagan" (1969) and "Plan for the Assassination of Jacquelyn Kennedy" (1969), each of which deals with psychotic fantasies about public figures in the mass media, and points to the intersection of psychology, mass media, and politics. In "The Subliminal Man" (1963) Ballard extends his analysis of politics and the media to advertising. This paranoid story depicts a late-capitalist world driven by consumer spending in which the drive for profit and excessive production have made subliminal advertising necessary. As one of the characters notes, "These subliminal techniques are the sort of last-ditch attempt you'd expect from an over-capitalized industrial system" (Ballard 2001: 422). Such stories about capitalism, politics, and mass media have contributed to Ballard's reputation as a writer of the postmodern condition. Interfaced with technology and media in a variety of ways, Ballard's characters recall Donna Haraway's cyborgs and William Gibson's cyberpunks, and the virtual world of simulacra in which they live resembles the late-capitalist world described by Jean Baudrillard, Guy Debord, Fredric Jameson, and other postmodern theorists.

Ballard's literary techniques have also contributed to his reputation as a postmodern writer. Over the course of his career he has been remarkably creative with the form of the short story. "Terminal Beach" (1964) and "The Atrocity Exhibition" are notable examples of Ballard's "compressed novels," short stories that emphasize images and juxtaposed narrative fragments with thematic titles. Traditional exposition and narrative transitions removed, these stories resemble the cut-up narratives of William Burroughs. In "Notes Towards a Mental Breakdown" (1976) Ballard presents a story through annotating an eighteen-word sentence, with one annotation for each word. Similarly, "Plan for the Assassination of Jacqueline Kennedy" and "Why I Want to Fuck Ronald Reagan" are oblique, fragmented narratives, the titles of each fragment constituting two sentences pointing toward the psychological and cultural themes of the respective story. "The Index" (1977) is the story of Henry Rhodes Hamilton told through the only remaining part of his autobiography, the index, while "Answers to a Questionnaire" (1985) is a story recounted through a series of 100 short answers to questions that have been elided from the text. "Time Passage" (1964) presents the story of James Falkner in reverse, from the exhuming of his corpse to his return to the womb. "The Beach Murders" is a kind of postmodern mystery in which a series of clues with a number of solutions has been arranged under alphabetical headings. "Theatre of War" (1977), finally, is cast in the form of a script for a TV documentary similar to "the type made popular by *World in Action*" (953). Assembled into remarkable short-story collections like *The Atrocity Exhibition* (1969), *Vermilion Sands* (1971), and *War Fever* (1999), such stories reveal the creativity of Ballard and the seemingly limitless possibilities of the short-story form, even as they help to secure Ballard's reputation as a postmodern writer.

Ballard's postmodernism, however, is rooted in his observations of the material realities of the twentieth century. His exploration of postmodern psychopathologies stems from his understanding of capitalism, information technology, advertising, science, mass politics, and the chilling historical realities of World War II, which he experienced first-hand as a child imprisoned in a Japanese concentration camp. The fantasies depicted in Ballard's stories are shaped by the peculiar conditions of the Space Age, whose unmatched technological sophistication has gone hand in hand with equally unprecedented irrational behavior. In the end, Ballard can be best understood as a psychoanalytic cultural critic because his work attempts to reveal the latent content of the manifest world of late capitalism in which reality has become a fantasy generated by the media landscape and animated by our deepest fears and desires.

REFERENCES AND FURTHER READING

Aldiss, B. and Wingrove, D. (2001). *Trillion Year Spree: The History of Science Fiction*, new edn. North Yorkshire: House of Stratus.

Ballard, J.G. (1988). *Vermilion Sands*. New York: Carroll & Graf Publishers.

Ballard, J.G. (1995). *The Best Short Stories of J.G. Ballard*. New York: Henry Holt and Company.

Ballard, J.G. (1996). *A User's Guide to the Millenium*. New York: Picador.

Ballard, J.G. (1999). *War Fever*. New York: Farrar, Straus and Giroux.

Ballard, J.G. (2001). *The Complete Short Stories*. London: Flamingo.

Ballard, J.G. (2005). *The Atrocity Exhibition*, rev. edn. San Francisco: RE/Search Publications.

Delville, M. (2000). *J.G. Ballard*. Plymouth, UK: Northcote House.

Freud, S. (1977). *Introductory Lectures on Psycho-Analysis*, trans. J. Strachey. New York: W.W. Norton (original work published 1916–17).

Goddard, J. and Pringle D. (eds) (1976). *J.G. Ballard: The First Twenty Years*. Hayes: Bran's Head Press.

G¹siorek, A. (2005). *J.G. Ballard*. Manchester: Manchester University Press.

Luckhurst, R. (1998). *The Angle between Two Walls: The Fiction of J.G. Ballard*. New York: St Martin's Press.

Pringle, D. (1984). *J.G. Ballard: A Primary and Secondary Bibliography*. Boston, Mass.: G.K. Hall.

Stephenson, G. (1991). *Out of the Night and into the Dream: A Thematic Study of the Fiction of J.G. Ballard*. Westport, Conn.: Greenwood Press.

Vale, V. (2005a). *Re/Search 8/9: J.G. Ballard*, new edn. San Francisco: Re/Search Publications.

Vale, V. (ed.) (2005b). *J.G. Ballard: Conversations*. San Francisco: Re/Search Publications.

Vale, V. and Ryan, M. (eds) (2005c). *J.G. Ballard: Quotes*. San Francisco: Re/Search Publications.

47

The Short Stories of Benjamin Okri

Wolfgang Görtschacher

The short fiction of Benjamin Okri (born 1959) has received considerably less serious critical attention than his eight novels, the latest – *Starbook* – published, after a hiatus of five years, in November 2007. This is still true, although Okri received both the Commonwealth Writers' Prize for Africa and the *Paris Review* Aga Khan Prize for Fiction for *Incidents at the Shrine* (1986), his first collection of short stories, in 1987.

In July 1986 Okri told Jane Wilkinson in an interview that at that time he felt he had "to go back to the basics." He had grown so distant from his first two novels, *Flowers and Shadows* (1980) and *The Landscapes Within* (1981), that he felt as if he was "just learning to write, as if I was writing for the first time." This change in his attitude to writing resulted in a change in his sense of both an audience and words and required "a radical alteration of perception" which "consisted of an atomization of the way I looked at craft. I had to look at words with new eyes." While the short story is – for Okri – one of the most neglected forms in African literature, it is the closest to what he defines as the essence of fiction, "legends, myths, fables." To him, the novel is a forest, but the short story is a seed, an atom that, he assumes, might contain "the secret of the universe" (Wilkinson 1992: 86). When interviewed by Stella Orakwue at the prize-giving ceremony for the inaugural Caine Prize for African Writing in 2000, he told her that he viewed the short story as "the most rigorous form in all literature apart from the sonnet. It's much more difficult to write a good short story than to write a novel." In *Dubliners* James Joyce provides a model, Okri believes, for both the construction of a short story and the demands placed on its readers. In "Fantasies Born in the Ghetto," Okri maintains that you "can't read Joyce's *Dubliners* casually: you'd be bored stiff" (Shakespeare 1986: 13). In an aphorism in "The Joys of Storytelling III", published in his collection of essays entitled *A Way of Being Free* (1988), Okri proclaims a "great challenge for our age," which is, for the writer, "to do for storytelling what Joyce did for language – to take it to the highest levels of enchantment and magic; to impact into story infinite richness and convergences" (Okri 1998: 111).

Thus his short-story collections, *Incidents at the Shrine* (1986), a slim volume of eight stories, and *Stars of the New Curfew* (1988), which comprises half a dozen, mark a new phase in Okri's artistic development, the first result of which would be his Booker Prize-winning novel *The Famished Road* (1991). Out of the fourteen short stories in the two collections, eleven focus on different aspects of city life and how it affects the protagonists living there. Two short stories deal with Okri's experiences during the Nigerian Civil War ("Laughter Beneath the Bridge," "In the Shadow of War"). One story ("What the Tapster Saw") does not seem to fit any of the categories developed by Helen Chukwuma in her essay "Two Decades of the Short Story in West Africa."

Of the stories published in *Incidents at the Shrine* five are set in Lagos ("Converging City," "Incidents at the Shrine," "Masquerades," "Crooked Prayer," "The Dream-vendor's August"), two in London ("Disparities," "A Hidden History"), and one is situated in an unspecified location in rural Nigeria ("Laughter Beneath the Bridge"). In his review of the collection published in *British Book News*, Geoffrey Parker argues that the characters in six stories are "losers, struggling impotently against the tide of filth, injustice and violence in slum or wartime life" (Parker 1986: 546). Okri seeks in these stories, which are unified by the image of the shrine, to explore as many layers of reality as possible. The title story, Okri told Wilkinson, refers to "a new orientation, a return to origins, a different set of perceptions" (Wilkinson 1992: 82). Anderson, the protagonist, is an employee in the Department of Antiquities situated in the capital. Although he draws his salary for knowing about the past, he knows hardly anything about the history of his own people. After having been sacked, he flees home to his village, where he undergoes a hermetic rite: has a meeting with the Image-maker, an encounter with the Image itself, and a skirmish with the Image-eaters, spirit-like figures living on the village boundaries. Anderson, an urban official, can only work vigorously in the city, if he retains (spiritual) contact with his village. "You must come home now and again," the Image-maker tells him, this "is where you derive power" (Okri 1986: 64).

Two of the stories, "Laughter Beneath the Bridge" and "Crooked Prayer", are related by a child who only half understands what he has witnessed. In the former, set at the outbreak of the Nigerian Civil War, this is made clear to the reader right from the start, when the narrator likens the turmoil around him to "an insane feast" and remembers it "as a beautiful time. I don't know how" (3). On a lorry journey in search of safety, mother and son reach the final checkpoint, where, to identify their ethnic origin, each passenger is obliged to recite the paternoster in his or her mother tongue, while a rape is going on behind the bushes. The mother is saved by saying it in her husband's tongue. The boy is rescued when he cries out the word for "shit" in his father's tongue. The most dramatic moment of the story is when the boy recognizes the rubbish in the narrow stream for what it really is: "The stream was full of corpses that had swollen, huge massive bodies with enormous eyes and bloated cheeks" (17–18). Alastair Niven is reminded of "those epiphanious moments in Joyce's *Dubliners* where children awake in a moment to the brutality and monstrousness of the adult world" (Niven 1989: 279). In "Crooked Prayer" the narrator is an admiring nephew, who functions as a go-between between his uncle Saba and a woman called Mary. Saba's relationship with her becomes more fixed when he moves in with her, once she has given him the child his infertile wife has been unable to produce. Fraser holds that both stories have affinities with Joyce, "in their deliberate omissions, their ear for dialogue, their blending of sweet and sour" (Fraser 2002: 51).

"Disparities" and "A Hidden History," both set in London, are remarkable for their "exaggerated treatment of the unspeakable, an accumulation of nastiness that flirts with bathos" (Melmoth 1986: 863). In "Disparities," which was first published by Peter Ackroyd in *PEN Fiction* 1 (1984) and six years later reprinted by Auberon Waugh in *Literary Review* 34 (1990), the reader accompanies the first-person narrator, a tramp-as-critic, on a tour of London in decline. He encounters the squalid living conditions of a bunch of undergraduates and enters a reeking pub, peopled with the "very cream of leftovers, kicked-outs, eternal trendies, hoboes, weirdoes, addicts and pedlars" (Okri 1986: 45). "A Hidden History," reminiscent of Okri's experience when living in New Cross, is an experimental nightmare portrait of the labyrinthine realities of modern London. The first-person narrator, a "black [. . .] angel [. . .], my wings heavy and black like all the sin" (1986: 90), focuses on "immigrants from lands whose destinies had been altered by slavery" (81).

For many of Okri's protagonists life in Lagos is similarly and extremely lacking in comfort and glamor. In "Converging City," defined by Robert Fraser as "an experiment of relative velocities" (Fraser 2002: 53), the third-person narrator watches the trader Agodi's response to commercial disappointments: he grows a reddish beard, wears his hair in tiny braids, founds a new church, and goes into business as a true prophet. In "Masquerades," a night-soil worker compensates for the vileness of his job by creating a spotless slum penthouse, "a curious slum paradise," smelling of "perfumed soaps, clean sheets, new clothes, leather, and velvet materials," with blue walls hung with "several large photographs of him [. . .], along with posters of London and Paris, Brazil with its Sango dancers, America with a saloon scene from the Wild West. [. . .] There was a Benin mask above the door; next to it was a picture of Jesus Christ" (Okri 1986: 72). The nameless protagonist copes with the "inchoate nihilism" (Melmoth 1986: 863), as John Melmoth put it, that goes with his job – "When I look at people I see nothing – what doesn't turn to shit turns to dust" (Okri 1986: 79) – by obsessively dousing himself with "the smells of lavender and jasmine" (72).

"The Dream-vendor's August," the longest and most complex story in the collection, is set during the rainy season. Ajegunle Joe combats futility with occultism, selling quack remedies by post, along with pamphlets on *How to Fight Witches and Wizards* and *How to Banish Poverty from Your Life*, and protecting himself from disaster with rings that belonged to Isaac Newton and King Solomon. Despite his lack of financial and personal success – he falls in love with a Ghanaian woman, but when they attempt to make love, he discovers that he is impotent – he finds happiness in disinterested serenity at the end: "Joe lay flat on his back and watched the clear sky" (Okri 1986: 133).

In *Stars of the New Curfew* (1988), Okri's second collection comprising six short stories, the influences are, according to Fraser, "fewer, far more intense, and largely African" (Fraser 2002: 57); Neil Bissoondath holds that these stories "resonate well beyond their immediate settings, striking chords of recognition in anyone with more than a nodding acquaintance with underdeveloped countries" (Bissoondath 1989: 12). "In the Shadow of War," dating from 1983, deals with a child's experience of the Civil War and is reminiscent of "Laughter Beneath the Bridge," especially at the moment when the boy Omovo notices that "the dead animals on the river were in fact the corpses of grown men" (Okri 1988: 8). Robert Fraser reads "Worlds That Flourish" as "an allegory of invisibility and the need to flee from limiting notions of identity [. . .] a quest to the land of the dead in search of a lost self" (Fraser 2002: 63). The first-person narrator undergoes experiences similar to Anderson's in "Incidents at the Shrine." He is sacked from his job, falsely imprisoned and, after his release, escapes by car and, after swimming across a river, reaches the village-of-the-dead where he meets his dead wife. Running back along the road, he comes to consciousness "in the wreckage of the car. [. . .] The twisted wreck of metal seemed to have grown on me." He trudges back towards the petrol shack "with the hope of reaching [it] before he died" (Okri 1988: 32).

For Neil Bissoondath, "In the City of Red Dust" is "a relentless tale of exploitation and degradation [. . .] a frightening picture of urban life in Nigeria [. . .], and one full of political commentary" (Bissoondath 1989: 12). The story, set in the eponymous city on the day of the military governor's fiftieth birthday, obeys all of the three classical unities of place, time, and action. Emokhai and Marjomi eke out an existence by "selling blood at Queen Mary's Memorial Hospital and by shifting the balances of people's pockets" (Okri 1988: 51). After Dede, Marjomi's former girlfriend, has avoided a gang rape by a group of soldiers by cutting herself in the neck, she is rushed to hospital. As they are in the same blood group, Marjomi gives her by transfusion his second glass tube of the day.

The title story "Stars of the New Curfew," the longest in the collection, is in Robert Fraser's view "a satirical-cum-surrealist treatment of the theme of the 1970s oil boom" (Fraser 2002: 60). The first-person narrator is hired as drugs salesman to promote a phoney panacea called POWER-DRUG: His selling it aboard a crowded molue bus to the driver leads to a first climax in the story when the driver loses control and the molue splashes into a lagoon. Successive auctions are the main principle the structure of the story is based upon. The first takes the form of a dream, in which bidders buy the stars in the sky by paying "either with huge sums of money, a special part of the human anatomy, or the decapitated heads of newly-dead children" (Okri 1988: 93). In a flashback of the narrator's schooldays two of his classmates died for his services as go-between with the prettiest girl in town. This is followed by a nightmare auction in which parts of the narrator's body are sold off. The climax is a nightmare contest by two millionaires in which the audience is tricked into fighting for joke currencies after bags of money have been emptied over them from a helicopter.

For Robert Fraser, "When the Lights Return" is Okri's "reworking of the classical Orpheus-Eurydice myth" (Fraser 2002: 59) to which he adds the motifs of the quest. The protagonists are Ede, a minor pop musician and – in Ato Quayson's view – a "male chauvinist," and his very attractive girlfriend Maria. After three weeks of ignoring her, Ede decides to walk to "her bungalow sinking in the depths of the Munshin ghetto" (Okri 1988: 156), which Fraser regards as equivalent to Hades in the Greek legend. Ede arrives to find Maria dying, attended by her herbalist, and walks back home. After Maria's death Ede wanders into a chaotic marketplace, where he is slain by marketwomen, a scene reminiscent, as Fraser notes, of "Orpheus' dismemberment by enraged Thracian women" (Fraser 2002: 59).

The last story in the volume, "What the Tapster Saw," is – according to Fraser – Okri's "transmutation" (Fraser 2002: 57) of Amos Tutuola's classic story *The Palm-Wine Drinkard and His Dead Palm-Wine Tapster in the Dead's Town* (1952). The tapster's creeks and palm groves have been taken over by the Delta Oil Company. He undertakes a quest after his provisional decease – he is unaware that is life is over – "without the faintest idea of where he [is] going" (Okri 1988: 185). With this quest "Okri seems to be suggesting," as Fraser believes, "a series of initiations into realms that lie outside one another, like the successive skins of a Russian doll" (Fraser 2002: 58).

One story that has been overlooked by critics – with the exception of Mariaconcetta Costantini (2002: 36–7) – is "In the Shadow of War" (Okri 1988: 3–9). However, it illustrates very well Okri's exceptional skills as a short-story writer.

Already in the first sentence Okri's narrator defines the setting as well as the theme of the text: "That afternoon three soldiers came to the village" (3). The determiner "that," used deictically in this context, carries the narrator's feeling of detached and critical distance and consequently draws readers immediately into the textual orbit, also because the subject of the sentence ("three soldiers") confirms their expectations raised by the title. The three simple parallelistic statements that follow – only the second, a coordinated sentence, is slightly more complex – create a rather hostile and frightening atmosphere: "They scattered the goats and chickens. They went to the palm-frond bar and ordered a calabash of palm-wine. They drank amidst the flies" (3). This first paragraph "beautifully illustrates," Neil Bissoondath holds, "the power of his [Okri's] writing. The language is simple, the details striking, the whole powerfully observed scene pulled together by the final sentence" (Bissoondath 1989: 12). The description of this scene seems to express Omovo's point of view without an external narrator's interference. This view is supported by the brevity of the sentences, the simple syntax, and the lexical range.

With the second paragraph the narrative situation changes. In the first sentence of the second paragraph the reader is introduced to the protagonist of the story:

"Omovo watched them from the window as he waited for his father to go out" (Okri 1988: 3). Although Omovo's passivity is described, in terms of narrative technique, from his point of view, it implies a third-person or heterodiegetic narrator, however impersonal. The opposition between the soldiers and Omovo is stressed by the local situation of outside versus inside. The physical distance is further reinforced by the paragraph break. The radio mentioned in the second sentence – "They both listened to the radio" (3) – provides the reason for a flashback that fills the reader in with some background information on the war: "His father had bought the old Grundig cheaply from a family that had to escape the city when the war broke out" (3).

The first sentence of the third paragraph takes up Omovo's position at the window again and is a variation of the first sentence of the second paragraph: "Omovo stared out of the window, irritated with his father" (3). These varied parallelisms are most effectively used as a stylistic leitmotif when Omovo dashes after the woman who, he has been told by the soldiers, "is a spy. She helps our enemies" (6). Thus the reader is guided through the various stages of Omovo's rite of passage: "He followed her through the dense vegetation. [. . .] He followed the woman till they came to a rough camp on the plain below. [. . .] He followed her till they came to a muddied river" (6–7). These stages are also stressed on the graphological level of the text, as each of the paralled sentences introduces a separate paragraph. Descending on to a Hades-like plain Omovo does not meet the dead (yet), but the refugees of the Nigerian Civil War: "Shadowy figures moved about in the half-light of the cave. The woman went to them. The figures surrounded her and touched her and led her into the cave. Children with kwashiorkor stomachs and women wearing rags led her half-way up the hill" (7). The description of the river reinforces the surreal nightmarish atmosphere, bears some resemblance to the river Styx and prepares the reader for the climax of the short story:

> Omovo saw capsized canoes and trailing water-logged clothes on the dark water. He saw floating items of sacrifice: loaves of bread in polythene wrappings, gourds of food, Coca-Cola cans. When he looked at the canoes again they had changed into the shapes of swollen dead animals. He saw outdated currencies on the riverbank. He noticed the terrible smell in the air. (Okri 1988: 7)

The pre-climax is a Joycean epiphany, introduced by a change of light over the forest: "for the first time Omovo saw that the dead animals on the river were in fact the corpses of grown men. Their bodies were tangled with river-weed and their eyes were bloated" (8). When he finally watches the woman being shot by one of the soldiers, Omovo is forced to give up his role as detached observer and has to look reality into its grisly face. However, he protests against the premature initiation forced upon him by the atrocities of the Civil War. His attempt at taking refuge from reality is, again, portrayed by Okri's narrator in four paralleled sentences: "He ran through the forest screaming. [. . .] He ran through a mist which seemed to have risen from the rocks.

As he ran he saw an owl staring at him from a canopy of leaves. He tripped over the roots of a tree and blacked out when his head hit the ground" (8–9). The world literally eclipses for Omovo. When he wakes up, he mistakes the darkness produced by the eclipse of the moon for blindness. Once Omovo has recovered his sight he observes his father's fraternizing with the soldiers, sitting outside drinking palm-wine with them. This situation again takes up the inside versus outside opposition from the beginning of the story. Although the father's explanation sounds more than reasonable ("'You must thank them,' his father said. 'They brought you back from the forest'" (9)), Omovo's experience cannot be regarded as mere fantasy. Mariaconcetta Costantini rightly points out that "its imaginary elements are inextricably intertwined with its crude real-life details." As he restricts the narrative stance to the boy's viewpoint, Okri problematizes, Costantini holds, "the reader's role as an interpreter of fictional events which, despite their implausibility, have a historical relevance that must by accounted for. The story's open-endedness is thus turned into a hermeneutic stimulus" (Costantini 2002: 37).

Foreshadowing is a traditional narrative device that is often foregrounded by Okri's narrator. For example, the forthcoming eclipse of the moon is described by Omovo's father as "That's when the world goes dark and strange things happen. [. . .] The dead start to walk about and sing" (4). The atmosphere in the village and the weather serve to foreshadow Omovo's crucial experience: "The heat was stupefying. Noises dimmed and lost their edges. The villagers stumbled about their various tasks as if they were sleep-walking. The three soldiers drank palm-wine and played draughts beneath the sun's oppressive glare" (5). When the woman leaves the cave the children touch her "as if they might not see her again" (7).

Okri told Wilkinson that he "wrote the stories the way poems are written" (Wilkinson 1992: 82), which nicely bears out John Melmoth's description of Okri's stories as "terse, poised, poetic." (Melmoth 1986: 863) Okri's dictum even holds true when the phonological level of the text is studied carefully. A good example of Okri's poetics can be found towards the end of the text:

> He found his way to the balcony, full of wonder that his sight had returned. But when
> he got there he was surprised to find his father sitting on the sunken cane chair,
> drinking palm-wine with the three soldiers. (Melmoth 1986: 9)

The alliterative patterns intricately interwoven, the consonance of [k] (sunken, cane, drinking), and the assonances of [aI] (sight, surprised, find, palm-wine) and [I] (his, sitting, drinking, with) produce a texture that fulfils the requirements of a carefully crafted poem.

Although Okri's output has been small so far, he has "found a voice and established a style of his own" (Melmoth 1986: 863). It is to be hoped that his short stories, which "ought to be read slowly, carefully" (Thomas 1989: 13), will receive the wider recognition, both by readers and by critics, which they indubitably deserve.

REFERENCES AND FURTHER READING

Bissoondath, N. (1989). "Rage and Sadness in Nigeria," *The New York Times Book Review* (August 13): 12.

Chukwuma, H. (1989). "Two Decades of the Short Story in West Africa," *WAACLALS* 1/1: 1–14.

Costantini, M. (2002). *Behind the Mask: A Study of Ben Okri's Fiction*. Rome: Carocci editore.

Fraser, R. (2002) *Ben Okri*. Horndon: Northcote House.

Melmoth, J. (1986). "From Ghetto to Badland," *Times Literary Supplement* (August 8): 863.

Moh, F.A. (2002). *Ben Okri: An Introduction to His Early Fiction*. Enugu: Fourth Dimensions.

Niven, A. (1989). "Achebe and Okri: Contrasts in the Response to Civil War," in J. Bardolph (ed.), *Short Fiction in the New Literatures in English*, pp. 277–83. Nice: Fac. des lettres & Sciences Humaines.

Okri, B. (1986). *Incidents at the Shrine*. London: Heinemann.

Okri, B. (1988). *Stars of the New Curfew*. London: Secker & Warburg.

Okri, B. (1998). *A Way of Being Free*. London: Weidenfeld & Nicholson.

Parker, G. (1986). Review of *Incidents at the Shrine*. *British Book News* (September): 546.

Quayson, A. (1997). *Strategic Transformations in Nigerian Writing: Rev. Samuel Johnson, Amos Tutuola, Wole Soynika, Ben Okri*. Oxford: James Curry.

Shakespeare, N. (1986). "Fantasies Born in the Ghetto," *The Times* (July 24): 13.

Thomas, M. (1989). "The Forest in the City," *Los Angeles Times Book Review* (September 24): 3, 13.

Wilkinson, J. (1992). "Ben Okri," in J. Wilkinson (ed.), *Talking with African Writers*, pp. 76–89. London: Currey/Portsmouth: Heinemann.

48

James Kelman:
Greyhound for Breakfast

Peter Clandfield

Near the end of James Kelman's short story "Forgetting to Mention Allende," from the 1987 collection *Greyhound for Breakfast*, the central character, a Glaswegian occupied with redecorating his family's new flat, is interrupted by door-to-door missionaries. They press him to defend his declaration of atheism, but he declines in words that illustrate not only his inability or reluctance to express himself fully but also Kelman's care in conveying the idiom and syntax of such hesitant and imperfectly-articulate utterances: "Naw, no really, I prefer taking a back seat I mean, it's all politics and that, eh, honest, I'll need to get back to the painting" (1987: 54). In recent interviews, Kelman, less reticent than his character, suggests that his more compact works have taken a back seat in the reception of his fiction: "I often get criticized by people who know me only from my key novels, whereas, Christ, I've written a hundred and fifty short stories, but they never seem to be on the agenda" (Toremans 2003: 572; see also Gardiner 2004: 102–3). While recent criticism has begun to remedy this deficit, even sympathetic and insightful assessments of Kelman's work have illustrated the tendency to which he refers. Cairns Craig, in a 1993 essay that remains a key reference point for discussions of Kelman's concerns and techniques, grounds his analysis exclusively in the three novels Kelman had then published. Craig mentions only the titles of the three full-length collections of short stories that Kelman had produced – *Not Not While the Giro* (1983); *Greyhound for Breakfast* (1987); *The Burn* (1991) – and says nothing of Kelman's contribution to the 1985 collection *Lean Tales*, which also features stories by Kelman's colleagues Agnes Owens and Alasdair Gray. Ian Haywood, in his 1997 survey *Working-class Fiction*, introduces a brief discussion of Kelman by stating that his "fiction has progressed from tiny vignettes of working-class experience to lengthy stream-of-consciousness narratives" (1997: 152). Though he offers a brief reading of one such Kelman "vignette," "Where but What," Haywood implies that short fiction has been essentially Kelman's apprenticeship for the more rigorous and significant work of producing novels such as *How Late It Was, How Late*, winner of the 1994 Booker

Prize. *How Late* has received extensive critical attention, in part because of debate arising from the objections of some commentators to the profanity-rich language of its focal character (on the debate see e.g. Gilbert 1999; Pitchford 2000). It is ironic that Kelman may be best known in connection with such supposed linguistic excess, since much of his work – from short stories like "Forgetting to Mention Allende" to, arguably, *How Late* itself (see, for example, Bittenbender 2000: 150–1) – features various forms of understatement and non-statement as both key techniques and central thematic preoccupations.

That critics have to some extent forgotten to mention Kelman's stories may reflect a general undervaluation of short fiction as a literary form, but it is also particularly strange given Kelman's consistent attention, in both his shorter and longer fictions, to the under-appreciated significance of things local, quotidian, or microcosmic. This focus is structural as well as thematic or ideological. Drew Milne characterizes Kelman's novels as "constructed through loosely linked short stories rather than through sustained plots" (2003: 159), and Craig suggests that Kelman may "be fulfilling Virginia Woolf's assertion that the novel ought to examine 'an ordinary mind on an ordinary day,' exploring . . . the 'incessant shower of innumerable atoms' that 'shape themselves into the life of Monday or Tuesday'" (1993: 104; see Woolf 1925/1966: 106). Craig is referring to Woolf's 1925 essay, "Modern Fiction," which offers additional terms in which to describe Kelman's approach, notably in the often-cited injunction that Woolf associates with the radically revised realism of James Joyce: "Let us not take it for granted that life exists more fully in what is commonly thought big than in what is commonly thought small" (1925/1966: 107). Stephen Bernstein, in another of the most valuable assessments of Kelman, observes that "The smallness of event in Kelman's fiction is a conscious strategy, part of a thoroughgoing socialist commitment" (2000: 52). Offering numerous useful readings of particular Kelman stories, Bernstein cites *Greyhound for Breakfast* as a "turning point" for Kelman's short fiction" (2000: 59). In fact, the collection can be ranked among Kelman's most important books, as this essay will aim to show by examining selected stories from the volume and by returning to "Forgetting to Mention Allende" as a particularly good illustration both of the nuances of Kelman's approach to short fiction and of the centrality of the form to his career.

In his 2004 book *James Kelman*, as of 2007 still the only full-length study of Kelman's work, H. Gustav Klaus proposes that Kelman's short stories are "an excellent point of entry into his oeuvre" (2004: 10). Yet, it seems equally valid to treat critical assessments of that oeuvre as points of entry into *Greyhound for Breakfast*. Craig suggests that "Kelman's narratives . . . are concerned fundamentally . . . not with the progress implied by a narrative sequence but with repetition–repetition as the systematisation and dehumanisation to which working-class people, above all others, are subjected" (1993: 105). This assessment is borne out by several of Kelman's novels, particularly his first, *The Busconductor Hines* (1984), whose title character struggles with the numbing routines of his job and with equally unpromising alternatives.

Craig's point about the way repetition is built into the worlds of Kelman's characters serves to counter critical objections such as those of Michiko Kakutani, whose *New York Times* review of *Greyhound for Breakfast* saw the "inability to come up with more than half a dozen situations" (quoted by Bernstein 2000: 45) as an indication of fundamental imaginative poverty on Kelman's part. Many of Kelman's stories – particularly those in *Not Not While the Giro* and *Lean Tales* – do contribute to his exploration of the dehumanizing rituals of exploitative employment, of chronic unemployment, and of pursuits such as drinking, gambling, and wandering that his characters often resort to. The title of one such story, "The same is here again," about a Glaswegian "washed up" homeless in London (*Lean Tales* 12), could describe the kind of response that Kakutani expresses, and the self-absorption of individual Kelman protagonists can be repellent. However, reading through Kelman's stories draws attention to the variation within their repetition. *Lean Tales* provides a case in point: while most of Kelman's 96-page portion of the volume consists of brief narratives about men marooned in idleness and vagrancy, the two longest pieces, "O jesus, here come the dwarfs" and "A Night Boilerman's Notes," both suggest that work can be even stranger than unemployment. The latter story's title character has hellish tasks – the boiler he must stoke inhabits a dangerous factory basement that contains mysterious "black holes, . . . cavities and short tunnels" (99) – yet he expresses a degree of job satisfaction that seems unusual, even perverse. He reflects, "It wasnt good when I had to sit by the black holes at first, some of my imaginings were horrible. I just had to stick it out and conquer myself" (99). The nightboilerman's description of this adjustment offers a metaphor for the way in which other Kelman focal characters endure circumstantial ordeals and confront existential "black holes," and in so doing it suggests that industrial employment and post-industrial unemployment are uncannily related conditions.

Klaus argues that "to seize only on the desolate and disturbing aspects of Kelman's world is to misread him" (2004: 59), and it is in the range of Kelman's stories that alternatives to the desolate and disturbing are most often represented. If the multiplicity of Kelman's stories serves as a metonym for his insistence on the value and diversity of ordinary lives, *Greyhound for Breakfast*, with forty-seven separate pieces, must be among his key books. Twenty-four of the volume's stories are fewer than two pages, and many of these are single paragraphs. Graeme Macdonald notes that in the absence of traditional "helpful, authoritative narrator[s]," these very short stories "turn on enigma, inference, speculation, and insecurity" (2006: 132) and thus invite the reader to assume interpretative responsibility. Two back-to-back examples of these very short pieces suggest the variety of ways in which they solicit active response. "An Old Story" (*Greyhound*, Kelman 1987: 185) is a dialog in which one speaker, who seems both anxious and reluctant to tell a story about a depressed young woman, is prompted by the other:

> But you've got to tell it. You've got to tell it. Unless . . . if it's no really a story at all.
> Oh aye Christ it's a story, dont worry about that.

The text ends here, leaving the reader to worry about precisely what kind of a story the piece may be. The "story" in question is perhaps, as Klaus suggests, that of "the first character's uneasiness, delusion, pain and self-reproach" (2004: 64), or more generally that of persistently problematic relations between women and men; yet possibly, too, this text can be read as Kelman's wry or even playful acknowledgement of his own reliance on the enigmatic and recurring emphasis on barriers to communication. More overtly provocative is the next story, "dear o dear" (*Greyhound*, Kelman 1987: 186), in which a 23-year-old man who is "going through a bad patch with the wife" describes a miniskirted, orange-haired woman who tempts him sexually. The piece draws on, in fact *with*, the techniques of concrete poetry: the words are arranged so as to form a recognizably detailed outline of a woman's skirted body poised in semi-profile. The reader, in looking the text up and down on the page, is made to mimic the speaker's act of gazing. In thus drawing attention to its male point of view, and appearing where it does in the volume, the story hints that men's tendency to objectify women may be an "old story" that continues to impede communication. Yet the story's form also dramatizes the resistance to totalizing interpretation and judgment that Macdonald points out in Kelman's work, since it serves to remind us that we, like the narrator, are seeing the woman only in outline.

Enigmatic brevity and implicit self-reflexivity are qualities that Kelman stories such as these share with some of the works of Franz Kafka (see Klaus 2004: 63–4). "In With the Doctor," one of the longer and seemingly more traditional stories in *Greyhound*, takes up Kelman's affinities with Kafka in a way that is more sustained and explicit, yet presents its own enigmas. The title refers both to the story's fairly ordinary basic situation, which has a man seeing a doctor about his sore back, and to the strange "in," or special status, that the man seems to have with the doctor. Instead of treating his patient, the doctor begins to discuss Kafka's story "The Country Doctor," whose title character he emulates in being oddly reluctant, perhaps unable or even afraid, to perform his professional duties. The doctor complains to the would-be patient about his job and his personal life, and the man grows inwardly restive. When he reveals that he is unemployed, class tensions surface: the patient accuses the doctor of being elitist; the doctor mocks the patient's presumptive socialism (125). The exchange becomes weirdly protracted, extending through a moment in which, in another echo of the Kafka story, the doctor attempts to dismiss the patient untreated (127; see Kafka 1919/1995: 238–9). The doctor continues to ramble about his own situation, and the patient finally explodes into a personal attack, but immediately begins to worry that in so doing he has "gone over the score" (Kelman 1987: 130). The final sentence could sum up the story's stance toward the reader: "He looked at me in an odd way, and I knew it was what to do next was the problem" (131). Like the doctor, the story declines to commit itself to a diagnosis.

As in the shorter works discussed above, the uncertain ending challenges – or trusts – the reader with the task of assessing an array of possible meanings. The Kafka intertext seems to be Kelman's implicit acknowledgement of the creative debt also evident in at least one other story in *Greyhound*, "Benson's Visitor," which, like "The

Country Doctor," depicts a mysteriously inexorable yet oddly matter-of-fact blurring of boundaries between the sick and the well. However, a reading of "In With The Doctor" as homage to Kafka is complicated by the fact that it is the dysfunctional doctor who is aligned with the author through his interest in classic short-story writers, while the understandably irritated patient seems increasingly keen to distance himself from these. The story implies that simply mentioning a distinctive figure like Kafka is not necessarily a constructive intellectual gesture; perhaps it even hints that literary allusiveness and inter-textuality are double-edged strategies for working-class writers, since they may carry associations with middle-class privilege or intellectual elitism. Yet the doctor's Kafka-like sensibilities might also be read as insinuating that disorientation, stagnation, and purposelessness can extend across class barriers, while the patient's concern that his belligerence has been excessive, and his overall uncertainty as to whose fault exactly the contretemps is, complicates any attempt to interpret the story as essentially a description of one incident in a class struggle. The story conveys a sense of balance and nuance that enhances Kelman's own general credibility as an oblique commentator on social or political matters.

Paradoxically, the recurrence of unresolved, ambiguous, and otherwise-uncertain communications helps to link the stories in *Greyhound*. The collection might be read as a primer on ways in which, and reasons why, individuals fail to speak meaningfully with one another. In "End of a Beginning" a naive young man who has migrated to London for work has a disastrous encounter with a fellow rooming-house inmate, who drunkenly misinterprets his innocuous question "Can one eat in one's room?" (Kelman 1987: 79) and stabs him in a rage. This story's focus on a conventionally dramatic event makes it atypical of Kelman and throws into relief the volume's prevailing emphasis on things that do not (quite, fully) occur. The title story, "Greyhound for Breakfast," offers a particularly sustained example of this emphasis. An unemployed Glaswegian, Ronnie, buys a racing greyhound on an impulse that he struggles to explain to pub cronies: "see if this fucking dog doesn't get me the holiday money I'll eat it for my fucking breakfast" (210). Interactions among men in pubs, and ways in which alcohol provokes the desire to communicate yet takes away the performance, are often featured in Kelman's work. Yet one of Ronnie's friends, McInnes, shrewdly diagnoses that the greyhound is connected to events in Ronnie's family life: "Your boy's fucked off to England and you've went out and bought a dog" (211). As the story continues and Ronnie walks the city, evidently unwilling to return home and face his wife, he seems better able to communicate with the patient, dignified animal than with fellow humans: "There was something about it; it made him feel a bit sorry as well, a kind of courage in the way it walked, its head quite high" (215); "The greyhound was looking at him. It had tugged on the leash to make him notice" (216). However, as the story, and the volume, ends, the extent to which Ronnie's regard for the dog is a hopeful sign remains unclear. (For a more detailed reading of the story, see Bernstein 2000: 59–60.) Ronnie, dwelling obsessively on dire possibilities that could await his son in London (and thus referring the reader back to "End of a Beginning"), lapses into incoherent, repetitive interior monologue: "it was just so fucking terrible you couldnt fucking man you fucking Jesus Christ trying to think about that . . ." (230). Liam McIlvanney describes a similar passage from *The Busconductor Hines* as representing "the syncopation of despair, the mind stuttering through a realization it can hardly bear to contemplate" (2002: 204). Language itself can fall among the things devalued or outworn for many Kelman characters, and passages in which profanity expresses impotence or exhaustion, rather than aggression, recur in Kelman's fiction; linguistic poverty stands for other kinds of deprivation, and the proliferation of profanity itself becomes a form of understatement.

The protagonist of "Forgetting to Mention Allende," Tommy McGoldrick, has much in common with Ronnie, yet is also significantly better off. McGoldrick is evidently unemployed, while his wife works as a supermarket cashier (54). Klaus focuses on this economic situation, linking it to the effects of "the twin forces of deindustrialization and privatization" which, since the 1970s, when the story is presumably set, have devalued traditional working-class jobs for men while creating new – and often exploitative – positions, particularly for women, "in the retail and service sector" (2004: 70). As Klaus notes, the story's attention to the effects of this process at a domestic level links it to the work of female writers such as Agnes Owens. Thus, "Allende" helps to offset and contextualize the masculine preoccupation of many other pieces in *Greyhound*. McGoldrick, though lacking paid employment, is not without meaningful work: he is both painting the flat and parenting his and his wife's three children, and the opening sentences provide more than a hint that these activities are a full-time job:

> The milk was bubbling over the sides of the saucepan. He rushed to the oven, grabbed the handle and held the pan in the air. The wean was pulling at his trouser-leg, she gripped the material. (Klaus 2004: 49)

In the relative absence of traditional plot, what is often gripping in Kelman's stories is the focal characters' negotiation of their various individual tasks. This passage exemplifies Kelman's own "grip on the material": his precise exploration of the intricate logistics of the everyday situations, or what McIlvanney, alluding to the story, calls the "intimate small-scale nightmares" (2002: 205; see also Klaus 2004: 7) that loom large in his protagonists' lives.

The sense of intimacy is extended for the reader by Kelman's distinctive handling of voice and narration. "Allende" illustrates multitasking as both a household and a textual operation. McGoldrick's parental tasks are compounded by the building's deficient soundproofing, which has been allowing a neighbor's record-playing to interfere with his daughter's naps: "He had tried; he had put her down and sat with her, read part of a story: it was hopeless but, the fucking music, blasting out" (Klaus 2004: 49). The use of *but* for *though*, like that of *wean* for *child* in the passage quoted above, exemplifies Kelman's unobtrusive way of making working-class Scots diction a distinctive but accessible feature of his style, while the combination of formal punctuation and f-word deftly expresses McGoldrick's inner condition of needing to maintain self-control yet also to register stress. More generally, the sentence illustrates Kelman's technique for moving past what he refers to in a 1989 interview as "'that standard third party narrative voice'" (quoted by Bernstein 2000: 54–5), whose conventional adherence to standard English implies a judgment on the idiomatic, idiosyncratic, or improper language of characters' voices as represented in dialog or interior monologue. As Craig observes, "Kelman's particular use of free indirect discourse" permits "the fusion of the spoken with the written, so that the narrative voice itself can take on the characteristics of a speaking voice" (1993: 103). True, characters and their voices remain Kelman's constructions (see Bernstein 2000: 55), but his work, along with that of Tom Leonard, his long-time colleague and ally among Glasgow writers, has succeeded in what Leonard calls the "presentation of voice as a fact" (1976/1995: 95) and more specifically in establishing the fact of working-class Scots as a valid literary idiom. (On the importance to recent Scottish writing of Kelman's treatment of voice, see e.g., Murphy 2006: 183–4.)

While "Forgetting to Mention Allende" pays close attention to McGoldrick's thoughts, the text also indicates that he remains engaged with his surroundings. Consideration for children is one of the more consistently positive traits of Kelman's focal characters, and McGoldrick's patience is conveyed as he feeds his daughter ("Thanks, he said, and bent to lift the pieces. The carpet loves broken biscuits. Daddy loves picking them up as well") and persuades her to keep trying to nap: "Just make stories out of the picture, he told her, indicating the wall" (50). McGoldrick's words here suggest that he recognizes a kind of solidarity between himself and the child, and they might also be read as linking him with his creator. Though McGoldrick is painting walls and not representational pictures, his gradual progress can be paralleled with Kelman's pursuit of a career in making stories while, as he puts it "Time was short and energy limited" by the demands of domesticity (Kelman 2002: 40). The title story of *Greyhound for Breakfast* emphasizes the familial stresses that economic uncertainty can exacerbate, and such matters are revisited even more traumatically in "By the Burn," the concluding story of Kelman's next collection, *The Burn* (1991). "Allende," however, contributes to a more hopeful view of family life as a basis for constructive engagement with the world, which also runs through Kelman's work and which finds particularly optimistic expression in "The Norwest Reaches," from Kelman's most recent collection, *The Good Times* (1998).

After McGoldrick succeeds in seeing off the missionaries, and their repetitive suggestions that his non-belief in God is a "big thing" that he ought to discuss with them, the story's title is explained: "Then he suddenly shook his head. He had forgotten to mention Allende. He always meant to mention Allende to the bastards. Fuck it" (55). The reference to Salvador Allende Gossens, the Marxist Chilean President elected in 1970 and killed after a military coup on September 11, 1973, serves, as Klaus notes, "to situate the story in the mid-1970s" (2004: 70). Since he identifies the missionaries as "Mormons probably" (54), McGoldrick presumably associates them with the global influence of the United States and with American support for the overthrow of the Chilean leader. McGoldrick himself may be disappointed in his failure to speak out, but it serves to dramatize one small way in which apparent apathy toward politics and other "big things" may develop from distraction and fatigue. Crucially, though it ends with the protagonist set to resume his domestic tasks, the story itself patently does not forget to mention Allende: the title both forecasts and contradicts the act of omission that will occur at the end. In dramatizing the act of forgetting to mention Allende, the story as a whole invites the reader to recall the Chilean leader – or to find out who he was – and to consider why he might be important to a working-class Glaswegian. Kelman's technique works to challenge not only hierarchies between narrator and character but also ones between author and reader: the story declines to preach explicitly about the political concerns that help to drive it, and its understatement implies respect for the intelligence and independence of its audience.

"Forgetting to Mention Allende" might be read as both a precursor and a supplement to Kelman's most recent novel, *You Have to Be Careful in the Land of the Free* (2004), whose first-person protagonist, an expatriate Scot in a dystopian, xenophobic United States of the near future (or perhaps the present), finds himself constantly on the brink of the kind of political confrontation that McGoldrick avoids. The novel implies, from its title on, that understatement may be a tactical necessity for those with dissident convictions. Kelman himself suggests in a 2003 interview that "My politics is really irrelevant to my work; there's no place for it" (Toremans 2003: 580). This remark, like the title of "Forgetting to Mention Allende," employs the ingeniously disingenuous rhetorical device known as paralipsis or preterition, whereby one draws attention to something in the very act of professing to omit reference to it. The place of politics in many of Kelman's best works is in readers' potential responses to his provocative understatements. Such pronouncements as the foregoing come perilously close to the kind of judgmental discourse that Kelman resists; acts of understatement, like jokes, can be betrayed by analysis. Yet a larger betrayal might be in opting not to explore the rich interpretative possibilities that Kelman's short fiction presents.

References and Further Reading

Bernstein, S. (2000). "James Kelman," *Review of Contemporary Fiction* 20/3: 42–80.

Bittenbender, J.C. (2000). "Silence, Censorship, and the Voices of *Skaz* in the Fiction of James Kelman," *Bucknell Review* 43/2: 150–65.

Craig, C. (1993). "Resisting Arrest: James Kelman," in G. Wallace and R. Stevenson (eds), *The Scottish Novel since the Seventies: New Visions, Old Dreams*, pp. 99–114. Edinburgh: Edinburgh University Press.

Gardiner, Michael (2004). "James Kelman Interviewed," *Scottish Studies Review* 5/1: 1–14.

Gilbert, Geoff (1999). "Can Fiction Swear? James Kelman and the Booker Prize," in R. Mengham (ed.), *An Introduction to Contemporary Fiction: International Writing in English since 1970*, pp. 219–34. Cambridge: Polity.

Haywood, I. (1997). *Working-class Fiction: From Chartism to Trainspotting*. Plymouth: Northcote House.

Kafka, F. (1995). "A Country Doctor," in *The Metamorphosis, In The Penal Colony, and Other Stories*, trans. J. Neugroschel, pp. 235–43. New York: Scribner (original work published 1919).

Kelman, James (1987). *Greyhound for Breakfast.* London: Picador.

Kelman, James (1991). *The Burn.* London: Minerva.

Kelman, James (1998). *The Good Times.* London: Vintage.

Kelman, James (2002). *"And the Judges Said . . .": Essays.* London: Vintage.

Kelman, James (2004). *You Have to be Careful in the Land of the Free.* London: Hamish Hamilton.

Kelman, J., Owens, A., and Gray, A. (1987). *Lean Tales.* London: Abacus (original work published 1985).

Klaus, H.G. (2004). *James Kelman.* Tavistock: Northcote House.

Leonard, T. (1995). "The Locust Tree in Flower, and Why It Had Difficulty Flowering in Britain," in *Intimate Voices: Selected Work 1965–1983*, pp. 95–102. London: Vintage (original work published 1976).

Macdonald, G. (2006). "James Kelman," in C.A. Malcolm and D. Malcolm (eds), *British and Irish Short-Fiction Writers, 1945–2000, Dictionary of Literary Biography*, vol. 319, pp. 128–36. Detroit, New York, San Francisco, San Diego, New Haven, Waterville, London and Munich: Thomson/Gale.

McIlvanney, L. (2002). "The Politics of Narrative in the Post-War Scottish Novel," in Z. Leader (ed), *On Modern British Fiction*, pp. 181–203. Oxford: Oxford University Press.

Milne, D. (2003). "The Fiction of James Kelman and Irvine Welsh: Accents, Speech and Writing," in R.J. Lane, R. Mengham and P. Tew (eds), *Contemporary British Fiction*, pp. 158–73. Cambridge: Polity.

Murphy, T.P. (2006). " 'Getting Rid of That Standard Third Party Narrative Voice': The Development of James Kelman's Early Authorial Style," *Language and Literature* 15/2: 183–99.

Pitchford, N. (2000). "How Late it was for England: James Kelman's Scottish Booker Prize," *Contemporary Literature* 41/4: 693–725.

Toremans, T. (2003). "An Interview with Alasdair Gray and James Kelman," *Contemporary Literature* 44/4: 564–86.

Woolf, Virginia (1966). "Modern Fiction," *Collected Essays*, vol. 2, pp. 103–10. London: Hogarth Press (original work published 1925).

49

Hanif Kureishi:
Love in a Blue Time

Patrick Lonergan

Love in a Blue Time is Hanif Kureishi's first collection of short fiction, gathering ten stories that explore identity and its relationship to sexuality, ethnicity, and gender. The stories are set in the post-Thatcher Britain of the mid-1990s, presenting a vision of a London depressed by economic stagnation, social disintegration, and the ubiquity of mass-mediated culture.

Although Kureishi's exploration of these themes is rooted in a specific space and time, his book has broader resonances. Its exploration of the radicalization of Muslim youth in Britain became particularly pertinent after September 11, 2001, and the subsequent wars in Afghanistan and Iraq. Its treatment of relationships would be developed in Kureishi's later work, notably his controversial 1998 novella *Intimacy*. Unlike much of his other writing, *Love in a Blue Time* reveals and pays homage to Kureishi's literary influences, featuring epigraphs from Robert Louis Stevenson and Italo Calvino, while modeling one story ("My Son the Fanatic") on a work by Philip Roth and another ("Lately") on Anton Chekhov's "The Duel." Furthermore, his representation of London as a site of chaos and *anomie* places his fiction in the tradition of urban realism, recalling the works of Zola and the later Dickens, while mapping territory also explored by Zadie Smith, Ian McEwan, and others. Finally, the book is important within Kureishi's own *oeuvre*, acting as a transition from his early works about ethnicity to his later period, which is characterized by a greater focus on individualism.

Kureishi's opening story defines the preoccupations that are explored throughout the collection. "In a Blue Time" focuses on a male artist-figure whose relationships with others are unsatisfying and frequently exploitative. This artist will attempt to distract himself from the resultant lack of fulfilment and guilt by abusing alcohol and drugs, and by seeking casual sexual encounters that are shown to be more satisfying when anticipated than they are when consummated.

Roy is a film-maker awaiting news about a proposal to direct a movie based on his own script. His sense of hope – and the likelihood of his failure – is revealed through

Roy's interactions with two characters: Jimmy, an old friend, and Clara, Roy's partner. Jimmy leads a directionless and often dangerous life of "alcoholism, unhappiness, failure, [and] ill-health" that Roy believes makes Jimmy attractive to women: Jimmy "showered them with despair and guiltlessly extracted as much concern as they might proffer" (Kureishi 1997: 9). Clara in contrast offers stability – albeit of a prosaic kind – to Roy. They have recently moved in together, and she is expecting his child; she appears to take for granted Roy's ability to achieve success, and plans carefully for their future.

Ironically, however, Roy's respect – and indeed his love – is reserved not for Clara but for Jimmy, whose hedonistic lifestyle he clearly desires for himself. Roy "decided that he loved his friend [and] envied his easy complacency" (14); earlier in the story, he thinks of Jimmy in relation to Montaigne's remark about friendship: "If I were pressed to say why I love him, I feel that my only reply could be "Because it was he, because it was I'" (9). He sees his relationship with Clara is considerably more nega-tive terms. He "disliked talking to his friends in front of her [because] she seemed to scrutinise him" (1). His attempts to seduce her involve having "scrupulously . . . to avoid her getting the right idea" about his intentions (12). And, when Roy finally recognizes that he "would have to live with himself as he was," he projects his sense of self-loathing on to his partner – "Clara would be ashamed of him", we are told – instead of acknowledging it himself (34). Roy therefore is capable of seeing people only in relation to himself.

His love for Jimmy arises from his inability to abandon the sense of identity he had constructed many years before:

> The problem was that at the back of Roy's world-view lay the Rolling Stones, and the delinquent dream of adolescence – the idea that vigour and spirit existed in excess, authenticity and the romantic unleashed self: a bourgeois idea that was strictly anti-bourgeois. It had never, finally, been Roy's way, though he'd played at it. But Jimmy had lived it to the end, for both of them. (Kureishi 1997: 38)

Jimmy's existence thus allows Roy to believe that he is fulfilling his dreams, albeit through identifying himself with someone else's life.

Likewise, Clara exists for Roy only as a manifestation of the responsibilities which he knows he ought to face but cannot. In seeing her in this way, he loses sight of her individuality, and is therefore frequently surprised when her actions fail to match his low expectations. Their sex-life, Roy claims, is "an amicable way of confirming that everything is all right," a statement which encapsulates her role in his life: she acts as a source of stability that Roy resents but also needs (23).

Notably, this story fails to reproduce exactly the title of the collection, omitting the word "love." Roy certainly exists in a "blue time," but his self-absorption makes love impossible: he professes to feel it for Jimmy because doing so costs him nothing, but can think of Clara only in terms of what she offers him. This is made explicit at the conclusion, which presents an apparently optimistic note: we are told that Roy "wanted to get back, to see what was between [him and Clara] and learn what it might give him" (40). Because we have seen no indication that Roy is capable of building a successful relationship with Clara – and because his interest remains in what their relationship would "give him" – it seems likely that his good intentions will not be realized.

This failure can be related to Roy's personality, but it is also pertinent to his environment: the "blue time" in which he lives should be seen as a moment in the life of his society. Roy may be an unlikeable character, but he is similar to many of the people in his immediate environment, who live in an "age when men and women with energy and restlessness but without much ability or persistence excelled" (16), their mediocrity evident in a lust for the impermanent and the superficial. Roy, like his fellow citizens,

> loved returning from the shops and opening the designer bags, removing the tissue, and trying on different combinations of clothes while playing the new CDs . . . He adored the new restaurants, bars, clubs, shops, galleries, made of black metal, chrome or neon, each remaining fashionable for a month, if it was lucky. Life had become like a party at the end of the world. (Kureishi 1997: 16)

These themes are further elaborated in "Blue Blue Pictures of You," a story about a photographer who is asked to create a portrait of two acquaintances having sex. When he brings the photographs to the couple, the woman speaks of her sense of boredom with life:

> London was full of drugged useless people who didn't listen to one another but merely thought all the time of how to distract themselves and never spoke of anything serious. She was tired of it; she was even tired of being in love; it had become another narcotic. (Kureishi 1997: 117)

The photographer likes to think of himself as an artist; his commission from his friends has made him fear he might be a pornographer. But this passage reveals he is something else: merely a distraction, another narcotic used by the couple for a fleeting sensation of participating in something unusual.

We therefore learn that the collection's title should be seen as interrogative rather than descriptive: *Love in a Blue Time* considers whether love is possible when personal identity has been undermined by the promotion of instant gratification through consumption. The "blue time" experienced by London society has reduced individuals to consumers, alienating them not only from each other, but most importantly, from their sense of personal identity. Roy in "In a Blue Time" is capable of understanding himself only through others and, in doing so, loses sight of how those people are important in their own right. His sense of individuality becomes fragmented, as his relationships become increasingly meaningless. This process will dominate the remainder of the collection.

Kureishi's interest in the instability of identity is most explicitly realized in his approach to narrative. Most of the stories in *Love in a Blue Time* are presented in a third-person narrative by an apparently omniscient narrator. However, the authorial point of view frequently matches that of each story's principal character, resulting in an accumulation of different and sometimes contradictory perspectives on similar events. This makes it difficult to determine the collection's moral or authorial center, to locate the presence of Kureishi himself. *Love in a Blue Time* may therefore be seen as presenting a vision of authorship that is as fragmentary as the identities of the characters in the stories themselves. This is particularly noticeable in "The Tale of the Turd," "The Flies," and "With Your Tongue Down My Throat."

"The Tale of the Turd" makes this process clear: we begin with an apparently realistic setting, in which an engaging first-person narrator describes an apparently everyday event: an introduction to his girlfriend's parents. It is revealed that his relationship with her is exploitative: he is considerably older than she, and appears to value her primarily for her youth, referring to her rather disturbingly as "my little girl" (134). He also maintains her dependency on him by providing her with heroin.

As the narrator's revelations become more distasteful, the tone shifts into a hallu-cinatory style that recalls the works of William Burroughs. The narrator has excused himself from his girlfriend's parents' dinner-party to use the bathroom; his attempts to flush away the "turd" referred to in the story's title fail repeatedly; he panics, and considers altering the entire course of his life before concluding that it is "too late for all that" (136). These considerations are interspersed by his growing fear of his "turd": "I glance at [it] and notice little teeth in its velvet head, and a little mouth opening. It's smiling at me, oh no . . . and, what's that, it's winking, yes" (136). By the story's conclusion, Kureishi's readers' perspective has been thoroughly destabilized: we begin by identifying with a narrator who is engagingly frank and unpretentious, but become confused by the rapid shifts to and from the irrational in his account of events.

A similar process of destabilization occurs in the collection's concluding story, "The Flies." In a narrative that begins with a familiar treatment of marital discord, we are introduced to the residents of an apartment block, who are attempting to deal with an infestation of flies. Doing so involves hiring a series of "Operatives," who issue threatening and increasingly bureaucratic instructions. The residents become suspicious and envious of each other as the story develops into a Kafkaesque nightmare. While we are encouraged to identify with the story's protagonists, we do not share their point of view; rather the tone of the narrative is as bureaucratic and clinical as that of the "Operatives" whose instructions torment the apartments' residents: the plot is revealed in a consistently reasonable tone, which carefully enumerates, cata-logues, and describes all of the story's most important details. As in "The Tale of the Turd," there is a shift from the rational to the irrational; but the reader must also share the perspective of the people who are responsible for the misery inflicted upon the characters. Both stories thus involve an approach to narrative that seeks to make the reader uncomfortable. Readers naturally aim to identify with and trust all narrators; Kureishi assumes this trust, builds upon it, and then turns it upon his readers, forcing them to question their own values.

The fragmentation of authorship is most evident in the collection's fourth story, "With Your Tongue Down my Throat," which is (ostensibly) told by Nina, a young British-Asian woman. The action is focused on Nina's relationship with her half-sister Nadia. In the story's first part, Nadia visits London, staying with Nina, Nina's mother, and her mother's partner Howard, who is described as a "radical {ha!} television writer and well-known toss-pot" (62). Later, Nina travels with Nadia to their father's home in Pakistan.

The story appears preoccupied with themes familiar from Kureishi's earlier work, notably the clash of values between immigrants living abroad and their compatriots at home. The two sisters appear to occupy opposite ends of the moral spectrum. Nina jokingly refers to her "smack addiction, my two abortions," and her suicidal tendencies (74), which are related in the story to her social status. Nadia describes herself (rather pompously) as dedicated to helping others: "I'm training to be a doctor, you see," she states. "My life is set against human harm" (71). This ambition is related to her father's status as a member of the social elite within Pakistan, and to Nadia's own sense of helplessness within a society that seeks to determine and limit her sexual behavior, her marital prospects, and almost everything else about her.

Despite these apparent differences, the sisters have much in common, particularly their attitudes towards relationships. In one crucial scene, both sisters' attitudes are revealed to be very similar when they make love with different men. Nadia tells the reader that when she kisses Billy, her lover:

> I get a renewal of this strange sensation that I've never felt before today: I feel it's Billy I'm kissing, not just his lips or body, but some inside thing, as if his skin is just a representative of all of him, his past and his blood. (Kureishi 1997: 97)

Moments later, she observes Nadia in a similar situation, and realizes that her sister "only wants to be held and kissed and touched" (98). The point being made here is that, although each woman is working against different social limitations and occupying different roles within her social hierarchy, both are prevented from expressing themselves fully by their societies.

Nina is perhaps the most engaging of Kureishi's narrators in *Love in a Blue Time.* Her tone and outlook contrast strongly with the narrators of the book's other stories: she is humorous and insightful, self-aware and self-possessed; she has a firm sense of her own identity, as well as a sensitivity to others. She is perhaps unstable, and will ultimately be rejected by her father's family, but one senses from the strength of character she displays that some progress will be possible for her. And the story's trajectory also appears more positive than in the rest of the book: Nina builds a meaningful relationship not only with Billy, but also forms a substantial connection with her sister. Nina's personality is perhaps best encapsulated by the story's title: "With Your Tongue Down My Throat" is frank and erotic, and (unlike the other stories in the book) suggests the possibility that two people can form a connection.

But that title has multiple meanings. It is revealed in the closing moments that the narrative voice and much of the plot are an invention: the story's final section opens with the following interpolation:

> Hello, reader. As I'm sure you've noticed by now, I, Howard, have written this Nina and Nadia stuff . . . all along, it's been me, pulling faces, speaking in tongues, posing and making an attempt on the truth through lies. (Kureishi 1997: 102)

"The tongue" down Nina's throat thus belongs to Howard: his voice has appropriated hers, both strangling and silencing her. Kureishi's sleight of hand it to have convinced the reader that this story is different to the others in the collection: in fact, we learn that we have simply witnessed another expression of the author as an exploitative, appropriative figure.

The theme of the instability of identity is broadened in a number of stories that consider issues of ethnicity, gender, and social class. The collection's second story, "We're not Jews," deals with ethnic identity in a tone that recalls Kureishi's earlier works, focusing on a British-Asian child who cannot fully identify himself with English society or the culture of his immigrant father. Azhar and his white mother Yvonne are being harassed on a bus journey by a racist father and son, Big and Little Billy: the two males persistently insult Azhar and his mother, making sexual references to Yvonne, and flinging racial stereotypes at the pair. Yvonne is upset by this and, having attempted to ignore the insults, is finally reduced to a surprising outburst: "Mother's lips were moving but her throat must have been dry: no words came, until she managed to say 'We're not Jews'" (45).

Yvonne's decision to use racism to defend herself against racism provides an interesting perspective on the issue of ethnic tension within Britain. The narrator of "We're Not Jews" explains that Yvonne "refused to allow the word 'immigrant' to be used about Father, since in her eyes it applied only to illiterate tiny men with downcast eyes and mismatched clothes" (45). Racial identity is therefore shown not to exist in terms of the binaries of black and white, or powerful and powerless. Instead, it is revealed as operating within a social hierarchy. Yvonne's identity is clearly based on a need to differentiate herself from others: by defining "immigrants" or the Jewish people as inferior, she asserts her own sense of value – her resistance to denigration is not based on a sense of her own worth, but instead a sense of her superiority to others.

Similar forms of discrimination are considered throughout the collection. The stories constantly reveal the extent to which male characters' difficulty in relating to women arises from their casual misogyny and an inability to see women as anything more than objects of sexual gratification. This theme is explored most thoroughly in "D'Accord Baby," in which Bill sets out to "fuck the daughter of the man who had fucked his wife" (52). This act of infidelity will be revenge both on the man who slept with Bill's wife Nicola, and on Nicola herself. Bill's vengeance offers him "a triumphant few days of gratification anticipated" (56), which allows him to alter his attitude to his wife: "As Nicola walked about the flat, dressing, cooking, reading, searching for her glasses, he could enjoy despising her" (56). When Bill's plan is finally realized, he feels no physical pleasure but instead "wanted nothing more than for his friends to see him" (59). The status of the woman with whom Bill sleeps is entirely irrelevant here.

The story "Nightlight" offers a different perspective on this form of objectification, describing a man and a woman who meet each Wednesday, and sleep with each other without ever speaking – never, in fact, knowing each other's name. There may be exploitation involved in such a relationship but, if so, it is an agreed exploitation: each of the participants is a mystery to the other, and their exchange is mutually beneficial.

Nevertheless, their relationship arises from failure. London, the narrator suggests, is a "city of love-vampires, turning from person to person, hunting the one who will make the difference" (142). The unnamed male protagonist is involved in the affair because of his difficult married life:

> He is starving for want of love. The shame of loneliness, a dingy affliction! There are few creatures more despised than middle-aged men with strong desires, and desire renews itself each day, returning like a recurrent illness, crying out, more life, more! (Kureishi 1997: 144)

Nothing is revealed of the woman however. "What wound or hopelessness," asks the narrator, "has made her want only this?" (141). Some speculation is provided, but we learn little about her motivations.

"Nightlight" is, thus, an example of the collection's treatment of sex, which is consistently presented not as the merging of two identities, but as the obliteration of selfhood. In "D'Accord Baby," Bill kisses his lover "until her forgot where he was, or who they both were, until there was nothing they wanted, and there was only the most satisfactory peace" (60). In "Tongue," Nina's sexual encounter with Billy involves their "bodies dissolving until we forget ourselves and think of nothing, thank fuck" (96). Sex thus offers freedom from identity, a longed-for forgetfulness that brings the characters peace.

This desire to flee reality through sensation is evident in other ways in the collection. Drug-taking and alcohol abuse are portrayed as offering a sense of liberation which, in some cases, actually makes the characters behave more positively towards each other. In "Lately," the central characters, Rocco and Lisa, are deeply unsatisfied with each other – but Lisa touchingly refers to one occasion when her partner "was kissing me . . . all over my face." She claims that he was unaware that he was doing it: "Rocco's at his sweetest when he's unconscious" (170).

This use of sensation to flee the tedium of existence is interestingly contextualized by "My Son the Fanatic," in which religion is presented as a narcotic that, like alcohol or marijuana, allows for the sublimation of the self. Modeled on Philip Roth's 1959 short story "Eli the Fanatic," the story presents the growing concern of Parvez, a Bradford taxi driver, for his son's welfare. The son "was outgrowing his teenage attitudes," disposing of his toys, clothes, and other possessions, while "parting from the English girlfriend who used to stop coming to the house. His friends had stopped ringing" (119). Parvez's fear, which is likely to be shared by the reader, is that his son has become addicted to drugs, a supposition made more likely given that the previous five stories have featured characters experiencing various forms of dependency on, and addiction, to narcotics.

Parvez soon discovers that his son has however become influenced by fundamentalist Islamic teachings:

> The Law of Islam would rule the world; the skin of the infidel would burn off again and again; the Jews and the Christians would be routed. The West was a sink of hypocrites, homosexuals, drug takers and prostitutes. (Kureishi 1997: 126)

Parvez's objections to these views arise from two causes. The first is that, in his own words, he "love[s] England" (126): his decision to ignore some of the rules of his religion initially arose from a desire to "fit in" to English society (124), but he enjoys doing so. And the second difficulty is that he objects to being "told by my own son that I am going to hell" (127). The story concludes with Parvez savagely beating up his son, asking "through his split lip 'So who's the fanatic now?'" (131).

Viewed in isolation, the story may be seen as an exploration of the radicalization of Islamic youth in the West; indeed, the story was later reprinted in Kureishi's *The Word and the Bomb* (2005), a collection of stories and essays about the post-9/11 world. Yet its relevance to the stories in *Love in a Blue Time* is also worth exploring. The response of Parvez's son to British society is unique within the book, but he is reacting to the same problems as the other characters: a feeling of deep dissatisfaction with his society, an objection to the meaningless of human relationships, and a desire to find something more substantial and lasting from his environment. The value of this comparison should not be underestimated: Kureishi displays that Islamic fundamentalism is not a problem of the Muslim Community, but that it arises from social problems that affect all sections of British (and indeed Western) society. The same is true of discrimination and racism, which is not simply enacted by the strong against the weak, but instead part of the system of human relationships within British society.

"My Son the Fanatic" has (perhaps unsurprisingly) gained more attention and praise than the other stories in the book, as evidenced not only in the reprinting referred to above, but also in its production as a 1997 film for the BBC. Patrice Chereau's 2001 film *Intimacy* is an adaptation of the novella of the same name, but draws substantially from "Nightlight." The success of both films has tended to overshadow responses to the other stories in *Love in a Blue Time*.

Indeed, critical responses to the collection were initially overshadowed by events in Kureishi's private life. His separation from Faber editor Tracey Scoffield, the mother of his two children, and his subsequent relationship with Monique Proudlove, received a great deal of press coverage during 1997 and 1998, the period of the book's release. The misogyny of many of the characters in *Love in a Blue Time* – not to mention the stories' apparent resemblances to events in Kureishi's life – led many critics to accuse him of exploiting personal experience (not to mention the pain of his former partner and their children) for artistic purposes. These criticisms intensified with the publication in 1998 of *Intimacy*. Even those critics who did not consider Kureishi's private life were ambivalent in their responses to the book. Many praised his exploration of contemporary consumerist culture, but there is a tendency in the reviews to criticize his characterization, which is seen as superficial and reductive.

There may be something in such views, but they ignore the fundamental achievement of *Love in a Blue Time*, which is its attempt to find a mode of narrative that can accommodate the experiences of the characters being described; the book also focuses clearly on the morality of an author using personal experience or interpersonal relationships for artistic gain. To read *Love in a Blue Time* involves being confronted with a series of voices that are at turns confusing and confused, amoral and apathetic; it involves facing a series of questions that are often too uncomfortable for us to ask; and it forces recognition of an important theme: that, despite these characters' differences, all are struggling against the same things: alienation, a lack of location, and the fact that their society offers them no hope. To see this achievement in reductively autobiographical terms involves missing the extent to which Kureishi has sought to excavate the truth about contemporary life from the chaos around us. As the author himself puts it, "I think when you're writing, you look for the bits that are difficult . . . You look for conflict. If you think, 'I shouldn't say that,' it's always the things you should say" (qtd by Brockes 2003).

REFERENCES AND FURTHER READING

Brockes, E. (2003). "When You're Writing You Look for Conflict," the *Guardian* (November 17).

Kaleta, K.C. (1998). *Hanif Kureishi: Postcolonial Storyteller*. Austin: University of Texas Press.

Kureishi, H. (1997). *Love in a Blue Time*. London: Faber and Faber.

Kureishi, H. (1998). *Intimacy*. London: Faber.

Kureishi, H. (2005). *The Word and the Bomb*. London: Faber.

Moore-Gilbert, B. (2001). *Hanif Kureishi*. Manchester: Manchester University Press.

Thomas, S. (ed.) (2005). *Hanif Kureishi: A Reader's Guide to Essential Criticism*. London: Palgrave.

Index

Ackroyd, Peter, 361
adventure story, 19–20, 68
Aldington, Richard, 36, 41, 44
  "At All Costs," 37–8
  "The Case of Lieutenant Hall," 36, 41
  Death of a Hero, 39
  "Meditation on a German Grave," 39–42
  Roads to Glory, 36
  "Sacrifice Post," 36, 38–9
Aldiss, Brian, 374, 380, 516–17, 519
  "The Impossible Star," 374–5
  Non-Stop, 517
  Trillion Year Spree, 519
Ali, Monica, 309
Allen, Grant, 88
  "Pallinghurst Barrow," 88
Allingham, Margery, 65–6, 71, 77–8
  Mr. Campion and Others, 77
  "The Case of the White Elephant," 78
  "The Frenchman's Gloves," 78
  "The Hat-Trick," 77
  "Safe As Houses," 78
  The White Cottage Mystery, 77
All the Year Round, 84, 91, *see also* Dickens, Charles
Ambler, Eric, 227
Amazing Stories, 372
Amis, Kingsley, 481
Amis, Martin, 325, 372
  Einstein's Monsters, 372

Anderson, Sherwood, 266
Anglo-Irish War (Irish War of Independence), 60–1, 211, 218
Anglo-Jewish short fiction, 330–41
anti-semitism, 334–5, 338–9, 427
Argosy, 90–1
Arrowsmith, Pat, 365
Astounding Science Fiction, 372
Attlee, Clement, 250–1
Atwood, Margaret, 309, 508
Austen, Jane, 54, 111, 286, 416–17

Babel, Isaac, 213
Baden-Powell, Robert, 27, 67–8
Bailey, Paul, 417, 421
Ballantyne, R.M., 25
Ballard, J.G., 255, 372, 374–6, 380, 516–23
  "Answers to a Questionnaire," 522
  The Atrocity Exhibition, 522
  "The Atrocity Exhibition," 522
  "The Beach Murders," 522
  "First Impressions of London" (essay), 520
  "The Gioconda of the Twilight Noon," 519
  "A Guide to Virtual Death," 521
  "The Illuminated Man," 517
  "The Index," 522
  "The Intensive Care Unit," 521
  "I Smile," 519

"Manhole 69," 376, 519
"Motel Architecture," 520–1
"Notes Towards a Mental Breakdown,"
   522
"Now Wakes the Sea," 519
"The Overloaded Man," 518–19, 521
"Plan for the Assassination of Jacquelyn
   Kennedy," 521–2
"Report from an Obscure Planet," 521
"The Secret History of World War 3,"
   521
"The Subliminal Man," 522
"Terminal Beach," 522
"Theatre of War," 522
"Thirteen to Centaurus," 517–18
"Time Passage," 522
"Venus Hunters," 519–20
Vermilion Sands, 522
"The Voices of Time," 520, 521
War Fever, 522
"Which Way to Inner Space?" 516
"Why I Want to Fuck Ronald Reagan,"
   521–2
Barker, Pat, 369
Barthes, Roland, 385, 500
Bartlett, Neil, 369
Bates, H.E., 11, 253
Baudelaire, Charles, 459
Baxter, Stephen, 380, 382
beast fable, 117–18, 126–7
Beckett, Mary, 342–4
   "A Belfast Woman," 343–4
   "The Excursion," 343
   A Literary Woman, 344
   "Theresa," 343
Beckett, Samuel, 59, 62–3, 184, 254–5,
   265, 384–5, 489, 495
   More Pricks Than Kicks, 62, 265
   Waiting for Godot, 489–91
   Watt, 489
Behan, Brendan, 267
The Bell, 60, 254, 267–8, 272, 448
Bell, Vanessa, 194
Bellerby, Frances, 96–8, 103–5, 111
   The Acorn and the Cup, 103
   A Breathless Child, 103

"The Carol," 104
Come to an End, 103
"Come to an End," 104
"The Cut Finger," 104
"The Doctor," 104
"Pre-War," 104
Bennett, Arnold, 198–9
Bergson, Henri, 490–1
Binchy, Maeve, 272–3
   Central Line, 272
   Dublin 4, 272
   The Lilac Bus, 272
   Victoria Line, 272
Blackwood, Algernon, 88, 91
   "A Case of Eavesdropping," 91
   "The Kit-bag," 88
   The Listener, 88
   Pan's Garden, 88
   "The Willows," 88
Blackwood's Magazine, 19
Boer War, 29–30, 119, 215
Bond, James, 230
Booker Prize, 309, 369, 472, 525, 532–3
Borges, Jorge Luis, 184, 385
Bowen, Elizabeth, 7, 10–11, 45–7, 59,
   62–3, 84, 86, 91–3, 96–8, 108, 111,
   236–43, 253, 265, 267, 360, 362–5,
   402, 421, 423, 480
   Ann Lee's and Other Stories, 105–7, 236,
      241
   "The Apple Tree," 365
   "Breakfast," 242
   "Careless Talk," 46
   The Cat Jumps, 105, 236
   "Coming Home," 105
   "Daffodils," 242
   "A Day in the Dark," 105–6
   The Demon Lover and Other Stories (US
      title: *Ivy Gripped the Steps and Other
      Stories*), 62, 84, 105–7, 236–7, 239,
      265
   "The Demon Lover," 47–8, 93, 237,
      238–40, 365, 421
   Encounters, 105, 236, 241
   "Gone Away," 242
   "Hand in Glove," 93, 105–6

Bowen, Elizabeth (*cont'd*)
  "Human Habitation," 106
  "The Happy Autumn Fields," 105, 365
  "Her Table Spread," 105–6
  In the Heat of the Day, 93
  Joining Charles, 105, 236
  "The Jungle," 365
  Look at All Those Roses, 105, 107, 236, 265
  "Love," 105
  "Mysterious Kôr," 46, 93, 107, 237,
    240–2, 365
  "Oh, Madam," 46–7
  "Pink May," 93
  "The Return," 242
  "The Shadowy Third," 93
  "The Short Story in England," 237
  "Summer Night," 45, 105
  "Sunday Afternoon," 45, 105–7
Boys' Own Paper (B.O.P.), 25–6, 30
Boyle, Patrick, 271–2
  All Looks Yellow to the Jaundiced Eye, 272
  At Night All Cats Are Gray, 272
  "Pastorale," 271–2
  A View from Calvary, 272
Braddon, Mary Elizabeth, 83, 91
Braine, John, 410
Brennan, Maeve, 62
British army, 13–4, 49, 401–8
British empire, 9, 19–20, 30, 42, 65, 81,
    84–5, 119, 132–4, 175–6, 178, 197,
    218, 249–52, 281–2, 308–9, 378,
    380, 520
Brontë, Charlotte, 326
Brontë, Emily, 381
Brooke, Jocelyn, 365
Brophy, Brigid, 367
Broughton, Rhoda, 91
Brown, Father, 68–70, *see also* Chesterton,
  G.K.
Browning, Robert, 456
Buchan, John, 20, 22, 24–5, 85–6
  "Basilissa," 24–5
  "Fountainblue," 22
  "The Green Wildebeest," 28
  "The Grove of Ashtaroth," 28
  The Moon Endureth: Tales and Fancies, 85

Burford, Barbara, 368
  "Dreaming the Sky Down," 368
  The Threshing Floor, 368
  "Miss Jessie," 368
Burgess, Anthony, 365
Burroughs, William, 380, 516, 522, 544
Burt, Simon, 369
  Floral Street, 369
Byatt. A.S., 343, 352–3
  "The Chinese Lobster," 353
  "The Story of the Eldest Princess," 353
  "Sugar," 362–53

Calvino, Italo, 541
Camus, Albert, 494
Carey, Peter, 309
Carleton, William, 52, 58, 272
  Traits and Stories of the Irish Peasantry, 52
  "Wildgoose Lodge," 58
Cather, Willa, 443
Carpenter, Edward, 359, 363
  Ioläus: An Anthology of Friendship, 359
Carson, Michael, 369
Carter, Angela, 255, 326, 343, 350–3, 379,
    507–15
  Angela Carter's Book of Fairy Tales,
    509–10
  "Black Venus," 352
  The Bloody Chamber, 507–15
  "The Bloody Chamber," 351
  "The Company of Wolves," 351–2, 511
  "The Courtship of Mr. Lyon," 511
  "The Erl-King," 508, 511, 513
  "The Lady of the House of Love,"
    510–11
  "The Loves of Lady Purple," 351
  Nights at the Circus, 514
  "Puss-in-Boots," 509
  The Sadeian Woman, 507, 510–11
  "Sleeping Beauty," 510
  "The Snow Child," 508, 511
  "The Tiger's Bride," 511
  "The Werewolf," 513–14
  Wise Children, 510
  "Wolf-Alice," 511–12
Cather, Willa, 443

censorship, 59, 62, 184, 191–2, 254, 264,
  266–8, 270, 448
Chandler, Raymond, 76
Chaudhuri, Nirad C., 119
Chekhov, Anton, 111, 202, 298, 376, 423,
  487, 541
Chesterton, G.K., 68–70, 78
  "The Blue Cross," 69
  "The Eye of Apollo," 69
  "The God of the Gongs," 69
  The Incredulity of Father Brown 68
  The Innocence of Father Brown, 68
  "The Queer Feet," 69
  The Scandal of Father Brown, 68
  The Secret of Father Brown, 68
  "The Sins of Prince Saradine," 69
  "The Wrong Shape," 69
Christie, Agatha, 65, 70–4, 77
  "The Adventure of 'The Western Star',"
    72
  "The Case of the Discontented Husband,"
    74
  The Hound of Death and Other Stories, 74
  "The Incredible Theft," 73
  The Listerdale Mystery and Other Stories, 74
  "The Man in the Mist," 73
  "The Million Dollar Bond Robbery," 73
  *Murder in the Mews and Three Other Poirot
    Cases*, 72
  The Mysterious Mr. Quin, 74
  Parker Pyne Investigates, 73–4
  Partners in Crime, 73
  Poirot Investigates, 72
  The Regatta Mystery and Other Stories, 72
  The Thirteen Problems, 73
  "The Tragedy at Marsdon Moor," 72
  The Under Dog and Other Mysteries, 72
Churchill, Winston, 250, 311
Clarke, Arthur C., 372–4, 382
  Childhood's End, 373
  "Loophole," 373
  "The Nine Billion Names of God,"
    373–4
  "The Star," 373–4
class, 14, 25, 30, 39, 53, 65, 67, 70, 75–8,
  83, 85, 90, 92, 100, 109, 115, 119,
  132, 138, 183, 185, 197, 200, 202–6,
  209, 275–6, 285–8, 409–10, 413–15,
  424–6, 428–9, 476, 480–1, 533–9
Cleland, John, 170
Clifford, Lucy, 89
  "A New Mother," 89
Coetzee, J.M., 309
Collins, William "Wilkie," 66, 91, 144
colonial adventure story (story of colonial
  adventure), 19–32, 59, 70, 116,
  150–1
colonialism, *see* British empire
Colum, Padraic, 56
  The King of Ireland's Son, 56
Compton-Burnett, Ivy, 360, 362
Conan Doyle, Arthur, 26, 27, 57, 65–9, 72,
  78, 88, 90–2
  "The Adventure of the Noble Bachelor,"
    67
  The Adventures of Sherlock Holmes, 66
  "The Boscombe Valley Mystery," 26–7
  "The Captain of the 'Pole Star'," 91
  The Case-Book of Sherlock Holmes, 66
  "The Engineer's Thumb," 68
  "The Final Problem," 67
  His Last Bow, 66
  The Hound of the Baskervilles, 66
  "The Man with the Twisted Lip," 67
  "Lot 249"
  The Memoirs of Sherlock Holmes, 66
  The Return of Sherlock Holmes, 66
  "A Scandal in Bohemia," 67
  The Sign of Four, 66
  A Study in Scarlet, 66
  The Valley of Fear, 66
Conlon, Evelyn, 342, 346–7
  "Taking Scarlet as a Real Colour, or And
    Also, Susan," 346
  "Park-going Days," 347
  "Telling," 346
Conrad, Joseph, 10, 20–4, 31–2, 120, 136,
  149–56, 179
  "Heart of Darkness," 150–1
  "The Lagoon," 24
  Lord Jim, 150–3
  The Mirror of the Sea, 154–5

Conrad, Joseph (*cont'd*)
  Nostromo, 155
  "An Outpost of Progress," 20–2, 149–52,
    155
  "The Planter of Malata," 155
  "The Secret Sharer," 149–56
  The Shadow Line, 150–4
  'Twixt Land and Sea, 151
  "Youth," 23–4, 32, 151
Coppard, A.E., 84
  "Ahoy, Sailor Boy," 84
  "The Kisstruck Bogie," 84
Corkery, Daniel, 59, 60, 63, 265
  Earth out of Earth, 60, 265
  The Hounds of Banba, 60
  A Munster Twilight, 60
  The Stormy Hills, 265
  Synge and Anglo-Irish Literature, 59
cosmopolitanism, in Irish fiction, 56–9, 63
Coward, Noël, 159, 366–7
  "Me and the Girls," 366
  "Pretty Polly Barlow," 366
  Star Quality, 366
  To Step Aside, 366
Cox, Anthony Berkeley, 71
Crackanthorpe, Hubert, 11–13, 115
  "Profiles," 12–13
  Wreckage, 11–12
Crawford, F. Marion, 87, 94
  "The Upper Berth," 94
Crichton Smith, Ian, 297–9, 304
  "Easter Sunday," 297
  The Village, 297
Croker, Bithia Mary, 85
  "To Let," 85

Dali, Salvador, 517
Dane, Clemence, 362
Darwin, Charles, 89, 175, 177, 519
Deane, Seamus, 273, 448
Derrida, Jacques, 385
Desai, Anita, 308
Descartes, René, 518
de Hamel, Herbert, 85
  "The House of Dust," 85
Deighton, Len, 227, 233

de la Mare, Walter, 82, 84, 88, 114
  "Seaton's Aunt," 82
  "The Promise," 84
de Sade, Marquis, 509
detective and crime fiction, 65–80, 83, 116,
    144, 189
  golden age of the detective story, 65,
    70–1, 73, 77
de Valera, Eamon, 264, 266–7, 272, 433
The Dial, 184, 364
Dickens, Charles, 9, 54, 75, 83–4, 138,
    335, 424, 495, 541
  A Christmas Carol, 84, 138
  "The Goblins Who Stole a Sexton,"
    83–4
Donisthorpe, G. Sheila, 362
  Loveliest of Friends, 362
doppelgänger, 82, 88, 91, 136, 200
Dorcey, Mary, 253, 275–6
  A Noise from the Woodshed, 275, 368
  "A Noise from the Woodshed," 276
  "The Husband," 276
Dostoevsky, Fyodor, 61, 509
Doyle, Roddy, 276
  Barrytown Trilogy, 276
  "The Photograph," 276
Drabble, Margaret, 365
Dreyfus Affair, 334
Dublin, 26, 54, 58–9, 165–73, 263–4, 269,
    273, 276, 326, 343
Dublin Magazine, 254
Duffy, Maureen, 365, 367
Duncker, Patricia, 255, 258–9, 311, 322–5,
    328, 368, 507
  Monsieur Shoushana's Lemon Trees, 322
  Seven Tales of Sex and Death, 258, 311
  "Small Arms," 323–5
  "Sophia Walters Shaw," 258–9, 322
  "Stalker," 322–3
  "The Strike," 325
Dunsany, Lord Edward, 84–5
  "Two Bottles of Relish," 84
  The Sword of Welleran and Other Stories,
    85
Dupin, C. Auguste, 65–7
dystopia, 116–18, 178, 257–8

Edgeworth, Maria, 52–3, 69
  Castle Rackrent, 52
Edwards, Amelia B., 91
Eliot, George, 111
Eliot, T.S., 109, 114, 478
Ellis, Havelock, 359
Enlightenment, The, 83, 518–20
Enright, Anne, 253, 275
  The Portable Virgin, 275
epiphany, 103–4, 165, 169, 171, 202–5,
  208–9, 298, 525, 529
espionage fiction, 116, 227–35
European Union, 250, 271, 273
exile (writers), 59, 96–7, 100, 111, 272,
  308, 339–41, 433
experimental writing, 193–4, 255, 275,
  343, 350, 353, 384–97

Faber, Michel, 255, 257–8
  "Fish," 257–8
  Some Rain Must Fall, 257
fable, 116–17, 126, 524
Fainlight, Ruth, 330
  "Another Survivor," 330–2
  Dr. Clock's Last Case and Other Stories, 331
fairy tale, 84, 131, 175, 180, 335, 509–10
fantastic, the/fantasy, 63, 82, 85, 91–2,
  104–5, 109, 175–6, 179–81, 257,
  350, 353, 372–83
  epic fantasy, 378–80
feminism, 68, 96, 98, 101, 109, 197–200,
  253, 342–3, 345–9, 351, 353, 362,
  419, 431, 507–8
femininity, feminization, 71–2, 75–6, 78,
  198
Firbank, Ronald, 358, 363, 366
  *Concerning the Eccentricities of Cardinal
    Pirelli*, 358, 363
  "A Study in Opal," 363
  "A Study in Temperament," 363
  "The Wavering Disciple: A Fantasia,"
    363
Flaubert, Gustave, 166
Fleetwood, Hugh, 255–6
  Fictional Lives, 255
  "A Wonderful Woman," 255–6

folk tale, 55–7, 131, 255, 257, 351, 508–15
Ford, Ford Madox, 110–11
Ford, John, 62, 222–3
  The Informer (film version), 222; *see also*
    O'Flaherty, Sean
  The Quiet Man (film version), 62; *see also*
    Walsh, Maurice
Forster, E.M., 361–3, 365–6
  "Arthur Snatchfold," 361
  "The Classical Annex," 361–2
  "Dr. Woolacott," 361–2
  The Life to Come and Other Stories, 361–2
  "The Life to Come," 361
  Maurice, 361
  "The Obelisk," 361–2
  "The Other Boat," 362
  "The Story of a Panic," 361
  "The Torque," 361
  "What Does It Matter? A Morality,"
    361–2
Frame, Ronald, 369
Freeman, R. Austin, 70
Freud, Sigmund, 81–2, 91, 147, 191,
  215–16, 359, 378, 380, 434, 513,
  519, 521
  "The Uncanny," 81, 434, 519
Friel, Brian, 62
Friel, George, 294–7, 479
  "A Friend of Humanity," 294–6
Fry, Roger, 196
Fry, Stephen, 369
Futrelle, Jacques, 70

Gaboriau, Émile, 66
Gaiman, Neil, 330, 339–41, 379
  Fragile Things: Short Fictions and Wonders,
    339
  "In the End," 339–41
Gale, Patrick, 369
Galloway, Janice, 343, 349–50
  "Bisex," 350
  Blood, 349–50
  "Fair Ellen and the Wanderer Returned,"
    350
  "Fearless," 349–50
  "It Was," 350

Galloway, Janice (*cont'd*)
  "Not Flu," 350
  "Scenes for the Life No. 26," 350
  "Scenes from the Life No. 27: Living In," 350
  "Scenes from the Life No. 29: Dianne," 350
  "Someone Had to," 350
  "Valentine," 350
  "Waiting for Marilyn," 350
  Where You Find It, 350
Galsworthy, John, 198–9
Gaskell, Elizabeth, 111
gay short fiction, 356–71
Gellner, Ernest, 280–1
gender, 65, 68, 71–2, 75–6, 94, 98, 99, 109, 112, 197–8, 200, 202, 206, 275–6, 322, 511
genre, 254–5, 259
genre mixture, 74, 114–18, 181
Gentle, Mary, 380
  "Human Waste," 381–2
ghost story (supernatural fiction), 47–8, 81–95, 115–16, 118, 131, 142, 145, 160, 176, 189, 238, 240, 457, 460–2
Gibson, William, 522
Gissing, George, 424, 429
Goethe, Johann Wolfgang, 352, 508
Gogol, Nikolai, 61, 212
golden age of the detective story, *see* detective and crime fiction
Golding, William, 314
Gordimer, Nadine, 309
gothic motifs and conventions, 57–8, 62, 72, 82–4, 86–7, 90, 105–6, 136, 142, 175–6, 180, 342, 349, 351, 375, 432–3, 508, 510, 519
Gould, Francis Carruthers, 158
Grassic Gibbon, Lewis (James Leslie Mitchell), 297
Graves, Robert, 478
Gray, Alasdair, 479, 532
Greene, Graham, 227, 367, 384, 423
  "Chagrin in Three Parts," 367
  May We Borrow Your Husband? And Other Comedies of the Sexual Life, 367
  "May We Borrow Your Husband?" 367

Gregory, Lady Augusta, 55–6, 84
  A Book of Saints and Wonders, 55
  A Kiltartan History Book, 55
Griffith, Nicola, 380

Haggard, H. Rider, 88, 94, 242
  She, 242
Haig, Sir Douglas, 36–7
Hall, Radclyffe, 192, 360–2
  Miss Ogilvy Finds Herself and Other Stories, 362–3
  "Miss Ogilvy Finds Herself," 362–63
  The Unlit Lamp, 362
  The Well of Loneliness, 360, 362
Hamilton, Hugo, 276
  Dublin Where the Palm Trees Grow, 276
Hamilton, Patrick, 71
Hammett, Dashiell, 76
Haraway, Donna, 522
Hardy, J.E., 368
  Stranger Than Fish, 368
Hardy, Thomas, 140–8, 184
  "Barbara of the House of Grebe," 142
  "The Distracted Preacher," 140–2, 147
  "Fellow Townsmen," 140, 142, 147
  A Group of Noble Dames," 142
  The Hand of Ethelberta, 142
  "An Imaginative Woman," 140
  Life's Little Ironies, 140
  "The Melancholy Hussar of the German Legion," 140–2
  The Return of the Native, 142
  "The Son's Veto," 142
  "The Three Strangers," 140–1, 143–5
  "A Tradition of Eighteen Hundred and Four," 140–1
  Wessex Tales, 140–8
  "The Withered Arm," 140–2, 145–7
Hawthorne, Nathaniel, 332
H.D. (Hilda Doolittle), 362
Heaney, Seamus, 218, 268, 273
Heinlein, Robert A., 517
Henry, O., 227
Henty, G.E., 25
Hiberno-English, 52, 56
historical fiction, 115–16, 118

Hitchcock, Alfred, 227, 521
   The Secret Agent (film version of *Ashenden*), 227
Hobbes, Thomas, 409
Hoffmann, E.T.A., 82, 519
Hogarth Press, 193–4
Hoggart, Richard, 414
Hollinghurst, Alan, 363, 369
Holmes, Sherlock, 26–9, 57, 66–8, 70, 75
Holocaust, 330–40
   survivor(s), 330–3, 338
Holtby, Winifred, 44
   "So Handy for the Fun Fair," 44
Homer, 59, 215
homosexuality, 97, 102, 108, 172, 276, 357–70
Hopkins, Gerard Manley, 476
Horizon, 10
Hornung, E.W., 70
horror story, 83, 90, 92–3
Household Words, 84, *see also* Dickens, Charles
Hulme, Kerri, 309
Hunt, Violet, 88
Huxley, T.H., 177
Hyde, Douglas, 84

Ireland, I.A., 86
   A Brief History of Nightmares, 86
   "Climax for a Ghost Story," 86
Ireland, Timothy, 369
identity, 99, 106, 150–1, 374–8, 461; (English) 65, 68–71, 75, 78, 86, 279–93; (Irish), 52, 59, 63–4, 84, 263–78, 309, 386–7, 448, 482–5
immigration, 28, 68, 78, 251–2, 273, 275–7, 281–5, 310, 330, 333, 337–8, 476, 478–9, 546
imperialism, *see* British empire
India, 121–4, 308–9, 317–19
Interzone, 372, 380–2
Irish Civil War, 10, 51, 61, 211, 213, 222–3, 266
Irish fiction, compared to British, 52, 54

Irish Free State, 51, 59, 252
Irish language (Gaelic), 52, 56
Irish Literary Revival/Renaissance, 51, 54–6, 84–5
Irish Press, 254
Irish Republic, 249, 252–3
Irish short story, 51–64, 263–78, 343–7
Irish Writing, 254, 268
Irisleabhar na Gaedhlige (journal), 55
Isherwood, Christopher, 365
Isler, Alan, 330, 333–5
   "The Affair," 333–5
   The Bacon Fancier: Four Tales, 334

Jacob, Naomi, 362
Jacobs, W.W., 90
   "The Toll-House," 90
Jacobson, Dan, 330, 337–9
   A Long Way from Home and Other Stories, 337
   "The Zulu and the Zeide," 337–9
James, Henry, 11, 93, 120, 184, 237, 423, 499
   "The Romance of Certain Old Clothes," 93
James, M.R., 84, 86–8, 92–3
   "The Ash-tree," 86
   "Casting the Runes," 86, 92
   "Count Magnus," 86, 88
   Ghost Stories of an Antiquary, 86
   "Lost Hearts," 91
   "Oh Whistle, and I'll Come to You, My Lad," 88
   "A School Story," 87
James, William, 90
Johnson, B.S., 390–3
   Aren't You Rather Young to be Writing Your Memoirs?, 390
   "Aren't You Rather Young to be Writing Your Memoirs?", 391–2
   "A Few Selected Sentences," 391
   "Instructions for the Use of Women," 391
   "Mean Points of Impact," 391
Johnson, Samuel, 493

Jordan, Neil, 253, 273–4
  Breakfast on Pluto (film), 274
  The Butcher Boy (film), 274
  The Crying Game (film), 274
  Night in Tunisia and Other Stories, 274
Josipovici, Gabriel, 255, 330, 333–4, 336
  "Goldberg," 394
  Goldberg: Variations, 394–6
  "He," 333–4
  In the Fertile Land, 333
  "Mobius the Stripper," 393
  "True Confessions of an Experimentalist,"
    393
Joyce, James, 25–6, 51, 58–9, 61, 165–73,
    202, 217, 264, 272, 275, 277, 298,
    326, 431, 433, 437, 485–6, 491,
    524–5, 529, 533
  "Araby," 167–9, 171
  "The Boarding House," 59, 170–2
  "Counterparts," 172
  "The Dead," 59, 61, 271
  Dubliners, 58, 165–73, 202, 217, 265,
    266, 485, 524–5
  "An Encounter," 25–6, 491
  "Eveline," 58, 168–70
  "Grace," 59
  "Little Chandler," 168, 170–1
  "A Little Cloud," 167, 170–2
  "A Painful Case," 58, 167, 171–3
  A Portrait of the Artist As a Young Man,
    264
  "The Sisters," 58, 166–7
  "Two Gallants," 59, 170–1, 486
  Ulysses, 275
Jung, Carl Gustav, 91, 381, 520
juvenile literature, 25–6, 30–1

Kafka, Franz, 404, 535–6
Kavanagh, Patrick, 266, 491
  The Great Hunger, 266, 491
Kay, Jackie, 237, 309, 325–8
  The Adoption Papers, 325
  "Blinds," 326
  "How to Get Away with Suicide," 326
  "My Daughter the Fox," 326–7
  Trumpet, 309, 327

  Wish I Was Here, 325–7
  "You Can Go When You Can No Longer
    Stay," 325–6
Kelman, James, 253, 255, 301–3, 479,
    532–40
  "Benson's Visitor," 535–6
  The Burn, 532, 538
  The Busconductor Hines, 533, 537
  "By the Burn," 538
  "dear o dear," 535
  "End of a Beginning," 536
  "Forgetting to Mention Allende," 532–3,
    537–8
  The Good Times, 538
  Greyhound for Breakfast, 532–40
  "Greyhound for Breakfast," 536–7
  How Late It Was, How Late, 532–3
  "The Importance of Glasgow in My
    Work," 302
  "In With the Doctor," 535
  Lean Tales, 532, 534
  "A Night Boilerman's Notes," 534
  "The Norwest Reaches," 538
  Not Not While the Giro, 301, 532, 534
  "O jesus, here come the dwarfs," 534
  "An Old Story," 534–5
  "Roofsliding," 301–2
  "The same is here again," 534
  "You Have to Be Careful in the Land of
    the Free," 539
Kennedy, A.L., 304–6
  "The Disaster," 305
  Night Geometry and the Garscadden Trains,
    304
  "Night Geometry and the Garscadden
    Trains," 304–5
  "Star Dust," 305
Kickham, Charles, 53
  Knocknagow, 53
Kiely, Benedict, 254, 263, 273
  A Ball of Malt and Madame Butterfly,
    263–4
  "A Ball of Malt and Madame Butterfly,"
    272
  A Cow in the House, 272
kindertransport, 331

Kipling, Rudyard, 20, 27–9, 86, 92,
    114–28, 158, 250, 407
  Actions and Reactions, 115–117, 120
  "The Bull That Thought," 126–7
  "The Comprehension of Private Copper,"
    30
  The Day's Work, 115–17, 120–1
  Debits and Credits, 115–18, 120–1, 126
  A Diversity of creatures, 115–17, 124
  "The Gardener," 115, 118
  In Black and White, 115–16, 119, 121
  The Jungle Book, 117, 119, 121
  Just So Stories, 117
  Life's Handicap, 116, 120
  Limits and Renewals, 115–17, 119, 121
  "The Man Who Would be King," 21–2
  Many Inventions, 115–17, 119
  "The Mark of the Beast," 85, 116, 120
  "Mary Postgate," 47, 115, 124–6
  "Miss Yougal's Sais," 27
  "Mrs Bathurst," 120
  "On the City Wall," 121–4
  The Phantom Rickshaw, 116
  Plain Tales from the Hills, 27, 29, 114–15,
    118–19, 121
  Puck of Pook's Hill, 115, 117, 121
  Rewards and Fairies, 115–17, 121
  "A Sahib's War," 29–30
  Stalky & Co., 116, 121
  "The Strange Ride of Morrowbie Jukes,"
    116, 120
  "They," 118, 121
  "Thrown Away," 28–9
  "To Be Filed for Reference," 28
  "Tod's Amendment," 29
  Traffics and Discoveries, 115, 117, 120
  Wee Willie Winkie, 115–16
  "The White Man's Burden," 250
  "Wireless," 92
Knox, Ronald A., 71
  "A Detective Story Decalogue," 71
Krafft-Ebing, Richard, 89, 359
Kristeva, Julia, 345, 352, 353, 436, 438
Kureishi, Hanif, 253, 311, 320–3, 541–9
  "Blue Pictures of You," 543
  "D'Accord Baby," 546–7

"The Flies," 544–5
"In a Blue Time," 320–1, 323, 541–3
Intimacy, 541; film version, 548
"Lately," 547
Love in a Blue Time, 311, 320–2, 541–9
"My Son the Fanatic," 547–8
"Nightlight," 547–8
"The Tale of the Turd," 544
"We're Not Jews," 321–2, 546
"With Your Tongue Down My Throat,"
    544–7
The Word and the Bomb, 548

Lacan, Jacques, 511
Laing, R.D., 300
Lane, John (The Bodley Head), 158
Lappin, Elena, 330, 335–7
  Foreign Brides, 336–7
  "Noa and Noah," 336–7
Lasdun, James, 255–7, 336–7
  "Ate/Menos *or* The Miracle," 336–7
  "Property," 256–7
  The Silver Age, 256
  Three Evenings and Other Stories, 336
Lavin, Mary, 62, 265, 268, 271
  At Sallygap and Other Stories, 268
  "At Sallygap," 268
  The Becker Wives and Other Stories, 268
  The Great Wave and Other Stories, 268
  The Long Ago and Other Stories, 268
  The Patriot Son and Other Stories, 268
  Selected Stories, 268
  A Single Lady, 268
  Tales from Bective Bridge, 62, 268
Lawrence, D.H., 42–3, 96, 183–92, 227,
    358, 363–4, 446
  "The Blind Man," 364
  "England, My England," 42–3
  "Fantasia of the Unconscious," 191
  The Fox, 364
  "The Horse Dealer's Daughter," 185–9
  "Jimmy and the desperate Woman," 364
  Lady Chatterley's Lover, 360
  "Love Among the Haystacks," 184
  "Parent Love," 191
  "Pornography and Obscenity," 363

Lawrence, D.H. (*cont'd*)
  "The Prelude," 183–4
  "The Prussian Officer," 364
  "Psychoanalysis and the Unconscious," 191
  The Rainbow, 364
  "The Rocking-Horse Winner," 189–92
  The White Peacock, 358
  "The White Stocking," 184
  Women in Love, 364
Lawrence, Margery, 93–4
  "The Mask of Sacrifice," 94
  "Robin's Rath," 94
le Carré, John, 227, 233
Lee, Tanith, 379
Lee, Vernon (Violet Paget), 88, 91, 94
  "Dionea," 88
Le Fanu, Joseph Sheridan, 52, 57, 84, 86
  "An Account of Some Strange
    Disturbances in Aungier Street," 84
  "The Ghost and the Bonesetter," 84
  In a Glass Darkly, 57, 84
  *Madam Crowl's Ghost and Other Tales of
    Mystery*, 84
legend, 116–19, 126, 524
Lehmann, John, 401
Lehmann, Rosamund, 362
Leonard, Tom, 300, 479, 538
Lewis, C.S., 378, 380
Le Queux, William, 227, 230
lesbian writing, 354
  British Asian/black lesbian writing,
    367–8
  lesbian short fiction, 356–71
Lessing, Doris, 342, 347–8, 384, 422,
  440–7
  African Stories, 440–7
  Five, 440
  "Flavours of Exile," 446
  "Flight," 446
  "Getting Off the Altitude," 444
  "A Home for the Highland Cattle," 445
  "How I Finally Lost My Heart," 348
  "Hunger," 441
  "A Letter from Home," 446
  "A Mild Attack of Locusts," 446
  "Mrs Fortescue," 348

"The Old Chief Mshlanga," 441–4,
  446–7
"Old John's Place," 444
"One Off the Shortlist," 348
"The Other Woman," 348
"Our Friend Judith," 348
"Plants and Girls," 446
"The Road to the Big City," 446
"Spies I Have Known," 440, 446
"The Story of a Non-Marrying Man,"
  440, 446
The Story of Two Dogs," 446
"The Sun between Their Feet," 446
This Was the Old Chief's Country, 440
"To Room Nineteen," 348, 422
"The Trinket Box," 446
"Winter in July," 347–8, 444
"The Words He Said," 446
Levy, Andrea, 309
Lewis, Alun, 11, 13–14, 49
  The Last Inspection, 13
  "The Last Inspection," 49
  "They Came," 13–14
Lewis, Matthew, 82
Libeskind, David, 498, 503
Litt, Toby, 292
  Adventures in Capitalism, 292
  Exhibitionism, 292
  "Mr. Kipling," 292
Livia, Anna, 368
  Saccharin Cyanide, 368
Lodge, David, 396
  "Hotel des Boobs," 396–7
London Journal, 90
Lorca, Federico García, 476
Lovecraft, H.P., 87–8
  "Supernatural Horror in Literature," 88
Lyotard, Jean-François, 385

Macaulay, Rose, 48–9, 105
  "Mrs Anstruther's Letters," 48–9
Machen, Arthur, 85, 94
  The Angels of Mons, 86
  "The Bowmen," 86
  "The Great God Pan," 88
  "The Soldier's Rest," 85–6

Mackay Brown, George, 296–7, 299, 472–9
  Beside the Ocean of Time, 472
  A Calendar of Love, 297, 474, 476–7
  Hawkfall, 296–7, 475
  "Master Halcrow, Priest," 297, 474–5
  "The Seller of Silk Shirts," 476, 478
  "The Tarn and the Rosary," 296–7,
    475–6
  A Time to Keep, 474
  "A Time to Keep," 472–4, 478
  "The Whaler's Return," 474
  "Witch," 477–8
Mackenzie, Compton, 362
Maclaren-Ross, Julian, 13, 289–90, 401–8
  "Ack Beer Charlie Don," 404
  "Action Nineteen-Thirty-Eight," 402,
    404
  "Are You Happy in Your Work?" 403–4
  Better Than a Kick in the Pants, 401–5
  "The Bird Man," 402–4
  "A Bit of a Smash in Madras," 402, 403,
    407
  "A Bit of a Stink," 403–4
  Bitten by the Tarantula, 401
  "Call a Policeman," 405
  "Civvy Street," 402, 404
  "Dead Men Do Tell Tales," 405
  "Dodging the Column," 405
  "Edward: A Detective Story," 405
  "The Far West," 404
  "Five Finger Exercises," 402
  The Funny Bone, 401–2, 404–5
  "Gas," 403–4
  "The Gem," 404
  "The Gold Fish," 405
  "The Gondolier of Death," 402, 404
  "The Great Writer," 405
  "Happy as the Day Is Long," 402, 405
  "The Hell of a Time," 402, 403
  "The High Jump," 405
  "The High Priest of Buddha," 404
  "The Honest Truth," 405
  "I Had to Go Sick," 403–4
  "I'm Not Asking You to Buy," 402
  "Invasion according to Plan," 404
  "Jankers," 404

  "London Is Soho," 402
  "Lulu," 402–4
  "The Man from Madagascar," 404–5
  "The Mandrake Root," 402
  "My Father Was Born in Havana," 403
  The Nine Men of Soho, 401–5
  Of Love and Hunger, 401–2
  "Old Ginger," 402, 404–5
  "The Oxford Manner," 403
  "Petty Cash," 402, 403, 405
  "Plots Ten-and-Six," 402
  "The Rubber Cheque," 402, 404
  "A Sentimental Story," 404
  "Seven Days of Heaven," 403–4
  "The Shoestring Budget," 405
  "The Soldier Who Had a Complex and
    the Psychiatrist Who Miraculously
    Cured Him," 405
  "The Spy Who Was a Character from
    Conrad," 404
  The Stuff to Give the Troops, 401–5
  "The Swag, the Spy and the Soldier,"
    402–5
  "The Tape," 403
  "They Can Have It," 403–4
  "They Put Me in Charge of a Squad,"
    405–7
  "This Mortal Coil," 404
  "The Triple Life of Major Trask," 402,
    404
  "The Virgin," 405
  "Welsh Rabbit of Soap," 404–5
  "Y List," 404
MacLaverty, Bernard, 253, 498–506
  Walking the Dog, 498
  "Walking the Dog," 498–506
Macleod, Fiona (William Sharp), 85
MacMahon, Bryan, 265, 268
  "The Exile's Return," 268
  Red Petticoat, 268
Macmillan, Harold, 410
Mankowitz, Wolf, 330, 335–6
  "The Finest Pipe-Maker in Russia,"
    335–6
  The Mendelman Fire, 335
  "A Village Like Yours," 335

Mansfield, Katherine, 85, 92, 96, 98–9,
    101, 104, 109–11, 202–10
Bliss, 98
"Bliss," 203
The Garden-Party and Other Stories, 98,
    202
"The Garden-Party," 100, 202–9
"Honeymoon," 98
In a German Pension, 98
"Je ne parle pas français," 99
"Marriage à la Mode," 202, 206–9
"Miss Brill," 98–100
"Pictures," 98–9
"The Prelude," 98–100, 203
"A Suburban Fairytale," 85
"Sun and Moon," 100
"The Tiredness of Rosabel," 98
marginality, 7, 72, 82, 96–7, 109–11, 138,
    183, 197, 208–9, 211, 224, 275,
    304–6, 309, 328, 352
Markham, E.A., 311–13, 328
"Digging," 312
"Mammie's Form at the Post Office,"
    312–13
Something Unusual, 311–12
Marple, Jane, 72–3
Marryat, Captain Frederick, 25
Marryat, Florence, 91
Marsh, Ngaio, 71
Mars-Jones, Adam, 255, 357, 369
"Bears in Mourning," 369
The Darker Proof: Stories from a Crisis,
    369
Monopolies of Loss, 357
"Summer Lightning," 369
Martin, Violet, *see* "Somerville and Ross"
Marx Brothers, 404
masculinity, 43–4, 67–8, 75–6, 78
Matthews, Brander, 9, 19
Maturin, Charles, 57
Maugham, W. Somerset, 20–2, 30, 31–2,
    44–5, 114, 227–35, 359
Ashenden: or The British Agent, 44,
    227–35
"The Door of Opportunity," 31
"The Fall of Edward Barnard," 31–2

"The Flip of a Coin," 228
"Footprints in the Jungle," 31
"Guilia Lazzari," 228, 230–3
"The Hairless Mexican," 228–30
"His Excellency," 228
"Mackintosh," 31
"Miss King," 228, 233–5
"Mr. Harrington's Washing," 228
"Neil MacAdam," 31
"The Outstation," 31
"Rain," 227
"Red," 32
"The Traitor," 44–5, 228
"The Vessel of Wrath," 32
Maupassant, Guy de, 11
McCabe, Brian, 300–1
"The Full Moon," 300–1
McCabe, Patrick, 274
McEwan, Ian, 253, 255, 288–9, 384,
    386–9, 541
"Disguises," 386
First Love, Last Rites, 288
"Homemade," 288–9
In Between the Sheets, 288, 386
"Psychopolis," 386–9
"Solid Geometry," 386
"Reflections of a Kept Ape," 386
McGahern, John, 253–4, 269, 271, 273–4,
    486, 488–97
"Christmas," 493
The Collected Stories, 270
"Coming into His Kingdom," 494
Creatures of the Earth, 495
The Dark, 270
Getting Through, 270
"Hearts of Oak and Bellies of Brass,"
    489–91
High Ground, 270
"The Image," 496
"Korea," 492–3
"Lavin," 491–2, 494–5
Memoir, 490
Nightlines, 269, 488–97
"Oldfashioned," 270
"Peaches," 491–2
The Pornographer, 489, 491, 495–6

"The Recruiting Officer," 496

"Sierra Leone," 269

"Strandhill, The Sea," 495

That They May Face the Rising Sun, 492

"Wheels," 269, 488–92, 494–6

"Why We're Here," 492, 495

McLaverty, Michael, 265, 267–68

   The Game Cock and Other Stories, 268

   The White Mare and Other Stories, 268

   "Six Weeks and Two Ashore," 268

McLellan, Robert, 302–3

   Linmill Stories, 302–3

Mew, Charlotte, 89, 91, 360, 362

   "White Night," 89

Miéville, China, 379–80

   King Rat, 379

   "Looking for Jake," 379–80

   Perdido Street Station, 379

Mills, Joseph, 369

   Obsessions, 369

modernism, 10, 35, 39, 49, 55, 96–7,
   100–1, 109, 111, 183, 199, 202, 204,
   208, 516

Moorcock, Michael, 253, 372, 374, 378–80,
   516

   "The Dreaming City," 378

   "Epic Pooh," 378–9

   "Islands," 376–7

   "The Singing Citadel," 378

   "While the Gods Laugh," 379

   Wizardry and Wild Romance, 378

Moore, George, 54–6, 59, 61–2, 265,
   267–8, 277

   "Homesickness," 268

   "In the Clay," 54

   "Patchwork," 54

   The Untilled Field 54–5, 265

   "The Wedding Feast," 54

   "The Window," 54

Morris, Kenneth, 85

Morrison, Arthur, 70, 115

Mulholland, Rosa, 58

   "The Hungry Death," 58

Mulkerns, Val, 267–8, 272

   Antiquities, 272

   An Idle Woman, 272

Munro, Hector Hugh ("Saki"), 85 157–64,
   360–1

   "Alice in Westminster," 158

   Beasts and Super-Beasts, 158, 160

   "Birds on the Western Front," 160

   "The Blood-feud of Toad-Water," 158

   The Chronicles of Clovis, 158, 160

   "Dogged," 158

   "For the Duration of the War," 160

   "Gabriel Ernest," 160, 360–1

   "The Hen," 162–3

   "The Political Junglebook," 158

   "Potted Parliament," 159

   Reginald in Russia, 158–9

   The Rise of the Russian Empire, 158

   "Shock Tactics," 162

   "The Soul of Laploshka," 85, 160

   The Square Egg, 158, 160–1

   "Sredni Vashtar," 160–2

   The Toys of Peace, 158, 160

   The Unbearable Bassington, 158

   "The Unrest-Cure," 162

   When William Came, 158

   "A Young Turkish Catastrophe," 160

Murdoch, Iris, 365

Murry, John Middleton, 96, 98

myth, 52, 55–7, 63, 84–5, 117, 215, 218,
   258, 478, 524, 528

Naipaul, V.S., 309

Natzler, Caroline, 368

   Water Wings, 368

neo-realism, 384, 510, 544; *see also* realism

Nesbit, E., 91

   "John Charrington's Wedding", 91, 93

   "Man-Size in Marble," 91

New Age, 98

The Newgate Calendar, 65

Newgate novels, 65

Newnes, George, 67, 90

"New Wave" science fiction, 372, 374–8,
   516

New Worlds, 372, 380, 382

New Yorker, The, 62, 89, 97, 416, 431

Nietzsche, Friedrich, 42, 172

Nordau, Max, 89, 359–60

Norris, Frank, 224
Northern Ireland, 51, 58, 249, 252–3, 271, 311, 498–506

O'Brien, Edna, 254, 265, 272, 274, 431–9
  "Cords," 433
  The Country Girls Trilogy, 270, 431, 433
  A Fanatic Heart: Selected Stories, 431
  "Irish Revel," 271, 431
  The Love Object, 270
  "The Love Object," 434
  Mother Ireland, 433–5
  Mrs Reinhardt and Other Stories, 271, 431
  "Paradise," 271
  "A Rose in the Heart of New York,"
    344–5, 431–8
  A Scandalous Woman, 271, 344
  "A Scandalous Woman," 344, 431
  "Sister Imelda," 433
O'Brien, Flann (Brian O'Nolan), 56, 62
  At-Swim-Two-Birds, 62
O'Casey, Sean, 60
Ó Conaire, Padraic, 55–6, 62
O'Connor, Frank, 7, 60–3, 209, 211–20,
  223–4, 265–6, 488
  The Common Cord, 266
  Domestic Relations, 266
  "First Confession," 266
  "The Genius," 266
  "Guests of the Nation," 60–1, 211–14,
    219
  The Lonely Voice, 212, 217, 266, 274
  "The Majesty of the Law," 61
  "My Oedipus Complex," 215–19, 266
  An Only Child, 214
  Traveller's Samples, 266
Ó Criomhthain, Tomás, 494
O'Donnell, Peadar, 267
O'Faolain, Julia, 342, 345–6
  Daughters of Passion, 346
  "Daughters of Passion," 346
  Man in the Cellar, 345
  "Man in the Cellar," 345
  "Oh My Monsters!," 345–6
O'Faoláin, Seán, 60–1, 223, 448–55, 488
  "The Faithless Wife," 60, 267

Foreign Affairs, 267
  "Liliput," 60
  "Lovers of the Lake," 60, 449–55
  The Man Who Invented Sin, 267
  "The Man Who Invented Sin," 60
  Midsummer Night Madness, 60
  "Midsummer Night Madness," 60
  A Purse of Coppers, 60
  The Short Story, 448, 453
  "Teresa," 267
O'Flaherty, Liam, 61–2, 221–6, 265
  "An Chulaith Nua," 61
  "The Arrest," 223–5
  Civil War, 265
  "The Cow's Death," 223–4
  Dúil, 61, 222
  Famine, 222–3
  "The Fanatic," 223–6
  "The Hawk," 223
  The Informer, 222–3
  The Mountain Tavern and Other Stories,
    222
  "The Pedlar's Revenge," 223–4
  "The Rockfish," 223
  The Short Stories of Liam O'Flaherty,
    222
  Skerrett, 222–3
  "The Sniper," 223
  Spring Sowing, 222, 224, 265
  The Stories of Liam O'Flaherty, 222
  "The Tavern," 61
  The Tent, 222, 265
  Two Lovely Beasts and Other Stories, 222
  "The Wave," 223–4
O'Kelley, Seamus, 55
  "The Weaver's Rest," 55
Okri, Ben, 253, 309, 311, 313–17, 322,
  328, 524–31
  "Converging City," 525–6
  "Crooked Prayer," 525–6
  "Disparities," 525–6
  "The Dream-vendor's August," 525–6
  The Famished Road, 525
  "Fantasies Born in the Ghetto," 524
  Flowers and Shadows, 524
  "A Hidden History," 314, 525–6

"In the City of Red Dust," 527
"In the Shadow of War," 525, 527–30
Incidents at the Shrine, 311, 313, 524–5
"Incidents at the Shrine," 525, 527
"The Joys of Storytelling III," 524
The Landscapes Within, 524
"Laughter Beneath the Bridge," 314–17,
    322, 525
"Masquerades," 525–6
Starbook, 524
Stars of the New Curfew, 525, 527
"Stars of the New Curfew," 527–8
"What the Tapster Saw," 525, 528
"When the Lights Return," 528
Ó Laoghair, Peadar, 55–6
O'Malley, Mary, 86
O'Neill, Jamie, 369
Orage, A.R., 98
Orczy, Baroness Emmuska, 70
Orel, Harold, 8–9
Orwell, George, 183, 410–11
Owen, Agnes, 532, 537

Paget, Sidney, 90
Pain, Barry, 88, 92
    "The Case of Vincent Pyrwhit," 92
Pall Mall Magazine, 91
Pall Mall Gazette, The, 89
Panter-Downes, Mollie, 47
    "Goodbye, My Love," 47
patriarchy, 198, 200; *see also* feminism,
    gender, masculinity
Penguin New Writing, 10, 237
Perrin, Alice, 85
Plomer, William, 356–7, 365
    "Local Colour," 357
Poe, Edgar Allan, 9, 65–6, 238, 375, 508
Poirot, Hercule, 72–3
pornography, 255, 258, 507, 510, *see also*
    censorship
postmodernism, 343, 349–54, 384, 522
Potts, Cherry, 368
    Mosaic of Air, 368
Powell, Anthony, 401–2
Pritchett, V.S., 114, 279–80, 284–5, 422,
    423–30, 481

"The Camberwell Beauty," 422
"The Fall," 279
"Handsome Is As Handsome Does,"
    285–6, 424, 427
'The Scapegoat," 424, 426–7
"Sense of Humour," 424–6
"Tea with Mrs Bitell," 284–5
"When My Girl Comes Home," 424,
    427–9
Why Do I Write?, 423
"X-ray," 424, 426
Proust, Marcel, 363, 366, 446, 495–6
publishing (in relation to short stories),
    9–10, 19, 25–6, 60, 66–7, 90–2, 174,
    184, 211, 253–4, 265, 267, 304,
    367–9, 372, 380, 382

race, 132–6, 251–2, 310, 343, 418, 427–8,
    440–7, 476, 546
Radcliffe, Ann, 82
realism, 35, 52, 67, 83–4, 89, 91, 104,
    118, 144, 181, 184–5, 195, 198–200,
    221, 223, 255, 257, 342–7, 350, 353,
    363, 384–5, 389–90, 432, 446, 480
neo-realism, 384, 510, 544
Reed, Henry, 401
Renault, Mary, 365
Rhys, Jean, 47, 96–8, 109–11, 464–71
    "At the Villa D'Or," 110
    "Fishy Waters," 111
    "From a French Prison," 110
    Good Morning, Midnight, 97, 469
    "Hunger," 111
    "I Spy a Stranger," 47
    "Illusion," 464
    "In a Café," 111
    "The Insect World," 111
    The Left Bank, 111
    "Let Them Call It Jazz," 110,
        464–71
    "Mannequin," 110–11
    "On Not Shooting Sitting Birds," 110,
        464, 467, 470
    Postures (Quartet), 97
    "Rapunzel, Rapunzel," 110
    "The Sidi," 110

Rhys, Jean (*cont'd*)
  Smile Please: An Unfinished Autobiography,
    468
  Voyage in the Dark, 467, 469
  Wide Sargasso Sea, 97, 464, 467
Richards, Grant, 165–6
Richardson, Tony, 415
Riddell, Charlotte, 84, 91
  "Hertford O'Donnell's Warning," 84
romance, 24, 70, 84, 90, 131, 142, 167,
    169, 175, 180
Rosenthal, Horst, 339
  Mickey au Camp de Gurs, 339
Roth, Philip, 541, 548
Royde-Smith, Naomi, 362
  The Island, 362
  The Tortoiseshell Cat, 362
Rushdie, Salman, 255, 308–9, 311,
    317–19, 328, 507, 509
  "Attenborough's *Gandhi*," 309
  East, West, 311, 317
  "The Courter," 317–19
  Midnight's Children, 308, 317
  "The New Empire within Britain," 308
  "Outside the Whale," 309
  Shame, 308

Saki (H.H. Munro), *see* Munro, H.H.
    ("Saki")
Sassoon, Siegfried, 39
Saturday Review, The, 89
Saxton, Josephine, 380
  "No Coward Soul," 380–1
Sayers, Dorothy L., 65, 71, 74–7, 362
  "The Adventurous Exploit of the Cave of
    Ali Baba," 76
  "The Bibulous Business of a Matter of
    Taste," 76
  "Bitter Almonds," 77
  "The Fascinating Problem of Uncle
    Meleager's Will," 75–6
  Hangman's Holiday, 75
  In the Teeth of Evidence, 75
  "In the Teeth of Evidence," 75
  "The Incredible Elopement of Lord Peter
    Wimsey," 76

"The Leopard Lady," 77
Lord Peter Views the Body, 75
"Nebuchadnezzar," 77
"The Poisoned Dow '08'," 77
Striding Folly, 75
"Tallboys," 75–6
"The Undignified Melodrama of the Bone
    of Contention," 75
Unnatural Death, 362
"The Vindictive Story of the Footsteps
    That Run," 76
science fiction, 92–3, 242, 255, 257,
    516–23
science fiction and fantasy, 372–83
scientific romance, 116–17, 174
Scotland, 252
Scots (language), 301–3, 537
Scott, Sir Walter, 54, 83, 239, 456
  Redgauntlet, 83
  "The Tapestried Chamber," 83
  "The Two Drovers," 239
  "Wandering Willie's Tale," 83
Scottish nationalism, 252–3, 294
Scottish short story (after 1945), 294–307,
    472–9, 532–40
sensation novel/fiction, 83, 90
Shakespeare, William, 39, 41, 102, 109,
    144, 208, 281–2, 324, 361, 434, 489
Sheehan, Ronan, 275
  "Paradise," 275
Shelley, Mary, 83, 375, 382
  Frankenstein, 83, 375, 382
Sheridan, Peter, 269
  44 Dublin Made me, 269
short story/fiction
  critical neglect, 5
  definition, 6–7, 174–5
  and genre, 7
  history before 1890s, 7–11
  post-1945 history in UK and Ireland,
    253–4
Sillitoe, Alan, 253, 286–8, 384, 409–15
  "The Bike," 287
  "The Disgrace of Jim Scarfedale," 288
  *The Loneliness of the Long-Distance Runner
    and Other Stories*, 287, 410

"The Loneliness of the Long-Distance Runner," 286–7, 409–15; film, 415
The Ragman's Daughter and Other Stories, 287
"On Saturday Afternoon," 287
Saturday Night and Sunday Morning, 410; film, 415
Sims, George
Sinclair, Clive, 330, 338–9
  "The Evolution of the Jews," 338–9
  Hearts of Gold, 338
Sinclair, May, 91, 93
Singer, Isaac Bashevis, 335
Smith, H. Greenough, 90
Smith, Zadie, 309, 541
Somerville, Edith, *see* "Somerville and Ross"
"Somerville and Ross," 53, 59, 60–1, 63
  All on the Irish Shore, 54
  The Irish R.M., 53–4, 61
  "Philipa's Fox Hunt," 53
  Some Irish Yesterdays, 54
Soyinka, Wole, 309
Spark, Muriel, 7, 280, 283–4, 456–63, 481
  "Alice's Long Dachshunds," 461
  All the Stories of Muriel Spark, 457
  Bang-Bang You're Dead and Other Stories, 457
  "Bang-Bang You're Dead," 460
  "The Black Madonna," 283–4
  Collected Stories I, 457
  The Comforters, 457
  Curriculum Vitae, 456
  "The Curtain Blown by the Breeze," 460
  "Come Along, Marjorie," 296, 461
  "The Dark Glasses," 461
  The Driver's Seat, 461
  "The Gentile Jewesses," 461
  The Ghost Stories of Muriel Spark, 457
  The Girls of Slender Means, 461
  The Go-Away Bird and Other Stories, 283, 296, 457
  "The Go-Away Bird," 291, 460–1
  The Mandelbaum Gate, 457
  "A Member of the Family," 461
  "One Hundred and Eleven Years without a Chauffeur," 457, 461
  The Only Problem, 458
  Open to the Public: New and Collected Stories, 457
  "The Pawnbroker's Wife," 460
  "The Portobello Road," 284, 422, 460–2
  The Prime of Miss Jean Brodie, 461
  "The Quest for Lavishes Ghast," 461
  "The Seraph and the Zambesi," 456–7, 459–62
  The Stories of Muriel Spark, 457
  The Takeover, 457
  "The Thing about Police Stations," 461
  Voices at Play, 457
  "You Should Have Seen the Mess," 296
Spence, Alan, 299–300
  "Auld Lang Syne," 300
  "Greensleeves," 299–300
  Its Colours They Are Fine, 299–300
  "Sheaves," 299
Spengler, Oswald, 520
"Speranza" (Lady Jane Wilde), 57, 84
  Ancient Legends, Mystic Charms, and Superstitions, 57
Spiegelman, Art, 339
  Maus, 339
spiritualism, 89–90, 92–3, 146
Stapledon, Olaf, 373
Stead, Christina, 85
Stephens, James, 56, 84, 88
  Here Are Ladies, 56
  Irish Fairy Tales, 56
Stevenson, Robert Louis, 20, 23–4, 31, 66, 88, 91–2, 131–9, 541
  "The Beach of Falesá," 23–4, 131–6
  "The Body Snatchers," 91
  "The Bottle Imp," 24, 131–2
  Island Night's Entertainments, 131
  "Markheim," 131, 136–8
  The Strange Case of Dr. Jekyll and Mr. Hyde, 136
Stoker, Bram, 57
  Dracula, 57
  Dracula's Guest and Other Weird Stories, 57

Storey, David, 410
  This Sporting Life, 410
Strand, The, 19, 66–7, 77, 81, 89–91
Suez crisis, 249–50, 410
supernatural motifs, *see* ghost story
surrealism, 375–6, 381, 507, 516, 519, 527
Swift, Graham, 254, 281–2, 389–90
  "Hotel," 390
  "The Hypochondriac," 390
  Learning to Swim and Other Stories, 281
  "Seraglio," 389
  "The Watch," 281–2
Symons, John Addington, 359, 370
Synge, John Millington, 51, 55

Taylor, Elizabeth, 416–22
  Angel, 417
  At Mrs Lippincote's, 416
  "The Blossoming," 416
  The Blush and Other Stories, 416
  "Crepes Flambees," 417, 421
  *Dangerous Calm: The Selected Stories of
    Elizabeth Taylor*, 417
  The Devastating Boys and Other Stories, 416,
    417, 421
  "The Devastating Boys," 418–19, 422
  "Excursion to the Source," 417, 421
  "Flesh," 417, 420–1
  "The Fly paper," 421
  Hester Lily and Twelve Short Stories, 416
  In a Summer Season, 421
  "In and Out of the House," 421
  "Hotel du Commerce," 417, 421
  "Miss A. and Miss M.," 421
  "Praises," 419
  "Sisters," 420
  "Tall Boy," 417, 419
  The Wedding Group, 421
  "The Wrong Order," 416
Temple Bar, 91
Thatcher, Margaret, 250–1, 309–11, 369
Tieck, Johann Ludwig, 82
Tolkien, J.R.R., 378, 380
Townsend Warner, Sylvia, 91, 96–7, 107–8,
  111, 362, 372, 379
  "The Cheese," 109

"The Golden Rose," 109
"How to Succeed in Life," 108
The Kingdoms of Elfin, 109, 372
"A Love Match," 108
A Moral Ending, 108–9
More Joy in Heaven, 108–9
The Museum of Cheats, 108–9
"The Nosegay," 108
"A Pigeon," 108–9
The Salutation, 109
Scenes of Childhood, 107–8
"Scenes of Childhood," 108
Selected Stories, 109
Winter in the Air, 109
"Winter in the Air," 108
travel writing, 116, 175
Trevor, William, 227, 253–4, 272, 274,
  277, 480–7
  "Access to the Children," 486
  After Rain, 486
  "After Rain," 486
  Angels at the Ritz, 272
  "Attracta," 484
  The Ballroom of Romance, 272, 482,
    484
  "The Ballroom of Romance," 272
  Beyond the Pale, 272, 485
  "Beyond the Pale," 482
  "A Bit of Business," 486
  "A Bit on the Side," 486
  Cheating at Canasta, 485
  "Cheating at Canasta," 486
  "Child's Play," 486
  "Cocktails at Doney's," 486
  Collected Stories, 272, 485
  The Day We Got Drunk on Cake, 290,
    485
  "Death in Jerusalem," 272, 486
  The Distant Past, 485
  "The Distant Past," 482
  "Downstairs at Fitzgerald's," 486
  "The Drawing-Room," 291
  "Faith," 486
  Felicia's Journey (film version), 486
  Fools of Fortune, 482
  "The General's Day," 486

"Gilbert's Mother," 486

The Hill Bachelors, 481

"Justina's Priest," 486

"Lost Ground," 486

Lovers of Their Time and Other Stories, 272, 290, 484

"Lovers of Their Time," 486

"Lunch in Winter," 486

"Matilda's England," 290

"Men of Ireland," 482

"Mrs Silly," 486

The News from Ireland, 485

"The News from Ireland," 482

"Of the Cloth," 482, 486

"Office Romances," 486

The Old Boys, 481

Outside Ireland, 485

The Oxford Book of Irish Short Stories, 277

"The Paradise Lounge," 486

"The Piano Tuner's Wives," 486

"Sacred Statues," 486

A Standard of Behaviour, 481

"The Summer-House," 290–1

"The Tennis Court," 290

"Teresa's wedding," 486

"Two More Gallants," 486

"The Virgin's Gift," 486

"The Wedding in the Garden," 486

"Widows," 486

A Writer's Ireland, 481

Trollope, Anthony, 52

Turgenev, Ivan, 54–5, 61, 212, 266

Tutuola, Amos, 528

uncanny, the, 81–3, 94; *see also* Freud, Sigmund

United States of America, 62, 69, 77, 198, 249–50, 311, 520–1, 538–9

and Irish short-story writers, 62, 211, 265–6

and lesbian fiction/publishing, 367–8

Updike, John, 458

utopia, 116–17, 175, 178, 180

Van Dine, S.S., 70, 71

Wain, John, 410

Wakefield, Tom, 369

Drifters, 369

Walcott, Derek, 309, 471

Wallace, Edgar, 70

Walpole, Horace, 82

Walsh, Maurice, 62

Green Rushes, 62

"The Quiet Man," 62

Wandor, Micheline, 330, 339–40

False Relations, 339

"The Song of the Jewish Princess," 339–40

war fiction, 35–50, 115, 118, 124–6, 160 211–14

Waters, Sarah, 369

Fingersmith, 369

Tipping the Velvet

Watson, Ian, 380

Waugh, Evelyn, 227, 481

Weil, Simone, 444

Welch, Denton, 366

"Alex Fairburn," 366

"Anna Dillon," 366

Brave and Cruel and Other Stories, 366

"The Fire in the Wood," 366

"The Hateful World," 366

"Weekend," 366

"When I Was Thirteen," 366

Weldon, Fay, 342, 348–9

"Down the Clinical Disco," 349

"A Gentle Tonic Effect," 349

"In the Great War," 349

Watching Me, Watching You, 349

"Weekend," 348

Wells, H.G., 86, 88, 90, 92, 114, 174–82, 198–9, 363, 424, 516–17

"The Beautiful Suit," 175–6

The Country of the Blind, 74

"The Country of the Blind," 175–9

"The Door in the Wall," 175–6, 179–80

"The Duration of Life," 179

"The Empire of the Ants," 175–6

"The Flowering of the Strange Orchid," 175, 177

"An Inexperienced Ghost," 90

Wells, H.G. (*cont'd*)
  "The Magic Shop," 175
  The Plattner Story and Others, 174
  "The Plattner Story," 175
  "The Sea Raiders," 175, 177
  "The Star," 517
  The Stolen Bacillus and Other Incidents, 174
  Tales of Space and Time, 174
  The Time Machine, 177
  Twelve Stories and a Dream, 174
  "The Valley of Spiders," 175–6
  "A Vision of Judgement," 179
  The War of the Worlds, 177
  "Zoological Regression," 176
Welsh, Irvine, 303–4, 306, 479
  The Acid House, 303
  "Granny's Old Junk," 303
  "Lisa's Mum Meets the Queen Mum," 304
  Trainspotting, 303–4
Welty, Eudora, 236
Wentworth, Patricia, 71
Wharton, Edith, 91–2
  "Afterward," 92
  "Kerfol," 92
  "Pomegranate Seed," 92
White, Edmund, 369
Whittaker Report, 252
Wilde, Lady Jane, *see* "Speranza"
Wilde, Oscar, 57, 59, 63, 68, 192, 202, 357–61, 363, 366
  "The Happy Prince," 57
  The Importance of Being Earnest, 361
  Intentions, 361
  Lord Arthur Savile's Crime and Other Stories, 361
  The Picture of Dorian Gray, 361
  "The Portrait of Mr. W.H.," 361
  Salomé, 361
  "A Sphinx Without a Secret," 57
Wilson, Angus, 227, 365–6, 384
  Hemlock and After, 365
  Such Darling Dodos, 365
  "Such Darling Dodos," 365–6

The Wrong Set, 365
Wilson, Edmund, 118–19, 227
Wilson, Jonathan, 330, 332–3
  "From Shanghai," 330, 332–3
  Schoom, 332
Wimsey, Lord Peter, 74–7
  and war trauma, 74–5
Winterson, Jeanette, 354, 369–70
  Oranges Are Not the Only Fruit, 370
  "The Poetics of Sex," 354
  The World and Other Places, 354
Wittgenstein, Ludwig, 102
Wodehouse, P.G., 75, 87
women short story writers, 96–113, 253, 342–55
Wonder Stories, 372
Woolf, Leonard, 194
  "Two Jews," 194
Woolf, Virginia, 10, 43–4, 85, 91–2, 96–8, 111, 193–201, 202, 362, 533
  Between the Acts, 194
  "Blue & Green," 101
  Monday or Tuesday, 101, 193, 202
  "Mr. Bennett and Mrs Brown," 198–200
  Mrs Dalloway, 97, 197, 200
  A Haunted House and Other Short Stories, 193, 198
  "A Haunted House," 85, 101
  "In the Orchard," 102
  Jacob's Room, 194
  "Kew Gardens," 102, 194–8, 200
  "Lapin and Lapinova," 102
  "The Legacy," 101, 198–200
  "The Mark on the Wall," 43–4, 100–1, 194
  "Modern Novels," 198–9
  Night and Day 194
  "On Re-reading Novels," 97
  "Phyllis and Rosamond," 101
  "Solid Objects," 102
  "The String Quartet," 101
  "Sympathy," 100
  Three Guineas, 198
  "Three Pictures," 102

Two Stories, 194

"An Unwritten Novel," 194

The Years, 198

Wood, Mrs Henry (Ellen), 83, 90–1

World War I, 10, 35–7, 39, 42, 43–5, 58, 75, 85–6, 91–2, 97, 103, 115, 124–6, 159, 189, 190, 197–8, 222, 225, 227, 238

World War II, 10–11, 35–6, 42, 45, 49, 51, 59, 62, 84, 92, 106–7, 217, 237, 240, 249–50, 254, 279–80, 292, 294, 309, 365, 408, 410, 516, 522

Wyndham, John, 517

Yeats, W.B. 51, 84, 171, 263–4, 478, 494, 501

Yellow Book, The, 11, 19, 89, 174

Zola, Émile, 224, 541

Zoline, Pamela, 516